ITALY AND HER INVADERS

PART FOUR

THE LOMBARD INVASION
LOMBARD KINGDOM
A.D. 600-744

THOMAS HODGKIN

BOOK VI.
THE LOMBARD INVASION.

I. THE ALAMANNIC BRETHREN.
II. THE RULE OF NARSES.
III. THE LANGOBARDIC FOREWORLD
1. Early Notices of the Langobardi by Greek and Roman Writers.
2. The Saga of the Langobardi
3. War with the Heruli
4. War with the Gepidae.
IV. ALBOIN IN ITALY.
V. THE INTERREGNUM.
VI. FLAVIUS AUTHARI.
VII. GREGORY THE GREAT.
VIII. GREGORY AND THE LOMBARDS.
IX. THE PAPAL PEACE.
X. THE LAST YEARS OF GREGORY
XI. THE ISTRIAN SCHISM.

BOOK VII
THE LOMBARD KINGDOM
A.D. 600-744

I. THE SEVENTH CENTURY.
II. THE FOUR GREAT DUCHIES.
I. The Duchy of Trient (Tridentum).
II. The Duchy of Friuli (Forum Julii).
III. The Duchy of Benevento (Beneventum).
IV. The Duchy of Spoleto (Spoletium).
Note A. Ecclesiastical notices of the Lombards of Spoleto in the Dialogues of Gregory the Great. Life of St. Cetheus.
III. SAINT COLUMBANUS.
IV. THEUDELINDA AND HER CHILDREN.
V. THE LEGISLATION OF ROTHARI.
VI. GRIMWALD AND CONSTANS.
The Story of St. Barbatus.
VII. THE BAVARIAN LINE RESTORED.
VIII. STORY OF THE DUCHIES, CONTINUED.
IX. THE PAPACY AND THE EMPIRE.
X. THE LAWS OF LIUTPRAND.
XI. ICONOCLASM.
XII. KING LIUTPRAND.
XIII. POLITICAL STATE OF IMPERIAL ITALY.
XIV. POLITICAL STATE OF LOMBARD ITALY.

BOOK V
THE LOMBARD INVASION
553-600

THE four invading nations whose history has been already related left no enduring memorial of their presence in Italy. The Visigoth, the Hun, the Vandal, the Ostrogoth failed to connect their names with even a single province or a single city of the Imperial land. What these mighty nations had failed to effect, an obscure and savage horde from Pannonia successfully accomplished. Coming last of all across the ridges of the Alps, the Lombards found the venerable Mother of empires exhausted by all her previous conflicts, and unable to offer any longer even the passive resistance of despair. Hence it came to pass that where others had but come in like a devouring flood and then vanished away, the Lombard remained. Hence it has arisen that he has written his name for ever on that marvel of the munificence of nature

'The waveless plain of Lombardy'.

Strange indeed is the contrast between the earlier and the later fortunes of this people, between the misty marshes of the Elbe and the purple Apennines of Italy, between the rude and lightly abandoned hut of the nomadic Langobard and the unsurpassed loveliness of the towers of Verona. From the warriors 'fiercer than even the ordinary fierceness of the Germans', what a change to the pale 'Master of Sentences', Peter the Lombard, intent on the endless distinctions which made up his system of philosophy. Nay, we may go a step further, and by a kind of spiritual ancestry connect London itself with the descendants of this strange and savage people. There is a street in London bearing the Lombard's name, trodden daily by millions of hurrying footsteps, a street the borders of which are more precious than if it were a river with golden sands. From the solitary Elbe pastures, occasionally roamed over by some savage Langobardic herdsman, there reaches a distinct historic chain of causes and effects, which connects those desolate moorlands with the fullness and the whirl of London's Lombard Street.

It was not however till the year 568 that the Lombards entered Italy. Between the defeat of Teias at Monte Lettere and that date, there intervened sixteen years of more or less trouble for Italy, the history of which will be told in the first two chapters of this volume. It will then be our duty to remount the stream of time through several centuries, in order to trace the early history of the Lombards.

CHAPTER I.

THE ALAMANNIC BRETHREN.

The Goths, who had fought under their last king, Teias, at the foot of Mount Vesuvius, made, as the reader will remember, a compact with their conqueror Narses that they should receive certain sums of money, and march forth out of Italy to live as free men, somewhere among their barbarian kinsmen. Either similar conditions were not offered to the other Goths scattered up and down through Italy, or having been offered and accepted they had been afterwards repented of, for when the history of Agathias commences, the curtain rises on a number of detachments of Gothic soldiers, some settled in Tuscia and Liguria, some wandering about from city to city of Venetia, all of them bent on remaining in Italy, and equally determined to abjure the service of the Emperor. With this intent, knowing themselves to be too weak to fight the Emperor single-handed, they decided to make one more desperate appeal to the Franks.

As the history of Italy now becomes almost inextricably intertwined with that of the Franks, and will so continue for a large part of the period embraced by this volume, it will be well briefly to summarize some of the chief events in Frankish history during the forty-three years which elapsed after the death of Clovis.

The founder of the Frankish monarchy, dying in 511, was succeeded by his four sons, who divided his unwieldy and ill-compacted kingdom between them. The division was conducted on a most singular plan: all kinds of outlying cities and districts being allotted to each brother. It was perhaps not desired, certainly it was not attempted, to give to each brother a well-rounded territory with a defensible frontier. But a mere approximation to the truth, we may say that the eldest son, Theodoric, received for his portion the country on both banks of the Rhine, Lorraine, Champagne and Auvergne, with the city of Metz for his capital. Chlodomir, from the city of Orleans, ruled the provinces watered by the Loire. Childebert had the country by the Seine, Brittany and Normandy, and Paris was his chief city. Chlotochar, the youngest of the brothers, but the one who was destined one day to reunite the whole inheritance, had his capital at Soissons, and governed the country by the Meuse and the plains of Flanders.

But the sons of Clovis had no intention of remaining satisfied with the ample dominions won by their father. In 523 the three younger brothers invaded the neighbouring kingdom of Burgundy, defeated its king, their cousin Sigismund, and seemed on the point of conquering the country. But the vigour of Sigismund's younger brother, Godomar averted for a time the threatened calamity. In the battle of Veseronce, Chlodomir, the eldest of the three brothers, was slain, and his fall so discouraged the Franks that they fled from the field, and their army retired from the rescued land.

Then followed a well-known domestic tragedy. The two royal brothers, Childebert and Chlotochar, determined to lay hands on the heritage of the dead Chlodomir, and for that purpose to put his little children out of the way. With cruel courtesy they sent a messenger to their mother, the aged Clotilda, to ask whether she would prefer that her grandchildren should receive the priestly tonsure or be slain with the sword, and when she in her agony cried out, "I would rather see them slain than shorn of their royal locks", they chose to consider this as sanctioning their crime, and slew the children with their own hands, the cold-blooded, saturnine Chlotochar preventing his brother, the weaker villain of the two, from faltering in the execution of their common purpose.

In 531 Theodoric overthrew the kingdom of the Thuringians, defeating and slaying Hermanfrid, who had married Amalaberga, the niece of the great Theodoric.

In 532 a fresh invasion of Burgundy was begun, Theodoric apparently now joining his younger brothers in the enterprise. This invasion was ultimately, though not immediately, successful. In 534, Godomar was defeated while attempting to raise the siege of Autun, and the Frankish kings divided his dominions between them. Henceforward Burgundy was 'a geographical expression'—of much historical interest indeed, and with wide and varying boundaries—but no longer a national kingdom.

The Frankish tribe had now subjected to themselves almost the whole of the fair land which today goes by their name, together with a vast extent of territory in what we now call Germany. We may omit for the present further reference, to the concerns of western Gaul, not troubling ourselves with the feuds and reconciliations of Childebert and Chlotochar, and may concentrate our attention on the kings of Metz, or, as they were perhaps already called, the kings of Austrasia (Eastern-land).

Theodoric died in 534, apparently before the conquest of Burgundy was completed, and was succeeded by his son Theudebert, who hastened home from his camp when he heard of his father's sickness, and by prompt action and timely liberality to his feudes (the warrior-chiefs who stood nearest to his throne), defeated his uncles' endeavours to possess themselves of his inheritance. For Theudebert was no puny boy, to be thrust contemptuously into a cloister, as had been done with St. Cloud, the only one of the sons of Chlodomir who escaped his uncles daggers. He was a bold and enterprising prince with far-reaching schemes of conquest and government, dreaming of invasions of Moesia and Thrace, accomplishing the subjection of his haughty Frankish warriors to a land-tax, and issuing—the first barbarian king who took so much upon him—gold coins like those of the Emperor, with his own name and effigy.

The sore troubles of the Ostrogothic people, caused by Belisarius' invasion of Italy, brought much increase of power to their Frankish neighbours. We have seen that Witigis in the autumn of 536, or ever he marched to his fatal siege of Rome, ceded to them Provence and all the countries on the lower course of the Rhone, which had formed part of the kingdom of Theodoric, and at the same time handed over £80,000 from the Gothic to the Frankish treasury. At this crisis also we have reason to believe that the protection which the Ostrogothic monarchy had afforded to the Alamanni and the Bavarians in the province of Raetia was withdrawn and that they too were absorbed in the great Frankish monarchy which now stretched over the larger part of southern Germany till it reached the frontier of Pannonia.

The long siege of Rome ended, as we have seen, in the spring of 538, disastrously for the Gothic besiegers. But the one event which shed a momentary gleam of prosperity 011 their cause was the capture of the great city of Milan (which had welcomed an imperial garrison), after a siege which lasted about half a year. This capture was accomplished by the aid of 10,000 Burgundians, subjects of king Theudebert, whom he had permitted to cross the Alps, and serve under the Ostrogothic standards, while representing to the ambassadors of Justinian that they went of their own free will, and that he was not responsible for their action. The very suggestion of such an excuse shows how little solidarity as yet existed in the great unwieldy mass of the Frankish dominion.

Soon, however, this pretence of feebleness was laid aside, and in the same year which witnessed the fall of Milan, Theudebert descended the Alps with 100.000 men, prepared to make war impartially on both the combatants, shedding Gothic and Greek blood with equal unconcern, but determined to pluck out of their calamities no small advantage for himself. Their savage deeds at Pavia, their rout of both armies under the walls of Tortona, the pestilence which carried off a third of then number, as they lay encamped on the plains of Liguria, and compelled their return to their own land, have already been described. It seems clear, however, that though Theudebert returned to the north of the Alps, he did not relinquish all the advantages which he had gained. It is true that Witigis in the supreme moment of the Gothic despair, just before 5the surrender of Ravenna, refused to avoid submission to Justinian by accepting the dangerous help of Theudebert, but that refusal did not compel the entire evacuation of Italy by the Franks. Even Procopius who dislikes that nation and seeks to minimize their success, admits that the larger part of Venetia, a good deal of Liguria, and the province known as Alpes Cottiae were retained by Theudebert.

A king whose unscrupulous energy had so great enlarged the borders of his realm, a king who, more than any other of his kindred, reproduced the type of character seen in their great ancestor Clovis, was probably obeyed with enthusiasm by his barbarous subjects, and was disposed to hold his head high among the monarchs of the world. He watched the gallant defence of the Gothic nation made by Totila perhaps with increasing sympathy, certainly with increasing dislike for the arrogant pretensions which, both in victory and in defeat, were urged by Justinian. For Justinian, so Theudebert was truly told, called himself (as in the well-known preface to the *Institutes*) victor of the Franks and the Alamanni, of the Gepidae and the Langobardi, and added many other proud titles derived from conquered and enslaved peoples. Why should this pampered Eastern despot, who had never himself set armies in the field, nor felt the shock of battle, give himself out as the lord of so many brave nations, the least of whose chieftains was a better man than he? Such were the self-colloquies that set the brain of Theudebert on fire. He contemplated a sort of league of the new barbarian kingdoms, Frankish, Gepid, Langobard, to quell the arrogance of the Emperor, and he would probably have led an army into Thrace or Illyria—who can say with what result; but that all his great projects were cut short by his early death. The authorities differ as to r cause of this premature ending of what might have been a great career. Both Procopius and Gregory of Tours attribute it to lingering disease; but Agathias who is singularly well informed on Frankish affairs says that when Theudebert was hunting in the forest, a buffalo, which he was about to pierce with his javelin, rushed towards him, overthrowing a tree by the fury of its onset. Not the stroke of the buffalo's horns, but the crash of a branch of the tree on the kind's head, gave him a fatal wound, of which he died on the same day.

But whatever the cause of death, the gallant king of the eastern Franks was dead, and his son, a sickly and feeble child named Theudebald, sat on his throne. To him, as we have seen, Justinian sent an embassy in 551, endeavouring to persuade him to recall his troops from northern Italy. The ambassador, Leontius, returned unsuccessful; but though the Frankish soldiers remained south of the Alps, guarding the territories which they had won, they do not appear to have rendered any effective assistance to Totila or Teias in the last struggle of those brave men for Gothic independence.

And now, in the early months of when Teias had met a warrior's death in sight of the cone of Vesuvius, another embassy came from the slender remnant of the Goths who still held out in Upper Italy, beseeching the Frankish king to undertake the championship of their cause. According to the report of the speech supplied—possibly from his own imagination—by Agathias, the ambassadors implored the Franks in their own interest not to allow this all-devouring Emperor to destroy the last relics of the Gothic name. If they did, they would soon have cause bitterly to repent it, for, the Goths once rooted out, it would be the turn of the Franks next. The Empire would never lack specious pretexts for a quarrel, but would go back, if need were, to the times of Camillus or Marius for a grievance against the inhabitants of Gaul. Even thus had the Emperors treated the Goths, permitting, nay inviting their King Theodoric to enter Italy and root out the followers of Odovacar, and then, 011 the most shadowy and unjust pretexts, invading their land, butchering their sons, and selling their wives and daughters into slavery. And yet these emperors called themselves wise and religious men, and boasted that they alone could rule a kingdom righteously. 'Help us,' said the Gothic orators, in conclusion, 'help us in this crisis of our fortunes; so shall you earn the everlasting gratitude of our nation, and enrich yourselves with enormous wealth, not only the spoils of the Romans, but the treasures of the great Gothic hoard, which we will gladly make over to you.'

The appeal of the Goths fell on unheeding ears, as far as the Frankish king was concerned. The timid and delicate Theudebald shrank from the hardships of war, and had none of his father's desire to measure his strength against Justinianus Francicus et Alamannicus. But there were two chieftains standing beside his throne, whose eyes gleamed at the mention of the spoils of Italy, and who—so loosely compacted was the great congeries of states which called itself the kingdom of the Franks—could venture to undertake on their own responsibility the war which Theudebald declined. These were two brothers named Leuthar and Butilin who were leaders of that great Alamannic tribe which as we have seen, after being protected by Theodoric against Clovis, had recently received the Frank instead of the Goth for their over-lord. A wild and savage people they were, still heathen, worshipping trees and mountains and waterfalls (in those Alamanni who dwelt in Switzerland, such nature-worship was perhaps excusable), cutting off the heads of horses and oxen, and offering them in sacrifice to their gods, but gradually becoming slightly more civilized owing to their contact with the Franks. Deep, indeed, must have been the barbarism of that nation which could gain any increased softness of manners from intercourse with the Franks of the sixth century.

Thus then, with high hopes and confident of victory, the two chiefs at the head of their barbarous hordes rushed down into Italy. Already they saw in imagination the whole fail peninsula their own; they discussed the question of the conquest of Sicily; they marvelled at the slackness of the Goths who had allowed themselves to be conquered by such a delicate and womanish thing, such a haunter of the thalamus, such a mere shadow of a man as the Eunuch Narses. The despised general was, however, meanwhile pressing on the war with the utmost vigour, in order to obtain the surrender of the fortresses still held for the Goths in Etruria and Campania, before their barbarian allies could appeal upon the scene. His chief endeavours were directed to procure the early surrender of Cumae, where Aligern, the brother of Teias, still guarded the Gothic hoard, and in order that no point in the game might be lost, he superintended the siege in person.

The city of Cumae, founded by settlers from Euboea on a promontory just outside the bay of Naples was for many generations the stronghold of Hellenic civilization in southern Italy, and it was from her walls that the emigrants went forth to found that colony of Neapolis which was one day so immeasurably to surpass the greatness of the mother-city. For two centuries (700-500 B.C.) Cumae successfully resisted the attacks of her Etrurian neighbors, but at last (about 420 B.C.) she was stormed by the Samnite mountaineers, and from that day her high place in history knew her no more. Now, after so many centuries, the hall forgotten Campanian city became once more the theatre of mighty deeds; and even as the fortress on the lonely promontory saw the waves of the Mediterranean breaking on the rocks at its foot, so were Narses and his Greek-speaking host now foiled by the very fortress which had once sheltered the Creek against the Etruscan.

The old city of Cumae, which stretched down into the plain, had probably vanished long before the Gothic war began: at any rate it seems to have been the rock-perched citadel, not the city, which Narses had now to besiege. The chief gate of the fortress was situated on its least inaccessible, south-eastern side, and against this the chief efforts of the besiegers were directed. The mighty engines of the Imperial army discharged their huge missiles, but were met by equally formidable preparations on the part of the besieged, who from their ramparts hurled great stones, trunks of trees, axes, whatever came readiest to hand, upon the ranks of the besiegers. It is strange that we hear nothing of Herodian, that deserter from the Imperial cause, whose utter despair of forgiveness must surely have made him one of the chief leaders of the fierce resistance. Aligern, the youngest brother of Teias, strode round the ramparts, not only cheering on the defenders but setting them an example of warlike prowess. The arrows shot from his terrible bow broke even stones to splinters: and when a certain Palladius, one of the chief officers of Narses, trusting too confidently in his iron breastplate, came rushing to the wall at the head of one of the storming parties, Aligern took careful aim at him from the ramparts, and transfixed him with an arrow which pierced both shield and breastplate.

This long delay before so comparatively insignificant a fortress chafed the Eunuch's soul, and he began to meditate other schemes for its reduction. The trachyte rock on which Cumae stands is still honeycombed with caves and grottoes, and one of these at the south-eastern corner of the cliffs, which bore the name of Virgil's Sibyl, was so situated that the wall of the fortress at that point actually rested on its roof. Into this grotto Narses sent a troop of sappers and miners, who with their mining tools hewed away the rock above them, till the foundation stones of the wall of the fortress were actually visible. They were of course careful to underpin the roof with wooden beams so that no premature subsidence should reveal their operations, and to prevent the noise of their tools from being heard the troops made perpetual alarums and excursions against that part of the wall while the work was proceeding. At length, when all was completed, the workmen set fire to a mass of dry leaves and other rubbish which they had collected within it and fled from the Sibyl's cave. As a piece of engineering the work was successful. The walls began slowly to sink into the ground: the great gate, tightly barred against the enemy, fell, carrying a large piece of the wall with it: base and wall, cornice and battlement, rolled down the cliffs into the gorge below. And yet, when the Imperial troops were hoping to press in through the breach thus made, and capture the fortress as if with a shout, they were baulked of their desire. For such was the nature of the igneous rock on which the citadel was built, so seamed with cracks and fissures, that when this piece of the wall was gone, there was still a narrow ravine, steep and untraversable, intervening between them and the towers in which lay hidden the Gothic hoard.

Foiled in this endeavour and in one more attempt to carry the fortress by storm, Narses was reluctantly compelled to turn the siege into a blockade. He left a considerable body of troops who surrounded the citadel with a deep ditch and watched, to cut off any of the garrison who might wander forth in search of fodder. Narses himself, still anxious to complete as far as possible the subjugation of Italy ere Leuthar and Butilin, who had already reached the Po, should penetrate further into the peninsula, marched into Tuscia to reduce the cities in that province, while he directed the other generals to cross the Apennines, occupy the strongest places in the valley of the Po, and, without risking a general engagement, harass the enemy as much as possible by skirmishing warfare.

These generals were of course chiefly those with whom we have already made acquaintance in the course of the Gothic war.

There was John, the nephew of Vitalian, the old ally of Narses against Belisarius, the kinsman of Justinian through his marriage with the daughter of Germanus. There were the ineffective Valerian, and Artabanes the Armenian prince whom Justinian had so generously forgiven for his share in a foul conspiracy against his life. But there was not the king of the Heruli, Philemuth, whose name had been so often coupled with theirs, for he had died of disease a few days previously and had been succeeded in the command of the 3,000 Herulian *foederati* by his nephew Phulcaris, a brave soldier but an unskilful general.

Most of the cities of Etruria surrendered speedily to the Imperial officers. Centumcellae, 'lordly Volaterrae,' Luna, Florence, Pisa, all opened their gates, on condition that they were to be treated as friends of their restored lord and not to suffer pillage from his troops. There was one exception which caused the impatient Narses some days of tedious delay. The garrison of Lucca had pledged themselves to surrender their city within thirty days if no succour reached them, and had given hostages for the fulfilment of their promise. But when the specified days had passed, being elated by the hope of the speedy arrival of the Alamannic host, they refused to keep their pledge. At this there were loud and angry voices in the Imperial camp, calling for the slaughter of the hostages. But Narses, though chafing at the delay, could not bring himself to kill these men for the fault of their fellows. He determined, however, to work upon the fears of the garrison and therefore ordered the hostages to be brought out into the plain beneath the city walls with their hands tied behind their backs, their heads bent forward, and all the appearance of criminals awaiting execution. As the threat of punishment did not shake the resolution of the garrison he proceeded to a sham execution of his prisoners. The soldiers on the walls could see their friends kneeling down as if for death, and the executioners with their bright blades standing over each. They could not see, for the comedy was enacted too far from their walls, that each prisoner had in fact a wooden lath fastened to the nape of his neck and covered with an apparent head-dress projecting above his real head. The town would not surrender, the bright swords flashed, the heads of the hostages apparently severed from their bodies: obedient to the word of command they fell prostrate on the ground and after a few well-feigned wrigglings all apparently was over.

Then arose from the walls of Lucca a cry of agony and indignation. The hostages were among the noblest of the Gothic host, and while their mothers and wives gashed their faces and rent their garments in their grief, the soldiers, with shrill cries, exclaimed against the hard and arrogant heart of the Eunuch who had put so many brave men to death, and against the disgusting hypocrisy of the votary of the Virgin, who had shed so much innocent Christian blood. Narses there-upon drew near to the walls and severely rebuked the garrison for the breach of faith which had been the cause of this slaughter. 'But even now,' said he, 'if you will repent of your evil deeds and surrender the city according to your promise, no harm shall happen to you, and you shall receive your friends once more alive from the dead'. 'Agreed! agreed!' shouted the garrison, 'the city shall be yours if thou canst call the dead back to life'. With that Narses bade his prostrate prisoners arise and marched them all up to the wall of the city. The garrison, who were dimly conscious of the trick hat had been played upon them, again went back from their plighted word and refused to surrender the city. Then Narses, with really astonishing magnanimity, sent the hostages all back, unharmed to their Gothic friends. Even the garrison marvelled, but he said to them, 'It is not my way to raise fond hopes and then to dash them to the ground. And it is not upon the hostages that I rely: it is this,' and therewith he touched his sword, 'which shall soon reduce you to submission'. But, in fact, the liberated and grateful hostages, moving about among their fellow-countrymen and telling every one of the courtesy and affability of their late captor and the mingled mercy and justice of his rule, soon formed a strong Imperialist party within the walls of Lucca and familiarized the minds of the garrison with the thought of surrender.

While Narses was still busied with the siege of Lucca, an unexpected disaster elsewhere befell a portion of his army. He had ordered his chief generals, John, Artabanes, Phulcaris, to concentrate their forces for the capture of Parma, in order that, from that strong city, placed as it was right across the great Aemilian Way, they might effectually bar the march of the Franks and Alamanni into central and southern Italy, and cover his own operations before the walls of Lucca. The other generals would seem to have performed at any rate part of their march in safety, but the unfortunate Herulian, Phulcaris, moving blindly forward, without making any proper reconnaissance, fell headlong into a trap prepared for him by Butilin, who had posted a considerable body of troops in the Amphitheatre near the town. At a given signal these men rushed forth and fell upon the Herulians who were marching along the great highway in careless disorder. Fearful butchery was followed by disgraceful flight: only the brave blunderer Phulcaris and his *comitatus* remained upon the field. They took up a position in front of a lofty tomb which bordered on the Aemilian, as that of Caecilia Metella borders on the Appian Way, and there prepared to die the death of soldiers. They made many a fierce and murderous onslaught on their foes, returning in an ever-narrower circle to the momentary shelter of their tomb. Still flight was possible, and some of the henchmen of Phulcaris advised him to fly. But he, who feared dishonour more than death, answered them, 'And how then should I abide the speech of Narses when he chides me for the carelessness which has brought about this calamity?'. And therewith he sallied forth again to the combat, but was speedily overpowered by numbers. His breast was pierced by many javelins, his head was cloven by a Frankish battle-axe, and he fell dead upon his unsurrendered shield. All his henchmen were soon lying dead around him, some having perished by their own swords and some by the weapons of the enemy.

The defeat and death of Phulcaris seemed as if it would turn the whole tide of war. The Franks were beyond measure elated by their success. The Goths of Aemilia and Liguria, who had before only corresponded with them in secret, now openly fell away to the invaders. And the Imperial generals, losing heart when they heard of the Herulian's misfortune, relinquished the march upon Parma and skulked off to Faventia, some hundred miles or so further down the Aemilian Way and almost in sight of Ravenna.

Great was the grief and indignation of Narses when he heard of the death of the brave Herulian and the cowardly retreat of the generals. It seemed as if he might have to raise the tedious siege of Lucca, deprived as he now was of his covering army; and what was worse, the dejection and discouragement of his own soldiers when they heard the fatal tidings, appeared to forebode yet further disasters. But the little withered Eunuch had in him a dauntless heart and was inclined by nature to follow the advice given to Aeneas by the Sibyl of Cumae—

'The mightier ills thy course oppose
Press the more boldly on thy foes.'

First he called his own troops together and addressed them in tones of rough but spirit-stirring eloquence. He told them that they had been spoiled by an unbroken course of victory, and were now ascribing an absurd importance to one solitary defeat, the result of a barbarian's neglect of the rules of scientific warfare. Nay, this very disaster if it taught them prudence and moderation in the hour of success would be well worth its cost. The Goths were really already subdued; they had only the Franks to deal with, strangers to the land, ill-supplied with provisions, and destitute of the shelter of fortified towns which the Imperial troops enjoyed. Only let them address themselves with vigour to the siege of Lucca, and they would soon see a satisfactory end to their labours. The words of the general revived the fainting spirits of his army, and the siege was pressed more closely than ever.

At the same time Narses sent a certain Stephanus of Dyrrhachium, with 200 horsemen, brave in battle, to chide the timid generals who were cowering behind the walls of Faventia. Stephanus had been charged with a message of fierce rebuke, and the sights and sounds which he saw as he marched through the devastated land, the ruined homesteads, the felled forests, the wailing of the peasantry, the lowing of the cattle driven from their stalls, all gave vehemence to his discourse: 'What spell has come upon you, good sirs? Where is the memory of your former deeds? How can Narses take Lucca and complete the subjugation of Etruria while you are selling the passage over Italy to the foe? I should not like to use the words "cowardice" and "treason", but be assured that others will be less fastidious, and if you do not at once march to Parma and take your allotted share in the campaign, it is not the indignation of Narses merely, but the heavy hand of the Emperor, that you may expect to encounter.'

The generals faltered out their excuses for their inaction. No pay had been received for the troops, and the entire failure of the commissariat, for which they blamed Antiochus, the Praetorian Prefect, who had not fulfilled his promises towards them, had compelled them to relinquish the camp at Parma. There was apparently some ground for these complaints, and accordingly Stephanus betook himself straightway to Ravenna. Having brought back with him Antiochus, and presumably some of the much needed *aurei*, having composed the differences between the civil and military authorities, and ordered the generals to march without further delay to Parma, Stephanus returned to the camp and assured Narses that he might now prosecute the siege with confidence as the returning generals would effectually secure him from the attacks of the barbarians. The Eunuch brought up his engines close to the walls, and poured a terrible shower of stones and darts upon the garrison who manned the battlements. There was division in the counsels of the besieged, the liberated hostages strongly urging the expediency of surrender to their magnanimous foe, while some

Frankish officers who happened to be in the city exhorted the Gothic garrison to resist with greater pertinacity than ever. But the complete failure of a sortie planned by the party of resistance, the terrible gaps made by the besiegers' engines in the ranks of the besieged, and the ruin of a portion of the city wall completed the victory of the party of surrender. Narses received their overtures gladly, showing no sign of resentment at the previous dishonourable conduct of the garrison. The siege, which had lasted three months, was ended; the Imperial troops entered the gates amid the acclamations of the inhabitants, and Lucca was once more a city of the Roman Empire.

The surrender of Lucca was followed by a more important event of the same kind, the surrender of Cumae. In the long hours of the blockade, Aligern had had leisure to reflect on the past and to ponder the future of the Gothic race in Italy, and he perceived more and more clearly that the Frankish alliance which his countrymen were so eager to accept meant not alliance but domination. The part which the great Transalpine nation would play in the affairs of Italy was already marked out for it, not by any great moral turpitude of its own, but by geographical position and by the inevitable laws of human conduct. They would offer themselves as champions and remain as masters, would undertake to free Italy from the Alps to the Adriatic, and would, if they were victorious, make it not free but Frankish1. Of the two lordships, the choice between which alone lay before him, Aligern preferred that which, though practically wielded from Constantinople, was exercised in the name of Rome, which rested on a legitimate foundation, and was still in accordance with the wishes of the people of the land. Influenced by these self-reasonings he signified to the besieging general his desire to visit Narses. A safe-conduct was gladly granted him and he repaired to Classis, where the Eunuch was then abiding. He produced the keys of his rock-fortress, handed them over to Narses, and promised to become the loyal subject of the Emperor, a promise which he faithfully kept, so that, as we shall see hereafter, in the decisive battle with the Alamannic invaders, Justinian had no braver champion than the Ostrogoth, the brother of Teias.

A portion of the army which had been besieging Cumae was ordered to occupy that fortress, the great Gothic hoard being of course handed over at once to the finance-ministers of the Empire. Aligern received the post of governor of Cesena, which is situated on the great Aemilian Way, about twenty miles south of Ravenna. Narses desired him to show himself conspicuously on the wall, that all men might know and perceive that the former champion of the Goths was now the champion of Rome. An excellent opportunity soon arrived for this display of himself in his new character. The Franco-Alamannic host arrived under the walls of Cesena, marching southward, intent on the plunder of Campania. They beheld to their astonishment the stalwart figure of Gothic Aligern erect upon the walls of this Imperial city, and heard his words of scorn shouted down from his airy pinnacle:

'You are going on a fool's errand, oh ye Franks, and are come a day after the feast. All the Gothic hoard has been taken by the Romans, yea, and the ensigns of the Gothic sovereignty. If we should ever hereafter proclaim a king of the Goths he will wear no crown or torque of gold, thanks to our Frankish allies, but will have to be dressed as a private soldier.'

Then the Franks upbraided him for a deserter and traitor; and they debated among themselves whether it was worthwhile to continue the war; but they decided in the end not to relinquish their project, and marched on for the Flaminian Way and the passage of the Apennines.

Winter was now coming on and the chief care of Narses was to house his troops in the fortified cities of Italy. He knew that he was thus surrendering the open country to the ravages of the Alamannic brethren, but this seemed a lesser evil than keeping his men, children of the south and dependent on warmth, shivering through the winter in the open fields, while the Franks, still fresh from the chilly north and from the marshes of the Scheldt, sustained no inconvenience and felt no hardship. He himself repaired to Rimini with his train of household troops in order to receive the military oath from Theudebald, king of the Warni (a namesake of the young king of the Austrasian Franks), who had just succeeded to the wandering royalty of his father Wakar, a chieftain in the Imperial army. Simultaneously with the administration of the oath, presents were given in the Emperor's name to the young king, and perhaps a donative to all the tribesmen who followed his standard, and thus the bond (for which it is difficult to find a suitable name) that united these Germans from the distant Elbe to 'the Roman Republic' was strengthened and renewed.

While Narses was still quartered at Rimini, a band of Franks, 2,000 in number, horsemen and foot-soldiers combined, poured over the plain busied in their work of rapine. From his chamber at the top of the house Narses, with indignant heart, beheld them ravaging the fields, driving off the oxen (those great dun-coloured oxen which plough the fields of Umbria), and carrying away the spoil from hamlet and villa. At length he could bear it no longer, but mounting his war-horse (high-couraged, but trained to perfect obedience) and gathering round him his followers to the number of 300 horsemen, he rode in pursuit of the marauders. Too wise in war to allow themselves to be vanquished in detail, the Franks left their work of spoliation and formed themselves into a compact mass, the infantry in the centre resting on a dense forest and the cavalry covering the two wings. Narses soon found that his horsemen could make no impression on this small but cleverly posted army, but rather that his own men were suffering from the discharge of the barbed Frankish spears. Hereupon he resorted to a stratagem which his admirer, Agathias, confesses to have been of the barbaric type, and more suited to a Hunnish chief than to an Imperial general. He ordered his men to feign panic and flight, and not to return till he gave the signal. The device, however barbaric, justified itself by its success. The Franks, thinking that they saw a chance of ending the war at one stroke by the capture of the great Imperial general, left the safe shelter of the wood and dashed forward in eager pursuit. When all, cavalry and infantry alike, were hurrying in disorder over the plain, Narses gave the signal for return, and the Franks, dreaming of easy victory, found themselves being butchered like sheep by the well-armed and well-mounted horsemen. The cavalry, indeed, made good their return to the wood, but of the infantry 900 fell and the rest with difficulty escaped, disheartened and panic-breeding, to the camp of their generals.

After this Narses returned to Ravenna, set in order whatever had gone wrong under the feeble rule of Antiochus, and went thence to Rome, where he passed the winter. For a few months, the land, though disquieted by the marauding invaders, had rest from actual war.

The interval of rest was employed by Narses in patient and systematic drill of his troops. The arm on which he most relied seems to have been his cavalry; at least, we hear how his men were taught to spring nimbly on their horses, and to wheel them to the right or to the left. But the pyrrhic dance, of which we also hear, was probably performed by the heavy-armed foot-soldier; and all, horsemen and foot-men alike, raised in unison the *barritus* (that proudly ascending war-song), when the spirit-stirring notes of the trumpet were heard challenging them to this martial melody. Meanwhile the barbarian armies, like two desolating streams of lava, were pouring over the unhappy peninsula. Keeping far from Rome and the fortresses in its neighbourhood, they marched in company as far as Samnium. There they separated, and Butilin, taking the western coast-road, ravaged Campania, Lucania, Bruttii, down to the very Straits of Messina; while Leuthar, marching down by the Adriatic, visited, in his destructive career, Apulia and Calabria, penetrating as far as the city of Otranto. All were bent on plunder, but a difference was observed between the two invading nationalities whenever they drew near to consecrated buildings. The Franks, mindful of their reputation for Christian orthodoxy, did, as a rule, spare the churches, while the heathen or heretic Alamanni seemed to delight in filling the sacred precincts with filth and gore and the unburied of their victims. They stripped off the roofs and shook the foundations of the churches, and the sacred bowls, the chalices, the patens, and the vessels for holy water, which were often of solid gold, were recklessly carried off to minister to the vulgar pomp of some barbarian chieftain.

Seven hundred and sixty-one years before, two brothers (but how different from this pair of blundering barbarians) had led two armies into Italy, hoping, by a combined effort, to crush out the name of Rome. Fortunately for the Imperial cause, the folly and the avarice of the Alamannic brethren brought about now that division of their forces which, in the case of Hannibal and Hasdrubal, was only accomplished by the desperately bold strategy of the consuls who conquered at the Metaurus. Leuthar was anxious to return to his barbarian home (perhaps somewhere in the Black Forest), and there store up in safety the spoils of Italy. Butilin, when he received his brother's message to this effect, refused to return, alleging the specious pretext of the alliance with the Goths, to which their oaths were plighted. The result was that Leuthar set forth on his northward march alone, intending, however, when he had safely housed his captives and his spoil, to return with an army to the help of his brother.

For some distance Leuthar and his army, though encumbered with spoil and captives, marched on in safety; but when they reached the Fane of Fortune, at the mouth of the Metaurus, disaster befell them. The Imperial generals, Artabanes and Uldac the Hun, were quartered in the little town of Pisaurum, about seven miles to the north of Fanum. When these generals saw the van of the Frankish host approaching and making their way with difficulty over the rocky headlands, they fell suddenly upon them, slew many with their swords, and forced the others to scramble down the steep and slippery sides of the cliff. The paths were so precipitous that a great number of the fugitives fell headlong into the Adriatic waves below. The few who did escape rushed back to Fanum and filled all the barbarian camp with their terrified shouts : 'The Romans are upon us'. Leuthar drew out his army in battle array, expecting an attack, but this the Imperial generals did not feel themselves strong enough to make. When, however, the soldiers, renouncing the thought of battle, returned to their quarters, they found that the greater number of their captives had taken advantage of the alarm to decamp, carrying with them no small part of the spoil.

Fearing the Imperial armies stationed in the fortresses of the Adriatic, Leuthar and his men turned inland and pursued their march along the base of the Apennines. At length they crossed the Po, and came into Venetia, which was now a recognized part of the Frankish kingdom. Here, at length, at Ceneda, under the shadow of the dolomites, the baneful career of Leuthar came to a fitting end. His army was attacked by a pestilence—the punishment, Agathias thinks, of their cruel and sacrilegious deeds.

Some showed symptoms of fever, some of apoplexy, some of other forms of brain-disease, but, whatever form the sickness might assume, it was invariably fatal. The leader was attacked as well as his men, and in his case some of the symptoms seem to point to delirium tremens. He rolled himself on the ground, uttering fearful cries; he tore the flesh of his own arms with his teeth; and then, like some savage beast, licked the flowing gore. Thus, in uttermost misery, he died—neither the first nor the last of the invaders upon whom the climate of Italy has taken a terrible revenge for her ravaged homesteads.

We have seen how the debased copy of Hasdrubal suffered defeat by the Metaurus; now we have to mark the reverse which befell the other brother near the equally fatal Capua. The army of Butilin, like that of Leuthar, suffered grievously from pestilence. Summer had now ripened into autumn, and the barbarians, unable to procure wholesome food in their marches—the country having been wasted by order of the provident Narses—partook too freely of the fruit which they found in the orchards and of the must which they pressed for themselves out of abundant clusters of the grapes of Campania. Butilin, seeing that his forces were simply wasting away under the influence of disease, determined to strike a blow for Rome, while he still had something that could be called an army. With this view, he marched northward and fixed his camp on the banks of the Vulturnus, not far from Capua.

A word or two must be said as to the topography of this city, the capital of Campania, once the second city of Italy, and one which, in the days of the Second Punic War, nourished ambitious hopes of outstripping even Rome. The Capua of mediaeval and modern times, the Capua which gave its title to a prince of the Royal Family of Naples, and which is surrounded by lunettes and bastions after the manner of Vauban, is situated close to the Vulturnus, on its left bank. This city, however, corresponds not to the Capua of Hannibal or of Narses, but to the little subject town of Casilinum. The older Capua lay about three miles to the south-east, away from the river, in the midst of the fruitful Campanian plain, and of course upon the great Appian Way. It had two spacious squares,—the Albana, the centre of the political life of the city, which contained the senate house and the place of popular assembly, and the Seplasia, the great commercial centre, where men bought and sold the earthenware, the wine, the oil, and pre-eminently the precious ointments for which Capua was famous on all the shores of the Mediterranean. Just outside the town, at its north-west corner, was the great amphitheatre, built, or, at any rate restored, by Hadrian, with dimensions closely corresponding to those of the Colosseum at Rome, and capable of accommodating 60,000 spectators, but the present ruins of which are less than half the height of the ruins of its Roman rival. All round the town are the multitudinous graves, in which archaeologists have been excavating for a century, leaving many still unexplored. The earthenware vases and ornaments of bronze and gold found in these sepulchres, and bearing witness to the three civilizations—Etruscan, Samnite, Roman—whose influence has passed over Capua, are to be found in large numbers in the museums of England and Italy. The city in old days abounded in temples, and one, the greatest of all, that of Diana, stood on the commanding eminence of Mount Tifata, some two or three miles to the north of Capua. The thick forests which surrounded it have long ago been felled; the substructures of the temple are still visible, but its pillars now (apparently) adorn the very interesting eleventh-century basilica of S. Angelo in Formis, which stands near the site of the ancient temple.

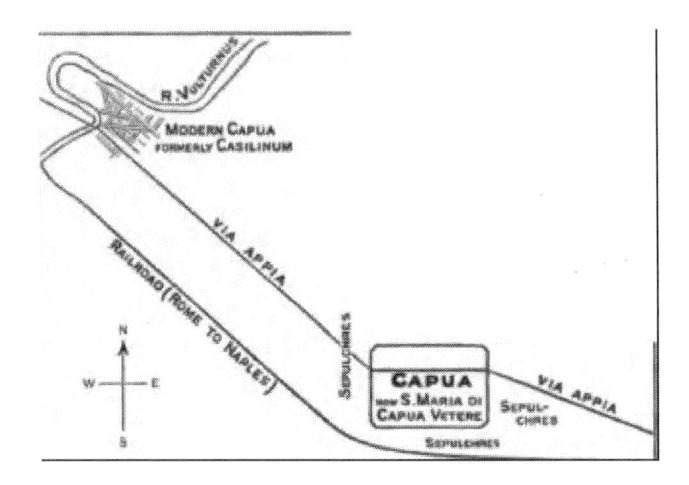

In this neighbourhood then Butilin pitched his camp, but as he was close to the river he was probably nearer to Casilinum (the site of modem Capua) than to Capua Vetere. Though he had 30,000 men under him and the army of Narses numbered only 18,000, he entrenched himself like one in presence of an overwhelming danger. All round his camp, except at one narrow gateway, he planted the heavy waggons which had thus far accompanied his army. To prevent the enemy from putting horses to these waggons and drawing them away, he ordered that they should be banked up with earth as high as the axles of the wheels, and the rude *agger* thus formed was further fortified with stakes. The river guarded his right flank, but in order to defend himself from an attack by way of the bridge he ordered a wooden tower to be erected, which he manned with some of the most warlike of his troops. Having made all these arrangements he waited for the arrival of the brother whom he was never again to behold.

Instead of Leuthar, Narses soon appeared upon the scene, having marched with all his army from Rome. Great was the excitement in both armies at the thought of the now imminent battle. Almost equally great was the excitement throughout the cities of Italy, at the prospect of the speedy decision of the question whether Justinian or Theudebald was to be their future lord. The engagement was hastened by an impulse of generous indignation. Narses could not bear to witness the Frankish ravage of the villages of Campania, and ordered Charanges the Armenian, a brave and war-wise officer, whose tents were pitched nearest to the foe, to chastise their presumption. The horsemen of Charanges easily overtook the creaking wains in which the Alamanni were carrying off the plunder of Campania, and slew their drivers. One of these waggons was filled with very dry hay, and by a happy inspiration Charanges ordered that it should be driven up close to the wooden bridge-tower and then set on fire. The fire caught, the garrison were obliged to evacuate the tower and rush to their comrades in the camp, and the bridge fell into the hands of the Romans. The mingled rage and terror which was thus engendered in the Frankish host compelled their generals to lead them forth to battle at once, though the day had been pronounced unlucky by the Alamannic soothsayers, who predicted, so we are told, that if Butilin fought on that day his troops would perish to a man.

The two armies which were now about to meet in deadly combat were strangely dissimilar in arms and equipments. The Franks were almost entirely infantry-soldiers: while Narses, like Belisarius, relied chiefly on his *Hippotoxotai*, the mounted archers whose Parthian tactics of flight and pursuit so often wrought deadly mischief to the heavy Teutonic hosts. Heavy armed, however, the Franks and Alamanni were not. Few of them wore either helmet or breastplate, and trousers of linen or leather were the only covering of their legs. A sword hung at each man's thigh and a shield covered his left side. They had neither bows nor slings, but sent their two-edged axes hurtling through the air, and above all they wielded the terrible *ango* of which a description has already been given.

While the two armies were striding to the encounter, Narses performed a signal act of retributive justice, which seemed at first as if it would lose, but which eventually gained him the day. A certain Herulian nobleman among his *foederati* had, for some trifling neglect of duty, put one of his slaves to death with circumstances of savage cruelty. News of the crime was brought to Narses after he had mounted his horse for battle, but wheeling swiftly round he sought the murderer and charged him with the deed. The Herulian neither denied nor excused his offence, but stoutly maintained that in all that he had done he had acted within his rights as a master, and added. that if his other slaves did not take warning by their comrades fate he would mete out to them the same punishment. The cruelty and insolence of the man raised the indignation of Narses, who also felt, moreover, that to shed the blood of such a monster would be an offering acceptable in the sight of heaven. He therefore ordered his guardsmen to slay the Herulian, who at once received a fatal sword-thrust in his side. His countrymen murmured loudly. They hung back from the march, and it seemed as if they would desert on the very eve of battle. Narses, however, would not change his tactics for them. He relied on the protection of Divine Providence, but he also reckoned on the unwillingness of a warlike tribe like the Herulians to melt away from the field of battle, when that battle was even now almost joined.

In arraying his troops for the combat, Narses repeated, perhaps not altogether of his own will, the tactics which had proved so successful in the battle of the Apennines. Again he left his centre weak and trusted to his flanks for victory. The barbarians on the other hand had formed themselves into a solid wedge shape, like a Greek *delta*, and meant to pierce the centre of the Imperial host and so to conquer. They were greatly stimulated to the encounter by the arrival of two deserters of the Herulian tribe, who assured Butilin that he would find the Imperial host all in confusion owing to the determination of the Herulians not to fight under the banners of the man who had slain their comrade.

The disposition of the two armies can be best explained by a diagram.

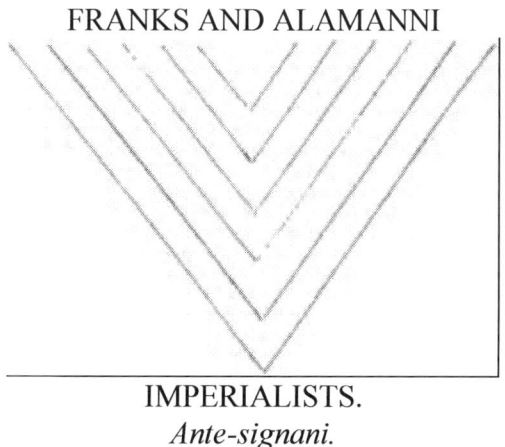

FRANKS AND ALAMANNI

IMPERIALISTS.
Ante-signani.

Woods] Valerian and   Infantry   NARSES.
Artabanes— Cavalry.   Cavalry Zamdalas and the
                                                 household of Kanes.

Light-armed troops, archers and slingers.
Heruli, slowly coming up.

In the van of the Roman host were the *Ante-signani*, picked troops, clothed in long coats of mail reaching down to their feet, and with stout helmets on their heads. Behind them stood, the light-armed troops, the archers and slingers, but all this centre of the host was weak by reason of the tardy movements of the angry Herulians who should have formed its core of resistance. Narses himself with a strong body of *Hippotoxotai* formed the right wing of the army; and just behind him stood his Majordomo Zandalas with all the slaves in his warlike household that were apt in war, for the family of Narses, like that of his great rival Belisarius, seems to have been a complete nursery of soldiers. On the left wing, partly resting on a dense wood and partly ambushed behind it, was another strong body of *Hippotoxotai* under Valerian and Artabanes.

The Frankish army came on with a wild cry and with all the dash and impetuosity of their nation. The *Ante-signani* were soon overpowered; the weak place in the centre of the line, where the Heruli should have been, but were not, was easily pierced: even the rear guard was scattered in flight, and the point of the attacking wedge was just touching the Imperial camp. But this apparently easy victory of the barbarians, if it had not been actually contrived by Narses, suited his plans exactly. Tranquilly he ordered his two wings to execute a manoeuvre which enabled them to enfold the barbarian host as in a bag. And now the over-confident Franks and Alamanni found themselves exposed to a destructive discharge of arrows aimed by invisible foes. For the orders given to the *Hippotoxotai* in each wing were to aim not at the breasts of the nearer but at the backs of the more distant enemies, and this they could easily do, because being on horseback they could see over the heads of the barbarian infantry. Thus the *Hippotoxotai* of Narses were raining their deadly shower upon the backs of the men who were fighting with Valerian, and in like manner the *Hippotoxotai* of Valerian were mowing down from behind the antagonists of Narses. In both cases the custom of the barbarians to wear no armour for the back made the manoeuvre more fatal. They could not see the foes by whose arrows they were falling, and even had they been able to confront them, the shorter range of their own missile weapons, the battle-axe and the *ango*, would have made the combat still unequal.

While this was going on in the broad part of the barbarian wedge, which was being rapidly thinned down as rank after rank fell under the back-piercing missiles of the Imperialists, the point of the wedge had also fallen into disaster. For now at last Sindual, king of the Heruli, with his tribesmen had appeared upon the field, to atone for the tardiness of his march by the ferocity of his onset upon the foe. The Franco-Alamannic van perceived that they had fallen into a trap, and rolled back in helpless disorder upon their beaten comrades. A few escaped and made for the river Vulturnus, but perished in its waters. The Roman infantry, both heavy and light-armed, closed in and completed the work of slaughter which had been begun by the *Hippotoxotai*. Soon, over all the battlefield were heard the groans of the dying barbarians. Butilin fell, the Herulian deserters who had fed him with such false hopes fell also. Undoubtedly the destruction of the Frankish host was complete, though we may refuse to give implicit belief to the statement of Agathias that only five men out of Butilin's 30,000 escaped to their own country.

The chief credit of so splendid a victory must undoubtedly be ascribed to Narses, that marvellous being who, after a lifetime spent in an emperor's dressing-room, emerged from an atmosphere of cosmetics and compliments to show himself 'a heaven-born general', a perfect master of tactics and most fertile in resource when the hurly-burly of battle was loudest. But the barbarian chiefs whose strong arms had executed what Narses planned, were deemed also worthy of commendation: and of these the men who most distinguished themselves were Sindual the Herulian and Aligern, brother of Teias, the erewhile enemy of Rome.

Great was the rejoicing in the Imperial host over the victory of Capua. Having buried their slain of the comrades and stripped the corpses of the foe, having swarmed over the waggon-rampart and plundered the Frankish camp, the soldiers marched to Rome, having their heads crowned with garlands and singing incessant paeans of victory. Quartered in Rome and deeming all the dangers and fatigues of war over for a lifetime, they began to abandon themselves to the sensual delights of a soldier's holiday. Here would you see one of the heroes of the late encounter who had sold his helmet for a lyre, there a brother in arms who had parted with his shield for an amphora of wine.

The general, however, soon perceived the growing demoralization of his troops, and knowing too surely that all danger from the Franks was not at an end, he called them together and addressed them with grave and earnest words, blaming their over-confidence, beseeching them to show themselves Romans, superior to the arrogant elation and panic fears of the barbarians, expressing his belief that the Franks would ere long renew the war, and exhorting them, whether that were so or not, in no case to relax that warlike discipline which alone could ensure success in the hour of danger. The army heard with shame the reproofs of their great commander, and laying aside their careless and self-indulgent ways, 'returned', says the historian, 'to the habits of their ancestors'. Those ancestors were of course supposed to be the men of Rome. It shows what magic yet lay in that mighty name, that this Armenian Eunuch, addressing his motley host of Huns, Heruli, Isaurians, Warni, could win them back from dissipation and self-indulgence by this single argument, 'They are unworthy of your Roman forefathers'.

For the present, notwithstanding the forebodings of Narses, the land had rest from foreign invasion. The sickly child Theudebald, king of Austrasia, died in 555, and his great-uncle Chlotochar, who succeeded to his kingdom, showed no sign of wishing to renew the war for the possession of Italy. Only a little band of Goths, 7,000 in number, who had not, like Aligern, renounced the alliance with the Franks and entered the service of the Emperor, still held out in the mountain fortress of Campsa. Their leader was Ragnaris the Hun, a much-aspiring man, eager to earn notoriety by the arts of the demagogue, by which he stirred up the Goths to continue a hopeless resistance. The fortress of Campsa was strong and the nature of the ground made it impossible to take it by assault, and Narses was therefore compelled to resort to blockade, a tedious process, as the garrison were well provisioned, and a dangerous one, as they showed their resentment by frequent and not altogether unsuccessful sallies.

In this blockade of Campsa the winter months wore away. In early spring Ragnaris called for a parley, and the two chiefs, the courtly old Armenian and the upstart Hunnish adventurer, met under the castle walls. However, the tone of Ragnaris was so arrogant and his demands were so preposterous that Narses soon broke up the conference in wrath. As each party was returning to its quarters Ragnaris stealthily fitted an arrow to the string, turned suddenly round, and discharged it at the Eunuch. But the treacherous heart had ill inspired his aim: the arrow missed Narses and fell harmlessly to the ground. The bodyguards of Narses, enraged at the felon deed, at once discharged their arrows at Ragnaris, who fell, having received a mortal wound. His followers carried him into the fortress, where he died after two days of agony. On his death real negotiations for surrender were begun by the garrison, who stipulated only that their lives should be spared. Narses, whose careful fidelity and his plighted word on all occasions excited the wonder of a degenerate age, would not allow one of the Goths to be put to death, but in order to guard against future disturbance to the peace of Italy, sent them all to Constantinople. Here, though we are not expressly told anything of their further fortunes, we may well imagine that the tallest and most soldier-like men among them would be enlisted in the bodyguards of the aged Justinian. Sixty-six years, or two generations of men, had passed away since Theodoric led his nation-army from Moesia into Italy, and now the last dwindled remnant of the Ostrogoths came back to dwell beside the Euxine of their forefathers and the Bosphorus of their unconquerable foe.

CHAPTER II.

THE RULE OF NARSES.

Of the twelve years during which the Eunuch Narses bore sway in Italy, after the last of the Goths had been driven forth, we possess very scanty memorials.

It was undoubtedly a time of general depression and misery. The fever of war was past, and the pain 0f Italy, of the sore wounds which twenty years of bloodshed had inflicted upon Italy was felt now perhaps more bitterly than ever. All over the land, doubtless, were cities lying desolate; the chasms still left in their walls, where the Gothic battering-rams had pounded into them; long streets of burnt houses, where the fiery bolts from the catapult had carried the wasting flame. To repair these ruined cities seems to have been the chief work of the busy Eunuch, whose official title seems to have been 'the Patrician'. The great city of Mediolanum, that Milan which has been more than once destroyed, and more than once has arisen in splendour from its ashes, felt especially the benefit of his restoring hand.

The great law-giving Emperor, too, contributed, after his manner, to the healing of the wounds of Italy. On the 13th of August, 554, he put forth a 'Pragmatic Sanction', the object of which was to bring back social peace into the chaos left by the expulsion of the Ostrogoths. All the legislative acts of Theodoric and his family, down to Theodahad, were thereby confirmed: only those of Witigis and his successors (but even these covered a period of sixteen years) were treated as absolutely null and void.

In the year 555, probably soon after his reduction of the Gothic stronghold of Campsa, Narses was called upon to take part in an ecclesiastical ceremony of an extraordinary kind, in connection with the newly consecrated pope, Pelagius I. It will be remembered that at the end of all his vacillations as to the miserable controversy of the Three Chapters, Pope Vigilius submitted himself to the Emperor's will, but there was still considerable delay before he was suffered to depart from Constantinople. After the defeat of Totila, the assembled clergy of Rome sought an audience with Narses, and, while congratulating him on the restoration of the Imperial rule, suggested (apparently) that the return of Vigilius, and of all the bishops who had gone into exile with him for their refusal to condemn the Three Chapters, would be a fitting acknowledgment of the Divine goodness which had thus blessed the arms of the Emperor. Justinian, on receiving this message from Narses, caused the banished bishops to be gathered together from Egypt, from the island of Proconnesus, and from all the various places of their exile, and asked them whether they were willing to recognize Vigilius (now, it must be remembered, a condemner of the Three Chapters) as their pope, or whether they would prefer the archdeacon Pelagius, the only other candidate whom he would permit them to choose. They replied with one accord, 'Restore to us Vigilius ; let him be pope again, and when it shall please God to remove him from this world, then, with your consent, archdeacon Pelagius shall succeed him'.

Then all those bishops were allowed to depart from Constantinople, and, setting sail for Italy, they touched at Syracuse, where, as has been already related, Vigilius died, after suffering much agony from the cruel malady with which he was afflicted, and which, as his biographers thought, was itself caused by his mental misery.

The archdeacon Pelagius, who was, in accordance with the declared wish of the Emperor, consecrated pope in the room of Vigilius, was the same whom we have seen bravely interceding for his fellow-citizens with the victorious Totila at the time of the siege of Rome. At that critical time he seemed to bear himself like an upright citizen and a patriotic Roman, but there must have been something in his character which suggested to onlookers the idea of a disposition to selfish intrigue. Under the pontificate of Silverius, who had appointed him his apocrisiarius (nuncio) at the Court of Constantinople, he was thought to have caballed with Theodora against that popes; and, under the pontificate of Vigilius, though he had followed that unhappy exile in all his waverings backwards and forwards about the Three Chapters, he was apparently suspected of having been all the while intriguing to supersede him, a suspicion to which the singular proposal of Justinian, which has just been quoted, seems to lend some probability. Now an even darker, and, it would seem, absolutely unjust suspicion of having in some way caused or hastened the death of Vigilius rested upon him. So nearly universal was the dislike and distrust with which he was regarded that only two bishops, John of Perugia and Bonus of Florence, could be found willing to consecrate him; and Andrew, a presbyter of Ostia, had to be joined with them in order to give the rite some semblance of canonical regularity. All the rest of the clergy, all the religious persons who filled the monasteries of Rome, all the more influential nobles of the city, shrank from communion with a man whom they openly accused of being responsible for the death of his predecessor.

In order to silence these calumnies and to reconcile the pontiff with the citizens of Rome, Narses and Pelagius together devised a striking ceremony. Starting from the Church of St. Pancratius on the Janiculan Hill, the two men, the chief of Italy and the chief of the Church, walked in solemn procession till they came to the great basilica of St. Peter. Up the long dim nave, lined with ninety-six columns taken from heathen temples, they proceeded till they came to the semicircular apse where, under the majestic figure of the Christ, displayed in mosaics on the vault, was placed the tomb of his boldest disciple. All the while that they were thus marching, Narses, Pelagius, and such of the priests as had been willing to join them, were chanting solemn litanies. Then Pelagius mounted the hexagonal pulpit or *ambo*, and, taking the Gospels in his hand and putting a cross upon his head, swore an awful oath that he had had neither part nor lot in the death of his predecessor. The earnest adjuration of the pontiff, made more impressive by the presence of the Patrician, who seems to have acted as a kind of compurgator of the accused man, appears to have satisfied the people. Pelagius proceeded to deliver one of those exhortations against simony which were becoming, by reason of the need for them, almost a commonplace in the mouth of an ecclesiastical ruler, and took measures for the restoration to the Roman churches of the golden vessels of which they had been plundered. As far as we can tell, the deep distrust and suspicion of the new pontiff, which had hitherto prevailed, were now laid aside. The chief occupation of his short pontificate was the endeavour to persuade the Western bishops that they might, without derogating from the authority of the Council of Chalcedon, accept the decree of the Council of Constantinople, condemn the Three Chapters, and anathematize the memory of the unfortunate Theodore, Ibas and Theodoret. In this labour, which was the price paid to the Emperor for his nomination to the pontificate, Pelagius was only partially successful, as we shall perceive in a later chapter, when we come to deal with the question of the Istrian schismatics. Though the period of the rule of Narses was generally peaceful, we still hear vaguely of conflicts with barbarian chiefs, the heavings of the ocean after the subsidence of the great storm of the Gothic war. A certain Aming, probably a Frankish chieftain, who had entered Italy in 539 with King Theudebert, returned or remained, and offered his assistance to a Gothic count, named Widin. They fell, however, before the victorious Eunuch. Aming was slain by the sword of Narses, and Widin was sent to Constantinople, whither so many captive barbarian chiefs had preceded him, all ministering to the pride of 'Justinianus Victor et Triumphator, semper Augustus.'

It may possibly have been in connection with this victory over Aming and Widin that, as we are told by Theophanes, 'letters of victory came from Rome, written by Narses the Patrician, announcing that he had taken two strong cities of the Goths, Verona and Brescia'. This event is placed by the chronicler in the year 563. It is hardly possible that such important cities can have been left untaken for ten years after the defeat of Totila, but either Widin the Gothic count, or some such champion of a lost cause, may have arisen and, collecting the scattered remnants of his countrymen, may have taken Verona and Brescia by surprise and held them for some time against the empire.

Two years later, Sindual, king of the Heruli, whom we last met with making a tardy but effectual charge on the army of Butilin, turned against Narses, from whom he had received many favours, and endeavoured to set up an independent barbarian sovereignty in Italy, or, as the Imperialist writers call it, to establish a 'tyranny'. Against him, too, the star of Narses prevailed. He was vanquished in war, taken prisoner, and hung from a lofty gallows.

This same year (565) witnessed the passing away of two great actors in the drama of the reconquest of Italy. Belisarius, who, after his last glorious campaign against the Kotrigur Huns, had fallen into disgrace at court, being accused of complicity in a plot against Justinian, and had then, after eight months' obscuration, been restored to the imperial favour, enjoyed his recovered honours for something less than two years, and died in the month of March, 565. Of him, as of Wolsey, might the words be used:

'An old man, broken with the storms of state,'

and yet, like Wolsey, he had not reached extreme old age, since, forty years before, he was still spoken of as in early youth

Eight months after Belisarius died his even more famous master. For thirty-eight years Justinian had governed the Roman world, filling a larger space in the eyes of men than any ruler since Theodosius, if not than any ruler since Constantine. He had restored much of the splendour of the Roman name, had reunited Rome and Carthage to the Empire, and had even displayed his victorious eagles on the coast of Spain. He had been an indefatigable student of theology, had called a General Council, and imposed the dogma which was the fruit of his midnight studies upon the conscience of a resisting pope. Above all, he had evoked from the chaos in which the laws of Rome had been tossing for centuries an orderly and harmonious system, which was to make the influence of Roman Law thenceforward coeval and conterminous with European civilization and with all that later civilization which, springing from it, was to overspread four continents. But there was a reverse to this brilliant picture on which perhaps sufficient emphasis has been laid in previous volumes of this book. The conquests of Justinian were not enduring. The financial exhaustion which was the result of his showy and extravagant policy left the provinces weak and anaemic, unable to resist the new forces which were about to be hurled upon them from the deserts of Arabia. The theological activity of the Emperor alienated many of his subjects, both in the East and West, and probably facilitated the conquests of Mohammed. Nor did even the Emperor's own theology, in the later years of his life, escape the charge of heretical error.

But were it good or bad, the work of Justinian was done and a new lord looked forth from the windows of the Anactoron, over the wide Propontis and the beautiful Horn of Gold. That lord was Justin the Second, a nephew of Justinian, who had consolidated his position at Court, and secured his succession to the throne by marrying Sophia, niece of the once all-powerful Theodora. In spite of the praises of the courtly poet, Corippus—who sought to re-awaken the lyre of Claudian and to sing the praises of Justin and his African general John, as the earlier poet had sung the praises of Honorius and Stilicho—the new Emperor was a narrow, small-minded man, just the kind of person who was likely to emerge, safe and successful, from the intrigues of a court like Justinian's, but not the man to guide aright the destinies of a mighty Empire. Moreover, when he had been eight years upon the throne the symptoms of a diseased brain were so manifest that it was necessary to provide him with a colleague, who was in fact a regent: and it is probable enough that even at the time of his accession he showed some deficiency of mental power. Whatever the cause, the result seems clear, that in the earlier years of the reign, Sophia, not Justin, was the true ruler of the Empire, and that this Empress, who possessed the ambition of Theodora without her genius governed feebly and unwisely, cutting away a branch here and there of the more unpopular parts of Justinian's administration, but neither resolutely upholding nor broadly remodelling the system which he had inaugurated.

It was, no doubt, in accordance with this general plan of change without reform that the Imperial pair decided on the recall of Narses. The popularity which the Patrician had won by the reconquest of Italy he had lost by his ten years' government of the peninsula, but whether justly or unjustly lost, who shall say? The full weight of the misery caused by a prolonged war is often not felt till the war is over, when the fever of fighting is followed by the collapse of bankruptcy and famine. This was the experience of our fathers in the decade which followed Waterloo, and it may well have been the experience of the Italians during the years which intervened between Totila and Alboin. Over such an emaciated and exhausted country Narses had to rule, squeezing out of it by his *rationales* and his *logothetes* the solidi which were to be transmitted to Constantinople—a miserable dividend (if so modem a comparison may be allowed) on the vast sums which Justinian had disbursed for the reconquest of Italy.

But did Narses plunder for his own private account as well as to fill the coffers of his master? That is the more or less open accusation of the later chroniclers, but though it is quite impossible now either to prove or disprove it, the charge does not altogether correspond with what we hear elsewhere of the character of Narses. Ambition rather than avarice seems to have been the master-passion of his soul, and he is represented as a free-handed and generous rewarder of the men who served him well.

But we have had enough of conjecture. Let us listen to the statement, poor and meagre as it is, given us by the Papal biographer, of the events which led up to the recall of Narses.

'Then the Romans, influenced by envy, sent representations to Justin and Sophia, that it would be more expedient for the Romans to serve the Goths than the Greeks. "Where Narses the Eunuch rules", said they, "he makes us subject to slavery. And the most devout Prince is ignorant of this. Either, therefore, free us and the City of Rome from his hand, or else we will assuredly become servants of the barbarians". Which, when Narses heard, he said "If I have done evil to the Romans I shall find myself in evil plight". Then going forth from Rome he came to Campania and wrote to the nation of the Langobardi that they should come and take possession of Italy'.

By the last sentence of this extract we are brought face to face with the accusation which is the heaviest charge that has been made against the character of Narses, the accusation that he, in revenge for his recall, invited the Lombard invaders into Italy. It is easy to show how slight is the basis of trustworthy evidence on which this accusation rests; but in order to show what the accusation is, it will be well to quote it in the fully developed and dramatic form which it assumed, two centuries after the event, in the pages of Paulus Diaconus, the great historian of the Lombard people. After copying the passage just quoted, from the Papal biographer, Paulus proceeds:

'Then the august Emperor was so greatly moved with anger against Narses that he immediately sent Longinus the praefect into Italy that he might take the place of Narses. But Narses, when he knew these things, was much afraid, and so much was he terrified by the same august Sophia that he did not dare to return to Constantinople. To whom, among other [insults], she is said to have sent a message that, as he was an eunuch, she would make him portion out the days' tasks of wool-work to the girls in the women's apartment1. To which words Narses is said to have given this answer, that he would spin her such a hank that she should not be able to lay it down so long as she lived. Therefore, being racked by fear and hatred, he departed to Naples, and soon sent ambassadors to the nation of the Langobardi, telling them to leave the poverty-stricken fields of Pannonia and come to possess Italy, teeming as it was with all sorts of wealth. At the same time he sent many kinds of fruit and samples of other produce in which Italy abounds, that he might tempt their souls to the journey. The Langobardi received with satisfaction the glad tidings, which corresponded with their own previous desires, and lifted up their hearts at the thought of their future prosperity'.

Such is, as I have said, the fully-developed story, and that which has succeeded in inscribing itself on the page of history. It contains some obvious improbabilities. The Langobardi, the flower of whose nation had served in Italy only fifteen years before, certainly needed no elaborate information as to the fruits and produce of that country. It would be strange, too, though not impossible, if just before sending so traitorous a message, Narses went southward from Ravenna to Naples, thereby at once adding to the labours of his messengers and lessening his own chances of deliverance from punishment by the hosts of the invading barbarians.

But, moreover, if we trace the tale backwards through the centuries, we shall find, as is so often the case, that the nearer we get to the date of the events, the less do the narrators know of these secret motives which are so freely imputed, and these dialogues of great personages which are so dramatically described. Paulus Diaconus wrote, as has been already said, about the middle of the eighth century. The chronicler, who is incorrectly quoted as 'Fredegarius' (who wrote about 642, and perhaps put the finishing touches to his history in 658), tells the story in nearly the same words, but, while he gives us the golden distaff, he takes away the fruits and other vegetable products. We then come back to the Spanish bishop, Isidore of Seville, who wrote a chronicle coming down to 615. He simply says, 'Narses the Patrician, after he had, under Justinianus Augustus, overcome Totila, king of the Goths in Italy, being terrified by the threats of Sophia Augusta, the wife of Justin, invited the Langobardi from Pannonia, and introduced them into Italy'. This sentence, written probably about fifty years after the recall of Narses, is, after the notice already quoted from the Papal biographer, the strongest support of the charge that Narses invited the Lombards into Italy. And if we accept, as we seem bound to do, the early date of the 'Papal Life,' we shall feel compelled to admit that there was a belief among his contemporaries that Narses had, at the end of his life, proved disloyal to the Empire. Only remembering the parallel case of Stilicho, we shall be careful to distinguish between popular suspicion and judicial evidence of such a crime1.

Our two best contemporary authorities are Marius of Aventicum and Gregory of Tours, both of whom died (having passed middle age) in or about the year 594. They are, therefore, strictly contemporary authorities for the events of 567. Neither of them makes any mention of Narses' invitation to the Lombards, though the former describes the recall of Narses (with some suppressed indignation at such a reward to so meritorious a servant of the Emperor), and both notice the entry of Alboin and the Lombards into Italy. Equally silent on the subject are the so-called Annals of Ravenna, though the ecclesiastical chronicler, writing in that Imperial capital, was just the person who would have been likely to utter the shrillest notes of execration at so signal an act of treachery by the Patrician towards the Empire.

Upon the whole, then, we conclude that there is hardly sufficient evidence for the far-famed vengeance of the Eunuch on the Empress. His recall, which took place in the year 567, was, probably enough, due to the advice of the ambitious and meddlesome Augusta, and it is in the highest degree likely that the removal of such a man from Ravenna, who had been not only the recoverer of Italy in war, but for twelve years the mainspring of the administrative machine in peace, may have led to a certain amount of confusion and disturbance, during which the barbarians on the north-eastern frontier perceived that their time had come to re-enter the beautiful land which they had so unwillingly quitted in 552, when Narses informed them that he had no further occasion for their services.

Of the later history of the great Eunuch-Patrician we have scarcely any trustworthy details. The 'Liber Pontificalis,' which, as we have seen, repeats the slander as to the invocation of the Lombards, goes on to describe a mysterious interview between Pope John III and Narses. 'The pope goes in haste to Naples, and asks the ex-governor to return to Rome. Narses says, "Tell me, most holy Pope, what mischief have I done to the Romans? I will go to the feet of him that sent me [the Emperor], that all Italy may know how I have laboured in its behalf." The pope answered, "I will go more quickly than thou canst return from this land." Therefore Narses returned to Rome with the most holy Pope John, and, after a considerable time, he died there; whose body was placed in a leaden chest, and all his riches were brought back to Constantinople. At the same time Pope John died also'

If this note of time is to be relied upon, the death of Narses must have happened about 573, or perhaps a year or two earlier; and, upon the whole, this seems to be the conclusion to which most of the authorities point: that he died in Rome early in the eighth decade of the sixth century. The statements as to his return to Constantinople and recovery of the favour of the Emperor probably proceed from a confusion between him and another Narses, who, thirty years later, was one of the bravest of the Imperial generals on the Persian frontier.

The vast wealth of the Eunuch was perhaps simply confiscated by the Imperial treasury, but in the next generation the following story concerning it reached the ears of

Gregory of Tours. Tiberius II (who, as we shall see, was first the colleague and then the successor of Justin II) was a man of generous disposition, and was frequently rebuked for this by his patroness, the Empress Sophia, who declared that he would bring the Imperial treasury to ruin. 'What I,' said she, 'have been many years in collecting, thou wilt disperse in a very short time.' Then he said, 'Our treasury will be none the poorer, but the poor must receive alms and the captives must be redeemed. Herein will be great treasure according to that saying of the Lord, "Lay up for yourselves treasures in heaven, where neither moth nor rust doth corrupt, and where thieves do not break through nor steal." Now Narses, that great Duke of Italy, who had had his palace in a certain city, went forth from Italy with a mighty treasure and came to the aforesaid city of Constantinople, and there, in a secret place in his house, he dug out great cisterns in which he stored up many hundred thousand pounds weight of gold and silver. Then, having slain all who were privy to his plans, he confided the secret of the hoard to one old man, under a solemn oath that he would reveal it to no man. On the death of Narses these treasures lay concealed under the earth. But when the afore said old man saw the daily charities of Tiberius, he went to him, and said, "If it may profit me, O Caesar, I can reveal to thee a great matter." "Say on, what thou wilt," answered Tiberius. "I have the secret of the hoard of Narses," said he, "and, being now at the extreme verge of life, I can conceal it no longer." Then Tiberius Caesar, being filled with joy, sent some servants, who followed the old man to the place with great astonishment. Having arrived at the cistern, they opened it, and entered within, and found there so great a quantity of gold and silver that it was hardly emptied after many days, though men were carrying it away continually. And after this, the Caesar went on more blithely than before, distributing money to the needy.'

So vanishes from history the mysterious figure of the great Eunuch-general.

CHAPTER III.

THE LANGOBARDIC FOREWORLD.

1.

Early notices of the Langobardi by Greek and Roman writers.

Most writers who have touched upon the early history of the Lombards have been struck with the curious hiatus which exists in the historical notices of that people. At the time of the Christian era, our information concerning them, if not very full, is clear and definite. At intervals throughout the first century their name reappears in the pages of the historians of the Empire, and we have one notice of them, brief but important, towards the end of the second century. From that date (*cir*. A.D. 167) to the reign of the Emperor Anastasius—an interval of more than three centuries—the Roman and Greek historians do not mention the name of the Lombards, and, as will be seen hereafter, we have to go to another source, and one of a very different kind, for any information as to their history during this period of obscuration.

Our chief authorities as to the geographical position of the Lombards, in their first settlement known to history are Strabo (who wrote about A. D. 20), Tacitus (*cir*. 61-177), and Ptolemy (*cir*. 100-161). On the combined testimony of these three authors we are safe in asserting that the Langobardi (such is the earliest form of their name) dwelt near the mouth of the Elbe, in frequent and close relations with the Hermunduri and Semnones, two great Suevic tribes which settled higher up the stream, on its western and eastern banks respectively. There is a little conflict of testimony between Strabo and Ptolemy as to the side of the Elbe on which the Langobardi dwelt. Strabo puts them on the further, Ptolemy on the hither shore. If the authority of the former prevail, we must look upon parts of Mecklenburg and Holstein as their home, if that of the latter, the eastern part of the Electorate of Hanover, from Luneburg to Salzwedel. Possibly enough both may be right for different periods of their history, for Strabo expressly points out that the common characteristic of all the dwellers in this part of Germany was the readiness with which they changed their homes, the result of the simplicity of their diet, and the pastoral rather than agricultural character of their occupations. He compares them herein to the Nomads of Scythia, in imitation of whom, as he says, they were wont to place all their household goods on waggons, and set their faces in any direction that pleased them, driving their cattle and sheep before them.

The Hermunduri and Semnones, the southern neighbours of the Langobardi, were important nations in their day, but their memory has perished, and they have left no lasting trace on the map of Europe. More interesting, at least to us, is the fact that among the neighbours of the Langobardi on the north are enumerated the tribe of the Angli, 'fenced in', as Tacitus says, 'by their forests or by their streams'. He goes on to tell us that the only thing noteworthy about the tribes (seven in number) north of the Langobardi—and the remark may possibly apply to the Langobardi themselves—is the worship which they all paid in common to the goddess Herthal, Mother Earth. Her chariot and her image were hidden in the recesses of a sacred grove, apart in an island of the ocean. Here dwelt the solitary priest who was allowed access to her shrine. At stated times he crossed the sea with the image of the goddess. Placed upon the consecrated chariot and covered by a sacred robe, it was drawn by cows from village to village, along the plains of Holstein. Wherever the sacred image went there was joy and feasting: peace reigned instead of the continual clashing of the swords of the sons of Odin; till at length the goddess, sated with the converse of mortals, returned to her island home. The chariot, the vest, and (some said) the image of Mother Earth herself, were washed in a sacred lake. The slaves who had been employed in this lustration were then themselves whelmed beneath its waters, and the lonely priest resumed his guard of the lonely deity whom it was death to behold. Such were the rites with which the Angle and the Langobard of the first century after Christ, the ancestors of Bede and of Anselm, of Shakespeare and of Dante, jointly adored the Mother of Mankind.

The origin of the name borne by the Langobardi has been a subject of some discussion. The national historian, as we shall see a little further on, derives it from their long beards, and tells a curious story to account for its first bestowal on the nation. As *bart* or *bard*, in some form or other, is the equivalent of the Latin *barba* in the chief Low-German languages, there can be no objection raised on the score of philology to this derivation. It has been urged, however, that the very fact of its resemblance to the Latin form may have suggested it too easily to an uncritical historian, and that since some other German tribes wore their hair and beards long, it is difficult to understand why the long beards of this one tribe should have been distinctive enough to entitle them to a separate name. It is, therefore, proposed to derive the name from the Old High-German word *barta*, an axe, the root which appears in hal*bert* and *part*izan. Again, another author argues for its derivation from the root *bord* (which we have preserved in the word sea-board, though custom forbids us to speak of a river-board), and contends that the Langobardi received their name from the long flat meadows by the Elbe where they had their dwelling. According as we adopt one or other of these suggestions, the tribe whose history we are considering will have been the Long-bearded men, the Long-halbert-bearing men, or the Long-shore-men. I confess that to me the first, the old-fashioned derivation, that which was accepted by Isidore and Paulus, still seems the most probable. In any case there is no doubt about the meaning of the first element of the name, and remembering the neighbourhood of the Langobardi and the Angli, we note with interest the true Teutonic form of the word, as it reappears in *Lang*dale, and *Lang*ley, and the Scotch phrase 'Auld *Lang* Syne', rather than in our modem Gallicized word *long*.

The tribe of the Langobards were early distinguished by their fierce and warlike disposition. Velleius Paterculus, the contemporary and flatterer of Tiberius, in speaking of the victories of his hero in Germany (*cir.* A. D. 6), says that 'nations whose very names were before almost unknown, were beaten down before him; the Langobardi, a race fierce with more than the ordinary fierceness of Germany, were broken by his arms, and the Roman legions with their standards were led from the Rhine to the Elbe'. So too, Tacitus, after describing the numerous and powerful nation of the Semnones, the head of the Suevic race, dwelling in a hundred *pagi*, passes on to their neighbours the Langobardi, and says that 'these may rather pride themselves on the smallness of their numbers, since, girt round by so many great and strong nationalities, they have preserved their existence, not by a humble obedience, but by perpetual fighting, and in peril have found safety.'

The two greatest names in the history of the German peoples during the first century of our era were undoubtedly Arminius and Maroboduus; Arminius, the patriot chief of the Cherusci, who stirred up his tribe t0 a successful resistance against the encroachments of Rome, and who annihilated the three legions of Varus in the

Teutoburgian forests; Maroboduus, the self-centred and crafty despot of the Marcomanni, who built up for himself a dominion of almost Oriental arrogance in the mountain-girdled realm of Bohemia; who gave succour and asylum to the enemies of Rome, and the shadow of whose ever-menacing might darkened with anxiety the last years of Augustus himself. In a fortunate hour for Rome, these two leaders of the German resistance to the Empire turned their arms against each other. The cause of the Cherusci, championed as it was by so popular a leader as Arminius, was looked upon by the Germans generally with greater favour than that of the Marcomanni under the autocratic Maroboduus, and hence it came to pass that on the eve of the conflict, two Suevic tribes, the Semnones and the Langobardi, separated themselves from the Marcomannic kingdom and joined the Cheruscan confederacy. In the battle which followed, and which, though nominally drawn, was virtually a defeat for Maroboduus (soon followed by the utter downfall of his power), the Langobardi are especially mentioned as doing great deeds of prowess by the side of their Cheruscan allies on behalf of their new-found liberty.

The Langobardi evidently adhered for one generation at least to their new alliance, and did not return within the orbit of the great Suevic monarchy. Thirty years after their revolt from Maroboduus, when the Cheruscan Italicus, the Romanized nephew of Arminius, was struggling, with diverse fortunes, to maintain himself in the royal position to which he had been raised by his countrymen, weary of anarchy, it was among the Langobardi that he took refuge after he had been defeated by the rebels; it was from them that he received help and comfort, and it was by their arms that he seems to have been once, at least, reseated on the forest-throne of the Cherusci.

From this point onwards our information as to the fortunes of the Langobardi becomes extremely meager. The indications of their geographical position given by Tacitus and by Ptolemy, show that they were still known to the Romans as occupying their previous dwellings on the Elbe, in the reigns of Nerva and the elder Antoninus. But soon after Ptolemy wrote, they must have quitted their old home in order to take part in that movement of the German tribes southwards which brought on the Marcomannic war, and involved the reluctant philosopher, Marcus Aurelius, in ten bloody and hard-fought campaigns.

In a somewhat obscure paragraph1 of the history written by Peter the Patrician (Justinian's ambassador to Theodahad), we are informed that 'six thousand Langibardi (*sic*) and Obii, having crossed the Danube, A.D. 165, were turned to utter rout by the cavalry under Vindex, aided by an attack from the infantry under Candidus. As the result of this defeat, the barbarians, desisting in terror from their first attempt, sent ambassadors to Aelius Bassus who was then administering Pannonia. The ambassadors were Vallomar, king of the Marcomanni, and ten others, one being chosen to represent each tribe. Peace was made, oaths were sworn to ratify it, and the barbarians returned to their home'.

Not much can be made out of a jejune fragment like this, but it is clear that the Langobardi have left the lower waters of the Elbe for the middle waters of the Danube. They are accompanied by the Obii, in whom some commentators see the same people as the Avieni, whom Tacitus makes next-door neighbours to the Langobardi, but of whose history we are otherwise entirely ignorant. They are evidently once more allies, perhaps subject-allies of their old masters the Marcomanni, since Vallomar the Marcomannic king heads the embassy to Aelius Bassus. Considering that the account of the campaign comes from a Roman source, we may probably infer with safety that the repulse sustained by the Langobardi and their confederates was not a serious one, and that though they did not maintain the position which they had taken up on the Roman shore of the Middle Danube, yet that in returning 'to their home' they withdrew to no great distance from the tempting plains of Pannonia.

After this notice, information from Greek or Roman writers as to the fortunes of the Langobardi entirely fails us, and for a space of 300 years (as was before to the said) their name disappears from history. It brings before us in a forcible manner the long space of time over which the downfall of the Empire extended, to remind ourselves that this mere gap in the story of one of its destined destroyers lasted for ten generations, for an interval as long as that which separates the Englishmen of today from their forefathers of the reign of Elizabeth.

To some small extent, however, we may fill up the interval by repeating what the national historian, Paulus Diaconus, has preserved of the old traditions of the Lombard race. Some of these traditions may possibly reach back to an earlier date than the notices of Strabo and Tacitus, but it is vain to attempt to fit the Saga (at least in its earlier portions) and the literary history into one continuous narrative. Far better does it seem to be to let the two streams of recital flow on unmingled, only eliminating from the pages of Paulus those paragraphs which evidently do not come from the treasure-house of the old national traditions, but are merely borrowed, and for the most part unnecessarily borrowed, from the pages of classical historians and geographers. The 'Origo Gentis Langobardorum' gives us the framework of the story, but the details come, for the most part, from the pages of Paulus Diaconus.

2.
The Saga of the Longbeards.

'In the Northern land, that fruitful mother of nations, whose hardy sons have so often poured down on Illyricum and Gaul, and especially upon unhappy Italy, lies a mighty island, washed, and owing to its flat shores, well-nigh washed away, by the sea, and named Scandinavia. Here dwelt long ago the little nation of the Winnili, afterwards known as the Langobards.

'Now the time came when this people found the island of Scandinavia too strait for them, and dividing themselves into three portions they cast lots which of the three it should be that must depart from their fatherland. Then that portion of the people upon which the lot had fallen, ordained two brothers to be their leaders, whose names were Ibor and Aio, men in the youthful vigour of their years, and sons of a woman named Gambara, in whose wise counsels they trusted greatly. Under these leaders they set forth to seek their new homes, and came to the region which is called Scaringa.

'Now, at that time, Ambri and Assi, the two chiefs of the Vandals, having won many victories, held all the countries round under the terror of their name. These men marched with an army against the Winnili, and said unto them, "Either pay us tribute, or prepare yourselves for battle and fight against us". Now the Winnili were all in the first flush and vigour of their youth, yet were they very few in number, being only the third part of the inhabitants of an island of no great size. Howbeit, Ibor and Aio having consulted with their mother Gambara, decided that it was better to defend their liberty by their arms than to soil it by the payment of tribute, and made answer accordingly, "We will prepare for battle". Then did both nations pray to the gods for victory. Ambri and Assi prayed to Odin, and he answered them : "Whomsoever I shall first look upon at sunrise, to that nation will I give the victory." But Gambara and her two sons prayed to Freya, the wife of Odin, that she would show favour unto them. Then Freya counselled them that at sunrise the Winnili should all assemble before Odin's eastern window, having their wives with them, and that the women should let down their hair and encircle their faces with it as if it were a beard. Then, when the sun was rising, Freya turned upon her couch, and awoke her husband, and bade him look forth from the eastern window. And he looked and saw the Winnili and their wives with their hair about their faces, and said, "Who are these long-bearded ones?" Then said Freya to Odin, "As thou hast given them the name Langobardi, so give them the victory." And he gave them the victory, and from that day the Winnili were called the Langobardi'.

'After this victory the Langobardi were sore pressed with famine, and moved forth from the province of Scoringa, intending to go into Mauringa. But when they reached the frontier, the Assipitti were drawn up determined to dispute the passage. When the Langobardi saw the multitude of the enemy, and knew that by reason of their own small numbers they could not engage with them, they hit upon the following device. They pretended that they had in their camp Cynocephali, that is dog-headed men. They made the enemy believe that these creatures followed the business of war with eagerness, being intent on drinking human blood, and that, if they could not drink the blood of an enemy, they would even drink their own. At the same time, to make their numbers appear larger than they were, they spread their tents wide and kindled very many fires in their camp. By these arts the enemy were so far dismayed that they did not dare to carry out their threat of battle; but, having in their ranks a champion who was very strong and whom they deemed invincible, they sent a messenger to propose that the dispute between the two peoples should be settled by single combat. If the champion of the Assipitti conquered, the Langobardi should return to the place from whence they came. But if the champion of the Langobardi prevailed, they should have liberty to march through the country of the Assipitti. Now when the Langobardi were in doubt whom they should choose for this encounter, a certain man, of servile origin, offered himself for the combat on condition that, if he were victorious, he and his offspring should be freed from the stain of slavery. His masters gladly promised to grant this request: he drew near to the enemy: he fought and conquered. The Langobardi had licence to pass through the country whither they would: and the champion obtained for himself and his children the rights of freedom. Thus, then, did the Langobardi succeed in reaching Mauringa, and there, that they might increase the number of their warriors, they gave liberty to many of their slaves. In order that the free condition of these might thenceforth be subject to no doubt, they ratified the enfranchisement in the accustomed manner by an arrow, murmuring at the same time certain words handed down from their forefathers for a solemn confirmation of the act.

'From Mauringa the Langobardi moved forward and came into Golanda, and there they possessed the regions of Anthaib and Bainaib and Burgundaib, and now, as Ibor and Aio were dead, who had brought them out of the land of Scandinavia, and as they wished no longer to be under chiefs [or dukes], they chose themselves a king, after the manner of the nations. This was AGELMUND, son of Aio, of the noble seed of the Gungingi; and he reigned over the Langobardi thirty-three years.

'In his time a certain woman of evil life brought forth seven children at a birth, and this mother, more cruel than the beasts, cast them all into a pond to be drowned. Now it happened that King Agelmund, on a journey, came to that very pond. Halting his horse, he marvelled at the unhappy babes, and, with the spear which he held in his hand, turned them over hither and thither. Then one of the children put forth its hand and grasped the royal spear. The king was stirred with pity, and, moreover, predicted a great future for the child, and at once ordered it to be lifted out of the pond, and handed over to a nurse, to be brought up with all possible care. And, as the child had been drawn out of a pond, which in their language is called *lama*, it received the name Lamissio.

'Lamissio, when he came to man's estate, proved to be so strong a youth and so apt in war that, upon the death of King Agelmund, he was chosen to guide the helm of the state. It is reported that before his accession, when Agelmund and his people were on their march, they found the passage of a certain river barred by Amazons. It was decided by the two armies that the dispute between them should be settled by single combat between Lamissio and one of the Amazons, a strong swimmer and a stalwart fighter. He surpassed her in swimming, and slew her in the fight, and thus obtained for his people passage across the stream.

'After this, the Langobardi, having crossed the stream and come into the lands beyond, dwelt there for some time in quietness and free from fear. The evil result of this security was seen when, by night, the Bulgarians suddenly fell upon them in their sleep, took and pillaged their camp, wounded many and slew many—among them Agelmund, their king, whose only daughter they carried off into captivity.

'On the death of Agelmund, as has been already said, Lamissio became king of the Langobardi. A young man, of eager soul, prompt for war, and longing to avenge the death of his benefactor Agelmund, he turned his arms against the Bulgarians. At the beginning of the first battle the Langobardi showed their backs to the enemy and sought refuge in their camp. Then Lamissio, seeing this, in a loud voice cried out to the whole army, bidding them remember the shame which they had before endured at the hands of these very enemies—their king slain, and his daughter, whom they had hoped to have for their queen, miserably carried off into captivity. He exhorted them to defend themselves and their families with their arms, saying it was better to die than to live as vile slaves, subject to the insults of such despicable foes. With threats and with promises he hardened the minds of his people for the fight, offering liberty and great rewards to any man of servile condition whom he saw forward in the fray, and thus, by his words and by his example (for he fought in the forefront of the battle), he so wrought upon the minds of his men that they at length made a deadly charge upon the enemy, whom they utterly routed, and wrought great slaughter upon them, thus avenging the death of their king. The great spoil which they gathered from this battle-field made them thence-forward keener and more bold in seeking the labours of war.

'On the death of Lamissio, LETHU was crowned the third king of the Langobardi. After he had reigned about forty years, he died, and was succeeded by his son HILDEOC; and on his death GUDEOC took the kingdom.

'In the reign of this, the fifth king of the Langobardi, happened that great overthrow of the Rugians and their king, Feletheus, by Odovacar, which had been foretold by the blessed Severinus, on account of the wickedness of Gisa, the Rugian queen. Then the Langobardi, going forth from their own regions, entered Rugiland (as the country of the Rugians was called in their language), and there, as the soil was fertile, they remained for several years.

'During this interval Gudeoc died, and was succeeded by CLAFFO, his son, and, on his death, TATO, his son, seventh king of the Langobardi, ascended the throne. Then the Langobardi, going forth from Rugiland, dwelt in the wide plains which are called, in barbarian speech, *Feld*. And as they were tarrying in that place, for a space of three years, war arose between Tato and Rodulf, king of the Heruli.'

We have now reached the point at which the two streams, of Roman-written history and of Lombard Saga, fall into one. The war between King Tato and King Rodulf is narrated by Procopius as well as by Paulus, and can be assigned without much risk of error to a definite date, A.D. 511 or 512.

In reading these early pages of Lombard history as narrated by their churchman-chronicler, one is forcibly impressed by the general similarity which they bear to the history of the Goths, as told by their churchman-chronicler, Jordanes. We have in both the same curious blending of Teutonic tradition and classical mythology, the same tendency to digress into geographical description, the same hesitating treatment of the legends of heathenism from the standpoint of Christianity. But there is one great and obvious difference between Paulus and Jordanes. The Gothic historian exhibits a pedigree showing fourteen generations before Theodoric, and thus reaching back very nearly to the Christian era. The Lombard historian gives us only five links of the chain before the time of Odovacar, the contemporary of Theodoric, and thus reaches back, at furthest, only to the era of Constantine. Doubtless this modesty of his claim somewhat increases our confidence in the genuineness of his traditions, since, had he been merely inventing, it would have been as easy to imagine twenty names as five. On the other hand, it seems to show that the Langobardi, 'fierce beyond even German ferocity', a brutal and savage people, had preserved fewer records of the deeds of their fathers, probably had been more complete strangers to the art of writing, than their more civilized Gothic contemporaries. Indeed, even with these latter, signs are not wanting that national consciousness and therefore national memory, were quickened and strengthened, if not altogether called into being, by their contact with the great civilized Empire of Rome.

However this may be, it is quite clear that it is hopeless to get any possible scheme of Lombard chronology out of these early chapters of Paulus. His narrative would place the migration from Scandinavia about A.D. 320, whereas it is certain that the Langobardi were dwelling on the southern shore of the Baltic at the time of the birth of Christ. And conversely he represents Agelmund the first king of the Langobardi, whose place in his narrative makes it impossible to fix his date later than 350, as slain in battle by the Bulgarians, who, as we know from another source, first appeared in Europe about 479. Thus, whatever genuine facts as to the early history of the people may be preserved in these curious traditions, they are like mountains seen through a mist, whose true size and distance we are unable to measure.

The chief of these dimly-discerned facts appear to be:—

(1) The primordial name of Winnili, applied to the nation which was afterwards known as Langobardi. There does not appear to be any motive of national vanity for inventing this change of name, and we may therefore accept it as true, though not coordinated with any other facts with which we are acquainted.

(2) The migration from the island of Scandinavia, by which Paulus appears to mean the southern part of the Swedish peninsula, intersected as it is with many lakes, and standing, so to speak, 'out of the water and in the water'. Few questions are more debated by ethnologists at the present day than this, whether the Teutonic nations are to be deduced from 'the common Aryan home' in Central Asia, or from the lands north of the Baltic: and, as far as the authority of Paulus and Jordanes is of any avail, it must be admitted to make in favour of the latter hypothesis.

3. *Scoringa*, the first home of the Langobards after their departure from Scandinavia, is probably named from a word related to our own word *shore*, and means the territory on the left bank of the Elbe near its mouth. Here is a considerable tract of country which late on in the Middle Ages still bore the name Bardengau, derived from that of the Langobards, and whose chief city, *Bardowyk*, played an eventful part in the history of the early German Emperors, till it was destroyed in a fit of rage by Henry the Lion in 1189.

Mauringa is also, on the authority of the Geographer of Ravenna, connected with the country near the mouth of the Elbe, probably on its right bank.

After this, however, we get into the region of mere conjecture. The hostile tribe of the Assipitti, the successive homes of the Langobard people in Anthaib, Bainaib and Burgundaib, are all matters of debate among the German inquirers who have written on the early history of the Lombards. The settlement of these questions, if settlement be possible, will depend on a minute acquaintance with German place-names and dialectic forms to which I can make no pretension, and therefore, while referring the curious reader to the note at the end of this chapter for a statement of some of the warring theories, I simply recall attention to the fact (hardly sufficiently noticed by some of them) that in the reign of the Emperor Marcus Aurelius, and about the year 166, we have a clear and trustworthy historical statement connecting the Langobards with an invasion of Pannonia. This movement from the Lower Elbe to the Middle Danube is quite accounted for by the facts that the Langobardi were more or less loosely attached to the great Suevic monarchy, which long had its centre and stronghold in that which is now Bohemia, that there was a general convergence of the tribes in Central Germany towards the Danube frontier of the Empire about the time of the Marcomannic War, and that the great migration of the Gothic nation to the Euxine, which was described at the outset of this history, and which probably occurred about the middle of the second century, may well have sucked some of the tribes of the Elbe into its vortex, causing them, if once bent on change, to turn their faces towards the Danube rather than the Rhine.

I see no reason to believe that the Langobardi, having once left the shores of the North Sea and reached the heart of Germany, ever retraced their steps to their old home, though undoubtedly the barbarian wave rolled back foiled from the Pannonian frontier. For the following three centuries, therefore, I prefer to think of them as hovering about the skirts of the Carpathians (perhaps sometimes pressed northwards into the upper valleys of the Oder and the Vistula) rather than as marching back across Germany to the once forsaken Bardengau. The fact that when they are next heard of they are occupying Rugiland, the district on the northern shore of the Danube which faces Noricum, entirely confirms the view here advocated.

As I have said, the fortunes of this obscure and unnoticed tribe for more than three hundred years (from 166 to 508) are a blank, as far as authentic history is concerned. They were subject probably in the fourth century to the rule of Hermanric the Ostrogoth, subject certainly in the fifth century to the rule of Attila the Hun, but are not mentioned by the historians who have written of either monarch. On the fall of the Rugian monarchy (if the statement of Paulus on this subject be correct) they made a successful attempt to obtain a footing on the northern bank of the Danube, opposite the Roman province of Noricum. But, possibly, owing to the consolidation of the power of Theodoric in these regions, they found that they had gained nothing by this movement, and that Noricum itself was still barred against them. They therefore went forth from

Rugiland and took up their abode in some part of the wide plains of Hungary, called by them in their own Teutonic dialect, *Feld*.

Through all the eventful years from 376 to 476 they remained in the second rank of barbarian nations. Other and stronger peoples, the Alamanni, the Thuringians, the Rugians, the Gepidae, the Heruli, ranged themselves close round the frontiers of the Empire, and, often overpassing its limits, watched with hungry eyes the death-throes of the Mistress of the World. The stalwart forms of these nations prevented the little Langobardic tribe from sharing the plunder or the excitement of the strife: and, for this reason doubtless, their name is not written in the Life of St. Severinus or in the letters of Cassiodorus.

But two events, separated by an interval of sixty years, yet displaying many points of similarity to one another, finally broke down this barrier and opened to the Langobardi the full career of rapine and of conquest. These were the war with the Heruli about 508 and the war with the Gepidae which ended in 567. The history of these two wars will now be related, on the joint authority of Procopius and of Paulus.

3.
War with the Heruli.

The tribe of the Heruli, with whom we have already made some acquaintance in the wars of Odovacar and of Belisarius, are a perpetual puzzle to ethnologists. Zeuss, the most careful of all our guides, says of them: 'The Heruli are the most unstable of German tribes and seem to have wandered over well-nigh the whole of Europe. They appear on the Dniester and the Rhine, they plunder in Greece and in Spain, they threaten Italy and Scandinavia'. It is clear that part at least of this 'instability' may be explained by the fact that the tribe was early split up into two great divisions, one of which moved towards the Black Sea, while the other, remaining nearer to the common home of both, eventually made its appearance on the banks of the Rhine. With the western branch of the nation we have no present concern, and only to a very limited extent with the eastern branch, which towards the close of the fifth century appears to have been situated in Hungary on the eastern shore of the Danube, south of the wide '*Feld*' which was occupied by the Langobardi.

Here, from of old, had dwelt the Herulian people, practising a number of strange and savage rites which Procopius (who loathed the race, having often had to endure their unpleasant companionship in camp and garrison) delights to describe to the discredit of their slightly less barbarous descendants. They propitiated their gods with human sacrifices, and the public opinion of the nation was hostile to the prolonged existence of the sick and the aged. As soon as a man found himself sinking into either of these two classes it was incumbent on him to ask his relations with the least possible delay to blot him out from the book of the living. Thereupon a great pile (apparently of pyramidal form) was built with logs of wood: the infirm man was seated on the top of it, and a fellow countryman, but not a kinsman of the victim, was sent up to despatch him with a short sword. When the executioner returned, having effected his purpose, the pious kinsmen set fire to the pile, beginning with the outer circle of logs, and when the whole pile was consumed and the flames had died down they collected their relative's charred bones and hid them in the earth. Not only was this form of *euthanasia* practised by the Heruli: the Hindu custom of *suttee* was also prevalent among them. On the death of a Herulian warrior, his wife, if she wished to preserve her good name, was virtually compelled to feign, if she did not feel, the emotions of a desolate widow, and to die, before many days had elapsed, at her husband's tomb. If instead of this self-sacrifice she chose to continue in life, her character was gone, and she was an object of jeering and derision to the relatives of her husband.

In the course of time the Heruli probably laid aside some of the more repulsive of these savage customs, but they appear to have remained heathens till their disappearance from history. Their power grew greater, and the terror inspired by them was such that many of the nations round them, including the Langobardi, consented to pay them tribute, a mark of subjection, as Procopius observes, unusual among Teutonic nations. At some time during the reign of the Emperor Anastasius, a singular interlude occurred in the savage annals of the Heruli, for it is recorded that having no one to fight with, they laid down their arms and for three years lived in peace. The warriors of the tribe, chafing at this inaction and having no instinct of discipline or subordination, constantly assailed their chieftain Rodulf with taunts and sneers, calling him womanish and soft-hearted. At length, unable any longer to bear these insults, Rodulf determined to make war upon the Langobardi, not alleging any pretext for the attack, but simply asserting that such was his sovereign will. Once, twice, thrice, did the Langobardi send their embassies to dissuade him from the meditated injustice. Submissively they pleaded that they had made no default in the payment of their tribute: yet even the tribute should be increased if the Heruli desired it. Most unwillingly would the Langobardi array their forces against their powerful neighbours, yet they could not believe that God, a single breath of whose power avails to overthrow all the haughtiness of man, would leave them unbefriended if battle was forced upon them. To the humble entreaty and the pious warnings Rodulf returned the same answer, simply driving the ambassadors from his presence with threats, and marching further into the Herulian territory.

At last came the inevitable collision, and Herul and Langobard met in battle-array. At that moment the sky above the Langobardic host was overcast with black clouds, while that above the Herulian army was magnificently clear, an omen (says Procopius) portending certain ruin to the latter nation. But of all this the Heruli took no heed, but, utterly despising their enemies, pressed on, thinking to decide the combat by mere weight of numbers. When, however, the hand-to-hand fight began, many of the Heruli were slain; Rodulf himself fell down dead, and his followers, forgetful of the duty of warriors, fled in headlong haste. Most of them were slain by the closely pursuing Langobardi, and only a few escaped.

Such is Procopius' account of the battle which practically blotted out the Heruli from the list of independent nations. We have another version of the same transactions from the pen of the Lombard historian, and curiously enough it is in many respects a version much less favourable to his people than that which Procopius heard, apparently from the Herulian mercenaries with whom he served in Italy. In the following words Paulus relates the story of the great encounter.

'After the Langobardi had abode in the open *Feld* for three years, war arose, upon the following occasion, between Tato, their seventh king, and Rodulf king of the Heruli. The brother of King Rodulf had gone to Tato for the purpose of cementing an alliance: and when, having accomplished his embassy, he was returning to his own land, it chanced that he passed before the house of the king's daughter who was named Rumetruda. She, beholding the multitude of men and his noble train of followers, asked who that man could be who had such illustrious attendance: and it was told her that the brother of King Rodulf was returning to his land after accomplishing his mission.

Thereupon the maiden sent to beg him to condescend to receive a cup of wine at her hand. He came, as he was asked, in all guilelessness; but because he was little of stature, the maiden looked down upon him in the haughtiness of her heart and uttered words of mockery against him. He, glowing at once with shame and indignation, replied in such wise, as brought yet greater confusion on the maiden. Then she, hot with a woman's rage and unable to repress the passion of her soul, at once set her mind on a wicked revenge. She feigned meekness, she put on a cheerful countenance, and soothing him with more pleasant words, she invited him to sit down and arranged that he should so sit as to have a window at his back. This window, apparently as a mark of honour, but really that his suspicions might not be excited, she had covered with a costly curtain: and then that cruellest she-monster commanded her servants, that when she said 'Mix' (as if speaking to the butler), they should pierce him in the back with their lances. It was done: the cruel woman gave the sign, her unjust commands were accomplished: her guest, pierced with many wounds, fell forward on the earth and expired.

'When these things were related to king Rodulf, he groaned at the cruel death of his brother, and impatient of his grief, burned to revenge so foul a murder. Breaking off, therefore, the league which he had made with Tato, he declared war against him. To be brief: the two armies met in the broad *Feld*. Rodulf drew up his men in battle array: then seating himself in his camp, having no doubt of the coming victory, he began to play at draughts. And in truth the Heruli of that day were well trained in the arts of war and already famous for the manifold slaughter of their foes: although (whether it were for nimbleness in the fight or that they might show their contempt of the wounds inflicted by the enemy) they fought entirely naked, save for a girdle round their loins. The king therefore, trusting without hesitation to the valour of his soldiers, while he comfortably continued his game, told one of his followers to climb a tree which happened to be near at hand, in order that he might have the earliest possible tidings of the victory. At the same time he threatened the man that he would cut off his head if he told him that the Herulian army was in flight. The man saw the ranks of the Heruli give way, he saw them being hard pressed by the Langobardi, but when asked again and again by the king, "How are my Heruli getting on?" always answered, "They are fighting splendidly." Nor did he dare to give utterance to the evil which he beheld until the whole army turned its back to the enemy. Then, at last, he broke forth into speech, "Woe to thee, wretched Herulia, who art chastened by the wrath of the Lord of Heaven!". At these words the king cried in consternation, "Is it possible that my Heruli are fleeing?". The soldier answered, "It is thou, O king, who hast said the word, not I." Then (as is wont to happen in such cases) the king and all his followers, perturbed and doubtful what to do, were sorely smitten by the in-rushing Langobardi, the king himself being slain notwithstanding a brave but fruitless resistance. The fleeing army of the Heruli—so great was the wrath of heaven upon them—when they beheld some green fields of flax, mistook them for lakes [covered with weed], and extending their arms and falling forward upon them as in act to swim were cruelly stricken by the swords of their enemies. When the victory was won, the Langobardi divided among themselves the vast spoil which they found in the enemy's camp : and Tato carried off the standard of Rodulf (which is called in their language *bandum*) and the helmet which he had been accustomed to wear in battle.

'From that time forward the valour of the Heruli so utterly collapsed that they never had a king over them again. The Langobardi, on the other hand, enriched with plunder and increasing their army out of the various nations which they overcame, began of their own accord to seek for occasions of war, and to push forward the renown of their valour in all directions.'

So far the Langobardic Saga as related by Paulus. As before said, it is less favourable to his own people than the story of the Byzantine historian. As a drama of providential retribution it entirely fails, since the cruel and treacherous deed of Rumetruda is left unavenged. It explains, however, some things which are left obscure in the narrative of Procopius. Well might the Herulian king—perhaps himself like his brother of small stature and unmartial appearance—fear the taunts of his subjects if he left that brother's murder unavenged; and well might he, with such provocation to harden his heart, refuse the threefold petition for peace offered by the Langobardi. They, on their part, may very probably have offered a money payment, not so much on account of augmented tribute as by way of *weregild* for the murdered prince, and the triple embassy may have been due to some barbaric bargaining as to what the amount of this *weregild* should be.

Though true in substance, the narrative of Paulus is not literally accurate in saying that the Heruli were kingless ever after this defeat. To lose the institution of kingship, to be without a leader in their glorious wars, was in that age a mark of the last stage of national decay and demoralization, and though this calamity did for a time befall the Herulian nation, the obscuration of the kingly office was only temporary. Procopius1 describes their miserable wanderings to and fro after their defeat by the Langobardi. They settled at first in Rugiland, evacuated as that country was by the Rugians when they went with the Ostrogoths into Italy. Driven thence, as the Langobardi before them had probably been driven, by hunger, they entered Pannonia and dwelt there as subjects of the Gepidae, paying tribute to those hard lords, and grievously oppressed by them. They then crossed the Danube, probably into Upper Moesia (which forms part of the modem kingdom of Servia), and there solicited and obtained permission from the Emperor Anastasius to dwell as his loyal *foederati*. We know, on the excellent authority of the chronicler, Marcellinus Comes, that this reception of the Heruli within the limits of the Roman Empire took place in the year 512, and we may therefore conjecturally assign the great battle between them and the Langobardi to a date a few years earlier, between 506 and 510.

Notwithstanding the hospitality which the Heruli had received from Anastasius, that savage people soon began their usual career of crime and outrage against their civilized neighbours. Anastasius sent an army against them which utterly routed and could easily have destroyed them, but in an evil hour the Emperor and his generals listened to their renewed supplications for mercy and suffered them to live. Procopius, whose bitter words we are here transcribing, regrets this clemency, for he says, 'the Heruli never were true allies to the Romans, and never did them a single good turn.' It is true that Justinian, who renewed the *foedus* with this people, brought them to make an outward profession of Christianity, and spread a little varnish of civilization over their inherent savagery. But they still remained bestial in their morality, fickle in their alliances, and in fact, says the loathing Procopius, 'they are the wickedest of all men, and utter and unredeemed scoundrels'. Before long they again fell out with the Empire, and the occasion of the quarrel was a curious one. They had suddenly conceived the idea that they would be henceforward kingless, and had therefore killed their king Ochon for no imaginable reason, for in truth he hardly deserved the name of king, since any of his subjects might sit down beside him, dine with him, or insult him with impunity. Then finding an absolutely anarchic existence insupportable, they changed their minds again, and sent to Thule for a prince of the blood royal to come and reign over them.

For, after the great catastrophe of the defeat of the Heruli by the Langobardi, certain of the former nation, not brooking the thought of dwelling with diminished might in the Illyrian lands, and cherishing the old national remembrance of their Scandinavian home, had set off under the leadership of men of the royal blood to seek a new habitation by the shores of the Northern Ocean. They had passed through the lands of the Sclavonians, and then, through a great wilderness, had reached the borders of the Warni, and had travelled through their land and through all the tribes of the Danes unmolested by any of these barbarians. Coming thus to the shores of the ocean, they crossed it in their barks and reached the island of Thule, where they took up their abode. Thule (by which Procopius probably wishes to designate not Iceland, but some part of the Scandinavian peninsula) is a marvellously great island, more than ten times the size of Britain, lying far off from it towards the north wind. The land is barren, but thirteen large nations, governed by as many kings, are settled therein. Procopius, though earnestly desiring to visit this remote land, had never in his busy life found opportunity to do so, but he had heard from accurate and trustworthy observers strange histories of the course of nature therein. For forty days, about the time of the summer solstice, the sun never sets over Thule, but appears, now in the eastern heaven, now in the western, and the inhabitants have to measure the day only by the reappearance of the sun in the same quarter where he shone before. Then, at the winter solstice, the sun is absolutely invisible for forty days. Endless night reigns and the inhabitants, cut off from all communication with one another, are plunged in dejection and sorrow. Though the event is of yearly occurrence, they fear each year that the sun will never return to them again; but at the expiration of thirty-five days (measured by the rising and setting of the moon) they send certain of their number to the tops of high mountains to catch a glimpse of his light. When these messengers return with the glad tidings that they have seen the sun, and that in five days he will shine upon them, the inhabitants of Thule give themselves to unbounded rejoicing, and hold, all in the darkness of their land, the greatest of their national festivals.

To this distant region, then, did the Heruli of the Danube send for a king after they had murdered the over-affable Ochon. The first who was chosen died in the country of the Danes, whereupon the ambassadors returned and persuaded Todasius to accept the distant crown. Todasius and his brother Aordus, with two hundred young men of the Heruli, set forth upon the immense journey: but long before they reached the Danubian lands, the fickle and unstable people, deeming it a disgrace to them to accept a king from Thule, had sought and obtained a king, a Herulian named Suartuas, from the Emperor Justinian. Civil war seemed imminent, but when the Arctic claimant had come within a day's journey of his rival, the minds of the people changed again. They all deserted by night to the camp of Todasius, and Suartuas with difficulty and alone, escaped to Constantinople. As Justinian seemed disposed to support his candidate by force of arms, the Heruli joined themselves to the confederacy of the Gepidae, who were at that time, notwithstanding their *foedus*, virtually the incessant enemies of the Empire.

It has seemed worthwhile to follow the fortunes of this remnant of a most savage and unattractive people, as the story illustrates what has been said in an earlier part of this history as to the relation between vigorous royalty and national success, among the Teutonic tribes. The soft and pliable character of Rodulf caused him to be hurried into an unjust war, which he had not sufficient generalship to bring to a successful issue, and the disastrous end of which was fatal to the greatness of his nation. Ruin demoralized the race, and the instinct of national dignity became so deadened that they delighted in flouting the king, the representative of the greatness of the nation, and at length crowned their insults by murdering him. The spasmodic attempts to replace him by pretenders fetched from distant Norway, or begged from haughty Byzantium, all failed, and the nation, kingless, soulless and decayed, sank into a mere appendage to the monarchy of the equally barbarous but more loyal Gepidae.

4.
War with the Gepidae.

Returning to the history of Paulus, we find these two sentences as to the succession to the rude throne of the Langobardi:—

'Tato was, shortly after the war with the Heruli, attacked and slain by his nephew Waccho, who succeeded him. Waccho left a son, the issue of his third marriage, named Waltari, who reigned for nine years. Then Audoin obtained the kingdom, who was succeeded by his son Alboin, the tenth king of the Langobardi'.

We see then that among the triumphant Langobardi also civil war and revolution soon broke out. It was not long after the great victory over the Heruli before king Tato was attacked, defeated, and slain by his nephew Waccho. The son of Tato, Risiulf, and his grandson Ildichis, who became at length refugees at the court of the king of the Gepidae, made apparently frequent attempts to recover the throne of their progenitor, but all these attempts were vain. For thirty years Waccho ruled the Langobardic nation in their settlement on the plains of Hungary, and he seems at last to have died in peace.

The long reign of Waccho is again nearly a blank the Langobardic annals. We are told that he brought the Suavi under subjection to his yoke but it is not easy to see what people are designated by this name. The Suavi, or Suevi, who dwelt in the south-western corner of Germany, called from them Suabia, are much too far off and too much involved in Frankish wars and alliances for any contest between them and the Langobardi to have been likely. More probably we have here another instance of the confusion pointed out in a previous volume between Suavia and Savia: and we are thus being told of the subjugation of the inhabitants of the region between the rivers Drave and Save. Such an event must have occurred after the Ostrogothic monarchy had begun to fall asunder in ruin, since, even in the days of Athalaric, Savia was still administered in his name in accordance with rescripts issued from Ravenna.

In the year 539, when Witigis the Ostrogoth found himself hard pressed by Belisarius, and began, too late, to cast about him for alliances to ward off his impending doom, he sent ambassadors to Waccho, offering him large sums of money if he would become his confederate. This, however, Waccho refused to do, having been, apparently throughout his reign, on cordial terms with the Court of Constantinople. In fact, we can see in the scanty notices concerning this king a determination to strengthen himself by alliances with all his more powerful neighbours, doubtless in order to resist the pretensions, either to dethrone, or to succeed him, which were put forward by the family of his predecessor. He was thrice married; the first time to a daughter of the king of the Thuringians, the second to a daughter of the king of the Gepidae, and the third to a daughter of the king of the Heruli. The last marriage only was fruitful in surviving male issue, but the two daughters of his second marriage were married to two successive kings of Austrasia, Theudebert and Theudebald: and thus these kings, who stood to one another in the relation of father and son, became brothers-in-law in right of their Langobardic wives. When at length Waccho died, probably somewhat advanced in years, he was succeeded by the child of his old age, his son by the Herulian princess Salinga, the boy-king Waltari.

For about seven years the nominal reign of Waltari, lasted, under the administration of the warrior Audoin, and then the young king died. It is distinctly stated that he died of disease, and we have none of those hints of foul play which are so usual when a young king dies and is succeeded by his guardian. Thus did the dynasty of the Lithingi, to which for sixty years or more the rulers of the Langobardi had belonged, cease to reign, and Audoin, father of the mighty Alboin, mounted the throne1.

It seems probable that the reign of Audoin lasted for about twenty years. During the greater part of that time there was a simmering feud between the Langobardi and the Gepidae, ever and anon boiling over into actual war. Mere neighbourhood was reason enough for bloodshed between two tribes so barbarous and so faithless. But in addition, there was the fact that the remnant of the conquered Heruli, henceforth the irreconcilable enemies of the Langobardi, had been received into the Gepid nationality, and there were also two pretenders to the throne of the rival nation, each one seated at the hearth of the hostile king. Ildichis, grandson of Tato, and the last descendant of the illustrious house of the Lithingi, in the intervals of his wanderings, which took him to the Sclavonian country, to Constantinople, even to the court of Totila, found his most abiding home in the palace of Thorisind, king of the Gepidae. On the other hand, Thorisind had himself a rival of whom he was in fear, the young Ustrigotthus, son of his predecessor Elemund, and this. pretender was a refugee at the court of Audoin.

To these two rival nations, whose power was so nearly equally balanced, the friendship and alliance of the great Caesar of Byzantium was a matter of supreme importance, and he was generally disposed to throw the weight of that alliance into the scale of the Langobardi, as slightly the weaker and the more remote of the two undesired neighbours. About the year 547, when the war between Totila and Justinian was dying down to its last embers, and when it was plain that either to hold or to conquer Italy alone was a task almost too heavy for either combatant, a great rearrangement of power took place in the countries under the shadow of the Alps. Without any trouble the Frankish kings took possession of the greater part of Venetia, neither Goths nor Romans being able to withstand them. On the other hand, the Gepidae pressed in from the north-east, resumed possession of their once held and long-coveted city of Sirmium, and spreading themselves thence across the Danube, wrested not from Goths, but from Romans, nearly the whole of the provinces which made up the diocese of Dacia. Irritated by this conduct of a people who still professed to call themselves *foederati* of the Empire, Justinian discontinued the subsidies which he had hitherto allowed them, and, as a counterpoise to the menacing Gepid power, invited the Langobardi across the Danube—not, however, to its southern, but to its western shore— and presented them with the city Noricum of Noricum and other fortresses over against the Pannonian settlements of the Gepidae. This migration, which is generally described as a migration into Pannonia, but which was probably as much into Noricum as into Pannonia, was a most important event in the history of the Langobardic nation. It brought them out of the distant Hungarian plains into the countries which we now know as Styria, Salzburg, and Carinthia. Henceforward the more adventurous huntsmen and warriors of the tribe were constantly scaling mountains from which at least other mountains could be seen that looked on Italy. As Theodosius brought Alaric, so now has Justinian brought the father of Alboin to the threshold of the Imperial land.

It would be a difficult and unprofitable task to endeavour to reduce into their precise chronological order the rude, chaotic struggles which took place between Langobard and Gepid during the reign of Audoin. Procopius gives us one series of facts relating to them, Paulus another; and as neither writer gives us any exact dates, it is impossible to arrange them with any certainty in a consecutive history. A few scenes, however, which illustrate the habits and modes of thought of these barbarians—immeasurably ruder and more anarchic than the Goths, to whom our attention has hitherto been chiefly directed—may here be recorded.

In the first place, at some uncertain date, but probably about the year 550, we have the two tribes, neighbours, and therefore enemies, earnestly desiring to go to war with one another, and fixing a definite time for the encounter. The Langobardi, who knew that they were outnumbered by the Gepidae, sought for a definite alliance with the Romans. The Gepidae, on the other hand, who claimed to be still *foederati* of the Empire, though the *foedus* did not restrain them from occupying Dacia, south of the Danube, and laying waste Dalmatia and Illyricum as far as the city of Dyrrhachium, insisted that the Romans were bound either to give them active assistance, or, at the very least, to stand aside and let them fight their battle with the Langobardi unhindered.

Ambassadors from the two nations arrived at Constantinople and received separate audience from e Justinian. The two harangues are given at great length by Procopius. There is much in them which savours of the Greek rhetorician and which is doubtless invented by him, but some of the pleas urged are so quaint and (in the case of the Gepidae) so impudent that we must believe that they were really uttered by the barbarians.

On the first day the Langobardi spoke. 'We are perfectly astounded' said they, 'at the presumption of these Gepidae, whose, embassy is the deadliest insult they could possibly have inflicted upon you. So long as the Ostrogoths were mighty, the Gepidae, cowering on the other side of the river, sought shelter in the Imperial alliance, received your yearly gifts, and were in all things the very humble servants of the Empire. As soon as the power of the Ostrogoths declined, when they saw them driven out of Dacia while you at the same time had your hands full with the Italian war, what did these faithful allies of yours do? They spurned the Roman rule, they broke all treaties, they swarmed across your frontier, they took Sirmium, they brought its citizens into bondage, and now they boast that they are making the whole of Dacia their own. Yet in their whole history they have committed no more scandalous action than in this embassy which they are now sending you. For as soon as they perceived that we were about to make war upon them, they dared to visit Byzantium and to come into the presence of the prince whom they have so grievously wronged. Perhaps also, in their abundant impudence, they will dare to invite you to an alliance against us, us your faithful friends. Should the condition of such an alliance be the restoration of the lands which they have wrested from you, the Roman gratitude will be due to the real authors of this late repentance, that is to the Langobardic nation. But if they propose to restore nothing, can anything be imagined more monstrous than their presumption?

'These things we have set forth with barbaric plainness of speech, and in unadorned language, quite inadequate to the offence of which we complain. Do you, Sire, carefully weigh our words and decide on such a course of action as shall be most for the interest, both of the Romans and of your own Langobardi. Especially remember this most important point, that in things pertaining to God we are at one with you in faith. The Gepidae are Arians, and for that very reason are sure to go into the opposite camp to yours, but we hold your creed, and have therefore, from of old, been justly treated by the Romans as their friends'.

Thus spoke the Langobardi. On the next day the Gepidae had audience of the Emperor. 'We admit, Sire', said they, 'that he who proposes to a neighbour that he should form an alliance with him, is bound to show that such alliance is just and expedient. That we shall have no difficulty in proving in the present instance. The alliance is a just one, for we have been of old the *foederati* of the Romans, while the Langobardi have only of late become friendly to the Empire. Moreover, we have constantly endeavoured to settle our differences with them by arbitration1; but this, in their braggart insolence, they have always refused till now, when perceiving that we are in earnest and recognizing their weakness they come whining to you for succour. And the alliance with us will be an expedient one, for anyone who is acquainted with the subject knows that in numbers and martial spirit the Gepidae far surpass the Langobardi. If you choose our alliance on this occasion, grateful for your present succour, we shall follow your standard against every other foe, and the abundance of our strength will ensure you victory.

'But then these robbers pretend that Sirmium and certain other parts of Dacia are a sufficient cause of war between us and you. On the contrary, there is such a superabundance of cities and territory in your great Empire, that you have rather to look out for men on whom to bestow a portion of them. To the Franks, to the Heruli, and even to these very Langobardi, you have given such store of cities and fields as no man can number. Relying in full confidence on your friendship, we anticipated your intentions. When a man has made up his mind to part with a certain possession, how much more highly does he value the friend who reads his thought and helps himself to the intended gift (always supposing there is nothing insulting in his way of doing it), than him who passively receives his favour. Now the former is exactly the position which the Gepidae have occupied towards the Romans.

'Lay these things to heart we entreat you. If it be possible, which we earnestly desire, join us with your whole force against the Langobardi. But if that be not possible, stand aside and leave us to fight out our own quarrels'.

So ended the extraordinary harangue of the Gepidae.

After long deliberation, Justinian decided to help the Langobardi, and sent to their aid 10,000 cavalry under the command of John, nephew of Vitalian, and three other officers whose names we have met with in the Gothic wars. The unstable and disorganized Heruli fought on both sides of the contest; three thousand of them, under their king's brother Aordus, helping their hosts the Gepidae, and seventeen hundred under Philemuth holding to their foedus with Rome and following the standards of John. Aordus and a large part of his Herulian army were slain by a detachment of the Imperial troops. Then, when the two rival nations perceived that Justinian's soldiers were really about to appear on the scene, the barbarians' dread and hatred of the great civilized Empire suddenly reassumed its old sway. The Gepid made proposals of peace and amity to the Langobard, the Langobard accepted them without the slightest reference to his Imperial ally; the quarrel was at an end, and the troops of Justinian, drawn far on into the barbarian territory and suddenly left without allies, were in imminent danger of destruction. Apparently they succeeded at length in making good their retreat, but we have no details of their escape, for Procopius leaves their story half-told.

The two nations, united by this patched-up peace, soon drifted again into war. Large bodies of troops, 'many myriads of men,' followed each king into the field. But before the armies were in sight of one another, a strange panic seized on either host. All the rank and file of the Langobardi, all the rank and file of the Gepidae, fled impetuously homeward, disregarding both the threats and blandishments of their leaders. Shame forbade these, the nobles of the nation, to fly; but Audoin, finding himself with only a trusty few around him, and ignorant that the enemy were in precisely the same condition, sent an embassy to Thorisind proposing conditions of peace. The ambassadors, finding this king also with only a staff and without an army, asked what had become of his people. 'They have fled,' was the answer, 'though no man pursued them'. 'The very same thing has befallen us', said the Langobardi. 'Come, then, since this has evidently happened by a Divine interposition to prevent two great nations from destroying one another, let us obey the will of God by putting an end to the war'. And accordingly a truce for two years was concluded between the two kings.

Again, perhaps at the end of this two years' truce, did the Gepid and the Langobard arm for the inevitable strife. Again, as before, both sides sought the help of Justinian, who, alarmed and angry at the conduct of Gepidae in ferrying his Sclavonic and Hunnish enemies across the Danube, and thus laying Thrace and Moesia open to their invasions, first, through fear, made a solemn treaty with that nation (which was ratified by the oaths of ten Senators of Byzantium), and then in his wrath made an equally solemn treaty with the Langobardi and sent an army to their assistance. The leaders of this expedition—Justinian seems, except in the case of Belisarius and Narses, to have shrunk from entrusting one man with the supreme command of an army—were Justin and Justinian, the two sons of Germanus, and great-nephews of the Emperor, Aratius, the Persarmenian, who had served under Belisarius in Italy, Suartuas, once king of the Heruli, who had been thrust aside by the returned wanderer from Thule, and Amalafrid, son of Hermanfrid, king of the Thuringians, and great-nephew of Theodoric. This Thuringian prince had been brought in the train of Witigis from Ravenna by Belisarius, had become a noble in the Court of Justinian and an officer in his army, and his sister had been given in marriage to Audoin, in order to cement the alliance between the Langobardi and the Empire

Of all this many-generalled host only Amalafrid with his *comitatus* reached the dominions of his brother-in-law. The rest of the generals with their troops tarried behind at Ulpiana, to settle in Imperial fashion some theological disputes which had broken out there, probably in connection with the controversy of the Three Chaptersl. Thus it came to pass that in the great, long-delayed and terrible battle between the Langobardi and the Gepidae, the former nation fought practically almost single-handed. They did indeed conquer and destroy multitudes of their foes, but king Audoin, in sending tidings of the victory to Justinian, took care to remind him that he had not fulfilled his duties as an ally, and had ill requited the loyalty with which the Langobardi had sent their soldiers, in large numbers, into Italy to fight under the banners of Narses against Totila. And in fact in that campaign, and at the decisive battle of the Apennines, Audoin himself had been present, as we have already seen, with 2500 warriors attended by their 3000 squires.

However, notwithstanding these complaints, the alliance between Justinian and the now victorious Langobardi lasted for the present unbroken, and the Gepidae, in a depressed and broken condition, suing for peace, were admitted to a humble place in the same confederacy. One condition, however, was needed to cement the alliance, and that was the surrender of the fugitive Ildichis, the last remnant of the old stock of the Lithingi. His life was a perpetual menace to the throne of the intruder Audoin, and, moreover, he had rendered himself obnoxious to Justinian, whose court he had deserted, whose stables he had robbed of some of their most valuable inmates, and whose officers he had slain in a well-contrived night attack on a detachment of the Imperial troops in an Illyrian forest. By both Emperor and King, therefore, the surrender of Ildichis was demanded as that of a common enemy, and the Gepidae were plainly informed that, without the fulfillment of this condition, no durable peace could be concluded with them. But when Thorisind assembled the chiefs of his people, and earnestly entreated their advice on the question whether he should yield to the demand of these two powerful princes, the assembly absolutely refused to entertain the proposition of surrender, declaring that it was better for the Gepidae to perish out of hand with their wives and children, than to consent to so impious an act as the betrayal of a guest and a fugitive. Thorisind, who was brought hereby into a most difficult dilemma, between fear of his victorious neighbours and fear of his own nobles, parried the difficulty for a time by making a counter demand from Audoin for the surrender of his rival claimant, Ustrigotthus, son of Elemund. The Langobard nobles were as unwilling to disgrace themselves by the abandonment of Ustrigotthus, as the Gepid nobles had been to countenance the abandonment of Ildichis, and so for the time both demands were refused, and the negotiation was at an end. A community of interest, however, drew the two usurpers together, and each privately got rid of the other's rival by secret assassination, in a manner so foul, that Procopius refuses to describe it. The whole story is a valuable illustration of the character of Teutonic royalty, the limitations which in theory restrained it, and the means which it practically possessed of rendering those limitations nugatory.

Amid these events Alboin, the son of Audoin by his first wife Rodelinda, was growing up to his memorable manhood. Tall of stature, and with a frame admirably knit for all martial exercises, he had also the strenuous aptitude for war of a born general. In the great battle with the Gepidae which has been already spoken of, while the fortune of war was still uncertain the sons of the two kings, Alboin and Thorismund, met in single combat. Drawing his great broad-sword, the Langobard prince cut down his Gepid rival, who fell from his horse lifeless. It was the sight of the death of this their bravest champion which struck terror into the hearts of the Gepidae and gave the victory and abundance of spoil to the Langobardi. When these returned in triumph to their homes they suggested to king Audoin that the son, by whose valour so conspicuous a victory had been wrought, was surely worthy now to take a seat at his father's table as King's Guest: and that he who had shared the royal peril might justly share in the royal conviviality. 'Not so', replied the tenacious king, 'lest I violate the customs of our nation. For ye know that it is not according to our manners that a king's son should dine with his father, until he has received his arms from the king of some foreign people'.

When Alboin heard these words of his father he took with him forty young men of his *comitatus* and rode to the court of Thorisind, his father's recent foe. Having explained the object of his visit, he was courteously received and placed at the king's table in the seat of honour on his right hand. But Thorisind, though he thus complied with the laws of barbaric courtesy and recognized Alboin's right to claim adoption at his hands, was filled with melancholy when he saw the slayer of Thorismund sitting in

Thorismund's seat. In one of the pauses of the long banquet he heaved a deep sigh and his grief broke forth in words :

'That place is to me ever to be loved, but the person who now sits in it is grievous to behold.'

Stirred by these words of his father, the king's surviving son began to taunt the Langobardi with clumsy sarcasms, derived from the white gaiters which they wore wrapped round the leg below the calf. 'You are like stinking white-legged mares', was the insult addressed to his father's guest by the Gepid prince. One of the Langobardi hurled back the taunt: 'Go,' said he, 'to the plain of Asfeld. There you will find out plainly enough how those mares can kick, when you see your brother's bones, like those in a knacker's yard, scattered over the meadows'. At these words the Gepidae started up trembling with rage: the Langobardi clustered together for defence: all hands were at the hilts of the swords. The king, however, leaped up from the table and threw himself between the combatants, threatening terrible vengeance on the first of his subjects who should begin the fray, and declaring that a victory earned over his guests in his own palace would be abomination in the sight of God. With these words he at length allayed the storm, and Gepid and Langobard returned with smoothed brows to the wassail bowl, the guttural-sounding song, and all the joys of the interrupted banquet. Thus did Alboin receive from Thorisind the arms of the dead Thorismund, and returning to his home was welcomed as a guest at his father's table, all voices being raised in praise of Alboin's valour and the faith—it is hard not to write the knightly faith—of Thorisind.

About ten years after these events (if we have read the chronology aright) Audoin died, and Alboin, on whom the nation's hopes were fastened, ascended the throne. Thorisind had meantime been succeeded by Cunimund, who was perhaps a brother of the deceased king of the Gepidae.

It was by a new political combination and by the aid of an altogether new actor on the scene, that the long duel between the two nations was terminated. In the closing years of the reign of Justinian, a fresh horde of Asiatics, apparently of Hunnish origin, but who assumed the name of Avars—a name which for some reason was already terrible—entered Europe, menaced the Empire, extorted large subsidies from the aged Emperor, and even penetrated westwards as far as Thuringia, bent on battle with the Frankish kings. These rude successors of Attila's warriors did, in fact, erect a kingdom far more enduring than his, for it was not till the close of the eighth century that the power of the Avars received its death-blow from the hands of Pippin, son of Charles the Great. The head of this barbarous race bore the title of Chagan (Khan), and the first Chagan of the Avars was named Baian. With him Alboin made a compact of a curious kind, and one which seems to show that hatred of the Gepidae had blunted the edge of the land-hunger of the barbarian. 'Let us combine to crush out of existence these Gepidae, who now lie between your territories and mine. If we win, yours shall be all their land and half of the spoils of war. Moreover, if I and my people cross over the Alps into Italy and conquer that land, all this province of Pannonia wherein we now dwell shall be yours also'. The league was made : the combined invasion took place: Cunimund heard that the terrible Avars had burst the barrier of the Eastern Carpathians, then that the Langobardi had crossed the Danube and the Theiss and were assailing him from the west. Broken in spirit and in sore distress from the difficulties of his position1 he turned to fight against the older and more hated foes. 'Let us fight,' said he to his warriors, 'with the Langobardi first, and if we vanquish them we shall without doubt drive the Huns forth out of our fatherland'. The battle was joined. Both sides put forth all their strength, and the Langobardi with such success and such fury that of all the Gepid host scarce one remained to tell the tale of his nation's overthrow.

Alboin himself slew Cunimund in a hand-to-hand encounter, and, like the untutored savage that he was, cut off his head and fashioned his skull into a drinking-cup, which ever after at solemn festivals was handed to the king full of wine, and recalled to his exultant heart the memory of that day's triumph.

Nor was this the only trophy carried from the land of the Gepidae to the palace of Alboin. His first wife, Chlotsuinda, daughter of the Frankish king Chlotochar, had died, and Rosamund, daughter of Cunimund, was selected by the conqueror to fill her place at the high-seat beside him. What seemed to the barbarians vast stores of wealth, taken from the Gepid dwellings, enriched the Langobardic homes. The Gepidae, on the other hand, were so depressed and enfeebled that they never thenceforward dared to choose a king of their own, but dragged out an inglorious existence either as subjects of the Langobardi, or in their own fatherland under the hard yoke of the brutal Avars.

Such was the fate of the third nation in the Gothic confederacy, which so many centuries ago, in its laggart ship, made the voyage from Scandinavia to the Livonian shore.

NOTE A.
On the Early Homes of the Langobardi.

In order not to encumber the text with the theories of German scholars on this subject, I insert the chief of them here.

I. *Zeuss* (*Die Germanen und die Nachbarstämme*) is so careful an enquirer, and is so well acquainted with the details given us by Greek and Roman geographers as to all the German tribes, that one always differs from him with reluctance.

He seems inclined to make Mauringa = the flat country eastward from the Elbe, connecting it with *Moor* and other kindred words. For *Golauda* he takes an alternative reading (not well supported by MS. authority), Rugulanda, and suggests that it may be the coast opposite the isle of Rugen. *Anthaib* is the *pagus* of the Antae who, on the authority of Ptolemy and Jordanes, are placed somewhere in the Ukraine, in the Dniester and Dnieper countries: *Banthaib* he gives up as hopeless, *Burgundaib* he connects with the Urugundi of Zosimus, whom he seems inclined to place in Red Russia, between the Vistula and the Bug. These names, he thinks, 'lead us in the direction of the Black Sea, far into the eastern steppes' and he connects this supposed eastward march of the Langobardi with their alleged combats with the Bulgarians.

II. Dr. Friedrich *Bluhme*, in his monograph 'Die Gens Langobardorum und ihre Herkunft' (Bonn, 1868), places the primeval home of the Langobardi in the extreme north of Denmark, in the peninsula or rather island formed by the Limfiord, which still bears the name *Wend-syssel*. (This he connects with the original name of the tribe, Winnili.) Thence he brings them to Bardengau on the left bank of the Elbe. I think he accepts the identification Scoringa = Bardengau. He places the Assipitti (the tribe who sought to bar the further progress of the Langobardi) in the neighbourhood of Asse, a wooded height near Wolfenbüttel. He rejects the identification of Mauringa with Holstein, and the reference to the Geographer of Ravenna, and thinks that we have a trace of the name in Moringen near Northeim, at the foot of the Harz Mountains. But he makes them wander still further westwards and Rhinewards, chiefly relying on the passage of Ptolemy, which places them in close neighbourhood with the Sigambri. He considers this allocation to be singularly confirmed by the *Chronicon Gothanum,* which says that they stayed long at Paderborn. Thus he contends for a general migration of the tribe from Eastphalia (Bardengau) to Westphalia; and considers this theory to be strengthened by the great resemblance between the family names of Middle Westphalia and those of Bardengau: between the legal customs of Soest (in Westphalia) and those of Lübeck, and between these two sets of customs and the Lombard Edict.

Bluhme does not offer much explanation of the difficult names Golanda, Anthaib, Banthaib, and Burgundaib, except that he thinks the last was the territory evacuated by the Burgundians when they moved westwards to the Middle Rhine. He puts the migration of the Langobardi to the borders of Bohemia about 373, and thinks that the election of their first king Agelmund was contemporary therewith. He observes that the ruins of the palace of king Waccho (who reigned at the beginning of the sixth century) were still to be seen at Beowinidis, i. e. in Bohemia, probably at Camberg, S.E. of Prague, in the year 805 *(Chronicon Moissiacense)*

Rugiland—Moravia. Feld=the March-feld bordering it on the south.

NOTE B.
Extract from the Codex Gothanus.

The opening and closing paragraphs of the Codex Gothanus are so utterly different from the Origo and the history of Paulus, that, instead of attempting to weave them into one narrative therewith, I prefer to give a separate translation of them here.

'1. The fore-elders of the Langobardi assert "per Gambaram parentem suam pro quid exitus aut movicio seu visitatio eorum fuisset, deinter serpentibus parentes eorum breviati exissent', a rough and bloody and lawless progeny. But coming into the land of Italy they found it flowing with milk and honey, and, what is more, they found there the salvation of baptism, and receiving the marks of the Holy Trinity, they were made of the number of the good. In them was fulfilled the saying, "Sin is not imputed where there is no law". At first they were ravening wolves, afterwards they became lambs feeding in the Lord's flock: therefore should great praise and thanks be brought to God who hath raised them from the dung-hill and set them in the number of the just, thereby fulfilling the prophecy of David, "He raiseth the needy from the dung-hill, and maketh him to sit with the princes of the earth". Thus did the aforesaid Gambara assert concerning them (not prophesying things which she knew not, but, like the Pythoness or Sibyl, speaking because a divine visitation moved her), that "the thorn should be turned into a rose". How this could be she knew not, unless it were shown to her by God. She asserts, therefore, that they will go forth, moved not by necessity, nor by hardness of heart, nor by the oppression of parents, but that they may obtain salvation from on high. It is a wonderful and unheard-of thing to behold such salvation shining forth, when there was no merit in their parents, so that from among the sharp blades of the thorns the odorous flowers of the churches were found. Even as the compassionate Son of God had preached before, "I came not to call the righteous, but sinners" [to repentance]. These were they of whom the Saviour Himself spoke in proverbs [parables] to the Jews, "I have other sheep, which are not of this fold: them also I must bring to seek for the living water".

'2. Here begins the origin and nation or parentage of the Langobardi, their going forth and their conversion, the wars and devastations made by their kings, and the countries which they laid waste.

There is a river which is called Vindilicus, on the extreme boundary of Gaul: near to this river was their first dwelling and possession. At first they were Winili by their own proper name and parentage: for, as Jerome asserts, their name was afterwards changed into the common word Langobardi, by reason of their profuse and always unshaven beards. This aforesaid river Ligurius flows into the channels of the river Elbe, and . loses its name. After the Langobardi went forth, as has been before said (?), from the same shore, they placed their new habitations at first at Scatenauge on the shore of the river Elbe: then still fighting, they reached the country of the Saxons, the place which is called Patespruna, where, as our ancient fathers assert, they dwelt a long time, and they encountered wars and dangers in many regions. Here too they first raised over them a king named Agelmund. With him they began to fight their way back to their own portion in their former country, wherefore in Beovinidis they moved their army by the sound of clanging trumpets to their own property : whence to the present day the house and dwelling of their king Wacho still appear as signs. Then requiring a country of greater fertility, they crossed over to the province of Thrace, and fixed their inheritance in the country of the city (sic) of Pannonia. Here they struggled with the Avars, and waging many wars with them with most ardent mind, they conquered Pannonia itself. And the Avars made with them a league of friendship, and for twenty-two years they are said to have lived there'.

From this point to the accession of Rothari, a.d. 636, the text of the Codex Gothanus coincides very nearly with that of the Origo. It then proceeds as follows:—

'7. Rothari reigned sixteen years: by whom laws and justice were begun for the Langobardi: and for the first time the judges went by a written code, for previously all causes were decided by custom (*cadarfada*) and the judge's will, or by ordeal (?) (*ritus*). In the days of the same king Rothari, light arose in the darkness: by whom the aforesaid Langobardi directed their endeavours to the canonical rule and became helpers of the priests'.

[8 contains the durations of the kings' reigns from Rodwald to Desiderius].

'9. Here was finished the kingdom of the Langobardi, and began the kingdom of Italy, by the most glorious Charles, king of the Franks, who, as helper and defender of lord Peter, the prince of the Apostles, had gone to demand justice for him from Italy. For no desire of gain caused him to wander, but he became the pious and compassionate helper of the good: and though he might have demolished all things, he became their clement and indulgent [preserver]. And in his pity he bestowed on the Langobardi the laws of his native land, adding laws of his own as he deemed fit for the necessities of the Langobardi: and he forgave the sins of innumerable men who sinned against him incessantly. For which Almighty God multiplied his riches a hundredfold. After he had conquered Italy he made Spain his boundary: then he subdued Saxony: afterwards he became lord of Bavaria, and over innumerable nations spread the terror of his name. But at last, as he was worthy of the Empire's honour, he obtained the Imperial crown; he received all the dignities of the Roman power, he was made the most dutiful son of lord Peter, the apostle, and he defended Peters property from his foes. But after all these things he handed over the kingdom of Italy to his great and glorious son, lord Pippin, the great king, and as Almighty God bestowed the grace of fortitude on the father, so did it abound in the son, through whom the province of Thrace (!), together with the Avars, was brought into subjection to the Franks. They, the aforesaid Avars, who were sprung from a stock which is the root of all evil, who had ever been enemies of the churches and persecutors of the Christians, were, as we have said, by the same lord Pippin, to his own great comfort and that of his father, expelled and overcome: the holy churches were defended, and many vessels of the saints which those cruel and impious men had carried off, were by the same defender restored to their proper homes. Then the cities of the Beneventan province, as they deserved for their violation of their plighted oath, were wasted and made desolate by fire, and their inhabitants underwent the capital sentence. After these things, he also went to Beowinidis (?) with his army and wasted it, and made the people of that land a prey, and carried them captive. Therefore also by his orders his army liberated the island of Corsica, which was oppressed by the Moors. At the present day by his aid Italy has shone forth as she did in the most ancient days. She has had laws, and fertility, and quietness, by the deserving of our lord [the Emperor], through the grace of our Lord Jesus Christ. Amen'

CHAPTER IV.

ALBOIN IN ITALY.

Thus have we followed the fortunes of the Langobardi, or, as I shall now for convenience call them, the Lombards, from their dim original on the shores of the Baltic, till they stood on the crest of the Julian Alps, looking down with lustful eyes on the land which had once been the Mistress of the World, but which now lay all but defenceless before them.

We may briefly summarize all that can be ascertained of their social and political condition on the day when, according to the Saga, the messengers of Narses appeared in Alboin's banqueting hall, bearing the grapes and the oranges of Italy. There is some difference of opinion as to the ethnological position of the Lombards. One German scholar, who, by his life-long devotion to philological study, claims our respectful attention, contends strongly for their Low-German character, basing his argument, not only on the traditions mentioned in the previous chapter, which connect them (in his opinion) with the Danish peninsula, but also (which is more especially interesting to us) on the extraordinary correspondence of Lombard words, customs and laws with those of the Anglo-Saxons. Another and younger authority (following, it is time, in the train of the venerable Jacob Grimm) says, in somewhat haughty tone, 'That the Lombards belonged to the West Germans, and to the High-German branch of that people, no one can now any longer deny'. Both he and Grimm were led to this conclusion chiefly by the High-German character of the Lombard names and the few relics which have been preserved to us of the language. The gift of the bridegroom to the bride, which was called in Low-German *Morgen-gabe*, is in the Lombard laws *morgin-cap*; the Anglo-Saxon *Alfwine* is apparently the same name as the Lombard Alboin; the judge who, in Gothic, is called *sculdhaita*, is, among the Lombards, *sculdhaizo*; and so with many other words. In all these the Lombard language seems to affect that form which, according to Grimm's well-known law, marks the High-German (say the Swabian or Bavarian) manner of speech, rather than the Low-German, which was practised by Goths, Frisians and Angles.

Where such authorities differ, it would be presumptuous in the present writer to express an opinion, but I may remark that to me the philological facts seem modified to correspond in a remarkable degree with what we have already learned from our authorities concerning the early history of the people. We have in the Lombards, as I venture to think, a race originally of Low-German origin, coming from the coasts and islands of the Baltic, and closely akin to our own Anglo-Saxon forefathers. So far, the case seems clear; and probably the Lombards spoke a pure Low-German dialect when they dwelt in Bardengau by the Elbe, and when they fought with the Vandals. But then, by about the middle of the second century after Christ, they gravitated towards the great Suevic confederation, and visited, in its train, the lands on the Middle Danube, where (if I read their history aright) they remained more or less persistently for nearly four hundred years.

This surely was a long enough time to give a Suevic, that is a Swabian or High-German, character to their speech, sufficient time for them to change their B's into P's, their G's into K's, and their T's into Z's, before they emerged into the world of book-writing and book-reading men.

Of the dress and appearance of the Lombards at the time of their invasion of Italy we have a most precious trace in the words of their great historian, and here again that connection, so interesting to us, between them and our own forefathers, comes into view.

'At Modicia,' says Paulus, 'queen Theudelinda built a palace for herself [about the year 600], in which she also caused some representation to be made of the deeds of the Lombards. In this picture it is clearly shown how at that time the Lombards cut the hair of their heads, and what was their dress, and what their habit. For, in truth, they made bare the neck, shaving it up to the back of the head, having their hair let down from the face as far as the mouth, and parting it on either side from the forehead. But their garments were loose and for the most part made of linen, such as the Anglo-Saxons are wont to wear, adorned with borders woven in various colours. Their boots were open almost to the extremity of the great toe, and kept together by crossing boot-laces. Later on, however, they began to use hosen, over which the riders drew waterproof leggings. But this fashion they copied from the Romans'. Would that the chroniclers of the early Middle Ages would more often have furnished us with details like these as to the dress and habits of the people! They would have been more valuable than many pages of controversy on the 'Three Chapters', or even than the usual notes of miracles, eclipses, and displays of Aurora Borealis, which are found in their annals.

Politically the organization of the Lombard people was evidently rude and barbarous. To use a phrase of the which has lately come into fashion among German historians, the tendency of political life among them was centrifugal rather than centripetal. The institution of kingship was imperfectly developed. There does not appear to have been any single family, like the Amals among the Ostrogoths or the Balthae among the Visigoths, towering high above the other noble families, and claiming the veneration of the people by the right of long descent. A king arises among them, and perhaps succeeds in transmitting his royal power to one or two generations of his descendants; but then there is a murder or a rebellion, and a member of an entirely different clan succeeds to the throne. Nor, for many generations, do any national leaders give proof of political genius or constructive statesmanship. Mere lust and love of plunder appear to be the determining motives of their ware. They produce no Alaric, with his consciousness of a divine mission to penetrate to the Eternal City; no Ataulfus and no Theodoric, longing to preserve the remnants of Roman civilization by the arms of the barbarian; no Gaiseric, able to stamp his own impress on the nation from which he sprang, and to turn the foresters of Pannonia into the daring mariners of Carthage. Everything about them, even for many years after they have entered upon the sacred soil of Italy, speaks of mere savage delight in bloodshed and the rudest forms of sensual indulgence; they are the anarchists of the *Volkerwanderung*, whose delight is only in destruction, and who seem incapable of culture. Yet this is the race from which, in the fullness of time, under the transmuting power of the old Italian civilization, were to spring Anselm and Lanfranc, Hildebrand and Dante Alighieri.

It is probable that the destructive ferocity of the invaders was partly due to the heterogeneous character of their army. For not only the Lombards, strictly so called, followed the standards of the son of Audoin. Twenty thousand Saxons (perhaps from the region which was afterwards called Swabia), mindful of their old alliance with the Lombards, came at Alboin's call to help in the conquest of Italy, and brought their wives and children with them, intending to make it their home1. Moreover in that motley host there were Gepidae, who had lost their own national existence, but were willing to help their victors to sack the cities of Italy; there were Bulgarians from the Lower Danube, Sarmatians or, as we should say, Sclaves from the plains of the Ukraine, and a mass of men of various nationalities (perhaps including the remnants of the Rugian and Herulian peoples), who called themselves after the provinces in which they dwelt—the men of Pannonia, of Savia, and of Noricum. Two centuries later, the names of these non-Lombard tribes were still preserved in some of the villages of Italy. At the time which we are now considering, it is easy to understand how the mixed character of the entering multitude may have added to the horrors of the invasion. Each barbarous tribe among the Germans had, so to speak, its own code of morality, as well as its own peculiar national vices; but when they were all united for one great ravaging inroad into the rich lands of the South, we can well believe that each tribe would contribute its worst elements to the common stock of savagery; the cruelty of one, the treachery of another, the lustfulness of a third, becoming the general character of all.

Among those loosely-connected nationalities, there were probably some which were still actually heathen. The Lombards, however, appear to have generally professed that Arian form of Christianity which, as we have seen, was common to nearly all the Teutonic invaders of the Empire. Of the time and manner of their conversion (if we may apply so noble a name to so slight and superficial a change) we know nothing.

Their Arianism, though it was sufficiently pronounced to make a chasm between them and the orthodox inhabitants of Italy, does not seem to have been of a militant type, like the bitter Arianism of the Vandals. Apparently they were not sufficiently in earnest about their faith to persecute its opponents; but, whether they were Arians or heathens, the divergence of their religion from that of the Roman provincials was excuse enough for sacking the churches, carrying off the costly communion chalices, and slaying the priests at the altar.

The muster of this manifold horde of barbarians was completed in the early spring of 568, and, on the second of April in that year, the day after Easter Sunday, Alboin set forth. He marched (if local tradition may be trusted), not precisely by the same road which Alaric had trodden before him, by Laybach and the Pear-tree Pass, but went somewhat higher up the valley of the Drave, near to the site of the modem city of Villach, and crossed the Julian Alps by that which is now known as the Predil Pass. A high hill rises here, to the southward of the road, which, at least from the eighth century onwards, has borne the name of the King's Mountain, for thither, it is said, the Lombard leader climbed, and from its height looked backward over the long train of his followers—the horsemen, the slowly moving waggons, the dusty foot-soldiers; and then, straining his eyes over the sea of hills to the south of him, he saw the longed-for Italy.

The march of the invader through the province of Venetia seems to have been practically unopposed. He reached the banks of the Piave and looked, it may be, towards the lagoons on the south-eastern horizon, where the descendants of the refugees from the wrath of Attila were leading their strange amphibious lives between the Adriatic and the mainland. But no message either of peace or war came to him from Torcello or Murano, and no Patrician from Ravenna stood ready to dispute his passage of the Piave. Only Felix, bishop of Tarvisium (Treviso), met the Lombard king and besought him to leave untouched the property of his church. The easy success of the invasion thus far had made Alboin generous. He granted the bishop's request, and ordered a charter to be prepared (called in the grand Byzantine style a Pragmatic) safeguarding all the rights and privileges of the church of Treviso.

Vicenza and Verona were conquered without difficulty, and now the whole province of Venetia, with the exception of Padua, Monselice and Mantua (to which must be added of course the little settlement in the Venetian lagoons), accepted the yoke of the invader.

It was probably while Alboin was spending the winter of 568-9 in one of the conquered cities of Venetia, that he took measures for closing the door by which he himself had entered Italy, against any future invader. With this purpose in view he appointed his nephew Gisulf first duke of Forum Julii. This city, now called Cividale, was the chief place of the district which still bears its name under a slightly altered form, that beautiful land of Friuli, whose barrier Alps are so memorable a feature in the northeastern horizon when we are looking forth from the palaces of Venice. Gisulf, whom he selected as duke of this outpost-country, was not only nephew of Alboin but also held the position of Master of the Horse in his uncle's household, a title which in the Lombard language was expressed by the word *Marpahis*. But though already famous for his warlike deeds, even he feared to undertake the onerous duty of guarding the passes of the Julian Alps, unless he might choose his retainers from among the pick of the Lombard army. To this condition Alboin assented, and some of the noblest and bravest *farae*, or kinships, of the Lombards were chosen to follow the standards of Gisulf and to settle under his government in the plains of Friuli. He also asked for and obtained a large number of the king's best brood-mares, that from them might spring the swift horses of his border-cavalry. As our historian's own lineage was derived from these Lombards of Friuli it is doubtless with a touch of family pride that he tells us of the foundation of this aristocratic colony.

The progress of the Lombard invaders was steady and rapid. In 569 Alboin overran the province 0f Liguria. Milan, so long the residence of the emperors, the city of Ambrose and of Theodosius, opened her gates to him on September 3, and all the cities of Liguria, and the neighbouring province of Alpes Cottiae, save Ticinum and those which were situated on the sea-coast, followed her example. From the day of the conquest of Milan, Alboin seems to have assumed the title of 'Lord of Italy' and from this event he dated the commencement of his reign.

As a rule we hear little of the resistance either of Byzantine garrisons or of citizens loyal to the Empire in any of these cities of Upper Italy. Nor, notwithstanding the general character for ferocity borne by the invaders, do we hear any particulars as to deeds of cruelty wrought by them after the capture of such cities. Possibly the very weakness of the garrisons and the panic terror of the inhabitants, caused by the reports which they had heard of Lombard barbarity, made the invaders' victory easy and inclined their hearts to mercy.

The one marked exception to this facility of conquest was afforded by the great city of Ticinum, or (to use the name which it acquired under Lombard domination) Pavia. This city, so strongly placed in the angle between the Ticino and the Po, was probably held by a numerous imperial garrison, and resisted the barbarian attack for more than three years. Alboin pitched his camp on the western side of the city and turned the siege into a blockade. Exasperated by its long and stubborn resistance, the king vowed that when he had taken it, he would put every one of the inhabitants to the sword. But when at length, doubtless owing to the pressure of hunger, the citizens surrendered, the cruel vow was recalled, owing to one of those strange occurrences in which Alboin, like Attila before him, read a marvel and a portent. The Lombard king in all his pride was riding in at the eastern gate of the city, the gate of St. John, when suddenly his horse fell in the middle of the gateway. Neither the spurs of his rider nor the spears with which he was abundantly beaten by the king's retinue availed to make him rise. Then one of the Lombard soldiers cried aloud, 'Remember, my lord the king! what manner of vow thou hast vowed. Break that cruel promise and thou shalt enter the town. For of a truth it is a Christian people that dwells in this city'. Alboin accepted his follower's counsel, recalled his vow and promised that none of the inhabitants should be harmed. Then the horse arose, and he rode on through the streets of the famine-stricken city to the palace built by the great Theodoric, where he took up his abode. The people, hearing of the cancelled vow, flocked to the palace to utter their joyful acclamations. Life, even under the savage Lombard, was sweet, and food was delightful after the years of hunger, and they let into their hearts a hope of better days to come after so many miseries which they had endured.

The city which had been able to make so long a defence was evidently worth holding. Pavia became, though perhaps not at once, the capital of the Lombard monarchy and the place of deposit of the royal hoard.

The three years from 569 to 572 were by no means exclusively occupied with the siege of Pavia. Alboin probably left the conduct of that operation to one of his trusted officers, while he himself with the mass of his followers wandered, ravaging and conquering, over northern and central Italy. We lack any precise chronological statement of his career, but we may conjecture that in the year 570 he completed (with a few exceptions, afterwards to be noted) the conquest of the valley of the Po, and that in 571 he crossed the Apennines and began the conquest of Tuscia and Umbria, of the Aemilian and Flaminian provinces. In the same year, as is generally believed, others of the Lombards pushed down through central to southern Italy, and by their conquests laid the foundation of the two great Lombard duchies of Spoleto and Benevento.

It was of great assistance to the cause of the invaders that they early obtained possession of Bologna, of Forum Cornelii (or Imola), and of the great fortress which guarded the tunnel-pass of Furlo. This latter fortress they burned to the ground, doubtless in order to prevent its again falling into the hands of the Imperialists and blocking the communication between north and south. If the reader will turn back to the previous pages of this history, in which the wars between the Ostrogoths and the Empire were recorded, he will see of what capital importance to the invading nation was the possession of these strongholds which guarded the great Flaminian Way, the main artery of traffic between the two centres of Imperial authority, Rome and Ravenna. It might seem as if communication between these two cities, except by sea, must have been henceforth entirely suspended: but the strong town of Perugia on its rocky perch still held out for the Emperor, and probably by means of this city, through difficult mountain roads, his faithful servants may have travelled between the two capitals.

To enumerate the conquests of the Lombards in these years would be to give a mere list of the chief cities of northern and central Italy. It will be more. the purpose to give the names of the principal cities which were yet held by the Empire. In Venetia, as already said, Padua and Monselice were still Imperial. Mantua fell to the Lombards, probably in the lifetime of Alboin, though we have no precise details of its capture and though it was soon reconquered by the Empire. In the valley of the Po, Cremona and Piacenza were still 'Roman': on the western coast, Genoa and probably several other cities of the Riviera: on the eastern, Ravenna and the five cities which formed the

Pentapolis (Rimini, Pesaro, Fano, Sinigaglia and Ancona); in central Italy, Perugia; in Latium, Rome itself and a certain, not very large, extent of territory round it; in southern Italy, Naples, Salerno, Paestum, and nearly all the towns of the province of Bruttii.

It will be seen that practically, with the single exception of Perugia, all the places of which the Empire retained possession were either on the sea-coast (like Genoa and Ancona), or surrounded by water (like Mantua), or accessible by a navigable river (like Cremona and Piacenza). On the other hand, the Lombards, an inland people, accustomed to traverse the high Alpine passes of Pannonia and Noricum, held the central ridge of the Apennines, from whence they swooped down at their pleasure upon the weakly garrisoned fortresses of Tuscia and Liguria. The invasion was thus—strange as the comparison would have seemed to the priests and 'Levites' of the Roman church—analogous to that which had occurred more than two thousand years before at the eastern end of the Mediterranean, when, under the leadership of Joshua, a nation, not less dreaded than the Lombards, came from over Jordan to occupy the high table-land of central Palestine, and to wage a war of generations with the more highly civilized inhabitants of the maritime plain, the citizens of the Philistine Pentapolis and the Canaanites of the Zidonian strand.

The victories of Alboin and his horde were doubtless somewhat aided by the terrible physical calamities which about this time afflicted Italy. Already, before the recall of Narses (probably about the year 566), a fearful pestilence had raged, chiefly in the province of Liguria. Its special symptom was the appearance on the patient of boils, about the size of a nut, the formation of which was followed by fever and intolerable heat, generally ending on the third day in the death of the sufferer. The Lombard historian draws a dismal picture of flocks deserted in the pastures, of farm-houses, once teeming with peasant life, abandoned to silence or only tenanted by troops of dogs: of parents left unburied by their children, and children by their parents. If some one, mindful of the ancient kindness between them, devoted himself to the burial of his neighbour, he would most probably himself fall to the ground plague-stricken and remain unburied. The harvests in vain expected the reaper's sickle : the purple clusters hung on the vine till winter drew nigh. An awful silence brooded over the fields where the shepherd's whistle and the sportsman's eager tread were alike unheard. And yet more dreadful than the silence were the sounds of a ghostly trumpet, the mysterious tramp of unseen multitudes which were heard at night by the solitary rustics who lay awaiting their doom1. This pestilence, as Paulus expressly tells us, was one cause of Alboin's easy victories : and another was the famine which raged in 570, following a year of extreme plenty in 569. This plenty was itself the result—so it was considered—of an abundant snowfall during the previous winter which had given the plains of Italy the semblance of the snow-fields of the Alps.

The career of Alboin had been brilliant and successful; in its savage style not unworthy to be ranked with the career of Alaric or of Attila, but it was destined to an even speedier ending than theirs. There were perhaps unextinguished jealousies and rivalries of the barbarian races under his command, which may have contributed to the fatal result, but the sagas of his nation—in which women had already played a leading part—attributed his death solely to the rage of an insulted woman. And thus the story was told:—

On a certain day (probably in the spring of 572) the king sat at the banquet in his palace-hall at Verona. Having drunk too freely of the wine-cup he bade bring forth the goblet which was fashioned out of the skull of king Cunimund; that same goblet, adorned with goodly pearls which near two centuries later the Lombard historian saw on a day of feasting exhibited by king Ratchis to his guests. He bade the cup-bearer carry this goblet (fashioned as it was out of her own father's skull) to queen Rosamund and invite her to drink merrily with her sire. The queen, it would seem, obeyed with no outward manifestation of repugnance, but in her heart she determined on a terrible revenge. With this intent she sought the aid of Helmechis the *scilpor* or armour-bearer of the king, and his foster-brother. She promised him her hand, she held out to him the dazzling prospect of the Lombard crown, and Helmechis entered into her treacherous designs. Only he stipulated that Peredeo, the chamberlain, should be made an accomplice in the plot. Doubtless Peredeo's help was indispensable to its successful execution, but also there may have been some reluctance on the part of Helmechis to strike the actual death-stroke against his foster-brother, and for this reason he may have desired to enlist the strong arm of Peredeo in the service of the infuriated queen. The chamberlain, however, when Rosamund sought to enlist his services in her scheme of revenge, refused to be partaker of so great wickedness. But he did not warn his master of the danger impending over him, and the queen, taking advantage of an intrigue between Peredeo and one of her waiting-women, by the sacrifice of her own honour, forced the unwilling chamberlain into a position in which he must either join the plot or be denounced to Alboin as the seducer of his wife. Peredeo chose the former alternative, and from that moment the success of the conspirators was assured. When Alboin had retired for his noon-tide slumber, a great silence was made all round his bedchamber; the tramping sentinels were, as we may suppose, removed by order of the chamberlain; and on some pretence or other the arms which hung in the room were taken away. Then, as Helmechis had counselled, the queen brought in Peredeo himself to strike the fatal blow. Suddenly aroused from slumber, Alboin stretched forth his hand to grasp the sword which always hung at his bed's head, but this by the cunning of the conspirators had been so tightly tied to its sheath that he could not draw it. He snatched up a footstool and for some time valiantly defended himself, but fell at last under the strokes of the assassins.

'Thus,' says Paulus, 'did that most warlike and courageous man, who had earned so great fame in war by the slaughter of multitudes of his foes, fall like a Nithing in his chamber by the stratagem of a miserable woman. His body, amid the abundant tears and lamentations of the Lombards, was buried under a certain flight of stairs which joined hard to the palace. He was tall of stature and his body was well knit for all warlike deeds. Now this tomb of his was opened in our own days by Giselpert, who had been duke of Verona, and who took away his sword and all the adornments that he found therein. Wherefore he was wont to boast with his accustomed folly, when he was surrounded by ignorant persons, that "he had seen Alboin".'

The hopes which Helmechis had entertained that he might be chosen king of the Lombards proved utterly vain. Instead of that elevation, he and the partners of his crime soon found that they must save themselves by flight from the vengeance of the kingless people. A secret message was conveyed to the Patrician Longinus, at Ravenna, who sent a ship to facilitate their escape. Helmechis and Rosamund, now husband and wife, went on board the Byzantine vessel, taking with them all the royal treasure and Albswinda, the daughter of Alboin by his first wife, a Frankish princess. Longinus, who, though the representative of the majesty of the Empire in Italy, achieved nothing for the defence of the peninsula that has been deemed worthy of notice by historians, showed himself an eager accomplice in the schemes of murderers and adulterers. He suggested to

Rosamund that she should rid herself of her newly-wedded husband and marry him. To the Gepid princess the temptation to become 'Lady of Ravenna' presented irresistible attractions; while to the Patrician the barbarian hoard, as well as the wicked loveliness of the barbarian bride, was doubtless an object of desire. When Helmechis was reclining in the *frigidarium* after enjoying the luxury of a Roman bath, his wife presented him with a goblet filled, as she averred, with some healthful potion. He drank half of the draught: then knowing himself to be poisoned, he stood over Rosamund with a drawn sword and compelled her to drink the remainder. Thus did the two guilty lovers die together, and the tragedy of Alboin's murder, which had begun with a cup of death at Verona, ended with a yet deadlier death-cup at Ravenna.

Albswinda was sent by the Patrician with the great Lombard hoard to Constantinople. There may have been some thought of keeping the daughter of Alboin as a hostage for the good behaviour of her father's people, but her name does not meet us in any subsequent negotiations, and she henceforth disappears from history.

There was a legend (for the truth of which our historian does not vouch) that Peredeo also was carried captive to Constantinople, and there, in the amphitheatre, slew a lion of marvellous size in the presence of the Emperor. Fearing lest a man of such great personal strength should work some damage to 'the royal cities,' the cowardly Emperor ordered him to be blinded. In the course of time he managed to provide himself with two sharp knives, and having secreted these in the sleeves of his mantle, he visited the palace and asked for an interview with the Augustus, asserting that he had some important secret to communicate. He was not, however, as he had hoped, admitted to the actual presence of the Emperor, but two counsellors, high in rank, came to learn his secret. As soon as he felt that they were before him, he went close up to them, as if to whisper his portentous news, and then at once struck right and left such fatal blows, that the two counsellors fell dead upon the spot. 'Thus, like Samson, he avenged his own cruel wrong, and for his two eyes of which he had been bereft, deprived the Emperor of two of his most useful counsellors'. Like Samson also, if there be any truth in the story, the revenge of Peredeo was, no doubt, fatal to its author.

CHAPTER V.

THE INTERREGNUM

The death of Alboin occurred, as has been already said, in the spring of the year, and that year was probably 572. The Lombard warriors, assembled, after some interval, at Pavia, which was perhaps, now for the first time, recognized as the capital of the new kingdom, chose Cleph, 'of the race of Beleo', one of the most nobly born among them, to be their king.

Of Cleph we really know hardly anything beyond his own name and that of his wife Masane. It is probable, though not distinctly stated, that, previous to his elevation to the throne, he was Duke of Bergamo. His rule bore hardly on the old Roman aristocracy, many of whom he slew with the sword, while he banished others from their native land.

At the end of eighteen months, that is, probably about the middle of 574, king Cleph was slain with the sword by a slave in his own household, whom he had probably exasperated by his overbearing temper.

Again the leaders of the Lombard nation were assembled at Pavia, but this time their meeting did not result in the choice of a king. King Cleph had left one son, Authari, who was apparently of tender years. The usual expedient of a maternal regency was probably not acceptable to a barbarous and warlike people. The chief nobles seem to have been all of nearly equal rank and power, so that it was difficult to single out one for supreme dominion. The debate (possibly a long and angry one) ended in a decision to elect no king, but to divide the royal power between the thirty-six chief nobles, who are known in history as the Lombard Dukes.

It was remarked, in an earlier chapter of this history, that the titles of Duke and Count came into the political vocabulary of Mediaeval Europe out of the Roman Imperial system, but were transposed on the way; 'Duke' being in the Middle Ages, as in modem times, always a title of higher honour than Count (or Earl), whereas in the *Notitia Utriusque Imperii*, *Comes* is a higher rank than Dux. Under the Empire both offices had to do with military administration, but the Comes had generally a larger or more important sphere of duties than the Dux, and in some cases the Comes of a diocese had directly under him the Duces of the various subordinate provinces.

It was probably through the German invaders of the Empire that the change in the relative value of the two titles was introduced, and, as far as we can trace it, the process of thought which led to that change seems to have been something like this. The word Dux, as implying him who led forth a tribe or a nation to battle, was chosen as the equivalent of *Heretoga*, or whatever might be the precise form then in use of the modem German *Herzog*. On the other hand, *Comes* (which, after all, meant only companion, and so might be applied to any member of a king's *comitatus* or band of henchmen) was chosen as the equivalent of the German *Graf*. This was an officer who probably did not exist when the Teutonic tribes were still in their native forests, but whom we meet with in the early Frankish State as the king's representative (exercising judicial as well as military functions) in the larger cities of Gaul.

The etymology of the two words seems to point to the conclusion indicated above. *Heretoga* is without doubt the leader of the host. The derivation of *Graf* is more doubtful, but one of our best German authorities thinks that it can be traced to a root denoting 'a companion'. However this may be, the meaning of these titles among the Teutonic invaders of the Empire is clear. Duke (*Dux*, *Herzog* or *Heretoga*) is a man who is looked upon as the natural leader in war of a nation or a large tribe. He is sometimes perhaps the descendant of earlier kings, and has only stooped to the condition of a Duke when his tribe lost its independence and became merged in some larger national unity. In other cases he has been chosen by some process of popular election or even by lot. At any rate he is no mere delegate of the king; but from old memories, as well as by right of his present power, he has a strong tendency to make the dukeship hereditary in his family, and even to break the bond of subordination which attaches him to royalty. Thus we get the Dukes of the Bavarians, the Saxons and the Swabians, who are already, in Merovingian times, not far short of sovereign princes. How unlike these great nobles are to the modest Duces of the 'Notitia', it is needless here to indicate.

On the other hand, the Count (*Garafio*, *Graf* or *Comes*) is at this period always essentially the king's representative. He governs a city, such as Tours, or Bourges, or Poitiers, acting as judge as well as administrator therein, and when summoned to do so, bringing that city's contingent of soldiers to swell the royal army. He often governs his city very badly—the counts who confront us in the pages of Gregory of Tours are for the most part grasping and unscrupulous barbarians—but, whether well or ill, he always governs it as the king's representative. He has generally a life-tenure of the office (differing herein from the easily displaced Roman *comes*), but he does not apparently, as yet, cherish any hope of making it hereditary. He shines by the reflected light of the king's dignity, having no inherent lustre of his own, whether derived from old traditions of kingship or from recent popular election.

After this little digression, it will be easier for us to understand the position of the Dukes at this period of Lombard history—a position to which, I think, we may safely assert there was nothing analogous in the Visigothic kingdom of Spain, or in the Frankish kingdom of Neustria.

Among the thirty-six Lombard dukes who were now about to share between them the sovereignty of Italy, six appear to have held somewhat higher rank than the others. These were Zaban, or Zafan, at Pavia, a second Alboin, or Alboni, at Milan, Wallari at Bergamo, Alichis at Brescia, Euin at Trient, and Gisulf at Friuli. Among these six, Zaban, as duke of Pavia, now the recognized Lombard capital, held the highest place, and was, to borrow a term from much more modern politics, President of the Lombard Confederation.

The form which this Teutonic aristocracy assumed deserves special attention, for it is, in a certain sense, typical of the whole mediaeval history of Italy. These Lombard leaders, fresh from the forests of Pannonia or the wide pastures of the *Feld*, were, doubtless, essentially men of the country; men who, like the old Scottish chief, 'would rather hear the lark sing than the mouse chirp'. Thus did Tacitus write of their ancestors, five centuries before the time with which we are now dealing: 'It is well known that none of the German tribes live in cities, nor can they even bear houses in a row. They dwell scattered and solitary, as a spring, a meadow or a grove may have taken the fancy of each'. Yet these rustic warriors, having come into the land of stately cities, at once succumbed to their fascinations, and became dwellers in cities themselves. Of course, military considerations, as well as sensual delights, determined such a change. The cities of Italy were there, erected at every point of vantage, covering the passage of rivers and the entrance into valleys; and, if they were not to be all levelled with the ground, it was needful that they should be held by Lombard garrisons. Still, whatever the cause, the result is clear and important. We see that the civic character of Italian life has conquered even its rough Pannonian conquerors. Lordship now, and for many long centuries in Italy, will be essentially lordship of a city. The Lombard dukes are turning the page on which great feudal nobles like the Estes, and clever and successful 'tyrants' like the Medici, will write their names in the centuries to come.

Historians have not informed us what were the thirty cities from which the lesser dukes took their titles. Probably a pretty correct idea concerning them may be derived from a study of the list of the Episcopal sees of Northern and Central Italy. We may also safely assume that the duke of a city governed, not only the city itself, but a certain extent, sometimes a pretty large extent, of surrounding country. Here also we have an anticipation of mediaeval geography, of the time when 'the Milanese', 'the Trevisan', 'the Bolognese', were well-known descriptions of territory.

The rule of these mailed aristocrats was, as might have been expected, hard and grasping, animated by the narrowest ideas of Lombard patriotism. Many of the Roman (that is, native Italian) nobility were slain by the sword, simply that their possessions might go to enrich some hungry Lombard warrior. The rest were reduced into a condition of semi-serfdom, still holding their lands, but only on condition of paying over one third of their produce to that one of the unwelcome 'guests' to whom they had been assigned. Harsh as this measure of spoliation was, the impoverished 'host' might console himself with the reflection that it might have been worse. Following the precedent set by Odovacar and Theodoric, the Lombards contented themselves (as has been said) with one third of the produce of the soil, while the Visigoths had taken two thirds, and the Burgundians a proportion varying between that fraction and a half.

Not only, however, did the refined Roman land-owner feel the weight of Lombard oppression in these years when there was no king in Italy. Among the barbarous tribes who had flocked to Alboin's standard, to share in the plunder of Italy, was a band of some 20,000 or 30,0003 Saxons, who had brought with them their wives and children, intending to settle in the conquered land. To their great disgust, however, they found that their confederates would only suffer this on condition of their abandoning the laws and customs of their fathers and becoming altogether subject to Lombard rule.

The decision of the Saxons was soon and firmly taken : that they would abandon their new settlements and march back, with their families, to the home of their forefathers, rather than abandon their Saxon nationality. The story of their return, though it does not strictly belong to the history of Italy, is worth studying for the light which it throws on the manners of the times, and the thoughts of the wild barbarians who had streamed into Italy.

The land to which the Saxons wished to return was, apparently, the country afterwards known as Swabia, and formed part of the dominions of Sigibert, the Frankish king of Austrasia. The Saxons adopted a peculiar method of recommending themselves to the favour of their new sovereign. Crossing the Cottian Alps by the Col de Genèvre, they poured down into the plains of Dauphiné, and pitched their camp there. The rich villas were sacked; the inhabitants were carried captive; everywhere they spread desolation and ruin. The brave Romano-Gallic general, Mummolus, to whom Guntram, the Frankish king of Burgundy, had entrusted the defence of this region, came upon them suddenly, found them unprepared, and slaughtered them till nightfall. When morning dawned, it seemed as if the battle would be renewed, but messengers arrived in the camp of Mummolus, bearing rich presents, and offering, on the part of the Saxons, to surrender all their booty if only they might be allowed to repass the Alps into Italy. The offer was accepted, and the Saxon warriors, as they marched away, declared that they meant to return, not as the foes, but as the loyal subjects of the Frankish kings.

Next year (apparently) the Saxons, finding their Lombard hosts inflexible, collected their wives and children and again marched into Gaul. They had divided themselves into two 'wedges', one of which marched along the Riviera to Nice and the other by the old road into Dauphiné. It was the time of the ingathering of fruits, and everywhere around them they saw the golden sheaves standing in the fields and all the fatness of the fruitful land. The simple barbarians, like felons let loose in London, could not keep their hands from plunder. They gorged themselves and then their horses with the crops of the peasants of Dauphiné, and they even set fire to some of the villages. But when they reached the banks of the Rhone, they found the terrible Mummolus ready to execute judgment upon them.' You shall not pass this stream', he said, 'till you have made satisfaction to my lord. See how you have laid waste his kingdom, have gathered the crops, trampled down the oliveyards and vineyards, slain the flocks, cast fire into the houses. You shall not pass till you have made atonement to those whom you have reduced to poverty. Otherwise I will put your wives and little ones to the sword, and will avenge the injury done to Guntram my king'. The brutal Saxons quaked with terror, paid down many thousand golden solidi for their redemption, and were suffered to march on into the kingdom of Sigibert1 on the east of the Rhine.

When they reached their old homes they found them filled up with Swabians, whom Sigibert had planted there when they themselves had started for Italy. The angry Saxons at once declared that they would sweep the intruders from the face of the earth. 'Take a third of our lands', humbly pleaded the Swabians; but the offer was indignantly refused. 'Half?'. 'Two thirds?'. 'We will add all our cattle if only we may have peace'. Every proposition that could be made was contemptuously spurned by the Saxons, who, confident of victory, were already dividing among themselves by anticipation the wives and property of the hated Swabians. 'But the mercy of a just God,' says Gregory, 'turned their thoughts into another direction. Of 26,000 Saxons who joined battle on that day, 20,000 were slain; of 6,000 Swabians only 480, and victory remained with their comrades. The survivors of the Saxons swore a great oath that they would cut neither hair nor beard till they had avenged them of their foes. But when they again rushed to battle they only incurred deadlier slaughter: and so at length there was rest from war'.

In the great work which lay before the Lombard nation, the conquest of the Italian peninsula and the expulsion of the officials who represented the majesty of the Eastern Augustus, but little progress was made by the confederated dukes. It is true that they were able grievously to harass the clergy and citizens of Rome. Already in 574 (perhaps before Cleph's assassination) such swarms of Lombards surrounded the Eternal City that communication with Constantinople was cut off, and after the death of Pope John III (13 July) more than ten months elapsed before his successor, Benedict I, could be chosen. Famine followed in the steps of the marauding invaders. Hearing of the sufferings of the Roman citizens from hunger, the Emperor Justin ordered a fleet of corn to sail from Egypt to the mouth of the Tiber. By this time the severity of the Lombard blockade must have been relaxed, for the mariners were able to ascend the Tiber and bring the longed-for relief to the hungering citizens.

In the year 575 a great Byzantine official appeared at the head of an army in Italy. This was Baduarius, the son-in-law of the Emperor and Count of the Imperial Stables. He had shortly before been strangely insulted by Justin, whose long latent insanity was then beginning to show itself openly. The Emperor ordered his chamberlains to assault and buffet his son-in-law and then to drag him into the wondering Consistory, while still bearing the marks of their blows. Sophia, having heard of this outburst of frenzy, was much distressed thereat and administered conjugal reproof to her husband. He too, now that the paroxysm was over, repented of his violence and sought Baduarius in the stables to make his apologies. When the Count of the Stables saw the Emperor approaching he feared that he was about to repeat his outrages and leaped from manger to manger in order to escape. But the Emperor adjured him in God's name to abide where he was, went up to him, caught him by the arm and covered him with kisses. 'I have sinned against thee', said he, 'but it was at the Devil's prompting. Now I pray thee receive me again as thy father and thy Emperor'. Then Baduarius fell at the Emperor's feet, which he watered with his tears, and said, 'My lord! in thy hands is supreme power over all of us : but as thou didst once treat thy servant contemptuously in the presence of thy counsellors, so now let these dumb creatures' (pointing to the horses) 'be witnesses of thy confession'. Whereupon the Emperor invited him to a banquet, and so he and his son-in-law were reconciled. This was the man who was now sent to try conclusions with the Lombards. We hear, however, very little of the course of the campaign, except that Baduarius was overcome by them in battle and shortly after ended his life

Again in 579 a vacancy in the Popedom is the cause of our being informed of that which was probably at this time the chronic condition of the regions round Rome, Lombard ravage and blockade. After a little more than four years' occupancy of the Papal throne Benedict I died and was succeeded by the Roman Pelagius (second of that name), who was ordained without the command of the Emperor, because the Lombards were besieging the City of Rome, and much devastation was being wrought by them in Italy. At the same time so great rains fell that all men said that the waters of the deluge were returning upon the earth, and so great was the loss of human life that the oldest inhabitant remembered nothing like it aforetime.

In their distress the citizens called upon the Emperor, their natural protector, for help. Two embassies, apparently in the years 577 and 579, bore to the New Rome the lamentable cry of the Old. The first was headed by the Patrician Pamphronius and carried a tribute of 3,000 pounds weight of gold (about £120,000 sterling); the second consisted of senators and ecclesiastics, one of the latter class being probably the man who was to be afterwards the world-famous Gregory the Great.

Neither embassy obtained the military help which was so urgently required. The Persian war pressed heavily on the resources of the state, and a somewhat feeble, though well-intentioned, ruler was at the helm. For in the year after his strange encounter with Baduarius the madness of Justin II assumed so outrageous a form that it was deemed necessary to confine him to his palace and to associate with him Tiberius a colleague who bore the humbler title of Caesar, but who was in reality supreme governor of the Empire. The new Caesar bore the ill-omened name of Tiberius, but was in character as unlike as possible to the suspicious and secluded tyrant of Capri. Open-handed and generous to a fault, he shocked his Imperial patroness Sophia by the profusion with which he lavished his treasure on the poor; but he was rewarded for his munificence, as was told in a previous chapter, by the opportune discovery of the buried hoards of the eunuch Narses. This good-tempered, but not strenuous monarch, before the second embassy reached Constantinople, had become in name as well as in fact supreme Augustus, by the death of his brainsick colleague Justin II. In neither capacity, however, could he be persuaded to send any adequate supply of soldiers for the deliverance of Italy, but, true to his character as a giver, he sent money—in the first case returning the tribute brought by Pamphronius—which money was to be employed in buying off individual Lombard dukes, or, if that resource should fail, in hiring Frankish generals to lend their arms for the liberation of Italy.

The policy thus pursued was not altogether ineffectual. Both on this and some later occasions Byzantine gold was found efficacious in detaching some members from the loosely-knit Lombard confederacy. Farwald, duke of Spoleto, who had probably hitherto taken the lead in the ravages of Roman territory, seems to have, in some measure, withdrawn his forces from her immediate neighbourhood. But it was only the recoil before a deadlier spring. It was probably in the year 579 that Farwald with his Lombards appeared before the town of Classis, the sea-port of Ravenna. We are not told how long a resistance it offered, but it was eventually taken and despoiled of all the treasures which had been accumulated within its walls during six centuries of security. After the sack the Lombards seem still to have held on to the city, hard as it was to do so in the face of the superior naval forces of the Empire.

The chief events of the Lombard interregnum that remain to be noticed relate to the Lombard invasions of Gaul. Some of these invasions were made in the lifetime of Alboin and therefore should strictly have been described in the preceding chapter, but in order to give a continuous narrative I have purposely reserved them for this portion of the history.

It has been well pointed out by a German historian that these attacks on their Frankish neighbours were utterly senseless and impolitic, mere robber-raids caused by nothing else than the freebooter's thirst for plunder. The one object which a Lombard statesman, whether he were called duke or king, should have set before himself was to consolidate the Lombard rule in Italy, to drive out the last representatives of the Empire, if possible to become master of the sea. Instead of firmly pursuing this aim, scarcely had the Lombards entered Italy when they began to swarm over the difficult passes of the Alps, to rob and ravage in Dauphiné and Provence. Thus did they make the old feud between themselves and the Franks, which a few generations of peaceful neighbourhood would perhaps have obliterated, an indelible national instinct, and, in fact, they thus prepared the levers which at length, after the lapse of two centuries, brought about the ruin of the Lombard monarchy at the hands of Frankish Charles.

When we were last concerned with Frankish history we reached the point where the divided monarchy was reunited by Chlotochar I. We must now glance at the well-known events which intervened between that reunion and the commencement of the Lombard interregnum.

For three years Chlotochar, the last surviving son of Clovis, reigned over the whole of the vast territory which had been won by the Frankish battle-axe. In 561 he died, and his kingdom was divided between his four sons. But the fourfold partition now, as in the previous generation, soon became threefold. Charibert, the king of Paris, died in 5672, and thus the well-known sentence of Caesar, 'Gallia est omnis divisa in partes tres,' was again true of Gaul and remained true for the rest of the century. It is true that, whatever might be the ostensible partition of the Gaulish territory, it was more and more tending to group itself into four—not three—great divisions, namely, Neustria, Austrasia, Burgundy and Aquitaine. But the last of these, the territory between the Loire and the Pyrenees, the territory which had been won from Alaric the Visigoth, and which was one day to give the Plantagenet princes their great vantage-ground for the conquest of France, was during the latter part of the sixth century so split up and so squabbled over by the lords of the other portions, that, for the sake of clearness, it will be well to leave it out of sight altogether. Let us briefly consider the three other divisions and their rulers.

I

BURGUNDY

The region which still bore the name of Burgundy was substantially that which had obeyed the shifty Gundobad and his unwise son, Sigismund. It embraced the later provinces of Burgundy, Franche Compté, Dauphiné, the greater part of Switzerland, Lyonnois, Nivemois and a considerable part of Languedoc. It was, in fact, 'the kingdom of the Rhone', including almost the whole territory watered by that noble river and its tributaries except—a notable exception—that thin strip of fruitful territory at the mouth of the Rhone which still bore the name of *Provincia*, and still keenly remembered that it had been the first and the last of the Roman provinces in Gaul. Though the nucleus of the new kingdom was the old Burgundian domain it included some lands in the centre of Gaul, south and west of the Loire, which had never belonged to the Burgundians, and the king's capital was Orleans, a city which had never owned the sway of Gundobad. The king of this territory, from 561 to 593, bore the uncouth name of Guntchramn, a name for which I will venture to substitute, as many have done before me, the easier form, Guntram. A good-tempered, easygoing man, who was not cruel, except when his interests seemed to call for cruelty, a man who took and put away wives and concubines with great facility, but was almost a moral man by comparison with the unbridled licentiousness of most of the Merovingian kings, Guntram has, by reason of his generosity to the Church and the comparative respectability of his character, obtained the honours of canonization, though it is not often that we meet with an historian sufficiently attentive to the rules of ecclesiastical etiquette to call him *Saint* Guntram.

Our Lombard historian, Paulus, describes Guntram as 'a peaceful king and one conspicuous by all goodness'. He then proceeds to tell concerning him a story which he had probably heard at Chalon-sur-Saone in the course of his travels through France, and which, as he states with a thrill of self-satisfaction, not even Gregory of Tours had related in his voluminous history of the Franks :—

'The good king Guntram went one day into the forest to hunt, and as his companions were scattered in various directions, he was left alone with one faithful henchman, on whose knees he, being weary, reclined his head and so fell fast asleep. From his mouth issued a little reptile, which ran along till it reached a tiny stream, and there it paused, as if pondering how to cross it. Then the henchman drew his sword out of its scabbard and laid it over the streamlet, and upon it the little creature crossed over to the other side. It entered into a certain cave of a mountain not far from thence, and returning after an interval again crossed the streamlet by the sword and re-entered the mouth of the sleeper. After these things Guntram, awaking from slumber, said that he had seen a marvellous vision. He dreamed that he crossed a river by an iron bridge, and entered a mountain in which he saw a vast weight of gold. Then he in whose lap his head had lain told him in their order the things which he had seen. Thereupon the king commanded an excavation to be made in that place, and treasures of inestimable value, which had been stowed away there in ancient days, were found therein. From this gold the king afterwards made a solid canopy of great size and weight, which he adorned with most precious stones, intending to send it to the sepulchre of the Lord at Jerusalem. But as he could not do this, he ordered it to be placed over the shrine of the blessed martyr Marcellus, at Cavallonum (Chalon-sur-Saone), and there it is to this day, a work incomparable in its kind'. As I have said, it was probably from the priests in the chapel of the martyr that Paulus, in his travels, heard the marvellous tale.

Treasures buried in long departed days by kings of old, mysterious caves, reptile guides or reptile guardians—are we not transported by this strange legend into the very atmosphere of the Nibelungen Lied? And if the good king Guntram passed for the fortunate finder of the Dragon-hoard, his brothers and their queens, by their wars, their reconciliations and their terrible avengings, must surely have suggested the main argument of that most tragical epic, the very name of one of whose heroines, Brunichildis, is identical with the name of the queen of Austrasia.

II
AUSTRASIA

This kingdom of Austrasia, the eastern land, the name of which first meets us about this time, is the same region with which we have already made acquaintance under the government of the Frankish Theodoric and his descendants; a region extending, it may be roughly said, from Rheims to the Rhine, but spreading across the Rhine an unknown distance into Germany, claiming the allegiance of Thuringians, Alamanni, and Bavarians, fitfully controlling the restless Saxons, touching with warlike weapons and sometimes vainly striving with the terrible Avars.

The capital of this kingdom was Metz—it is noteworthy how these royal partners always strove to fix their seats as near as possible to the centre of Gaul, as if to keep close watch on one another's designs—and the son of Chlotochar who reigned there as king was Sigibert.

Sigibert was the youngest, but the most capable and least vicious, of the royal brotherhood. Disgusted at the profligacy of all his brothers, who disgraced themselves by adulterous unions with the handmaids of their lawful wives, he determined to wed a princess of his own rank, and accordingly he wooed and won Brunichildis, daughter of Athanagild, the Visigothic king of Spain. A brave and high-spirited woman, Brunichildis, in the course of her long and strong career, became hard and unpitying as the rocks upon which she was dashed by the waves of her destiny; but the ten years of her union with Sigibert were the brightest portion of her life. The young Austrasian king and queen seem to have loved one another with true and pure affection, and their story is an oasis in the desert of Frankish profligacy and shame.

III
NEUSTRIA

The kingdom of Chilperic (who was half-brother to his three royal colleagues) is generally spoken of as the realm of Neustria. This name strictly belongs to a somewhat later period than that which we have yet reached, but as 'the western kingdom', in antithesis to Austrasia, it conveniently expresses the territory ruled over by Chilperic, which was in fact the old kingdom of the Salian Franks, and comprised the Netherlands,

Picardy, Normandy, and Maine, with perhaps some ill-defined sovereignty over the virtually independent Celts of Brittany. The capital of this kingdom was the ancestral seat of dominion, Soissons.

Chilperic's character is one of the strangest products of the strange anarchic period in which he lived. Cruel, lustful, avaricious—a man whom the kindly Gregory calls 'the Nero and Herod of our time'—he nevertheless was, after the fashion of his age, a religious man—wrote sacred histories in verse, after the manner of Sedulius (it is true that his hexameters limped fearfully)—composed masses and hymns, and wrote a treatise on the Trinity, which he hoped to impose, Justinian-like, on his bishops and clergy, but the theology of which was so grossly heretical, that the prelates to whom he showed it could hardly be restrained from tearing it in pieces before his face.

Chilperic had already taken to himself many mistresses, whom he dignified with the name of wives; but when he heard of the rich and lovely young princess whom his younger brother had won for his bride, he was seized with jealousy, and vowed that he too would have a princess for his wife. An embassy to Athanagild, bearing the promise of a rich dower for the future queen in case she survived her husband, and an assurance that the palace should be purged of the concubines who then polluted it, was successful in obtaining the hand of a sister of Brunichildis, named Galswintha. The princess, who might almost seem to have had some forebodings of the dark fate reserved for her, clung to her home and her parents, and begged for delay; but the ambassadors insisted on her immediate return with them. State reasons prevailed, and the weeping Galswintha set forth upon her long journey, accompanied by her fond mother as far as the Pyrenees. There the mother and daughter parted; and the latter journeyed in a kind of triumphal procession through Gothic Gaul, and then through the territory of her future husband, till she reached the city of Rouen. She was received with all honour by Chilperic, by whom she was loved with great affection, 'for' (says Gregory) 'she had brought with her great treasures'. On the day after the marriage, according to old Teutonic custom, he gave her as 'moming-gift' (*morgane-gyba*) Bordeaux and four other cities in the south-west of Gaul. These were to form her dower in case she survived her husband.

For a short time all went well. Then one of concubines, Fredegundis, succeeded in recovering her lost footing in the palace; the king's old passion for her was rekindled, and the poor young Spanish bride was made to suffer daily insults and mortifications, such as, eleven centuries later, her countrywoman, the queen of Louis XIV, had to endure when she saw Montespan or La Vallière preferred before her. With pitiful pleading, Galswintha besought that she might leave her treasures behind her and return across the Pyrenees. Chilperic soothed her with kind words, but not many days after she was found dead in her bed, strangled by a slave, in obedience her husband's orders. The royal hymn-writer professed to mourn for her for a few days, and then married Fredegundis.

The wedding, the murder, the second marriage, all happened in the year 567. And now began that long duel between two beautiful and angry queens which for thirty years kept the Frankish kingdoms in turmoil. Of Brunichildis I have already spoken. She was not by nature cruel, and might, perhaps, have passed through life with fair reputation, had not the longing for vengeance, first for a murdered sister, and then for a murdered husband, transformed her nature and turned her into a Fury. Fredegundis, evil from the first, utterly remorseless and cruel, had yet a magnetic power of attracting to herself those whom she would make the ministers of her wicked will. She ruled her husband with absolute sway, though strongly suspected of unfaithfulness to her own marriage vows. And whenever there was a rival to be disposed of, a brother-in-law, a step-son, a dangerous confidant to be murdered, there was always to be found some young enthusiast, willing, nay eager, to do the deed, going to certain death for the sake of winning a smile from Fredegundis. In her marvellous power of fascination over men, she resembled a woman with whom, in all other respects, it would be a calumny to couple her name, Mary, Queen of Scots. With all her wickedness, Fredegundis must have been a brilliant and seductive Frenchwoman; and there is something about her strange demoniac power which reminds us of the evil heroines of the Renaissance.

The murder of Galswintha, followed by the marriage with her low-born rival, aroused the anger of the Franks, and Chilperic's brothers endeavoured to eject so atrocious an offender from their royal partnership. In this, however, they do not seem to have been successful. If war was actually waged by Sigibert against the murderer (which is not clearly stated), it was terminated by a more peaceful civil process, in which Guntram acted as arbiter between his brethren. The result of this process was as follows: but both its terms and the principles on which it was based would have been utterly unintelligible to any of the Roman jurisconsults who, two centuries before, abounded in the great cities of Gaul. 'The *morgane-gyba* of Galswintha was to form the *weregild* of Brunichildis'. In other words, the five cities of Aquitaine, which Chilperic had assigned to the murdered queen as her dower, were to be handed over to her sister and next of kin in atonement for the crime. It would, seem as if the decision had scarcely been given when the faithless Chilperic sought to overturn it; at any rate, it is in Bordeaux (one of the cities of the 'morning-gift') and its neighbourhood that we find him constantly attacking his brother of Austrasia, in the obscure wars which fill up the interval between 567 and 575. At length the dispute came to a crisis. The fierce Austrasian warriors, Sigibert's subjects, were only too ready to pour themselves westwards into Neustria, and enjoy the plunder of its cities. Sigibert was a warrior and Chilperic apparently was not, though he shrank from no deed of cowardly violence. And Guntram, though the most uncertain and untrustworthy of allies, was at this time ranged, with some appearance of earnestness, on the side of Sigibert. The campaign went entirely in favour of the Austrasian army. It pressed on to Paris, to Rouen: Chilperic, beaten and cowed, was shut up in Tournay (his capital now, instead of Soissons) : a large part of the Neustrian Franks consented to acclaim Sigibert as their sovereign instead of the unwarlike and tyrannical Chilperic. The ceremony took place at Vitry, near Arras, not far from the border of the two realms. Sigibert was raised on the shield and hailed king by the whole army of the Franks; but almost in the moment of his triumph, two serving-men rushed upon him and dealt him a mortal wound on either side with their strong knives, which went by the name of *scaramaxes*. The weapons, it was said, had been steeped in poison by the hands of Fredegundis; the servants had been 'bewitched' by the terrible queen. There can be little doubt that for this murder, at, least, she was justly held answerable by her contemporaries.

So fell, in the prime of his life and vigour, the gallant Sigibert—

'Titus, the youngest Tarquin: too good for such a brood.'

Had he lived and attained, as he well might have done, to the sole dominion of the Franks, the course of European history might have been changed. He would hardly, one thinks, have propagated so feeble a race as the *fainéant kings* who issued from the loins of the kings of Neustria; he would almost certainly have checked the growing audacity, and resisted the overweening pretensions, of the nobles of Austrasia.

Brunichildis, with her children, was at Paris (the capital of the late king Charibert) when the terrible news reached her of the murder of Sigibert—a crime which utterly reversed the position of affairs, and made her a helpless outcast in the land of her deadly foe. Her little son Childebert, a child of five years old, was carried off by one of Sigibert's generals, who succeeded in conveying him safely to Metz, where he was accepted by the Austrasian warriors as his father's successor. Thus began a reign which lasted for twenty-one years—one which was upon the whole prosperous, and which had many points of contact with the history of the Lombard neighbours of Austrasia. As Childebert, however, was only twenty-six when he died, it is evident that during the greater part of his nominal reign, the actual might of royalty must have been in other hands than his. In fact it seems to have been during his long minority that the power of the great Austrasian nobles (who must have formed a sort of self-constituted Council of Regency) began distinctly to overshadow the power of the crown. Our justification for lingering over these events, which apparently belong to purely Frankish history, is that we are here watching the beginnings of that singular dynasty of officials, the Mayors of the Palace, whose descendant was one day to overthrow the Lombard monarchy.

As for Brunichildis, she, like the Kriemhild of the great German poem after the death of her glorious young hero Siegfried, lived but to avenge his death; and, like Kriemhild, she sought to compass her revenge by a second marriage, the natural resource of a young and beautiful woman in a lawless generation, which was ready to trample under foot the rights of the widow and the fatherless. It was, perhaps, for this reason that she did not attempt to return to Austrasia. Taken prisoner by Chilperic, she was despoiled of all her treasures and sent to live in banishment at Rouen. Thither, before long, came Merovech, the son of Chilperic by one of the many wives whom he had married before Galswintha. He saw the beautiful widow and loved her, and, though she as his uncle's wife was within the forbidden degrees of relationship, he was married to her within a few months of her first husband's death, by Praetextatus, bishop of Rouen. Great was the wrath of Chilperic, greater still probably the rage of Fredegundis, when they heard that the hated Gothic princess had thus made good her footing in their own family, and was the wife of the young warrior to whom all Franks looked forward as chief of the descendants of Clovis in the next generation. Chilperic marched to Rouen, intending to arrest the newly-wedded pair, but they fled to the church of St. Martin at Tours, whose inviolable sanctity Chilperic was forced to respect. On receiving his promise that he would not separate them 'if such were the will of God', Merovech and his wife came forth. The kiss of peace was exchanged, and the king, his son and his new daughter-in-law banqueted together. Notwithstanding his oath, however, Chilperic insisted on his son's accompanying him to Soissons, while Brunichildis appears to have returned to Austrasia. Merovech fell under suspicion, perhaps just suspicion, of complicity with some rebels who attacked the city of Soissons, where Fredegundis was then dwelling. He was again arrested, shorn of the long hair which was the glory of a Merovingian prince, and forcibly turned into an ecclesiastic. Another escape, a long sojourn in the sanctuary at Tours, a visit to Austrasia (where he was coldly received by the nobles, who desired the presence of no full-grown scion of the royal house among them), and then an ill-judged expedition into his father's kingdom followed. He was again taken prisoner and lodged in an inn, while his captors sent messengers to his father to ask what should be done with him. But meanwhile he had said to his henchman Gailen, 'Thou and I have hitherto had but one mind and one purpose. I pray thee let me not fall into the hands of mine enemies, but take this sword and rush with it upon me'.

This Gailen did; and when Chilperic arrived he found his son dead. But some said that Merovech never space those words to his henchman, but that the fatal blow was struck by order of Fredegundis.

The romance of Brunichildis' second marriage—at any rate in the fragmentary shape in which it exists in the pages of Gregory—is a disappointing one. Even Brunichildis seems to falter and hesitate in her great purpose of revenge for the death of Sigibert, and Merovech seems to spend most of his time cowering as a suppliant by the tomb of St. Martin. And the least romantic part of the story is the calmness with which the newly-wedded couple bear their separation from one another; a separation which it was apparently in their power at any time to have ended.

The remainder of the reign of Chilperic was chiefly memorable for the afflictions which befell him in his family. One after another of the sons of his earlier marriage, young men just entering upon manhood, fell victims to the jealous hatred of their stepmother; and as if to punish her for her cruelty, one after another of her own sons died in infancy. The sons of Guntram also perished in their prime; it seemed as if the whole lineage of Clovis might soon fail from off the earth. Wars, purposeless but desolating, were waged between the three Frankish kingdoms, and in some of these wars, strange to say, Childebert—that is to say the counsellors of Childebert—were found siding with Chilperic, his father's murderer, against the easy-tempered Guntram. This, however, was only a passing phase; as a rule Austrasia and Burgundy stood together against Neustria. The chief characteristic of the rule of Chilperic was the increasing stringency of his financial exactions, not merely from his Roman, but from his Frankish subjects, and the jealousy, a well-grounded jealousy, with which he regarded the growing power and possessions of the Church. 'He would often say, "Behold! our treasury remains poor; behold! our riches are transferred to the churches; none reign at all save the bishops; our honour perishes and is all carried over to the bishops of the cities". With this thought in his mind, he continually quashed the wills which were drawn up in favour of the churches, and thus he trampled under foot his own father's commands, thinking that there was now none left to guard their observance'. No wonder that such a prince—whom even secular historians must hold to have been a profoundly wicked man—figures in an ecclesiastic's pages as 'the Nero and Herod of our time.'

At length, in the fifty-second year of his age, Chilperic met that violent death, which in the sixth century was almost as much as the long hair that floated around their shoulders—the note of a Merovingian prince. He went to his country-house at Chelles, about twelve miles from Paris, and there amused himself with hunting. Coming back one evening in the twilight from the chase, he was about to dismount from his horse, and had already put one hand on the shoulder of his groom, when some one rushed out of the darkness and stabbed him with a knife, striking one blow under the armpit, and one in his belly. 'The blood gushed out from his mouth and from the two wounds, and so his wicked spirit fled.'

The author and the motive of the assassination of Chilperic remained a mystery. We do not even hear the usual details as to the death by torture of the murderer, and it seems possible that in the obscurity of the night and the loneliness of the forest he may have succeeded in escaping. Fredegundis was accused of this, as of so many other murders. It was said that Chilperic had discovered her infidelity to her marriage vows, and that she forestalled his inevitable revenge by the hand of a hired assassin. This explanation, however, seems in the highest degree improbable. No one lost so much by the death of Chilperic as his widow; hurled, like her rival Brunichildis, in one hour from the height of power to helplessness and exile, and obliged to seek temporary shelter at the court of the hospitable Guntram.

After all its vicissitudes, the family of Chilperic at his death consisted only of one babe of three years old, named, after its grandfather, Chlotochar. This child, who was destined one day to reunite all the Frankish dominions under his single sceptre, was at once proclaimed king, the reins of government being assumed, not by Fredegundis, but by some of the more powerful nobles, and thus Neustria had to pass through even a longer minority than that from which Austrasia was now slowly emerging. There can be little doubt that these long periods of obscuration of the royal power, however welcome to the great nobles who exercised or controlled the authority of the regent, were deplored by the poorer Franks and by the Gallo-Roman. population, to whom even the worst king afforded some protection from the lawless violence of the aristocracy.

But our rapid review of Frankish history, which began with the eleventh year of the government of Narses, has taken us on to the end of the Lombard Interregnum. It is time now to turn back and fit the Lombard invasions of Gaul into the framework of Frankish history.

The year of the Lombard irruption into Italy was, it will be remembered, 568. This was one year after the murder of Galswintha, and at a time therefore when the relations between Sigibert and Chilperic were probably strained to the utmost; and yet, strange to say, it was rather against Burgundy than against Neustria that the arms of Austrasia were at this time directed. Sigibert wrested Arles from his brother Guntram; then he lost Avignon: but these struggles, purposeless and resultless as they were, perhaps distracted the attention of the Burgundian generals and made a Lombard invasion possible. We are vaguely told that 'in this year the Lombards dared to enter the neighbouring regions of Gaul, where multitude of captives of that nation [*i. e.* the Lombards] were sold into slavery'. Evidently the invasion, whithersoever directed, was a failure. Probably it was only by isolated bands of marauders without concert or leadership.

The next invasion which was made, probably in the year 570, was more successful. The Lombards made their way probably by one of the passes of the Maritime Alps into Provence. Amatus (whose name makes it probable that he was a man of Gallo-Roman extraction) held that region for king Guntram, wearing the Roman title of Patrician. He delivered battle to the Lombards, was defeated and fled. A countless number of Burgundians lay dead upon the field, and the Lombards, enriched with booty, the value of which their barbarous arithmetic could not calculate, returned to Italy.

In the room of the defeated, perhaps slain, Amatus, king Guntram conferred the dignity of Patrician on Eunius, surnamed Mummolus, and with his appointment an immediate change came over the scene. Though a grasping and selfish man, Mummolus was a brave soldier, and if, as seems probable, he too, like Amatus, was a Gallo-Roman by birth, his career was a proof that there was still some martial spirit left in the descendants of the old provincials of Gaul. His father, Peonius, had been count of Auxerre, and entrusted to Mummolus the usual gifts by which— perhaps on the accession of Guntram—he hoped to obtain the renewal of his office. The faithless son, however, obtained the dignity, not for his father, but for himself, and having thus placed his foot on the official ladder, continued to mount step by step till he reached, as we have seen, the dignity of the Patriciate, which was probably still considered the highest that could be bestowed on a subject.

In the following year (apparently) the Lombards again invaded Gaul, not now by the Maritime Alps, but by the Col de Genève. They reached a point near to Embrun1 in the valley of the Durance; but here they were met by Mummolus, who drew his army all round them, blocked up with *abattis* the main roads by which they might have escaped, and then felling upon them by devious forest paths took them at such disadvantage as to accomplish their entire defeat. A great number of the Lombards were slain; some were taken captive and sent to king Guntram, probably to be sold as slaves: only a few escaped to their own land to tell the story of this, the first of many Lombard defeats which were to attest the military skill of Mummolus. Ecclesiastics heard with horror that in this battle two brothers and brother- prelates, Salonius and Sagittarius—the former bishop of Embrun and the latter of Gap—had borne an active part, 'armed, not with the heavenly cross, but with helmet and coat of mail', and, which was worse, had slain many with their own hands. But this was only one, and in fact the least censurable, of many irregularities and crimes committed by this lawless pair, who had already a few years before (in 566) been deprived of their sees by the Council of Lyons, but had been replaced therein by the Pope. Again, at a later period, deposed and confined in separate monasteries, they were once more let out by the good-natured Guntram and again condemned by a council. The end of Salonius is unknown. Sagittarius, as we shall shortly see, came to a violent end in consequence of joining a conspiracy against king Guntram. Such were some of the bishops of Gaul in the sixth century, though it must be admitted that few were as wildly brutal and licentious as Salonius and Sagittarius.

In the years immediately following the invasion, Mummolus distinguished himself by that successful campaign against the Saxon immigrants of which mention was made in the earlier part of this chapter. Then somewhat later still, in the year which witnessed the assassination of Cleph the Lombard king, a large army of Lombards under the command of duke Zaban again entered the dominions of king Guntram. This time, however, it was not against Dauphiné but against Switzerland that their ravages were directed. They went, doubtless, northward by the Great St. Bernard Pass from Aosta to Martigny, and descended into that long Alp-bounded parallelogram through which the young Rhone flows, and which then as now bore preeminently the name of 'the Valley'. They reached the great monastery of Agaunum (now St. Maurice), scene of the devotions and the vain penitence of Burgundian Sigismund, and there they tamed many days, perhaps engaged in pillaging the convent, though this is not expressly stated by the monkish chronicler from whom we derive our information. At length, at the town of Bex, a little way down the valley from St. Maurice, they suffered so crushing a defeat at the hands of the Frankish generals, that but a few fugitives, duke Zaban among the number, succeeded in recrossing the mountains and reaching Italian soil.

Undaunted by this terrible reverse, in the next year the Lombards resumed their irritating inroads into Gaul. This time Zaban was accompanied by two dukes, other dukes, Amo and Rodan, the names of whose cities have not been recorded. The three armies all went by the same road till they had crossed the Alps. This was that to which allusion has already been made, which is still the well-known pass of the Mont Genèvre. Though one of the lowest in the great chain the Alps and frequently traversed by Roman generals, it is, at the summit, nearly 6,500 feet high. Leaving the city of Turin in the great plain of Piedmont, the road ascends the beautiful valley of the Dora Susa till it reaches the little town of Susa, where a triumphal arch still preserves the memory of Augustus, the founder of the Colony of Segusio. A steep climb of several hours leads to the summit of the pass and the watershed between the two streams, the

Dora Riparia which flows eventually into the Po, and the Clairet which flows into the Durance. The Roman road from this point turned sharply to the south and followed the course of the Durance till it reached the neighbourhood of Arles. In doing so it passed the little cities of Ebrodunum (*Embrun*) and Vapincum (*Gap*), the seats of the two bellicose bishops, Salonius and Sagittarius. In all the story of these campaigns Embrun in the valley of the Durance plays an important part. It was apparently a sort of mustering place for the invaders both after crossing and before recrossing the Cottian Alps.

From this starting-point the three dukes diverged in order to make three separate raids into south-eastern Gaul.

(1) Amo, keeping to the great Roman road, descended into 'the province of Arles', which he ravaged and perhaps hoped to subdue. He paid a hostile visit to a villa in the neighbourhood of Avignon which Mummolus had received as a present from his grateful king.

He threatened Aquae Sextiae (*Aix*) with a siege, but on receiving 22 lbs. of silver, he marched away from the place. He did not penetrate as far as Marseilles itself, but only to the 'Stony Plain', which adjoined that ancient seaport, and he carried off large herds of cattle as well as many captives from the Massilian territory.

(2) Duke Zaban took the road which branched off March. from Gap and led north-westward through Dea (*Die*) to Valentia (*Valence*) at the confluence of the Isère and the Rhone, and there he pitched his camp.

(3) Higher up on the course of the Isère, in a splendid March of amphitheatre of hills, lies the stately city of Grenoble, recalling by its Roman name Gratianopolis the memory of the brilliant young Emperor Gratian. To this city duke Rodan laid regular siege. Mummolus, hearing these tidings, moved southwards with a strong army and first attacked the besiegers of Grenoble. 'While his army was laboriously crossing the turbid Isère, an animal, by the command of God, entered the river and showed them a ford, and thus the whole army got easily through to the opposite shores'. The Lombards flocked to meet them with drawn swords, but were defeated, and duke Rodan, wounded by a lance, fled to the tops of the mountains. With 500 faithful followers he made his way to Valence through the trackless Dauphiné forests—the high road by the Isère being of course blocked by Mummolus. He told his brother-duke Zaban all that had occurred, and they jointly decided on retreat. Burning and plundering they had made their way into the valleys of the Rhone and the Isère: burning and plundering they returned to Embrun.

At Embrun Zaban and Rodan were met by Mummolus at the head of a 'countless' army. Battle was joined; the 'phalanxes' of the Lombards were absolutely cut to pieces, and with a few of their officers, but far fewer, relatively, of the rank and file, the two dukes made their way back over the mountains into Italy. When they reached Susa they were coldly and ungraciously received by the inhabitants. The reason for this coldness, which does not seem to have passed into actual hostility, was that Sisinnius, Master of the Soldiery, was then in the city as the representative of the Emperor. There was no bloodshed, but a little southern astuteness freed the good town of Susa from its unwelcome visitors. While Zaban was conferring with Sisinnius (perhaps arranging as to the billeting of the remnant of the Lombard army), a man entered who feigned himself to be the slave of Mummolus. He greeted Sisinnius in his master's name, handed him letters, and said, 'These are for thee from Mummolus. He is even now at hand'. At these words (though in truth Mummolus was nowhere in the neighbourhood) Zaban and Rodan left the city with all speed and retreated panic-stricken to their homes.

When tidings of all these disasters were brought to Amo in the province of Arles, he collected his plunder, and sought to return across the mountains. The snow, however, had now begun to fall on the Mont Genèvre, and so blocked his passage that he had to leave all his booty and many of his soldiers behind. With much difficulty and accompanied by only a few of his followers, Amo succeeded in returning to his own land. So disastrously ended the expedition of the three dukes. 'For', as the Frankish historian truly says, they were all terrified by the valour of Mummolus.

After the failure of this expedition we hear of no futher invasion of Gaul by the Lombard dukes. The only result of these invasions (except memories which must long have made the name of Lombard hateful to the inhabitants of Dauphiné and Provence) was an extension of territory over the crest of the Alps in favour of the Franks of Burgundy, and at the expense of the Lombards. Ecclesiastical charters prove that about the year 588, the upper valley of the Dora Baltea, with its chief city Aosta, and that of the Dora Susa, with its chief city Susa, were treated as undoubted portions of the dominions of king Guntram, and were spoken of as having been formerly in Italy, but annexed by him. These two cities and the regions surrounding them occupied the Italian side of the two great practicable passes of that time—the Great St. Bernard and the Mont Genèvre. There can be little doubt that their occupation by Frankish generals was at once the result of the campaigns which have been just described, and the cause that the Lombard invasions of Gaul were not renewed.

The after-career of Mummolus, the brave champion of Burgundy against the invading Lombards, forms one of the most striking pages in Gregory's history of the Franks, but is too remote from our subject to be related here in any detail. In an evil hour for himself he deserted the master whom he had hitherto served so faithfully, and took up with a pretender, probably base-born and certainly mean-spirited, who was named Gundovald and called himself son of Chlotochar. The soldiers of the pretender, led by Mummolus, obtained some temporary successes, but in 585 Guntram sent a powerful army against him, and, at the mere rumour of its approach, Gundovald's party began to crumble, and he and Mummolus were forced to take refuge in Convenae (now Comminges), a little city perched on one of the outlying buttresses of the Pyrenees. Gundovald made a plaintive appeal to the Burgundian general, Leudegisclus, that he might be allowed to return to Constantinople, where he had left his wife and children. The general only scoffed at the meek petition of 'the painting man, who used in the time of king Chlotochar to daub his pictures on the walls of oratories and bed-chambers'. After the siege of Convenae had lasted fifteen days, secret communications passed between Leudegisclus and Mummolus, the result of which was that the latter persuaded or forced Gundovald to go forth and trust himself to the faintly hoped for mercies of the foe. Vain was the hope : no sooner was he outside the city than one of Guntram's generals gave him a push, which sent him headlong down the steep hill on which Convenae was built. The fall did not kill him, but a stone from the hand of one of his former adherents broke the pretender's skull and ended his sorrows. Vengeance was not long in overtaking his betrayers; one of whom was that same turbulent Bishop Sagittarius, whom we have already seen fighting with carnal weapons against the Lombard invaders. Leudegisclus sent a secret message to his king, asking how he was to dispose of them. 'Slay them all' was the answer of 'good king Guntram'. Mummolus, having received some hint of his danger, went forth, armed, to the hut where Leudegisclus had his head-quarters.

'Why dost thou come thus like a fugitive?' said the Burgundian general.

'As far as I can see', he answered, 'none of the promises made to us are being kept, for I perceive myself to be in imminent danger of death'.

Leudegisclus said, 'I will go forth and put all right'. And going forth, he ordered his soldiers to surround the house and slay Mummolus. The veteran long kept his assailants at bay, but at length, coming to the door, he was pierced in the right and left sides by two lances, and fell to the earth dead. When Bishop Sagittarius, who had apparently accompanied Mummolus to the hut, saw this, he covered his head with his hood, and sought to flee to a neighbouring forest; but one of the soldiers followed him, drew his sword, and cut off the hooded head. Such was the ignoble end of Mummolus, who at one time bade fair to be the hero of Merovingian Gaul. The story is a miserable record of brutality and bad faith. Not one of the actors keeps a solemnly plighted promise or shows a trace of compassion to a fallen foe. These Frankish and Gallo-Roman savages, with a thin varnish of ecclesiastical Christianity over their natural ferocity, have not only no conception of what their descendants will one day reverence as knightly honour, but do not even rise to the usual level of truthfulness attained by their heathen forefathers in the days of Tacitus.

The treasures of Mummolus came into the hands of king Guntram, who out of them caused fifteen massive silver dishes to be wrought, all of which, save two, he presented to various churches. And the residue of the confiscated property he 'bestowed upon the necessities of the churches and the poor'.

It is now time to return to the affairs of the Lombards, round whom the clouds were gathering in menacing fashion a year before the death of Mummolus. In the year 582, the Emperor Tiberius II, the generous and easy-tempered, had died and had been succeeded by his son-in-law Maurice, who as a general had won notable victories over the Persians, though he was eventually unsuccessful as a ruler, owing to his riding with a sharper curb than the demoralized army and nobles of Constantinople could tolerate.

The eternal quarrel with Persia wore during these years a favourable aspect for the Empire, whose standards were generally victorious on the Tigris and the mountains of Media, and the wild Avars on the Danubian frontier were for the moment at peace with their southern neighbours. Thus freed from his most pressing cares, Maurice began to scheme for the attainment of that object which could never be long absent from a Roman Emperor's thought—the recovery of Italy.

Already, before the death of Tiberius, an Austrasian army under duke Chramnichis had, from the Bavarian side, attacked the Lombards in the valley of the Adige; but after winning a signal victory it had at last been defeated and expelled from the country by Euin, duke of Trient. The court of Constantinople had doubtless heard of this invasion, and knew that it would find in the nobles, who governed Austrasia during Childebert's minority, willing helpers against the hated Lombards. Troops indeed could not yet be spared from the Persian war, but money, as in the days of the lavish Tiberius, could still be sent. The ambassadors of Neustrian Chilperic had received from Tiberius certain wonderful gold medals, each a pound in weight, bearing on the obverse side the Emperor's effigy, with the inscription "Tiberii Constantini Perpetui Augusti", and on the reverse, a chariot and its driver, with the motto "Gloria Romanorum". A more useful, if less showy gift, now (in the year 584) reached the court of the Australian king. The ambassadors of Maurice brought him a subsidy of 50,000 solidi (£30,000) and a request 'that he would rush with his army upon the Lombards and utterly exterminate them out of Italy'. The young Childebert, now about fourteen years of age, was permitted by his counsellors to lead his army across the Alps. The force which poured in from Austrasia (probably by the Brenner or some other of the eastern passes of the Alps) was too overwhelming for the Lombards to cope with it. They shut themselves up in their cities (whose fortifications, wiser than the Vandals, they had not destroyed) and saw the hostile multitudes sweep over the desolated plains. But though unable to meet the Franks in arms, they had other weapons which, as they probably knew, would be more efficacious with the greedy nobles of the Austrasian Court. They sent ambassadors who offered costly gifts, and, tempted by these, Childebert and his army retired. As a pecuniary speculation the invasion had been a complete success for the Franks. The 50,000 *solidi* were still almost untouched in the treasury of Metz, and though the Emperor Maurice loudly demanded the return of the money, he demanded in vain. To the same treasury were now carried the gifts of the Lombard dukes, gifts which doubtless consisted chiefly of their own plunder from the palaces of the Roman nobles, the work of generations of cunning craftsmen, while the Lombards were still wandering through Pannonian wildernesses. These gifts could, of course, be easily represented as tribute, and the returning Austrasians might boast that the Lombards had professed themselves servants of king Childebert. There was none to say them nay; and such is the colour put upon the treaty of peace by Frankish Gregory, but which disappears .from the pages of his Lombard copyist.

CHAPTER VI.

FLAVIUS AUTHARI.

The attempt of the Lombard dukes to keep the government of the new state in their own hands, after ten years of trial, had proved a failure. Their enemies were drawing together into an alliance which might easily bring upon the Lombard kingdom the same ruin that had befallen its Ostrogothic predecessor, and internally the condition of the subject population, which called itself Roman, was probably both miserable and menacing. Though we greatly lack precise details as to the real position of these subject Italians, there are many indications that their lot was harder during the ten years of 'the kingless time' than at any period before or after. We can well understand that the yoke of these thirty-six barbarous chiefs, each one a little despot in his own domain, would be far more galling than that of one supreme lord, who, both for the sake of his revenues and in order to prevent a dangerous rivalry, would be disposed to defend the peasant and the handicraftsman from the too grievous exactions of a domineering neighbour. But there is no need to labour at this demonstration: it is one of the commonplaces of medieval history that the power of the king was generally the shield of the commoner against the oppression of the noble.

Whether it was the fear of external war or of internal discontent that caused the return to monarchy, we know not; all our information on the subject is contained in the following words of Paulus :—

'But when the Lombards had been for ten years under the power of their dukes, at length by common consent they appointed to themselves as king, Authari, the son of the above-mentioned sovereign, Cleph. On account of his dignity they called him Flavius, a forename which all the kings of the Lombards who followed him used auspiciously. In his days, on account of the restoration of the kingdom, the then ruling dukes contributed half of all their possessions to the royal exchequer, that there might be a fund for the maintenance of the king himself, and of those who were attached to him by the liability to perform the various offices of his household. [In this division] the subject populations who had been assigned to their several Lombard guests were also included. In truth this was a marvellous fact in the kingdom of the Lombards; there was no evidence, no plots were devised, no one oppressed another with unjust exactions, none despoiled his neighbour; there were no thefts, no robberies with violence: every man went about his business as he pleased, in fearless security'.

In this brilliant, but doubtless over-painted picture of the golden days of Flavius Authari, let us try to discover such lines of hard prosaic fact as the labour of archaeologists and commentators have been able to decipher.

It was said in the previous chapter that there was some reason to suppose that Cleph was the first Lombard duke of Bergamo. If this were so, probably his son Authari passed his boyhood at that place under the guardianship of his mother, Queen Masane.

Most of the great cities of Lombardy are built in the plain; but Bergamo, at least the older city of Bergamo, stands on a hill, an outlier of the great Alpine range which, even to the far Bernina, towers majestically behind her. Her territory in those far-off days, when she still gave birth to kings, was more extensive than in later centuries, reaching back to the deep trough of the Valtelline, through which the early waters of the Adda are poured, resting on the two lakes of Iseo and Como to the east and west, and coming far down into the plain within eight miles of the unfortunate Cremona,— Cremona, which as still loyal to the Empire, had to see her territories retrenched for the benefit of her more submissive neighbours.

As we have seen, Authari assumed the title Flavius, that title which, endeared to the memories of the subject Roman population by dim remembrance of the glories of the Flavian line, was looked upon as in some sort putting the seal of Roman legitimacy upon barbaric conquest. Odovacar, the captain of Herulian mercenaries, had called himself Flavius, a century before the accession of Authari. Recared, the Visigothic king of Spain, who was just at this time coming over to the orthodox creed, and generally reconciling himself to the old order of things, assumed the same title. There can be little doubt that the poor downtrodden Roman colonists heaved a sigh of relief and lifted up his eyes with faint hopes of the coming of a better day, when he heard that the king of these fierce barbarians from the Danube condescended to call himself Flavius. And upon the whole, the promise implied in Authari's new title was fulfilled, and the expectations formed of him by the nobles who raised him to the throne were justified. In the letters of popes and emperors, he and his people are still 'most unspeakable' (*nefandissimi*); but we hear less, in fact we hardly hear anything at all, of mere barbaric plunder of the cities and villas of Italy; the senseless invasions of Gaul are not resumed; the dukes are kept well in hand, and apparently the resources of the young kingdom are directed with wisdom and foresight to the necessary work of its defence against the threatening combination of its foreign foes. And thus, though we certainly cannot accept the picture of millennial happiness under Authari's sway drawn for us by Paulus, we can believe that his was, in the main, a rule which made for righteousness, and that life was more endurable in his days than during the barbarous 'kingless time', or during the feeble reigns of some of his successors.

The figure of this bright and forceful young king, whose reign was too short for his people's desires (for he was only six years upon the throne), impressed the imaginations of the Lombard people, and their Sagas were more busy with his fame than with that of most of the dwellers in the palace at Pavia. Minstrels told how he marched victoriously through the regions which were formed into the two great duchies of Spoleto and Benevento, how he arrived finally at the city of Reggio, at the extreme end of the peninsula which looks across over Scylla and Charybdis at the white walls of Messina, and seeing there certain columns (perhaps of a submerged temple) placed in the very waters of the straits, he rode up towards them, and hurling his spear said, 'Thus far shall come the boundaries of the Lombards'. Wherefore to this day (says Paulus) that column is called 'the column of Authari'.

The story of his wooing belongs to the latest years of his life, but it may be related here, in order to show the popular conception of his character. Authari had asked for and obtained the promise of the hand of Chlodosinda, daughter of Brunichildis, sister of Childebert, king of Austrasia. But when news arrived in Gaul of the conversion of Recared of Spain to the Catholic faith, Brunichildis, who was herself a convert from Arianism and a fervent Catholic, broke off her daughter's engagement to Authari, and betrothed Chlodosinda to Recared. Hereupon Authari turned his thought to a nearer neighbour and determined to woo Theudelinda, the daughter of Garibald, duke of the Bavarians. Theudelinda, whose fame as a beautiful and accomplished princess had probably been widely spread abroad, had been herself betrothed to the youthful Childebert, but that alliance had also been broken by the influence of Brunichildis, who probably dreaded the ascendency of such a woman over her feeble son. The sister of Theudelinda had been already some ten or fifteen years the wife of a Lombard duke, the stouthearted and successful soldier Euin of Trient.

To Bavaria accordingly king Authari sent his ambassadors to ask for the hand of the daughter of Garibald. They returned with a favourable answer, and the young king determined to seize an opportunity for gazing on the features of his future bride before she entered his kingdom as its queen. Choosing out therefore few of his most trusty followers, he journeyed with slight equipment to the Bavarian court. A grave and reverend 'senior,' upon whom was devolved the apparent headship of the mission, spoke some words of diplomatic courtesy to Garibald, and then Authari himself (of course preserving his incognito) stepped up to the Bavarian and said, 'My master Authari has sent me that I may behold the face of his betrothed, our future mistress, and may make report of her beauty to my lord'. Garibald then ordered his daughter to approach, and Authari gazed long in silence on the blender form and beautiful face of his betrothed. Thereafter he said to the Bavarian duke, 'In good sooth we behold that your daughter is such a person that she is well worthy to be our queen. Command, therefore, I pray, that we may receive a goblet of wine from her hand, as we hope often to do in the years that are to come'. Garibald gave the word and Theudelinda brought the goblet of wine and offered it first to the older man, the apparent chief of the embassy. Then she handed it to Authari, all unwitting that he was her future husband, and he in returning the cup secretly intertwined her fingers with his, and bending low, guided them over the profile of his face from the forehead to the chin. When the ambassadors had left the presence-chamber, Theudelinda, with a blush of shame, told her nurse of the strange behaviour of the Lombard. 'Assuredly,' said the aged crone, 'he must be the king thy betrothed suitor, or he would never have dared to do this unto thee. But let us be silent about the matter lest it come to the knowledge of thy father. And in truth he is a comely person, worthy of the kingdom and of thee'. For the young king, in the flower of his age, with his tall stature and waves of yellow hair, had won the hearts of all the beholders.

A banquet followed, and the Lombard messengers, escorted by some of the Bavarian nobles, set forth upon their homeward journey. When they were just crossing the frontiers of Noricum and their horses' feet touched the soil of his Italy, Authari, rising high in his saddle, whirled his battle-axe through the air and fixed it deep in the trunk of a tree, where he left it, shouting as he threw, 'So Authari is wont to strike his blow'. Then the Bavarian escort understood that he was indeed the king.

A short time elapsed. Childebert, probably alarmed at the tidings of the alliance between the Bavarians, his doubtful subjects, and the Lombards, his frequent foes, moved his army against Garibald. There is one reason to think that either at this time or soon after, Garibald was dethroned and his duchy given to a relative, perhaps a son or a nephew, named Tassilo; but however that may be, it is certain that Theudelinda fled from her country (her young brother, Gundwald being the companion of her exile), and notified to her betrothed her arrival in Italy. Authari received her with great pomp on the shores of the beautiful Lake Garda, and the marriage was celebrated amid general rejoicings in the neighbouring city of Verona the 15th of May (589).

The union so romantically brought about was apparently a happy one, but its happiness was short-lived, for in September of the following year Authari died. But having thus related all that is to be known as to the personal history of the young king, let us turn back to consider the chief public events of his short but important reign.

For some time the occupants of St. Peter's chair had been uttering to all the potentates of the Catholic world plaintive cries for help against the violence of the Lombards. In a letter written by Pope Pelagius II to Aunacharius, bishop of Auxerre, the writer bewails 'the shedding of innocent blood, the violation of the holy altars, the insults offered to the Catholic faith by these idolaters'. 'Not without some great purpose', continues the Pope, 'has it been ordained by Divine Providence that your [Frankish] kings should share with the Roman Empire in the confession of the orthodox faith. Assuredly this was brought to pass in order that they might be so to speak neighbours and helpers of this City of Rome, whence that confession took its birth, and of the whole of Italy. Beware then lest through levity of purpose your kings should fail in their high mission. Persuade them as earnestly as you can to keep themselves from all friendship and alliance with our most unspeakable enemies the Lombards, lest when the day of vengeance dawns (which we trust in the Divine mercy it will do speedily), your kings should share in the Lombard's punishment'.

Again, in 585 the same Pope addressed a letter to the deacon Gregory, his representative at the court of Byzantium, urging him to bring under the notice of the Emperor Maurice the cruel hardships of his Italian subjects. 'Such calamities and tribulations are brought upon us by the perfidy of the Lombard, contrary to his own plighted oath, that no one can avail to relate them. Tell our most pious lord the Emperor of our dangers and necessities, and consult with him how they may be most speedily relieved: because so straitened is the Republic that, unless God shall put it into the heart of our most pious sovereign to bestow his wonted compassion upon his servants, and to relieve our troubles by sending us one Master of the Soldiery and one Duke, we shall be brought to the extremity of distress, since at present the region around Rome is still for the most part quite undefended.

'The Exarch writes that he can give us no remedy, since he avers that he has not sufficient force even to defend that part of the country [the neighbourhood of Ravenna]. May God therefore direct him speedily to succour our perils before the army of that most unspeakable nation succeeds (which God forbid) in occupying the districts still held by the Republic'.

If the Emperor could not spare any large number of soldiers in response to these plaintive appeals, he could at least place the existing Italian army under more efficient leadership than that of the incapable Longinus, who, during the eighteen years of his government, had performed no memorable action, except abetting the flight of the murderess Rosamund and shipping off Alboin's daughter and her treasures to Constantinople. Smaragdus was now appointed governor of Italy, with a title which was afterwards to become famous, but of which we now meet with the first undoubted mention, the title of Exarch. It was probably in the early part of the year 585 that the new governor arrived in Italy. His name (a curious one to be borne by a Roman governor) is the Greek word for an emerald. By no means a flawless jewel, and a man with some strange streaks of madness in his composition, Smaragdus was nevertheless an active and energetic soldier, and the fact that he twice held the great post of Exarch of Italy shows the high value which the Imperial Consistory placed on his services.

The efforts of the new Exarch were powerfully seconded by those of a deserter from the Lombard camp. This was a certain Droctulf, by birth belonging to the Suavic or Alamannic nation, who had grown to manhood among the Lombards, and being a man of comely presence and evidently of some military talent, had received the honour of a dukedom among them. He had apparently been taken prisoner in some battle by the Imperial troops, and nurtured a feeling of resentment against the other Lombard generals, to whose languid support he considered that he owed his captivity. In this captivity at Ravenna, he, like so many barbarian chiefs before him, was fascinated by the splendid civilization—splendid even in its ruins—of the great Roman 'Republic'. The barbarous Suave of the Black Forest, the more barbarous Lombard of Pavia—what were these beside the magnificent officials who sat in Theodoric's palace at Ravenna, issuing the decrees and bestowing on loyal allies the endless golden *solidi* of the great World-Emperor? As he worshipped in the glorious basilica of St. Vitalis, and gazed upon the yet existing mosaic pictures of that martyred praetorian, father of two sons, Gervasius and Protasius, soldiers and martyrs like their sire, he took that warrior-saint for his patron, and in the visions of the night he seemed to see Jesus Christ himself giving to him, as to Constantine, a banner to be reared in the service of Christ and of Rome.

This was the man who, as it seems, early in the reign of Authari openly attached himself to the party of the Empire, gathered a band of soldiers together, and seizing the little town of Brixellum (*Brescello*) on the Po, raised there the Christ-given banner of Rome against the unspeakable Lombard. Brescello is only about twelve miles from Parma on the Aemilian way, and Droctulf's object in seizing this position was doubtless to hamper the communications of the Lombards along that great highway between Parma, Placentia and Modena, while he himself by the swift sailing-ships (*dromones*), which sailed up and down the river Po, kept open his own communications with the Adriatic. However, the young Authari led the Lombard host against Droctulf, and, after a long siege took Brixellum, razed its walls to the ground, and forced Droctulf to flee to Ravenna.

Hereupon a truce for three years (555-558) was concluded between the Lombard king and the Exarch; a truce which was probably employed by both parties in completing their preparations for further war. It was perhaps before the full completion of the third year that hostilities of a desultory kind were resumed both on the east and west of the Lombard kingdom. In the extreme north-east, Authari's future brother-in-law, Euin, duke of Trient, invaded the wealthy province of Istria. After much pillaging and burning he concluded peace—doubtless a special, local peace—with the governor of the province for one year and returned bearing great spoil to Authari. In the west, the shouts of battle were heard on the shores of the Lake of Como, where for twenty years there had been a strange survival of Roman rule in a part of Italy otherwise entirely subjugated by the barbarians.

At the present day, a traveller sailing or steaming up the western branch of the Lake of Como, perhaps scarcely notices a little island—the only one which the lake can boast—lying on his left hand as he is nearing Bellaggio. The hills of the mainland rise high above him, bearing aloft the shrine of Our Lady of Succour, to which many a boatman has looked for help when the suddenly arising storm has threatened to fill his bark. But the little island itself, which is about half a mile long and two to three hundred yards broad, rises to no great elevation, though its cliffs are in one place somewhat steep, and there are slight traces of the walls which once rose above them. Still the Isola Comacina, as Paulus calls it, suggests to us in these modem days little of the idea of a stronghold, nor has it ever been such since the invention of gunpowder. But before that great change in the art of war, the simple fact that it was separated by a deep strait, some quarter of a mile wide, from the mainland rendered it inaccessible to any power which had not naval supremacy on the lake and made its possession an object of desire to contending potentates. Here, as we shall see, came Imperial generals and rebel Lombard dukes bent on defying the arms of the lord of Pavia. In the twelfth century, in those fierce intestine wars which preceded the formation of the Lombard League, the little island threw in her lot with Milan against Como, shared the earlier reverses and the final victory of her mightier ally, but was at last, some forty years later, utterly destroyed by the neighbour whose power she had braved. The sacristan of the small and lonely church of St. John tells one in dejected tones that the little island once counted its 7000 inhabitants, but that in the time of Frederick Barbarossa 'everything was burnt', and the island has since remained desolate. Apparently, however, it was not from the terrible Emperor, but from their own burgher neighbours of Como, that the vengeance and the destruction came. Last of all, in our own days, in the war of Italian Liberation in 1848, Charles Albert confined a number of his Austrian prisoners on the island. At night they slept in the church; in the day they were allowed to scramble about the rocks and thickets of their prison, looking over the narrow strait which divided them from the shore and longing in vain for their Tyrolese or Croatian home

Hither then to this 'home of lost causes' came an Imperial *magister militum*, Francio by name, when Alboin entered Italy, and here for twenty years he had kept the flag of the Empire flying. But now at length Authari directed the whole forces of his kingdom against Francio, and after six months' siege captured his island-fortress and took possession of the vast stores of treasure deposited there by refugees from almost all the cities of Italy. To Francio himself terms were accorded worthy of so brave a foe, and he was allowed to depart for Ravenna with his wife and all his household possessions.

It was probably just after the expiration of the three years' truce that the port of Classis, which had been for at least nine years in the occupation of the Lombards was recaptured for the Empire. The hero of this reconquest was Droctulf, who was no doubt well supported by the Exarch Smaragdus. He prepared a swarm of vessels of small draft, with which he covered the shallow streams and lagunes between Ravenna and Classis, and by their aid he overcame the large Lombard host which Farwald of Spoleto had sent to maintain his important conquest.

This is all that is told us of the deeds of Droctulf in Italy. He seems, after his first Romanization, to have lived and died a faithful servant of the Empire, and to have fought her battles in the Danubian lands against the savage Avars. We know not the year of his death, but we learn that he was buried in the church of his patron-saint Vitalis at Ravenna, where for many generations might be seen his epitaph in thirteen elegiac couplets, which may be thus somewhat freely translated:—

'Droctulf here lies; his body, not his soul;
Droctulf, whose fame doth round the wide world roll

Though leagued with Bardi, Suavia gave him birth,
And suave his mood to all men upon earth.

Kind was his heart, though terrible his frown,
And his long beard o'er his broad breast flowed down.

On Rome's great commonwealth his love he placed,
And for that love's sake laid his brethren waste.

He scorned his fathers, prayed with us to stand,
And chose Ravenna for his fatherland.

Brixellum captured was his earliest feat;
There, feared by all his foes, he fixed his seat.

Christ gave the banner which he stoutly bore,
After Rome's standards thenceforth evermore.

When Farwald Classis won by foul deceit,
He for the Fleet-town's conquest armed his fleet.

Up Badrin's stream his shallops fought their way,
And made the countless Bardic hosts their prey.

Taming, in Eastern lands, the Avar hordes,
He won the glorious laurel for his lords.

The soldier-saint, Vitalis, gave him might,
Triumph on triumph thus to earn in fight;

And in Vitalis' holy home to lie
He prayed, when 'twas the warrior's turn to die.

This of Johannes was his last request,
Whose loving hands here fold him to his rest.'

The rest of the political events in the life of Authari were chiefly connected with Frankish invasions, threatened, accomplished, or averted; and to understand their somewhat obscure and tortuous course, we must once more cross the Alps and visit the hill-girt city of Metz, whence the young king Childebert, son of Sigibert and Brunichildis, rules his kingdom of Austrasia. In the courtly language of contemporary ecclesiastics he is 'gloriosissimus dominus Childeberthus rex'; but to us he is a somewhat pale and uninteresting figure, always acting under the impulse of some stronger will, ruled either by his mother or by one of the great nobles and prelates, who, as already said, claimed the right to advise—a right not easily distinguishable from the right to rule—their youthful monarch.

Childebert was generally on good terms with his uncle, the easy-tempered Guntram of Burgundy, and he was in fact, three years after the accession of Authari, formally recognized as his heir by the Treaty of Andelot: but occasional misunderstandings arose between them, nor was it easy to direct their combined resources to one common end.

The old fierce feud between Brunichildis and Fredegundis, though not healed, was during these years slumbering. Ever and anon the wicked queen of Neustria despatched one of her emissaries on the forlorn hope of murdering Guntram or Childebert: but the plot was always discovered; the would-be murderer confessed under torture the name of his inciter; he was put to death: Fredegundis bestowed some of her vast wealth on his surviving relatives, and all went on as before. Generally speaking, it may be said that the period from 584 to 600 was the time of the greatest obscuration of the Neustrian kingdom. Its king, Chlotochar II, was, at the beginning of this period, a mere infant, and Neustria was shorn of a considerable part of its former territory for the benefit of Austrasia and Burgundy.

The 'most glorious lord Childebert' having once crossed the Alps at the head of an army, and won but little renown there, was not disposed to repeat the experiment. The court of Constantinople, however, unceasingly demanded either the return of its 50,000 *solidi* or the accomplishment of the expedition of which they were the wages. And, in addition to this pecuniary claim, there was a personal motive towards friendliness with Constantinople, operating at this time with peculiar force both on Brunichildis and on Childebert. To understand its bearings we must go back three or four years, and must glance at the history of Spain and the tragedy of the rebellion of Hermenigild

We have seen that two kings of the Franks married two daughters of Athanagild, king of the Visigoths. That monarch died shortly after he had despatched the hapless Galswintha on that nuptial journey which proved to be the road to death, and he was succeeded, after a short interval, by the last and well-nigh the greatest of the Arian kings of the Visigoths, Leovigild. Lion-like by name and by nature, this Visigoths, champion of a falling cause stoutly defended the land and the faith 0f his Arian forefathers. Against the generals of the Empire who had gained a footing in Murcia and Andalusia, and against the hereditary Suevic enemy in Gallicia and Lusitania, he dealt his swashing blows. He fought the Basques (that irreconcilable remnant of the dim aboriginal race which once peopled the Peninsula), and sent them flying across the Pyrenees. He repressed the anarchic movements of his own turbulent nobility, and made them feel that they had now indeed a king.

True, however, to the policy of his predecessor Athanagild (whose widow Goisvintha he had married after the death of his own first wife), Leovigild desired to conciliate as much as possible his mighty Frankish neighbours on the north. Accordingly, he asked and obtained for his son Hermenigild the hand of the young Austrasian princess Ingunthis, sister of Childebert. The little princess—she was scarcely more than a child—thus recrossed the Pyrenees which her mother had crossed on a similar errand fourteen years before. She was attended by a brilliant retinue; but she came bringing dissension into the palace of the Visigoths, and to herself exile and untimely death.

The cause of dissension was—need it be said?—the difference of creed between the two royal families to which the bride and bridegroom belonged. In the previous generation both Brunichildis and Galswintha had easily conformed to the Catholic faith of their affianced husbands. Probably the counsellors of Leovigild expected that a mere child like Ingunthis would, without difficulty, make the converse change from Catholicism back into Arianism. This was ever the capital fault of the Arian statesmen that, with all their religious bitterness, they could not comprehend that the profession of faith, which was hardly more than a fashion to most of themselves, was a matter of life and death to their Catholic rivals. Here, for instance, was their own princess Brunichildis, reared in Arianism, converted to the orthodox creed, clinging to it tenaciously through all the perils and adversities of her own stormy career, and able to imbue the child-bride, her daughter, with such an unyielding devotion to the faith of Nicaea that not one of all the formidable personages whom she met in her new husband's home could avail to move her by one hair's breadth towards 'the Arian pravity'.

Chief of all these baffled proselytisers was Queen Goisvintha, own grandmother to the bride and step-mother to the bridegroom. This ancient dame was a bitter Arian, who had inflicted some humiliations on the ecclesiastics of the opposite party, and whose one blinded eye, covered with the white film of cataract, was hailed by the Catholics as a Divine judgment on her wickedness. It was at first with soft and fair speeches that the aged grandmother—who had received Ingunthis with real gladness—sought to persuade her to quit the Catholic fold and to be baptized as an Arian. But the child-wife answered with manly spirit, 'It is sufficient for me to have been washed from the stain of original sin by baptism, and to have confessed the Trinity in one equality. This doctrine I avow that I believe with my whole heart, nor will I ever go back from this faith'. By this stubborn refusal the wrath of Goisvintha was aroused. She seized the child—so says the Catholic Gregory—by the hair of her head and dashed her to the ground; she trampled her under foot and beat her till the blood spirted forth; she ordered her to be stripped and thrown into a pond: but all these outrages failed to shake the constancy of the heroic princess.

Of these proceedings, on the part of his wife, Leovigild seems to have been a passive, probably an unwilling spectator, and it was perhaps in order to deliver his daughter-in-law from such persecution, that he assigned the city of Seville, far from his own new capital Toledo, as the residence of the youthful pair; associating Hermenigild with himself in the kingdom.

In their new home by the Guadalquivir Ingunthis began to ply her husband with entreaties that he would leave the falsehood of heresy and recognize the verity of the Catholic law. Although Hermenigild came by the mother's side from a Catholic family, his maternal uncle being the celebrated Leander, bishop of Seville, he long resisted the arguments of his wife, but at length he yielded and received Catholic baptism, perhaps from Leander's own hands; changing his name to John.

After this defection of the young prince from the ancestral creed there was of course 'doubt, misconception, and pain' in the royal palace. The father invited the son to a friendly conference. The son refused, as he said, 'because thou art hostile to me on account of my being a Catholic'. He called upon 'the Greeks' that is the generals of the Empire, to protect him from his father's anger; but as their succour had not arrived when the royal army was approaching, he accepted the mediation of his brother Recared, entered the hostile camp, and cast himself at the feet of Leovigild. The king raised him by the hand, kissed him and spoke to him kindly; but afterwards, 'forgetful' (says Gregory) 'of his plighted oath, sent him into exile, removing from him all his usual attendants except one young slave'.

It is not easy to trace the exact course of subsequent events, but it is clear that Hermenigild must have escaped from exile, and renewed his rebellion, or, as the annalists (though of the Catholic party) call it, his 'tyranny'. The war seems to have lasted for two years. 'The Greeks', as far as we can see, brought little effectual help to

Hermenigild, but the Catholic Suevi put forth all their strength on his behalf. Their king perished in a vain attempt to raise the siege of Seville, and the war ended in the triumph of Leovigild, the captivity of Hermenigild, and the final overthrow of the Suevic kingdom.

Once again the king's son was sent into confinement; this time at Valencia. Possibly he escaped thence, for a few months afterwards we hear of his being slain at Tarragona. The Gaulish historian says that his father put him to death; but a somewhat better informed Spanish annalist attributes the murder to a certain man named Sisbert, without hinting at Leovigild's approval of the deed.

The unfortunate Ingunthis was thus made a widow in her nineteenth year and left with one orphaned child, a boy, already it would seem three or four years old, whom she had named Athanagild, after her maternal grandfather. She had been apparently separated from her husband during these years of war, for when the rebellion first broke out he had left his wife and child under the care of his Greek allies. Those allies, however, fully recognized the value of such a hostage as Ingunthis, sister of the king of the Franks, and daughter-in-law of the king of the Visigoths, bearing in her bosom one who one day sit on the throne of Leovigild. In all the subsequent negotiations, reconciliations, wars, between Leovigild and his son, neither of them could ever recover Ingunthis from 'the Greeks'. And now, after her husband's death, she was not restored to her home by the Moselle, but sent in a kind of honourable captivity over the wide Mediterranean, her destination being Constantinople: so little consideration or sympathy did the orthodox Greeks exhibit for one who had in her tender youth done and suffered so much on behalf of the Creed of Nicaea. As it turned out, Ingunthis never reached the city of the Bosphorus, but died, probably worn out by home-sickness and sorrow, at Carthage, and was buried there. The little Athanagild was sent on to Constantinople, where it is probable that he eventually died, as we never hear of his return to the West of Europe, though that return was the subject of much diplomatic discussion.

It was by the captivity of Ingunthis and her child that the tragedy of Hermenigild was connected with the history of Italy, but it is worthwhile to devote a few sentences to the sequel of that tragedy in Spain. The stout-hearted Leovigild died in the spring of 586, not many months after the murder of his eldest son. His second son, Recared, who then ascended the throne, promptly put his brother's murderer to death, and by another striking exercise of his royal power proved that the example of that brother, the courage of his young sister-in-law, the exhortations of his uncle Leander, had not been lost upon him. In 587 he assembled a conference of prelates, both Catholic and Arian. They argued with one another and the heretics were unconvinced; but when they appealed to miracles the orthodox won a signal victory. Recared openly avowed himself a believer in the Three Equal Persons of the Godhead, and before many years were passed he had, by gentle compulsion, brought the whole Visigothic nation to share his change of faith. Thus was the last of the great Arian kingdoms, except the Lombard, brought into communion with that form of Christianity which was professed by the Empire, and thus was, if not the 'Eldest Son of the Church', perhaps the most obedient of her children brought into the fold.

In the opinion of some scholars, it is to Recared that we should assign, if not the composition, at any rate the authoritative publication of that great battle-hymn of orthodoxy the 'Quicunque vult', which is generally known by the incorrect name of 'The Creed of Saint Athanasius'.

In his father's lifetime Recared had been betrothed to the young Regunthis, daughter of the Neustrian Chilperic and Fredegundis; but on her father's assassination this matrimonial project fell through, though the bride had already arrived on her nuptial journey almost at the borders of the Visigothic kingdom. After his conversion Recared obtained, as we have seen, the promise of the hand of Chlotoswinda, sister of Childebert, thus depriving Authari of the coveted Frankish alliance. In fact, however, this betrothal also came to naught, and the wife whom Recared eventually married was a Visigothic lady named Baddo. Certainly the Merovings and the kings of the Visigoths were not happy in their matrimonial diplomacies.

We return to the court of Childebert, whither came messengers from the Emperor Maurice with the usual request that the Frankish king would send an army to Italy to fight against the Lombards. Childebert, supposing that his widowed sister was still alive and in the Emperor's power, complied the more readily with the Imperial request, and sent an expedition across the Alps. But the heterogeneous character of the state which obeyed the rule of the Austrasian king reflected itself disastrously in his army. So great a dissension arose between the Franks and Alamanni serving under his standards, that, without any gain of booty for themselves or conquest of territory for their master, they were obliged to return home.

At length, perhaps early in the year 588, the tidings of the death of Ingunthis reached the court of Metz, but at the same time probably came the news that the little Athanagild was detained at Constantinople. Thereupon all the resources of Austrasian diplomacy were employed to procure his liberation. Four ambassadors were sent to Constantinople: their names and titles were Sennodius the 'Optimate', Grippo the king's Sword-bearer, Radan the Chamberlain, and Eusebius the Notary. They took with them a whole packet of letters, sixteen of which have been preserved. Though written, of course, not by their reputed authors, but by some clerk—probably an ecclesiastic—in the royal chancery, they are interesting for the light which they throw on the ways of European diplomacy in the sixth century, and especially on the relations existing between the barbarian kings of Western Europe and the Imperial Court. There are letters to the Emperor's father, the veteran Paulus; to his little son Theodosius, a child of about the same age as Athanagild; to the Patriarch of Constantinople; to the Master of the Offices, the Quaestor and the Curator of the Palace, beseeching the good offices of all these illustrious persons on behalf of the ambassadors, sent as they were to establish a firm peace between the Frankish monarchy and the Empire. In these letters we hear but little of the true, the personal object of the embassy; but those addressed by Childebert to Maurice, and by Brunichildis to the Empress, are more outspoken, and plead earnestly for the liberation of the little orphan who, by the waves of a cruel destiny, had been drifted so far from his home. Two of the letters are addressed to Athanagild himself. In the letter of Brunichildis to her grandson, notwithstanding the stilted style of its address, there is something really pathetic. Though the prattling child is called 'the glorious lord, king Athanagild', he is also 'my sweetest grandson whom I long after with inexpressible desire'; and we read that the vanished Ingunthis will not seem altogether lost, if only Brunichildis may gaze upon her offspring.

The whole correspondence, and the way in which this little one's captivity among 'the Greeks' influences the movements of armies, and accomplishes results which thousands of solidi had been vain to procure, give us a favourable idea of the strength of the family tie among these otherwise unattractive Merovingian monarchs. Even the apathetic Childebert seems to show some concern for the safety of his nephew: but doubtless Brunichildis was the moving spirit in the whole negotiation. That fierce old Spanish lioness, though her life was spent in fray, had something of the lioness's longing to recover her captured whelp.

The embassy to Constantinople was hindered by various causes, which will shortly be mentioned, and did not finally return to Metz till near two years after it had set forth; but meanwhile Childebert, anxious to show his zeal in the Emperor's service, sent an army into Italy, probably in the early summer of 588. Over this invading host Authari and his warriors won a signal victory. They felt that the very existence of the Lombards as an independent nation was at stake, and thus, fighting for their freedom, they triumphed. It is admitted by Gregory that the slaughter of Frankish soldiers was greater than that on any former battlefield whereof the memory was preserved. Many captives were taken, and only a few fugitives returned, with difficulty, to their native land. This victory was the chief event of Authari's reign, and, notwithstanding some subsequent reverses, obtained for him an enduring place in the grateful recollection of his countrymen.

During the year 589 warlike operations seem to have slumbered. The year was memorable to the of inhabitants of Italy for other ravages than those of war. Throughout the north of Italy the streams fed by the Alpine snows rushed down in such destructive abundance that men said to one another in terror that Noah's deluge was returning upon the earth. Whole farms were washed away by the raging streams, and in those villas which remained might everywhere be seen the corpses of men and cattle. The stately Roman roads were in many places broken down (and what a Roman Emperor had built a rough Lombard king would find it hard to replace), and some of the smaller paths were quite obliterated. Impetuous Adige rose so high that a large part of the walls of Verona was undermined and fell in ruin, and the beautiful church of San Zenone outside the city was surrounded by water reaching up to the highest tier of windows; but men noted with awe-struck wonder that not a drop penetrated into the building itself. This most terrible storm of a stormy season raged on the 17th of October, the thunder rolling and the lightning flashing in such fashion as was rarely witnessed even in the middle of summer. And only two months later the unhappy city of Verona, which had suffered so severely from the plague of great waters, was well-nigh reduced to ruin by the opposite enemy, fire.

At Rome the Tiber rose so high that it overtopped the walls which lined its banks, and filled all the lower quarters of the City. 'Through the channel of the same river,' says our historian, 'not only a multitude of serpents, but also a dragon of vast size, passed through the City and descended to the sea.'

One reason why there were no great warlike operations in the year 589[1] may have been that Pavia was busy with the marriage festivities of Authari and Theudelinda, and that Ravenna was witnessing the departure of Smaragdus and the advent of his successor in the office of Exarch. A bitter ecclesiastical quarrel, the result of the miserable controversy about the Three Chapters, was raging in the churches of Istria. The energetic but hot-tempered Smaragdus could not refrain from interfering in this quarrel. Laying violent hands on the patriarch of Aquileia he dragged him and three other bishops to Ravenna, and forced them by threats and violence to communicate with the bishop of that city. It was, in the general opinion, a fitting punishment for this high-handed treatment of the Lords anointed, that Smaragdus was shortly afterwards 'attacked by a demon' (in other words, became insane), and had to be recalled to

Constantinople. His successor, Romanus, held the office of Exarch for about eight years (589-597).

In the year 590 Grippo, the ambassador who had been sent to Constantinople to plead for the liberation of the young Athanagild, returned to Metz, having a strange and terrible story to tell of his mission. It seems, on the whole, most probable that the little prince was already dead when the embassy of 588 arrived at Constantinople, that Grippo had returned to his master with these tidings, and had then, in the year 589, been sent forth on another embassy to the same court, his companions this time being two Gallo-Roman noblemen, Bodigisil, son of Mummolinus of Soissons, and Evantius, son of Dynamius of Arles. For some reason quite unknown to us, but probably connected with the closing scenes in the life of Ingunthis, these ambassadors went first to the great city, the metropolis of Roman Africa, which was called Magna Carthago, to distinguish her from her lesser namesake in Spain.

While the ambassadors were tarrying here, waiting the commands of the Prefect as to the order of their journey to the Imperial Presence, a tragedy was enacted, which affords us one of our few glimpses of the condition of the great African city in the century and a half that elapsed between her liberation from the yoke of the Vandals and her conquest by the sword-preachers of Islam. One of the body-servants of Evantius saw in the market-place some piece of merchandise which caught his fancy, and following 'the simple plan,' laid hold of it and took it with him to the inn where the ambassadors were lodging. The shopkeeper, thus defrauded of his goods, demanded daily, with ever more clamorous entreaties, the return of his property, and at length, one day, meeting the servant in the street, laid hold of his raiment and said, 'I will not let you go till you have returned that which you stole from me'. At this the Frank drew his sword and slew the importunate creditor. He then returned to the inn, but gave no hint to any of his companions of what he had done. The chief magistrate of the city1, when he heard of the murder, collected his soldiers and some of the common people, whom he hastily armed, and went at their head to the inn where the ambassadors were then enjoying their siesta after the midday meal. Hearing an uproar the Franks looked out and were at once called upon by the city magistrate to come forth and assist in the investigation into an act of homicide which had just been committed. Perplexed and alarmed, they asked for some security for their lives before laying down their arms. Meanwhile the angry and excited mob began to rush into the house. First Bodigisil, and then Evantius stepped out and were slain at the inn-door. Then Grippo, fully armed and at the head of his retainers, sallied forth and said, 'What the crime may be, about which you say that you are come to enquire, I know not; but here are my two colleagues, who were sent on an embassy to the Emperor, slain by the swords of your citizens. We came for peace and for the common benefit of your state and ours; but now there will never be peace between our kings and your Emperor. I call God to witness of your crime, and He will judge between us and you'. At this the Carthaginian levy was dismissed, and the Prefect of the city, coming to Grippo's lodging, endeavoured to soothe him and began again to discuss the old question of the formalities which were to be observed in their visit to the Imperial court.

The Carthaginian outrages on the Frankish embassy had at least the effect of making the surviving ambassador's work easier at Constantinople. The Emperor laid aside his usual haughty isolation of manner, received Grippo as an honoured guest, and promised that ample satisfaction should be made to his master for the wound given to his dignity by the outrages at Carthage. In fact, however, this 'ample satisfaction' consisted in arresting, some months later, twelve men who were said to have been guilty of the murder, and sending them bound to the court of Childebert, who was told that he might put them to death if he thought fit, or else allow them to redeem their lives at the rate of 300 *aurei* apiece. The Frankish king took reasonable objection to this mode of settling the dispute. 'There was no proof that these twelve men had anything to do with the murder. They might be slaves of some Greek courtier, who allowed them to be cheaply sacrificed in this manner, while the king's ambassadors, who had been slain at Carthage, were men of noble birth'. Grippo too, who was standing by, said, 'The Prefect of that city collected two or three thousand men, came against us, and killed my colleagues. Ay, and he would have killed me too, if I had not known how to defend myself like a man. If I go to the place myself, I can pick out the men who did the deed, on whom your master will have to take vengeance, if he desires peace as much as he professes to desire it'. King Childebert gave the word : the captives were allowed to depart, and, with provoking reticence, the historian never tells us how the affair ended.

This last incident, however, of the sham satisfaction for the outrage belongs to the later stages of the business. On the return of Grippo, in the early months of 590, with his first friendly message from the Emperor, and his promise of ample justice on the authors of the outrage, Childebert—so mighty were still a few courteous words from the great Roman Emperor to a barbarian king—at once prepared an army, the fourth that he had put in the field for the invasion of Italy.

Twenty dukes were the officers of this new army, acting under three leaders, whom we should call generals of division, and whose names were Audovald, Olo and Chedin. All three divisions of the army, according to the usual Frankish custom, robbed and murdered to their hearts' content, long ere they passed the frontiers of their own land, beginning this work of devastation in the immediate neighbourhood of Metz.

When they had crossed the Alps, Audovald with seven1 dukes encamped over against Milan. Olo with no ducal subordinate marched against Bellinzona. Chedin, with thirteen dukes, descending, the valley of the Adige, threatened Verona.

Olo, approaching incautiously too near to the walls of Bellinzona, was pierced in the breast by a javelin and died of the wound. His soldiers probably joined the main body under Audovald, who was pressing the siege of Milan. The Franks, ravaging the country in all directions, found themselves continually liable to be cut off by detachments of the Lombard army, issuing forth from the fortresses, in which they had Audovald taken refuge. At length, however, the two hosts were drawn up in battle array on the western side of Lake Lugano, where the small but deep stream of the Tresa issues from the lake, carrying its waters to the broader expanse of Maggiore. On the banks of this stream stood a Lombard warrior, armed with helmet and breastplate, and brandishing a spear, who shouted, 'This day will it appear to which side God will grant the victory'. A few of the Franks crossed the stream, set upon the Lombard champion and overthrew him, whereupon his countrymen, who had apparently staked all their hopes on the rude ordeal of this unequal combat, took to flight. The Franks then crossed the stream, but the operation occupied some time, and when they entered the Lombard camp they found nothing there but the ovens and the marks of the tent-poles.

One cause of the discouragement and flight of the Lombard army was doubtless the near approach of the Exarch's forces, which seemed to be on the point of effecting a junction with the Franks. Messengers arrived from the Imperial camp to announce this approach to Audovald, and to say that they hoped in three days' time to reach the camp of their allies. The signal of their arrival on the scene was to be the wreaths of smoke arising from a certain villa on the hill to which the envoys pointed and which they promised to set on fire. For six days the Franks waited, but no smoke was seen to arise from the doomed villa. Apparently the failure to effect this junction was the death-blow to the hopes of the western division, and they returned home at the end of the sixth day.

In the north-east, Chedin, with his thirteen dukes, took five border-fortresses in the Tridentine duchy, from the inhabitants of which he received oaths of fidelity to King Childebert, permanently annexing, or rather restoring, the surrounding territory to the Austrasian kingdom. He also took ten towns or villages in the valley of the Adige, two in the Valsugana, and one in the immediate neighbourhood of Verona. Verona itself saw the Frankish host encamped beneath its walls, but apparently resisted the siege with success, if any regular siege there were.

The fortress of Verruca, erected, or at any rate greatly strengthened, by Theodoric the Ostrogoth, was saved by the intercession of two bishops, Ingenuinus of Seben and Agnellus of Trient, and the inhabitants were permitted to redeem themselves at rates varying from one to 600 solidi. From all the conquered towns a long train of captives was carried back into Gaul, though in many cases their surrender had been obtained by the solemn oath of the generals, that the liberty and property as well as the lives of the citizens should be spared. In fact, to any one who studies the obscure notices which we possess of this campaign, it will be clear that the Franks, burning, murdering and pillaging, were more terrible to the miserable inhabitants of Italy than even the Lombards themselves.

But now, as so often before and since, the climate of Italy, especially her climate in the later months of summer, proved the best friend to her afflicted inhabitants. The terrible deluges of 589 were succeeded by pestilence in the following year, pestilence which carried off the venerable Pope Pelagius II, and which, in the form of dysentery, so terribly wasted the invading army that Chedin, as well as Audovald, found himself obliged to abandon the campaign.

After three months of destructive wandering over Return the plains of northern Italy, the whole Frankish army returned into its own country, having practically accomplished nothing. It had not been able to force the Lombards to fight, for they had remained behind the walls of their fortresses. It had not, as it once hoped to do, captured Authari himself, for he had tarried in his strongly fortified capital of Pavia. It had not succeeded in collecting great spoil, for the soldiers had to sell their clothes and even their arms for bread, before they reached their native land. Plague-stricken, ragged and desperate, the great army of the Twenty Dukes disappeared from the soil of Italy.

The Byzantine version of this campaign of 590—agreeing as to the main result, but differing as to the cause of the failure—was given by the Exarch of Italy, who wrote to Childebert two letters (still extant) bitterly complaining of the incapacity of the Franks in war, and of their cruel conduct towards the Roman provincials. The following are the most important sentences in these letters:—

'We heard from your messenger, the Vir Magnificus, Andreas, how earnestly your Glory desired to stop the effusion of Christian blood and to liberate Italy from the unspeakable Lombards. We heard and reported to the most clement Emperor and to his Augusta (your most serene sister) that for this purpose you had ordered the most flourishing army of the Franks to descend into Italy.

'Even before their arrival God gave us, in answer to your prayers, the cities of Modena, Altino and Mantua, which we won in fight and beat down their walls, hastening as we did to prevent the unspeakable ones from attacking the Franks before our arrival1.

'Then we heard that the Vir Magnificus (your general) Chedin was encamped with 2000 men near the city of Verona, and had sent an ambassador to Authari with some talk about terms of peace. That king had shut himself up in Ticinum; the other dukes and all their armies had sought the shelter of divers fortresses; we saw ourselves on the point of joining the Roman army to the 20,000 of Chedin, supporting them by our cutters on the river, besieging Ticinum and taking captive king Authari, whose capture would have been the greatest prize of victory. While we were urging Chedin to this course and anxiously consulting your dukes as to each step to be taken against God's enemies and ours, what was our amazement to find that they, without any consultation with us, had made a ten months' truce with the Lombards, abandoned the opportunities for booty, and marched suddenly out of the country.

If they had only had a little patience, today Italy would be found free from the hateful race, and all the wealth of the unspeakable Authari would have been brought into your treasury; for the campaign had reached such a point that the Lombards did not consider themselves safe from the Franks even behind the walls of their cities.

'For ourselves (besides the previously mentioned successes) Parma, Rhegium and Placentia were promptly surrendered by their dukes to the Holy Roman Republic, when we marched to besiege these cities. We received their sons as hostages, returned to Ravenna, and marched into the province of Istria against our enemy Grasulf. His son, the magnificent Duke, Gisulf, wishing to show himself a better man than his father, came with his nobles and his entire army, and submitted himself to the Holy Republic. The glorious patrician, Nordulf, having come by the favour of our Lords into Italy, gathered his men together again and in concert with the glorious Osso and his Roman army recovered several cities.

'Now, as we know that your anger is kindled by the return of your generals, leaving their mission unaccomplished, we pray you to send speedily other generals, more worthy of your trust, who may fulfill the promises made by you and your pious ancestors. Let them come at such a time that they may find all the enemy's harvests in the field. Tell them to inform us by what routes and at what dates we may expect them. And, above all things, we hope that when, with good luck, the Frankish army descends from the Alps, the Romans, on whose behalf we ask your aid, may not be subjected to pillage and captivity; that you will liberate those who have been already carried off into bondage; and that you will direct your generals not to bum our workshops, so that it may be clearly seen that it is a Christian nation which has come to the defence of Italy'.

There is much which, owing to our imperfect knowedge of persons and events, is obscure in these letters of the Exarch, but we can see in them quite enough of bitterness and misunderstanding to account for the failure of the coalition to accomplish its full purpose and drive the Lombards out of Italy. At the same time it is clear that the Lombards were in great danger, and that Authari had a narrow escape of being carried in chains to the Austrasian capital and visiting the court of Childebert, not as brother-in-law, but as captive. A considerable tract of country on the southern bank of the Po was recovered for the Empire; but this was won more through the disloyalty of the Lombard dukes—perhaps weary of the strict rule of Authari—than by any bravery of the Byzantine soldiers. Still, a hundred miles of the great Aemilian way had been cleared from the presence of the invader; the frontier of the Empire had been pushed up to within twenty miles of the Lombard capital, and the delusive hope of once more extending the dominions of 'the Republic', from the Adriatic to the Gulf of Genoa, floated before the eyes of the Imperial governor.

Before the summer of 590 was ended, Authari sent an embassy first to the king of Burgundy and then to the king of Austrasia, praying, in somewhat humble fashion, for peace and alliance with the nation of the Franks. The ambassadors were courteously received by Guntram and terms of peace between the Lombards and the Franks of Burgundy were agreed upon. They were still at the court of Childebert when they heard the unexpected tidings of their master's death.

King Authari died at Pavia on the 5th of September, 590, being still in the prime of youthful manhood and having reigned less than seven years. His death was by some attributed to poison, but, as pestilence was ravaging Italy in that year, and he had been living for months in the unwholesome atmosphere of a blockaded city, it seems more reasonable to attribute the event to natural causes, especially as no author and no motive is suggested for the crime.

Though the last few months of Authari's reign were clouded by adversity, it is evident that he guided the fortunes of the Lombard state with vigour and success. Some of the constitutional changes connected with his assumption of royal power, and especially with that arrangement whereby the Lombard dukes surrendered half of their territory in order to endow the new kingdom with a royal domain, are reserved for consideration in a later chapter.

CHAPTER VII.

GREGORY THE GREAT.

'King Authari dying: left no seed. Then all the Lombards', says Paulus, 'since the queen Theudelinda pleased them well, decided that she should remain queen, and that whosoever of the Lombards should be chosen by her as husband should wear the royal crown. She, therefore, taking counsel with the wise men of the realm, chose Agilulf, duke of Turin, for this double honour. For he was a strong man and a warrior and well fitted by manly beauty, as well as by courage, to grasp the helm of the kingdom.

'Now this Agilulf (who was also called Ago) was with the rest of the Lombard nobles at Verona, when Theudelinda came thither amid the rejoicings of the people to wed her first husband, Authari. And it so happened at that time that the air was greatly disturbed, and that a certain tree in the royal garden was struck by lightning, accompanied with a mighty thunder-crash. Agilulf then, having among his servants a certain youth with a spirit of divination, who, by diabolical arts, could foretell things to come, was secretly told by him, "That woman, who has just been wedded to our king, will after no long time be thy wife". Which, when Agilulf heard, he told the boy that he would cut off his head, if he said anything more of that matter. "I may be killed," quoth the boy, "but it is none the less certain that woman has come into this land to be thy wife'.

'And now behold, after the death of Authari, Theudelinda ordered Agilulf to come into her presence, and she herself hastened as far as the town of Laumellum to meet him. And when they had met, after some words spoken, she ordered wine to be brought, and after she had first drunk of it, she ordered the residue to be handed to Agilulf. Then he, receiving the cup from the queen, reverently kissed her hand; but she with a blush and a smile said, "He ought not to kiss my hand who has the right to kiss my lips". So, raising him up to her salute, she opened to him her intentions concerning her re-marriage and the royal dignity.

'The wedding was celebrated amid great rejoicings. Agilulf, who was a kinsman of the late King Authari, assumed the royal dignity in the beginning of the month of November (590), and afterwards in the month of May, when all the Lombards were gathered together into one place, he was solemnly raised to the kingdom at Milan'.

So runs the Saga of Theudelinda and Agilulf in the pages of Paulus. Modern criticism, which would rob history of every touch of poetry, suggests doubts as to the accuracy of the story; but there seems no reason why it should not be strictly true. Of course the tale as to the divining boy, coupled with the suspicions as to the unnatural character of Authari's death, might easily suggest that the second marriage of Theudelinda was the climax of some dark domestic tragedy; but no contemporary writer makes this obvious suggestion, while the high and noble character of the great queen herself, and (as far as we can discern) of her second husband also, utterly negatives any such suggestion.

Let us look a little more closely at this newly-wedded pair, who are to play so important a part in the history of Lombard Italy. Agilulf, late duke of Turin, now entering on a victorious career which is to last for a quarter of a century, is of Thuringian extraction, though a relative of his predecessor, Authari. He is sprung, therefore, from the great nation settled in the centre of Germany, whose king, Hermanfrid, married Theodoric's niece, and whose state was, about the middle of the sixth century, swallowed up by the all-devouring Austrasian monarchy. He is a man capable in war and of manly beauty, the ideal leader of a still semi-barbarous people.

Theudelinda, daughter of the king (or duke) of the Bavarians, is descended on her father's side from the warlike nation of the Marcomanni, who so often saw the legions of Imperial Rome flee before their onset, and who, after long sojourn in the country which we now call Bohemia, entered, about the year 500, that fair and wide land which now bears their name.

But, on the mother's side, Theudelinda was descended from the old Langobardic kings, for Walderada, wife of Garibald, was daughter of Waccho, who so long ruled the nation in its Pannonian home. Undoubtedly this alliance with the old family of the Lithingi, together with the fame of Theudelinda's beauty and accomplishments, was a powerful motive with Authari when he sought her hand in marriage, and the same remembrance made the chiefs of the proud Lombard nation willing to leave the decision as to the choice of their king in the hands of one who, though foreign-born, was not a stranger in blood.

And in fact Theudelinda is a central figure in the history of the Lombards. As I have said, she reached back through her mother's ancestry to the old barbarous Langobardic kings. She virtually established a new, a Bavarian dynasty in Italy, her descendants and those of her brother, the exiled Gundwald, occupying the Lombard throne with little intermission to the fifth generation. And lastly, she was the main agent in that great change of creed which at last brought the Lombard nation into line with the other Teutonic monarchies of Western Europe, and made it possible—though even then not easy—to establish a *modus vivendi* between the Lombard kings and the successors of St. Peter.

Looking to her later history, we can hardly doubt that so fervent a Catholic as Theudelinda sought to use her influence, even with her first husband, to mitigate the bitterness of his Arianism. But the time was too short for her to accomplish anything noteworthy, and so late as the spring of 590 we find Authari putting forth an edict whereby he forbade the sons of the Lombards to be baptized at Easter according to the Catholic rite. For this act of oppression Pope Gregory saw a righteous retribution in the sudden death which prevented Authari himself from witnessing the celebration of another Easter. Over Agilulf, however, the man whom she had herself exalted to the throne, Theudelinda exercised a more potent influence; and though it cannot be positively stated that he ever formally renounced the creed of his forefathers, he cultivated the friendship of the rulers of the Catholic Church, and seems to have witnessed with complacency the baptism of Theudelinda's son by an adherent of the Creed of Nicaea.

In this great change Theudelinda was powerfully aided by the man who was placed in the chair of St. Peter, about the same time when Agilulf saluted his queenly bride at Lomello; a man who more than all other pontiffs who have received that title merited the epithet of the Great.

Gregory was born, about the year 540, of a noble Roman family, which had already given one Pope to the Church, and many Senators to the State. His father, Gordianus, a tall, grave-visaged Roman noble-man, who lived in a stately palace on the Coelian Hill, held the post of *Regionarius*, a civil office which seems to have represented the secular side of the duties of the seven deacons, each one of whom administered the vast charities of the Roman Church in one of the seven regions into which, for ecclesiastical purposes, the City was divided.

Three of Gregory's aunts on one and the same day embraced with enthusiasm the conventual life, now made illustrious by the fame of Benedict and Scholastica: and though one of them, Gordiana, fell away from that early fervour of faith, returned into the world, and even married her steward, the other two, Aemiliana and Tharsilla, persevered, and died in early life worn out by their pious austerities.

Gregory himself received a good education in Latin literature—the Greek language he never mastered—and apparently had sufficient acquaintance with the ordinary course of instruction pursued by the teachers of rhetoric to despise and avoid their frivolous pedantry. We hear, however, very little about his youth or early manhood, until we find him, about the year 573, filling the high office of Prefect of the City.

The dignity of this office, which brought with it presidency of the Senate, the right to wear a robe of Imperial purple and to be drawn through the streets of Rome in a four-horsed chariot, has been described in an earlier volume of this history. We have also, in following the fortunes of Sidonius and Cassiodorus, had a glimpse of the anxious responsibilities, especially in respect to the food-supplies of the City, which almost outweighed even its dignity. It is probable that when Gregory held the office its duties were lighter and its splendour less than half a century earlier. The Lombards had now been for some years in Italy, and we can perceive that, in presence of this continued danger, there was a tendency in the Imperial government to circumscribe the powers of the merely civil magistrates, and to concentrate all authority in the hands of the military chiefs. But there can be no doubt that the Prefect of the City was still an important personage, and great therefore must have been the marvelling of the populace in the Forum when, one day, the news was spread abroad that the Prefect of the City was about to lay aside his silken robe, decked with jewels, to don the coarse sackcloth of the monk, and to minister as a pauper to his pauper brethren. This, however, was the truth. Gregory laid down his high office (perhaps at the expiration of his its usual term), founded and endowed six Benedictine convents in Sicily (then from various causes the especial asylum and Paradise of the Church), and divided all the residue of his property among the poor, except one possession, the ancestral palace on the Coelian Mount. This abode he turned into a monastery, which he dedicated to St. Andrew, and into this new monastery the descendant of so many Senators entered in mean attire, not as its abbot, but as the humblest of its brethren.

It was apparently in the year 575 that this great change occurred in the life of Gregory. For the next three years he remained in the monastery, enjoying its deep repose and practising its austerities. His food consisted chiefly of uncooked vegetables, which his mother supplied to him on a silver dish, sole relic of the former splendours of the Coelian palace. This silver dish itself was at last given away to one who bore the appearance of a shipwrecked mariner, and who came for three days in succession, asking for alms. A student of these monastic biographies already knows the sequel. Long afterwards the self-styled shipwrecked mariner appeared again as a glorious angel, and told his benefactor that for him was reserved the honour of sitting in the chair of St. Peter and guiding the Church of God.

Of more interest for us, sons of the Saxons, than the conventional stories of the faintings, the fastings, and the macerations of the body, which, notwithstanding the wise caution of St. Benedict, still filled too large a place in the life of a young and earnest monk, is the story (too well known to need more than an allusion here) of the incident which first kindled Gregory's missionary zeal on behalf of the island of Britain. It was during his residence as a monk in the monastery of St. Andrew that Gregory took that memorable walk through the Forum, in the course of which he saw, exposed for sale, the fair-haired and fresh-faced Yorkshire lads, whose angelic beauty suggested to him the mission to the Angles and the hope of rescuing from the wrath to come the heathen inhabitants of Deira, and teaching the subjects of King Aelle to sing Alleluia.

Gregory himself sought and obtained from Pope Benedict I leave to undertake this great mission, and had already accomplished three days' journey towards Britain when, during the noonday halt, a grasshopper lighted on the page of the scriptures which he was reading. His mind at this time, perhaps throughout his life, seems to have been singularly attuned to that pleasant figure of speech which has been so often an 'infirmity of noble minds,' and which grammarians term *paronomasia*. '*Ecce Locusta*!' said he. 'Does this mean "*Loco sta*" ("Abide still in the place where thou art")? Know ye, my companions, that we shall not be suffered to proceed on our journey'. And even while they were talking, before the hot and tired mules were saddled for the next stage of the journey, messengers arrived who told them that the Pope had withdrawn his permission, and commanded Gregory to return. For the people of Rome, who perhaps thought that Benedict had seen without regret the departure of a man whose sanctity overshadowed his own, gathered round the Papal palace, and shouted with terrible voices, 'Ah, Apostolic one! what hast thou done? Thou hast offended Peter; thou hast destroyed Rome in suffering Gregory to depart'.

Thus then Gregory returned to the great City, but not to his convent: for Pope Benedict, whose attention had perhaps, by this very event of his attempted flight and recall, been attracted to the great power and Deacon.' popularity of the former Prefect, now appointed him to the office of 'Seventh Deacon': thus associating him with his own cares and labours. The seven deacons of Rome, as has been already said, super-intended—each one with the assistance of a *Regionarius* and his staff—the distribution of the alms of the Church to the poorer classes of the seven regions of the city. The cares of the public 'annona', which had formerly devolved on the Imperial officers, and pre-eminently on the Prefect of the City, were thus, in great part, if not altogether, now discharged by the officers of the Church. We are not able exactly to state what is meant by the expression 'Seventh Deacon,' but if, as seems probable, it means the Arch-deacon, that office was already looked upon as a frequent stepping-stone to the Papacy.

Soon, apparently, after Benedict I had thus called Gregory to his side, his own pontificate was ended by his death. The choice of a successor fell not, as yet, upon Greg0ry but upon Pelagius II, some of whose letters against the Lombards were quoted in the last chapter. It may have been partly some jealousy of the popularity of Gregory, but more probably a praise-worthy desire to employ his great practical ability on behalf of the Church in a sphere where all that ability was sorely needed, that led the new Pope to send Gregory as his Nuncio, or (as it was then called) his Apocrisiarius to the Imperial court of Constantinople.

The years, probably not more than six in number, during which Gregory remained at Constantinople were important both for the Empire and the Church. He heard a new Emperor proclaimed, and saw a new Patriarch consecrated. On the 14th of August, 582, the over-generous Emperor Tiberius was succeeded by the unconciliatory Maurice; and four months previously the aged Eutychius had been succeeded as bishop of Constantinople by the aspiring John the Faster, a man with whom Gregory was one day to wage a long and difficult spiritual combat. With Eutychius his personal relations appear to have been friendly, but with him too he had a sharp discussion, turning on the mysterious question of the resurrection-body of the saints. Eutychius maintained that this body will be more subtile than aether, and too rare to be perceived by our present bodily senses. Gregory met him with the words of Christ, "Handle Me and see, for a spirit hath not flesh and bones, as ye see me have". Eutychius answered that this was a body specially assumed by the Saviour in order to reassure the doubting hearts of his disciples; a suggestion which Gregory met by some obvious arguments against such a Docetic resurrection. Eutychius quoted, 'Flesh and blood shall not inherit the kingdom of God', and Gregory replied by distinguishing between two different senses of the word 'flesh' in the New Testament. The debate grew warm, and, as such discussions are wont to do, left neither party convinced by the arguments of the other. The good Tiberius visited each of the disputants separately, and tried in vain to reconcile them; but, convinced himself by the arguments of Gregory, committed the treatise of Eutychius to the flames. Ere any open breach had been caused, both the Patriarch and the Nuncio fell sick. Gregory, though his health had been thoroughly broken by his monastic austerities, recovered of this malady, a sharp attack of fever; but Eutychius, who had the burden of seventy years upon him, died of his sickness. On his death-bed he touched his skin, and said to the friends who surrounded him, 'I acknowledge that in this flesh I shall see God'; an allusion to the celebrated passage in Job, which was accepted by Gregory as a recantation of his former errors.

It was on this same book of Job that Gregory, in the intervals of his busy diplomatic life at Constantinople, found leisure to write the voluminous commentary which goes by the name of the *Magna Moralia*, that marvellous treatise the object of which was to show that 'the book of Job comprehended in itself all natural, all Christian theology, and all morals. It was at once a true and wonderful history, an allegory containing in its secret sense the whole theory of the Christian Church and Christian sacraments, and a moral philosophy applicable to all mankind.

For our present purpose it is not the religious but the political results of Gregory's residence at Constantinople which are most important. Though I am not aware that he ever gave utterance to the feeling, we can well believe that a Roman noble, one who had seen from his childhood the triumphal arches, the *fora* and the palaces of Rome, glorious even in their desolation, viewed with some impatience the pinchbeck splendours of the new Rome by the Bosphorus, already, it is true, near three centuries old, but still marked with somewhat of the ineffaceable brand of a *parvenu* among cities.

Gregory made some warm friendships with members of the Imperial family and household. Constantina, the wife, and Theoctista, the sister, of the Emperor; his imperial cousin Domitian, Metropolitan of Armenia; Theodore, the Imperial physician; Narses, a general who not only bore the name, but in some degree shared the fame, of the mightier Narses of a previous generation; these and some others were admitted into the innermost circle of the friends of the Roman Apocrisiarius. But with Maurice himself, though that Emperor paid him the compliment of asking him to stand sponsor for his son, the infant Theodosius, it would seem that his relations were not cordial. We can imagine that the Emperor was worried by repeated applications from Rome for help in men and money against the Lombards; applications with which he felt himself unable to comply. We can imagine also that Gregory, in whose eyes 'Roma caput mundi' was the one absolutely priceless jewel of the Empire, was irritated by seeing the resources of the State muddled away, as he deemed it, in somewhat inglorious campaigns against the Persians and the Avars. With his undoubted genius for affairs, he probably despised the wordy inefficiency of the Greek statesmen; with his old Roman pride he scorned the Byzantine servility. Whatever the cause may have been, and though undoubtedly his residence at Constantinople largely increased his knowledge of the great game of politics, and was an invaluable preparation for his own future political career, it seems clear that he left the Thracian capital with no great love in his heart either for the city or the Caesar. After he became Pope he was still outwardly the loyal subject of the Emperor, but 'the little rift within the lute' was already beginning to mar the harmony of their relations. We seem able to trace here that little crack in the earth which, two centuries later, was to widen into a mighty chasm, separating the successor of St. Peter from the successor of Divus Augustus.

It was probably in 585 or 586 that Gregory returned to Rome, and re-entered the monastery of St. Andrew; not now as a humble monk, but as head of the community. We hear scarcely anything of his life during these years of his second residence in the convent (585-590), except that, during this time, his pen seems to have been put at the service of the Pope, in the interminable controversy with the bishops of Istria, about the condemnation of the Three Chapters. We are also told that he inflicted signal punishment on one of his monks who had sinned against the monastic rule that all things were to be in common. This monk, Justus by name, had some knowledge of the art of a physician, and had in that capacity tended Gregory himself in his frequent illnesses. But he had, apparently by the exercise of his profession, earned three golden solidi, which, against the rule of his order, he kept secreted in his medicine chest. He was attacked by a mortal disease, and his brother Copiosus, a physician outside the monastery, who tended him in his sickness, discovered his secret and reported it to the Abbot. All beside Copiosus were ordered to absent themselves from the sick man's cell. He died almost alone, with the brand of ignominy upon him, in deep penitence for his sin. At his burial his body was laid in unhallowed earth, and a monk threw the three solidi after him into his grave, crying with a loud voice, 'Thy money perish with thee'. But after thirty days the heart of Abbot Gregory relented, and he ordered mass to be said without intermission during thirty days more for the soul of Justus, who at the end of the appointed time appeared in a dream to Copiosus, his countenance radiant with joy, and assured him that hell's torment was ended and that he was now received into the communion of the blessed.

In such cares as these passed away the years of Gregory's abbotship. In 589 came the terrible inundations, at the beginning of 590 the more terrible pestilence which ravaged Italy. On the eighth of February Pope Pelagius II died; the clergy and people of Rome flocked to the gate of the monastery of St. Andrew and insisted that Gregory should fill the vacant chair.

He resisted and wrote a letter to the Emperor Maurice, imploring him to withhold that Imperial assent which in those days was deemed necessary ere the Pope elected by the people and clergy could receive consecration. But the Prefect of the City, who was himself, according to one account, a brother of the Pontiff elect sent a swift messenger, who overtook the bearer of Gregory's letter, suppressed that document, and substituted for it the earnest petition of the people that Gregory should be made Pope.

The answer from the Imperial court was long in arriving, and meanwhile the pestilence raged fearfully in the City. The eyes of all the citizens were turned towards the Abbot of St. Andrew's, who came forth from his seclusion, and, like another John the Baptist, preached a sermon of repentance and conversion to the people.

'The judgments of God are upon us, dearest on the brethren. Let grief and fear open the path of pestilence. Our hearts, for it is indeed with us as the prophet Jeremiah said of old, "The sword reacheth unto the very soul." Lo! the whole people is smitten with the sword of the divine anger and a sudden mortality lays waste the city. The languor of disease does not precede death, for death itself cuts short all its lingering pains. Each one who is struck down is hurried off before he has had time to turn to repentance. The dwellers in the city are not cut off one by one, but in whole companies do they hurry to the grave. The houses are left empty: parents have to behold the funerals of their sons, and their own heirs die before them.

'Let us then turn to Him who hath said that He willeth not the death of a sinner. Let us imitate the three days' penitence of the men of Nineveh and beseech our merciful God to turn away His anger from us. Therefore, dearest brethren, let us come, with contrite hearts and pure hands and minds prepared for tears, to the Sevenfold Litany, to which I now invite you, and the celebration of which will begin at dawn on the fourth day of the week, according to the following order.'

Then followed the programme of the great procession, which gives us an interesting glimpse of the 'regions' and churches of Rome at the close of the sixth century:—

(1) In the church of SS. Cosmas and Damian (in the Roman Forum) were to assemble the great body of the clergy, with the priests of the sixth region.

(2) The abbots and monks of Rome with the priests of the fourth region, in the church of SS. Gervasius and Protasius, on the southern slope of the Quirinal.

(3) The abbesses and their nuns with the priests of the first region, in the church of SS. Marcellinus and Peter, two miles out of Rome on the eastward leading Via Labicana.

(4) All the children, with the priests of the second region, in the church of the martyrs John and Paul, on the Coelian Hill, very near to Gregory's own monastery.

(5) All the laymen, with the priests of the seventh region, in the church of the Protomartyr Stephen, that quaint round building which, with its strange and ghastly modem frescoes representing the torments of the martyrs, still stands, a little to the west of the Lateran.

(6) All the widows, with the priests of the fifth region, in the church of St. Euphemia.

(7) All the married women, with the priests of the third region, in the church of the holy martyr Clement, that church between the Colosseum and the Lateran, the

successive stages of whose development have been recently laid bare and form one of the most interesting monuments of Christian antiquity in Rome.

From their several places of assembly these seven troops of suppliants were to march in solemn procession, with prayers and tears, to the great basilica on the Esquiline, now known as S. Maria Maggiore, and there for three days in succession (Wednesday to Friday) were to implore the pardon of the Lord for the sins of the people.

The assembling took place at dawn, the march through the streets at the third hour of the day, and all as they went sang loud the great penitential hymn Kyrie Eleison. A deacon of Tours, who was present at the ceremony, informed his bishop (the chronicler) that in one hour, while the procession was moving through the streets, eighty men fell to the earth and gave up the ghost; a proof of the severity of the pestilence, but also an event which raises a doubt whether the great concourse, and the excitement of soul caused by the Sevenfold Litany, were the best means of staying its ravages.

With this solemn act of intercession ordered by the chosen of the people, the imagination of much later ages coupled a beautiful legend, which changed the name of one of the best-known monuments of ancient Rome. In the course of the three days' procession, so it was said, Gregory was about to march with the seven groups of chanting penitents over the bridge of Hadrian, in order to worship at the tomb of St. Peter, when, lifting up his eyes, he saw standing on the top of the mighty Mausoleum of Hadrian the Archangel Michael with a flaming sword, which was in the act of returning to its sheath; thereby showing that the penitential Litany was accepted in Heaven, and that the pestilence was about to cease.

From this story the Mausoleum received the name of the Angel's Castle, which it bore already in the tenth century. In later days Pope Benedict XIV fixed the legend for ever in the memories of all pilgrims to Rome, by erecting that statue of St. Michael which has now stood for a century and a half on the summit of 'The Castle of Sant' Angelo.

It seems that seven months elapsed before the Imperial assent to the consecration of the new Pope arrived in Rome. Possibly the wretched state of the City and 0f Italy, distracted both by pestilence and by the ravages of the Lombards, caused delays to the messengers, alike in going and returning. But the assent came at length; probably about the end of August: and Gregory began to prepare for flight, in order to avert the dreaded honour. Legend said that he was carried forth from one of the City gates in a basket of merchandise, and that he hid himself in some solitude of the Campagna, but that his hiding- place was revealed by a light from heaven. His contemporary and namesake, Gregory of Tours, knows nothing of all this. He says simply—and this is no doubt the true account of the matter—that 'while he was preparing for flight and concealment, he was taken prisoner, dragged to the basilica of St. Peter, and having there been consecrated to the Pontifical office, was given as a Pope to the City'.

The letters of Gregory I, for some time after his elevation to the Papacy, are full of lamentations over this disastrous change in his life. 'It is an old and terribly shaken ship,' he writes to the Patriarch of Constantinople, 'the command whereof has been entrusted to my weak and unworthy hands. At every seam the waves are entering, and the rotten planks, shaken by daily and fierce tempests, creak out the word "shipwreck." I pray you, in the Almighty's name, stretch out the hand of your prayers to help me'.

To Theoctista, sister of the Emperor, he writes: 'Under the colourable pretext of bishopric, I am in truth brought back into secular life; for in this office I am in bondage to so many worldly cares, that in no part of my career as a layman can I remember to have been in equal slavery. I have lost the deep joys of my old quietness, and while I seem to have risen into a higher station, internally I am in a state of collapse. Thus must I bewail that I am driven far from the face of my Creator. I was endeavoring each day to put myself outside of the world, outside of the flesh, to banish all the phantasms of the body from the eyes of the mind, and to look with disembodied gaze on the joys of heaven. Not in words only, but in my inmost soul did I pant for the countenance of God, saying with the Psalmist, "Thy face, Lord, will I seek". Naught desiring in this world, naught fearing, I seemed to myself to stand, as it were, at the summit of all things, so that I could almost believe that in me was fulfilled the Lord's promise to His prophet, "I will cause thee to ride upon the high places of the earth". Then suddenly, being caught by the whirlwind of temptation, I have been dashed down from this high pinnacle, and plunged into all sorts of fears and terrors, since, though I have no fear for myself, for those committed to my charge I do greatly tremble.'

Then the Pope goes on, in that vein of mystical commentary which was the fashion of the age, to explain that a contemplative life was the Rachel of his tenderest affections, barren, it might be, of visible result, but lovely beyond telling in his eyes. Homely, blear-eyed Leah, the life of activity and affairs, was doubtless more fruitful in offspring, but she possessed none of his love. Yet now that the veil of night was removed, it was to this bride, unlovely and unloved, that he found himself hopelessly united.

After many more reflections of this kind, he ends a long and interesting letter with a grotesque piece of self-disparagement. 'Behold! the most serene Emperor has ordered an ape to become a lion. A lion indeed it may be called at the Imperial command, but a lion it cannot become'.

In reading these many similar utterances of the greatest Pope who ever sat in the chair of St. Peter, we are forced to ask ourselves, 'Is this passionate reiteration of the formula *Nolo episcopari* quite sincere? Gregory could not but know and feel that he had capacities for the great office of the Popedom, such as no other man then living upon the earth possessed. He belonged to the Imperial race of Rome, and showed forth its noblest qualities, as scarce any Roman had done since Trajan died. Is it possible that he was wholly indifferent to the master-passion of his countrymen, Ambition? Must we not rather believe that even in the days of his Prefecture he had perceived that the office of Pope was the only one which brought with it real power, or which was worthy of a Roman's acceptance? And the successive stages of 'the Great Renunciation' which followed, the laying aside of the purple robe, the conversion of the paternal palace into a monastery, the fastings, the austerities, the self-humiliations,—were they not all parts of a subtle and unavowed canvass for that splendid prize?

As in the cases of Mohammed, of Savonarola, and of Cromwell, this easy hypothesis of conscious hypocrisy seems to me to be a quite inadequate solution of the problem. Rather is the solution to be found in a frank recognition of that dual nature which many men who have played a great part on the stage of the world have evidently possessed. There were two men, not one, within the visible enwrapping of this great Aristocrat Bishop. One man, seeing keenly the follies and vanities of the world, longing after the joys of Heaven, disliking the petty routine of daily business, and cherishing ardent aspirations after that clear vision of the Most High which was thought to be the peculiar guerdon of a life of contemplation:—this man was happy in the cloisters of the Coelian, and had no desire to quit their grateful shade. Another man, inhabiting the same fleshly tabernacle, and thinking through the same brain, saw, as has been said, that none of the offices of the effete and decaying Empire, neither Exarchate, Prefecture, nor Duchy, was, for real power over the wills and inclinations of men, to be compared with the Bishopric of Rome. He saw that the holder of this office had an opportunity of conferring incalculable benefits on powerful races and vast kingdoms of men, and of winning for the half-ruined city by the Tiber a wider and more enduring empire than had been swayed by Titus or by Aurelius. This man, full of a noble ambition, longed to be Pope, and was, perhaps, dimly conscious that the austerities, the generosities, the humiliations of his other self were all bringing him nearer to that splendid goal. But when the goal was reached, satiety began to reign in his soul, and to poison all the joys of possession. Though the strong and vigorous intellect at once set itself to grapple with the difficulties of the situation and overcame them with brilliant success, the body, enfeebled by monastic austerities and tortured by gout, longed for the ordered life and the inviolable repose of the cloister; and the soul, weary of the sordid cares of the administration of the vast Papal Patrimony, yearned for the mystic joys and the serene contemplative happiness which had once been hers. In short, to use his own metaphor, the man was truly wedded to two wives. The Rachel of ascetic holiness was his best beloved, but the Leah of practical beneficence had also a share of his affections, and it was through her progeny, through such facts as the conversion of England, the remodelling of the liturgy, the spiritual conquest of the Lombards, that Gregory most powerfully influenced the world.

The chief monument of Gregory's life of practical statesmanship is the Epistles, composed by him during the fourteen years of his pontificate, arranged in fourteen books corresponding to those years, and filling nearly 500 closely printed pages. Though the writer despised all rhetorical artifices, and even allowed himself to speak disrespectfully of the rules of the grammarians, he wrote in a vigorous style, and his generally correct, if not polished, Latinity was utterly unlike the grammatical chaos which we find in the writings of his namesake of Tours. It is probably the very fact that he did not care to write rhetorically, which makes his letters so much pleasanter reading than the prolixities of Cassiodorus or the pompous obscurities of Ennodius. He does not, like the scholars of the Renaissance period, labour to give all his sentences a hexameter ending, but they are often instinct with manly and simple eloquence. Thus there is in them no affected imitation of Cicero, but often a true echo of Caesar.

These fourteen books of the *Epistles* of Gregory are a vast quarry, out of which the student of early mediaeval history may hew almost endless material. While the letters of the heathen Prefect, Symmachus, give us little beside hollow compliments and literary inanities, almost every letter of Gregory affords some information as to the politics, the morals, or the economics of his age. In this respect it would be hardly too much to say that *Gregorii Epistolae* are only surpassed, and not far surpassed, by the two great Codes of Theodosius and Justinian. It is of course impossible in a single chapter of this book to give any proper idea of a correspondence, for an adequate description of which two volumes like the present would not more than suffice; but a few samples culled almost at random throughout the mighty collection may give some faint idea of the world-wide activity of the Second Founder of the Papacy.

If not the most anxious of the new Pope's duties, of one of the most troublesome to a man who had any longings after contemplative repose, must have been the care of the vast estates which went by the name of the Patrimony of St. Peter. These estates, the proofs of the liberality of the faithful during four or five centuries, had probably been much increased during the last two hundred years by the financial burdens and military perils to which the landowners in outlying districts found themselves exposed. When the demands of the Imperial tax-gatherer were trenching more and more closely on the narrow margin of profit left to the owner of the soil; when the barbarian henchmen of Alaric or Alboin were burning the villas and liberating the slaves in Picenum or Campania, the pleasures of possession began to be outweighed by its anxieties, and the devout landowner felt a strong inducement to make over his threatened domains to the Church and to save his soul by retirement into a monastery, or his body by flight to Constantinople. Notwithstanding all the troubles of the times, the Church had armour of defence both against the tax-gatherer and the barbarian, such as no lay proprietor possessed, and we may well believe that of all the real estate thus surrendered to the Bishops of Rome, they succeeded in retaining by far the largest portion.

The Patrimony of St. Peter (we may well marvel what would have been the feelings of the simple-hearted fisherman of Bethsaida, could he have surveyed the lordly lands which were said to be his inheritance) was largest and richest in the island of Sicily; but it also embraced considerable estates in Rome and its environs, in the country of the Sabines, in Picenum, in the neighbourhood of Ravenna, in Campania, Apulia and Bruttii, in Gaul and Illyricum, and in the islands of Sardinia and Corsica. The precise extent of all these widely scattered possessions can only be approximately stated, but a careful German enquirer[1] estimates it at 1800 square miles. These wide domains, it must be remembered, were not ruled, but owned, as an English nobleman owns his estate, and the revenue accruing therefrom is calculated at £300,000 a year.

The care of this magnificent property, though administered by able and generally by conscientious stewards, was evidently a heavy burden on the shoulders of an ascetic Pope, to whom great revenues and large estates could, in themselves, bring no pleasure.

In the first eighteen months of his pontificate Gregory wrote fourteen letters (some of them extremely long ones, touching on a great variety of topics) to the subdeacon Peter, the steward whom he had set over the Apostolic Patrimony in Sicily, in succession, but not in immediate succession, to a layman, Antoninus the *defensor*. Antoninus, it seems, had in several instances pushed the claims of the Roman Church both against its neighbours and its serfs (*coloni*) beyond what justice and humanity warranted. The new Pope shows in his letters a praiseworthy anxiety that all these wrongs shall be redressed by his representative. Peter, however, as far as we can judge from the letters addressed to him, though an honest man and a personal friend of Gregory's, seems to have been somewhat weak, forgetful and procrastinating. A few passages selected from the fourteen letters just mentioned will help the reader to imagine their general tenour.

'It has come to my ears that during the past ten years, from the times of Antoninus the *defensor*, many persons have suffered violence and wrong at the hands of the Roman Church, and that men openly complain that their borders have been invaded, their slaves enticed away, their moveable property taken from them by the strong hand with no pretence of judicial process. Pray, in all these things, let your Experience exercise the most strenuous vigilance, and let this letter be your warrant for the restoration of whatever you may find to have been violently taken away or wrongfully detained in the Church's name during these ten years: that he who has suffered wrong may not be forced to come to us, undertaking the toil of so long a journey, when, after all, the truth of his story cannot be so well tested here as there. Considering, then, the awfulness of the coming Judgment, restore all things that have been sinfully taken away, being assured that you will bring me in a more profitable return if you accumulate the reward of a good conscience than if you bring back great riches.

'We are informed also that many complain of the loss of slaves, saying that any runaway slave who professes himself to be under ecclesiastical law is at once claimed and kept by the Church's bailiffs (*rectores*), who, without any judicial decision in their favour, back up the slave's assertions by violence. All this displeases me as much as it is abhorrent to the spirit of justice and truth. Wherefore I desire that your Experience should shake off all sloth and correct all misdeeds of this kind which you may discover. Let any slaves now in the Church's power, who were taken away without a judge's order, be restored before any proceedings are taken; and if any such do lawfully belong to the Holy Church, let the right to them be asserted against their alleged owners in a regular and orderly action.

'Amend all these abuses with firmness, for you will thus approve yourself a true soldier of the blessed Apostle Peter, if in causes where he is concerned, you do anxiously maintain truth, without suspicion of partiality even towards Peter himself. But if, on the other hand, you see some piece of property which you think justly belongs to the Church, beware of defending our right even to this with the strong hand; especially since we have published a decree, forbidding, under the penalty of our anathema, the affixing of notices of claim to any property, either urban or rural, by our Church. Whatever reasonably belongs to the poor ought to be defended by reason, lest otherwise our unrighteous action in a good cause should make even our just claims seem unjust in the sight of Almighty God. May the noble laymen and the glorious Praetor love you for your humility and not abhor you for your pride. So act that your humility may not make you slack, nor your authority rigid; but that the righteousness of your purpose may give a seasoning to your humility, and your humility may impart mildness even to your righteousness'.

In another letter, Gregory says that he has been informed that the monks of a city in the south of Italy dispersed by barbaric violence (probably some raid made by the Lombards of the Duchy of Benevento), are wandering over Sicily without a ruler, without any care as to the health of their souls, without the habit of their order. These vagabond monks are all to be collected into the monastery of St. Theodore at Messina, and there placed under proper discipline.

In another long and extremely interesting, but difficult letter, Gregory describes the various unjust exactions to which the peasants on the farms of the Sicilian Patrimony had been subjected, and orders the immediate reformation of these abuses. These peasants (called *rustici Eclaesiae*) had to pay a corn-rent to the Church, that is the equivalent in golden *solidi* of a certain number of pecks of corn; and Gregory enjoins that they shall not have the value of the peck oppressively beaten down in times of plenty. Thus, if there were a bountiful harvest, the Church under Gregory's liberal management of her estates would leave to her tenants the whole of the profit which the favourable year had brought them. It would certainly seem, however, as if an unvarying price fixed for the *modius* must have borne hardly upon the rustic in years of scarcity.

The iniquitous oppressions of the farmers of the ecclesiastical revenue, some of whom insisted on the peasants supplying 25 *sextarii* to the *modius* instead of the normal 16, were rigorously suppressed, a margin of 2 *sextarii* only (or 18 to the *modius*) being left to allow for shrinkage or short measurement. The unjust weights which, according to the report of a previous administrator, were found to be in use in some parts of the Patrimony, were to be at once broken, and new and righteous weights made in their stead. To prevent the recurrence of any similar exactions after Pope Gregory's death, each tenant was to receive a document called his *libellus securitatis,* in which the exact sum that might be legally claimed from him was to be clearly set forth.

Besides these and many other ordinances of a general kind for the regulation of the estate, a great number of cases of individual hardship were dealt with in this letter, which gave orders for their relief.

Both Antoninus the *defensor*, and a certain Theodosius (who was perhaps a subordinate in the Patrimonial Estate-office), seem to have died in debt to the Church. The legacies left by Antoninus were to be in part discharged by Peter out of his sequestered property. From the goods of Theodosius a return was to be made to the unfortunate peasants who had been forced to pay their taxes to the Imperial government twice over, Theodosius having collected the money from them and then made default in his payments to the treasury. 'If, after repayment of the sum required for this purpose, amounting to 507 *solidi* [£304], there are still left, as you reckon, 40 *solidi* [£24], they may be handed over to the daughter of Theodosius, that she may redeem her property which is in pawn. And we wish also that her father's drinking-cup be restored to her.'

Almost every word of this long and carefully-written letter, of some forty paragraphs, is in favour of a wise and generous liberality towards the tenants, the servants and the debtors of St. Peter. Yet that the Pope could, on occasion, use sharpness is clearly seen, not only by the command, twice or thrice repeated, 'Lay aside all sluggishness,' and fulfill this or that commission, but also by the following caustic paragraph about an order which Gregory had given with reference to a member of his own family, and which Peter had apparently forgotten :—

'We must express our great thanks to your Anxiety, since I desired, in respect to my brother's affairs, that you should retransmit his money [hither], which injunction you have treated with as complete forgetfulness as if it had proceeded from the meanest of your slaves. Now then, let—I will not say your Experience, but—your Negligence set about obeying my commands. Anything of his which you may find to have been lodged with Antoninus, retransmit [hither] with all speed.'

At last the long letter, the fruit probably of many days of toil, ends thus:

'Carefully read over all these commands and lay aside that too fondly indulged habit of negligence. Cause my writings which I have addressed to the rustics to be read to them on every farm; that they may know how they ought to defend themselves by our authority against the violence of their superiors, and let authentic copies be given to every one of them. See that you keep all these precepts in their integrity, for I, who write them for the preservation of justice, am thereby freed from responsibility, and you, if you neglect my words, remain bound. Consider the terrible Judge who is coming, and let that consideration cause you to tremble now before His Advent, lest you should then fear, and have no plea to urge in your behalf, when before His presence Heaven and Earth shall tremble. You have heard what I wish: see that you perform it'.

In other letters of this series Gregory gives orders that the son of a certain Godischalcus being blind and poor, shall receive annually 24 pecks of wheat, 12 pecks of beans, and 20 *decimatae* (?) of wine, at the charge of the Patrimony: while Pastor, a man apparently of somewhat higher rank, formerly on the staff of the Magister Militum, who is also afflicted with blindness, having a wife and two servants, is to receive annually 300 pecks of wheat and 300 of beans out of the same revenues.

Joanna, the wife of Cyriacus, a woman who was converted from Judaism to Christianity after her betrothal, has been subjected to some annoyance in the courts of law, probably by her Jewish relatives, from whom she is to be protected in future. The possessions of the Church of Tauromenium (beautiful Taormina), which border on the Patrimony of St. Peter, are said to have been unjustly invaded by the bailiffs of the Roman Church, and it is ordered that these wrongs shall be redressed.

The correspondence closes with another long letter, the receipt of which, we may be sure, caused some bitter heart-stabs to the procrastinating sub-deacon. After directing that the Jewish tenants on the Church's farms, if they are willing to become Christians, shall receive some mitigation of their pecuniary burdens, the Pope passes on to ordinary landlord's business: 'Let the cows that are too old to calve, and the bulls which appear to be useless, be sold, so that at least their price may serve some good purpose. I wish all those herds of horses which we keep in very useless style, to be disposed of, and only 400 of the younger mares to be kept for breeding. Of these, one is to be sent to the tenant of each farm, who is each year to make some return on its behalf, for it is a very hard thing that we should be paying 60 *solidi* [£36] a year to our stud-grooms, and not receiving 60 denarii [£2 10s.] from our stud.'

Towards the end of the letter, the Pope says, 'You have moreover sent us one wretched horse and five good asses. The horse I cannot ride, because it is a wretch, nor the asses, good as they are, because they are asses. I pray you, if you are disposed to serve me, to bring with you something worthy of my acceptance.'

The reason why the Pope tells Peter to bring the horse with him is because he has already, in an earlier part of the letter, summoned him to Rome. Gregory himself is sick, but he desires the sub-deacon to come to him with all speed before St. Cyprian's day, that he may escape the equinoctial storms. He wishes to consult with Peter whether it will be better that he should return to Sicily or that some one else shall be appointed in his place. Several sentences reveal the Pontiff's deep dissatisfaction with his subordinate.

'If you have an atom of sense, you will be able to arrange this matter so as to perform my will without displeasing the bishop of Syracuse. I wrote to you to pay the legacies of Antoninus. I cannot think why your Experience has delayed the execution of my orders. I desire you to attend to these payments at once, that you may not, when you come to visit me, leave behind you the groans of the poor.'

'Abbot Martinianus tells me that the storehousl in the Praetoritan monastery is not yet half finished. Wherefore, what can I do but praise the zeal of your Experience? Even now, being thus warned, rouse yourself and show what you can do towards the construction of that monastery.'

'I am further informed that you have ascertained that some [moveable] things and many farms [in our possession] belong of right to other owners, but that, owing to the entreaties of certain persons or your fear of them, you hesitate to restore these things to their lawful owners. But if you were truly a Christian, you would fear the judgment of God more than the voices of men. Give your mind to this business, about which I have incessantly warned you. If you fail to fulfill it, my words will rise up as witnesses against you at the last day.'

Such being the mood of mind to which eighteen months of Peter's administration had brought his master, it is not surprising that his official career soon came to an end. The letter from which these extracts have been taken, virtually contained his dismissal, and we have no more epistles of Gregory addressed to Peter the sub-deacon of Sicily.

Of course, not only the receipt, but also the expenditure, of the large income derived from the Papal Patrimony imposed severe labour on so conscientious a steward of his wealth as Pope Gregory. Hints of his discriminating liberality to the poor have reached us in the few letters already quoted. The description of his public benefactions given by Joannes Diaconus, though written nearly three centuries after his death, seems vouched for in a way that entitles it to credit:—

'He turned into money the revenues of all the *patrimonia* and farms, according to the ledger of [Pope] Gelasius, of whom he seems to have been a most studious follower: and then, having collected all the officials of the Church, the palace, the monasteries, the lesser churches, the cemeteries, the deaconriess, the reception-houses for strangers, in the city and suburbs, he decided from the ledger (in accordance with which, distribution is still made) how many solidi, out of the above-named receipts in gold and silver, should be given to each person four times in the year, namely, at Easter, on the birthday of the Apostles, on the birthday of St. Andrew, and his own birthday. At the first dawn of the day of the Lord's resurrection, in the basilica of Pope Vigilius, near to which he dwelt, he gave to all bishops, presbyters, deacons, and other dignitaries of the Church, an *aureus* a-piece, after bestowing on them the kiss of peace.

'On the first day of each week, he distributed to the poor generally, the same kinds of produce which were collected from the rents. Thus corn in its season, and in their several seasons, wine, cheese, pulse, bacon or other wholesome flesh, fish and oil, were most discreetly distributed by that father of the family of God. But pigments and other delicate articles of commerce were courteously offered by him to the nobles of the City, so that the Church came to be regarded as the warehouse of the whole community.'

'To three thousand maids of God (whom the Greeks call *monastriae*) he gave 15 lbs. of gold for bed-furniture1 and bestowed upon them for their daily stipends 80 lbs. annually.'

' Moreover, every day, by means of charioteers appointed to the office, he sent out cooked rations to all the sick and infirm poor throughout the streets and lanes of the City. To those who had seen better days he would send a dish from his own table, to be delivered at their doors with his Apostolic blessing.'

The biographer then goes on to tell us of Gregory's grief on learning that a poor man in one of the common lodging-houses of Rome had died of hunger. He blamed himself as if he had killed the man with his own hands, and for some days he would not permit himself to celebrate mass.

'There exists to this day,' Joannes continues, 'in the most holy muniment room of the Lateran Palace, a very great paper volume, compiled in his times, wherein the circumstances of all persons of either sex, of all ages and professions, whether at Rome or in the suburbs, in the neighbouring towns, or even in the far-off cities of the coast, are described in detail, with their names, ages, and the *remunerationes* which they received.'

Certainly in all these philanthropic engagements there was abundance of work, abundance of drudging and wearisome routine, to fill up the hours of a studious and meditative Pope. Leah's progeny came with quick-thronging steps, with loud and importunate voices, to call the *Paterfamilias Dei* away from communion with the Rachel in whom his soul delighted.

In addition to the cares of the largest landowner in Italy and the greatest almsgiver in Rome, there were those cares which came upon Gregory as the Metropolitan Bishop of the West. In reading his correspondence we realize how thoroughly monarchical the constitution of the great Latin Patriarchate had now become. For generations the tendency of events had been in this direction, and when a man of Gregory's saintly character and intellectual force entered the Lateran Palace, the transformation was complete. The chair of St. Peter was now indeed a throne. Though desirous to preserve the dignity of his brother bishops unimpaired, Gregory would assert, upon occasion, almost with severity, the right of the Bishop of Rome to the unquestioning obedience of all the bishops of the West, and even to receive appeals from the East and to reverse the judgments of the Patriarch of Constantinople himself. So wide a spiritual Empire necessarily brought a vast accession of care to him who ruled it, especially when the ruler was such a man as Gregory, in Africa.

In Africa he organized a system of firm and quiet ecclesiastical pressure, which, with the frequently invoked assistance of the secular arm, at length extinguished the schism of the Donatists—a schism which had lasted for three centuries and which the Catholic Church in Africa vanquished, only just in time to enjoy the honours of victory before she and her rivals were swept together into destruction by the followers of Mohammed.

In Sardinia Gregory stirred up the clergy to undertake the conversion of the idolatrous Barbaricini, and set himself to control the vagaries of the bishop of Cagliari, the white-haired Januarius, who crowned the eccentricities of a lifetime by going forth into his neighbours' corn-fields, and ploughing them on the Lord's Day, both before and immediately after his celebration of mass.

In France, by his correspondence with his somewhat in lethargic vicar, Vergilius, bishop of Arles, he laboured, with more zeal than success, to correct that barbarization of the Gallican Church, of which the pages of 'Gregory of Tours' furnish so terrible a picture, to uproot the simony which was destroying the Church's life, to induce the bishops to resume their almost abandoned custom of assembling in national and provincial councils for the reform of abuses, and to combat the disorders which were making the Frankish monastery, and yet more the Frankish nunnery, a scandal to Christendom.

With Visigothic Spain, which (as has been related), after nearly two centuries of uncompromising Arianism, had entered the Catholic fold three years before Gregory's elevation to the Papacy, the correspondence is somewhat less active than might have been expected, from the splendour of such a conquest and from the ties of old friendship which bound the Pope to the most conspicuous actor in the drama, Leander the Metropolitan of Seville. In a letter, written just after his consecration, Gregory, while expressing his joy at the conversion of his 'most glorious son Recared' to the Catholic faith, entreats Leander to warn his nephew against the snares of the devil, which, in his case, will probably take the shape of temptations to spiritual pride. The correspondence then seems to languish. Perhaps Recared expected a more enthusiastic welcome from the pontiff. Perhaps he was engaged in suppressing some revolt of the discontented Arians. At any rate the first letter from the Visigothic king to the Pope is assigned to so late a date as the ninth year of Gregory's pontificate. In this letter, written in somewhat halting and barbarous Latin (possibly the consciousness of these defects had something to do with the King's silence), Recared excuses himself for having so long delayed to express his reverence to the head of the Christian priesthood. Hindered for three years by the cares of his kingdom, he had at last chosen certain abbots and charged them to bear his gifts to St. Peter. But when already within sight of the shores of Italy they were overtaken by the violence of the sea, thrown back on the rocks near Marseilles, and barely escaped with life. Now at last Recared sends another messenger, with a golden chalice studded with gems for the Apostolic treasury, and the expression of his profound reverence for the Pope, whom he has already learned to love through his conversations with his uncle Leander. Apparently this letter was accompanied or followed by a communication of a more political nature.

King Recared desired to establish a *modus vivendi* with the Emperor, who had acquired (as we have seen) a footing on both sides of the Peninsula, and, with this loathe view, asked for a sight of the treaty between Justinian Empire and an earlier Visigothic king, a copy of which he believed to be stored in the archives of the Holy See. The request gives us a glimpse into the still lingering barbarism of the court of Toledo, which, for a document so vitally affecting its own interests, had to depend on the presumed superior accuracy of the Papal chancery, though that body had really no immediate concern in the affair. In this case, however, Gregory replied that the archives of the See had suffered so severely from fire in the time of Justinian, that scarcely a single paper of that time was still extant.

As some compensation for this disappointment, and an indication of good-will, 'we send you', says the Pontiff, 'a little key from the most holy body of the blessed Apostle Peter, in which is enclosed some iron from his chains, so that the same metal which bound his neck to the cross of his martyrdom may loose you from all your sins. The bearer of these presents will also offer you a crucifix, wherein is some of the wood of our Lord's cross, and some hairs of the blessed John the Baptist: so that by means of this cross you may also have the consolations of Christ, through the intercession of his Forerunner'.

The spiritual conquest of Spain was glorious, but it had been achieved before Gregory mounted the Papal throne. The conquest of England was all his own work, his own daring thought translated into action. In 596 he sent forth Augustine, Abbot of his own beloved monastery of St. Andrew, on his memorable mission, armed with letters of introduction to all the chief prelates of Gaul, requesting them to speed the missionaries on their way. But whatever might be the outward professions of respect and obedience tendered by these eminent ecclesiastics, so weak was their faith, and so alarming the picture which they drew of the savage temper of our Saxon forefathers, that the timid monks, accustomed as they were to the stormless atmosphere of the convent, shrank from encountering the perils before them, and Augustine actually returned to Rome to beseech permission to abandon the difficult enterprise. Then it was that Gregory's singleness of purpose and inflexibility of will saved the endangered project, and he who had once, in obedience to a Pope, left the path to Britain untrodden, now, as Pope, claimed the obedience of Augustine, sent him forth again on his great mission, and forced upon the timid Abbot of St. Andrew's the glory of being the first Archbishop of Canterbury.

The success of that mission, the conversion of Ethelbert and the larger part of his nobles and people to Christianity, are events which lie beyond our present province, and are too well known to need more than a passing allusion here. All that we are here concerned with is the fresh burden of toil, fruitful and triumphant, but still toil, which the conduct of this great enterprise must have brought upon the pain-racked Pope. In 601 he sent out a second mission under Mellitus, to reinforce Augustine and his fellow-labourers. These also had to be sped upon their difficult way; letters of commendation had to be written for them to the Gaulish bishops, and protection had to be claimed from the Frankish kings. In the same year a letter was sent to Augustine, in which, at great length, Gregory replied to eleven questions which the English missionary had addressed to him as to the government of the new province won from heathenism. The questions travelled over a wide range of subjects, touching on the division of the Church revenues, the punishment of sacrilege, the degrees of affinity within which marriage was prohibited, the consecration of bishops, the ceremonial defilements which operated as a bar to holy communion, and so forth. Gregory's answers were upon the whole wise and statesmanlike, especially in reference to varying ecclesiastical usages. 'Your Brotherhood knows already the custom of the Roman Church in which you remember that you were nourished. But my pleasure is that you should carefully select, not only from the Roman, but also from the Gallican, or any other Church, whatsoever you can find that is pleasing to Almighty God, and in the Church of the Angles, which is still new to the faith, implant all that you have thus collected from various Churches. For we ought not to value a thing because of the place from which it has sprung, but value places according to the things which they produce. From the several Churches, therefore, select all customs which are godly, religious, just, and, weaving them all into one wreath, crown with them the souls of the Angles.'

Besides that which came upon Gregory daily, the care of all the Churches, he laboured also at that reformation (if it were in truth a reformation) of the music of the Church, which has perpetuated his fame in some quarters where his other great deeds are little remembered. He remodelled the Roman Liturgy, composing a new *Sacramentarium* and *Antiphonarius*, and giving to the service of the Mass nearly the same form which it bears at the present day in the Roman ritual. He established and endowed two schools of singers, one at the Lateran, the other under the steps of the basilica of St. Peter at which the pupils were taught the Gregorian ' plain song' which now superseded the Ambrosian chants, and the musical scale divided into octaves, which superseded the eighteen *tones* or five tetrachords of the Greeks. Three centuries after his death, men still looked with veneration upon the memorials of Gregory's musical enthusiasm which were preserved in the Lateran Palace, not only the authentic copy of his *Antiphonarius*, but the bed on which he reclined when, racked with gout and dyspeptic pains, he still persisted in giving his lessons to the choir, and the rod with which he corrected the youthful singers, when they failed to render a passage in one of his chants correctly.

As diligently as he laboured to cultivate the musical sense of his people, even so diligently did he reorganize his own household at the Lateran on the strictest monastic and Roman models. All the lay servants who had ministered to the pride and luxury of former pontiffs were banished from his palace. None but monks and clergy were to be found in attendance on the visible head of the Church. The Pope led, with these, his brethren in religion, that life in common which was the characteristic of the convent, and we may fairly infer that he, though lord of such mighty resources, submitted himself to that stern prohibition against private property which he had enforced so rigidly against the unfortunate Justus.

This change applied not merely to the personal attendants of the Pontiff. He first, apparently, inaugurated that strict rule that the Church's possessions should be governed by churchmen, which prevailed with few exceptions down to the fall of the temporal power of the Popes in our own day. 'No layman could administer any part of the Church's patrimony, but all ecclesiastical charges were held by ecclesiastical men, laymen being relegated to the profession of arms or the occupations of agriculture'.

And not only was the lay element excluded from even the outer courts of the Church's service; the descendants of so many Roman Senators also barred his doors against the all-pervading influence of the barbarians. 'None,' says his biographer, 'of those who were in the Pope's service, from the lowest to the highest, ever showed anything barbarous either in speech or attire, but the purest Latinity of speech, and the constant use of the *toga* of the Quirites or the *trabea* [of the old Consuls] preserved, as it were, an inviolate Latium in the dwelling of the Latin Pope.'

From his palace in the ancient domain of the Senator Lateranus, the gift of Constantine to the Roman See, Gregory doubtless often wandered to his own ancestral home on the slope of the Coelian Hill, scarcely more than half a mile distant, that palace which had become the monastery of St. Andrew. There are still shown his marble chair and a recess in the wall, in which, if the inscription speak truly, the great Pope often passed the night. There undoubtedly, for centuries after his death, were visible the contemporary portraits, in fresco, of himself and his parents, with which the liberality of Gregory had adorned the walls of the convent. Near the fountain in the courtyard were two doors, on one of which St. Peter, in a sitting posture, was represented as holding out an encouraging right hand to the *regionarius*, Gordian, father of Gregory. Gordian was depicted as tall of stature, with somewhat solemn face but penetrating eyes, with short hair and scanty beard. His feet were shod with the military *caliga*, and over his dalmatic was thrown a mantle (*planeta*) of a chestnut colour.

Silvia, the mother of Gregory, was painted as also tall, but with a round and cheerful face, beautiful notwithstanding the wrinkles of age, and with the large grey eye of genius. On her head she wore the turban of a Roman matron, and over her milk-coloured tunic a white veil flowed in ample folds from her shoulders to her feet. With two fingers of her right hand she made the sign of the cross, while her left hand held the Psalter, open at the words, 'My soul liveth and it shall praise thee, and thy judgments shall help me.' A scroll in the background of the picture, running from the right shoulder to the left, bore the words, 'GREGORIUS SILVIAE MATRI FECIT.'

In an apse behind the monks' *cellarium* (cupboard) was the likeness of Gregory himself, designed by the same artist—a namesake of his own—who had painted the portraits of his parents. A face which combined in comely proportions the length of his father's, and the roundness of his mother's, countenance; a high and noble forehead crowned with two little curls bending towards the right; a head, bald above but with a wisp of nearly black hair, brushed back behind his ears; dark and small eyes, and a slightly aquiline nose; fresh-coloured cheeks, which became even high-coloured towards the close of his life; moderate stature and a goodly figure: long taper fingers which seemed well adapted to handle the pen of the writer;— such was the guise in which, 270 years after his death, John the Deacon beheld the mightiest of the Popes, the converter to Christianity of our Saxon forefathers.

CHAPTER VIII.

GREGORY AND THE LOMBARDS, 590-595.

From the deeds of the great founder of the mediaeval Papacy we must turn to follow for a little while the far humbler fortunes of the Lombard king.

Immediately on his elevation to the throne, Agilulf turned his attention to that which was the most pressing necessity of the Lombard state, the conclusion of peace with the Franks. Two missions were dispatched with this object to the Austrasian court, both going from the Duchy of Trient, and both doubtless proceeding by the pass of the Brenner, through what had once been the Roman provinces of Rhaetia and Vindelicia. Agnellus, bishop of Trient, went to negotiate for the return of the prisoners whom the Franks had carried off from his diocese in the cruel raid of the previous year. It seems doubtful whether complete success crowned his efforts, but he had at least the joy of bringing back to their homes many captives whom the Austrasian queen-mother had herself redeemed from bondage. In the difficult task of assaying the strangely compounded character of Brunichildis, let at least this good deed be remembered to her credit.

The other, a more directly political mission, was entrusted to Euin, duke of Trient, and brother-in-law of Queen Theudelinda. We have no details as to his journey; we are only told that 'he went to Gaul to obtain peace, and having obtained it, returned home'. The Austrasian king had perhaps perceived by this time that he could not conquer, could only ravage, Italy, and that, in unduly weakening the Lombards, he was but playing the game of the Emperor. The hostility of Neustria was becoming more dangerous, as the son of Fredegundis was growing out of infancy into boyhood. The old actors, too, were soon to pass away from the scene. The easy-tempered Guntram of Burgundy died early in 593. Childebert, who of united that kingdom to his paternal inheritance of Austrasia, enjoyed his wide-reaching sway but three years, and died in 596, having only attained his twenty-sixth year. His sons, children of nine and ten years old, succeeded him, Theodoric in Burgundy, and Theudebert in Austrasia. There were thus, now, minors on all the three Frankish thrones. Brunichildis hoped to govern two kingdoms as regent in her grandsons' names, but her hope was disappointed. Expelled from Austrasia, she took refuge in Burgundy, and sought to avenge herself by Burgundian arms on the

Austrasian rebels. Civil war and domestic confusion became the normal condition of Gaul, and for the twenty-five years during which Agilulf was consolidating the Lombard throne, the Frankish monarchy was in a state of partial eclipse. These were, perhaps, some of the causes of the change which now came over the relations of the two peoples. The change itself is undoubted; with the accession of Agilulf the hostilities between Frank and Lombard—so irritating to the student by their want of plan, and so lamentable for the sufferers by their purposeless barbarity—cease, and for many generations Italy is left to work out her own destinies, undisturbed by any interference on the side of Gaul.

The next duty of Agilulf was to assert his royal authority against the subject dukes, who could look back to a still recent time when they had no king over them, and some of whom had seen with anger the elevation of a Thuringian stranger over their heads by a woman's favour.

One of these was Mimulf, who in the recent campaign had traitorously surrendered himself to the Frankish dukes. His stronghold was the island of St. Julian in the Lake of Orta. Notwithstanding his watery defence he was captured and slain. Ulfari, duke of Treviso, who had also rebelled (perhaps had gone over to his Imperial neighbours), was besieged and taken prisoner.

The most powerful and the most obstinate of all the rebel nobles was Gaidulf1, duke of Bergamo. By right of his important duchy, possibly also by right of some relationship with Authari of Bergamo, Gaidulf had probably himself aspired to the kingdom. Agilulf, however, marched against him, received his submission, and forced him to give hostages for his future fidelity. How long he remained loyal we know not; but next time that he broke out into rebellion we find him not behind the walls of Bergamo, but in that cave of Adullam, the island in the Lake of Como. This island, after the defeat of the Byzantine general Francio, had apparently been annexed to the territory of Bergamo, and the rich treasure found there had been entrusted to Gaidulf's keeping. The island was now successfully attacked, Gaidulf's soldiers expelled, and the treasure carried off to safer keeping at Pavia. Gaidulf fled to Bergamo, was there taken prisoner by Agilulf, a second time pardoned and a second time listened to when he repeated his promises of loyalty. We shall see at a future time how these promises were kept.

These domestic disturbances being quelled, Agilulf, doubtless at the earliest moment of leisure, turned his thoughts towards the long struggle with the Empire; a struggle which was now passing into a chronic stage and involving a second generation of combatants. Rome, Ravenna, Naples, Genoa; these four cities were Empire's grasp, and so long as these cities and the territories round them were in hostile hands, could any king of the Lombards feel that his possession of the remaining three-fourths of Italy was secure? Rome and Ravenna especially, the old and the new capitals of Emperors, were always alluring and always defying the Lombard attack. The Pope at Rome, the Exarch at Ravenna, held perilous communication with one another by the long nerve-filament of the Flaminian Way. Might it not be possible for the Lombard marauders to destroy that communication, to isolate the two capitals from one another and then to conquer them in detail? It seemed doubtless feasible enough to a Lombard duke; but it was never wholly done, and even its partial accomplishment was only attained towards the very end of the Lombard domination. Instead of the Lombard king being able to separate Rome from Ravenna, the Via Flaminia practically separated him from his fellow-countrymen in the South. The duchies of Spoleto and Benevento (whose histories will be hereafter described more in detail) became more and more detached from the great body of the monarchy, whose heart was in Pavia; and the Empire, though powerless to expel the Lombards from Italy, was powerful to divide and to scatter them.

The impression made by the events which we are now considering, on the political condition of Italy was deep and long-enduring. In our own day a new generation is arising which is accustomed to the appearance of United Italy on the map: but all men of middle age remember how the maps of their boyhood showed a great irregularly-shaped region called 'The States of the Church', reaching across the waist of Italy, from the north-east to the south-west: almost within sight of Venice, where it touched the Adriatic, almost within sight of Naples, where it touched the open Mediterranean. That strange rhomboidal figure, which once seemed to present so hopeless a barrier to the unity of Italy, was a direct survival from the age when Rome and Ravenna were the two great strongholds of the Empire in the Italian peninsula, and when the Flaminian Way was the all-important line of communication between the city of the Pope and the city of the Exarch.

There was, however, one station on the Flaminian Way which had been occupied by the invaders, and by the which a Lombard duke had made the seat of power. This was Spoletium, now Spoleto, almost exactly half-way between the Tyrrhene Sea and the Adriatic. Here Farwald had reigned, and here in 591 *Ariulf* was reigning, drawing ever nearer and nearer to Rome, so that it seemed, in those early days of Gregory's pontificate, as if the great prize of the World-City's capture might after all fall into the hands, not even of a king, but of a mere duke of the Lombards. To Gregory himself, and all true Roman hearts within the City, the outlook must have seemed indeed a dreary one. As far as they were concerned, Roman territory, once deemed world-wide had shrunk into limits little wider than those of the early days of the Republic. Latium with a corner of Etruria and a few square miles of Sabine territory—this was the *Ducatus Romae*: this was all the territory in which the citizens could move about, and even then only with a precarious and menaced freedom. As they looked forth from the walls of their City, they knew that the *Ducatus Romae* was almost bounded by the visible horizon. North-westward the Cassian Road led up to the dark brow of the Ciminian Mount. Just over the shoulder of that forest-crowned hill was Viterbium, and in Viterbium reigned a Lombard duke. On the northern horizon were the Sabine hills, at whose foot lay Interamna with its waterfalls, and Interamna was an outpost of Lombard Spoletium. Far nearer and even within sight of Rome were the towers of Tibur and Praenestes, high up on their hills against the sunrise; and though these towns were still Roman, they were now frontier towns, looking forth on Lombard territory. It was only towards the south-east, where stretched the old Volscian land, and towards the west, where rolled the friendly sea, that the Roman could gaze without feeling that he was gazing towards the near dominions of a foe.

The letters of Gregory, in the early years of his pontificate, give us a vivid picture of his anxieties and distresses, hemmed in as he was within such narrow bounds, daily hearing of, and all but seeing, the desolation wrought by the invaders. Writing to one of his old friends at Constantinople, the Patrician and Quaestor John, in the beginning of 591, he says, 'You have intended to do me a kindness [in assisting my elevation to the papacy], and may God repay you for your good mind towards me, but you have brought me, the lover of quietness, into a state of continual disquiet. For my sins I find myself bishop, not of the Romans but of the Lombards; men whose promises stab like swords, and whose kindness is bitter punishment. Hither has your patronage led me. But do you, who still have the power, fly from the business of this world, because, as far as I see, the more progress a man makes in this, the more he falls off from the love of God. Moreover, I send you a most sacred key, from the body of the blessed Apostle Peter, Prince of the Apostles, made illustrious by the many miracles performed by its means on the bodies of many sick persons, and enclosing some filings from his chains. Let those chains therefore, which once clasped that holy neck, now be hung round your neck and sanctify it.'

In another letter to the Judicial Assessor Paulus, Gregory begs his correspondent to come and assist in the extreme need of the Roman City, 'because outside the walls we are incessantly molested by the swords of the enemy, and within we are threatened by the yet graver peril of a mutiny of the soldiers'.

The effect of all the ravages, not only of the Lombards during the recent years, but of their predecessors during the two previous centuries, was already seen in reducing the fertile regions of the Campagna to a desert. The two towns of Mintumae and Formiae (both in our own day represented only by ruins) were to be joined under one bishop (the bishop of Formiae), 'because we have learned' says the Pope, 'that the Church of Mintumae is, owing to the desolate condition of the country, utterly stripped both of clergy and of people'.

The ecclesiastical administrator of Campania (Anthemius the subdeacon) was enjoined to prevent the dwellers on the Papal patrimonies, who with their wives were fleeing from barbarian savagery, from taking refuge on the Insula Eumorphiana, on which was erected an oratory to St. Peter. 'There are other places of refuge in the neighbourhood, and I think it highly inopportune that women should be dwelling on the same island with monks.'

So far, however, up to the end of the first year of Gregory's papacy, the tide of battle had not rolled close up to the walls of Rome. But with September, 591, when his second year of office began, hostilities became more active. The terrible pestilence, from which Pope Pelagius had died, was still raging in Italy, and Gregory, writing to the bishop of Narni, exhorts him to turn the panic caused by its ravages in that city to good account spiritually, by labouring among the Lombards as well as Romans within its walls, and persuading the heathens and the heretics to turn to the true Catholic faith. Narni was emphatically a frontier city, but there is perhaps room for a doubt whether the Lombards here referred to were conquerors who had carried the city by a surprise, or the remnant of some of the Lombard armies, who, under various generals, had deserted to the Empire in recent years.

The next letter, however (written on the twenty-seventh of September, 591), gives no uncertain sound of war. It is addressed to Velox, Master of the Soldiery, stationed probably at Perugia, certainly somewhere on the road between Ravenna and Rome.

'I told your Glory some time ago that I had soldiers ready to come to you at your present quarters : but as your letter informed me that the enemy were assembled and were making inroads in this direction, I decided to keep them back. Now, however, it seems expedient to send some of them to you, praying your Glory to give them suitable exhortations, that they may be ready to undertake the labour which falls upon them. . . . And do you, finding a convenient opportunity, have a conference with our glorious sons, Maurice and Vitalian: and whatever, by God's help, you shall jointly decide on for the benefit of the Republic, that do. . . .. And if you shall discover that the unutterable Ariulf is breaking forth either towards Ravenna or in our direction, do you fall upon his rear and exert yourselves as becomes brave men, that so, by God's help, the high opinion which the Republic already holds of you may be raised yet higher by your glorious labours.'

The autumn and the winter of 591 passed away, apparently, without bringing the dreaded invasion. But the Pontiff was looking anxiously towards his northern frontier, desiring to strengthen himself against attack from the side of Tuscany. Here, about thirty miles from Rome, south of the Ciminian Mountain, stood the two little towns of Sutrium and Nepe. These towns, which, in the infancy of the Republic, had been won for her by the valour of Camillus, were now part of her northern barrier against invasion. Sutrium and Nepe under Maurice were thus what the Firths of Forth and Clyde had been under Antoninus. The Pope, who as one grasping the helm of the State at a moment of extreme peril spoke with all the authority of a king, addressed a short letter 'to the clergy, council, and commonalty dwelling at Nepe.'

'To the clarissimus Leontius, bearer of these presents, we have entrusted the care and responsibility for your city, that by his vigilance in all things he may make such arrangements as shall be for your advantage and that of the Republic. We therefore admonish you by these presents to render to him in all things due obedience, that none may dare to despise him, when he is toiling for your benefit. Whosoever shall resist his lawful commands will be deemed to rebel against us; and whosoever listens to him listens to us. If any should venture—which we do not expect—after this admonition to think that he may treat Leontius with contempt, let him clearly understand that he does so at his peril.'

It is easy to see from one short letter like this how the distance from the seat of Empire, the interruption of communication with Ravenna, the lordship of the vast Patrimony of St. Peter, were all tending to turn the Pope, with his will or against his will, into a temporal sovereign. Not only would Pope Symmachus not have so written under the strong rule of Theodoric, but under the weakest of the phantom emperors who flitted across the stage in the middle of the fifth century, it is inconceivable that such a letter could have been addressed even by the mighty Pope Leo to the inhabitants of the most insignificant village in the Campagna.

As the spring drew on, Ariulf again showed unwelcome signs of life. In April, Gregory, writing to the bishop of Ravenna, asked him to examine into the case of certain bishops in the obedience of the Roman see, 'who cannot come hither by reason of the interposition of the enemy'. Then, in June, we find Gregory writing as follows to the Masters of the Soldiery, Maurice and Vitalian, who, notwithstanding their high official titles, seem to have been really his generals, responsible to him and not to the Exarch.

'The magnificent Aldio, after the arrival of your messengers, wrote to us that Ariulf was now very near, and we feared lest the soldiers who are being dispatched by you should fall into his hands. But, by God's help, our son, the glorious Master of the Soldiery, has made his preparations to meet him. And let your Glories also, if the enemy should march hither, fall upon his rear and, with God's help, do what you can according to your wonted valour. For we trust in the power of Almighty God and of the blessed Peter, Prince of the Apostles, on whose natal day they hope to shed our blood, that they will find him too strong for them, and that immediately.'

Soon after the dispatch of this letter Vitalian came to Rome, had a personal interview with the Pope, and carried back his commands, both oral and written, to his comrades. Then another person appeared upon the scene—a messenger from the Lombard host, bearing a letter written by Ariulf himself, and dated the 11th of June. In this letter he mentioned, probably by way of boast, and in order to show how closely he was drawing his net round the City of Rome, that the inhabitants of Suana had promised to surrender to him. Suana, now the miserable little village of Sovana in the Etruscan Maremma, was a strongly fortified town as late as the thirteenth century, though its chief celebrity was derived from the fact that there was born the only other Pope who could for a moment contest with the first of the name the title of Gregory the Great. In the year 592 it can only have been an outlying fortress of the Empire, being fully forty miles beyond the frontier of the *Ducatus Romae*, and the marvel is that it should have resisted the Lombard attack so long.

With the despatch which the Pope now sent to the two generals, Maurice and Vitalian, he enclosed the letter of Ariulf, and continued, 'Do you therefore carefully read this letter, and see if the citizens of Suana have persevered in the faith which they promised to the Republic. Take from them important hostages, the possession of whom may give you confidence in the fulfilment of their promises; and bind them moreover with fresh oaths, returning to them that which you have already taken by way of pledge, and healing their spirits by your speeches.'

So far had spoken the monarch and the statesman, but then came in the churchman's fear of doing anything that might put the souls of his flock in jeopardy. If the Suanese had sworn, even to the hurt of the State, they must not be encouraged to break their oaths. 'But if you shall clearly ascertain that they have treated with Ariulf for their city, or even have given him hostages with that intent— a point as to which his enclosed letter leaves us in doubt—then give the whole matter your most careful consideration, that neither your souls nor ours may come under any burden by reason of [violated] oaths. Accomplish then whatsoever you may deem advantageous to the Republic. Let your Glories so act that on the one hand we give no occasion for blame to our adversaries [at the Imperial Court], nor on the other hand neglect God while looking to the welfare of the State. Be careful, my glorious sons, because, as far as I can ascertain, Ariulf has collected his hostile forces, and he is said to be now quartered at Nardiae, and if, through God's anger against him, he should choose to direct his course hither, do you, by the Lord's help, lay waste his own territory1, or at least let those whom you send carefully post their sentinels lest some serious mishap should befall you.'

How the affair of Suana ended we are not informed, but the most probable conjecture is that Ariulf's was no vain boast, and that the Etrurian outpost did at this time fall into the hands of the Lombards.

All round the horizon the sky seemed darkening. Arichis, duke of Beneventum, was cooperating with his countryman Ariulf and pressing hard on Naples. As the Pope could not stir up the Exarch to provide for the defence of that important city by sending an Imperial duke with sufficient reinforcements, he took upon himself to send the 'magnificent' tribune, Constantius, to bear military rule in the city, and wrote a letter ordering all the soldiers quartered there to render him due obedience. What troubled him most was the apparent indifference of the Exarch, Romanus, who seemed heedless to all the misery which the fury of Ariulf and his Lombards was bringing on the peasants of Campania. On behalf of Romanus it may be urged that the one all-important matter was to keep the communications open between Rome and Ravenna, and that every soldier who could be spared was needed for the defence of Perugia, which had become the vital point in these communications. But, whether justly or unjustly, Gregory was now thoroughly out of temper with Romanus, and the project, the momentous project, of forming a separate peace with Ariulf and cultivating the friendship of Spoleto, since Ravenna was so callous and unjust, was already taking shape in the Pope's mind. It was with such thoughts stirring in his soul that he wrote to John, bishop of Ravenna, probably in the month of July, 592.

'Set it not down to indolence but to ill-health that I have made such scant reply to the numerous letters of your Blessedness. For my sins, when Ariulf came [close up] to the City of Rome, slaying some of our people and mutilating others, I was smitten with such sadness that I suffered from an attack of colic. Much did I marvel what could be the reason why the well-known solicitude of your Holiness on our behalf did not profit this City nor relieve my necessities. But when I got your letters which went astray, I recognized that you do indeed act zealously for me, but that you have to deal with a man with whom such zeal is of no avail. It must be, therefore, to punish me for my sins that he who is now concerned only pretends to fight against our enemies, and at the same time forbids us to make peace, although now we should be quite unable to do so even if we wished it, because Ariulf, having with him the army of Auctarit and Nordulf, claims that gratuities for them shall be handed over to him before he will condescend to say anything about peace'.

Gregory then goes on to speak about the schismatical bishops of Istria and the Three Chapters Controversy, and continues, 'Be assured that I shall not cease to write to our most serene lords [the Emperor and his son] on that matter with perfect freedom and earnestness. But you need not be distressed by the animosity of the aforesaid most excellent Patrician Romanus [against me], because as far as I am superior to him in place and dignity, with so much the more patience and gravity I ought to bear his impertinence.

'If, however, there is any chance of getting a hearing, let your Brotherhood deal with him, so that we may make peace with Ariulf, should there be any hope, however faint, of accomplishing that result. The regular soldiery, as he himself knows, have been removed from Rome. Only the Theodosians remain, and as they have not received their donative, they will scarce consent to do sentry duty on the walls. Since the City is thus bereft of all its defenders, if it have not peace, how shall it continue to exist?

'As to the city of Naples, you must press the most excellent Exarch hard. For Arichis, as we have heard, has joined himself to Ariulf, and in violation of his promise has gone against the Republic. He is plotting deeply against that city, and if a duke be not speedily sent to its relief, it may be absolutely given up for lost.

'As for your suggestion about sending alms to the burnt city of Severus the schismatic, your Brotherhood would not have made it if you had known what bribes he has been sending to the palace to inflame persons against us. And even had he not been thus active, we must remember that our pity is primarily due to the faithful, and only in the second place to the enemies of the Church. All the more so, as hard by is the city of Fanum, many of whose inhabitants have been carried captive, and to which in the past year I wished to send remittances, but could not on account of the interposition of the enemy. It seems to me, therefore, that you ought to send the abbot Claudius thither with a pretty large sum of money, to redeem all such free persons as he may find to be there held in bondage for their ransoms, or to be still in captivity. Make your mind easy about the sum of money to be transmitted to you [for this purpose], because whatever you decide upon I shall be glad to pay. But if you can convince the most excellent Patrician Romanus that we ought to make peace with Ariulf, I am ready to send you another person with whom these matters of ransom can be better arranged.'

After this letter, the name of Ariulf fades for a time out of Gregory's correspondence. Evidently the stress of war and the fear of the capture of the City were soon lightened, and we may assert with little fear of contradiction that the cause of this change was a separate peace concluded between Rome and Spoleto about the end of July 592. In negotiating this peace, the Papal coffers were probably put under contribution, in order to satisfy the demands of Ariulf, since Gregory himself, in alluding to the transaction three years later, says that the peace was made 'without any cost to the Republic'.

Having thus carefully traced the course of events as revealed to us by the Papal letters we may now listen to a story told by Paulus Diaconus in his life of Gregory in which, though Ariulf's name is not mentioned, the similarity of events is so great that we can hardly doubt that Ariulf is the person alluded to.

'There was a certain tyrant who greatly oppressed the Roman Church, troubling its repose by his unbearable importunity, laying waste its possessions, and treating the serfs belonging thereto with the utmost cruelty. For which wrongs the blessed Pope admonished him by means of messengers, but he was made all the more furious by this reproof, and came, mad with rage, to depopulate the City itself. But on his arrival, he was met in conference by the blessed Gregory. His heart was touched by Divine grace, and he perceived that there was so much force in the Pontiff's words that with most humble courtesy he made satisfaction to the pious successor of the Apostles, and promised that he would ever after be the subject and devoted servant of the Roman Church. Finally, he being afterwards sick [apparently] unto death, besought the prayers of the venerable Pope, and received for answer that God would grant unto him further space for repentance.'

It seems clear that, as here described, the raging enemy of the Church was converted by this interview, if not into a subject ally, at least into a respectful and courteous antagonist. The moral miracle of Leo I's subjugation of Attila was thus repeated after the lapse of a century and a half, by the greatest of his successors. That Ariulf, rough warrior as he might be, was not insensible to influences which may be called religious or superstitious according to the narrator's point of view, is shown by a story told of him by Paulus in the Lombard history. When warring against the Romans at Camerinum (possibly in that very expedition which caused the captivity of the citizens of Fanum), he enquired of his men, after they had gotten the victory, who was that warrior whom he had seen fighting so valiantly. 'There was no braver warrior than yourself,' said his soldiers. 'No, assuredly, there was one better than I, who, whenever one of the opposite party wished to strike me, guarded me with his shield'. Soon after they came near to the basilica in which rests the venerable body of the blessed martyr St. Sabinus; and Ariulf asked, 'Whose is that ample house?' Some Catholics in his suite answered, 'There rests the martyr Sabinus, whose help Christians are wont to invoke when they go forth to war'. Ariulf, who was still a heathen, reasoned, 'How can a dead man give help to the living?'. Having so said, he leaped from his horse and went in to view the basilica; and while the others were praying, he strolled round the church admiring the pictures on the walls. As soon as he saw the blessed martyr's portrait, he exclaimed, with an oath, 'That is the face and that is the figure of the man who guarded me in the fight'. Then all understood that Sabinus himself had been Ariulf's defender'.

So runs the story in the pages of Ariulf's countryman Paulus. What the Emperor or the Exarch said of such a miraculous interference on behalf of an enemy of the Roman Republic no Byzantine chronicler informs us.

The separate peace thus concluded by Gregory with Ariulf aroused great indignation, when the tidings of it reached Ravenna and Constantinople. Though probably a wise and statesmanlike measure, there can be no doubt that—to use a legal phrase—it was quite *ultra vires*, being entirely beyond any legal competency yet possessed by the bishop of Rome in 'the Roman Republic'. An archbishop of Canterbury negotiating for himself a separate peace with Napoleon I, at the time of his meditated Boulogne invasion, or, to take a less improbable contingency—a bishop of Durham making private terms for himself and the territories of St. Cuthbert with the king of Scots, on the eve of the battle of Flodden; these hypothetical cases offer fair analogies to the conduct of Gregory on this occasion, on which he did indeed make a memorable stride towards complete independence. It appears to have been at this time, and was possibly in order to undo Gregory's work, that Romanus at last marched with an army from Ravenna to Rome. It would seem as if the independent action of the Pope accomplished that which his piteous entreaties had failed to effect, in stirring up the Exarch to action. His campaign was evidently a victorious one. The towns of Sutrium, Polimartium, Horta, Tuder, Ameria, Luceoli, and Perugia1, were all recovered from the Lombards, and the Exarch returned in triumph to Ravenna.

This expedition of Romanus is usually represented as a mere outbreak of temper on his part, a petulant explosion of wrath on the part of a man 'who could make neither war nor peace', and who, by this ill-timed display of energy, sacrificed all the fruits of Gregory's diplomacy. It is not clear, however, that we are right in so regarding it. If we look at the map, we shall see that the loss of these places (which had probably all fallen during Ariulf's campaign of 592) fatally jeopardized the line of communication between Rome and Ravenna. Luceoli, Tuder, Ameria, were all important stages on the Via Flaminia, while Sutrium, Polimartium and Horta were towns within the border of the *Ducatus Romae*, as it remained for the next century. Gregory's desire for peace, and his pity for the sufferings of the war-worried *coloni*, were praiseworthy and Christian, but Romanus was justified in thinking that a peace concluded on the basis of the *status quo* in July 592, would leave the Imperial possessions in Italy at the mercy of the barbarians.

The case of Perugia was peculiar. That old Etruscan city, on her high Umbrian hill, held, probably, the true key of the position; but we are, unfortunately, not able fully to follow her varying fortunes. It is now pretty generally agreed that up to the year 592 the city had remained in the uninterrupted possession of the Empire. In that year it was taken, perhaps by Ariulf, perhaps by a Lombard duke named Maurisio, who was entrusted with the government of the city. This man, however, surrendered his post to Romanus, deserted his countrymen, entered the service of the Empire, and, in that capacity, held Perugia for the Exarch in 593. As we shall see, it was almost immediately won back by the Lombards, but it was probably restored to the Empire at the general peace in 599, for it was certainly Imperial in 735, and probably during the whole course of the preceding century.

This successful campaign of Romanus brought king Agilulf into the field. The rebellion of the dukes had probably kept him fully employed in 592, while Ariulf and Arichis were carrying on the war in the centre and south of Italy, but now, apparently in the spring of 593, he took the field, crossed the river Po, and marched with a powerful army to Perugia. After a siege of some days, the city surrendered, and Duke Maurisio, for his treason to the cause of the Lombards, was at once put to death.

Agilulf then marched on Rome, where Gregory was at that time engaged in giving daily homilies on woe, which exactly harmonized with the mood of mind of the melancholy Pope, who sincerely believed—and it is the key to much of his conduct—that the end of the world was visibly approaching. He had already, in his sixth homily, bewailed the overthrown cities, the desolated country, the departed glory of the senate and people, the stately buildings of Rome herself daily toppling in decay. 'After the men have failed, even the walls fall. Where are they who aforetime rejoiced in her magnificence? Where is all their pomp, their pride, their frequent disordered revelry? Lo, she sitteth desolate, she is trodden down, she is filled with groaning. Now, no one hastens to her that he may get forward in the world: not one of her mighty and violent men remaineth to oppress the poor and to divide the spoil.'

So was Gregory daily haranguing from the pulpit when the news came that Agilulf had crossed the Po. Then, after a few days, came the manifest and miserable signs of war. Some citizens crept back to Rome, their hands having been chopped off by the savage foe; others were reported to be taken prisoners; others slain. Gregory himself, from the battlements of the threatened City, saw the captive Romans driven over the Campagna, with halters round their necks, roped together like dogs, on their way to slavery in the land of the Franks. He closed the great uncial manuscript of Ezekiel with a sigh, descended from the pulpit, and preached no more homilies on the prophet. Perhaps he called to mind that even so had St. Jerome been labouring to expound the mysteries of Ezekiel when he received the news of the capture of the City by Alaric; an event, the horrors of which, after nearly two centuries, seemed likely to be repeated by the more barbarous Agilulf. However this may be, the Pope turned from his spiritual labours as expositor of the Bible, and, aided by his namesake Gregory, the Prefect of the City, and by Castus, the Master of the Soldiery, set himself vigorously to work to provide for the defence of Rome.

After all, the City was not stormed, was perhaps not even subjected to a long blockade, though there are indications of something like a famine having prevailed within its walls. How was it that Agilulf did not write his name in the list of Rome-capturers, where Alaric, Gaiseric and Totila had written theirs? It is a curious illustration of the sparsely-scattered lights by which the history of this period has to be written, that the answer to this important question comes to us from far Copenhagen. In the continuation of Prosper's Chronicle, which has been frequently referred to in these pages, and which is known as *Codex Havniensis*, we find it recorded that 'Agilulf at last, with the whole force of his army, set forth for the siege of the City of Rome; but on his arrival he found the Blessed Gregory, who was then gloriously ruling the Church, ready to meet him at the steps of the basilica of St. Peter, Prince of the Apostles. Being melted by Gregory's prayers, and greatly moved by the wisdom and the religious gravity of so great a man, he relinquished the siege of the City. He kept, however, the spoil which he had already taken, and, returning, betook himself to Milan'.

Other causes may have concurred to produce this result; the fear of fever, the remembrance of the long and disastrous Gothic siege, disaffection, or even rebellion, on the part of some of the Lombard dukes. But, as in the case of Attila, so here the venerable personality of the recognized head of Christendom seems to have been the main instrument in procuring peace.

But the reconciliation between Pope and King, if it was to lead to a durable peace for Italy, must necessarily be followed by a reconciliation between King and Emperor. For this the Pope seems at once to have begun working, since we find him, in a letter written in September, 593, urging the bishop of Milan to use his good offices to reconcile Agilulf and Romanus, and even empowering him to offer something like a

Papal guarantee for the Lombard's good behaviour. Moreover, it was just about this time (October, 593) that Gregory gave orders for a diligent search to be made for the vessels of Church plate, that had been carried into Sicily by bishops fleeing from their sees in Italy, which were menaced by the Lombard ravagers. These vessels were to be all collected into one place and carefully labelled, in order that when peace was reestablished—a contingency which the Pope then regarded as probable— they might be restored to the Churches which were their rightful owners.

But peace between two such essentially antagonistic powers as the Lombard and the Greek was not easily to be obtained, nor was the Pope in these years in such favour at Constantinople as to be an acceptable mediator. The Emperor had issued an edict, which seemed to be rendered necessary by the increasing tendency of the servants of the State to evade their patriotic obligations by hiding themselves in a monastery, or assuming the office of the priesthood. The terms of this now lost edict appear to have been, 'That no one who is engaged in the administration of public business shall undertake ecclesiastical duty: nor shall it be lawful for him to change his condition and enter a monastery. The same prohibition applies to all officers and to every private soldier who has once been marked on the hand as belonging to the army, until his term of service is expired'.

Against this edict Gregory remonstrated in which is perhaps the most famous of all his Epistles, full as it is of holy indignation and couched in terms of bold rebuke, such as the Emperors never heard from the pliant Patriarchs of Constantinople. To the first part of the law, forbidding civil servants to accept office in the Church, the Pope made no objection. The result of his own sorrowful observation was that 'Whosoever shall doff the secular habit from a desire to scramble into ecclesiastical office, wants to change his world, not to leave it.' But the prohibition to enter a monastery was a widely different matter. It could not be justified by any supposed loss to the State, for any claims which it might have on the estate of a civil servant would be defrayed out of the property of the monastery. And as for the soldiers, why was the way of salvation to be closed up to them by Imperial decree? There were many who could not possibly lead a religious life, while still clothed with the secular habit. Was the Emperor's soldier to be forbidden to become a soldier of Christ?

Then, like another Bossuet or Bourdaloue, confronting Louis XIV in the plenitude of his power, Gregory turns and addresses these daring words to 'the Master of all things':—

'Lo! thus to thee, through me the lowest of his and thy servants, Christ makes answer, saying, "From a notary I made thee Captain of the Guard, from Captain of the Guard Caesar, from Caesar Emperor, and not only that, but father of Emperors yet to be. I have committed My priests to thy keeping, and wouldest thou withdraw thy soldiers from My service?". Most pious lord! I pray thee answer thy servant what reply wilt thou make to thy Lord, when He comes and says these things to thee at the Judgment?

'But perhaps you think that there is no such thing as the honest conversion of a soldier to the monastic life. I, your unworthy servant, know how many converted soldiers in my days have wrought miracles in the monasteries which they have entered. But by this law, not even one such soldier is to be allowed the privilege of conversion.

'I beg my lord to enquire, what previous Emperor gave forth such a law, and then let him carefully consider if that Emperor [Julian] set an example which he ought to follow. Let him consider this also, that he is hereby forbidding men to renounce the world at the very time when the world's own end is drawing near. For lo! there will be no delay: the time is at hand when, while the sky is burning, burning too the earth and the elements flashing fire, with angels and archangels, with thrones and dominations, with principalities and powers, the terrible Judge shall come. If He shall have forgiven all thy other sins, and shall allege against thee but this one law which thou hast promulgated, what, I pray, will be thy excuse? Wherefore, by the same terrible Judge I adjure thee, not to allow all thy tears, thy prayers, thy fastings, and thine alms, for the sake of some supposed advantage, to be clouded over before the eyes of Almighty God: but either by some fresh interpretation or by some open change to turn aside the rigour of that law. For then does my lord's army prevail most against his enemies when God's army grows strongest in prayer.

'I verily, as becomes one subject to your orders, have caused that law to be transmitted to various parts of your dominions: but I hereby announce to my Most Serene Lords by the pages of this memorandum that the law itself is utterly repugnant to Almighty God. Thus have I paid the debt which I owe to each, to the Emperor obedience, to God the assertion of His rights'

What was the result of these energetic remonstrances by the Pope we are not distinctly informed, but it is probable that the obnoxious edict, if not formally rescinded, was allowed to slumber unenforced in the Statute-book, and silently passed into oblivion.

If some soreness was left in the Emperor's mind by Gregory's vigorous protest, this was not likely to be allayed by his chief ecclesiastical adviser. John the Faster, Patriarch of Constantinople, was one the few eminent ecclesiastics who might conceivably claim to rival Gregory in the severity of his asceticism; and it is evident that the relations were never cordial between these two holy men, both so celebrated for the rigorous treatment of their bodies, and both really contending for the first place in the Christian hierarchy. It seems probable, though the fact is not expressly stated, that a certain letter addressed by the Empress Constantina to the Pope in the spring of 594, was secretly prompted by John of Constantinople. This letter contained the really astounding request that the head of St. Paul might be severed from his body, which was believed to repose in his stately basilica by the Ostian road, and might be sent to Constantinople to enrich a chapel which Constantina was building in the Imperial palace in honour of the Apostle. If John the Faster was consulted about this letter, he must have known that it was quite impossible that the Empress's petition should be granted, and he may have calculated that the inevitable refusal would place his rival at some disadvantage in the competition for Imperial favour. Gregory replied to the Empress that her request was one which he could not and dared not comply with. 'For the bodies of the holy Apostles Peter and Paul, reposing in their churches, gleam with such miracles and such terrors that we cannot approach them, even for prayer, without great fear. When my predecessor [Pelagius II], of blessed memory, wished to change the silver [canopy] which was over the most holy body of St. Peter, though it was at a distance of fifteen feet from the corpse, a sign of no small terror appeared unto him. I, too, wished to make a similar improvement in connection with the most holy body of St. Paul, and found it necessary to dig somewhat deeply near the sepulchre. But the superintendent of the place having found certain bones not in immediate contact with the tomb, and having dared to lift them and remove them to another place, beheld certain sad signs and died by a sudden death'. The Pope then proceeds to relate a number of similar occurrences which showed the anger of the saints against those who ventured to disturb their bones. Some of his stories admit of an obvious physical explanation, but not all. The whole letter is an extraordinary one, proceeding as it does from the pen of one who had been a great Roman magistrate, accustomed to the careful weighing of evidence : and we rise from its perusal as from our study of the same author's life of St. Benedict, with the painful question in our minds, 'Is it possible that this man of clear and shrewd intellect really believed all that he has here recorded?'

Another root of bitterness between the Pope and the Emperor was the election of a certain Maximus as bishop of Salona, that Dalmatian city which a century and a half before this time saw a fallen Emperor officiating in its cathedral. Honoratus the archdeacon was the candidate for this see favoured by Gregory, who disliked the character of Maximus, and suspected him of winning the votes of his most influential supporters by simony. The contest was a long one (593-599), and ended after six years in something that resembled a Papal surrender; and meanwhile Maximus, secure in the favour of the Imperial court, ventured on acts of the most outrageous defiance to the see of Rome, and even dared to accuse the saintly Gregory of murder, because a Dalmatian bishop named Malchus, who had been summoned to Italy to account for his maladministration of the Papal Patrimony, had died suddenly in exile. 'It has come to my ears' said the Pope, 'that Maximus has sent a certain cleric [to the Emperor] to tell him that the bishop Malchus was killed while in custody on a charge of embezzlement. On this matter I have only one brief suggestion to make to my Most Serene Lords, that if I, their humble servant, had chosen to mix myself up with the murder even of a Lombard, at this day the Lombard nation would have neither king, duke, nor count, but would be all split up in hopeless confusion. But because I fear God I shrink from imbruing my hands in the blood of any man.

'As for Malchus, he was neither in custody nor under any kind of duresse; but on the day on which he pleaded his cause and lost it, he was without my knowledge taken home by Boniface the notary, who invited him to dinner. He was treated at the banquet as an honoured guest, but died suddenly in the night, as I think that you, dear friend, have already heard.'

At the beginning of 595 the relations seem to have become somewhat more friendly. On the 12th of March in that year we find the Pope writing to the Emperor, thanking him for a remittance of 30 lbs. of gold [£1200] 'brought by my fellow-servant, the Treasury-clerk, Busa', for distribution among the priests, the poor, and especially the nuns who had flocked to Rome from the various parts of Italy that were invaded by the Lombards, and were now eking out a bare subsistence in the convents and other places wherein they were quartered. He also reports that Castus, the Master of the Soldiery, has distributed the donative to the soldiers out of the funds brought by the same messenger: that this gift has been gratefully received by the soldiers and has put an end to the murmurs and indiscipline which were before prevalent in the ranks.

Two months later (May, 595) Gregory wrote to Severus, the Assessor of Exarch Romanus, entreating him to use his influence with his chief in favour of peace. He says that those who sit by the side of rulers and who love them with pure affection, ought to make to them such suggestions as, without detracting from their own reputation for wisdom, may tend to the salvation of the ruler's soul. 'Therefore, as I know what faithful love you bear to the Most Excellent Exarch, I desire to inform your Greatness of the course of affairs, that you, being in possession of this knowledge, may use your influence with him on behalf of reasonable proposals.

'Know, then, that Agilulf, king of the Lombards, is not unwilling to make a general peace, if my Lord the Patrician is of the same mind. He complains that many things have been done in his district contrary to the terms of the truce. He claims that compensation shall be made to him for these wrongs, if they are proved to the satisfaction of the judges, and on the other hand he is willing to make the fullest reparation if any breach of the peace can be proved against his side. As this request is reasonable, judges should be appointed to take cognizance of acts of violence committed by either party; and let us hope that thus, by God's favour, a general peace may be firmly made. How necessary such a peace is to all of us you well know. Act, therefore, with your usual wisdom, that the Most Excellent Exarch may be induced to come in to this proposal without delay, and may not prove himself to be the one obstacle to a peace which is so expedient for the State. If he will not consent, Agilulf again promises to make a separate peace with us; but we know that in that case several islands and other places will necessarily be lost. Let the Exarch then consider these points and hasten to make peace, that we may at least have a little interval in which we may enjoy a moderate amount of rest, and, by the Lord's help, may recruit the strength of the Republic for future resistance.'

But the Pope's noble persistence in the cause of peace was not yet to be crowned with success. Hardly had this epistle been dispatched when he received a letter from the Emperor, the sharpest and the hardest to bear of all that had reached him from that quarter. The contents of that letter, itself lost, may easily be conjectured from the reply. All the transactions with the Lombards for the five preceding years were passed in review, and Gregory found himself accused of disloyalty, of presumption, of prodigality and—hardest stroke of all—of stupidity, all in one breath. The letter of reply is so important that it is necessary to quote it almost entire.

'GREGORY TO MAURICE, AUGUSTUS.

'In their most serene commands the Piety of my Lords, whilst rebuking me for certain faults, has with an appearance of sparing, not spared me at all. For in your letter, though you politely use the word "simplehearted", you do in fact call me "a fool". Now, in the Scriptures we are always exhorted to let our simplicity be mingled with prudence, as it is said of Job, He was a man simple and righteous": as the Apostle Paul says, "I would have you wise unto that which is good and simple concerning evil," and as the Truth Himself says in the gospel, "Be ye wise as serpents and harmless as doves." It follows, therefore, that when I, in my Lords' most serene letters, am said to have been deceived by the wiles of Ariulf, and am called "simple," without the addition of "prudent," your meaning, without doubt, must be that I am a fool. And I myself must confess that you are right. Even if your Piety did not use the word, my very circumstances cry aloud "He is a fool." If I were not, I should never have consented to suffer those things which I have suffered here from the swords of the Lombards. As for my report concerning Ariulf, that he was ready with his whole heart to come over to the Republic, you do not believe me. That means that I am accused of telling lies. But even if I am not worthy to be considered a priest, I know this much about the priest's office, that he is bound to render service to the truth, and that it is a deadly insult to call him a liar. I have long perceived, however, that more confidence is reposed in Norduulf or in Leo than in me, and now those who come between us receive more credence than is given to my assertions.

'And in truth if the captivity of our land were not daily and hourly increasing, I would gladly hold my peace as to the contempt and derision that are poured upon me.

But this sorely afflicts me, that the same temper which accuses me of falsehood permits Italy to be daily led captive under the Lombard yoke, and that while no confidence is reposed in my assertions the forces of the enemy are enormously increasing. I would suggest, however, to my Most Pious Lord, that he may think of me all the evil that he pleases: but for the good of the Republic and for the cause of the liberation of Italy, let him not easily lend his pious ears to the first comer, but let him trust facts rather than words.

'Do not let my Lord, in the consciousness of his earthly power, be quick to take offence with bishops, but let him remember Whose servants they are, that he may show them fitting reverence. God Himself, speaking through the mouth of Moses, calls priests "gods", and the prophet Malachi says, "The priest's lips should keep knowledge and they should seek the law at his mouth, for he is the angel [messenger] of the Lord of Hosts". The history of the Church bears witness that when the bishops were assembled in council [at Nicaea] Constantine burned the indictments preferred against some of them, before their faces, saying, "Ye are gods, appointed by the true God. Go and judge your own causes yourselves, for it is not fitting that we should be the judges of gods." In which sentence, pious Lord! he gained more honour for himself by his humility than he conferred on the bishops by his reverence. Even the pagan Emperors of old, who worshipped gods of wood and stone, gave highest honour to their priests, and surely a Christian Emperor should not do less to his bishops.

'These suggestions I make to my pious Lords, not for mine own sake, but for the sake of other bishops. For I am but a sinful man, and as I am incessantly failing in my duty towards Almighty God, so I trust that the strokes which I am now daily and hourly receiving may somewhat lighten my sentence at His awful Judgment-day : and I think that you may even please the Almighty the better, the more harshly you deal with His unworthy servant. For I have already received many strokes, and when my Lords' orders came, I found some consolations that I did not hope for. If possible, I will briefly enumerate these strokes to which I refer.

'The first was that the peace which, without any cost to the Republic, I had concluded with the the bards encamped in Tuscia, was wrested from me.

'Then, when peace had been broken, the soldiers were removed from Rome. Some were slain by the enemy, others quartered at Narni and Perugia, and that Perugia might still be held, Rome was left unguarded.

'A heavier stroke after this was the arrival of Agilulf, when, with my own eyes, I saw Romans coupled together like dogs, with ropes round their necks, being led away to be sold in France.

'Then, as we who were within the City by God's protection escaped his hands, an attempt was made to show that we were responsible for the failure of the corn-supplies, which cannot possibly be stored in any great quantity or for a long time in this City, as I have shown more fully in another memorandum.

'For myself, I am not harassed by any of these things, because my conscience bears me witness that I am ready to suffer any adversity, if only I may escape all these evils without peril to my soul. But for the Glorious persons, Gregory the Prefect [of the City], and Castus, Master of the Soldiery, I am distressed, greatly distressed, since they neglected no possible precaution, but endured the toils of police-duty and sentry-duty during the aforesaid siege with the greatest alacrity, and then, after all, are struck by the severe indignation of My Lords. All which plainly shows that it is not their own conduct, but their connection with me, that brings them into trouble, and that as they laboured together with me in our tribulations, so they are to be tribulated together with me after our labours are ended.

'As for my pious Lords reminding me of the awful and terrible judgment of Almighty God, I pray them in the same Almighty Name not to do that again. We do not yet know how each man will appear on that day. As the illustrious preacher Paul says, "Judge nothing before the time, till the Lord cometh who shall illuminate the hidden things of darkness, and make manifest the secrets of all hearts." I will say this, however, briefly, that as an unworthy sinner I have more hope from the mercy of Jesus when He comes, than I have from the justice of your Piety. Men know little about His judgment, and perchance the things which you praise He will blame, and those which you blame He will praise. Therefore, amid all this uncertainty, I can but have recourse to tears, and pray that the same Almighty God may guide our most pious lord by His own hand, and that in that dread day He may find me free from fault, having enabled me so to please men (if that be necessary) as not to forfeit His everlasting favour'.

This letter of Gregory, bold almost to insolence, marks the 'dead point' of his strivings after peace with the Lombards. He had now occupied the chair of St. Peter, and Agilulf the throne of Pavia, for nearly five years. Peace was their common interest, but the relation in which Gregory stood to Constantinople made that peace as yet unattainable. The Emperor, though powerless to win back Italy, and not too sure of being able to defend even the fragments of it which were left to him, would not recognize, and thereby seem to legalese, the past conquests of the Lombards. For his attempt to persuade him to adopt that course the Pope had now received a sharp reprimand, which, had Maurice been Justinian and Gregory Vigilius, would probably have been followed by deportation to an island in the Propontis, and a formal charge of *laesa majestas*.

CHAPTER IX.

THE PAPAL PEACE.

The year 595 has been generally looked upon as a turning-point in the history of Gregory's papacy. It was not only in that year that he began seriously to prepare his scheme for the conversion of England, but it was also then that he formally entered the lists to dispute the pretensions of the Patriarch of Constantinople. For we must always bear in mind the double character of the warfare which a Bishop of Rome, at that period of the world's history, deemed himself bound to wage. Locally, as the first citizen of Rome, as one who looked forth from her walls on the Sabine hills and the Ciminian forest, he felt himself to be, as he continually repeats, 'between the swords of the Lombards;' but, ecclesiastically, he had to defend the contest so-called rights of Peter, Prince of the Apostles, against the ever-menacing encroachments of the see of Constantinople. It has been already shown, and the proof need not be repeated here, how the claim of Old Rome to the ecclesiastical primacy of the world was interwoven with her old Imperial dominion, and how this claim was threatened when Constantinople became the political centre of the Empire, and her bishops the intimate friends and spiritual advisers of the Emperor. Now, the very fact that Italy was becoming more and more hopelessly lost to the Empire, and that the Bishop of Rome, if he retained any connection whatever with 'the Roman Republic,' must live a most precarious life 'between the swords of the Lombards,' to some extent imperilled even his ecclesiastical position. Pope and Exarch already found their interests diverging; those interests would probably diverge yet more in future. Yet greater in all probability would be the ever-widening gulf between Pope and Emperor; while, on the other hand, the Bishop of Constantinople, living under the shadow of the Imperial greatness, and with the hard fate of the outspoken Chrysostom ever present to his mind, tended more and more to become the mere private chaplain of the Byzantine Augustus. No wonder, therefore, that whenever a dispute arose between the First and the Second in authority in the Universal Church, the Emperor was always ready to look askance at the pretensions of Rome and to favour those of Constantinople.

The holy man, John the Faster, whose elevation to the patriarchal throne Gregory had witnessed in 582 during his residence at Constantinople, had revived for his own benefit a dormant claim to a title which had been conceded, as a matter of courtesy, to some of his predecessors, that of Ecumenical, or Universal, Bishop. In the year 588 (two years before Gregory's accession) a synod was held at Constantinople in reference to the affairs of the see of Antioch, and when the Acts of this synod were received at Rome they were found to contain frequent mention of the name of John of

Constantinople, with the unwelcome addition 'Universal Bishop'. Against this title Pelagius II, probably by the advice of Gregory, who knew the temper of the Eastern Patriarch, energetically protested, forbade his *responsalis* to communicate with the usurping prelate, and even went so far as to declare the Acts of the Council null and void by reason of this irregularity.

Apparently the controversy slumbered during the first five years of Gregory's pontificate; but in 595, John the Faster, with an ingenuity in annoyance such as might be looked for in a man so holy and so abstinent, addressed to his brother of Rome a letter in which 'almost in every line he called himself Ecumenical Patriarch'. By this letter all the wrath of Gregory—not naturally a sweet-tempered man, and already sufficiently tortured by dyspepsia, gout and Lombards—was aroused against the aspiring Patriarch. The messenger who was speedily dispatched to the Imperial court took with him a heavy packet of letters, all relating to this 'wicked word' ecumenical.

To the offending Patriarch himself Gregory wrote, as he says, sweetly and humbly admonishing him to cure his desire of vainglory. Yet even this sweet and humble letter cannot have been altogether pleasant to receive.

'I am astonished' says the Pope, 'that you, who fled in order that you might escape the honour of the Patriarchate, should now bear yourself in it so proudly that you will be thought to have coveted it with ambitious desire. In the days of my predecessor, Pelagius, a letter was sent to you in which the acts of the synod about Bishop Gregory were disallowed because of the proud title attributed to you therein, and the Archdeacon sent to the Emperor was forbidden to celebrate mass with you on account of it. That prohibition I now repeat: my *responsalis* Sabinianus is not to communicate with you till you have amended this error.

'The Apostle Paul rebuked the spirit which would shout, "I am of Paul and I of Apollos." You are reviving that spirit and rending the unity of the body of Christ. The Council of Chalcedon offered this title of *universalis* to the Roman Pontiff, but he refused to accept it, lest he should seem thereby to derogate from the honour of his brother bishops.

'It is the last hour: Pestilence and the sword are raging in the world. Nation is rising against nation, the whole fabric of things is being shaken. Cities with their inhabitants are swallowed up by the yawning earth. All the prophecies are being fulfilled. The King of Pride is nigh at hand, and—inexpressible shame—priests are serving in his army. Yes, they are raising the haughty neck of pride who were chosen that they might set an example of humility.

'Our Lord humbled Himself for our sakes, and He who was inconceivably great wore the lowly form of manhood, yet we bishops are imitating, not His humility, but the pride of His great foe. Remember that He said to His disciples, Be not called Rabbi, for one is your Master, even Christ, and all ye are brethren." He said, "Woe to the world because of offences! Woe to him by whom the offence cometh!" Lo! from this wicked word of pride offence has come, and the hearts of all the brethren are provoked to stumbling by it'.

Gregory then quotes the words of Christ (Matt, XVIII. 15-17) about telling a brother his fault 'between him and thee alone,' and continues, 'I have, by my *responsalis*, once and twice told you your fault, and am now writing to you myself. If I am despised in this endeavour to correct you, it will only remain to call in the Church.

'I have received the very sweet and kind letters of your Holiness about the causes of John and Athanasius, about which, with the Lord's help, I will reply to you in my next, because under the weight of so great tribulations, surrounded as I am by the swords of the barbarians, I am so oppressed that I cannot say much, nay can hardly breathe.'

So ran the letter to the arch-offender. To his *responsalis*, Sabinianus, the Pope wrote, saying that he had addressed his most reverend brother John with a proper admixture of frankness and courtesy, but, if he persisted, another letter would be addressed to him which his pride would not relish. 'But I hope in Almighty God,' said Gregory, 'that his hypocrisy will soon be brought to nought by the Supernal Majesty. I marvel, however, that he should have been able so to deceive you, dear friend, that you should allow our Lord the Emperor to be persuaded to write, admonishing me to live in peace with the Patriarch. If he would act justly, he should rather admonish him to give up that proud title, and then there would be peace between us at once. You little thought, I can see, how craftily this was managed by our aforesaid brother John. Evidently he did it in order to put me in this dilemma. Either I must listen to our Lord the Emperor, and so confirm the Patriarch in his vanity, or not listen, and so rouse the Imperial mind against me.

'But we shall steer a straight course in this matter, fearing none save God Almighty. Wherefore, dear friend, tremble before no man; for the truth's sake despise all whom you may see exalting themselves against the truth in this world; confide in the favour of Almighty God and the help of the blessed Peter; remember the voice of Truth which says, "Greater is He that is in you than he that is in the world and do with fullest authority, as from us, whatever has to be done in this affair.

'For after we have found that we could in no way be defended [by the Greeks] from the swords of our enemies, after we have lost, for our devotion to the Republic, silver, gold, slaves and raiment, it is too disgraceful that we should, through them, lose our faith also. But to consent to that wicked word is nothing else than to lose our faith. Wherefore, as I have written to you in previous letters, you must never presume to communicate with him.'

It will be seen from this letter that the aspiring Patriarch had invoked the assistance of the Emperor against the Pope, even before the latter had received the extreme provocation of the letter which bristled with the obnoxious word 'ecumenical'. Evidently John of Constantinople had represented his brother of Rome—not altogether without truth—as exacting and quarrelsome; and Maurice, sincerely desirous for peace in the Church, had addressed Pope Gregory in language similar to that which Constantine employed to the contending prelates at Nicaea. To Maurice, therefore, the Pope addressed a long and eloquent letter praising his zeal for the peace of the Church, but insisting that the whole trouble arose from the pride of the Patriarch of Constantinople. Yes, the pride of the clergy was the real cause of the disasters of the Empire, of the triumphs of the barbarians. To disarm criticism, Gregory appears to associate himself with the sins of which he accuses his rival, but this is evidently a mere rhetorical artifice, and when he says 'we', he means the obnoxious Faster alone.

'When we leave the position which befits us, and devise for ourselves unbecoming honours, we ally our own sins to the forces of the barbarians; we depress the strength of the Republic and sharpen against us the swords of her enemies. How can we excuse ourselves, who are preaching one thing to our flocks, and ourselves practising the opposite? Our bones are worn away with fasting and our hearts are swollen with pride: our body is clothed with vile raiment, and in the elation of our souls we surpass the purple of emperors. We lie in ashes, and we nourish proud fancies. Teachers of the lowly and generals of pride, we hide a wolf's teeth behind a sheep's visage. But God sees our spirits, and is putting it into the heart of the Most Pious Emperor to restore peace to the Church.

'This is not my cause, but the cause of God Himself. It was to Peter, the Prince of the Apostles, that the Lord said, "Thou art Peter, and on this rock will I build my Church." He who received the keys of the kingdom of heaven, he to whom the power of binding and loosing was entrusted, was never called the Universal Apostle; and yet that most holy man, my fellow-bishop John, strives to get himself called the Universal Bishop. When I see this I am compelled to cry out, "*O tempora! O mores!*"

'Lo! all Europe is handed over to the power of the barbarians; cities are destroyed, villages overthrown, provinces depopulated; no tiller cultivates the soil; idolaters rage and rule, daily murdering the faithful; and yet the priests, who alone should have thrown themselves on the pavement and wept in sackcloth and ashes, are seeking for themselves names of vanity and flaunting new and profane titles.'

The Pope then enlarges on the undoubted fact that Bishops of Constantinople had been more than once convicted of heresy[1], and after touching on some of the arguments brought forward in the accompanying letters, he tries to excite the Emperor's resentment by hinting that the hated word implied a covert attack on his own crown and dignity.

'We are all suffering from the scandal of this thing. My Most Pious Lord must coerce this proud man, who is disobeying the canons of the Church, and is even setting himself up against the honour of your Imperial dignity by this proud private word.

'Let the author of this scandal return to a right life and all the quarrels of bishops will cease. I am myself the servant of priests, so long as they live priest-like lives. But as for this man, who in his swelling vainglory raises his neck against Almighty God and against the statutes of the fathers, I trust in God that he shall never bend my neck, no, not with swords'.

So wrote the first citizen of Old Home to the Monarch of the New; and his words, though uttered in the bland tone of the Churchman, had in them a ring which reminds us of Regulus and Coriolanus.

Lastly, Gregory wrote to the Empress Constantina, thanking her for having thrown her influence on the side of St. Peter against some who were proudly humble and feignedly meek. For this she would be rewarded both in this life and in the life to come, when she would find the benefit of having made him who had the power of binding and loosing, her debtor. 'Do not let any hypocrisy,' he says, 'prevail against the truth. There are some who, by sweet speeches and fair words, deceive the hearts of the simple: shabby in dress, but proud in heart, they seem as if they despised everything in this world, yet they are scheming to obtain all this world's treasures. They profess themselves the unworthiest of men, yet they are trying to acquire titles which proclaim them worthier than all others.

'I have received my Most Pious Lord's letters, telling me to live peaceably with my brother John. It is quite fitting that a religious Emperor should send such instructions to his bishops. But when my brother, by a new and unheard-of presumption, calls himself "Universal Bishop," it is a hard thing in my Most Serene Lord to correct, not him whose pride is the cause of all the trouble, but me, who am defending the rights of the Apostle Peter and the canons of the Church.

'In my brother's pride I can only see a sign that the days of Antichrist are at hand. He seems to imitate him who said, "I will set my throne above the stars of heaven : I will sit on the mount of the covenant on the sides of the north, I will ascend above the heights of the clouds. I will be like the Most High." Do not suffer this perverse word to be used. Perhaps the sins of Gregory may have deserved such a humiliation, but Peter has not sinned; and it is Peter who will be the sufferer again I say: see that the honour paid by your pious predecessors to Peter suffers no diminution, and Peter will be your helper here in all things, and hereafter will discharge your sins.

'It is now seven and twenty years that we have been living in this City between the swords of the Lombards. How much we have had to pay daily from the Church's treasury, in order that we might be able even to live among them, cannot be calculated. Briefly, I will say that as my Lords have at Ravenna an officer called Paymaster of the First Army of Italy, who, as necessity arises, provides for the daily expenditure, so in this City in such matters I am their Paymaster. Yet this Church, which is incessantly spending such vast sums on the clerics, on the monasteries, on the poor, on the people, and on the Lombards also, must be further oppressed by the affliction of the other Churches, all of which groan over this man's pride, though they do not dare to express their feelings'.

Such was the tenor of the letter to the Empress. Let it not be thought that in drawing so largely from this correspondence we are devoting too much time to a mere ecclesiastical squabble, which might find a place in the history of the Church but scarcely concerns the history of Italy. Besides its valuable incidental allusions to the miseries inflicted by the ravages of the Lombards, this correspondence is of truly 'ecumenical' importance in its bearing on the relations of East and West, of the Tiber and the Bosphorus. It was the growing estrangement between the Churches which prepared the way for the separation of the Empires. Had there been any real cordiality through the sixth, seventh and eighth centuries between Pope and Patriarch, it is not probable that the descendant of a Frankish Mayor of the Palace would ever have been hailed as Augustus in the streets of Rome.

In this particular case the dispute between the two sees ended in something like a drawn battle. In the very year in which the fierce correspondence quoted above had taken place, perhaps only a few weeks after Gregory's angriest letter had arrived at Constantinople, John the Faster died. When the Universal Conqueror had thus mowed down the Universal Bishop, one element which had lent peculiar acrimony to the dispute, namely, the emulation of austerity between the two chief combatants, disappeared. The Emperor, sincerely anxious for the peace of the Church, lingered for some time over his choice of a successor to the Faster, and at length selected Cyriacus, a man apparently of gentle and unassuming nature, who had been a friend of Gregory during his residence at Constantinople. The two *responsales* whom the new Patriarch dispatched to Rome were cordially received, and unhesitatingly admitted to communion with the Pontiff; 'for why,' as Gregory himself argued, 'should the fact that I forbade my representative to accept the sacred mysteries at the hands of one who had fallen into the sin of pride and elation, or who had failed to correct that sin in others, prevent his ministers from receiving them at the hands of one who, like myself, has not fallen into that sin?'. After five months' residence at Rome the messengers of Constantinople were at length reluctantly and affectionately dismissed.

To the Emperor Gregory wrote thanking him for his delay in choosing John's successor, and for his final appointment of Cyriacus. To the new Patriarch himself the Pope wrote a few letters, in a gradually diminishing tone of affection, as it became more and more manifest that the 'wicked word' Ecumenical, though not obtruded by him, would not be abandoned. But though Gregory still emphatically asserted that whoever called himself 'Ecumenical Bishop' was the precursor of Antichrist, the correspondence on the subject lost much of its former heat, and we may perhaps say that, the title having been claimed by Cyriacus for the honour of Constantinople, and protested against by Gregory for the honour of Rome, the personal relations of the two Patriarchs became friendly, if not cordial.

The issue of the controversy, which shall be finally stated here, was so illogical as to be almost amusing. Notwithstanding a decree of Phocas, the successor of Maurice, confirming in strong terms the primacy of the see of Rome, the Patriarchs of Constantinople continued to use the objectionable title, and at length the Roman Pontiffs, finding that they could not inhibit the use of it by their rivals, decided to adopt it for themselves. About the year 682 the Popes began to style themselves, and to allow others to style them, Ecumenical Bishops or Ecumenical Popes; and in the two succeeding centuries the title, as used by or of the bishops of Rome, was of frequent occurrence. The world had thus the curious spectacle of two rulers of the Church, each of whom claimed universal jurisdiction, though not yet at open war with one another; and the Church of Rome saw Pope after Pope assuming a title which, in the judgment of their greatest predecessor, was a distinct note of the precursor of Antichrist.

So much for the ecclesiastical war of Patriarchates. We return to the endeavours which Gregory was making, with praiseworthy perseverance, to secure peace to Italy. Throughout the year 595, and at least the first half of 596, he was sore in spirit because of the continued hostility of the Exarch Romanus. 'Most Exarch holy brother,' he wrote to Bishop Sebastian, 'the things which we suffer in this country from the influence of your friend, the lord Romanus, are such as we cannot describe. Briefly, I may say that his malice towards us is decidedly worse than the swords of the Lombards, so that the enemies who slay us outright seem kind in comparison with the rulers (*judices*) of the Republic who consume us by their spite, their rapine, and the treachery of their hearts. But to have simultaneously to support the care of the bishops and clergy, of the monasteries and the people, to watch with anxious vigilance against the snares of the enemy, to have always to defend oneself as a suspected person against the tricks and malice of the [Imperial] generals:—what labour and what grief this is, your Brotherhood who loves me so well and so purely, will be able truly to conjecture.'

Moreover the cowardice or the licentiousness of the clergy demoralised their flocks, and so made the work of the invaders easier. In the beginning of 596 Gregory wrote to his representative in Campania that it had come to his ears that Pimenius, bishop of Amalfi, was not content to dwell in his own Church, but was roaming about to different places, and that his flock, following his bad example, were deserting their own village. All this was simply inviting the enemy to make depredations on their homes, and therefore Pimenius must be sharply rebuked and ordered to remain thenceforward in his own Church, where a bishop ought to be. If disobedient, he was to be shut up in a monastery, in which case Gregory would take measures for the appointment of a successor.

Castorius the Papal chartularius, who was much employed by the Pope about this time in certain ecclesiastical matters concerning the succession to the see of Ravenna, became also a person of considerable political importance, as one acquainted with the views of the Pope on the subject of peace, and as the intermediary between him and Agilulf. It was he who brought to Rome the report of the negotiations which his colleague Secundus had been carrying on with the Lombard king. But his activity in this negotiation did not render him popular with the citizens of Ravenna. Shut up in their impregnable city, they could afford to despise the sufferings of the *coloni* of Campania—those sufferings which tore the heart of Gregory—and could boast, with easy courage, that they would have nothing to do with any surrender to the barbarian. A curious letter of the Pope's, which was probably written in the spring of 596, states that 'some person, at the instigation of a malign spirit, has in the silence of the night affixed a placard in a public place at Ravenna, speaking of Castorius in libellous terms, and even bringing crafty insinuations against ourselves in reference to the conclusion of peace. Hereupon all the priests and Levites, the generals, the nobles, the clerics, the monks, the soldiers and the people of Ravenna, at home or abroad, are called solemnly to witness that the author of this libel, unless he shall come forth in public and confess his sin, is excluded from participation in the body and blood of Jesus Christ. If he presume to partake thereof after this denunciation, it shall be anathema unto him, and if the unknown writer be a person to whom, in our ignorance, we have sent letters of congratulation, the good wishes contained in those letters will be null and void. The only condition upon which the offender can be restored to the communion of the Church, and relieved from this awful curse, is that he shall come forth in public either to prove his assertions or to retract them.'

As the ill-timed obstinacy of the Imperial government, backed up as it evidently was by the public opinion of Ravenna, still prevented the conclusion of the peace so necessary for Italy, Gregory exerted himself at least to lessen the miseries of war by promoting the redemption of some out of the many captives carried off in the train of each Lombard army. Writing to his Campanian representative Anthemius, he said1, 'How great is the sorrow and affliction of our heart, arising from the events which have happened in the regions of Campania, we cannot describe, but you will imagine, from the greatness of the calamity. To remedy this, we are sending you money by the hands of Stephen, Vir magnificus, which we desire you diligently to employ in the immediate liberation of such freemen as are not able to pay their own ransoms, also of all those slaves whose masters are too poor to redeem them, and especially of such slaves on the Church's estates as have perished [fallen into the hands of the enemy] through your negligence. Make a careful list of the names, occupations, dwelling-places, birthplaces, of all whom you redeem. Give your best attention to this work, that those who are to be redeemed may not incur any peril through your negligence, nor you hereafter undergo our vehement displeasure. Especially strive to redeem the captives at as low a price as possible, and send us the list above mentioned with all speed.'

For this pious work of the liberation of captives, Gregory thankfully accepted the help of the powerful and wealthy friends whom he had made at Constantinople. In two letters, written about the middle of June 597 to his old allies, Theoctista, the Emperor's sister, and Theodore, his physician, he gratefully acknowledges the large sums which they have sent him for the redemption of captives and the relief of the poor. The physician's contribution is not mentioned; that of Theoctista amounted to 30 lbs. of gold (£1200). In his letters to the latter, after congratulating her on her generosity, and pitying himself for the added responsibility thus brought upon him, he says :—

'I will mention to you, however, that from the city of Crotona on the Adriatic, which was taken by the Lombards in the past year, many men and many noble women were led away as booty: and sons were divided from their parents, husbands from their wives: but because they ask heavy ransoms for them, many to this hour have remained among the unutterable Lombards. However, I at once remitted for their liberation half of the money which I received from you, but out of the other half I have arranged to buy bed-clothes for the maids of God (whom you call in Greek monastriae), because they suffer sadly from the cold in our City from the scantiness of their bedclothes. Of these maids there are many in this City, for according to the memorandum of distribution there have been found 3000 of them, and they receive from the Patrimony of St. Peter 80 lbs. (£3200) annually. But what is that among such a multitude, especially in this City, where everything is sold at such a high price? But their life is of such a kind, so strictly passed in fasting and in tears, that we believe if it were not for them, none of us would have been able to exist for so many years between the swords of the Lombards [i.e. we owe our lives to their sanctity and prayers]'.

To each of his friends, in return for their munificent offerings, Gregory sent his usual present of a golden key which had lain by the body of St. Peter, and which contained some filings from his chains; and to Theoctista he told the story of a miracle which connected her key with the Lombard king Authari:—

'A certain Lombard who had entered a city beyond the Po, found this key, and despised it as being a key of St. Peter, but seeing that it was golden desired to make something out of it, and took out his knife that he might cut it. But at once, being arrested by the Spirit, he stuck that same knife into his throat and fell dead the same hour. Autharith [sic], king of the Lombards, came up, with many of his men, found the dead man lying on the ground, and the key lying by itself, and they were all at once struck with grievous fear, so that none of them dared to lift that key from the earth. Then a certain Catholic Lombard, Mimiulf by name, who was known to be given to prayer and almsgiving, was called, and he raised it from the ground. But in remembrance of such a miracle, Autharith caused another golden key to be made, and sent it along with this one to my predecessor of blessed memory, relating what a miracle it had wrought. I therefore wished to send it to your Excellency, that the same instrument through which Almighty God killed a proud infidel may bring present and eternal salvation to you who love and fear Him.'

The letter to Theoctista, a very long one, from which these quotations have been made, is also interesting, not only as containing some of Gregory's most beautiful thoughts, and a specimen of his most extravagantly allegorizing1 interpretation of Scripture, but also as giving us a glimpse of the Imperial nursery as presided over by the Patricia, the aunt of the young princes:—

'I beg also that you will take care to train the little lords whom you are nursing, in excellent morals, and to warn the Glorious Eunuchs, who are charged with their education, to speak to them in such fashion, that their hearts may be softened towards one another in mutual love and tenderness, and that if they have conceived any passion of hatred among themselves, it should not break forth into a quarrel.'

In the same year, probably, in which these letters were written to Constantinople, one great obstacle to peace was removed by the death of the Exarch Romanus. He was succeeded by a man of less difficult disposition, and more statesmanlike intellect, whose true name was Callinicus; but it is characteristic of the increasing divergence between the two divisions of the Empire that this regularly formed Greek name, which had been borne by rhetoricians, martyrs, and bishops in the eastern world, was now evidently a stumbling-block to western Romans, and was gradually converted by them into the barbarous Gallicinus.

Already, in May 597, we find a more hopeful tone in Gregory's letters. Writing to his representative in Sicily, the deacon Cyprian, he mentions the case of a certain

Libertinus, *Vir magnificus,* who had apparently filled the office of Praetor of Sicily, and had received a hostile summons to Ravenna, there to give an account of his stewardship. Gregory's language is not very clear, but he seems to say, 'Do not let Libertinus distress himself. We have received a letter from Ravenna which we enclose for your perusal, and which shows that his enemies will not get the upper hand. Bid him therefore to be of good cheer, for we believe that our most excellent son the Exarch will do nothing to grieve him. We did not forget to write about his business; but as the said Exarch is now busied in the valley of the Po, we have not yet received his reply'. There can be little doubt that we are here dealing with a new regime. The Pope's 'most excellent son' is the new and friendly Exarch Callinicus, and his occupations in the valley of the Po have possibly something to do with negotiations for peace.

But all the members of the new Exarch's suite were not equally friendly with himself, and in a letter written about the same time as the last to his old ally the *scholasticus* Andreas at Ravenna, we find Gregory saying : 'Moreover, I thank you for putting me on my guard about two persons who have come with the Glorious Callinicus, although we have already had some very disagreeable experience of the person first named by your Excellency. But inasmuch as the times are evil, we bear all things—with a groan'.

In the year 598 no great change seems to have occurred in the position of affairs. Pope Gregory's letters for this year are few in number, suggesting the probability that communications with the other parts of Italy may have been unusually disturbed by hovering swarms of Lombards. Certainly the language employed by the Pope to the bishop of Terracina shows that the inhabitants of that city, though only sixty miles from Rome, and close to the friendly sea, were still harassed by war's alarms :— 'We have heard that many are excusing themselves from sentry duty on the walls : and we therefore wish you to take anxious heed that no one, either in our own name or in that of the Church, obtains exemption from this duty, but that all collectively be compelled to undertake it: so that by the vigilance of all, and by Divine help, the guarding of the city may be secured.'

In the midst of all the terror which filled the rest of Italy, the City of Rome itself remained not only unharmed, but apparently unmenaced; an immunity which was doubtless due to the spiritual ascendency which Gregory had obtained over the minds of Ariulf and Agilulf. This special security granted to Rome is much insisted upon by the Pope in a letter written the summer of 598 to Rusticiana, a great lady of Constantinople. He thanks her for the 10 lbs. of gold (£400) which she has sent him for the redemption of captives. He gently chides her for tarrying so long at Constantinople, and postponing indefinitely her visit to Rome, 'a visit which would greatly redound to her profit hereafter in the life eternal'. (And here we observe in passing that Rome, the Babylon of the Apocalypse, which was to become the hold of every unclean and hateful bird, is already, by the end of the sixth century, become a sacred City, a pilgrimage to which confers spiritual benefits on the traveller.) 'The Gospel orders us,' says Gregory, 'to love even our enemies. Think then what a grave fault it must be to love too little those who love us. Your servant will tell you how great desire we all have to behold your face. If any one tells us that he loves us, we know very well that no one loves those whom he does not care to visit. But if you are afraid of the swords and the wars of Italy, you ought to see for yourself how great is the protection vouchsafed by Peter, prince of Apostles, to this City, in which, without any great number of people, and without help from soldiers, we have by God's help been preserved for so many years unhurt between the swords of the enemy. All this we say to you because we love you. May Almighty God grant you whatsoever He may see to be for the everlasting benefit of your soul, as well as for the present reputation of your household.'

In the autumn of 598 the long pending negotiations for peace at length began to assume a favourable aspect. Gregory's representative at the Lombard court was now the abbot Probus, and the Pope heard from him in the month of September that the terms of the peace might be considered as settled, both King and Exarch having given their consent. Our chief information as to this crisis of the negotiations is derived, curiously enough, from a letter of the Pope to Januarius, bishop of Sardinia. That strange and silly old man had not only to be restrained from sallying forth from his cathedral just after the celebration of mass to plough up his neighbour's harvest-field—but also to be warned of the continued necessity of vigilance against the Lombards. Both he and Gennadius the Exarch of Africa, to whose province Sardinia belonged, had been already in vain admonished by the Pope to put the island in a proper state of defence; and their carelessness had been punished by an attack of the barbarians (possibly on Caralis the capital), by which, though no permanent settlement had been effected, much injury had been done to the property of the islanders. The Pope expressed his hope that Januarius would learn a lesson from this misadventure, and keep a better guard in future, and he promised that for his part he would omit nothing which might be of service to the islanders in their preparations for defence. 'Know, however,' said he, 'that the abbot, whom a long time ago we sent to Agilulf, has by God's favour arranged a peace with him according to the most excellent Exarch's letters to us. And therefore till the actual signing of the articles for the confirmation of peace, cause the sentinels on your walls to discharge their duty with anxious vigilance, lest by chance in this time of delay our enemies should think to make another visit to your parts. We trust in our Redeemer's power that the assaults or the stratagems of our adversaries will work you no further harm.'

In a later letter the Pope seems to speak of the peace as now actually concluded. But as it was for a limited time—we learn from other sources that it was only concluded for two years—he warns Januarius of the probability that at the end of that time Agilulf would renew the war :—

'As we have no less concern for your safety than for our own, we thought it right at once to point out to you that when this peace is ended, Agilulf, king of the Lombards, will not make [another] peace. Wherefore it is necessary that your Brotherhood, while you still have liberty, should cause your city and other places to be more strongly fortified, and should take care that abundant store of provisions be laid up in them, so that when the enemy, by God's wrath against him, arrives there, he may not find anything that he can injure, but may go away disappointed.'

The peace negotiations seem after all not to have been finally concluded till the spring of 599. The the reason for such an inordinate delay (which reminds us of the prolonged negotiations of Munster or of Utrecht), is partly disclosed to us by a letter of the Pope to Theodore the Curator (or, as we should say, the Mayor) of Ravenna. From this we learn that after Agilulf the King and Callinicus the Exarch had been brought to agree as to the terms of peace, a difficulty arose as to its signature on the part of Ariulf and Arichis, the Dukes of Spoleto and Benevento, and strange to say on the part of Gregory also, who, when the object of his earnest strivings for seven years seemed at length within his grasp, displayed either a strain of morbid conscientiousness left in him by his cloister life, or else an ignoble desire to shield himself from responsibility, and make others his instruments for extracting the advantage by which he was to profit. Whatever the motive, he declined himself to sign the peace, offering one of his suffragan bishops, or at any rate an archdeacon, as a substitute. The part of the letter which is important for our purpose is as follows:—

'Our *responsales* have always brought us tidings about you which have gladdened our hearts, but now preeminently our son the abbot Probus has told us so much about your Glory's liberal expenditure on behalf of peace, and the earnest desire which you have manifested for the same (a desire which was never displayed by any previous citizen of Ravenna), that we can only pray that your labours for the common weal may be abundantly repaid to your own soul hereafter. We observe therefore that Ariulf has sworn for the preservation of peace not [unconditionally] as the king himself swore, but only on condition (1) that there shall be no act of violence committed against him, and (2) that no one shall march against the army of Arichis. As this is altogether unfair and deceitful, we look upon the case precisely as if he had not sworn at all, for he will always find something to complain of as "an act of violence against himself," and the less suspicious we are of him the more easily he will deceive us. Wamilfrida too, by whose counsel, or as I might say no-counsel, Ariulf is ruled in all things, absolutely refused to swear. And thus it has come to pass that from that peace from which we expected so much, we in these parts shall receive practically no remedy, because the enemies by whom we have hitherto been chiefly suspected will in future continue to suspect us.

'Your Glory ought also to know that the king's men who have been passed on hither insist that we ought to sign the agreement for peace. But remembering the reproaches which Agilulf is said to have addressed to Basilius, Vir clarissimus, tending through us to the injury of blessed Peter (though Agilulf himself entirely denies having thus spoken), we nevertheless decide to abstain from signing, lest we who have been suitors and mediators between him and our most excellent son the lord Exarch, if by chance anything is privately carried off, should seem to fail in any point, and so our own promise should be brought into doubt. Thus should any similar occasion arise in future (which God forbid), he will make an excuse for not granting our petition. We therefore beg of you, as we have already begged of our aforesaid most Excellent son, that you will, with your wonted goodness to us, bring it to pass that when the king's men return from Arichis he shall speedily send them writings which are to be brought to us, and in which he shall command them not to ask for our signature. If that be conceded we will cause our brother Gloriosus, or one of the bishops, or at any rate an archdeacon, to sign the pact.'

In reading this letter we cannot but be struck by the distrust of Ariulf which is evidently displayed by the Pope. Had he himself come round to the opinion of the Emperor and did he look upon himself as fatuus for having seven years before listened to the fair words of the duke of Spoleto? The Pope's relations with King Agilulf, too, seem far from friendly. The Vir clarissimus Basilius, whoever he may have been—probably some great Byzantine official—had made mischief between King and Pontiff by repeating some unguarded words of the former which Gregory chose to understand as reflecting injuriously on his honour, and through him on that of the blessed Peter.

But this was not the permanent relation of the two potentates The influence of the devout Theudelinda was being ever exerted to smooth away asperities and to make her husband and her unknown friend Gregory kindly disposed one towards the other. It was probably through her influence that the difficulties which had arisen at the last moment, and which seemed so menacing, were smoothed away. The dukes of Spoleto and Benevento must have been persuaded to acquiesce in the proposed arrangement; the Pope's guarantee must have been either obtained or dispensed with. In some way or other the weary negotiations were brought to a close and peace was concluded between Agilulf and Callinicus.

This chapter, devoted to the story of a peace which formed a turning-point in the history of Lombard Italy, may be fittingly ended by a translation of the two letters which the Pope addressed shortly before the conclusion of the peace to the king and queen of the Lombards.

'To Agilulf, king of the Lombards:—

'We render thanks to your Excellency that you have heard our petition, and justified the confidence which we had in you, by arranging a peace which will be profitable to both parties. Wherefore we greatly praise the wisdom and goodness of your Excellency, because in loving peace you have proved that you love God who is the author of peace. For if it had unhappily not been made, what else could have followed but the sin and danger of both parties, accompanied by the shedding of the blood of the miserable peasants whose labour is serviceable to both? But in order that we may feel that peace, as you have made it, we pray, while saluting you with fatherly love—that whenever opportunity offers, you will by your letters order your Dukes who are commanding in various districts. But especially in these parts, to keep this peace in its integrity, according to your promise, and not to look out for occasions of strife or unpleasantness. Thus doing you will earn from us yet ampler gratitude.

'We have received the bearers of these presents, as being truly your servants, with proper affection: since it was right that we should give a loving greeting and farewell to wise men who announced the peace made by the favour of Almighty God.'

'To Theudelinda, queen of the Lombards:—

' We have learned, by the report of our son the abbot Probus, how kindly and zealously, according your wont, you have exerted yourself for the conclusion of peace. We knew that we might reckon on your Christianity for this, that you would by all means apply your labour and your goodness to the cause of peace. Therefore we render thanks to Almighty God, who has so ruled your heart as not only to bestow on you the true faith, but to cause you to accomplish His own decrees.

'Do not think, most excellent daughter, that it is any trifling reward which you will reap from staying the effusion of blood on both sides. Therefore while thanking you for your willing help in this thing, we pray our compassionate God to give you His recompense for your good deeds both in body and soul, both here and hereafter.

'Saluting you, moreover, with fatherly love, we exhort you to use your influence with your most excellent consort that he may not reject the alliance of the Christian Republic. For, as we think you know, it is in many ways expedient that he should be willing to accept its friendship. Do you therefore, according to your custom, ever study all that tends to grace and the reconciliation of foes, and when you have such an opportunity of earning reward, labour that you may yet more conspicuously recommend your good deeds before the eyes of Almighty God.'

CHAPTER X.

THE LAST YEARS OF GREGORY.

The peace of 599, though not final, marks the transition to a different, and more settled, state of affairs in Italy. Hitherto war had been the relation between the Empire and the Lombard invaders: henceforward peace, though doubtless a turbulent and often interrupted peace, prevailed. Both Empire and Papacy now recognized the fact that the presence of the intruders, however unwelcome and 'unspeakable' they might be, was no mere passing misery; that there was no hope of expelling them from the peninsula; little prospect even of inducing them to accept the nominal subordination of *foederati*; that they were settled in Italy as the Franks and Burgundians were settled in Gaul, and the Visigoths in Spain; and that the only thing now to be done was to defend the fragments of coast line, and the chain of posts along the Flaminian Way, which still owned the sway of the Roman Republic.

It would seem therefore that no more fitting place could be found for ending the history of Lombard Invasion, and beginning that of Lombard Rule in Italy, than this same year 599, which has also the advantage of coming at the close of a century. But there are two men, an Emperor and a Pope, whose names have occurred so frequently in my later pages, that for their sakes I shall include in this period the few years by which their lives overlap the six hundredth year from the birth of Christ.

One consideration, which probably weighed with the Emperor in favour of the peace so long urged by Gregory, and so long refused by him, was the fact that the Avars, those Huns of the sixth century, were keeping up desultory but worrying hostilities in the provinces south of the Danube; twice besieging the key-city of Singidunum (Belgrade), invading Dalmatia, and on one occasion (597) penetrating as far south as Thessalonica. There was probably some connection between these invasions and an embassy which the great Chagan of the Avars sent to Milan in order to 'make peace', by which we are probably to understand a treaty of alliance with King Agilulf. The movements of these Tartar swarms evidently exercised a powerful influence on the politics of Europe at this time, and, as in the days of Attila, a century and a half previously, inclined the earlier invaders of the Empire to seek for peace with one another and with 'the Republic'. Issuing westwards from their quarters in Pannonia, they invaded Thuringia, and waged grievous war with the Franks, who were now overlords of that country.

As with the Empire so also with the Franks, harassed by these sons of the wilderness, King Agilulf concluded a treaty of peace which was perhaps in their case a treaty of alliance. As we have seen, all the kings of the Franks were now in their infancy. Guntram, the uncle, king of Burgundy, had died in 593 : Childebert, the nephew, in 596. His two children, Theudebert II and Theodoric II, ruled in Austrasia and Burgundy. Their grandmother Brunichildis, expelled from Austrasia by the nobles, swayed the sceptre of Burgundy as regent over her infant grandson, and it was of course by her influence, though in the name of Theodoric, that a 'perpetual' peace was concluded between the Lombards and the Franks of the southern kingdom.

The Lombard king had in truth need of peace with his foreign foes in order to deal with domestic treason. Or perhaps we should state cause and effect in a different relation, and say that the conclusion of peace and the relaxation of the grasp on the forces of the State which the 'war-power' gave to the king, brought its opportunity to rebellion. Three dukes revolted: the irrepressible Gaidulf of Bergamo, already twice pardoned; Zangrulf of Verona, and Warnecaut, who was perhaps duke of Pavia. All were defeated and slain by the energetic Agilulf, who wisely forbore from leaving Gaidulf under temptation to a fourth act of treason.

To Gregory the conclusion of the long wished for activity, peace brought in one sense rest, in another an immense increase of labour. Now was the time, when the roads were clear, and the Papal messengers could travel in safety, to order the affairs of the Churches, many of which had been lapsing into anarchy under the pressure of the times. Never probably, during the whole pontificate of Gregory, was the Papal chancery so busy as during this year of restored peace, 598-599. Of the 851 letters which make up the collection *Gregorii Epistolae*, 238, or more than one quarter of the whole, belong to this year.

A great number of these letters are addressed to the *defensores*, and relate to disputes about boundaries, the recovery of fugitive slaves, the administration of the estates of deceased persons, and matters of that kind. Many also are addressed to the sub-deacons, who had charge of the Papal Patrimony. The affairs to Sicily occupied a large amount of the Pope's attention, now no longer fixed with anxious gaze upon swords of the Lombards.' In Naples party-spirit was running high between two groups of citizens, and a grasping bishop was claiming privileges which properly belonged to the 'patron' of the city. In Gaul there were the ever-recurring difficulties, the licentious lives of the clergy, the wide prevalence of simony, the impossibility of getting the bishops to assemble in a synod; an impossibility which was probably due to the fact that the majority of them were conscious of deeds of their own, which would not bear the light of a judicial investigation. These are some of the subjects which were touched upon in the 240 letters of 'the Second Indiction'.

In one letter addressed by the Pope to the pay-master Donellus, entreating him to come without delay and pay the half-mutinous garrison of Rome their wages, we have a sentence which sounds like the sigh of an Italian patriot of our own times under Austrian domination. 'We grieve to hear that you have been troubled by sickness: but we trust in the Divine compassion that He, who has made you to love our miserable and depressed Italy, will both restore to you bodily health, and reward you with eternal life.'

The same letter concludes—'The city of Rome, doubtless owing to our sins, is so reduced by the languor of various diseases, that there are hardly men enough left to guard the walls'. And in another letter of about the same date, the Pope says:—'Such grievous febrile languors have attacked the clergy and people of this city, that scarce any man remains, free or slave, able to undertake any charge or duty. From the neighbouring cities also we hear daily reports of destructive mortality. And how Africa is being wasted by disease and death you doubtless know more accurately than we, as being closer to the scene of events. They, too, who come from the East report yet more terrible desolations there. All these things point to the approaching end of the world'.

We hear from Paulus that this pestilence was especially severe at Ravenna and all along the sea-coast (probably therefore ravaging Roman Italy more grievously than the mountainous interior which was in the hands of the Lombards); and that in the following year a terrible mortality laid waste the inhabitants of the district round Verona.

Gregory himself, though he apparently escaped the fever, was more cruelly than ever racked by gout. We may perhaps infer that the busy energy of the summer of 599, during all of which time he was fighting against this persistent enemy, brought him at last to so low a point that work became almost impossible; for the 240 letters of 'the Second Indiction' are succeeded by only twenty letters in the following year; one of the poorest harvests in the whole collection. He himself says to his correspondents[1] in Sicily,

'For my sins I have now for eleven months been able only very rarely to rise from my bed. Such are the pains inflicted upon me by gout and other infirmities, that life is to me the heaviest of punishments. Every day I faint with the pain and wait with sighing for the remedy of death.' And again, in a later letter, July 600, addressed to the Patriarch of Alexandria, he says:—

'I received last year the very sweet letters of your Holiness, which I have not hitherto been able to answer, on account of my exceeding sickness. For behold! it is now all but two years that I have been confined to my bed, and so tortured with the pains of gout, that scarcely on festival days have I been able to rise for the space of three hours to celebrate the rites of the Mass. Then I am forced to lie down, in such severe pain, that only an occasional groan enables me to bear my agony. This pain in my case is sometimes gentle, sometimes intense, but never so gentle as to depart, nor so intense as to kill me. Hence I am daily dying, and daily driven back from death.'

So the two years of peace wore away in Italy. There were fears of an invasion of Alamanni, but they were not fulfilled. The dukes of Benevento and Spoleto seem to have come in to the peace, and to have lived on friendly terms with their Roman neighbour. It is even thought by some that Arichis, the duke of Benevento, renounced his Arianism, and became a member 0f the Catholic Church; but this is perhaps too large an inference to draw from the fact that in the only letter which the Pope addressed to him, and which was probably written in the year 599, he accosts him 'as in truth our son'.

At length the two years' peace came to an end. Notwithstanding the anxious fears of Gregory, it would perhaps have been renewed by Agilulf, for the perfidious act of the Exarch, who thought by the seizure of a hostage to force the Lombard king to renew the peace on less favourable terms. A daughter of Agilulf by his first wife was dwelling with her husband Gottschalk at Parma, of which place Gottschalk was probably duke. It may have been owing to the security born of the two years' peace (though we are not expressly told that this was the case), that the princely couple were taken unawares by the soldiers of Callinicus, who suddenly appeared before the city, and carried them off to Ravenna.

It seems to have been a felon stroke, and it utterly missed its aim. Far from being intimidated by his daughter's danger, Agilulf was roused to a more vigorous prosecution of the war. He made overtures for a fresh league with the Chagan of the terrible Avars, and sent him shipwrights, from the Italian ports under his sway, to help him to construct ships for warlike operations against Thrace. Agilulf himself then moved against the great city of Patavium (Padua), which till this time had successfully resisted the arms of the Lombards. He succeeded in kindling a conflagration by means of fiery bolts hurled into the city. The garrison saw that they could no longer hold the place, and surrendered to Agilulf, who, honouring their bravery, allowed them to depart uninjured to Ravenna. The city itself, we are told, was levelled with the ground; the second time within two centuries that this fate had befallen the proud city of Livy.

At this time the ambassadors who had been sent to the Chagan of the Avars returned, announcing that he had graciously concluded a perpetual peace with the Lombards. The great barbarian sent also an ambassador of his own, who proceeded to the courts of the Frankish kings, and announced to them his master's pleasure that they should dwell at peace with his Lombard friend.

The next year was a prosperous one for Agilulf. The Lombards, with their Avar and Sclavonic allies, entered Istria, which they laid waste with fire and sword. In the Po valley, the arms of the Lombards achieved a signal success by the reduction of the Mountain of Flint (*Monselice*), which had been one of the few islands rising above the flood of barbarian conquest.

There was great joy also in the new palace at Modicia (*Monza*), which Queen Theudelinda had built and adorned with paintings of the victories of the Lombards. Here in this barbaric Versailles, Queen Theudelinda, after eleven years of married life, gave birth to her firstborn son, who was named Adalwald, and who was baptized according to the Catholic rite by Secundus of Trient, the historian to whom Paulus was indebted for most of his knowledge of this period. This was a signal triumph for Catholicism. Agilulf's predecessor had sternly forbidden the Lombard nobles to have their children baptized by Catholic bishops, and now King Agilulf himself, though probably still making profession of Arianism, permitted his own son to be held over the baptismal font by a Catholic ecclesiastic.

The year of Adalwald's birth also witnessed the reconciliation of the two great dukes, Gaidwald of Trient, and Gisulf of Friuli, who had before been estranged from Agilulf, if not actually in rebellion against him, but who now came in and submitted themselves to his rule.

Meanwhile there was a change in the occupants of the Imperial palace at Constantinople and of the Exarch's palace at Ravenna. The year 602 saw downfall of the Emperor Maurice, with circumstances which will shortly be related, and also saw the removal of Callinicus, who was replaced as Exarch by Smaragdus, the same capable, but somewhat headstrong official, who had been recalled from Ravenna thirteen years before for his too harsh treatment of the Istrian schismatics. The recall of Callinicus at this juncture may have been connected with the revolution at Constantinople, but seems sufficiently accounted for by the conspicuous failure of his dastardly blow at the family of the Lombard king, and by an actual defeat which he is said to have suffered under the walls of Ravenna.

The change of rulers did not, however, make any difference in the fortunes of the war. The year 603 beheld the most triumphant of all the campaigns of Agilulf. Going forth from Milan in the month of July, he laid siege to the city of Cremona. There were among his troops a number of Sclavonic barbarians, whom his great ally, the Chagan of the Avars, had sent to serve under his banners. On the 21st of August Cremona was taken, and, according to Paulus, was levelled with the ground. It is hardly likely, however, that the Lombard king would thus utterly destroy a large and wealthy city just added to his dominions. It seems more probable that it was only the fortifications that were destroyed, as in the case of the African and cities taken by Gaiseric. From

Cremona he marched against its old neighbour Mantua, beat down its walls with battering-rams, and entered the city on the 13th of September, having admitted the garrison to an honourable surrender, and allowed them to return to Ravenna. He also captured the little town of Vulturina, the position of which is unknown, but which was probably situated upon the northern bank of the Po, not far from Parma, for we are told that the garrison in their flight from Vulturina set the town of Brixellum on fire. Brixellum (now Brescello) was the town on the south bank of the Po, about ten miles from Parma, which as the reader may remember, the Alaman Droctulf had long held for the Empire against the Lombards. It was, however, at last surrendered to King Authari, and, as a Lombard town, was now set on fire by the fleeing garrison of Vulturina.

The fortune of war was so evidently going against the Imperial arms that, in September of this year, Smaragdus was glad to make peace with Agilulf. Hostilities were to cease for eighteen months, till the 1st of April, 605. King Agilulf evidently retained all his conquests, and—most striking confession of Imperial failure—his daughter was restored with her husband and children. The princess returned to her home of Parma, but the story of her captivity had an unhappy ending. She died in child-bed almost immediately after her return from Ravenna. Would that we knew more of this strange and pathetic little incident in the meagre annals of the time! The princess, whose very name is hidden from us, dwelt probably for two years and a half with her husband and children in captivity at Ravenna. How gladly would we hear something of the effect which the imperial and ecclesiastical splendours of the city by the Ronco produced on the daughter of the Thuringians; of her relations with the two Exarchs who successively ruled there; of the terms of her captivity, whether easy or severe; of the Exarch's announcement to her that she was free; of the scene of her restoration to her father's arms, and of his emotions when he heard that a mightier than the Exarch had carried her off into the captivity from which there is no returning!

The total effect of these operations of 601-603 was greatly to enlarge the Lombard boundary. The whole valley of the Po was now in the possession of the invaders; the communication by land with the cities of the Venetian lagunes was cut off; there was now no Imperial city of importance in Italy north of the latitude of Ravenna. No change of frontier occurred for a generation of equal extent with that which followed on the abduction of the daughter of Agilulf.

We have followed the course of events in Italy down to the autumn of 603; but we must now return to the close of the preceding year in order to notice the revolution which, in November, 602, was accomplished at Constantinople.

From his correspondence with Gregory, the reader will probably have already formed a fair estimate of the character of Flavius Tiberius Mauricius Augustus. He was neither a bad nor a foolish man, but he often did the right things in the wrong way, and he had not that power of achieving personal popularity which has been possessed by many rulers of far inferior capacity. A skillful general and author of a book of some authority on Strategics, Maurice was nevertheless unpopular with the army. An orthodox Churchman, he, nevertheless, on account of his quarrel with Pope Gregory, earned a bad name in ecclesiastical history. Inheriting an exhausted treasury from his lavish predecessor Tiberius, he failed to make his subjects understand that 'his poverty, and not his will, consented' to retrenchments which they thought mean and unworthy of the Imperial dignity. In civic politics Maurice leaned to the faction of the Blues, which seems to have been weaker than that of the Greens, and at a critical period of the revolution he unwisely armed both factions in order to form a city-guard against the mutinous soldiers. The remote cause of his downfall appears to have been his refusal (in the year 600) to ransom 12,000 soldiers (possibly deserters), who were in the power of the Chagan of the Avars, and who, being unransomed, were put to death by the barbarian. This refusal, which was perhaps due in part to absolute poverty, in part to notions of military discipline, like those which prompted the well-known speech of Regulus to the Roman Senate, sank deep into the hearts of the soldiery; and when, in 602, Maurice issued orders that to save the expense of their rations the Danubian army should spend the winter in the cold and inhospitable regions inhabited by the Sclavonians, the long-suppressed anger of the legions burst into a flame. They defied the Emperor's power, refused to cross the Danube, and raising one of their officers, the centurion Phocas, on a shield, after the fashion of the barbarians, they saluted him, not indeed as yet with the title of Imperator, but with the only less splendid name of Exarch.

The full details of the revolution need not be given here, as they belong rather to the history of the East than of Italy, and they have been already to some extent anticipated in connection with the history of Germanus Postumus, the great-grandson of Theodoric, and the great-nephew of Justinian, who was for a time an unwilling candidate for the Imperial dignity, but who was eventually put to death by the usurper, after he had used that venerated name as a cloak for his own ambition.

It may not, however, be out of place to give the outlines of the story of the fall of Maurice as it is told by Joannes Diaconus, who probably preserves that version which early obtained credence in Italy.

Through the barbarous and obscure Latinity of the biographer we can discern something of the internal struggle in the Emperor's mind, distracted between his duty to the State and his fear for the safety of his soul if he continued in opposition to the Pope. 'Most of covetous and most tenacious of Emperors,' (says the Deacon),—Maurice perceived that Gregory, who had been raised to the pontificate by his vote, no longer needed the Emperor's defence against the tumults of the time, but relied on spiritual help, on the force of the canon law, on his own holiness and prudence to overcome the dangers by which he was surrounded. While partly admiring his courage, Maurice was drawn away more and more to hatred and detraction of the great Pontiff, and at length wrote him that sharp letter of rebuke for wasting the stores of corn [and listening to the peace propositions of Ariulf], to which Gregory replied in the famous letter beginning 'In serenissimis jussionibus' which was quoted in an earlier chapter.

The boldness of this reply moved Maurice both to admiration and to anger, and he would probably have proceeded to some act of tyrannical oppression against the Pope, but for a strange scene which was enacted in the streets of Constantinople. A certain man, clothed in monastic garb, and endued with superhuman energy, walked, bearing a drawn sword in his hand, from the Forum to the brazen statue of the gladiator, proclaiming to all the bystanders that the Emperor should die by the sword. (The biographer's manner of telling the story leaves us in doubt whether he is describing a supernatural appearance or the bold deed of some enthusiast.) When Maurice heard this prediction he at once forbore all further acts of violence against Gregory, and set himself with earnestness to avert the coming judgment. He sent not only to Gregory, but to all the Patriarchs, bishops, and abbots in his dominions messengers bearing costly gifts, money, tapers, and frankincense, accompanied by his written petition, to which he besought them to add their suffrages, that it would please God to punish him for his sins in this life, and to deliver him from endless torment. This for long was the burden of his tearful prayer. At length one night in his slumbers he saw himself standing with a great multitude by the brazen statue of the Saviour, at the brazen gate of the palace. Lo! a voice, a terrible voice, issued from the mouth of the Incarnate Word, 'Bring Maurice hither and the ministers of judgment brought him, and laid him down before the Judge. With the same terrible voice the statue said, 'Where dost thou wish that I should requite to thee the ills that thou hast wrought in this world?' 'Oh! Lover of men,' the Emperor answered, 'Oh! Lord, and righteous Judge, requite me here, and not in the world to come.' At once the divine voice ordered that 'Maurice and his wife Constantina, with their sons and daughters, and all their kinship, should be handed over to Phocas the soldier'. When the Emperor awoke, he sent a chamberlain to summon his son-in-law Philippicus, whom he had long suspected of treasonable designs upon the throne. Philippicus came in, trembling, having taken, as he supposed, a last embrace of his wife Gordia, and having fortified himself with the Holy Communion. When he entered the Emperor's sleeping apartment, and, according to custom, prostrated himself at his feet, Maurice raised him up, and, performing the same prostration, said, 'Pardon me, I pray, for I now know, by a revelation from God, that thou hast harboured none of the evil designs against me, of which I suspected thee. But tell me if in all our armies thou knowest a man who passes by the name of Phocas'. Then Philippicus, after long musing, answered, 'One man called Phocas I do know, who was lately named procurator by the army, and who was murmuring against your rule'. 'What manner of man is he?' said the Emperor. 'Young and rash,' answered Philippicus, 'but timid withal.' Then said Maurice, 'If he is timid, he will also be a murderer.'

While he was still in doubt and fear over this business an Imperial messenger[1] brought back the answer of some holy hermits to whom he had been sent—'God has accepted thy repentance. Thou and all thy house shall be saved, and shall have your dwelling with the saints above, but thou shalt fall from the throne with disgrace and danger.'

When Maurice heard these words he thanked God and continued his acts of penitence. His covetousness, however, he could not eradicate, and thus it came to pass that he ordered his troops to winter in perilous places, crossing over the Danube to seek their food at the risk of their lives in the country of the Sclavonians, that they might not eat their rations at the expense of the State. These orders were conveyed to the general Peter (brother of the Emperor), who, summoning his officers, said, 'These orders of the Emperor that we should winter in the enemy's country seem to me too hard. I am placed in a most difficult position. Disobedience to orders is disastrous, but obedience seems more disastrous still. Nothing good comes out of avarice, which is the mother of all the vices; and that is the disease under which the Emperor is now suffering, and which makes him the author of such grievous ills to the Romans.'

Then came, as has been already said, the open mutiny of the army, their elevation of Phocas on the shield, his proclamation as Exarch. The mutineers offered the diadem successively to Theodosius, son of the Emperor, and to Germanus, the father-in-law of Theodosius, who both refused it, and acquainted Maurice with the offer that had been made them. Germanus, however, seeing that he had roused the Emperor's suspicions, took refuge in the church of the Theotokos. Maurice looked upon his son as a traitor, and ordered him to be flogged, and he then sent many persons to draw Germanus forth from the shelter of the church of St. Sophia, to which he had removed from that of the Theotokos. The multitude, however, would not permit Germanus to be removed, and broke out into shouts of invective against Maurice, calling, him a Marcionite heretic. Unnerved by the tumult, Maurice went on board a swift cutter with his wife and children, and reached the sanctuary of the martyr Autonomus, on the Bithynian coast. Meanwhile Phocas arrived at the palace of the Hebdomon, outside the gate of Constantinople, and, after some little dallying and delay, during which the claims of Germanus to the vacant throne were advocated by the Blue faction, Phocas himself was proclaimed Emperor.

Possibly Maurice might have been left unmolested in his sanctuary, but for the injudicious cry of the offended Blues at the coronation of the new Empress Leontia:— 'Begone: understand the position: Maurice is not dead'. An officer was sent to Chalcedon to slay the Emperor and his four younger sons; Theodosius, the eldest, having started on the eastward road to seek the assistance of the Persian king. As each of the young princes yielded up his life, the fallen Emperor, determined to drink the cup of his punishment to the dregs, repeated the verse, 'Thou art just, Oh! Lord, and true are thy judgments'. The youngest of the tribe was but a baby, and the nurse, who was rearing him, with 'splendid mendacity' tried to substitute her own child for the Imperial nurseling, but Maurice, as nobly unselfish, insisted on proclaiming the truth, and gave his own little one to the sword. Last of all, the Emperor himself was slain. His martyr death revealed the essential nobleness of his nature, and seems to demand a merciful judgment on a life marked indeed by many mistakes, but, as far as we can see, stained by no crime.

The young and attractive prince Theodosius, returning from his eastern journey, at its first stage fell into the hands of the usurper's creatures and was slain. The widowed Empress Constantina, her daughters, and Germanus, were put to death about three years afterwards. By the end of 605 there was no scion left of the once flourishing house of Mauricius Augustus.

Too soon the soldiers and the people of Constantinople found out the terrible mistake which they had made in exchanging a just and noble-hearted, if somewhat unsympathetic, ruler for that monster of lust and cruelty, the imbecile and brutal Phocas, whose reign is perhaps the darkest page in all the annals of Byzantium. We are indeed bound to read with some caution the character of a monarch, written by the courtiers of the rival who dethroned him. The dynasty of Heraclius, who in 610 ended the horrible nightmare of the reign of Phocas, wore the imperial purple for the greater part of a century; and we, therefore, ought to treat the history of Phocas, as told by the meagre historians of that century, in something of the same spirit in which modern critics treat the Tudor historians' description of the deeds and character of Richard III; but after every deduction has been made, there can be no doubt that Phocas was a jealous, lecherous and cruel tyrant, besides being intellectually quite unfit to wield the sceptre of a great empire, and that the eight years of his reign were one of the gloomiest and most disastrous periods in Byzantine history.

The death of Maurice took place on the 27th of November, 602. Probably some indistinct rumours of the revolution reached Rome before the formal Embassy, but it was on the 25th of April, 603, that the statues of the August Phocas and Leontia were brought to Rome, accompanied by letters in which the crowned trooper addressed the Senate and People of Rome in terms of the utmost condescension. The clergy and the Senate assembled in the great Julian basilica, near the Papal palace of the Lateran, and shouted the customary acclamations to the new Augustus and the new Augusta. The statues were then carried, by order of the Pope, into the oratory of S. Caesarius, in the Lateran Palace, and erected there; and then Pope Gregory sat down to compose his answer to the Imperial proclamation.

It might have seemed that he had a difficult task before him. He had himself, in the earlier stages of his career, been somewhat indebted to the deceased Emperor's friendship. Of later years it is true that the relations between them had been much strained, and the angry correspondence of the years 595 to 597 had apparently been succeeded by an angrier silence. But if the Pope's relations with Maurice himself had of late been hostile, with his family he had ever been on terms of friendship. He had written letters of fatherly love and tenderness to the Empress Constantina; he had raised her eldest son, Theodosius, from the baptismal font; he had interested himself in the education of the little occupants of the Imperial nursery. And now Constantina was in forced seclusion; Theodosius, if yet living, was a fugitive; the other princes, down to the youngest of them, had been slain in their innocent childhood by the order of an usurper. And to that usurper Gregory had now to address congratulatory letters on his accession. As has been already said, the task, to an ordinary man of the world, might have seemed a difficult one. To the infinite disappointment and disgust of all honest champions of the great Pope's reputation, it must be admitted that he found in the task no difficulty at all. He could not rise to the level of the Jewish chieftain who poured forth his glorious song of lamentation over the relentless enemy who had fallen on Mount Gilboa. The thought of the desolate widow and murdered infants seems never to have crossed his mind; he only remembered the slights offered to his priestly dignity, the monarch who had dared to call him fatuous; the Patriarch who had used the abhorred word 'ecumenical'; and, because Phocas had trampled on the man who dared to use the one word and to defend the other, he addressed that murderous usurper with Hosannas like those uttered by the crowd at Christ's entry into Jerusalem:—

'Glory to God in the highest—to Him who according to the Scripture changeth times and transferreth kingdoms. For He hath made all men to perceive that which He deigned to speak by the mouth of His prophet:—"The Most High ruleth in the kingdoms of men, and giveth it to whomsoever He will". In the incomprehensible providence of Almighty God the destinies of our mortal lives alternate one with another. Sometimes, when the sins of many have to be punished, one is exalted, by whose sternness the necks of his subjects are pressed under the yoke of tribulation; and this we have experienced in our own long afflictions. Then again, when the merciful God decides to cheer the sorrowing hearts of many by His own consolation, He raises one man to the height of power, by whose tender compassion He pours the oil of His own gladness into the hearts of all men. With this abounding gladness we are persuaded that we shall soon be refreshed, we who do already rejoice that the kindness of your Piety has arrived at the summit of Imperial greatness. "Let the heavens rejoice and let the earth be glad." By your benign actions may all the citizens of our Republic, till now so grievously afflicted, regain their cheerfulness of soul. Under the yoke of your rule may the proud minds of our enemies be pressed down. By your compassion may the contrite and dejected hearts of your subjects be raised up again—may the power of the heavenly grace make you terrible to your enemies; may your piety make you merciful to your subjects. In your most happy days may the whole Republic have rest, an end being put to those ravages of peace which are made under the guise of law. May the ambuscade of testaments, may the pretence of voluntary gifts exacted by violence be done away. Let all men have once again secure possession of their own property, that they may enjoy without trembling that which they have honestly acquired. Under the yoke of a pious Emperor let liberty be fashioned anew for every man. For this it is which makes the difference between the kings of the nations and the Emperors of the Republic, that the former are lords of slaves, and the latter of free men.

' But we can say all this better in prayer than in exhortation. May Almighty God in every thought and word hold the heart of your Piety in the hand of His grace, and whatever is to be done with justice, whatever is to be done with clemency, may the Holy Spirit, inhabiting your breast, direct you to these things, so that your Clemency may be made sublime by your temporal reign, and that after many years have run their course you may attain to the Heavenly Kingdom'.

Again two months later, in sending an *apocrisiarius* to represent him at the Imperial Court, the Pope continued in the same strain of virulent abuse of the fallen, and fulsome flattery of the reigning, Emperor:—

'I delight to think, with a grateful heart, what praise is due to Almighty God for removing the yoke of our sadness, and bringing us to days of liberty under the pious rule of your Imperial kindness.

'That your Serenity did not find a deacon from the Apostolic See dwelling in your palace according to ancient custom, must be ascribed not to my negligence, but to our sore need. For as all the ministers of our Church shunned and declined such hard times [as had to be endured by our *apocrisiarius* at Constantinople], I could not lay upon them the burden of going to the royal city to abide in the palace. But as soon as they knew that, by the disposing grace of Almighty God, your Clemency had arrived at the summit of the Empire, they who had hitherto trembled, were now eager in the promptings of their joy, to hasten to your feet. But as some of them are prevented by the infirmity of age, and others by the cares of the Church, from undertaking this duty, I have chosen the bearer of these presents [Bonifacius], who is the first of all our *defensor* of long tried diligence, and fit by his life, faith, and manners, to wait upon the footsteps of your Piety. I have therefore ordained him deacon, and sent him with all speed, that he may at a fitting time convey to your Clemency tidings of all that is going on here. May your Serenity deign to incline your pious ears to him, and so be the more quickly moved to pity our affliction, by hearing from him the true relation of it. For in what fashion we have now for the long space of thirty-five years been oppressed by the daily swords of the Lombards, and how their inroads have afflicted us, no words of ours are adequate to express.

'But we trust in the Almighty Lord, that He will perfect for us those good gifts of His consolation which He has already begun, and that He who has raised up pious rulers for the Republic will also extinguish her cruel foes. May the Holy Trinity long guard your life, that we may have the longer fruition of the blessing of your Piety, which we have so late received'.

At the same time Gregory wrote thus to the new Empress Leontia, who was inhabiting doubtless the very rooms which had witnessed the orisons of the pious Constantina, and echoed to the prattle of the children whom the husband of Leontia had murdered:—

'What tongue can utter, what heart can conceive, the thanks which we owe to Almighty God for the serenity of your Empire, that the hard weight which so long pressed upon us is removed from our necks, and that light yoke of the Imperial majesty which the subjects love to bear, has taken its place? Let glory therefore be given to the Creator of all by the hymning choirs on high:—let thanks be brought by men upon the earth:—because the whole Republic, which has borne so many sorrowful wounds, has now found the fomentings of your consolation'

Gregory then goes on to pray that God, who holds the hearts of kings in His right hand, may turn the hearts of Phocas and Leontia into His service, and make them as zealous defenders of the Catholic faith as they are benign rulers of the state; that Leontia may be another Pulcheria in clemency—another Helena in zeal for the true religion. As they love the Creator of all, so are they bound to love the Church of that Apostle, to whom it was said, 'Thou art Peter, and on this rock I will build my church'. May they give their relieved subjects joy on earth, and themselves receive, after a long reign, the eternal joys of heaven.

These letters, written in July, 603, are nearly the last that we shall have to notice as proceeding from the pen of the great Pontiff.

In December of the same year he wrote to Queen Theudelinda thanking her for a letter which she had written from Genoa announcing the Catholic baptism of her son Adalwald. The tortures of gout prevented him from replying at that time to the doubts which had been instilled into her mind by her spiritual adviser Secundus, with reference to the 'Three Chapters' controversy; but he sent the Acts of the Fifth General Council in order to show that nothing had really been done thereat in derogation of the council of Chalcedon. He sent, moreover, certain presents which may have fascinated the gaze of the baby convert.

'We send our most excellent son, Adalwald the king, certain charms, namely, a cross with the wood of our Lord's cross, a manuscript of the Holy Gospel enclosed in an embroidered case. To his sister, my daughter, I send three rings, two with jacinths and one with an onyx, and I pray you to hand these presents to your children, that so your Excellency may foster their love towards us. Saluting you with fatherly love, we pray you to give thanks to our most excellent son the king your consort, for the peace which has been made. As your manner has ever been, incline his heart by all means to peace in the future, that so, besides your many other good actions, you may earn from God the reward of an innocent people saved, who might otherwise have perished unshriven'.

During all this time the Pope's bodily infirmities were increasing. His once portly frame was shrunken and withered by the gout, and by the daily worries of his life. Sometimes he was simply tortured with pain, and at other times a strange fire seemed to spread along with the pain through his body: the fire and the pain seemed to fight together, and body and mind alike gave way under the

In February, 603 he wrote:—'I live in such wailing and worry that I regret to see the light of each fresh day; and my only comfort is the expectation of death. Wherefore, I beg you to pray for me, that I may be the sooner led forth from this prison-house of the flesh, and that I be not any longer tortured by such agonies.'

It is pleasant to have to record that almost the last letter which we have from Gregory's pen is one which shows his thoughtfulness for others in the midst of his own daily sufferings. In January, 604, he wrote to the bishop of Perugia that he heard that 'our brother and fellow-bishop' Ecclesius was suffering from the cold, because he had no winter garment. He had asked the Pope to send him something, and accordingly Gregory sent a two-ply wrapper, a tunic and a waistcoat, which were to be forwarded from Perugia with all speed to the shivering bishop. 'Be sure that you lose no time in executing this commission, and write to us at once that you have done it, for the cold is intense.'

Soon after writing this letter, the great Pontiff's long struggle with life was ended. He died on March 11, 604, and was buried on the following day at the east end of the basilica of St. Peter. After the death of the man, who for fourteen years had been indisputably the foremost figure in the Italian peninsula, there was some trace of that reaction which is so often perceived when a commanding personality, such as that of Augustus, of Elizabeth, of Cromwell, is removed from the world; and, strange to say, it was the open-handed liberality of the deceased Pope which was chosen as the point of attack by his calumniators. The stories of what happened in Rome after his death are obscure, and reach us only through authors who lived two or three centuries after the event; but there is probably in them some vague echo of the truth. Paulus Diaconus tells us that Sabinianus, Pope Gregory's successor, refused to continue his predecessors lavish charities to the people, averring that if he did, the corn-magazines would be exhausted and they would all die of hunger. Thrice did Gregory appear to him in a vision to warn him to repent and change his course, but in vain. A fourth time he appeared, and vehemently rebuked him, and struck him on the head with his staff. Soon after (in February, 606) Sabinianus died.

According to the story told by Joannes Diaconus, Gregory's later biographer, the Pope's death was followed almost immediately by a famine in Rome. (This at least seems to be an undoubted fact.) Certain calumnious persons (Sabinianus' name is not expressly mentioned) stirred up the people, alleging that Gregory had been a spendthrift, and had wasted the treasures of his patriarchate. Hereupon the mob assembled with tumultuous cries, and began to talk of burning the late Pope's books. His friend the deacon Peter ran in among the crowd and earnestly sought to dissuade them, declaring that he had often seen the Holy Spirit hovering over the late Pope's head in the form of a dove, while he was writing his books. The people shouted, 'Swear to this till death, and we will not burn the books'. Hereupon Peter ascended the 'ambo' with the Gospels in his hand, swore the required oath, and 'breathed out his spirit amid his true confession'.

The character of Pope Gregory, truly called the Great, has been sufficiently indicated by what has been here recorded of his deeds, and quoted of his words. The one great blot upon his escutcheon, his jubilation over the downfall of Maurice, and his fulsome praise of the tyrant his successor, can be palliated by no lover of truth and justice; and it is grievous to think how much more stainless his record would have been had his cruel enemy, the gout, carried him off only one year before the actual date of his death. We must admit, however, that a man of deep spiritual discernment, thoroughly imbued with the spirit of his Master, would not have written either the congratulatory epistles to Phocas, or many another letter in the great collection, which denotes impatience and an angry temper. On the whole, it seems safer to judge him as a great Roman, than as a great saint;—and thus considered, his generosity, his justice, his courage, entitle him to a high place among the noblest names of his imperial race. In estimating his character we must never forget that, during all his public life, he was almost incessantly tortured by disease. That little passage in his biography which describes how he used to train the choir in the convent which had been his father's house, seems to me emblematic of much in the life of Gregory. In the midst of a tumultuous and discordant generation, it is his to bear witness to the eternal harmony. But he is stretched upon the bed of sickness; his frame is racked by pain; he holds the rod of discipline in his hand, and ever and anon, as he starts up to chastise the offender, he feels a sharper twinge than usual of his ever-present agony; and this gives an energy to his stroke, and a bitterness to his words, of which he himself is hardly conscious. At any rate, there can be no doubt of the world-historical importance of this man, the last of the great Romans of the Empire, the true founder of the Mediaeval Papacy.

CHAPTER XI.

THE ISTRIAN SCHISM.

I have postponed to this place the description of some ecclesiastical events which took place in the North of Italy during the latter part of the sixth century, and which exercised a powerful influence over the political condition of the cities of the Northern Adriatic, especially over that of the rising Venetian Commonwealth, during the greater part of the Lombard rule.

It is necessary to remind the reluctant reader of that dreary page in ecclesiastical history known as the controversy of the Three Chapters. Most futile and most inept of all the arguments that even ecclesiastics ever wrangled over, that controversy nominally turned on the question whether three Syrian bishops of irreproachable lives, Theodore of Mopsuestia, Theodoret of Cyrrhus, and Ibas of Edessa, were to be stigmatized, a century or more after their deaths, as suffering the punishment of everlasting fire, because the Emperor Justinian, sitting in the library of his palace at the dead of night, and ceaselessly turning over the rolls of the writings of the Fathers, had discovered in the works of these three men the germs of the Nestorian heresy. That was nominally the issue, but, as all men knew, something more than this trifling matter was really involved. The writings of these three Syrians had been received without condemnation, if not with actual applause, at the great Council of Chalcedon; and the real question was whether the Eastern Emperors should be allowed to inflict a backhanded blow on the authority of that Council by throwing out the souls of these three hapless Syrians to the Monophysite wolves of Egypt and of Asia, who were forever howling after the Imperial chariot. The Council of Chalcedon was dear to the Western, especially dear to the Roman, heart. In it a check had been inflicted on the audacious speculations of Oriental ascetics; by it the Tome of the great pontiff Leo had been accepted almost as a fresh revelation, or (it would perhaps be better to say) as the best expression of Christian common sense on the matters in dispute, and had been used as a bulwark against the ever-rising tide of irreverent speculation into which the Fullers and the Weasels and the other grotesquely-named theologians of Alexandria delighted to plunge.

No Roman Pope would willingly connive at anything which seemed like disrespect to the Council of Chalcedon. Vigilius had struggled, we have seen how desperately, to avoid the slight on that Council which was involved in the condemnation of the Three Chapters; but having obeyed the Imperial summons to Constantinople, he had found that he was in the power of one stronger than himself, and, after doubling backwards and forwards like a frightened hare, he had at last yielded his reluctant but final consent to the proceedings of the Fifth Council, by which the Three Chapters were condemned.

After the Holy See had once irrevocably committed itself to the propositions of Justinian, it could not be accused of lukewarmness in its newly-adopted cause. No partisans are more bitter than those who have a position which they declared they would never surrender, and who in their secret hearts envy the courage of its remaining defenders; a courage which they themselves have not dared to imitate. And thus it came to pass that for something like a century and a half the Roman Pontiffs oppressed with unusual bitterness and acrimony the men who were called the defenders of the Three Chapters, and who still struggled to maintain the position which a Pope had once fought for, and which was almost universally held in the Western Church when Justinian first started his idle controversy.

As far as we can discern, the condemnation of the Three Chapters was for a generation or more an unpopular measure in Italy generally as well as in Africa, but the peculiar geographical position and political circumstances of one province, that of Istria, caused the opposition there to be more stubborn and long-enduring, and to assume more completely the character of schism than in other parts of Italy.

The peninsula of Istria, stretching forth into the Adriatic Sea at its northern end, whose coast, during the sixth century, was still lined with fair cities which owned the sway of the Empire, formed one province with the mainland and islands to the West which bore the name of Venetia1. But this province was now so circumscribed by the conquests of the Lombards, especially in the Western portion, that its full name, 'Venetia et Istria', was often abbreviated, and it was called 'Istria' alone. The chief city of the province was Aquileia, for which, notwithstanding its awful destruction by Attila, its ecclesiastical supremacy had procured a fresh lease of life, though doubtless with greatly diminished splendour.

The Patriarch of Aquileia was still therefore an important ecclesiastical personage, perhaps the most important between Ravenna and Constantinople. Paulinus, who was Patriarch of Aquileia from about 558 to 570, raised the standard of ecclesiastical rebellion against the Fifth Council and the condemnation of the Three Chapters, and refused to communicate with Pope Pelagius, the successor of Vigilius, whom he regarded as a betrayer of the faith. The Pope retorted by urging Narses, who was then ruling Italy with an all-powerful hand, to seize both Paulinus of Aquileia and the bishop of Milan (who had consecrated Paulinus in defiance of a Papal mandate, and who probably shared his views), and to carry both these ecclesiastics to Constantinople, where they were no doubt to be subjected to the same gentle arguments which had enlightened the mind of Vigilius as to the damnation of the three Syrians. Narses, however, seems to have wisely refused to meddle in such matters; and though the schism was now formally begun, and was apparently shared by all the bishops of Istria, the dispute seems to have slumbered, till in 568 the Lombard avalanche descended upon Italy.

It was probably very soon after this event that Paulinus, fearing the barbarity of the Lombards, fled the island of Grado, taking with him all the treasures of the Church. He died soon after, about the year 570, very likely worn out with the terrors of the times and the hardships incidental to his new abode, for Grado is a poor little island at the mouth of the Isonzo, and probably offered no accommodation for a Patriarch and his retinue at all comparable to that which they had enjoyed in the neighbouring Aquileia. His successor Probinus also died, after a very short enjoyment of his dignity (about 570-571), and a man bearing the name of the prophet Elias was elected in his stead (571-586). In his days a step was taken which gave a new importance to the little island of Grado. For ten years or so the settlement in that island had been considered a mere temporary expedient. The Istrian clergy, like so many other subjects of the Emperor, looked upon the Lombard invasion as the overflow of a barbaric flood, which would soon pass away, allowing the dry land of the Roman Republic once again to appear. But by the year 579 this cherished hope had been of necessity abandoned, and on the third of November in that year a Council was held at Grado, under the presidency of Council of Elias, at which it was formally decreed that the city of Grado should receive the title of 'the new Aquileia,' and should be declared in perpetuity the metropolis of the whole province of Venetia and Istria. The alleged proceedings of this Council are unfortunately regarded with much suspicion by scholars. If genuine, they present an interesting picture of the times. We see in them the bishops of the whole important province assembled. Padua and Verona in the Venetian plain; Concordia and Opitergium (Oderzo) in the neighbourhood of the lagunes, Trieste, Pola, and Parenzo on the Istrian coast, Aemona (Laybach) in Camiola, Celeia (Cilli) in Styria; and Avoricium, which is perhaps Avronzo, the well-known resort of travellers, under the shadow of the Dolomites: all of them sent their representatives to the Council, which assemble in the new basilica of St. Euphemia. Then, while the bishops and presbyters sat, the deacons stood round them, and a copy of the Gospels having been placed in the middle of the assembly, Elias stood forth to explain his reasons for summoning the Council. 'Unspeakable,' said he, 'is the mercy of the Lord Jesus Christ, who condescends to help our weakness. Amid the pangs of the Church of God, and the fierce massacres of the heathen who cease not to shake and devastate the remnants of our miserable province, I confess that it was beyond my hopes to see you all collected in this venerable assembly. For I feared lest anything should thwart the fulfillment of our common prayers; but now that by the mercy of Christ we are all met together, let me tell you wherefore I have summoned you. Long ago, by Attila, king of the Huns, our city of Aquileia was destroyed from top to bottom. Shaken afterwards by the inroads of the Goths and other barbarians, it had scarcely time to recover its breath under the rule of Narses, and now it absolutely cannot bear the daily scourge of the unutterable nation of the Lombards. Therefore with the consent of the blessed Pope Pelagius of the Apostolic See before whom I have laid our case, I ask, does it please your Holinesses to confirm this city of Gradus as our metropolis for ever, and to call it the new Aquileia?'

The presbyter Laurentius, legate of the Apostolic See, handed in the Papal 'privilegium', bestowing the new dignity on Grado; and when this was read by the notary Epiphanius, the bishops all shouted, 'Hear, O Christ: grant long life to Pelagius', and unanimously ratified the proposal of Elias. Epiphanius read the Nicene Creed as contained in the acts of the Council of Chalcedon : and the members of the synod then all affixed their signatures to the record, Patriarch Elias first, the Pope's legate next, then the bishops, probably in order of age, and then the presbyters.

If we have here a genuine record of the acts of the Council of 579, it is clear that some sort of reconciliation must have taken place between the sees of Rome and Aquileia, or such a letter as the 'privilegium' handed in by the legate Laurentius could never have left the Roman chancery. Possibly the deaths of both the original disputants (Pelagius I having died in 560, and Paulinus in 570) may have smoothed the way of peace. No doubt also the Roman pontiffs saw the great advantage which would accrue to the cause of orthodoxy from the transference of the patriarchal see. At Aquileia the heretical defenders of the Three Chapters could shelter themselves under the wing of those deadlier heretics, the Lombards, and defy both Pope and Emperor. At Grado they were of necessity the obedient servants of the Empire, and a visit from the Imperial galleys could at any time reinforce the cause of orthodoxy. And in fact, not many years had elapsed after the meeting of the Council at Grado, before the Patriarch of New Aquileia received an earnest admonition from the Pope as to the necessity of no longer delaying his condemnation of the Three Chapters.

In this letter the Pope said that he took advantage of the interval of peace procured by the anxious labours of the Exarch Smaragdus to write to the bishop Elias, and the rest of his dear brethren the bishops of Istria, exhorting them no longer to continue in schism from the Church. He solemnly protested his unwavering faith in the decisions of the four great Councils, Nicaea, Constantinople, Ephesus, and Chalcedon; his veneration for the Tome of his great predecessor Leo, and his determination to uphold its authority unimpaired. He did not in this letter condescend to the details of the Three Chapters controversy, but desired the Istrians to choose out from among themselves bishops or presbyters whom they might send to Rome, and he promised to receive such messengers with love, meekly to offer them satisfaction on all the points as to which they were in doubt, and to allow them to return unhindered to their homes.

The messengers were sent; but they brought what seemed to the Pope neither submission to his will, nor an answer to his arguments, nor open minds to receive his explanations, but a short and sharp definition of the Istrian position; in fact a summons to the Pope himself to surrender, under pain of interdict from Elias and his brethren.

The receipt of this letter filled Pelagius with such grief that, as he told the Schismatics, he 'kept silence even from good words'. In his second letter he told them that they did not understand what they were talking about. He had shown, he said, to the envoys the passages which they had quoted from the proceedings of the Councils, as they stood in the ancient documents still preserved in the Papal chancery, and had argued that when taken in their proper connection, and not read in garbled extracts in the Encyclicals of hostile bishops, they by no means sustained the contention of the defenders of the Chapters. Especially with much diplomatic skill, but hardly equal candour, he laid stress on some reservations of the great Leo, who, in assenting to the decrees of Chalcedon, had expressly stated that he only ratified that which was therein decided with reference to the faith. Doubtless Pope Leo himself, if he could have been questioned, would have replied that this exception did not refer to the alleged Nestorianism of Theodore, Ibas, and Theodoret (which was a question of faith), but did refer to the rash attempt of the Council of Chalcedon to raise the see of Constantinople to an equality with the see of Rome. Long extracts followed from Augustine and Cyprian on the necessity of keeping in unity with the visible Church, founded on the rock of St. Peter; and the letter closed with a somewhat peremptory demand that instructed persons, able to give and to receive a reason in the debate, should be sent to Rome, or (if they feared the length of the journey and the unsettlement of the times) to Ravenna, where they would be met by envoys from the Pope.

The Istrian bishops, however, were quite immovable; refused to come either to Rome or Ravenna, and sent another letter in which, as the Pope declared, they hardly condescended to argue, but announced their own authoritative decision, and seemed to command the Pontiff to accept it. That there were, however, some arguments in this letter (now lost, like almost all the documents on that side of the controversy), we may infer from the reply which Paulus Diaconus calls 'a very useful Epistle, composed by the blessed Gregory while he was still deacon, and sent by Pelagius to Elias, bishop of Aquileia'.

In the interval between the second and third letters dispatched by Pelagius II, Gregory had returned from Constantinople, and even without the express statement of

Paulus, we could hardly be mistaken in attributing to him the altered tone now assumed by the Pope at whose elbow he was standing.

'I have hitherto', he says, 'written to you words full of sweetness, and rather by prayer than by admonition have sought to guide you into the right way. But I now see with grieving wonder the lengths to which you dare to proceed, confiding in your own wisdom, and I have to confess to myself that my example of humility has been wasted upon you. Like Jeremiah I must say, "We would have healed Babylon, but she is not healed". I have tried to kindle the fire of charity, and burn off your schismatic rust, but with the same prophet I must say "the bellows are burned, the lead is consumed of the fire, the blower bloweth in vain: his ashes are not consumed".'

The Pope, or rather the deacon by his side (for in these passages we recognize all the characteristics of Gregory, his familiarity with the old prophets, and his desperate love of allegorical interpretation), proceeds to ply the recalcitrant bishops with passages from Jeremiah, Paul and Ezekiel to convince them of their error.

"Is there no resin in Gilead, is there no physician there? Why then is not the scar of the daughter of my people healed?". What does he mean by *resin*, which feeds the flames, and which for the adornment of a palace cements together severed marbles? What can he mean but charity, which kindles our hearts to love, and binds together the discordant minds of men by the longing after peace, for the adornment of Holy Church? And *Gilead*, which is by interpretation the heap of witness—what can he mean by that but the mass of sentences piled up on high in Holy Scripture? The *physician*, is not he the preacher? The *daughter's scar*, is not that the fault of the erring multitude laid bare before the eyes of God?'

After a few more remarks of this kind the Papal champion plunges into the thick of the controversy, and goes over all the weary battlefield, whither we need not follow him, showing that Leo had not confirmed all the decrees of the Council of Chalcedon, but had expressly reserved private and personal matters; that the case of the three Syrian bishops might be considered as included in these private and personal matters : that Chalcedon must have implicitly condemned them, since it approved of Cyril and the Council of Ephesus which they opposed : that there was good patristic authority for anathematizing heretics even after their death: and that the long reluctance of Vigilius and the western bishops to accept the decrees of the Fifth Council arose from their ignorance of Greek, and gave all the more value to the sentence which they at last, after such rigorous scrutiny, consented to pronounce.

On the whole, if the course taken by the Popes in this dismal controversy had to be defended, it was probably impossible to put forth a better defence than that here made by Gregory, and he did well in sending a copy of it six years later, when he was himself Pope, to each of the schismatic bishops, inviting their candid and unprejudiced study of its contents, and predicting that they would then speedily return to the bosom of the Church.

This was not the effect, however, of the 'useful letter', when issued either by Pope Gregory or his of predecessor. In 5862 the Patriarch Elias died, apparently unreconciled, and was succeeded by Severus, who for twenty years ruled the Church of Aquileia. Soon after his accession, to end this troublesome business, the Exarch Smaragdus came (probably with a few Imperial ships) from Ravenna to Grado, dragged the new Patriarch forth with his own right arm from the basilica itself, and carried him off in ignominious captivity to Ravenna. Severus went not alone, for there were carried off with him three bishops, John of Parenzo, Severus of Trieste, and Vindemius of Cissa, and an aged defensor of the Church of Grado named Antonius. At Ravenna the captive ecclesiastics were detained for a year till their spirit was broken by the violence used, and the further exile threatened; and they consented, doubtless with heavy hearts, to communicate with John, bishop of Ravenna, who was on the now winning side, and condemned the Three Chapters.

Violence, however, now, as so often before and since in affairs of the conscience, failed of its purpose. When the bishops were at length at the year's end allowed to return to Grado, neither their brother bishops nor the lay multitude would have ought to say to them: and thus the end of the schism was as far off as ever. Smaragdus, the audacious violator of the sanctity of the Church of Grado, became insane, and men saw in his mental disease the work of a demon to whom he was given over for his crime. He returned to Constantinople, and Romanus, as we have seen, was sent as his successor to Ravenna.

A Council was now held at Marano, a place on the mainland, but overlooking a broad lagune, and about twelve miles west of Aquileia. From this place, where the Lombard rather than the Byzantine was supreme, the Schismatics could venture to hurl unabated defiance both at Constantinople and at Rome. The names of the sees represented at this Council are not quite the same as those which took part in the former one. They wear a more Venetian, and less Istrian character, as might be expected from the fact that the men who bore them were now leaning on Lombard protection, and somewhat estranged from the rule of the Empire. We find the bishops of Verona, Vicenza, Treviso, Belluno, Feltre, and Zuglio from continental Venetia, to which names must be added Asolo, which I mention separately for the sake of its Cypriote queen, and its English poet. Altino and Concordia on the shores of the lagunes, Trient and Seben from the country which we now call Tyrol, all sent bishops to the Council. The Istrian peninsula was apparently represented by Pola alone. At this Council the Patriarch Severus handed in a paper in which he humbly confessed his error in having communicated with the condemners of the Three Chapters. He was hereupon received again into fellowship with his suffragans.

This Council of Marano was probably held in 589, during a pause of something like peace in Italy. Next year the great Gregory ascended the pontifical Gregory throne, and one of his earliest acts was to write a letter, short, sad, and stern, to the Patriarch of Aquileia, lamenting his willful departure from the way of truth (of which, having once walked in it, he could no longer pretend ignorance), and summoning him, with his followers, to the threshold of St. Peter, there to be judged by a synod concerning all the matters about which doubt had arisen.

This summons purported to be issued in accordance with the commands of 'the most Christian and most Serene lord of all things', but in point of fact, since the substitution of Romanus for Smaragdus, the Pope had neither the Emperor nor the Exarch at his back.

On the receipt of this Papal summons two Councils were assembled, one of the bishops in Lombard territory, and one of those who dwelt in the Imperial cities on the coast. From these two Councils and from Severus in his individual capacity three letters were sent to the Emperor. Of these only the first has been preserved but the contents of all were probably similar. The bishops who were under the Lombard yoke expressed their unshaken loyalty to the Empire, recalled with a sigh the happy days of peace which they had once passed under its shadow, congratulated Maurice on the recent successes of his arms in Italy, and predicted the speedy arrival of the day when the

'Gentiles' would be suppressed, and all would be once more subject to the beneficent rule of the 'Holy Roman Republic'. When that day should come they would gladly present themselves before a synod in the sacred city of Constantinople. Meanwhile, however, let a religious truce be proclaimed, and let them not be compelled to appear before Gregory, who was really a party to the cause, since they had renounced communion with him, and could not accept him as their judge. In all that they were now doing, they were only upholding the authority of Chalcedon, and maintaining the position which Pope Vigilius had himself ordered them to take up when he anathematized the condemners of the Three Chapters. If their enemies were allowed to persecute them, and destroy the rights of the Metropolitan Church of Aquileia, the inevitable result would be that on the death of the present occupants of the Venetian and Rhaetian sees, their successors would be appointed by a Gaulish Metropolitan, and would transfer their allegiance to him (a thing which had already happened in three churches of the Province): and where ecclesiastical obedience had gone, political obedience would probably follow. Thus even from a political point of view it was important for Maurice to uphold the rights of the struggling Church of Aquileia.

This, and the kindred petitions drew forth a letter addressed 'In the name of our Lord Jesus Christ', by 'the Emperor Caesar Flavius Mauritius Tiberius, the faithful in Christ, the Peaceful, the Mild, the Mightiest, the Beneficent, the victor of the Alamanni;—to the very holy Gregorius, most Blessed Archbishop of the fair City of Rome, and Pope'. After referring to the three petitions, the Emperor says that he has learned from them (one imagines with some surprise) that the Pope has himself sent a tribune and a guardsman to enforce his summons on Severus and his brother bishops. He also mentions their prayer for a religious truce, and concludes, 'Since therefore your Holiness is aware of the present confusion in Italian affairs, and knows that we must adapt ourselves to the times, we order your Holiness to give no further molestation to those bishops, but to allow them to live quietly until by the providence of God the regions of Italy be in all other respects restored to peace, and the other bishops of Istria and Venetia be again brought back to the old order. Then, by the help of your prayers, all measures will be better taken for the restoration of peace, and the removal of differences in doctrine'. To which the Emperor added in his own handwriting, 'May God preserve you for many years, holiest and most blessed Father!'.

Gregory had certainly some reason to complain of such a mandate as this. The question of the Three Chapters was none of Rome's raising. It was an Emperor at Constantinople who had dug up the bones of Theodore, Theodoret and Ibas, and set the whole Christian world at variance over the question of their damnation. The Popes had been merely the instruments, at first the most unwilling instruments, of the State in enforcing conformity with the decrees of the Fifth Council on their suffragans, and now, when the unity of the Western Church was endangered, and Rome was threatened with the uprising of a new and insolent rival at Aquileia, Constantinople intervened, and would not allow the use of one tribune and one life-guardsman in order to put pressure on the Schismatics. Doubtless the remembrance of that letter about the Istrian bishops was one of the things which rankled in the breast of Gregory, when, eleven years after, he sang his lamentable hosannas over the murder of Maurice and his sons. However, for the present the Pope bowed his head to the hard necessity of the times, and, as far as we can see, during the whole Exarchate of Romanus (that is till 597) made no attempt to invoke the powers of the State in order to end the Istrian schism.

It was during this interval that, as has been said, he reissued the 'useful letter' which he had himself composed for his predecessor Pelagius, and sent a copy to each of the schismatic bishops, informing them that if, after reading that document, they still remained unconvinced, their error could only be imputed to sheer obstinacy. He also pointed out to them that they were entirely in error in saying that they were 'persecuted'. Persecution, martyrdom and words of that kind can only be rightly used of those who hold the truth. Men who are in error have no right to claim them. This reasoning would have been cheerfully adopted by Diocletian or Galerius.

Towards the end of this period (July 595), two bishops, Peter of Altinum, and Providentius of an unknown see, made overtures for reconciliation to the Pope, and were invited to visit him at Rome. We are not informed, however, of the result of the negociations. A little later on (June 596), we find one solitary monk, Joannes by name, returning from the schismatic fold. He takes refuge in Sicily, and Gregory makes him a small annual allowance from the Church patrimony; but his conversion cannot be considered a signal triumph for the cause of orthodoxy.

With the appointment of Callinicus to the office of Exarch a slight change comes over the scene. The Imperial veto on compulsory conversion remains in force, but it is evidently felt that the man in power at Ravenna is now more friendly to the Roman See, and that the Istrians may have a harder struggle to maintain their position of independence. A certain Magister Militum with the barbaric name of Gulfaris receives the warm thanks of Gregory for his watchful care over the souls of those under his rule, and his desire to bring them back from schism into the bosom of the Church.

But our attention is especially attracted by the case of the *Insula Capritana*, which appears to be the island in the lagunes at the mouth of the Piave, upon which was soon to arise the city of Heraclea, the precursor of Venice. The story is somewhat obscurely told us in Gregory's letters, but seems to have been something like this. A certain man named John, coming from Pannonia, had been appointed bishop of the Venetian 'Newcastle', (Castellum ad Novas), and had violently annexed to his diocese the adjoining island of Caprea, expelling its bishop. He had then temporarily abjured his schismatic profession, and had, together with the laity on the island, sought through the Exarch Callinicus reconciliation with the Roman Church. Before long, however, the bishop relapsed into schism, while the congregation, or at least a considerable portion of them, still desired to re-enter the Catholic fold. The expelled bishop also, who had made his way to Sicily, that chosen home of all the Roman 'emigration', showed some signs of willingness to condemn the Three Chapters. A deputation from his late flock having arrived in Rome, Gregory invited the bishop to come himself to the 'threshold of the Apostles' in order to be confirmed in his new faith. Whether he accepted the invitation or not, a meeting was to be arranged between the Istrians and their bishop, and the new converts were sped upon their homeward way (the journey being apparently accomplished by water, and therefore taking them round by Sicily), and were supplied with letters of amplest commendation to the Exarch, to the bishop of Ravenna, and to all their fellow countrymen of the island of Caprea. The result of this affair, as of so many others which have been opened to us by the Papal correspondence, does not seem to be anywhere disclosed. But there is an interesting passage in the first of Gregory's letters to the Exarch about these poor returning Capritans. Two pieces of news have just been communicated by the Exarch which have equally gladdened the Pope's heart. One is a series of victories over the Sclavonians, and the other this return of the inhabitants of Caprea to their ecclesiastical obedience. The Pope assures him that his victory over the enemies of the State is the reward of his exertions to bring back the enemies of God under the yoke of their true Lord. But Callinicus had some doubts whether he was not transgressing the Emperor's commands in going even as far as he had gone to meet the returning heretics. To this Gregory answers that the Imperial prohibition, itself obtained under false pretences, only restrained the Exarch 'during this time of uncertainty', from forcibly compelling the unwilling, and by no means ordered him to repel those who were willing to return to the unity of the Church; 'wherefore it is necessary that you should hasten to make this suggestion to our most pious Emperors, so that they may understand that under their reign, by the help of Almighty God, and of your labours, the Schismatics are of their own accord returning to the Church.

'Know, however, that it caused me no little sorrow that your Intendant [Major Domus], who had received the petition of a bishop desirous to return, professes to have lost it, and that it afterwards fell by accident into the hands of the adversaries of the Church. I think this was done, not through negligence, but for a bribe: wherefore I wonder that your Excellency should have so slightly punished such a fault. But after saying "I wonder", I at once corrected myself, for where my lord Justin is allowed to give advice, a man who is himself out of the peace of the Catholic Church, one cannot expect that heretics will be punished'. Dark hints these as to cabals in the Exarch's cabinet, to which we have no further clue.

In May 602, as we find from another letter of Pope Gregory, Firminus, bishop of Tergeste (Trieste), returned to his obedience to the Roman See. He suffered, we are told, many things at the hands of his schismatic Metropolitan Severus, who even endeavoured to stir up an insurrection against him in his own city. The conversion of the bishop of so important a city was doubtless a great triumph for the condemners of the Three Chapters, and we are not surprised to find Pope Gregory earnestly entreating the Exarch Smaragdus to protect the new convert.

It was not only on the shores of the Northern Adriatic that this miserable controversy about the the Three Chapters disturbed the peace of the Church. Constantius, bishop of Milan, the firm friend and adherent of Gregory, was beset by entreaties, both from above and below, that he would separate himself from the see of Rome in this matter. The bishop and citizens of Brescia called upon him to write them a letter, in which he was to assert upon oath that he had never condemned the Three Chapters. Pope Gregory forbade him to give them any assurances of the sort. Three of his suffragan bishops solemnly informed him that they renounced his communion because he had condemned the Chapters, and had given a bond for his perpetual adhesion to the Fifth Council. And not only so, but the pious Theudelinda herself, 'seduced by the words of evil men', consented to the course pursued by the three bishops, and withdrew for a time from communion with Constantius. Here was indeed a blow for the Catholic cause, if the royal influence so hardly won, after the long contest with Arianism, was to be lost again over the souls of the three Syrians. Gregory wrote to the queen expressing his regret that she should endanger the result of all her good works and all her pious tears by listening to the talk of 'unskilled and foolish men, who not only were ignorant of what they were talking about, but could scarce understand what they heard,' and at their persuasion separating herself from the communion of the Catholic Church. He assured her that whatever had been done 'in the times of the pious Emperor Justinian, had been so done as in no degree to impair the authority of the great council of Chalcedon'. This letter was sent to Constantius for delivery, but was prudently suppressed by him, for he knew that an allusion to the Fifth Council, however faint and indirect, would ruin all chance of its reception by Theudelinda. Thus warned, the Pope wrote another letter, in which he dwelt with earnest emphasis on his adhesion to the four councils (the number of which, like that of the four gospels, the four living creatures in the Apocalypse, the four rivers of Eden, had a charm for devout minds), and, in slightly different words, renewed his entreaties that she would submit herself to the judgment of the priests of God.

The entreaties of the Pope probably availed to induce Theudelinda to resume her communion with Constantius, and her relations with Pope Gregory seem thenceforward to have been those of unbroken friendship. He sent her a copy of his marvellous 'Dialogues' with the deacon Peter, and in 599 he wrote to her that letter of congratulation, which has been already quoted, on the great peace obtained through her mediation.

One last letter, as we have seen, Pope Gregory wrote to the Lombard queen in December 603, only three months before his death. In it, while congratulating her on the birth and Catholic baptism of her son Adalwald, he excused himself on the plea of sickness from writing an elaborate answer to the paper sent him by 'his dearest son the abbot Secundus'. We have here an interesting glimpse of the Tridentine Ecclesiastic, to whom we are indirectly indebted for so much of the early history of the Lombards. It is evident that Secundus was on the side of the vindicators of the Three Chapters, and we are thus enabled to understand why the allusions to the controversy in the pages of his copyist Paulus are written with so obvious a bias towards the schismatic side. We may conjecture also that Secundus, who, according to Paulus, lived on till the year 612, exerted his influence till the close of his life on behalf of the defenders of the Three Chapters. Theudelinda would seem, at any rate after the year 594, to have occupied a middle position, heartily cooperating with the Pope in all good works, but not renouncing the communion of the Istrian schismatics, perhaps at heart well inclined to their cause.

Along with the letter just referred to, Gregory sent a copy of the Acts of the Fifth Council, which the royal infant was, at some future time, to read and thereby convince himself that all that was alleged against the Apostolic See was utterly false, and that the Popes had deviated in nothing from the Tome of the sainted Leo. There is evidently here some change in the relations of the two parties from the time when the Pope did not venture even to mention the name of the Fifth Council to Theudelinda.

At the time of Gregory's death the Schism was not closed, but had assumed a geographical character. All becomes round the coast of Istria, at Grado itself, and probably among the lagunes of Venetia—in fact, wherever the galleys of Constantinople could penetrate—churchmen were desirous to return into unity with the Emperor and the Pope, and were willing to admit that Theodoret, Theodore and Ibas were suffering the vengeance of eternal fire. On the mainland, at Aquileia itself, in the great old desolate Venetian cities, Padua, Vicenza, and the like, in the little towns under the shadow of the Dolomites, wherever the swords of the Lombards flashed, men took a more hopeful view of the spiritual prospects of the three Syrians. At the death of Severus, in 606, the divergence became manifest. The abbot John was chosen by one set of ecclesiastics, assembled at old Aquileia, as their Patriarch, and the champion of the Three Chapters, while the bishop Marcianus, and, after him, Candidianus, both in full communion with the Pope, were chosen Patriarchs of Grado by the bishops and clergy of the coast.

'And from henceforth' as Paulus relates, 'there were two patriarchs'. The detailed history of the schism after this point does not greatly interest us, nor indeed are there many materials from which it could be written. Its effect, however, in throwing the defenders of the Three Chapters into the arms of the Lombard invaders is vividly shown by a letter from the Aquileian Patriarch John to King Agilulf. In it the Patriarch complains bitterly of the severities practised by the 'Greeks' and asks what sort of unity is that which is obtained at the point of the sword, by imprisonment, by the blows of the cudgel, by long and dreary banishment. The old grievance of the forcible abduction of the bishops to Ravenna by Exarch Smaragdus is again brought up, and the king is informed that in more recent times three Istrian bishops have been dragged away by the soldiers of the Empire from their churches, and forced to communicate with Candidianus at Grado. Now, however, at the hour of writing, that worthless prelate has departed this life and gone to the place of eternal torment, and Agilulf is entreated to interpose on behalf of the Catholic faith and prevent another unjust ordination of a Patriarch from taking place in the village of Grado. However, the election was held, and the schism continued. Some years later, a certain Fortunatus, though a secret champion of the Three Chapters, was chosen Patriarch of orthodox Grado. He soon found his position untenable, and fled, with all the Church's treasure, to the mainland, where the Lombard duke of Friuli obtained for him the Patriarchate of Aquileia. In vain was application made to the Lombards by his successor Primogenius (a faithful adherent of the Pope) for the surrender of the fugitive Patriarch, or at least of the stolen treasure. Both were steadfastly refused, and, on the 'lamentable petition' of Primogenius to the Emperor Heraclius, setting forth the sad condition of the Church of Grado, bereft of all her wonted ornaments, a large sum was transmitted from the Imperial treasury to enable the Patriarch to make good the deficiency.

So the Schism smouldered on till near the very end of the seventh century, when the reigning Lombard king Cunincpert summoned a council at Pavia, which was attended by a full representation from the lately schismatic Patriarchate of Aquileia. With shouts of triumph they entered the church, declaring that they renounced the heresy of Theodore and his companions, and wished to be restored to the unity of the Church. Tears and sobs expressed the overpowering emotion with which the spectators, Catholics and Schismatics alike, witnessed this ending of so long a struggle. Legates were sent to bear the joyful news to Pope Sergius, who returned for answer to King Cunincpert, 'He which converteth a sinner from the error of his way shall save his soul from death, and shall cover a multitude of sins.' At the same time he gave orders that all the MSS. setting forth the doctrines of the now defeated sect should be burned, lest their errors should ever again infect the souls of the new converts.

So ended the heresy of the Three Chapters; a heresy which at one time had all that was best and wisest in the Western Church, including the Pope's own authority, on its side. But not even thus was peace restored to the Church, nor were occasions of strife between Rome and Constantinople done away. The Monotheletic word-war had already tormented Christendom for half a century, and the dispute about the worship of images was shortly to ascend above the horizon.

BOOK VI
THE LOMBARD KINGDOM
A.D. 600-744

CHAPTER I.

THE SEVENTH CENTURY.

The century whose early years witnessed the death of Pope Gregory the Great, and the establishment of something like peaceful relations between the Empire and the Lombards in Italy, was one of a strangely mingled character. As far as Western Europe was concerned (perhaps we might say as far as the Aryan races were concerned) it was, on the whole, monotonous, uneventful, unimportant; but the changes wrought during its course in the regions of the East, the immense spiritual revolution which it witnessed among the Semitic peoples, and which has profoundly modified the condition of a quarter of the human race at the present day,—these characteristics entitle the seventh century to a place in the very foremost rank of the great epochs of the world's history.

Let us briefly survey the events which were happening in the rest of Europe and round the Mediterranean Sea during the hundred years which now lie before us.

In England, the great achievement of Gregory (the introduction of Christianity) was carried triumphantly forward. Edwin of Deira, in his youth the hunted outlaw, in his manhood the king of Northumbria, and the mightiest in all the land of Britain, wrought with brain and sword for the supremacy of the faith which he had learned from Paulinus. Benedict Biscop introduced into the barbarous land the architecture and the mosaics of Italy. The statesman-archbishop Wilfrid of York won for Rome that victory over the usages and teaching of Iona which even the memory of the saintly Aidan was unable long to postpone. When the century closed, the body of St. Cuthbert, monk and bishop, had been for thirteen years lying in its first resting place at Lindisfarne; and the chief herald of his fame, that Beda who was to be known by the title of Venerable, was still a young deacon of twenty-seven years of age. The great Northumbrian kingdom to which they both belonged, and of which the seventh century had beheld the glory, was already slowly falling into ruins.

In France the chief characteristic of the century was the decay of the Merovingian race, and the ever-increasing importance of the Mayors of the Palace. The Frankish kingdoms were indeed for a few years reunited under Chlotochar II, the son of Fredegundis, and both that king himself and his son Dagobert (628-638) showed some traces of the old daemonic energy which had made the first Merovingians terrible, if not beloved.

But the realm was soon again parted asunder, the 'Germany' and the 'France' of a future day already beginning to reveal themselves, as Austrasia on the one hand, and Neustria with Burgundy on the other. The kings of this divided realm, a wearisome succession of Chilperics and Childeberts and Theodorics, scarcely exhibit even a vice which can help us to distinguish them from one another. They are already 'rois fainéants', for the possession of whose persons rival Mayors of the Palace fight and conspire, but who have no self-determining character of their own.

Of these Mayors of the Palace we, of course, watch with most interest the 'Arnulfings', who will one day be known as the 'Karlings', the descendants of two Austrasian grandees, Pippin, and Arnulf, bishop of Metz, whose combined desertion (as will be hereafter told) delivered over Brunechildis and her great-grandchildren into the hands of her hereditary enemy. But owing to the premature clutch at the name as well as the reality of the kingly power, made by Grimwald, son of Pippin (656), the fortunes of the Arnulfings were for a time during the latter part of the century under a cloud, and other figures fill the confused picture. Ebroin, Mayor of the Palace for the three kingdoms, governs with a strong and grasping hand, is imprisoned, emerges from confinement, gets hold of one of the royal puppets, and again rules in his name. A bewildering succession of Mayors of the Palace, for Neustria, for Austrasia, even for a mere section of Austrasia, such as Champagne, pass before us, and civil war and assassination supply the staple of the dreary annals of the chronicler.

At length (689) the waters of chaos begin to subside. The Arnulfings reappear on the scene. Pippin, second of the name, grandson of Arnulf on the paternal, of the first Pippin on the maternal side, becomes Mayor of the Palace of all the three kingdoms; and, in the strong hands of that able general and administrator, the Frankish realm enjoys some degree of rest from tumult, and peace from external enemies when the seventh century closes.

Already we have to note in these Arnulfing statesmen, sprung as they were from the loins of a man who in later life became a bishop, and even a monk, a strong tendency to link their cause with that of the Church, perhaps to oppose to the ghastly licentiousness of the later Merovingian kings something of that higher standard of morality and religion, for which the barbarized Church of the Franks was dimly and fitfully striving.

In Spain the seventh century was a period of dreary and scarce interrupted decline. The Visigothic nation, which had, under Recared (589), solemnly renounced the Arian heresy, now rushed into the other extreme of narrowest and most bigoted orthodoxy. The king was an elected ruler, who never succeeded in founding; a dynasty that lasted for more than two generations. The nobles, turbulent and rapacious, were perpetually conspiring against their king, or oppressing their poorer neighbours. The bishops were now the most powerful order in the state: their assemblies, the councils of Toledo, of which fourteen were held during the seventh century, were the real Parliaments of the realm. There was a scanty infusion of the lay nobility in these councils, but the predominant voice belonged to the ecclesiastics, whose influence was seen in the ever sterner and more cruel legislation directed against the unhappy Jews (so long the faithful clients of the Arian Goths), and in the sickening adulation with which usurper after usurper, if only successful and subservient to the Church, was addressed by the Council, and assured of the Divine favour and protection.

Every symptom showed that the Visigothic kingdom in Spain was 'rotten before it was ripe'. Eleven years after the seventh century had closed, judgment was pronounced upon the earth-cumbering monarchy. The Moors, that is, the Saracen conquerors of Africa, crossed the straits of Gibraltar; and in one victorious battle brought the whole fabric of the Gothic state to the dust. A slender remnant of the nation fled for shelter to the mountain fastnesses of the Asturias, but the great mass of the Spanish population bowed beneath the Moorish yoke, and repeated the prayer of Islam when the voice of the muezzin was heard from the minaret. The work of the Scipios was undone, and Spain, lost to the Aryan world, had once more a Semite lord. The same fate had previously overtaken Egypt, Cyrene, and Carthage. These fair provinces, once the granary of Rome, were now for ever lost to her Empire, and only in our own century have the civilization and religion of Europe been able to exert an influence, and that but a superficial influence, on the great Orientalised, Mohammedanised regions of Northern Africa.

The rapid conquests of the Saracens along the Southern shore of the Mediterranean invite us to give a brief glance at the events which had meanwhile been occurring at Constantinople and in the regions of the East. The seventh century, in the story of the Roman Empire, must be remembered as the period of the dynasty of Heraclius.

We left Phocas, the murderer of Maurice, wearing the Imperial diadem, and receiving the shameful congratulations of Pope Gregory. For eight years this coarse and brutal soldier filled the highest place in the civilized world. We are bound to look with some distrust on the record of the crimes of a fallen sovereign when written by the servants of a hostile dynasty; but after making every deduction on this score we cannot doubt that Phocas was a cruel and jealous tyrant, as well as an utterly incapable ruler, and that the Empire passed through one of its deepest gulfs of humiliation while he was presiding over its destinies.

At length deliverance for Constantinople came from distant Carthage, still a member of the great Roman Republic, though not long to remain in that condition. Heraclius, Exarch of Africa, after two years of preparation, sent two armaments forth for the delivery of the Empire. One, embarked on high, castle-like ships, went by sea; the other, consisting chiefly of infantry, assembled at Alexandria, and went by land. Each was under the command of a young general; the navy under Heraclius, junior, the Exarch's son,—the land force under his nephew Nicetas; and it was understood that the diadem was to be worn by him who first arrived at Constantinople. The winds were favourable to the sailors, and in this race for Empire the young Heraclius won. The servants of the hated Phocas made but a feeble and faint-hearted resistance. Heraclius tarried for a while at Abydos, where a host of exiles driven into banishment by the tyrant gathered round him.

The brother of Phocas, to whom the custody of the lone walls had been committed, fled with precipitation, and soon Heraclius, with his castled ships, was anchored in the harbour of St. Sophia. A short battle, perhaps a naval engagement, followed. The African troops won a complete victory, and Phocas, deserted by all his followers, was brought into the presence of his conqueror with his arms tied behind his back. According to the well-known story, a short dialogue took place between them. Heraclius said, "Is it thus, oh! miserable man, that you have governed the Empire?". Phocas answered, "May you be able to govern it better!" Heraclius, seated on his *curule* chair, kicked the fallen tyrant, and ordered him to be cut up like dogs' meat.

His body, and those of his brother and two of his most hated ministers, were then burned in a place called the Bull.

The young Heraclius, as liberator of the Empire, has something about him which attracts our sympathy and admiration; but when we are reading his story, as told by John of Antioch or the monk chronicler Theophanes, it is impossible not to feel how thoroughly barbarized were all, even the best men of this epoch of the Empire. The same thought strikes us when we look upon the grotesquely barbarous coins of Heraclius. The Greek Republics had had their young and chivalrous tyrannicides, their Aristogeitons and their Timoleons; but great as is the descent from the glorious *stater* of Rhodes or Cyxicus to the strange *aureus* of Heraclius, so great is the fall from the tragic beauty of the deeds of the Greek tyrannicides to the coarse brutality of the murderers of Phocas.

It was indeed at a perilous and difficult crisis that Heraclius seized the helm of the state. The Avars, who about this time made a terrible raid into Italy, almost obliterating Friuli from the list of Lombard duchies, were now at the height of their power, and were able to roam over Thrace unchecked right up to the long wall of Anastasius. On the other hand the Persian king Chosroes, grandson of the great Nushirvan, under pretence of avenging the death of his benefactor Maurice (who had won for him the throne), had not only overrun Syria, but had sent a victorious army through the heart of Asia Minor, to encamp finally at Chalcedon, within sight of Constantinople. Thus the Roman Empire, though still owning in theory the fairest part of three continents, was in danger of seeing itself confined within the narrow limits of the capital. The overthrow of Phocas and consequent change of dynasty at Constantinople did not arrest the Persian career of conquest.

The overtures for peace made by Heraclius resulted only in an insulting answer from "the noblest of the gods, the king and master of the whole earth, Chosroes, to Heraclius, his vile and insensate slave". Syria was again overrun, Egypt was turned into a Persian province, the army of the Persians was again seen encamped at Chalcedon. None of the Persian triumphs, not even the conquest of Egypt (which involved the loss of the chief corn supplies of Constantinople), affected either Emperor or people so profoundly as the capture of Jerusalem, and, with it, of that identical Holy Cross which Helena believed herself to have discovered three centuries before, and which had given its name to so many churches in Italy and in every province of the Empire. Nevertheless, for twelve years Heraclius seemed to be sunk in lethargy, and to endure with patience the insolence of the Persians. It is probable that he was really during this time consolidating his power, disciplining his forces, and persuading the factious nobles of the state to acquiesce in his assuming something like an ancient dictatorship for the salvation of the Republic.

At length, in 622, a fateful year for Asia and the world, Heraclius, having completed his preparations, and having coaxed the Chagan of the Avars into temporary good humour, set forth on the first of his great Persian campaigns. These campaigns were six in number, and presented some of the strangest vicissitudes recorded in history; but through all, the untiring patience, the resourceful generalship, the unfaltering courage of Heraclius, revealed themselves, and once again, as eleven hundred years before, the disciplined armies of Greece proved themselves mightier than the servile hordes of Persia.

Heraclius, after penitential exercises and in reliance on the virtue of a heavenly picture of the Virgin, set sail from Constantinople on the day after Easter, and voyaged through the Archipelago, and along the southern coast of Asia Minor till he reached the shores of Cilicia and the neighbourhood of Issus, already memorable for one great victory of Hellas over Iran. From thence he plunged into the defiles of Taurus, succeeded by a series of brilliant manoeuvres in utterly baffling the Persian generals, and at length won a decisive victory in the highlands of Cappadocia. He was thus encamped upon the line of communication between the Persian king and his generals at Chalcedon, hoping doubtless to compel the retreat of the latter. But for some years the Persian standards were still visible at Chalcedon, and once, half way through the war, Constantinople was straightly besieged by the combined forces of Persians and Avars. But not all their endeavours could recall Heraclius from his career of conquest, nor force the Roman mastiff to relinquish his hold of the Persian leopard. At one time he would be wintering in the passes of the Caucasus, forming a network of alliances with the rough tribes of Colchis and Albania. Then he would descend into Media, lay waste the plains of Azerbaijan, and avenge the desecration of Jerusalem by burning the birthplace of Zoroaster.

Then would follow a campaign by the upper waters of the Euphrates, or among the difficult ranges of Taurus, and in almost all of these campaigns victory followed the Roman eagles, and the Persian generals, serving a suspicious and unreasonable master, grew more and more disheartened and bewildered by the strategy of their foe. At length a decisive victory within sight of Nineveh, followed by the capture and spoliation of the royal palace of Dastagherd, completed the ruin of the Persian king. The long-stifled rage of his subjects broke forth against a tyrant who was safe only while he was presumed to be irresistible. Chosroes fled: his son Siroes, whom he had sought to exclude from the succession to the throne, conspired against him; eighteen of his other sons were slain before his eyes, and he himself perished miserably in the Tower of Oblivion, to which he had been consigned by his unnatural offspring. Heraclius had little to do but to look on at the death-throes of the Persian kingdom. He was able to dictate his own terms, which were just and moderate: the restoration of the conquered provinces of the Empire, and of the precious Cross, which he brought in triumph to Constantinople, and next year carried back in pilgrim fashion to Jerusalem. In all the long duel between the Republic and the Arsacids of Parthia, between the Empire and the Sassanids of Persia, a duel which had been going on since the days of Crassus the Triumvir, no victory had been won, so brilliant, so complete, apparently so final, as these wonderful victories of Heraclius.

And yet these seeming brilliant triumphs of western civilization were only the prelude to its most disastrous and irreparable defeat. The darkly brooding East renounced the worship of Ormuzd, and the belief in Ahriman, she abandoned the attempt to substitute a Monophysite creed for the cautious compromise of Chalcedon; but it was only in order to emerge from the burning deserts of Arabia with blood-dripping scimitar in her hand, and with this cry upon her fanatic lips, "There is no God but God: Mohammed is the Prophet of God"

The career of the Saracen conquerors, though in after years it was to include Sicily, and even parts of Italy within its orbit, did not immediately exercise any direct influence on the Hesperian land. The Arabs are not among the invaders whose deeds this history has undertaken to describe; and therefore it will be sufficient here to enumerate a few dates which indicate their onward whirlwind course of conquest through the seventh century.

In 622, the year when Heraclius set forth for his death-grapple with Persia, Mohammed made that celebrated retreat from Mecca to Medina, which has been, ever since, the great chronological landmark for the world of Islam. In 628, he wrote to the Emperor, as well as to the Kings of Persia and Abyssinia, calling upon all to accept the new divinely given creed. In 629 was the first shock of battle between the Empire and the Children of the Desert, when Khalid, 'the Sword of God', won a doubtful victory. In 630, Mohammed returned in triumph to Mecca, where he died on the 8th of June, 632.

Under Mohammed's successor, the Caliph Abu Bekr, though he only reigned two years, great part of Syria was overrun by the Arab swarms, the decisive battle of Yermuk was won by Khalid in 634, and in the year after Abu Bekr's death (635), Damascus was taken. Omar, the next Caliph (634-643), saw the conquest of Syria and Palestine completed, Jerusalem itself taken (637), and Egypt wrested from the Roman Empire. Heraclius himself, so lately the brave and resourceful general, seemed struck by mental impotence, and fled in terror to Chalcedon (638), bent apparently only on saving his own imperial person, and the precious wood of the Holy Cross which he carried with him from Jerusalem. In the midst of the ruin of his Empire, with provinces which had once been kingdoms wrested from the grasp of his nerveless arm by the followers of an Arabian camel-driver, it seems to have been a consoling thought that at least that precious relic would not fall again into the hands of the infidel.

Meanwhile, Persia, enfeebled by her disastrous struggle with Heraclius, and having no energy of religious conviction in her people which could struggle against the faith of the Arabians, hot as the sand of their own deserts, fell, but not quite so speedily as Syria and Egypt. The war of Saracen conquest began in 632. In 636 the great battle of Cadesia was lost by the Persians, and their famous banner, the jewel-loaded leathern apron of a blacksmith, fell into the hands of the invader. But the struggle was still continued by the sons of Iran, and it was not till 641 that the battle of Nehavend destroyed their last hopes of successful resistance.

The conquest of Northern Africa seems to have been one of the hardest tasks that were undertaken by the followers of the prophet. Carthage was not taken till 697: it was retaken by the Imperial general, and not finally captured till 698, two years before the close of the century. But if the conquest was slow, it was sure, and the path of the conquerors was prepared for that final onrush which, in 711, added the great peninsula of Spain to the dominions of the Caliph.

In one generation, not the conquering power, but the fervour of faith, the absolute oneness of purpose which at first animated all the followers of Mohammed, had departed. Omar's successor, Othman (644-655), was more of a worldly king and less of an apostle than any of his predecessors, and he perished in a rebellion caused by his weak favouritism, and fomented by the ambitious and intriguing Ayesha, widow of the Prophet. The murder of Othman was used, most unjustly, to stir up popular feeling against Ali the next Caliph (655-659), the brave, pious, simple-hearted son-in-law of the Prophet. Schism and civil war followed, and the student who has followed with any sympathetic interest the story of the early believers in Islam, finds with indignation that the story ends with the assassination of Ali, and the murder of his two sons Hassan and Hosein, grandsons of the Prophet, by order of the descendants of his most persistent enemy (661-680). In the person of Moawiyah this hostile family ascended the throne (now indeed a throne) of the Caliphs, and fixed their luxurious abode among the gardens of Damascus. The faith of Islam, like the faith of Christ, but with a far more rapid decline, had fallen away from its first fervour, and was accepting the kingdoms of this world and the glory of them at the hands of the Dark Spirit. Like Christianity also, but again with swifter development, it was rent asunder by a mighty schism. The well-known division between the Shiites, who venerate the memory of Hassan and Hosein, and the Sunnites, who at least condone the guilt of their murderers, still cleaves the Moslem world with a chasm quite as deep as that which separates the Latin Church from the Greek, or the Protestant from the Catholic.

Still, notwithstanding its spiritual decay, the spirit of Islam was a mighty force in that effete world of Hellenic Christianity. Still, as the drilled and uniformed Jacobins of France carried far the standards of Napoleon, did the Saracen warriors, with the religious maxims of the Koran on their lips, do the bidding of the sensual and worldly-minded Ommiade Caliph at Damascus. It was in the year 672, fifty years after the Hegira, under the reign of the great-grandson of Heraclius, that the fleets and armies of Moawiyah set sail for Constantinople, eager to earn the great blessing promised by the Prophet: "The sins of the first army that takes the city of Caesar are forgiven". But not yet, nor for near eight centuries to come, was the fulfilment of that promise to be claimed. For five years (673-677) (magnified by tradition to seven) did the Arab wave dash itself in vain against the walls of Constantinople. The fire-ships of the Greeks carried havoc into their great Armada, the land army sustained a disastrous defeat with the loss of 30,000 men, and at last the baffled armament returned, not without fatal storm and shipwreck, to the Syrian waters. Then was peace made on terms most honourable to the Empire, including the restoration of captives, and a yearly tribute from Damascus to Constantinople; and for a generation peace in the Eastern waters of the Mediterranean seems to have been maintained, though North Africa was during this very time witnessing the steady progress of the Saracen arms.

Monotheletism.

While such tremendous conflicts as these were going forward, conflicts in which the very existence of the Empire, the mere continuance of the Christian Church, would seem to have been at stake, it might have been supposed that theological metaphysics would at least be silent, that all who professed and called themselves Christians would be drawn together by the sense of a common danger, and would agree at least to postpone, if they could not absolutely relinquish, the verbal disputations on which they had wasted so much energy. On the contrary, the seventh century was disastrously distinguished by the fury of one of the bitterest and least intelligible of all these disputes. Monophysitism had filled the world with turmoil for nearly two hundred years. Now Monotheletism took its place as chief disturber of the nations.

It was in that eventful year 622, which witnessed the withdrawal of Mohammed to Medina, and the departure of Heraclius for the Persian war, that the Emperor seems to have first conceived the idea that the Monophysite dissenters might after all be reconciled with the Church, which accepted the decrees of Chalcedon, by a confession on the part of the latter that, though the Savior had two natures, he had only one will, "only one theandric energy". Through all the later events of his chequered reign, his successes against the Fire-worshippers of Persia, his defeats by the Allah-worshippers of Arabia, he seems to have held fast to this scheme of reuniting the Church by the profession of *Monothelete* doctrine.

Sergius, Pyrrhus, and Paul, the successive Patriarchs of Constantinople, zealously and ably abetted his designs. The Patriarchs of Antioch and Alexandria subscribed to the same doctrine: even the Pope Honorius I, when appealed to give judgment in words which might be understood as at least permitting, if not ordaining, the teaching of the Monothelete faith. For a time only Sophronius, the Patriarch of Jerusalem, stood, like another Athanasius, alone against the world. But the current soon began to set in the contrary direction. The very willingness of the Monophysite schismatic to accept the new doctrine aroused suspicion among those who had been for two centuries fighting the battle of Chalcedon; and the Popes of Rome, far from the fascination of the Imperial presence, and under no political compulsion to propitiate the Monophysites of Egypt and Syria, resisted with vehemence the new *Eirenicon.*

The Emperor, however, still persevered in his plan, though he tried to broaden the issue by withdrawing from it one or two terms of technical theology which appeared unnecessary. In 638, the year after the loss of Jerusalem, the year before the Saracen invasion of Egypt, there appeared at Constantinople an *Ecthesis*, or exposition of the Faith, which was affixed by the orders of Heraclius to the great gates of the church of St. Sophia. This document, after repeating in orthodox terms the doctrines of the Trinity, of the Incarnation, of the two natures in Christ, declared that many were scandalized by the thought of two operations, two warring wills of the Saviour, that not even Nestorius in his madness, though he had divided Christ into two persons, had dared to say that their wills were contrary one to the other. "Wherefore", said the *Ecthesis*, "following the holy Fathers in this and in all things, we confess one will of our Lord Jesus Christ, the very God, so that there was never a separate will in His body when animated by the intellect, which worked by a contrary motion natural to itself, but only such a will as operated when and how, and to what extent the God who was the Word willed".

Then followed the usual profession of faith in the five great Councils, including Chalcedon, and the usual anathema of all the great heretics, from Novatus and Sabellius to Theodore, Theodoret, and Ibas.

This new declaration of faith, accepted generally in the East, except by the Patriarch of Jerusalem, was energetically repudiated at Rome, where Honorius. the peaceful and the unmetaphysical, no longer filled the Papal chair. First Severinus and then John IV set themselves to combat the new doctrine, and latter Pope, while piously shielding the memory of Honorius, visited with absolute anathema the Ecthesis of Heraclius. The tidings of this condemnation, however, can hardly have reached the ears of the Imperial theologian. The anathema was probably pronounced in January, 641, and on the eleventh of February in the same year, Heraclius, who had long been suffering from a painful disease, died; thus ending one of the most glorious and one of the most disastrous reigns in the whole long history of the Eastern Caesars.

With the death of Heraclius, a dispute, which had probably been long foreseen, broke out concerning the succession to the throne. Heraclius, after the death of his first wife Eudocia, had married his niece, the beautiful but ambitious Martina. Such a union, forbidden by Church law, and repugnant to the general feeling of Christendom, had been denounced even by the friendly Green faction in the Circus, and the Patriarch Sergius, who was ever the loyal henchman of Heraclius, wrote him a long letter, entreating him not thus to sully his fair fame; but passion won the day, and, in spite of all remonstrances, Martina became the Augusta of the Romans. Now, however, when after the death of her husband the middle-aged woman, whose beauty was probably faded, presented herself in the Hippodrome before the citizens of Constantinople, and claimed under her husband's will the right to administer the Empire as the senior partner of two Emperors, her stepson Constantine and her own son Heraclonas, the voices of the multitude clamoured against such a partition of power, crying out (as if Pulcheria and Theodora had been forgotten names), "You are honored as the mother of the Emperors, but they as our Emperors and lords".

For the moment Martina retired into the background, and Constantine, third of that name, was recognized as Emperor, with Heraclonas for his younger colleague. After three months and a half, Constantine, apparently a weak and delicate man, died at Chalcedon, not without suspicion of foul play; and then Martina, as mother of Heraclonas, became again the chief person in the Empire. Neither she nor her children, however, were popular in Constantinople, and a large part of the army supported the claims of the young Heraclius, a boy of ten years old, son of the lately deceased Constantine. For a short time Heraclonas and the young Heraclius, whose name was changed to Constans, reigned together in apparent harmony; but there were mutual suspicions and jealousies, a sort of veiled civil war, and a popular insurrection. The upshot of the whole business was that Martina and her son Heraclonas were banished, after punishments of that barbarous kind which was becoming characteristic of the Eastern Empire had been inflicted upon them. The tongue of the widowed Empress was cut out and her son's nose was slit. These punishments were inflicted by order of the Senate (September 641), by whose vote the child Constans became sole ruler of the Roman Empire. We shall meet with him again in a future chapter, and shall see his heavy hand laid on the Pope of Rome and on the people of Italy.

Constans reigned from 641 to 668, and was succeeded by his son Constantine IV (or V), who in 685 was followed by his son Justinian II. With this strange, powerful, savage man, who, though named Justinian, resembled much more closely Nero or Commodus than the astute, diplomatic legislator whose name he bore, the dynasty of Heraclius came to an end (711). Something will have to be said in future chapters about all these three Emperors. It will be enough for our present purpose to repeat and emphasize the fact that the seventh century, which in the history of religion will ever be remembered as the century of Mohammed, was, in Imperial history, the century of the dynasty of Heraclius.

CHAPTER II.

THE FOUR GREAT DUCHIES.

I.
The Duchy of Trent.

We are already confronted with that difficulty of treating the history of Italy from one central point of view, which recurs in a far more embarrassing form in the history of the Italian Republics of the Middle Ages.

The Lombard Monarchy, as the reader must have already perceived, was a very loosely aggregated body; the great Duchies were always tending to fly off from the central mass, and to revolve in orbits of their own. Two of them, Spoleto and Benevento, did in the end succeed in establishing a virtual independence of the Kingdom which had its seat at Pavia. There were two others, Trent and Friuli, which never quite succeeded in accomplishing the same result, being nearer to the heart of the monarchy, and not being liable, as the southern duchies were, to have their communication with the Lombard capital intercepted by bodies of Imperial troops moving between Rome and Ravenna. But though these great northern dukes did not achieve their independence, there can be little doubt that they desired it, and there is, to say the least, sufficient evidence of a separate political life in their states to make it desirable to treat their histories separately, though this course will involve us in some unavoidable repetition.

DUKES OF TRIDENTUM.
EUIN or EVIN,
569-595 (?),
married a daughter of Garibald, duke of the Bavarians.
GAIDWALD,
595
ALAHIS,
circa 680-690.

TRIDENTUM, which I generally speak of under its modern name Trent, has made a great mark in the position ecclesiastical history of the last three centuries, owing to the choice that was made of this city as the seat of the Council that was summoned to define the faith, and so regulate the practice of the Churches still obedient to the see of Rome after the storms of the Reformation.

In Roman times, and in the centuries with which we are now dealing, its importance was derived from the fact that it was one of the chief border towns of

Northern Italy, an outpost of Latin civilization far up under the shadow of the Alps, and the capital of the district watered by the upper Adige.

The modern province of Tyrol, as every traveller among the Eastern Alps knows, is composed of two main valleys, one running East and West, the valley of the Inn, and another running in the main North and South, the valley of the impetuous Adige. With the former, which constitutes Northern Tyrol, we have here no concern, and we have not to deal with quite the whole of the latter. The Adige descends from the narrow-watershed which separates it from the Inn, and flows through the long trough of the Vintschgau (called in old times Venosta) to Meran, situated at the confluence of the stone-laden Passeyer, and proud of its memories of the Tyrolese patriot Hofer. Here in the days of the Emperors was the Roman station Castrum Magense (the modern Mais). About twenty miles further down the valley, the Adige, which here flows over dark slabs of porphyry rock, is joined by the Eisach, coming down from Brixen, and from the long Pusterthal. The next important stream that joins it is the Noce, which falls in from the West, after flowing round the base of the mighty mountain mass of the Adamello, and through the interesting valleys of Italian-speaking people known as the Val di Sole and the Val di Non. A little lower down, the Avisio, which has risen at the foot of the noble Dolomitic Mountain, the Marmolata, after then flowing through the Val di Cembra, joins the Adige from the East. Soon afterwards we reach at last the battlemented walls of the city of Trent, the true centre, as has been before said, of the Adige valley, being about equally distant from Meran in the North, and from Verona in the South. An unimportant stream, the Fersina, is all that here brings its contribution to the central river; but the position of Tridentum is important for this reason, that only a few miles off, and across a low watershed, we enter the broad valley which is known as the Val Sugana, and through which flows the stream of the Brenta, a stream that takes its own independent course past Bassano and Padua to the Adriatic, and there, more than any other single river, has been 'the maker of Venice'.

For the rest of its course the Adige flows through the narrow Val Lagarina, shut in by high hills on either side, and receiving no affluent of importance till it emerges upon the great Lombard plain, and darts under the embattled bridges of Verona, beyond which city we must not now follow its fortunes.

On the west, however, side by side with the Adige, during the last thirty miles of its course above Verona, but studiously concealed from it by the high barrier of Monte Baldo, stretches the long Lago di Garcia, largest if not loveliest of all the Italian lakes; the sheet of water whose sea-like billows and angry roar when lashed by the tempest were sung by the great bard of not far distant Mantua. Into this lake at its northern end pours the comparatively unimportant stream of the Sarco, which draws its waters from the melted snows of the southern sides of Monte Adamello, as the Noce draws its waters from the North and West of the same great mountain-chain.

Every one who has travelled in the Tyrol knows that it is emphatically a land of mountain ridges and intervening valleys. Lakes like those of Switzerland are hardly to be met with there, but we find instead a cluster of long sequestered valleys, each of which is a little world in itself, and which, but for the artificial necessities of the tourist, would have little communication one with another. In order, therefore, to describe the territory of the Duchy of Trent under the Lombards, we have only to enumerate the chief valleys of which it was composed.

According to Malfatti (whose guidance I am here following), when the Lombards first entered this region (probably in the year 569), and established themselves there under the rule of their duke Euin (or Evin), they took possession of the central valley of the Adige, about as far northward as the *Mansio* of Euna (represented by the modern town of Neumarkt), and southward to a point not far from the present Austro-Italian frontier, where the mountains are just beginning to slope down to the Lombard plain.

Of the lateral valleys, those watered by the Noce, the Avisio and the Sarco were probably included in the Duchy; and with the Sarco may have been also included the whole of the long and narrow valley of the Giudicarie, which touches that stream at its lower end. The short valley of the Fersina, of course, went with Tridentum, and probably also some portion, it is impossible to say how much, of the Val Sugana.

The boundary to the north is that which is most difficult to determine. As has been said, Malfatti fixes it in the earliest period at Euna. At that time we are to think of Bauzanum (Botzen), Castrum Magense (in the neighbourhood of Meran), and the valley of Venosta (Vintschgau), as all in the possession of the Bavarians, who were subject to the overlordship of the kings of the Austrasian Franks. But as the tide of war ebbed and flowed, the Lombard dominion sometimes reached perhaps as far north as Meran in the valley of the Adige, and Brixen in the valley of the Eisach; and the Venostan region may have seen the squadrons of the Lombards, though it hardly can have owned them as its abiding lords.

The first duke of Tridentum, as has been said, was Duke *Euin* or *Evin* (569-595?), who seems to have been a brave and capable man, and a successful ruler. It was he who began that system of alliance with the Bavarian neighbors on the north which was afterwards carried further by Authari and Agilulf: for he, too, married a daughter of Duke Garibald, and a sister of Theudelinda.

It was probably a short time after Duke Euin's marriage (which we may date approximately at 575), that an army of the Franks, under a leader named Chramnichis, entered the Tridentine territory, apparently in order to avenge the Lombard invasion of Gaul by the three dukes Amo, Zaban, and Bodan, which had been valiantly repelled by Mummolus. The Franks captured the town of Anagnis (above Trent, on the confines of Italy), which seems to be reasonably identified with Nano in the Val di Non. The inhabitants, who had surrendered the town, seem to have been considered traitors to their Lombard lords, and a Lombard count named Ragilo, who (under Euin, doubtless) ruled the long Val Lagarina south of Trent, coming upon Anagnis in the absence of the Franks, retook the town and plundered its citizens. Retribution was not long in coming. In the Campus Rotalianus, the meadow plain at the confluence of the Noce and the Adige, Chramnichis met Ragilo returning with his booty, and slew him, with a great number of his followers. The Frankish general then, we are told, laid waste Tridentum, by which we are probably to understand the territory round the town rather than the town itself, as the capture of so important a place would have been more clearly indicated by the historian. For Chramnichis also the avenger was nigh at hand. Duke Euin met him and his allies, possibly some Roman inhabitants of the Tridentine who, like the citizens of Anagnis, had embraced the cause of the Catholic invader. The battlefield was Salurn on the Adige, a little north of the Campus Rotalianus. This time fortune favored the Lombards. Chramnichis and his allies were slain, the booty was recaptured, and Euin recovered the whole Tridentine territory.

Not only did Euin resume possession of his Duchy after the Frankish inroad, but he seems to have extended its limits; for when the Franks next invade the country, all the valley of the Adige as far as Meran, and that of the Eisach nearly up to Brixen, appear to be in the keeping of the Lombards. It is a probable conjecture, but nothing more, that this extension of the territory of the Lombards may have been connected in some way with the domestic trouble of their Bavarian neighbors, when Garibald their duke was attacked, possibly deposed, by his Frankish overlords.

In the year 587, Duke Euin commanded the army sent by Authari into Istria. Conflagration and pillage marked his steps, and after concluding a peace with the Imperialists for one year, he returned to his king at Pavia, bearing vast spoils.

The next Frankish invasion of the Tridentine duchy was in 590, the year of Authari's death, when, as we under have already seen, the Austrasian king and Roman Emperor joined forces for the destruction of the unspeakable Lombards. We need not here repeat what the generals of the western armies, Audovald and Olo, accomplished, or failed to accomplish, against Bellinzona and Milan. Chedin, the third Frankish general, with thirteen 'dukes' under him, invaded the Lombard kingdom by way of the valley of the Adige, coming probably through the Engadine and down the Vintschgau to Meran. Thirteen strong places were taken by them: the sworn conditions upon which the garrisons or the inhabitants surrendered these towns were disregarded with characteristic Frankish faithlessness, and the citizens were all led away into captivity. The names of these captured fortresses can for the most part be identified, and enable us to trace the southward progress of the invaders through the whole Tridentine territory. Tesana and Sermiana (Tiseno and Sirmian) are placed on the right bank of the Adige, some ten or twelve miles south of Meran. The position of Maletum is uncertain, but it was probably at Male, in the Val di Sole. Appianum is the castle of Hoch Eppan on the mountains opposite Botzen. Fagitana is probably Faedo on the hilly promontory between the Adige and the Avisio, overlooking the former battlefield of the Rotalian plain. Cimbra must be placed somewhere in the lower part of the valley of the Avisio, which is still known as the Val di Cembra. Vitianum is Vezzano, a few miles west of Trent. Bremtonicum is Brentonico between the Adige and the Lago di Garda, nearly on a level with the head of the latter. Volaenes is Volano, a little north of Boveredo. The site of Ennemase must remain doubtful. If it is intended for Euna Mansio it is mentioned out of its natural order, as that station, whether rightly placed at Neumarkt or not, was certainly not far south of Botzen. The names of the other three camps captured are not given us, but we are told that two were in Alsuca (the Val Sugana), and one in the territory of Verona.

But where during this inflowing of the Frankish tide was the warlike duke of Tridentum? We are not expressly told, but, remembering that the letter of the Exarch of Italy to Childebert mentions not only that Authari had shut himself up in Pavia, but that the other dukes and all his armies had enclosed themselves in their various castles, we may conjecture that Euin, in obedience to the plan of defence devised for the whole kingdom, was holding Trent with a strong force, ready to resist a siege, but renouncing the attempt to prevent the ravage of his territory.

Over against the capital city of Trent on its western side stood the high hill-fortress of Verruca, as to the construction and repair of which, under Theodoric, we have some interesting information in the letters of Cassiodorus. This castle probably it was which the historian calls *Ferruge castrum*, and which underwent a rigorous siege by the invading army. The fortress would have been compelled to surrender, but two bishops, Agnellus of Tridentum and Ingenuinus of Savio, interceded for the garrison, who were permitted to ransom themselves at the rate of a solidus a head. The total ransom amounted to 600 solidi.

It will be remembered that the campaign of the allied powers in 590 ended in a treaty between the Franks and the Lombards, which the Imperialists viewed with deep disgust, but the conclusion of which they were powerless to prevent. Probably the ransom of the garrison of Verruca was arranged for in these negotiations. The Frankish historian mentions the unwonted heat of the Italian summer as having exercised an unfavorable influence on the health of the invaders, and describes them as returning to their homes, decimated by dysentery, worn by hunger, and compelled to part with their raiment, and even with their arms, in order to procure necessary food. We can well understand that the Tridentine duchy was not at this time a highly cultivated or wealthy district, and that after three months of ravage not even the license of a brutal soldiery could extract any more plunder from the exhausted peasantry.

This, however, was the last invasion—as far as we know—that the Tridentine territory had to undergo for more than a century. The peace concluded by Agilulf with the Frankish kings must have been an especial blessing to this district, which had no other foes to fear except those who might enter their country from the north; since high mountain ranges secured them from invasion on the east and west, and on the south was the friendly territory of Verona.

It was probably about five years after the Frankish invasion that Duke Euin died, and was succeeded by *Gaidwald*, perhaps not a member of Euin's family, but who is spoken of as "a good man and a Catholic". With peace, and probably some measure of prosperity, the relations between the Lombards and the Romano-Rhaetian population in the valley of the Adige were growing more friendly, and now both ruler and people were no longer divided by the difference of creed.

The centrifugal tendency, as it has been well called, so often to be found in these Teutonic states, and so especially characteristic of the Lombards, carried both Gaidwald of Trent and his neighbor of Friuli into opposition, estrangement, perhaps, rather than open rebellion, against King Agilulf. How long this estrangement may have lasted, or in what overt acts it may have borne fruit, we cannot say. All that we know is that the joyful year 603, perhaps the very Eastertide which witnessed the baptism of Theudelinda's son in the basilica of Monza, saw also the reconciliation of Gaidwald and his brother duke with Agilulf.

From this point we hear very little more of the separate history of the Adige valley. We know neither the date of Gaidwald's death, nor the names of any of his successors save one. That one is a certain Alahis, who about the year 680 fought with the Count (Gravio) of the Bavarians, and won great victories over him, obtaining possession of Botzen (which had evidently therefore passed out of Lombard hands), and of many other strong places. These successes so inflated his pride that he rebelled against the then reigning king Cunincpert (688-700), with results which will have to be recorded when we come to that king's reign in the course of general Lombard history.

For the earliest period of the Lombard monarchy our information as to the duchy of Trent, doubtless derived from its citizen, 'the servant of Christ', Secundus, is fairly full and satisfactory; but after his death (612) this source dries up, and none other is opened to us in its stead.

II.
Duchy of Friuli.

From the Armenian convent, or from any island on situate the north of Venice, the traveler on a clear afternoon in spring sees the beautiful outline of a long chain of mountains encircling the northeastern horizon. He enquires their names, and is told that they are the mountains of Friuli. Possibly the lovely lines of Byron's *Childe Harold* recur to his memory:

The moon is up, and yet it is not night;
Sunset divides the sky with her; a sea
Of glory streams along the Alpine height
Of blue Friuli's mountains;

and the very name Friuli bears to his ears a sound of idyllic beauty and peace. Yet the name really speaks of war and of prosaic trade; of the march of legions and the passage of long caravans over dusty Alpine roads to the busy and enterprising Aquileia. Friuli, once Forum Julii, derived its name, perhaps its origin, from the greatest of the Caesars, who probably established here a market for the exchange of the productions of Italy with those of the neighboring Noricum, with which it communicated by means of the Pass of the Predil. Reading as we do in Caesar's Commentaries so much about his operations in Trans-Alpine Gaul and in Britain, we are in danger of forgetting the vast amount of quiet work of an organizing kind which he achieved while tarrying in winter quarters in his other two provinces, Cisalpine Gaul (that is, Northern Italy), and Illyricum, This northeastern corner of Italy is eloquent of the memory of that work. The mountains which part it off from the tributaries of the Danube are called the Julian Alps; the sequestered valley of the Gail is said to have been named Vallis Julia, and two towns, Julium Carnicum, north of Tolmezzo, and this Forum Julii, in the valley of the Natisone, also tell of the presence of the great dictator.

This place, Forum Julii, now known not as Friuli but as *Cividale* (as having been the chief *Civitas* of the district), was chosen as the capital of the great frontier duchy. Aquileia had been the chief city of the province, and the high roads which still converged towards that Venice of the Empire, the Pontebba and Predil Passes, the Pass of the Pear Tree, the road which skirted the Istrian coast—all these gave its distinctive character to the region. But Aquileia, though, as we have seen, it still retained its ecclesiastical importance, was not the place chosen for the seat of the Lombard duke. It was probably too near the sea to be altogether safe from the galleys of Byzantium; it was perhaps already beginning to be tainted with malaria; it was possibly considered not the best place for watching the passes over the mountains. Whatever the cause, the place chosen by the Lombards was, as has been said, Forum Julii, a town which held a respectable position under the Empire, but which attained its highest pitch of prosperity and importance under its Lombard rulers. Though now shorn of its old glory, Cividale is still one of the most interesting and picturesque cities of the Venetian mainland. It is situated on the north-eastern margin of that great alluvial plain, and clings, as it were, to the skirts of the mountains which are climbed by the highway of the Predil Pass. The city is divided from one of its suburbs by a deep gorge, through which, blue as a turquoise, flow the waters of the river Natisone on their way to the ruins of desolate Aquileia. The gorge is spanned by a noble bridge (Il ponte del Diavolo), and its steep cliffs are crowned by the tower of the church of St. Francesco, and—more interesting to an archaeologist—by the quaint little building called Il Tempietto. This was once a Roman temple, dedicated, it is said, to Juno, but afterwards converted into a Christian basilica. The low marble screen which separates the choir from the nave, and the six statues at the west end, stiff and Byzantine in the faces, but with some remembrance of classical grace in the fall of their draperies, give a decidedly archaic character to the little edifice, and may perhaps date from the days of the Lombards.

The museum of Cividale is rich in objects of interest; a Roman inscription of the end of the second century making mention of *Colonia Forojuliensis*; a very early codex of the Four Gospels, with autographs of Theudelinda and other illustrious personages of the Middle Ages; the Pax of St. Ursus, and ivory slab about six inches by three, representing the Crucifixion and set in a silver-gilt frame, which used to be handed to strangers to kiss, in token of peace; and many other valuable relics of antiquity. But the relic which is most important for our present purpose is the so-called Tomb of Gisulf. This is an enormous sarcophagus, which, when opened, was found to contain a skeleton, a gold breast-plate, the golden boss of a shield, a sword, a dagger, the end of a lance, and a pair of silver spurs. There was also an Arian cross of gold with eight effigies of Christ, and a gold ring with a coin of Tiberius I attached to it, which perhaps served as a seal. Undoubtedly this is the tomb of some great barbarian chief; but, moreover, there are rudely carved upon the lid the letters GISULG, which are thought by some to indicate that we have here the tomb of Alboin's nephew, Gisulf I, or his great-nephew, Gisulf II. This opinion is, however, by no means universally accepted, and it has been even asked by a German critic whether local& patriotism may not have so far misled some enthusiastic antiquary as to induce him in clever fashion to forge the name of the city's hero, Gisulf.

Such then is the present aspect of the little city which now bears the proud name of Cividale, and which once bore the even greater name of Forum Julii. No doubt the chief reason for making this a stronghold of Lombard dominion was to prevent that dominion from being in its turn overthrown by a fresh horde of barbarians descending from the mountains of Noricum. Alboin remembered but too well that entrancing view of Italy which he had obtained from the summit of the royal mountain, and desired not that any Avar Khan or Slovene chieftain should undergo the same temptation, and stretch out his hand for the same glittering prize.

It was then with this view that (as has been already related) Alboin selected his nephew and master of the horse, Gisulf, a capable man, probably of middle age, and made him duke of Forum Julii, assigning to him at his request some of the noblest and most warlike *faras*, or clans, of the Lombards for his comrades and his subjects. Horses also were needed, that their riders might scour the Venetian plain and bring swift tidings of the advance of a foe; and accordingly Gisulf received from his sovereign a large troop of brood mares of high courage and endurance.

The boundaries of the duchy of Forum Julii cannot be ascertained with even the same approximation to accuracy which may be reached in the case of the duchy of Tridentum. Northwards it probably reached to the Carnic, and eastwards to the Julian Alps, including, therefore, the two deep gorges from which issue the Tagliamento and the Isonzo. Southwards it drew as near to the coast-line as it dared, but was limited by the hostile operations of the Byzantine galleys. The desolate Aquileia, however, as we have already seen, was entirely under Lombard, that is, under *Forojulian* domination, and Concordia was won from the Empire about 615. Opitergium (Oderzo) was a stronghold of the Empire in these parts till about the year 642. The Lombard king (Rothari), who then captured the city, beat down its fortifications, and a later king, Grimwald, about 667, having personal reasons of his own for holding Opitergium in abhorrence, razed it to the ground, and divided its inhabitants among the three duchies of Friuli, Treviso and Ceneda. The fact of this threefold division gives us some idea how far westward the duchy of Forojulii extended. In this direction it was bounded neither by the Alps nor by the unfriendly sea, but by other Lombard territory, and especially by the duchy of Ceneta (Ceneda). The frontier line between them is drawn by some down the broad and stony valley of the Tagliamento, by others at the smaller stream of the Livenza.

On the latter hypothesis Gisulf and his successors ruled a block of territory something like fifty miles from west to east and forty miles from north to south. Broadly speaking, while Aquileia and the roads leading to it gave the distinctive character to this duchy, the necessity of guarding the passes against barbarous neighbors on the north gave its dukes their chief employment. It was emphatically a border principality, and *markgraf* was the title of its chief in a later century. The neighbors in question were perhaps the Bavarians at the northwest corner of the duchy; but far more emphatically all round its northeastern and eastern frontiers, the Slavonians, from whom are descended the Slovenic inhabitants of the modern duchy of Carniola. Behind these men, in the recesses of Pannonia, roamed their yet more barbarous lords, the Asiatic Avars, the fear of whose terrible raids lay for centuries as a nightmare upon Europe.

For a reason which will shortly be stated, the information vouchsafed to us by Paulus as to the earliest history of the duchy of Friuli is less complete than that which he gives us as to the neighboring duchy of Trent; an inferiority which is all the more noticeable since the Lombard historian saw in Friuli the cradle of his own race. From the year 568 till about 610, we have only two or three meager notices of the history of Forum Julii in the pages of Paulus; but some hints let fall in the correspondence of the Exarch of Ravenna with the Frankish king enable us partly to supply the deficiency. *Gisulf*, the nephew of Alboin, was, as we are expressly informed, still living at the time of the commencement of the interregnum (575). His reign, however, was apparently not a very long one, for in the year 589 we find another person playing a prominent part in the politics of northeastern Italy, by name *Grasulf*; and this man, who was in all probability a brother of Gisulf I, was almost certainly duke of Forum Julii. To this Grasulf, who was evidently an influential personage as he was addressed by the title Your Highness', a strange but important letter was addressed in the name of the Frankish king Childebert by a secretary or other official named Gogo. In this letter the Frankish secretary acts as a sort of 'honest broker' between the Emperor and the Lombard chief. He says in brief: "Your Highness has made known to us by your relation Biliulf a certain proposition very desirable for all parties, which ought to be put into shape at once, that we may break the obstinacy of our foes. The most pious Emperor has signified that he is going to send a special embassy, and we may expect its arrival any day; but as time presses we will lay before you two courses and leave it to you to decide between them.

I. If you can give the Republic sufficient security for the fulfillment of your promises, we are prepared to hand over to you the whole sum of money in hard cash. Thus the injuries done to God will cease; the blood of our poor Roman relations will be avenged and a perpetual peace will be established between you and the Empire.

II. But if you are not satisfied with the authority of the document which conveys to you the Emperor's offer, and therefore cannot yet come to terms, the most pious Emperor will send plenipotentiaries, and you also should send men to meet them somewhere in our territory. Only we beg that there may be no more delay than such as is necessarily caused by a sea voyage in this winter season; and that you will send persons who have full power finally to settle everything with the representatives of the Emperor.

Do this promptly, and we are prepared to join our forces with yours for the purpose of revenge [on the common foe], and to show by our actions that we are worthy to be received by the most pious Emperor into the number of his sons".

Obscure as is the wording of this letter, there can be no doubt as to its general purport. Grasulf, evidently a man of high rank and great power, is a traitor to the national Lombard cause, and is preparing to enter into some sort of federate relation with the Empire, if he can receive a sufficiently large sum of money; and for some reason with which we are not acquainted, the Frankish king, or rather his secretary, is employed as the go-between to settle the price of Grasulf's fidelity, and the terms of payment.

If the intending traitor was, as I believe him to have been, a nephew of Alboin, and the duke of the great frontier-province of the new kingdom, it is evident that we have here a negotiation which might have been of the utmost importance to the destinies of Italy. And the suggestion that one motive for Grasulf's meditated treason may have been resentment at his own exclusion from the throne when, at the end of the interregnum, he, Alboin's nephew, was passed over, and the young Authari was invested with the robes of the restored kingship, seems to me one which has much to recommend it on the score of probability, though we can produce no authority in its favor.

However, the negotiations for some reason or other fell through, and Grasulf did not surrender the duchy of Forum Julii to the Empire. For in the year 590, the Exarch Romanus, writing to King Childebert, and describing the course of the war, says: "Returning [from Mantua] to Ravenna, we decided to march into the province of Istria against the enemy Grasulf. When we arrived in this province Duke Gisulf, *vir magnificus*, son of Grasulf, desiring to show himself in his youthful manhood better than his father, came to meet us that he might submit himself, his chiefs, and his entire army with all devotion to the holy Republic".

Here again, though we have no express identification of the actors in the drama with the ducal family of Friuli, everything agrees with the theory that they are the persons concerned. Duke Grasulf, as we may reasonably conjecture, was only half-hearted in his treachery to the Lombard cause. When it came to the point of actually surrendering fortresses, or giving any other sufficient security for the fulfillment of his compact with the Roman Republic, the negotiation broke down. His son Gisulf, who had perhaps succeeded his father Grasulf in the course of this campaign of the Exarch's, took an opposite line of policy to his father, and professed that he would do that which Grasulf had failed to do. He would show himself more loyal to the Empire than his father, and would bring over all the heads of the Lombard *faras*, who were serving under him, and all their men, to the holy Republic.

However, as far as we can discern the misty movements of these Sub-Alpine princes, Gisulf did not in the end prove himself any more capable friend to the Empire than Grasulf had done. If there had been any wholesale surrender of Forojulian fortresses to the Exarch we should probably have heard of it from Paulus. As it is, all that the Lombard historian tells us is that Gisulf of Friuli, as well as his brother-duke Gaidwald of Trent, having previously stood aloof from the alliance of King Agilulf, was received by him in peace after the birth of his son, and that Gisulf concurred with the king in promoting the election of Abbot John as the schismatic Patriarch of Aquileia after the death of Severus in 606.

But terrible disaster from an unexpected quarter, was impending over the house of Gisulf and the duchy of Friuli. We have seen that hitherto, from the tie of the Lombards' departure from Pannonia, their relations with the Avar lords of Hungary had been of the most friendly character. There had been treaties of alliance; menacing cautions to the Frankish kings that if they would have peace with the Avars they must be at peace with the Lombards also; joint invasions of Istria; help given by Agilulf to the Great Khan by furnishing shipwrights to fit out his vessels for a naval expedition against the Empire. Now, for some reason or other, possibly because the Lombards were growing too civilized and too wealthy for the taste of their barbarous neighbors, the relations between the two peoples underwent a disastrous change. Somewhere about the year 610, the Khan of the Avars mustered his squalid host, and with 'an innumerable multitude' of followers appeared on the frontier of Friuli. Duke Gisulf set his army in array, and went boldly forth against the enemy, but all his Lombard *farax* were few in number in comparison with that multitudinous Tartar horde: they were surrounded and cut to pieces; few fugitives escaped from that terrible combat, and Gisulf himself was not among the number. There was nothing left for the remnant of the Lombards but to shut themselves up in their stronghold, and to wait for the help which doubtless they implored from King Agilulf. Seven strong fortresses, partly in the valley of the Tagliamento and partly under the shadow of the Julian Alps, are expressly mentioned as having been thus occupied by the Lombards, besides the capital and several smaller castles.

But the kernel of the national defence was, of siege of course, Forum Julii itself, where the few survivors of Gisulf's host, with the women and the lads who had been too young for the battle, manned the walls, whence they looked forth with angry, but trembling hearts on the Avar hordes wandering wide over the fair land, burning, robbing and murdering. Hardly more than a generation had passed since the Lombards had been even thus laying waste the dwellings of the Romans, and now they were themselves suffering the same treatment at the hands of a yet more savage foe. The family of the dead warrior Gisulf, as they stood on the battlements of Forum Julii, consisted of his widow Romilda and his four sons, of whom two, Taso and Cacco, were grown up, while Radwald and Grimwald were still boys. There were also four daughters, two of whom were named Appa and Gaila, but the names of the other two have perished.

The Avar host of course besieged Forum Julii, and bent all their energies to its capture. While the Grand Khan was riding round the walls of the city, seeking to espy the weakest point in its fortifications, Romilda looked forth from the battlements, and seeing him in his youthful beauty, felt her heart burn with a shameful passion for the enemy of her people, and sent him a secret message, that if he would promise to take her for his wife she would surrender to him the city with all that it contained. The Khan, with guile in his heart, accepted the treacherous proposal; Romilda caused the gates to be opened; and the Avars were within the city. Every house was, of course, plundered, and the citizens were collected outside the walls that they might be carried off into captivity. The city itself was then given to the flames. As for Romilda, whose lustful heart had been the cause of all this misery, the Khan, in fulfillment of his plighted oath, took her to his tent, and for one night treated her as his wife; but afterwards handed her over to the indiscriminate embraces of his followers, and finally impaled her on a stake in the middle of the plain, saying that this was the only husband of whom Romilda was worthy. The daughters of the traitress, who did not inherit her vile nature, succeeded by strange devices in preserving their maiden honor; and though sold as slaves and forced to wander through strange lands, eventually obtained husbands worthy of their birth, one of them being married to the king of the Alamanni, and another to the duke of the Bavarians.

As for the unhappy citizens of Forum Julii, their the captors at first somewhat soothed their fears by telling them that they were only going to lead them back to their own former home in Pannonia. But when in the eastward journey they had arrived as far as the Sacred Plain, the Avars either changed their minds, or revealed the murderous purpose which they had always cherished, and slaughtered in cold blood the Lombard males who were of full age, dividing the women and children among them as their slaves. The sons of duke Gisulf, seeing the wicked work begun, sprang on their horses, and were about to take flight. But it was only Taso, Cacco, and Radwald who were yet practiced horsemen, and the question arose what should be done with the little Grimwald, who was thought to be yet too young to keep his seat on a galloping horse. It seemed a kinder deed to take his life than to leave him to the squalid misery of captivity amongst the Avars; and accordingly one of his older brothers lifted his lance to slay him. But the boy cried out with tears, "Do not pierce me with thy lance; I, too, can sit on horseback". Thereupon the elder brother stooped down, and catching Grimwald by the arm, swung him up on to the bare back of a horse, and told him to stick on if he could. The lad caught hold of the bridle, and for some distance followed his brothers in their flight. But soon the Avars, who had discovered the escape of the princes, were seen in pursuit. The three elder brothers, thanks to the swiftness of their steeds, escaped, but the little Grimwald fell into the hands of the foremost of the band. The captor deemed it unworthy of him to smite with the sword so young an enemy, and determined rather to keep him, and use him as a slave. He therefore caught hold of his bridle, and moved slowly back to the camp, delighting in the thought of his noble prize : for the slender figure of the princely boy, his gleaming eyes, and thick clustering locks of flaxen hair were fair to behold, especially to one accustomed to nought but the mean Kalmuck visages of the swarthy Avars. But while the captor's heart was swelling with pride, grief at his captivity burned in the soul of Grimwald.

'And mighty thoughts stirred in that tiny breast'.

He quietly drew from its sheath the little sword which he carried as the child of a Lombard chief, and watching his opportunity dealt with all his might a blow on the crown of the head of his Avar captor. Wonderful to tell, the stripling's stroke was fatal. The Avar fell dead from his horse, and Grimwald, turning the head of his steed rode fast after his brothers, whom he overtook, and who hailed him with shouts of delight both at his escape, and at his first slaughter of a foe.

So runs the story of Grimwald's escape as told in the pages of Paulus. It is Saga of course; and in order to magnify the deeds of one who became in after years the foremost man of the Lombard nation, it is very possible that the bards have somewhat diminished the age of the youthful warrior. But it is not worthwhile to attempt the now hopeless task of disentangling poetry from prose. A historian who is so often compelled to lay before his readers mere names of kings and dukes without one touch of portraiture to make them live in the memory, may be excused for wishing that many more such Sagas had been preserved by the Lombard chronicler.

Happily at this point Paulus interrupts the course of the general history, in order to give us some information as to the fortunes of his own forefathers; and this little chapter of family history helps us to understand the immense and terrible importance of the Avar raid into Friuli, a raid which in many ways reminds us of the Danish invasions of Anglo-Saxon England in the ninth and tenth centuries; like them blighting a young and tender civilization, and like them probably destroying many of the records of the past.

The first of his ancestors mentioned by Paulus is Leupchis, who came into Italy in the year 568 at the same time with the great body of his countrymen. After living many years in Italy he died, leaving behind him five young sons, who having apparently escaped death by reason of their tender age, were all swept by the tempest of the invasion from Friuli into Avar-land. Here they groaned under the yoke of their captivity for some years; but when they had reached man's estate, the youngest, named Lopichis, by an inspiration from above, conceived the thought of returning to Italy, and regaining his freedom. Having resolved on flight he started, taking with him only his quiver and his bow, and as much food as he could carry. He was utterly ignorant of the road, but, strange to say, a wolf was his guide through the mountain solitudes. When he halted the wolf halted too: when he lagged behind, the creature looked around to see if he were following, and thus he at length perceived that the wild beast was his divinely appointed guide. But after some days' wandering amid the desolate mountains (probably in the district of the Kavawanken Alps) his provisions came to an end, and his death seemed nigh at hand. Faint with hunger, he fitted an arrow to the string and aimed at his heaven sent guide, thinking that even its flesh might save him from starvation. The wolf, however, seeing what he meditated, vanished from his sight. Then Lopichis, despairing of life, fell to the ground and slept; but in his slumber he saw a man who seemed to say to him, "Arise! why sleepest thou? Resume thy journey in the opposite direction to that in which thy feet are now pointing, for there lies the Italy of thy desire". He arose at once, journeyed in the direction indicated, and soon came among the dwellings of men. It was a little Slavonic village that he entered; and there he found a kindly woman who, perceiving that he was a fugitive, received him into her cottage, and hid him there, and perceiving moreover that he was nearly dead with hunger, gave him food gradually and in small quantities as he was able to bear it. At length, when he had sufficiently recovered his strength, she gave him provisions for the journey, and pointed out to him the road to Italy, which country he entered after certain days. He at once sought his old home, but found no trace of the ancestral dwelling left, only a vast tangle of thorns and briers. Having cleared these away, he came upon a large elm growing within the old enclosure of his home, and in this tree he hung up his quiver. Some of his relatives and friends gave him presents which enabled him to rebuild his house and to marry a wife; but the property which had once been his father's he could not recover, as the men who had occupied it pleaded successfully the rights of long possession. Lopichis was the father of Arichis, Arichis of Warnefrit, and Warnefrit, by his wife Theudelinda (named no doubt in honor of the great Lombard queen) had two sons, one of whom was the historian, and the other (named after his grandfather) was his brother Arichis.

We return to the history of the duchy of Friuli, of which, after the death of Gisulf, and the withdrawal of the Avars, Taso and Cacco, the two eldest sons of Gisulf, became joint lords. They seem to have been valiant in fight, for they pushed the boundaries of their territory northward as far as Windisch-Matrei, adding the whole long valley of the Gail to their dominions, and compelling the Slovene inhabitants of that region to pay tribute, which they continued to do for more than a century.

It seems probable that Paulus has omitted some links in the family genealogy. Three generations are very few to cover the period between the Avar invasion and Charles the Great, between Leupchis, who came (presumably as a full-grown man) into Italy in 568, and Paulus himself, who was born about 720. Besides, it is strange that Leupchis, a grown man in 568, should leave five little children ('pueruli') at the time of the Avar invasion in 610. Most likely, then, owing to the destruction of records during that invasion, a generation has been omitted from the historian's own pedigree, as well as from that of duke Gisulf. Even after Lopichis' return the number of generations (say three to 120 years if Lopichis was born in 600) is somewhat scanty, though not impossibly so.

But the two sons of Gisulf, who had escaped from the swords of the Avars, fell before the vile treachery of a Byzantine official. The Exarch Gregory invited young duke Taso to come and meet him at the Venetian town Opitergium (*Oderzo*), which was still subject to the Empire, promising to adopt him as his "*filius per arma*", the symbol of which new relationship was the cutting off of the first downy beard of the young warrior by his adoptive father. Fearing no evil, Taso went accordingly to Opitergium with Cacco, and a band of chosen youthful warriors. As soon as they had entered the city, the treacherous governor caused the gates to be shut, and sent a band of armed men to attack the young Forojulian chiefs. Seeing that death was inevitable, they resolved to sell their lives dearly, and having given one another a last farewell, the two dukes and their comrades rushed through the streets and squares of the city slaying all whom they met. The slaughter of Roman citizens was terrible, but in the end all the Lombards were left dead upon the pavement of Opitergium. The Exarch ordered the head of Taso to be brought to him, and with traitorous fidelity cut off the beard of the young chieftain, so fulfilling his promise.

Fredegarius (so-called) tells a story which seems to be derived from this, as to the murder of Taso, duke of Tuscany, by the Patrician Isaac. According to him Charoald (Ariwald), king of the Lombards, offers Isaac that he will remit one of the three hundredweights of gold which the Empire pays yearly to the Lombards if he will put Taso out of the way. Isaac accordingly invites Taso to Ravenna, offering to help him against Charoald, whom Taso knows that he has displeased. Taso repairs to Ravenna with a troop of warriors, who, through fear of the Emperor's displeasure, are prevailed upon to leave their arms outside the walls. They enter the city, and the prepared assassins at once rush upon and kill them. Thenceforward the yearly beneficia from the Empire to the Lombards are reduced from three hundredweights of gold to two. Soon after Charoald dies. As Ariwald's reign lasted from 626 to 636, and as Isaac did not become Exarch till 620, it seems to me absolutely impossible in any way to reconcile this wild story with the events described by Paulus, which must have happened many years earlier. Either Fredegarius, who is a most unsafe guide, has got hold of an utterly inaccurate version of the death of Taso, son of Gisulf II, or the coincidence of name is accidental, and the story of Fredegarius relates to some completely different series of events to which we have lost the clue.

Such is the story of the massacre of Opitergium as related to us by the Lombard historian. It is possible that there is another side to the story, and that some excesses of Taso's henchmen may have provoked a tumult, in which he and his brother perished; but as it is told to us the affair reminds us of the meditated massacre of Marcianople; and like that massacre it was bitterly avenged.

The two young dukes of Friuli being thus cut off in their prime, their uncle Grasulf, brother of Gisulf, succeeded to the vacant duchy. Badwald and Grimwald, sore at heart at being thus passed over, took ship, and sailed for Benevento, where, as we shall see, they had an old friend in the person of the reigning duke. We, too, will follow their example and leave Friuli for Benevento, for there is nothing further recorded of the history of the former duchy for half a century after the invasion of the Avars.

III.
Duchy of Benevento.

Benevento stands in an amphitheatre of hills overlooking the two rivers Calove and Sabato, which meet near its western extremity, and flowing on together for about thirty miles, pour their waters into the channel which bears the name of the Voltorno, and so pass out by Capua to the sea.

The city of Beneventum, as we have already seen, laid claim to a high antiquity, professing to have been founded by Diomed, and to show the tusks of the monstrous boar, which in the days of his grandfather ravaged the territory of Calydon. Leaving these mythical glories on one side, we remark only that it was a city of the Samnites possibly at one time inhabited by the Etruscans of Campania, and that about the time of the Third Samnite War (BC 298-290 it passed under the dominion of Rome. In its neighborhood (BC 275) Manius Curius won that decisive victory over Pyrrhus, which settled the question whether the Roman or the Greek was to be master in the Italian peninsula. Seven years after this (BC 268) the Romans, true to their constant policy of pinning down newly conquered territories by the establishment of miniature Roman republics among them, sent a colony to the city by the Calore; and on this occasion that city, which had previously been called Maleventum, had that name of evil omen, which it had accidentally received, changed into the more auspicious Beneventum, by which it has thence forth been known in history. The chief importance of Beneventum arose from its being situated on the great *Via Appia*, which led front Rome through Capua to Tarentum and Brundisium. Many a schoolboy has read the passage in the *Iter Brundusinum* in which Horace describes the officious zeal of the innkeeper at Beneventum, who, while blowing up his fire to roast a few lean thrushes for his illustrious guests, narrowly escaped burning down his own house. Some portion of the bridge by which the Appian Way crossed the river Sabato is still standing, and is known by the somewhat mysterious name of *Il Ponte Lebbroso* (The Leprous Bridge).

But a century after Horace's Brundisian journey the greatest of the Roman Emperors stamped his name on Beneventum by a noble work of public utility, and by a stately monument. The old road to Brundisium, over which Horace travelled, had apparently been a mere mule-track where it crossed the Apennines, the road which was passable by wheeled carriages making a bend to the south, and circling round by Tarentum. In order to avoid this deviation, and to save a day in the through journey from Rome to the east, the Emperor made the new and splendid road across the mountains which thenceforward bore the name of Via Trajana.

To commemorate this great engineering work there was erected on the north side of the city in the year 114, a triumphal arch dedicated to '*Nerva Trajanus Optimus Augustus, Germanicus et Dacicus*' by the Senate and people of Rome. This noble work, which has hardly yet received from archaeologists the attention which it deserves, though it has suffered much at the hands of sportive barbarians, still casts a light upon the reign of the best of Roman Emperors, only less bright than that thrown by the celebrated column at Rome. It is like the same Emperor's Arch at Ancona, but not despoiled of its bas-reliefs; like the Arch of Constantine, but with its best works of art restored to their rightful owner; like the Arch of Titus save for the incidental interest which the latter derives from the fact that it records the calamity of the chosen people. Here, notwithstanding the irritating amputations effected by the mischievous hands of boys of many generations, we can still discover the representation of the chief scenes in the life of Trajan, his adoption by Nerva, his triumphal entry into Rome, his victory over the Dacian chief Decebalus. Here we can see him achieving some of his great peaceful triumphs, giving the '*congiarium*' to the citizens of Rome, founding an asylum for orphans, and hailed by the Senate's enthusiastic acclamations as *Optimus Princeps*. And lastly, here we see the Roman sculptor's conception of an Imperial apotheosis: Trajan's sister Marciana welcomed into the assembly of the Immortals by Capitolian Jupiter, while Minerva and Ceres, Bacchus and Mercury, look on approvingly.

It was not only the Via Appia and the Via Trajana that entered the gates of Beneventum. A branch of the other great southern road, the Via Latina, led off to it from the neighborhood of Teanum, and another road skirting the northern side of Mons Tifernus connected it with Aesernia and the northeast end of Latium. The more we study the Roman itineraries the more are we impressed with the importance of Beneventum as a military position for the Lombards commanding the southern portion of Italy, watching as from a hostile outpost the movements of the duke of Neapolis, blocking the great highroad between Rome and Constantinople, and cutting off the Romans on the Adriatic from the Romans on the Tyrrhenian Sea. Yet though doubtless strategic considerations weighed heaviest in the scale when the Lombard chiefs were choosing their southern capital, the character of the climate had also probably something to do with their selection. Children of the north, and denizens of the forest and the moorland, the Lombards (or at any rate some of the Lombards) shrank at first from fixing their homes in the sultry alluvial plains. The cooler air of the uplands, the near neighborhood of the great Apennine chain, even the boisterous wind which blustered round the walls of Beneventum were all additional recommendations in the eyes of the first generation of invaders who had crossed the Alps with Alboin.

The duchy of Benevento is often spoken of by Paulus as the duchy of the Samnites. At first the use of so archaic a term of geography strikes us as a piece of mere pedantry, and only provokes a smile; but when we look a little more closely into the matter our objection to it almost disappears. The attitude of the old Samnite mountaineers to the lowlanders of Campania, Greek, Etruscan, Oscan, or Roman, seems reproduced in the attitude of the Lombards of Benevento to the Imperialist duke of Neapolis, and the citizens of Salernum and Paestum. The pass of the Caudine Forks, the scene of Rome's greatest humiliation (whether it be placed at S. Agata dei Goti or at Arpaia), was within fifteen miles of Benevento. Though wars, proscriptions and the horrors of the Roman *latifundia* may have well-nigh exterminated all the population in whose veins ran a drop of the old Samnite blood, the faithful memory of the mountaineer may have retained some trace of those great wars, which once made each pass of the Apennines memorable; and even as the Vandals of Carthage avenged the wrongs of their long vanished Punic predecessors, so possibly some faint tradition of the ungenerous treatment of that noble Samnite general C. Pontius of Telesia by his

Roman conquerors may have reached the ears of Arichis or Grimwald, and nerved them to more bitter battle against the Roman dwellers in the plain below.

I have briefly touched on the history of Beneventum before it became the seat of a Lombard duchy. The chief architectural monuments of Lombard domination belong to the reign of Arichis II, and are therefore outside the limits of this volume. But having followed the fortunes of the city so far, I may here record the fact that the Lombard duchy of Benevento lasted as an independent state till the latter part of the eleventh century, when the Norman conquest of Southern Italy, contemporaneous with the Norman conquest of England, extinguished its existence along with that of its old Greek or Imperial foes. The city of Benevento itself, in the troubles connected with the Norman invasion, became a part of the Papal territory (1053), though entirely surrounded by the dominions of the Neapolitan kings, and seventy miles distant from the frontier of the States of the Church. In the plain below the city walls, on the banks of the river Galore, was fought in 1266 that fatal battle in which Manfred, the last the Hohenstaufen princes, was defeated by Charles of Anjou, the first, but by no means the last, of the French lords of Southern Italy. From various causes Benevento lost much of the importance which had belonged to it at the beginning of the Middle Ages. During the Saracen invasions of the ninth and tenth centuries the old Roman roads fell into decay, and the great Via Appia and Via Trajana no longer brought traders to its gates. When Naples ceased to be under a Byzantine ruler, it naturally took the place of Benevento as capital of Southern Italy. Later on the position of the city as a mere enclave of the Popes, surrounded by the territory of sometimes unfriendly princes, was doubtless unfavorable to its commercial growth. Thus it has come to pass that Benevento now possesses only a little over 20,000 inhabitants, and has played no important part in the later history of Italy. In fact the historian of the nineteenth century will perhaps find his chief reason for remembering it in the fact that in the short-lived Empire of Napoleon it gave the title of Prince to that strange and shifty intriguer, the Sisyphus of modern politics, Bishop or Citizen Talleyrand. It now, however, of course, forms part of the kingdom of Italy, and is capital of a province. With good roads, and becoming again by the construction of two or three converging railroads, somewhat of a focus of communication for Southern Italy, it is likely to be an important agricultural centre, and may perhaps regain by trade some of the importance which it lost by politics and war.

But we have wandered thirteen centuries away from our proper subject. We must return to the middle of the sixth century. The still existing city walls, to a large extent of Roman workmanship, the eight gates by which they are pierced, the arch immediately outside them, the remains of the baths and amphitheatre, the ruins of a vast warehouse outside the city, all help us to imagine its appearance as it lay in desolate grandeur for some twenty years or more after Totila had thrown down its walls, and before the "unspeakable Lombard" came marching along the Appian Way to ravage and to rule.

It was probably about the year 571, three years after Alboin's first entrance into Italy, that a Lombard chief named Zotto entered the city—an easy prey by reason of its ruined walls—and established himself there as its duke. From this centre, in the course of his twenty years' reign, he extended his dominions far and wide over Southern Italy. Naples, which was no doubt the chief object of his desire, he never succeeded in capturing, though he besieged it in 581. But Aquinum, more than sixty miles north-west of Benevento (that little Volscian town which was one day to become famous as the birthplace of a great theologian and philosopher), was laid waste about the year 577 by the swords of barbarians, who were probably the soldiers of Zotto. And towards the end of Zotto's reign, about the year 590, the little town of Atina, somewhat north of Aquinum, and not far from Arpinum (the birthplace of Marius and Cicero), was entered by the ruthless Lombards, and its bishop, Felix, after an episcopate of thirty years, died as a martyr under the hands of the Beneventan duke, the city and the great church being also destroyed at the same time.

It was apparently about the same time, or perhaps a year earlier (589), that the great convent, which the saintly Benedict had reared sixty years before on Monte Cassino, was stormed in the night by Zotto's savage followers. They laid hands on everything valuable that they could find in that abode of willing poverty, probably not much besides the vessels of divine service, and perhaps some ornaments of the founder's tomb. Not one of the monks, however, was taken, and thus was fulfilled the prophecy of their father Benedict, who long before, predicting the coming calamity, had said, "With difficulty have I obtained of the Lord that from this place the persons alone should be granted me". The fugitive monks escaped to Rome, carrying with them the original manuscript of the Benedictine Rule, and some other writings; the regulation weight for the bread, and measure for the wine, and such scanty bed furniture as they could save from the general ruin.

It was under the fourth successor of St. Benedict that this ruin of the great convent took place, and notwithstanding all the softened conditions of life in Italy during the generations that were to follow, it was 130 years before the *Coenobium* of Monte Cassino rose again from its ruins.

In the year 591 Duke Zotto died, having pushed the terror of his ravages, as we can see from the early letters of Pope Gregory, far into Apulia, Lucania and Calabria. In all this career of conquest he had been apparently acting on his own responsibility, with very little regard to the central power, such as it was, in Northern Italy; and indeed, during half of his reign there 'had been no king over Israel', only that loose confederacy of dukes of which he must have been nearly, if not quite, the most powerful member. But either Zotto left none of his own family to succeed him, or the obvious danger to the Lombard state, involved in the independence of Benevento, stirred up the new king, Agilulf, to a vigorous assertion of the right which was undoubtedly his in theory, to nominate Zotto's successor. His choice fell on Arichis, who was a kinsman of Gisulf, duke of Friuli, and who had, according to Paulus, acted for some time as instructor of his younger sons in all manly exercises.

The reign of Arichis I lasted fifty years, from 591 to 641, and was an important period in the history of the new duchy. I have called it a reign advisedly, for whatever may have been the theory of his relation to Arichis, the Lombard king ruling at Pavia, it is clear that in practice Arichis acted as an independent sovereign. We have seen him, in a previous chapter, making war on his own account with Naples and Rome: nay more, we have seen that King Agilulf himself could not conclude a peace with the Empire till Arichis was graciously pleased to come in and give his assent to the treaty. It is suggested that if Agilulf, on Zotto's death, had taken proper measures for ensuring the dependence of the duchy of Benevento on the central monarchy, he might still have accomplished that result; but whether this be so or no, it is clear that the long and successful reign of a great warrior like Arichis, a reign, too, which coincided with many weak and short reigns of his nominal superiors at Pavia, established the virtual independence of the southern duchy. There was apparently no royal domain reserved in all that long reach of territory; there were no officers acting in the king's name, or appointed by him; and when at last the reign of Arichis came to an end his successor was chosen without even a pretence of consulting the Lombard sovereign.

It was during this reign that the duchy of Benevento received that geographical extension which, in the main, it kept for centuries. Roughly speaking, it included the old Italian provinces of Samnium, Apulia, Campania, Lucania, and Bruttii, except such parts of the coast—and they were considerable, and included all the best harbors—as were still held by the Empire. The capital and heart of the duchy were in the province of Samnium, and 'the people of the Samnites' is, as we have seen, the phrase generally used by Paulus when he is speaking of the Lombards of Benevento. It is certainly with a strange feeling of the return of some great historic cycle that we find Rome engaged in a breathless struggle for her very existence with Carthage in the fifth century after Christ, and with 'the Samnites' in the sixth.

The limits of the Samnite duchy cannot now be very exactly defined. On the northwest the frontier must have run for some distance side by side with that of the *Ducatus Romae* along the river Liris, and under the Volscian hills. In the Sabine territory and Picenum, the Fucine lake and the river Pescara probably formed the boundary with the other great Lombard duchy of Central Italy, that of Spoleto. The easternmost peninsula (sometimes called the heel of Italy), which lies between the gulf of Taranto and the Adriatic, and which includes Taranto itself, Otranto and Brindisi, was still held by the Empire at the death of Arichis. So did the extreme south, the toe of Italy, forming large part of the ancient province of Bruttii. Consentiae (Cosenza) seems here to have been close to the border line between the Imperial and the Lombard dominions. Rossano was still Imperial, and a line drawn across the peninsula from that city to Amantia formed the frontier between 'Romania and Varbaricum'. The patient monks of Cassiodorus therefore, in their convent at Squillace, could study theology and grammar, and transcribe the treatises of their founder, undisturbed under the aegis of the Empire. Further north all the lovely bay of Naples, with its fine harbors and flourishing cities, owned the sway of the Roman Augustus. It was not till towards the end of the reign of Arichis (probably about 640) that the city of Salerno passed, apparently by peaceful means, into the keeping of the Lombards.

The few facts which illustrate the internal history of the duchy, and especially those which throw any light on the condition of the conquered Roman inhabitants, will come under our notice in later chapters. It will be enough to say here that all the symptoms would seem to show that the oppression was harder, the robbery of cities and churches more ruthless, the general relation of the two nations more unnatural, in the duchy of Benevento (and probably in that of Spoleto also) than in the northern kingdom. No Theudelinda was at work here to help forward the blessed work of amalgamation between the races. It is true that in the spring of 599 we find Pope Gregory writing to Arichis, and asking for help in the felling of timber in the forests of Bruttii for the repairs of the churches of St. Peter and St. Paul. As before said, we must not conclude that because the Pope in this letter addresses 'Arogis' as his son, he had joined the Catholic Church. It is true that Gregory would hardly have used this mode of address to a notorious idolater, perhaps hardly to a bitter Arian persecutor; but these Lombard conquerors were not as a rule sufficiently interested in theology to be persecutors. They were simply rough, sensual, boorish children of the forest, men who, if there were any object to be gained, would address the great bishop of Rome as 'Father', and would be glad to be addressed by him as 'Glorious Son', but would not surrender an ounce of church plate, nor recall a single bishop from the exile into which their suspicions had driven him, for all the loving exhortations of the Holy Father.

Thus it came to pass that all through the long reign of Arichis, the Catholics of his duchy were in a lamentable state of spiritual destitution. The unusually large number of episcopal cities which were once to be found in Southern Italy seem to have remained widowed of their bishops, and the convents, like Monte Cassino itself, lay, probably for the greater part of the seventh century, in ruins. Even Benevento, the capital of the duchy, had perhaps no resident bishop till shortly before St. Barbatus came to it (in 663) to restore the ruins of many generations. The life of this saint (from which some quotations will be made in a note to a later chapter) draws a lamentable picture of the foolish and degrading superstitions by which the people of Benevento, though calling themselves baptized Christians, were still held in bondage. Salerno seems to be the only city in this region (except those that remained in the possession of the Empire) which can show an absolutely unbroken line of bishops during all this troubled time; and this exceptional prosperity is probably accounted for by the fact of its peaceful surrender to the conquerors.

Arichis had probably been reigning some twenty or five-and-twenty years when (as was told in the last section) his young kinsmen, Radwald and Grimwald, having left Friuli in disdain, landed from their little bark, and made their way to the court of Benevento. They were received by Arichis with the utmost cordiality, and brought up as his own sons. He had indeed one son of his own named Aio, but over him there hung a mystery which clouded the last years of the life of Arichis. When the great King Rothari took his seat on the Lombard throne, Arichis ordered his son to repair to Pavia, probably with a message of dutiful submission from one who, though in fact king of all Southern Italy, yet owned the king of the Lombards as his lord. On his way, the young prince tarried at Ravenna. Whether he ever completed his journey to Pavia we are not informed, but when he returned to Benevento all men noted a strange alteration in his behavior. Dark rumors were spread abroad that by the malice of the Romans some maddening potion had been brewed for him at Ravenna. Perhaps we may conjecture that the maddening potion was only that Circean cup of enchantment which the dissolute cities of the Romans have so often held out to the easily-tempted sons of the Teutons; but, whatever the cause, Aio from that time forth was never again in full mental health.

Seeing this fatal change, Arichis, when he felt his last hour approaching, commended Radwald and Grimwald to the Lombards as his own sons, and advised that one of them rather than Aio should be his successor. The advice, however, was disregarded, and on the death of Arichis, the brain-sick Aio became 'leader of the Samnites'. Neither chief nor people seem to have taken any heed of the right which the king of the Lombards must have in theory possessed to name the new duke of Benevento. We are told that Radwald and Grimwald, not murmuring at their exclusion from the throne, to which the will of Arichis had seemed to open the way, obeyed Aio in all things as their elder brother and lord. His reign, however, was not to be of long duration. A year and five months after his accession, a cloud of Slavonic invaders descended on Apulia. They came by way of the sea, with a multitude of ships, and landed at Sipontum; a city which has now disappeared from the face of the earth, but which stood under the peninsular mount of Garganus, near to the spot where, six centuries later, the last of the Hohenstaufens built out of its ruins his capital of Manfredonia. Here the Slavonians pitched their camp, which they fortified with pits dug all round it, and covered probably with brushwood. Thither came Aio with an army, but unaccompanied by his two friends. Riding rashly forward, he fell into one of the hidden pits, and was killed, with many of his followers, by the on-rushing Slavonians. The news was brought to Radwald, who, in order to avenge his patron's death, dealt wilily. He had not forgotten the Slavonic speech which he had learned long ago in the mountains of Friuli, and, approaching the camp of the invaders, he spoke to them friendly words in their own tongue. Having thus lulled their suspicions to sleep, and made them less eager for the battle, he fell upon them at unawares, and wrought great slaughter in their ranks. Thus was Aio's death avenged, and the remnant of the Slavonians returned in haste to their own land. Radwald, who now became without dispute duke of Benevento, reigned for five years only, and at his death was succeeded by his brother Grimwald. The only event which is recorded of the latter's reign as mere duke of Benevento is that 'the Greeks' (as the Romans of the East are now beginning to be called) came to plunder the sanctuary of the Archangel Michael on Mount Garganus; a deed which recalls the ignoble raid upon Apulia made by the ships of Anastasius in the days of Theodoric the Ostrogoth. Grimwald, however, fell upon the sacrilegious invaders with his army, and destroyed them with a great destruction.

At this point we rejoin for a time the main stream of Lombard history: for Grimwald, who is certainly its greatest name in the seventh century, became, as we shall see, in the latter years of his life, king of all the Lombards. Thus the history of the lad who so marvellously escaped from his Avar captors binds together the two duchies of Friuli and Benevento, and the kingdom of Pavia. The eventful story of that last stage of the life of Grimwald must be reserved for a future chapter.

IV.
The Duchy of Spoleto.

The geographical importance of the duchy of Spoleto has been already brought before the reader's notice. We have seen that it represented that struggle for the possession of the Flaminian Way which, since Rome and Ravenna were the two great foci of Imperial dominion in Italy, must have been always going on with more or less vigour for nearly two centuries.

It is true that the great Via Flaminia itself went from Narnia to Mevania, and so passed about twenty miles west of Spoletium; but the road which branched off from Narnia to the east, and led through Interamna, Spoletium and Fulginium northward, and so on through Petra Pertusa to Ariminum, was also a great highway, and we have seen reason in the course of the previous history to believe that it was looked upon, at any rate so long as the tunnel of the Petra Pertusa was open, as the great highway between Rome and Ravenna. Evidently the object of the Lombard dukes who placed their capital at Spoleto was to keep their hands on the throttle-valve of the Empire, and they probably always nourished the hope of being able to close all the three roads across the Apennines which lay in their immediate neighborhood, and so to conquer Rome.

Spoleto itself, a city rich in historical associations of widely-parted centuries, and standing in the midst of one of the loveliest landscapes of Italy, was well worthy of the high place which it held in the early Middle Ages, and deserves far more careful study than it has yet received either from the artist or the historian. It stands upon a high hill, half encircled by the little stream of the Tessino. Faintly seen on the northern horizon are the long terraces of Assisi and the high rock-citadel of Perugia. Round it on all sides rise the beautiful hills of Umbria, with all that charm of outline and of color which assuredly helped to train the eyes of Raffaele and Perugino to discern the Beautiful. The traveler winds his way under the city walls, whose Cyclopean masonry tells of races that fought and built in the peninsula while the hills of Rome were still a sheep-walk. He climbs under many an intersecting archway up the steep lanes which lead him to the heart of the city. Bright-eyed little children and gaily-kerchiefed women come out to look at *the forestiere*: a little tired, he reaches the top, and suddenly, between two picturesque street-lines, he sees a bit of the beautiful amphitheatre of plain, a bit of the deep purple of the mountains of Umbria.

Yet, as so often in Italy, the visitor to Spoleto finds the historic interest even more powerful to attract him than the beauty of landscape with which Nature woos his regards. Here, near the bottom of the city wall, stands an arch bearing the name of the Porta Fuga, and commemorating the memorable repulse of Hannibal on that day when, flushed with his victory by Lake Trasymene, he marched up to its walls, expecting an immediate surrender; but, beaten back with heavy loss, began to understand, from the resistance of that one brave colony, how great a task he had taken in hand when he set himself to war down Rome.

We mount higher to the crest of the hill, and find ourselves under an arch erected probably twenty-one years after the birth of Christ, bearing an inscription on its front, which states that it is dedicated to Germanicus and Drusus, the adopted and the real sons of Tiberius. The palace of the Municipality, which stands on the highest ground of the city, is erected over the remains of a spacious Roman house which is believed, apparently on sufficient evidence, to have belonged to the mother of Vespasian.

We leave the city by one of its eastern gateways and we find ourselves under the splendid mass of the citadel (fitly called by the townspeople La Rocca), which, standing on its great promontory of cliff, towers above us on our left. Round the base of the cliff far below us circles the tiny torrent of the Tessino. But another, an artificial river, calls away our attention from the natural streamlet. For before us rise the ten lofty and narrow arches of a noble aqueduct, which, at a height of nearly 300 feet, spans the valley and bridges the stream, carrying the pure water from the mountains into the heart of the city. It is called the Ponte delle Torri, and it carries a roadway at a little lower level than the channel of the aqueduct. Both these two splendid structures speak to us of the Teutonic invaders of Italy. The citadel is undoubtedly on the site of the fortress raised by Theodoric, though there may be none of the actual work of the great Ostrogoth in the present building, which was reared in the fourteenth century by Cardinal Albornoz. A very strong local tradition connects the aqueduct with Theudelap, who, as we shall see, was the Lombard duke of Spoleto during the greater part of the seventh century. The pointed character of the arches makes it scarcely possible that they, at least, are of so early a period, and probably much of the grand structure which we now behold dates from the thirteenth century or even later; but cautious and accurate enquirers are inclined to admit that there is some value in the tradition which I have mentioned, and that at least in the great stone piers which support the brick arches, we may see the actual work of the subjects of Duke Theudelap.

This is not the place for anything like a complete enumeration of the monuments of medieval antiquity at Spoleto; and I must leave undescribed the Doric columns of some Pagan temple which now form part of the church of the Crucified One, the joyously grotesque bas-reliefs on the exterior of S. Pietro, and the gigantic stones—

surely of pre-Roman workmanship—which form the base of the tower of S. Gregorio. But as illustrating what was said above as to the wealth of various memories that is stored up in these Italian cities, I may observe that the cathedral—not in itself extremely interesting, having suffered much transformation at the hands of Renaissance architects—is connected with the tragic story of Fra Filippo Lippi. His half-faded frescoes telling the story of the Virgin, line the choir of the church. His sepulchral monument, erected by Lorenzo dei Medici with an inscription in Politian's finest Latinity, is to be seen in a chapel on the north side of the choir. In this city it was that the artist monk won the love of a nobly-born lady, Lucrezia Buti, and here it was—so men said—that her indignant relatives mixed for him the fatal cup which ended his stormy life.

If we descend to our own times we learn that in 1860 the fortress of Theodoric and Albornoz was one of the last positions that held out for the Pope-King when all Italy was rallying round the standard of Victor Emmanuel. The garrison, chiefly composed of Irishmen, bravely resisted the besiegers, but was at last forced to capitulate by a cannonade from the surrounding heights.

At present Spoleto, which contains about 11,000 inhabitants, has suffered some diminution of its importance, owing to having lost its position as *capo luogo* of the province, and this has led to a decay of interest in its antiquities. But, as I before said, there are probably few cities in Italy which would better reward the spade of the excavator or the brush of the artist.

At the time when the savage hordes of the Lombards swarmed through the gateways of Spoleto, the minds of the citizens were still tilled with the memory of a certain holy hermit named Isaac, who many years before came from Syria, and suddenly appearing in Spoleto, craved from the guardians of the great church permission to remain there as long as he might desire, in order to oiler up his prayers. So small a request was readily granted; but when the holy man had remained standing for three days and nights in the attitude of prayer, one of the attendants, deeming him an impostor, slapped him on the cheek, and ordered him out of the church. At once a foul spirit seized the too hasty custodian, and caused him to fall prostrate at the feet of the unknown hermit, crying out, "Isaac is casting me forth". The holy man—whose name the unclean spirit alone knew—delivered his assailant from the evil one, and at once the news of his spiritual victory spread through the city. Men and women, noble and ignoble, flocked into the church to behold him, besought him to take up his abode with them, offered him houses and lands for the erection of a monastery. But Isaac, who feared peril to his poverty as the miser fears peril to his wealth, refused all their offers, saying continually, "The monk who seeks for possessions in this world is no monk", and built himself a humble cell in a desert place not far from the city. Here he abode many years, performing many wonderful works, the recital of which may be read in the Dialogues of Gregory the Great, from which the preceding narrative is taken. As we are told that he continued almost to the very end of the Gothic domination, the fame of his sanctity must still have been fresh when Spoletium was severed from the Empire, and when her churches were profaned by the tread of the 'unspeakable Lombard'.

Such then was the city which became the capital of the Lombard domination in Central Italy. Its dukes ruled over a territory bounded by the Adriatic on the east, and by the Tiber valley (or the hills which enclosed it) on the west. On the south, a line drawn across from Subiaco by the Fucine Lake, and along the river Pescara, may roughly represent the boundary between Spoleto and Benevento. On the north the little river Musone was perhaps the boundary which separated the Spoletine dukes from hostile Ancona, while the Imperial garrisons along the Flaminian Way probably disputed with varying success the possession of all the territory northward of Tadino. Thus, stated in terms of classical geography, the dukes of Spoleto ruled the southern wedge of Umbria, the greater part of Picenum, and almost the whole of the territory which upon the maps is usually allotted to the Sabines.

Duke Farwald, 571-591

The first duke of Spoleto was *Farwald*, who, if it be true that Zotto was ruling in Beneventum in 571, had probably established himself at least as early in his more northern capital.

The chief exploit of Farwald's reign was the capture of Classis, which occurred probably about 579 or 580 while the inefficient Longinus was still the Imperial governor of Italy. A great achievement truly this must have been, and one which, had the Lombards possessed the same fertility of resource which was shown by their Vandal kinsfolk, might have turned Classis into a second Carthage, and given them the empire of the Mediterranean. As it was, it seems difficult to suppose that they ever seriously interrupted the communications even of Ravenna, and Constantinople; for Exarchs came and went, and letters seem to have been freely interchanged between the Emperor and his representatives. It was therefore probably only the town, not the whole even of the harbor of Classis, of which the Lombards kept possession; but even so, it must have been a galling thing for the 'Romans' of Ravenna to feel that the invaders had established themselves in that place, which with Caesarea was joined by one continuous line of houses to their own city, that the domes and towers from which in its pictured semblance on the walls of S. Apollinare, the procession of Virgin martyrs set forth to adore the Holy Child were now in the hands of heretics and idolaters.

Classis seems to have been held by the Lombards of Spoleto for eight or nine years, and was finally reconquered for the Empire (perhaps in the year 588), by that Romanized Teuton Droctulf, on whose tomb, as we have seen, this military operation was recorded as one of the proudest of his triumphs.

Against the older and more venerable capital by the Tiber, it is possible that Farwald also urged his savage soldiery. When we hear that before the consecration of Pope Benedict I, there was an interval of more than ten months and three days, during which the Papal throne remained unoccupied; we may reasonably conjecture that Lombard pressure, either from the side of Tuscany, or from that of Spoleto, was the cause of this long delay. At the next vacancy, when, after an interval of nearly four months, Pelagius II was chosen without the leave of the Emperor, we are expressly told that this was done because Rome was being besieged by the Lombards, and they were making great ravages in Italy. And this besieger of Rome is more likely to have been Farwald than any other of the Lombard dukes.

Duke Ariulf. 591-601

Farwald died about the year 591, possibly of the pestilence which was then ravaging Italy. He was succeeded by *Ariulf,* apparently not a relation; certainly not a son. Possibly in this case the theoretical right of the king to nominate all the dukes was successfully claimed by the new sovereign Agilulf. Thanks to the letters of Pope Gregory, this duke of Spoleto is to us something more than a mere name. We saw him, in the summer of 592, addressing that boastful letter to Gregory about the promised surrender of Suana which caused the Pope such strange searchings of heart, whether he should advise the Suanese citizens to keep or to break their promise. Soon after, negotiations for peace followed with Gregory himself; but Ariulf still kept up his somewhat swaggering tone, and insisted that the gratuities for his allies (or subordinates), Auctarit and Nordulf, should be handed over to him before he would say one word about peace. While Ariulf appears to make war and peace with sublime independence of his nominal overlord at Pavia, he throughout cooperates loyally with his brother duke Arichis of Benevento, and whenever the latter attacks Naples he helps him to the utmost of his power by a demonstration against Rome, or against one of the outposts on the Flaminian Way.

But Ariulf's campaign of 592, including, as it probably did, a virtual siege of Rome, ended in a partial peace concluded by Gregory with the Lombard duke; and this concession on Ariulf's part seems to have been due to the feelings of veneration aroused in his heart by a personal interview with the pontiff. And though the peace itself was disavowed at Ravenna, and exposed the Pope to bitter reproaches at Constantinople for his 'fatuity' in listening to the promises of such an one as Ariulf, the good understanding thus established between Pope and Duke seems never to have been entirely destroyed; and in a dangerous sickness the Lombard chief asked for and obtained the prayers of Gregory for his recovery. In the final negotiations, however, which at last resulted in the great peace of 599, the Pope complained with some bitterness of the hindrances which came from the side of Ariulf. To Gregory the duke of Spoleto's stipulations that there should be no act of violence committed against himself, and no movement against the army of Arichis, seemed altogether unfair and deceitful and the fact that a certain Warnilfrida, by whose counsel Ariulf was ruled in all things, refused to swear to the peace, confirmed his suspicions. It is, of course, impossible for us to apportion the precise share of praise and blame due to each of the parties to these obscure negotiations; and, as I before remarked, the change of Gregory's tone with regard to Ariulf between 592 and 599 is an important feature in the case. But, on the other hand, it may fairly be urged on Ariulf's behalf, (1) that his previous dealings with the Imperial court had taught him caution, since he had seen, a treaty which had been concluded by him with Rome torn up at Ravenna, and followed by an aggressive movement on the part of the Exarch; and (2) that his stipulations on behalf of Arichis showed his steadfast truth to the duke of Benevento, and his determination not to make himself safe by the sacrifice of that faithful ally.

The only other incident in the life of Ariulf that has been recorded is that curious story which has been already extracted from the pages of Paulus, and which seems like a barbaric version of the share taken by the Great Twin Brethren in the battle of the Lake Regillus. It was when he was warring against Caraerinum that Ariulf saw a champion, unseen by others, fighting bravely by his side, and it was soon after the battle that he identified his ghostly defender with St. Sabinus, whose figure he saw depicted on the walls of his basilica. Paulus assigns no date to this story, which is connected with his obituary notice of Ariulf. Seeing how near Camerinum is to Spoletium, we should feel inclined to *put* the campaign against the former city early in the victorious reign of Ariulf : indeed, it is difficult to understand why his predecessor should have penetrated as far north as Chassis, leaving such a stronghold as Camerinum in his immediate neighborhood untaken.

Ariulf's reign, though a memorable, was not a long one. He died in 601, about ten years after his accession; and on his death a contest arose between the two sons of his predecessor Farwald, which should succeed to the vacant dignity. The dispute was decided by the sword—we have again to note how little voice King Agilulf seems to have had in regulating the succession to these great duchies—and Theudelap, the victor in the fight, was crowned duke on the field of battle. We know neither the name nor the fate of his unsuccessful rival.

Theudelap. 601-653

Theudelap wore for more than half a century the ducal crown of Spoleto. This long reign, which during the greater part of its course coincided with that of Arichis at Benevento (591-641), had doubtless an important influence in rendering both of the southern duchies more independent of the northern kingdom. At Pavia during this half century four kings bore sway; two of whom were able and successful rulers, but the other two were an infant and an usurper. It cannot be doubted that, during this long period, that part of Lombard Italy which lay south and east of the Flaminian Way would be growing less and less disposed to respond to any effectual control on the part of the kings who dwelt north of the Apennines.

Of the events of the long reign of Theudelap we are absolutely ignorant. It is generally supposed to have been peaceful; but this may be only because record fails us of the wars in which he may have been engaged. Some of the early mediaeval buildings of Spoleto are traditionally attributed to his reign; but of this also there appears to be no clear proof; though (as I have already said) there is some reason to think that popular tradition is not altogether wrong in assigning to Theudelap some share at least in the construction of that noble aqueduct which is the great glory of the city of Spoleto. There has been, to use a geological term, a complete denudation of all this part of the history of Lombard Italy; and if we know little of Theudelap himself, we know still less of his successor *Atto,* who is to us a mere name in the pages of Paulus Diaconus. The story of the later dukes will be told chiefly in connection with that of the Lombard kings, against whom they were frequently found in rebellion.

NOTE
ECCLESIASTICAL NOTICES OF THE LOMBARDS OF SPOLETO.

We have some hints as to the proceedings of the Lombards in Central Italy, furnished to us by the church writers of the period, which from their character we cannot accept as sober history, and yet which supply us with too vivid a picture of the times to be altogether omitted.

I. Chief among these are the marvelous stories told by Pope Gregory in his strange wonder-book the *Dialogues.* This book was composed in 593, in the early years of his pontificate, before he had tamed Ariulf, or corresponded with Theudelinda, or hurled meek defiance at the Emperor Maurice. Possibly in the later years of his life, after peace with the invaders had been brought about by his means, he might have spoken with rather less bitterness concerning them. The geographical indications furnished by the

Dialogues all point, as we might have expected, to the Lombards of the duchy of Spoleto as the ravagers with whom Gregory's friends were chiefly brought in contact. In one place we hear (and it is an almost solitary instance of religious persecution) of their putting four hundred captives to death because they refused to worship a goat's head, round which the Lombards themselves circled in rapid dance, singing an unholy hymn. Of course, these barbarians must have been mere idolaters, who did not pretend to the name even of Arian Christianity. We may perhaps be allowed to conjecture that they belonged rather to that *colluries gentium,* Bulgarians, Sarmatians, Gepidae, who came with the Lombards into Italy, than to the Lombards properly so called.

At Spoleto itself, the Arian bishop of the Lombards demanded of the bishop of the city a church which he might dedicate to his error. On the firm refusal of the Catholic prelate he announced that he should come next day and forcibly enter the church of St. Paul. The guardian of that church hastened to it, closed and bolted the doors, extinguished all the lights at eventide, hid himself in the recesses of the church, and awaited the result. In the early morning twilight the Arian bishop came with a multitude of men prepared to break open the doors of the church. Suddenly, by an unseen hand, all the bolts of the doors were loosed, the doors opened with a crash, the extinguished lamps burst into flame, and the intruding bishop, seeking to pass the threshold of the church, was struck with sudden blindness and had to be led back by a guide to his home. The miracle of light at the same instant given to the church, and taken away from the heretical bishop struck all the Lombards in that region with awe, and there was no further attempt to deprive the Catholics of their churches.

Some of Gregory's most characteristic stories are told us concerning a certain presbyter of the province of Nursia, named Sanctulus, who had recently died and appeared to him in vision at the hour of his departure. This Sanctulus passing by saw some Lombards toiling in vain at an olive-press, from which no oil would run forth. He brought a skin and told them to fill it for him. The barbarians, already chafed by their wasted labor, answered him with angry and threatening words; but the holy man called for water, which he blessed and cast into the press, and now there gushed forth such a stream of oil that the laboring Lombards filled not their own vessels only, but his bladder also.

In a similar way he fed the workmen employed in rebuilding the church of St. Lawrence destroyed by the Lombards, with a large and beautiful white loaf miraculously hidden in that which was supposed to be an empty oven. All these miracles seem to have procured for him a certain amount of favor from the barbarians, and when a deacon was brought into the city, whom some Lombards had taken prisoner, and were about to put to death, they consented to hand him over to the custody of Sanctulus, but only on condition that he should answer for his safe keeping with his own life. At midnight, when the Lombards were all wrapt in slumber, the saint aroused the deacon and commanded him to fly, saying that he was in the hands of God and feared not the consequences for himself. Next morning, when the Lombards came and found their bird flown, they were of course vehemently enraged.

'You know', said they, 'what was agreed upon between us'.

'I know it', he answered.

'But you are a good man: we would not willingly torture you. Choose by what death you will die'.

'I am in God's hands: slay me in any manner that He shall permit'.

Then they consulted together and decided that his head should be cut off by the stroke of a strong Lombard swordsman. At the news that so great a saint and one whom they so highly reverenced was to be put to death, the Lombards gathered from far and near to witness the famous sight. The saint asked leave to pray, which was granted him; but as he remained a long time on the ground prostrate in prayer, the executioner gave him a kick and said, "Rise, kneel down, and stretch out your neck". He obeyed; he stretched out his neck; he saw the flashing sword drawn to slay him, and uttered only the prayer : "Saint John, receive my soul". The executioner swung his sword high in air, but there it remained, for his stiffened arm was unable to bring it down again. Then all the Lombards crowded round the holy man and begged him to arise. He arose. They begged him to release the executioner's arrested arm, but he replied, "I will in no wise pray for him, unless he will swear never to slay a Christian man with that hand". The penitent executioner swore the oath, and at the saint's word of command brought down his arm, and plunged the sword back into its sheath. The miracle struck a deep awe into the hearts of all the barbarians, who crowded round the saint and sought to buy his favor by presents of horses and cattle which they had plundered from the country-folk; but he refused all these and only claimed, and this successfully, that all the captives whom they had taken should be restored to freedom.

Less fortunate, or less strong in faith, was a certain abbot named Soranus, who, having at the news of the approach of the Lombards given away all the stores laid up in the monastery and therefore having nothing to give when the barbarians came round him, clamoring for gold, was carried off by them to a forest among the mountains. He succeeded in escaping, but one of the Lombards finding him, drew his sword and slew him. When his body fell to the ground the mountain and the forest were shaken together as though the trembling earth confessed herself unable to bear the weight of his holiness.

A deacon in the land of the Marsi being beheaded by a Lombard, the foul fiend at once entered into the murderer, who fell prostrate at the feet of his victim. Two monks in the province of Valeria being taken by the raging Lombards were hung on the branches of a tree and died the same clay. At evening the two dead monks began to sing with clear and sweet voices, to the joy of their fellow-captives who yet remained alive, but to the terror and confusion of the barbarians who had murdered them.

Such are the chief stories told by the great Pope concerning the evil deeds of the Lombards of Central Italy.

Life of St. Cetheus.

Another source of information of a similar kind is opened to us by the Life of St. Cetheus (or Peregrinus), bishop of Amiternum, a city now destroyed, which once stood about forty miles southeast of Spoleto, at the foot of the Gran Sasso d'Italia.

In the time of Pope Gregory, Emperor Phocas, and Farwald duke of Spolelo, the Lombards entered Italy and overflowed the boundaries of the Romans, Samnites and Spoletines. Of this nation, two most evil and ignoble men, sons of concubines, named Alais and Umbolus, came to the city of Amiternum, which they ravaged and plundered in their usual barbaric fashion. Unable to bear their cruelty, Cetheus bishop of the city fled to Rome and besought the protection of Pope Gregory, who assured him that in no long time the Lombards would repent and seek the Papal blessing. For this Cetheus prayed, and before long his prayer was granted, the Lombards from Amiternum coming to implore the Pope's benediction, which he would only grant them on condition of their receiving back their bishop. All the priests and other clergy poured forth from the gate of the city to meet him on his return and welcomed him in the name of the Lord.

Now dissensions arose between the two Lombard dukes, of whom Alais held the eastern and Umbolus the western gate. Each sought to kill the other, and there was great sadness among the Christians in that city. Alais, plotting with his friends the ruin of the city, sent messengers to Vesilianus [the Roman] count of Orta, praying him to make a midnight attack on the city of Amiternum, and utterly destroy it. Of this design the blessed bishop Cetheus, abiding in his cell, was utterly ignorant. Now there were in that city a Godfearing couple named Fredo and Bona, who went at eventide into the church and prayed, and then having received the bishop's blessing returned to their home. When bed-time came, Fredo did not take off his clothes, but lay down as he was. On his wife asking him the reason he answered, "I am shaken with an immense trembling and I greatly fear that tonight this city will perish". "God will forbid it", said she; but he said, "Bring me my weapons of war and place them by my head, and then we shall sleep secure". This he said, being warned by the Holy Ghost, for he knew naught of the counsels of Alais.

At midnight a cry was heard, "Arise, arise, an enemy attacks the city!". The most Christian Fredo rose from his wife's side, and donning his arms, ran through the streets crying, "Rise most holy father Cetheus, rise and pray for us! The city perisheth, we shall lose all our goods and shall ere daybreak be slain with the sword". Bishop Cetheus arose, and rushed into the street, calling aloud on Christ who delivered Daniel from the lions and the Three Children from the fiery furnace, to save the people of Amiternum from their foes. The prayer was heard, the invaders were struck with panic and retired having lost many of their number.

Next day all the citizens came together to see by what means the enemy could have entered the city. They found ladders raised near the church of St. Thomas, and discovered that all this had been done by the counsel of Alais. He was brought bound into the midst of the people, who thundered forth the words, "Death to the traitor!" and began to consider how best to torture him. But Cetheus besought them not to lay hands on him but to cast him into prison and call a meeting of all in that city, both small and great, who should lay upon him a penance lasting many days, that his spirit might be saved in the day of the Lord Jesus.

At once uprose the impious Umbolus in wrath and fury, and said, "Thou too, O Cetheus, was certainly privy to this treacherous scheme, for the ladder set against the church of St. Thomas was placed there by thy magic arts. Thou art unworthy to be bishop any longer". The blessed Cetheus swore by the crucified Son of God, by the undivided Trinity, and by the holy Gospels, that he was innocent of any such design; but Umbolus, stopping his ears, ordered him and Alais to be led bound into the midst of the city and there beheaded in the sight of all the people. On the road to execution Cetheus sang Psalms with such a loud and triumphant voice that the awe-stricken guardsman, though he gladly struck off the head of Alais, refused to strike a blow at the holy man. Full of fury, Umbolus ordered Cetheus to be brought before him and began to taunt him with his bonds. The bishop declared that the curse of Cain the fratricide should rest upon him, and that he should dwell for ever with the Evil One. Turning then to his guards he said, "Why, oh sons of iniquity and servants of darkness, do ye keep me thus in chains? Is it because ye recognize in me a servant of the true God? In His name I will gladly bear not chains only, but death itself: but you, Arians and infidels that ye are, shall have your mansions with Judas Iscariot in the unquenchable Tartarus, and among the wandering spirits shall be your portion : yea, and cursed for ever shall ye be, because ye have scorned my preaching and have refused to listen to the corrections of Truth. But to thee Umbolus, most unutterable of men, none shall ever give the kiss of peace. He who blesses thee shall be accursed, for the curser of Satan curses thee". Filled with rage, Umbolus ordered him to be bound and led away to the river Pescara and thrown into it from the marble bridge. So was he thrown in, but by the blessing of God he came to shore safe and sound. Again and again was he thrown in at the tyrant's command by the raging people, but always came safely to the shore. Then the most impious Umbolus ordered them to bring the holy man into his presence, and to fasten under his feet a millstone weighing live hundredweight, and drown him in the deepest part of the river. Then after another prayer he was thrown into the stream, and at once yielded up his breath, but his body was carried [down the river and across the Adriatic] to the city of Jaterna [Zara in Dalmatia], where a fisherman found it with the millstone still attached to it and surrounded by a holy light. News of the discovery was brought to the bishop and clergy of Zara, who at once perceived that it was the body of a holy man, and buried it near the shore in the odour of sanctity. Often at night was a light like that of a lamp seen to hover round the corpse's head; and a blind man received sight by visiting the tomb. But as none knew the martyr's name, the men of Zara called him only by this name, Peregrinus.

With all the marks of the handiwork of the conventional martyrologist, there are some touches in this narrative which indicate a real knowledge of the circumstances of the time, and point to a nearly contemporary origin. The Lombards are still 'unspeakable': the split between the two Lombard dukes and the intrigue of one of the rivals with the Imperial general are events of only too frequent occurrence in Lombard history: and lastly the martyrdom as it is called, is not due to religious intolerance on the part of the Lombards, but to merely political causes. Bishop Cetheus is drowned, not because he upholds the creed of Nicaea, but because he is suspected of complicity in the betrayal of the city to the Greeks, and various circumstances suggest even to us the thought that the suspicion was not altogether without foundation.

CHAPTER III.

SAINT COLUMBANUS.

IN relating the history of the four great duchies, we have travelled far down through the seventh century. We must now retrace our steps to the very beginning of that century, and follow the fortunes of the Lombard kingdom established at Pavia, from the year 603 onwards. It will be remembered that this year witnessed the greatest of King Agilulf's triumph. Cremona, Mantua, Brexillum, all surrendered to his generals; the whole valley of the Po became a Lombard possession; the Exarch Smaragdus was forced to conclude peace on terms humiliating to the Empire; the kidnapped daughter of Agilulf, with her husband Gottschalk, was restored to her father; and, most fortunate event, as it seemed, of all, the new dynasty was consolidated by the birth of Theudelinda's son Adalwald, who was baptized according to the Catholic rite by Bishop Secundus of Trient.

Agilulf lived for twelve or thirteen years after this year of triumph, but, with one exception, that period seems to have been marked by no political events of great importance for the Lombard kingdom. The exception referred to—and it was a lamentable one—was that terrible invasion of the once friendly Avars which (as was told in the last chapter) blasted the reviving prosperity of the border duchy of Friuli.

Relations with the Empire consisted chiefly of a series of renewals of the peace of 603. It had been arranged that that peace should endure till the first of April, 605. In the summer of that year we must suppose the war to have been in some measure renewed, and the Lombards to have been successful, for two cities on the east of Lake Bolsena, Orvieto and Bagnorea, were lost by the Empire. In November of this year (605) Smaragdus was fain to conclude a year's peace with Agilulf at a cost of 12,000 solidi. In 606 the peace was renewed for three years more. It was, perhaps, in 609, at the end of this interval that Agilulf sent a great officer of the household to the Emperor Phocas. He returned, accompanied by the Imperial ambassadors, who brought gifts from their master, and renewed the yearly peace. And so the diplomatic game went on, somewhat in the same fashion as between Spain and the United Provinces in the early part of the seventeenth century. The Roman Emperor could not recognize the Lombards as lawful possessors of any part of the soil of Italy, but he was willing to postpone from year to year the effort to expel them; and the Lombard king, sometimes by the inducement of a large payment of money, was made willing to allow the operation to be so postponed. Emperor succeeded Emperor at Constantinople—the revolution which placed Heraclius on the Imperial throne broke out in the autumn of 610—and Exarch succeeded Exarch at Ravenna, but the long-delayed war never came during that generation.

With his powerful neighbors on the west, the relations of Agilulf were also in the main peaceful. When in July, 604, the infant Adalwald was solemnly raised upon the shield in the Roman hippodrome at Milan, and declared king over the Lombards, the ambassadors of the Austrasian king, Theudebert II, were standing by, and in their master's name they swore to a perpetual peace between the Lombards and the Franks, to be sealed by the marriage of the royal babe with their master's daughter.

A few years later we hear of Agilulf as joining a quadruple alliance against Theodoric II of Burgundy. This young king, sensual and profligate like all the Merovingian brood, had repudiated with insult the daughter of the Visigothic king, Witterich. Some said that the divorce was suggested by Theodoric's grandmother Brunichildis, who in her eager clutch of regal power would rather that her descendant wallowed in sinful lusts than that she herself should be confronted in the palace by the influence of a lawful queen. But however this may be—and Brunichildis, struggling against the increasing power of the great nobles of the Court, was bitterly assailed by the calumnies of her foes—the offence seemed likely not to go unpunished. A powerful combination was formed. The insulted Witterich obtained the alliance of the culprit's brother, Theudebert of Austrasia, of his cousin Chlotochar of Neustria, and even, strange to say, of Agilulf of Italy, who perhaps considered himself bound to follow his ally Theudebert wheresoever he might lead him. However, this formidable combination led to no results, and the meager annals of the time do not even inform us whether Burgundy was ever invaded by the confederate kings. Evidently Theodoric II, the resources of whose kingdom were directed by the wary old politician Brunichildis, was the most powerful of all the Frankish monarchs. The long-smoldering feud between him and his brother broke out in 612 into open hostilities. Theodoric was twice victorious, took his brother prisoner, and put him, together with his infant son, to death. What became of the little princess, the affianced bride of Adalwald, we are not informed. Theodoric then turned against the only remaining Frankish king, Chlotochar of Neustria, whose neutrality in the previous struggle he had purchased by a promised cession of territory. It seemed as if the long rivalry between the offspring of Fredegundis and that of Brunichildis was about to end in the triumph of the latter, and as if the grandson of Sigibert was to reunite under his scepter all the wide dominions of Clovis and Chlotochar I. But just at this critical moment Theodoric II died, leaving four infant, but bastard, children behind him. In the name of her great-grandson Sigibert, eldest of the four, Brunichildis aspired to rule over Burgundy and Austrasia, and hoped to conquer Neustria. But the deadly enmity of the Austrasian nobles to the old queen prevented this consummation. Two great nobles, Arnulf, bishop of Metz, and Pippin, went over to the party of Chlotochar, and by their defection determined the result of the campaign. The battle, which was to have been fought near the banks of the Aisne, was only a sham fight. the armies of Austrasia and Burgundy turning their backs without striking a blow. Brunichildis and her great-grandchildren were captured. Two of the latter were put to death; one escaped, but vanished from the eyes of men; the life of the fourth was spared because he was the godson of the conqueror. Brunichildis herself, after being—so it is said—tormented for three days, and then paraded through the Frankish camp on a camel, was tied by her hair, her hands and her feet to a vicious horse, and so dragged and trampled to death. The long strife between the two houses was at an end, and while Fredegundis, unquestionably the most wicked of the two queens, had died quietly in her bed sixteen years before, the able, unscrupulous, and beautiful Brunichildis lived on into old age only to meet this shameful and terrible end.

With the unfortunate Frankish queen and her descendants is closely connected the name of one who exercised a mighty influence on the spiritual history of Theudelinda, and, through her, on the religious history of Italy—the Irish saint Columbanus.

Columbanus or Columba (the second) was born in West Leinster probably in 543, the same year which saw the death of the greatest of monks, St. Benedict. He was well born, and was educated in those arts and sciences a knowledge of which still lingered in Ireland while Gaul and Italy were almost submerged under the flood of barbarian invasion. When the fair and noble youth was growing up into his comely manhood, visions of beautiful women began to haunt his imagination. Marriage was hopeless, for he had been in some sort vowed by his mother to the service of the Church. Renewed earnestness in his studies, devotion to grammar, rhetoric, geometry, the reading of the Scriptures, failed to banish the alluring dream. At length, by the advice of a pious nun, though against the earnest entreaties of his mother, he resolved to leave his paternal home in Leinster; and, after spending some time in the school (which was probably also a monastery) taught by St. Sinell on an island in Lough Erne, he entered the great monastery which had then been recently founded by St. Comgall at Benchor or Bangor in the county of Down. Here, too, he was doubtless still engaged in intellectual labor, for this was one of the most learned monasteries of the time. Ovid and Virgil were studied within its walls; music was held in high honor; some, probably, of those beautiful Irish MSS. which are among the most precious possessions of our great libraries were illuminated by the monks of Bangor.

Columbanus, however, though no foe to liberal culture, was possessed by the missionary spirit, and, after spending many years at Bangor, he set forth with twelve companions, bent on preaching the Gospel, but not knowing whether they should go. They reached the shores of Brittany; and after they had pursued their missionary career in this country for some time, the fame of St. Columbanus reached the ears of Sigibert, king of Austrasia, the husband of Brunichildis. He sent for the Irish saint, begged him to remain in his kingdom, and at length overcame his reluctance to do so by the gift of a ruined village named Anagratis, in a wild and rocky region of the Vosges.

Here Columbanus established his monastery, and here he dwelt in peace during the stormy years that followed the death of Sigibert. There was nothing in his possessions to tempt the cupidity of the fierce dukes and simoniacal bishops of the Frankish kingdoms. The diet of Columbanus and his monks was for some time the bark of trees, wild herbs, and little crab apples, but, as we afterwards hear of the monks ploughing and reaping, we may infer that, at any rate from their second season onwards, they were not destitute of bread. For the saint himself, even the austerities of the coenobitic life were not sufficient. Leaving his monastery to govern itself for a time, he retired to a cave in the rocks, which was already the abode of a bear. On hearing the word of command from the saint, "Depart hence, and never again travel along these paths", the wild beast meekly obeyed. The fame of the preaching of the saint, and, still more, the fame of his miracles and exorcisms, drew so large a number of postulants to Anagratis that Columbanus found it necessary to establish another monastery, larger and more famous, at Luxovium (now Luxeuil), which was situated within the dominion of Guntram of Burgundy, and was eight miles south of Anagratis. This place, though a ruin like the other, was the ruin of a larger and less sequestered settlement. It still shows the remains of a Roman aqueduct, and when Columbanus and his companions settled within its walls, the hot springs which had supplied its baths were still flowing, and the marble limbs of the once-worshipped gods of the heathen gleamed through the thickets which had been growing there probably since the days of Attila. Eventually, even Luxovium was found to be insufficient to hold all the monks who flocked to its holy shelter, and a third monastery was reared on the neighboring site of Ad Fontanas.

But all this fame and popularity brought its inevitable Nemesis of jealousy and dislike. Columbanus was revered by the common people, but with the high ecclesiastics of Gaul his relations were probably unfriendly from the first. We can see that there was not, and could not be, sympathy between the high-wrought, mystical Irish saint, and the coarse and greedy prelates of Merovingian Gaul. He was, intensely, that which they only pretended to be. To him the kingdom of God was the only joy, the awful judgment of Christ the only terror. They were thinking the while of the sensual delights to be derived from the revenues of the bishoprics which they had obtained by simony. If they trembled, it was at the thought of the probable vengeance of the heirs of some blood-feud, the next of kin of some Frankish warrior whom they had lawlessly put to death. Intellectually, too, the gulf between the Gaulish bishops and Columbanus was almost as wide as the moral divergence. He retained to the end of his days that considerable tincture of classical learning which he had imbibed under Sinell and Comgall. He and his Irish companions were steeped in Virgil and Horace. When they sat down to write even on religious subjects, quotations from the Aeneid flowed with only too great copiousness from their pens; and the Latin prose of Columbanus himself, though often stilted and somewhat obscure, is almost always strictly grammatical. Comparing him with one of the most learned of his Gaulish contemporaries, Gregory of Tours, whose countless grammatical blunders would be terribly avenged on an English schoolboy, we see that the Irish saint moved in an altogether different intellectual plane from his Gaulish episcopal neighbors, and we can easily believe that he did not conceal his contempt for their ignorance and barbarism.

Another cause of difference between Columbanus and his Frankish neighbors, and one which could be decorously put forward by the latter as the reason for their dislike, was the divergence between him and them as to the correct time for keeping Easter. In this matter the Irish ecclesiastics, with true Celtic conservatism, adhered to the form of cycle which had been universal in the West for almost two centuries, while the Frankish bishops reckoned their Easter-day according to the table which was published by Victorius in the year 457, and which, though advocating the old Roman usage, noted also that of Alexandria, and in cases of divergent Easters left the ultimate decision to the Pope. The difference, much and earnestly insisted upon in the letters of Columbanus, turned chiefly on two points: (1) The Irish churchmen insisted that in no case could it be right to celebrate Easter before the 25th of March, on which they placed the vernal equinox, while the rest of Christendom had adopted the 21st; (2) they maintained that since the Passover had been ordained to fall on the 14th day of the lunar month, it was right to celebrate Easter upon it, and they consequently allowed the great festival to range between that and the 20th day. The Alexandrian Church restricted the celebration to the interval between the 15th and 21st days: Victorius, in conformity with the old Latin rule, to that between the 16th and 22nd. In theory it would probably be admitted that the Irishmen were nearer to the primitive idea of a Christian festival based on the Jewish Passover; but in practice—to say nothing of the unreasonableness of perpetuating discord on a point of such infinitely small importance—by harping as they did continually on the words the "14th day" they gave their opponents the opportunity of fastening upon them the name of *Quartodeciman,* and thereby bringing them under the anathema pronounced by the Nicene Council on an entirely different form of dissent.

On this subject, the celebration of Easter, which absorbed an absurdly large amount of his time and thoughts, Columbanus addressed a letter to Pope Gregory the Great. The dedication is too characteristic not to be given in full:

"To the holy lord and father in Christ, the most comely ornament of the Roman Church, the most august flower, so to speak, of all this languishing Europe, the illustrious overseer, to him who is skilled to enquire into the theory of the Divine causality, I Bar-Jonah (a mean dove) send greeting in Christ".

It will be seen that Columbanus, here, as in several other places, indulges in a kind of bilingual pun on his own name. The Hebrew equivalent of Columba, a dove, is Jonah. So here he makes Columbanus equivalent to Bar-Jonah, which in his modesty he translates "vilis Columba"; and elsewhere he recognizes that it is his fate to be thrown overboard like his namesake Jonah, for the peace and safety of the Church.

The letter itself argues with much boldness and some skill against the practice of celebrating Easter at a time when the moon does not rise till after two watches of the night are past, and when darkness is thus triumphing over light. He warns the Pope not to set himself in opposition to the great Jerome by condemning the Paschal calculations of Anatolius, whom Jerome had praised as a man of marvelous learning. He asks for advice on two points, (1) whether he ought to communicate with simoniacal and adulterous bishops, and (2) what is to be done with monks who, through desire of greater holiness, leave the monasteries in which they have taken the vows, and retire to desert places, without the leave of their abbot. He expresses his deep regret at not being able to visit Rome for the sake of seeing Gregory, and asks to have some of the Pope's commentary on Ezekiel sent to him, having already perused with extreme pleasure his book, sweeter than honey, on the *Regula Pastoralis*.

It would be interesting to know what reply the great Roman Pope made to the great Irish abbot, but Gregory's letter to Columbanus, if written, has not come down to us. Some years later, about 603 or 604, a synod was held (probably at Chalons-sur-Saone) at which the question of the schismatical observance of Easter in Luxovium and the sister monasteries was the chief subject of discussion. To the Gaulish bishops "his holy fathers and brethren in Christ, Columba the sinner" addressed a remarkable letter. He praised them for at last assembling in council, even though it was in order to judge him; and this praise recalls Gregory's oft-repeated censure of the Gaulish bishops for their neglect of synodal action. After exhorting them to the practice of humility, he discusses at some length the great Paschal question, and begs them not to celebrate the Resurrection before the Passion by allowing Easter to fall before the equinox, and not to overpass the 20th day of the lunar month, "lest they should perform the sacrament of the New Testament without the authority of the Old". Then he turns to more personal affairs, and utters a pathetic prayer for peace. "In the name of Him who said, 'Depart from Me : I never knew you', suffer me, while keeping your peace and friendship, to be silent in these woods, and to live near the bones of my seventeen departed brethren. Suffer me still to live among you as I have done for these past twelve years, and to continue praying for you as I have ever done and ought to do. Let Gaul, I pray you, contain both you and me, since the kingdom of heaven will contain us if we are of good desert, and fulfill the hope of our one calling in Christ Jesus. Far be it from me to contend with you and to give our enemies, the Pagans and the Jews, occasion to triumph in our dissensions. For if it be in God's ordering that ye should expel me from this desert place, whither I came from across the seas for the love of my Lord Jesus Christ, I can only say with the prophet [Jonah] : 'If for my sake this tempest come upon you, take me and cast me into the sea, that this turmoil may cease'."

Thus not only amid the increasing cares of his three great monasteries, but amid increasing conflicts with the hostile bishops of Gaul, passed the middle years of the life of Columbanus. If men hated him, the brute creation loved him. Many of the stories told of him reveal that mysterious sympathy with the lower animals which he shared with an even greater religious revivalist, St. Francis of Assisi. One of his disciples long after told his biographer that often when he had been walking lonely in the desert, his lips moving in prayer, he had been seen to call birds or wild creatures to him, who never disobeyed the call. Then would the saint stroke or pat them, and the shy, wild things rejoiced like a little dog in his caresses. Thus, too, would he call down the little squirrels from the tops of the trees, and they would nestle close to his neck, or play hide and seek in the folds of his great white scapular.

We have already heard how the bear at the summons of Columbanus quietly yielded up to him its dwelling in the cave. One day when he was walking through the forest, with his Bible hung by a strap to his shoulder, he pondered the question whether it were worse to fall into the hands of wild beasts or of evil men. Suddenly, as if to solve the problem, twelve wolves rushed forth, and surrounded him on the rip-lit hand and on the left. He remained immovable, but cried aloud, "Oh! Lord, make haste to help me". The savage creatures came near, and gathered round him, smelling at his garments; but, finding him unmoved, left him unharmed, and disappeared in the forest. When he came forth from the wood, he thought that he heard the voices of Suevic robbers roaming: through the desolate region, but he saw not their forms, and whether the sounds were real, or an illusion of the Evil One to try his constancy, he never knew.

One day, when he came into the monastery at Luxovium to take some food, he laid aside the gloves which had shielded his hands while working in the field. A mischievous raven carried off the gloves from the stone before the monastery doors on which the saint had laid them. When the meal was ended, and the monks came forth, the gloves were nowhere to be found. Questions at once arose who had done this thing. Said the saint, "The thief is none other than that bird which Noah sent forth out of the ark, and which wandered to and fro over the earth, nor ever returned. And that bird shall not rear its young unless it speedily bring back that which it has stolen". Suddenly the raven appeared in the midst of the crowd, bearing the gloves in its beak, and, having laid them down, stood there meekly awaiting the chastisement which it was conscious of having deserved. But the saint ordered it to fly away unharmed. Once upon a time a bear lusted after the apples which formed the sole fruit of the saint and his companions. But when Columbanus directed his servant, Magnoald, to divide the apples into two portions, assigning one to the bear, and reserving the other for the use of the saint, the beast, with wonderful docility, obeyed, and, contenting itself with its own portion, never dared to touch the apples which were reserved for the man of God. Another bear, howling round the dead body of a stag, obeyed his bidding, and left the hide untouched, that out of it might be made shoes for the use of the brotherhood; and the wolves, which gathered at the scent of the savoury morsel, stood afar off with their noses in the air, not daring to approach the carcass on which the mysterious spell had been laid.

But the time came when the saint had to solve his own riddle, by proof that men, and still more women, could be harder and more unpitying even than the wolves. The young king of Burgundy, Theodoric, already, at the age of fourteen, had a bastard son born to him, and by the year 610 he had several children, none of them the issue of his lawful wife. These little ones their great-grandmother, Brunichildis, brought one day into the holy man's presence, when he visited her at the royal villa of Brocoriacum. Said Columbanus," What do you mean by bringing these children here?". "They are the sons of a king", answered Brunichildis, "fortify them with your blessing". "Never", said he, "shall these children, the offspring of the brothel, inherit the royal scepter". In a rage, the old queen ordered the little ones to depart. As the saint crossed the threshold of the palace, a thunderstorm or an earthquake shook the fabric, striking terror into the souls of all, but not even so was the fierce heart of Brunichildis turned from her purpose of revenge.

There were negotiations and conversations between the saint and the sovereign. Theodoric, who throughout seems to have been less embittered against the saint than his grandmother, said one day, in answer to a torrent of angry rebuke for his profligacy, "Do you hope to win from me the crown of martyrdom? I am not so mad as to perpetrate such a crime". But the austere, unsocial habits of the saint had made him many enemies. There was a long unsettled debt of hatred from the bishops of Gaul for the schismatical Easter and many other causes of offence; and the courtiers with one voice declared that they would not tolerate the continued presence among them of one who did not deem them worthy of his companionship. Thus, though the harsh words concerning the royal bastards may have been the torch which finally kindled the flame, it is clear that there was much smoldering indignation against the saint in the hearts of nobles and churchmen before ever these words were spoken. By the common people, on the other hand, Columbanus seems to have been generally beloved.

The resultant of all these conflicting forces was an order from the Court that Columbanus should leave his monastery of Luxovium, and take up his residence in a sort of *libera custodia* at Vesontio *(Besançon)*. Finding himself laxly guarded, he went up one Sunday to the top of the mountain which overlooks the city of Besançon and the winding Doubs. He remained till noon, half expecting that his keepers would come to fetch him; but, as none appeared, he descended the mountain on the other side, and took the road to Luxovium. By this daring defiance of the royal orders he filled up the measure of his offences, and Brunichildis at once sent a cohort of soldiers to arrest the holy man and expel him from the kingdom. They found him in the church of the monastery, singing psalms with the congregation of the brethren. It seemed as if force would have to be used in order to tear him from his beloved Luxovium, but at length, yielding to the earnest entreaties of his monks, and of the soldiers, who prayed for forgiveness even while laying hold of the saint's garments, he consented to go with them quietly. The monks all wished to follow him, but only his Irish fellow-countrymen and their Breton comrades were allowed to do so, while those of Gaulish birth were ordered to remain behind. He was taken by way of Besançon and Autun to Nevers, and there was put on shipboard and conveyed down the Loire to Nantes. Many miracles, especially the cure of those afflicted with evil spirits, marked his progress. At Auxerre he said to a certain Ragamund, who came to act as his escort, "Remember, oh! Ragamund, that this Chlotochar, whom you now despise, will within three years be your lord and master". The prophecy was the more remarkable because the king of Neustria was at that time much the weakest member of the Frankish partnership, and quite overshadowed by his cousins of Austrasia and Burgundy. Theodoric, especially, was then at the zenith of his power; and the route traversed by Columbanus and his guards shows that something like three-quarters of that which is now France must have owned his dominion. When, in their voyage down the stream, they came opposite the shrine of the blessed Martin of Tours, Columbanus earnestly besought his keepers to let him land and pay his devotions at the holy sepulcher. The inexorable guards refused, and Columbanus stood upon the deck, raising sad eyes to heaven in mute protest against their cruelty. But suddenly the vessel stopped in her course, as though she had let down her anchor, and then began mysteriously to turn her head towards the watergate of Tours. Awed by this portent, the guards made no further resistance to his will; and Columbanus, landing, spent the night in vigils at the tomb of St. Martin. It was a memorable scene, and one worthy to be celebrated by an artist's or a poet's genius; for there the greatest Gaulish saint of the sixth century knelt by the tomb of his greatest predecessor of the fourth century, the upbraider of Brunichildis communed with the spirit of the vanquisher of Maximus.

When day dawned Columbanus was invited by Leuparius, bishop of Tours, to share his hospitality. For the sake of his weary brethren he accepted the invitation, though it came from a Gaulish bishop, and spent the day at the Episcopal palace. At the evening meal, when many guests were present, Leuparius, either through ignorance or want of tact, asked him why he was returning to his native country. "Because that dog, Theodoric, has forced me away from my brethren", said the hot-tempered saint. At the table was a guest named Chrodoald, a kinsman by marriage of Theudebert, but loyal to Theodoric. He, with demure face, said to the man of God, "Methinks it is better to drink milk than wormwood", thus gently hinting that such bitter words ill became saintly lips. Columbanus said, "I suppose you are a liege man of Theodoric?". "I am", he answered, "and will keep my plighted faith so long as I live". "Then you will doubtless be glad to take a message from me to your master and friend. Go, tell him that within three years he and all his race shall be utterly rooted up by the Lord of Hosts". "Oh! servant of God", said Chrodoald, "why dost thou utter such terrible words?". "Because I cannot keep silence when the Lord God would have me speak". Like another Jeremiah denouncing woe on the impious Jehoiakim was this Irish saint, as he hurled his fierce predictions among the trembling courtiers of Theodoric.

After all, the dauntless Irishman was not carried back to his native land. When he arrived at Nantes, the bishop and count of that city, in obedience to the king's orders, set him on board a merchant vessel carrying cargo to "the Scots", that is to the inhabitants of Ireland. But though the ship, impelled by the rowers and by favoring gales, was carried out some way from the land, great rolling waves soon forced her back to the shore. The ship-master perceived that his saintly cargo was the reason of his disappointment. He put Columbanus and his friends ashore, and the ship proceeded on her voyage without difficulty.

Columbanus, who seems to have been left at liberty to go whither he would, so long as he did not return to Burgundy, visited Chlotochar in his Neustrian capital, gently chided him for his Merovingian immoralities, and advised him to remain neutral in the war which had now broken out between Theodoric and Theudebert. Under the protection of an escort given him by Chlotochar he reached the dominions of Theudebert, who gave him a hearty welcome, and invited him to choose some place in the Austrasian territory suitable for the erection of a monastery, which might serve as a base of operations for the missionary work planned by him among the pagans on the border. (In the course of this journey he arrived at the villa of Vulciacum on the banks of the Marne, where he was welcomed by its lord, Autharius, and his wife Aiga. He gave his blessing to their children Ado and Dado, who afterwards rose high in the service of the kings Chlotochar and Dagobert, but retired from the world, and founded monasteries in the Jura according to the rule of Columbanus. Note here the names of this Austrasian nobleman and his wife, so similar to those of two successive Lombard kings, Authari and Ago = Agilulf). Such a retreat, after two abortive attempts by the lake of Zurich and at Arbon, he found finally at Bregenz, by the Lake of Constance, whither he travelled up the Rhine, doubtless with much toil of oar to the rowers assigned him by the king. The barbarous Alamanni who dwelt by the banks of the Upper Rhine were still worshippers of Wodan, and filled a large barrel, holding ten gallons, with the beer which they brewed and drunk in his honor. When the saint heard from the idolaters what hateful work they were engaged in, he drew near and breathed upon the barrel, which suddenly burst asunder with a loud crash, spilling all the liquor on the ground.

In the 'temple' of Bregenz (a ruined Christian oratory once dedicated to St. Aurelia) the stranger found three brazen images fixed to the wall. These images received the idolatrous worship of the people, who said, "These are our ancient gods, by whose help and comfort we have been preserved alive to this day". His friend and follower, Gallus, who was able to preach not only in Latin, but in the "barbaric tongue", exhorted the multitude who had assembled in the temple to turn from these vain idols and worship the Father and the Son. Then, in the sight of all, Columbanus seized the images, hammered them into fragments, and threw the pieces into the lake. Some of the bystanders were enraged at this insult to their gods, but the more part were converted by the preaching of Gallus. Columbanus sprinkled the temple with holy water, and, moving through it in procession with his monks chanting a psalm, dedicated it afresh to God and St. Aurelia.

This Gallus, whose knowledge of the Suevic tongue proved so helpful on this occasion, was the same St. Gall who, by the monastery which he founded, has given his name to one of the cantons of Switzerland. He was an Irishman of noble birth who came with Columbanus to the country of the Franks, and accompanied him in all his journeys but the last. From his life we learn some comparatively unimportant particulars about the life of the saint and his followers in Switzerland which need not be repeated here. But it would be wrong to omit one narrative which has in it a touch of poetry, and which shows how the grandeurs of the Swiss landscape blended themselves with those thoughts of the spirit world which were ever uppermost in the souls of these denizens of the convent. St. Gallus, who was the chief fisherman of the party, and who in fact provided all their food except the wild fowl and the fruits of the wilderness, was once, in the silence of the night, casting his nets into the waters of Lake Constance, when he heard the Demon of the mountain calling from the cliffs with a loud voice to the Demon of the lake. "Arise", said he, for my help, and let us cast forth these strangers from their haunts; for, coming from afar, they have expelled me from my temple, have ground my images to powder, and drawn away all my people after them". Then the Demon of the Lake answered, "All that thou complainest of I know too well. There is one of them who ever harasses me here in the water, and lays waste my realm. His nets I can never break, nor himself can I deceive, because the divine name which he invokes is ever on his lips; and by this continual watchfulness he frustrates all our snares". Hearing these words, the man of God fortified himself with the sign of the cross, and said, "In the name of the Lord Jesus Christ I command you that ye depart from this place, and do not presume to injure any one here". Then he returned and told the abbot what he had heard. The brethren were assembled at once in the church, though it was the dead of night, and their voices filled the air with psalmody. But even before they began the holy song, there were heard dread voices of the Demons floating about from summit to summit of the mountains, cries and wails as of those who departed in sadness from their home, and confused shrieks as of those who were pursued by the avenger.

About this time visions of missionary service among the Slavonic tribes on the border or Venetia began to float before the mind of Columbanus, but an angel appeared to him in a dream, and, holding forth a map of the world, indicated to him Italy as the scene of his future labors. Not yet, however, he was told, was the time come for this enterprise: meanwhile he was to wait in patience till the way should open for his leaving Austrasia. It was by the bloody sword of fratricidal war that the way to the saint's last harvest-field was laid open. It has been told how the long grudge between the two grandsons of Brunichildis burst at last into a flame, and hostilities began. Columbanus, with prophetic foresight of the result, perhaps also with statesmanlike insight into the comparative strength of the two kingdoms, left his solitude, sought the Court of Theudebert, and exhorted him to decline the contest and at once enter the ranks of the clergy. The king and all his courtiers raised a shout of indignant derision. "Never was it heard that a Merovingian, once raised to the throne, of his own will became a priest". "He who will not voluntarily accept the clerical honor", said Columbanus, "will soon find himself a clergyman in his own despite"; and therewith he departed to his hermitage. The prophecy was soon fulfilled. The two armies met on the field of Toul. Theudebert was defeated, fled, gathered a fresh army, and was again defeated on the field of Tolbiac, where a terrible slaughter was made in the ranks of both armies. Betrayed by his friends, he was captured by his brother and carried into the presence of their grandmother, who had never forgiven him or his for her exile from Austrasia. She at once shore his long Merovingian locks, and turned him into a tonsured cleric; and not many days after, she or Theodoric ordered him to be put to death. Close upon these events followed, as has been already related, the sudden death of Theodoric II, the murder of his children, and the reunion of the whole Frankish monarchy under the scepter of the lately despised and flouted Chlotochar.

The bloody day of Tolbiac was seen in a dream by Columbanus, overtaken by sudden slumber as he was sitting reading on the rotten trunk of a fallen oak tree in his beloved wilderness. The disciple who listened to his story of the battle said, "Oh, my father, pray for Theudebert, that he may conquer his and our enemy, Theodoric". "Unwise and irreligious is thy advice", said Columbanus. "Not thus hath the Lord commanded us, who told us to pray even for our enemies". Afterwards, when the tidings came of the great encounter, the disciple learned that it had been fought at the very day and hour when the saint beheld it in his vision.

The battle of Tolbiac broke the last thread that connected Columbanus with the kingdom of the Franks, and accordingly, leaving Gaul and Germany behind him, he pressed forward into Italy. One only of his faithful hand of followers did not accompany him. Gallus, who had sickened with fever, and who perhaps felt that his special gifts as a missionary to the Suevi would be wasted when he had crossed the Alps, remained behind on the shores of Lake Constance, which he had learned to love. As St. Paul with Mark when he departed from him and Barnabas at Perga, so was Columbanus deeply grieved with the slackness of spirit of his disciple, upon whom he laid a solemn injunction never to presume to celebrate mass during the lifetime of his master.

Columbanus was received with every mark of honor and esteem by Agilulf and Theudelinda. He remained apparently for some months at Milan, arguing with the Arian ecclesiastics who still haunted the Lombard Court. "By the cautery of the Scriptures", as his biographer quaintly says, "he dissected and destroyed the deceits of the Arian infidelity, and he moreover published against them a book of marvelous Science". But all men who knew Columbanus knew that he would not be content to dwell long in palaces or cities, but that he must be sighing for the solitude of the wilderness and the silence of the convent. It was doubtless from a knowledge of this desire that a certain man named Jocundus came one day to King Agilulf, and began to expatiate on the advantages for a monastic life afforded by the little village of Bobium (Bobbio), about twenty-five miles from Placentia. This place, situated on the banks of the little river Trebia (which witnessed the first of Hannibal's great victories over the Romans), lies away from the great high-roads of the Lombard plain, its cities and its broad river, and nestles in a fertile valley shut in by the peaks of the central Apennine chain. It has its own little stream, the Bobbio, confluent with the Trebia and abounding in fish. Everything marked it out as being, according to the description of Jocundus, a place well suited for the cultivation of monastic excellence; and thither Columbanus joyfully retired. He found there a half-ruined basilica of St. Peter, which he at once began to restore with the help of his followers. The tall firs of the Apennines were felled, and their trunks were transported over rough and devious ways down into the fertile valley. The alacrity of the aged saint, who personally helped in the pious toil, became in the next generation the subject of a miracle. There was a beam which, if placed on level ground, thirty or forty men would have drawn with difficulty. The man of God, coming up to it, placed the immense weight on the shoulders of himself and two or three of his friends; and where before, on account of the roughness of the road, they had, though unencumbered, walked with difficulty, they now, laden with the beam's weight, moved rapidly forward. The parts seemed reversed, and they who were bearing the burden walked with triumphant ease, as if they were being borne along by others.

Such were the beginnings of the great monastic house of Bobbio. It has for us a special interest (and this is our justification for spending so long a time over the life of its founder), for there can be little doubt that the monastery of Bobbio, even more than the holiness and popularity of Queen Theudelinda, was the means of accomplishing that conversion of the Lombards to the Catholic form of Christianity, which at last, though not in the first or second generation, ended the religious duality of Italy. True to his early literary and philosophical instincts, Columbanus seems, with all his austerities, ever to have preserved the character of an educated Churchman. Learned as the Order of Benedict became in after years, we shall probably not err in supposing that at this time it was surpassed in learning by the Order of Columbanus. The library of Bobbio was for many centuries one of the richest, probably *the* richest, in Italy, and many of the most precious treasures now deposited in the Ambrosian library at Milan have been taken thither from the monastery of Columbanus.

It is noteworthy that among these treasures are to be found some considerable fragments of the Gothic Bible of Ulfilas, and of his Commentary on the Gospel of John. Apparently Columbanus, in his controversies with the Arians at Milan, did not neglect the wholesome practice of studying his opponents' arguments in their own books, and to this wise liberality of thought may have been due some portion of his success. Nor was the secular, Pagan side of literature unrepresented in the library of Bobbio. The great palimpsest now in the Vatican, in which Cardinal Mai discovered, under St. Augustine's Commentary on the Psalms (119-140), Cicero's lost treatise, *De Republica*, bears yet this inscription on one of its pages, "Liber Sancti Columbani de Boboi".

A quaint exemplification of the saint's unextinguished love for classical literature is furnished by the verses which, at the age of seventy-two, and probably within a few months of his death, he addressed to a certain friend of his named Fedolius. They are written in a metre which he calls Sapphic, but which a modern scholar would rather call Adonic, being entirely composed of those short lines (dactyl and trochee) with which the Sapphic verse terminates :—

Take, I beseech you,
Now from my hands this
Trumpery gift of
Two-footed verses;
And for your own part
Frequently send us
Verses of yours by
Way of repayment.
For as the sun-baked
Fields when the winds change
Joy in the soft shower,
So has your page oft
Gladdened my spirit.

Columbanus then proceeds through about eighty lines to warn his friend against avarice. The examples of the curse of riches are all drawn from classical mythology. The Golden Fleece, the Golden Apple, the Golden Shower, Pygmalion, Polydorus, Amphiaraus, Achilles, are all pressed into the poet's service: and as the easy and, on the whole, creditable lines flow on, the idea is suggested to the reader's mind that probably Fedolius was no more inclined to avarice than his adviser, but that the commonplaces about avarice expressed themselves so easily in the Adonic metre that the saint had not the heart to deny himself the pleasant exercise. He ends at last thus:—

"Be it enough, then,
Thus to have spun my
Garrulous verses.
For when you read them,
Haply the metre
May to you seem strange.
Yet 'tis the same which
She, the renowned bard
Sappho, the Greek, once
Used for her verses.
You, too (the fancy
Haply may seize you
Thus to compose verse).
Note my instructions :
Always a dactyl
Stands in the first place;
After it comes nex
Strictly a trochee,

> But you may always
> End with a spondee.
> Now then, my loved one,
> Brother Fedolis,
> Who when you choose are
> Sweeter than nectar,
> Leave the more pompous
> Songs of the sages,
> And with a meek mind
> Bear with my trifling.
> So may the World-King,
> Christ, the alone
> Son Of the Eternal,
> Crown you with Life's joys.
> He in his Sire's name
> Reigneth o'er all things
> Now and for ever.
> Such is the verse I have framed, though tortured by cruel diseases,
> Born of this feeble frame, born too of the sadness of old age.
> For while the years of my life have hurried me downward and onward,
> Lo! I have passed e'en now the eighteenth Olympian milestone.
> All things are passing away : Time flies and the traitor returns not.
> Live : farewell. In joy or in grief remember that Age comes".

These dallyings with the classic Muse surprise us, not unpleasantly, in the life of so great a saint, who was the founder of a rule more austere than that of St. Benedict. Still greater becomes our surprise when we learn that, according to a tradition which, though late, seems to be not wholly unworthy of belief, even monastic austerity was not sufficient for the saint in these years of his failing strength, and that he must needs resume the life of a hermit. To this day a cave is pointed out in a mountain gorge a few miles from Bobbio, to which Columbanus is said to have retired—for the last few months, perhaps years, of his life, only returning to the monastery on Sundays and saints' days to spend those seasons of gladness with his brethren.

We hear more of Columbanus in the monastery and in the cave than in the palace, but there can be no doubt that his interviews with Agilulf and Theudelinda were frequent and important, he helped the Bavarian queen with all the energy of his Celtic nature in fighting against Arianism, but he also (unfortunately for his reputation with the ultraorthodox) threw himself with some vehemence into her party in the dismal controversy of the Three Chapters. For Theudelinda, it is evident, notwithstanding the pious exhortations of popes and archbishops, still remained unconvinced of the damnation of the three Syrian ecclesiastics; and now, finding that the new light which had risen upon Italy was in the same quarter of the theological heaven with herself, she determined to use his influence on behalf of the cause which she held dear. At her request and Agilulf's, Columbanus addressed a long letter to Pope Boniface IV, the third successor of Gregory the Great in St. Pete's chair.

The address of his letter is peculiar. Columbanus often alludes to the garrulity which has been for centuries the characteristic of his race, and as we seem to hear the words of this fulsome dedication, uttered in the rich, soft Irish brogue, an epithet unknown to the dignity of history seems the only one which will describe the saintly communication :—

"To the most beautiful Head of all the Churches of Europe, to the sweetest Pope, to the lofty Chief, to the Shepherd of Shepherds, to the most reverend Sentinel, the humblest to the highest, the least to the greatest, the rustic to the citizen, the mean speaker to the very eloquent, the last to the first, the foreigner to the native, the beggar to the very powerful: Oh, the new and strange marvel! a rare bird, even a Dove, dares to write to his father Bonifacius".

However, when Columbanus has fairly commenced the letter thus strangely preluded, no one can accuse him of indulging in "blarney". He speaks to the Pope with noble independence, recognizing fully the importance of his position as representative of St. Peter and St. Paul, but telling him plainly that he, the Pope, has incurred suspicion of heresy, and exhorting him not to slumber, as his predecessor Vigilius did, who by his lack of vigilance has brought all this confusion upon the Church.

It is not very clear what Columbanus desired the Pope to do, for the letter, which is inordinately long and shows traces of the garrulity of age as well as of the eloquence of the Irishman, is singularly destitute of practical suggestions, and evinces no grasp at all of the theological problem. It appears, however, that he recommends the Pope to summon a council, and that he does not recognise "a certain so-called fifth council in which Vigilius was said to have received those ancient heretics, Eutyches, Nestorius, and Dioscorus". What we are concerned with, however, is the information afforded us by this letter as to the sentiments of the Lombard king and queen; and this is so important that it will be well to extract the sentences containing it in full. "If I am accused of presumption, and asked as Moses was : Who made thee a judge and a ruler over us?, I answer that it is not presumption to speak when the edification of the Church requires it; and if the person of the speaker be caviled at, consider not who I, the speaker, am, but what it is that I say. For why should the Christian foreigner hold his peace when his *Arian neighbor* has long said in a loud voice that which he wishes to say, "For better are the wounds of a friend than the deceitful kisses of an enemy?"... I, who have come from the end of the world, am struck with terror at what I behold, and turn in my perplexity to thee, who are the only hope of princes through the honor of the holy Apostle Peter. But when the frail bark of my intellect could not, in the language of the Scriptures, "launch out into the deep", but rather remained fixed in one place (for the paper cannot hold all that my mind from various causes desires to include in the narrow limits of a letter), I found myself in addition *entreated by the king* to suggest in detail to your pious ears the whole story of his grief; for he mourns for the schism of his people, for his queen, for his son, perchance also for himself: since h*e is reported to have said that he, too, would believe if he could know the certainty of the matter...* Pardon me, I pray, who may seem to you an obscure prater, too free and rough with his tongue, but who cannot write otherwise than he has done in such a cause. I have proved my loyalty, and the zeal of my faith, when I have chosen to give opportunity to my rebukers rather than to close my mouth, however unlearned it be, in such a cause. These rebukers are the men of whom Jeremiah has said, "They bend their tongues like their bow for lies"... But *when a "Gentile king begs a foreigner, when a Lombard begs a dull Scot to write,* when the wave of an ancient torrent thus flows backward to its source, who would not feel his wonder overcome his fear of calumny? I at any rate will not tremble, nor fear the tongues of men when I am engaged in the cause of God.

"Such, then, are my suggestions. They come, I admit, from one who is torpid in action, from one who says rather than does; from one who is called Jonah in Hebrew, Peristera in Greek, Columba in Latin; and though I am generally known only by the name which I bear in your language, let me now use my old Hebrew name, since I have almost suffered Jonah's shipwreck. But grant me the pardon which I have often craved, since I have been forced to write by necessity, not from self-conceit. For almost at my first entrance into this land I was met by the letters of a certain person, who said that I must beware of you, for you had fallen away into the error of Nestorius. Whom I answered briefly and with astonishment that I did not believe his allegation; but lest by any chance I should be opposing the truth, I afterwards varied my reply, and sent it along with his letter to you for perusal.

"After this, another occasion for writing was laid upon me *by the command of Agilulf,* whose request threw me into a strangely blended state of wonder and anxiety, for what had occurred seemed to me hardly possible without a miracle. For these kings have long strengthened the Arian pestilence in this land by trampling on the Catholic faith; but now they ask that *our* faith shall be strengthened. Haply Christ, from whose favor every good gift comes, has looked upon us with pitying eye. We certainly are most miserable, if the scandal is continued any longer by our means. Therefore *the king asks you,* and the queen asks you, and all men ask you, that as speedily as possible all may become one; that there may be peace in the country, peace among the faithful; finally, that all may become one flock, of which Christ shall be the shepherd. Oh, king of kings! do thou follow Peter, and let all the Church follow thee. What is sweeter than peace after war? What more delightful than the union of brethren long separated? How pleasant to waiting parents the return of the long-absent son! Even so, to God the Father the peace of His sons will be a joy for countless ages, and the gladness of our mother the Church will be a sempiternal triumph".

The letter ends with an entreaty for the prayers of the Pope on behalf of the writer, "the vilest of sinners".

Now I must ask the reader to set over against this letter of Columbanus, written probably about 613 or 614, very shortly before Agilulf's death, the following statement of Paulus, which occurs at an early point in the history of his reign :—"By means of this queen [Theudelinda] the Church of God obtained much advantage. For the Lombards, when they were still involved in the error of heathenism, plundered all the property of the Churches. But the king, being influenced by this queen's healthful intercession, *both held the Catholic faith*, and bestowed many possessions on the Church of Christ, and restored the bishops, who were in a depressed and abject condition, to the honor of their wonted dignity".

These words certainly seem to imply that Agilulf was persuaded by his wife to embrace her form of faith. We should indeed have expected some other word than "held" to describe the conversion of a heretic, and throughout the paragraph the historian is thinking more of the outward and visible effects of the king's conversion than of the internal process. Still, the passage cannot, as it seems to me, be made to assert anything less than the catholicity of Agilulf, and it does not describe a deathbed conversion, but the whole character of his reign.

On the other hand, the letters of Gregory for the first fourteen years of that reign, and this letter of Columbanus within a couple of years of its close, bring before us an entirely different mental state. The Agilulf whom they disclose to us is tolerant, and more than tolerant, of the religion of the queen who has invited him to share her throne.

He allows his son, the heir to the Lombard crown, to be baptized with Catholic rites. He is anxious that the Three Chapters Schism should be ended, and that there should be religious peace in his land. If the orthodox would but agree among themselves, and not worry him about the damnation of Theodore, Ibas, and Theodoret, he is almost ready himself to believe as they believe, but meanwhile he is still "vicinus Arius"; and in the Arian faith, for anything that the contemporary correspondence shows us, he died as well as lived. Different readers will perhaps come to different conclusions on such conflicting evidence, but upon the whole I am inclined to disbelieve the alleged conversion of Agilulf.

The whole discussion is to my mind another evidence of the loose, limp hold which the Lombards had on any form of Christian faith. The Vandals, in the bitterness of their Arianism, made the lives of their Catholic subjects in Africa miserable to them. Visigothic Alaric, Arian though he was, would rather lose a campaign than fight on Easter Day; and his successors, when they at length embraced the orthodox form of faith, became such ardent Catholics that they virtually handed over the government of the state to the councils of bishops. But the Lombards, though heterodox or heathen enough to plunder and harry the Church, had no interest in the theological battle, and whether their greatest king was Arian or orthodox was probably more than many of his counselors knew, perhaps more than he could himself have told them.

The last event recorded in the life of Columbanus was the visit of Eustasius, his dear friend, disciple, and successor in the Abbotship of Luxovium. He came on an embassy from Chlotochar, now, after the death of Theodoric, unquestioned lord of all the Frankish kingdoms. Chlotochar knew well how the saint had been harassed by their common foe, Brunichildis, and how in the days of his own humiliation Columbanus had predicted his coming triumph. Gladly, therefore, would the king have had him return to Luxovium, that all things might go on as aforetime in the Burgundian monastery. But Columbanus probably felt himself too old and weary to undertake a second transplantation. He kept Eustasius with him for some time, giving him divers counsels as to the government of the monastery, and then dismissed him with a grateful message to Chlotochar, commending Luxovium to his special protection.

After a year's residence at Bobbio Columbanus died, on the 21st of November, 615, having on his death-bed handed his staff to a deacon, with orders to carry it to Gallus as a sign that he was forgiven for his old offence, and was now at liberty to resume his ministrations at the altar. The rule of Columbanus, somewhat harsher than that of Benedict, both in respect of abstinence from food and of corporal chastisement tor trivial offences, spread far and wide over Gaul. Luxovium (or Luxeuil) became the mother of many vast monasteries, the schools of which were especially renowned for the admirable education which the sons of Frankish nobles there received from the disciples of Columbanus. In Italy, already preoccupied by the followers of Benedict, the spread of the Columbanian rule was probably less universal, as Bobbio does not seem to have vied with Luxeuil in the number of her daughter convents. But in all, whether Gaulish or Italian, the rule of Columbanus early gave way to that of Benedict, in whose monastic code there was perhaps less of the wild Celtic genius, more Roman common sense, less attempt to wind men up to an unattainable ideal of holiness, more consideration for human weakness than in that of the Irish saint. Above all—and this was perhaps the chief reason for the speedy triumph of the Benedictine rule—Gregory the Great had given the full, final, and emphatic sanction of Papal authority to the code of his master, Benedict; while in Columbanus, with all his holiness of life and undoubted loyalty to the chair of St. Peter, there had been a touch of independence and originality, a slight evidence of a disposition to set the Pope right (in reference both to the keeping of Easter and the controversy about the Three Chapters), which perhaps prevented the name of the Irish saint from being held in grateful remembrance at the Lateran. Whatever the cause, in Burgundy at any rate, at the Council of Autun in 670, the rule of Benedict was spoken of as that which all persons who had entered into religion were bound to obey. Thus little more than fifty years after his death the white scapular of Columbanus was disappearing before the black robe of Benedict.

We have seen that Columbanus died in the year 615. In the same or possibly the following year, Agilulf king of the Lombards, died also, and Theudelinda was a second time left a widow.

CHAPTER IV.

THEUDELINDA AND HER CHILDREN.

The story of the joint reign of Theudelinda and Adalwald, after the death of the strong and statesmanlike Agilulf, is obscure and melancholy. We might conjecture that we should find in it a repetition of the tragedy of Amalasunta and her son; but there is no trace in our authorities of those domestic dissensions which brought the dynasty of Theodoric to ruin. We might also with more reason conjecture that the fervent zeal of Theudelinda for the Catholic faith provoked a reaction among her Arian subjects; and certainly the fact that the rival who succeeded in hurling Adalwald from his throne was a zealous Arian would lend some probability to the hypothesis. But, though it is true that Paulus tells us that "under this reign the churches were restored, and many gifts were bestowed on sacred places", there is no evidence of anything like aggressive war being waged by the royal rulers against the Arian sect. On the contrary, we may still read a most curious letter in which Sisebut, king of the Visigoths, exhorts the young king to greater zeal in "cutting off the putrid errors of the heretics by the knife of experience", inveighing with all the zeal of a recent convert against the Arian contagion, and lamenting that so renowned a nation as the Lombards, so wise, so elegant, and so dignified, should sit down contented under the yoke of a dead and buried heresy. Of course it is possible that this and similar exhortations may have lashed the young ruler into a fury of persecution on behalf of the now fashionable orthodoxy, and that this may have been one of the things which cost him his crown; but our scanty historical evidence tells rather against than in favor of that suggestion. The historian of the Lombards distinctly attributes the fall of Adalwald to his own insanity. A strange but contemporary story connects that insanity in a mysterious way with the influence of the court of Ravenna; and this will therefore be a fitting place to piece together the scanty notices that we possess of the Byzantine governors of Imperial Italy during the first quarter of the seventh century.

We have already seen how the ineffectual Longinus was superseded, probably in 585, and his place given to the energetic but hot-headed Smaragdus; how Smaragdus, interfering too violently in the Istrian schism, was recalled in 589, and was succeeded by Romanus, the Exarch whose apparent indifference to the fate of Rome aroused the indignation of Pope Gregory; how, on the recall of Romanus, Callinicus succeeded to the government, and administered the affairs of Italy, generally in a friendly spirit to the Pope, from 597 to 602, and then, on the downfall of the Emperor Maurice, was

superseded in favor of Smaragdus, who a second time sat as Exarch on the tribunal of Ravenna. The second administration of Smaragdus lasted in all probability from 602 to 611. Its chief political events, the dastardly abduction of the daughter of the Lombard king with her family, and the heavy price which the Empire had to pay for that blundering crime, in the loss of its last foothold in the valley of the Po, have already been related. One proof of Smaragdus' servile loyalty to the usurper Phocas (fitting master of such a man) has not been mentioned. All visitors to Rome know the lonely pillar with a Corinthian capital, which stands in the Forum, near the Arch of Severus, and which, when Byron wrote his fourth canto of *Childe Harold* was still
"the nameless column with the buried base".

They know also how, in 1816, an English nobleman's wife caused the base to be unburied, and recovered the forgotten name. It was then found that the inscription on the base recorded the fact that Smaragdus, the Exarch of Italy, raised the column in honor of an Emperor whose innumerable benefits to an Italy, free and peaceful through his endeavors, were set forth in pompous terms. The Emperor's name had been obliterated by some zealous adherent of his successful rival; but there could be no doubt that the name which was originally engraved there in the year 608 was Phocas.

Not to Smaragdus himself was left the humiliating task of thus effacing the memorials of his former devotion to a base and cruel prince. It was on the 5th of October, 610, that the brave young African governor, Heraclius, was crowned as Emperor by the Patriarch of Constantinople, and it was probably early in the following year that Smaragdus was recalled for the last time, and a new governor, Joannes, took his place. The five years of this Exarch's rule were marked by no brilliant achievement. He renewed the peace with Agilulf (probably from year to year; he saw probably the Lombard fugitives from the terrible Avar invasion of Istria sweep across the plain, but we hear nothing of this, and are told only of the disastrous termination of his rule. An insurrection seems to have taken place at Ravenna, and Joannes was killed in the tumult. Eleutherius was appointed to succeed him; but when he arrived he found all his district in a flame, and the last remains of Imperial government in Italy apparently on the verge of Rebellion ruin. For Joannes of Compsa, either a general in the Imperial army, or possibly a wealthy Samnite landowner (if any such men were still left in Italy), seeing the apparent dissolution of all the bonds of Imperial authority, took military possession of Naples, and declared himself—Emperor, Exarch, Duke, Ave know not what—but it was such an usurpation of authority as justified the chronicler from whom we get these facts in calling him "tyrannus". His usurped rule, however, lasted not long, for after not many days we are told the Patrician Eleutherius expelled and slew him. On his march to the scene of conflict, the new Exarch had passed through Rome, and had there been graciously received by the reigning pontiff Deusdedit, from whose life we derive this information. After the Neapolitan revolt came a renewal of the Lombard war. Agilulf was now dead, but Sundrar, the Lombard general, who had been thoroughly trained by Agilulf in all the arts of war, valiantly upheld the cause of his nation, and struck the Imperial armies with blow upon blow. At last the Exarch found himself obliged to sue for peace, but only obtained it on condition of punctually paying the yearly tribute of five hundred pounds weight of gold, which (as we are now told) had been promised to Agilulf to induce him to raise the siege of Rome.

When peace was thus concluded with the Lombards, Eleutherius, who well knew the necessities of the Emperor Heraclius, at that time hard pressed by the Avars on the North, as well as by the Persians on the East, began to entertain treasonable thoughts of independent sovereignty. In the fourth year of his rule (619) he assumed the diadem and proclaimed himself Emperor. Though wielding the great powers of Exarch, he was himself but an Eunuch of the Imperial household. That such a man should aspire to be Emperor of the Romans seemed to bring back the shameful days of Eutropius and Arcadius. Eleutherius set forth from Ravenna at the head of his troops for Rome, intending probably to get himself crowned by the Pope and to sit in what remained of the palace of the Caesars on the Palatine. But the ignominy of such a rule was too great even for the degenerate Byzantines who made up the "Roman" army in the seventh century. When the Eunuch-Emperor had reached the village of Luceoli on the Flaminian Way (a few miles north of the place where his great prototype the Eunuch Narses won his victory over Totila), the soldiers revolted, and slew the usurping Exarch, whose head they sent as a welcome present to Constantinople

The next Exarch of whom we have any certain and satisfactory information is Isaac the Armenian, but as he died in 644, and his epitaph records that he ruled Italy for eighteen years, we have about five years unaccounted for, between 620, when we may consider that a new Exarch in succession to Eleutherius would have arrived at Ravenna, and 626 (or rather, probably 625), when the rule of Armenian Isaac seems to have begun. It is possible that this gap should be filled by the name of a certain Eusebius, who comes before us as the representative of the Emperor in that dark, mysterious story to which I have already referred as containing almost our only information as to the causes of the fall of the young king, Adalwald. The story is thus delivered to us by the anonymous Burgundian historian who is conventionally known as Fredegarius. In that same fortieth year of Chlotharius [Chlotochar II, king of the Franks, whose accession was in 584], Adloald, king of the Lombards, son of king Ago [Agilulf], after he had succeeded his father in the kingdom, received with kindness an ambassador of the Emperor Maurice named Eusebius, who came to him in guile. Being anointed in the bath with certain unguents whose nature I know not, he thenceforward could do nothing else but follow the counsels of Eusebius. Under his persuasion he set himself to slay all the chief men and nobles in the kingdom of the Lombards, intending, when they were put out of the way, to hand over to the Empire himself and all the Lombard nation. But after he had thus slain with the sword twelve of their number for no fault assigned, the rest of the nobles, seeing that their life was in danger, chose Charoald [= Ariwald], duke of Turin, who had to wife Gundeberga, sister of King Adloald, and all the oldest and noblest of the Lombards conspiring in one design raised this man to the kingdom. King Adloald, having received poison, perished.

And at this point we get a side-light on these mysterious events from the correspondence in the Papal chancery. Pope Honorius I, who succeeded Boniface V in November, 625, addressed a letter, apparently in the early months of his pontificate to Isaac, the new Exarch of Ravenna. In this letter the Pope says that he has learned with regret that some bishops in the regions beyond the Po have embraced the cause of the usurper so warmly that they have spoken most unepiscopal words to Peter, son of Paul, declaring that they will take on their consciences the guilt of his perjury if he will agree with them not to follow Adulubald, but the tyrant Ariopalt. The glorious Peter (he is evidently some layman high in office) has scorned their words, and persists in holding fast the faith which he swore to Ago, father of the aforesaid Adulubald; but the crime of the bishops, whose advice should have been given on the other side to strengthen him in his observance of his oath, is none the less odious to the Pope; and as soon as, by the decree of Providence, Adulubald has been restored to his kingdom, he desires the

Exarch to send the offending bishops into the regions of Rome, that they may be dealt with according to their sins. But the pious hopes of Honorious for the triumph of the righteous cause were not fulfilled. King Adalwald died of poison, and a modern historian unkindly insinuates that the fatal draught was administered by order of Isaac, desirous to rid himself of a guest whose unwelcome presence at his court was certain to involve him in disputes with the new Lombard king. Of this, however, we have no hint in our authorities, and we must be careful not to record our imaginations as facts.

Only so much can we safely say as to this mysterious passage in Lombard history, that the young king fell in some strange way under the power of a certain Eusebius, who is called an ambassador, but who may have been sent as an Exarch into Italy; that the voluptuous character of Roman civilization (not idle here is the allusion to the *bath* as the medium of enchantment) proved too much for the brain of the Teuton lad, who lent himself with fatuous readiness to all the sinister purposes of his treacherous friend. It was not a case of Catholic against Arian, otherwise the Transpadane bishops (though probably upholders of the Three Chapters) could hardly have supported so vigorously the cause of the usurper. But it probably was a plan such as Theodahad the Ostrogoth, Huneric the Vandal, Hermenigild the Visigoth, conceived, and such as very likely other weak-brained barbarian kings had often dallied with, of surrendering the national independence, and bartering a thorny crown for the fattened ease of a Byzantine noble. The plan, however, failed. Adalwald lost his crown and life. The Exarch Eusebius (if Exarch he were) was recalled to Constantinople, and succeeded by Armenian Isaac, and Ariwald, son-in-law of Agilulf and Theudelinda, sat, apparently with the full consent of the people, on the Lombard throne. The chronology of all these events is somewhat uncertain; but on the whole it seems probable—that the strife between Adalwald and his successor, if it began in 624, lasted for about two years, and that it was not till 626 that the death of the former left Ariwald unquestioned ruler of the Lombard people.

And Theudelinda, the mother of the dethroned and murdered king, what was her part in the tragedy? It is impossible to say. No hint of interference by her for or against her unhappy son has reached our ears. If it is true, as Fredegarius tells us, that the successful claimant was husband of her daughter, it is easy to conjecture the motives which may have kept her neutral in the strife. But she did not long survive her son. On the 22nd of February, 628, the great queen passed away. She left her mark doubtless on many other Italian cities, but preeminently on the little town of Modicia (*Monza*), where she and her husband loved to spend the summer for the sake of the coolness which came to them from the melting snows of Monte Rosa. Here she built the palace on whose pictured walls were seen the Lombards in that Anglo-Saxon garb which they brought from their Pannonian home. Here, too, she reared a basilica in honor of John the Baptist, which she adorned with many precious ornaments of gold and silver, and enriched with many farms. The church has been more than once rebuilt, but there may perhaps still remain in it some portions of the original seventh-century edifice of Theudelinda, and in its sacristy are still to be seen not only the Iron Crown of the Lombards but the gold-handled comb of Theudelinda, and the silver-gilt effigies of a hen and chickens which once probably served as a centerpiece for her banquet table.

Of the ten years' reign of Ariwald after his rival's death Paulus honestly confesses that he has nothing to relate. We have again to draw on the inaccurate but contemporary historian Fredegarius for information as to two events which made some stir in the court of Pavia during his reign, the degradation of a queen, and the murder of a Lombard duke.

Gundiperga (as Paulus calls the wife of Arlwald) was a lovely and popular queen, zealous for the faith, and abounding in works of charity to the poor. But there was a certain Lombard nobleman named Adalulf, who was frequently in the palace, being busied in the king's service; and of this man the queen in the innocence of her heart chanced one day to say that Adalulf was a man of goodly stature. The favored courtier hearing these words, and misreading the queen's character, presumed to propose to her that she should be unfaithful to her marriage vow, but she indignantly scorned the proposal, and spat in the face of the tempter. Hereupon, fearing that his life would be in danger, Adalulf determined to be beforehand with his accuser, and charged the queen with having three days previously granted a secret interview to Taso, the ambitious duke of Tuscany, and having at that interview promised to poison her present husband, and raise Taso to the throne. Ariwald (or Charoald, as Fredegarius calls him), believing the foul calumny, banished his queen from the court, and imprisoned her in a fortress at Lomello.

More than two years Gundiperga languished in confinement; then deliverance reached her from a perhaps unexpected quarter. Chlotochar II, king of the Franks, sent ambassadors to Ariwald, to ask why such indignities were offered to the Lombard queen, who was, as they said, a relation of the Franks. In reply Ariwald repeated the lies of Adalulf as if they were true. Then one of the Frankish ambassadors, Answald by name, suggested on his own account, and not as a part of his master's commission, that the judgment of God should be ascertained by two armed men fighting in the lists, and that the reputation of Gundiperga should be cleared or clouded according to the issue. The counsel pleased Ariwald and all the nobles of his court. The cause of Gundiperga was now taken up by her two cousins, Gundipert and Aripert (the sons of her mother's brother Gundwald), and, perhaps hired by them, an armed man named Pitto entered the lists against Adalulf. The queen's champion was victorious; her traducer was slain, and she, in the third year of her captivity, was restored to her royal dignity.

But though King Ariwald was convinced that he had done his gentle queen injustice, his suspicion of the treasonable designs of the Tuscan Duke Taso remained, and was perhaps not without foundation. In the year 631 he sent ambassadors to the patrician Isaac, asking him to kill Duke Taso by any means that were in his power. If the Exarch would confer this favor upon him, the Lombard king would remit one of the three hundred-weights of gold which the Empire was now by treaty bound to pay to him. The proposition stirred the avaricious soul of Isaac, who at once began to cast about for means to accomplish the suggested crime. He sent men to Taso, bearing this message: "I know that you are out of favor with King Ariwald, but come to me and I will help you against him". Too easily believing in the Exarch's goodwill, Taso set out for Ravenna, and with fatal imprudence left his armed followers outside the gate of the city. As soon as he was well within the walls, the assassins prepared for the purpose rushed upon him and slew him. News of the murder was brought to King Ariwald, who thereupon fulfilled his promise, and graciously consented to remit one third of the usual tribute "to Isaac and the Empire". Soon after these events King Ariwald died.

No doubt there are some improbabilities in the story thus told by Fredegarius as to the murder of Taso, and possibly Pabst is right in rejecting it altogether. The name and the circumstances look suspiciously like a repetition of the story told by Paulus of the assassination of Taso of Friuli. and the title "Dux Tusciae" is almost certainly wrong, for, at any rate a little later on, there was more than one duke in "Tuscia". On the other hand, it is possible that two men of the name of Taso (not an uncommon name among the Lombards) may have been murdered by a treacherous Roman governor, and it is also possible, if the two stories describe the same event, that the contemporary though alien Fredegarius may have heard a more correct version than the native but much later historian Paulus.

On the death of Ariwald, if we may, trust Fredegarius, the precedent set in the case of Theudelinda was repeated, and the widowed queen was asked to decide for the Lombard nation as to his successor. Her choice fell on Rothari, duke of Brescia, whom she invited to put away his wife and to be joined with her in holy matrimony. Rothari swore by all the saints to love and honor Gundiperga alone, and thereupon by unanimous consent of the nobles was raised to the throne. Both queen and nobles, however, if Fredegarius is to be believed, had soon reason to repent of their choice. He drew tight the reins of discipline (which had probably been relaxed under the reign of the usurper Ariwald), and, in pursuit of peace, struck terror into the hearts of the Lombards, and slew many of the nobles, whom he perceived to be contumacious. Forgetful also of his solemn promises to Gundiperga, and perhaps partly influenced by dislike to her Catholic ways (he being himself an Arian), he confined her in one little room in the palace of Pavia, and forced her to live there in privacy, whilst he himself held high revel with his concubines. She however, "as she was a Christian woman", blessed God even in this tribulation, and devoted herself continually to fasting and prayer. The chronicler makes no mention of the earlier divorced wife of Rothari, but one would fain hope that the remembrance of that injured woman's wrongs helped to reconcile Gundiperga to her own fate, and gave reality and truth to her words of penitence. At length, after five years of seclusion, an embassy from the Frankish king, Clovis II, again brought the wrongs of this "relation of the Franks" before the notice of the Lombard ruler. Again the Frankish intercession prevailed, and Gundiperga, being brought forth from her seclusion, wore once more her regal ornaments, and sat in the high seat by the side of her lord. All the farms and other possessions of the royal fisc belonging to her, which had been apparently impounded during her seclusion, were restored to her, and to the day of her death she lived in queenly splendor and opulence. Aubedo, the Frankish ambassador who had so successfully pleaded her cause, received in secret large rewards from the restored queen. This is the last that we hear of Queen Gundiperga, who probably died some about the middle of the seventh century. As her mother had done at Monza, so she at Pavia reared a basilica in honor of St. John the Baptist, which she adorned with lavish wealth of gold and silver and precious vestments. There, too, her corpse was interred.

The careers of these two women, mother and daughter, Theudelinda and Gundiperga, present some points of resemblance and some of striking contrast. Each was twice married to a Lombard king; each was entrusted by the nation with the choice of a successor to the throne; one saw a son exiled and slain, the other a brother; each was the Catholic wife of an Arian husband, but one apparently preserved to her death the unswerving loyalty of the Lombard people, while the other had twice to undergo imprisonment, and once at least the stabs of cruel calumny. Their united lives extended from Alboin to Rothari, from the first to the last Arian king of Italy, and covered the whole period of an important ecclesiastical revolution—the conversion of the Lombards to the Catholic form of Christianity.

We have hitherto seen only the unfavorable side of the character of Gundiperga's second husband. We may now listen to the more favorable testimony of Paulus, who says:

"The kingship of the Lombards was assumed by Rothari, by birth an Arodus. He was a man of strong character, and one who followed the path of justice, though he held not the right line of the Christian faith, being stained by the infidelity of the Arian heresy. For in truth the Arians, to their own great harm and loss, assert that the Son is inferior to the Father, and the Holy Spirit inferior to the Father and the Son; but we Catholics confess the Father, and the Son, and the Holy Spirit to be one true God in three persons, with equal power and the same glory. At this time in almost all the cities of the realm there were two bishops, one a Catholic, the other an Arian. In the city of Ticinum the place is still shown where the Arian bishop had his baptistery, residing near the basilica of St, Eusebius, while another bishop resided at the Catholic church. However, the Arian bishop who was in that city, Anastasius by name, being converted to the Catholic faith, afterwards ruled the Church of Christ. This King Rothari arranged in a series of writings the laws of the Lombards, which they were retaining only in memory and by practice, and ordered that the Edict thus prepared should be called a *Code*. But it was now the seventy-seventh year since the Lombards had come into Italy, as the same king has testified in the prologue to his edict".

"Now King Rothari took all the cities of the Romans which are situated on the sea-coast from Luna in Tuscany up to the boundary of the Fanks. In the same way also he took and destroyed Opitergium (*Oderzo*) a city placed between Treviso and Friuli; and with the Romans of Ravenna he waged war at the river of Aemilia, which is called Scultenna (*Panaro*). In which war 8000 fell on the side of the Romans, the rest taking flight".

It is evident that we are here listening to the exploits of one who, however harsh a ruler either of his nobles or of his wife, did at least know how to rule successfully. His conquests from the Empire are hardly less extensive than those of Agilulf. Genoa and the coast of the Riviera ("di Ponente" and "di Levante") are wrested finally from the grasp of Constantinople. Oderzo is taken, and its walls are demolished. So must we understand the word used by Paulus in this place, since the utter destruction of Opitergium is placed by him about twenty-five years later, and is attributed to another king of the Lombards, Grimwald. Finally, Rothari wins a great victory over the forces of the Exarch on the banks of the river which flows past Modena, and perhaps at the very point where it intersects the great Emilian highway.

These victories were probably won at the expense of Isaac of Armenia, whose eighteen years' tenure of the Exarchate (625-644) included one half of the reign of Rothari. Visitors to Ravenna may still see the stately sarcophagus of this Byzantine governor of fragments of Italy, which is placed in a little alcove behind the church of S. Vitale. Upon the tomb is carved an inscription in twelve rather halting Greek iambics, with a poor modern Latin translation. The inscription may be rendered into English thus:

> A noble general here is laid to rest,
> Who kept unharmed Rome and the Roman West.
> For thrice six years he served his gentle lords,
> Isaac, ally of kings, this stone records.
> The wide Armenia glories in his fame.
> For from Armenia his high lineage came.
> Nobly he died. The sharer of his love,
> The chaste Susanka, like a widowed dove

Will spend her rest of life in ceaseless sighs.
She mourns, but his long toil hath won its prize,
Glory alike in East and Western Land,
For either army owned his strong command.

It is not difficult to read through the conventional phrases of this vapid epitaph the unsuccessful character of Isaac's Exarchate. Had there been any gleam of victory over the Lombard army, the inscription would have been sure to record it. As it is, the utmost that can be said of him is that he "kept Rome and the West unharmed", but if our reading of his history be correct, he probably kept the beautiful Riviera unravaged by surrendering it to the enemy.

Some of the events of Isaac's government of Italy, to which his epitaph makes no allusion, are brought before us by the meager narratives of the Papal biographer

It was in 638, six years before the death of Isaac, that his old correspondent, Pope Honorius, died. A Roman ecclesiastic, Severinus, was chosen as his successor, and the Exarch, who had at this time the right of strange approval of the Papal election, sent the *Chartularius*, Maurice (by whose advice, we are told, he wrought him much evil), as his representative to Rome. Maurice, taking counsel with some ill-disposed persons, stirred up "the Roman army" (that is, probably, the civic militia) by an inflammatory harangue concerning the wealth of the Papacy. Pointing to the episcopal palace of the Lateran, he exclaimed, "What marvel that you are poor when in that building is the hoarded wealth of Honorius, to whom the Emperor, time after time, sent your arrears of pay, which he, holy man that he was, heaped up in the treasure-chambers of yon stately palace". At these words burning resentment against the Church filled all hearts, and the whole body of citizens, from the greybeard down to the stripling, rushed with arms in their hands to the Lateran palace. They were, however, unable to force an entrance, so strongly was it guarded by the adherents of Severinus. For three days the armed band besieged the Lateran, and at the end of that time Maurice, having persuaded the "Judges" (that is, the civil authorities of the City) to accompany him, claimed and obtained admission to the palace. Then he sealed up all the rich vestments which he found in the Church's wardrobe and all the treasures of the Lateran palace, "which Emperors, Patricians and Consuls had left, for the redemption of their souls, to the Apostle Peter, to be employed in almsgiving and the redemption of captives". Having done this, he wrote to the Exarch Isaac that all was ready and he might now come and help himself at his leisure to the splendid spoil. Soon Isaac arrived, and immediately banished the leading clergy to various cities of Italy. Having thus disarmed ecclesiastical opposition, he proceeded to take up his dwelling in the Lateran palace, where he abode eight days, calmly appropriating its wealth of centuries. To the indignant members of the Papal household the spoliation must have seemed not less cruel and even more scandalous (as being wrought in the name of a Roman Emperor) than that celebrated fortnight of plunder when Gaiseric and his Vandals stripped the gilded tiles from the roof of the Capitol. Part of the booty Maurice sent to Heraclius, thus making the Emperor an accomplice in his deed. The soldiers may have received their arrears of pay out of the proceeds of the plunder, but assuredly no contemptible portion found its way to the Exarch's palace at Ravenna, whence it may have been transported by the widowed dove Susanna, after her husband's death, to their Armenian home.

Pope Severinus, after this act of spoliation, was installed by the Exarch in St. Peter's chair, but died little more than two months after his elevation. Another short pontificate followed, and then Theodore, 642-649, a Greek by birth, but as stout as any Roman for the defence of the Roman see against the Patriarchs of Constantinople. In his pontificate Isaac and Maurice reappear upon the scene in changed characters. The *Chartularius* again visited Rome, again allied himself with the men who had helped him in his raid upon the treasures of the Church, and persuaded the soldiers in the City and the surrounding villages to swear fidelity to him and renounce their allegiance to Isaac, whom he accused of seeking to establish an independent throne. The Exarch, however, whether loyal or not to the Emperor, showed himself able to cope with his own rebellious subordinate. He sent Donus the *Magister Militum* and his treasurer to Rome, doubtless with a considerable body of troops. At once all the "Judges" and the Roman militia, who had just sworn fealty to Maurice, struck with fear, abandoned his cause and gave in their adhesion to his enemy. On this Maurice fled for refuge to the church of S. Maria Maggiore, but being either forced or enticed from that sanctuary was sent, with all his accomplices, heavily chained with collars of iron to Ravenna. By the Exarch's orders, however, he was not suffered to enter the city, but was beheaded at a place twelve miles distant, and his head, the sight of which gladdened the heart of the Armenian, was exhibited in the circus of Ravenna. His followers, with the iron collars still round their necks were led away into strict confinement while Isaac revolved in his mind the question of their punishment. But before he had decided on their fate, he himself died, "smitten by the stroke of Death of God", and the liberated captives returned to their several homes. Isaac was succeeded in the Exarchate Exarch by Theodore Calliopas, who was twice the occupant of the palace at Ravenna. In his second tenure of office, 653-664, Italy witnessed strange scenes—the banishment of a Pope and the arrival of an Emperor; but the description of these events must be reserved for a future chapter.

CHAPTER V.

THE LEGISLATION OF ROTHARI

In the last chapter we were concerned with the external events of the reign of Rothari, who for sixteen years (636-652) wore the Lombard crown. Our information as to those events is certainly meager and unsatisfactory enough, but the main interest of the reign for us is derived from a feature of its internal politics, the fact, namely, that Rothari was the first great legislator of his people.

The Lombards had now been for two generations encamped on the soil of Italy, yet during all that time, as Paulus tells us, their laws had lived but in the memory of unlettered judges, who remembered only so much as frequent practice rendered familiar; and this, in a country which had been subject to the most scientific system of jurisprudence that the world has ever seen, and had witnessed its gradual development from the Laws of the Twelve Tables to the Code, the Institutes, and the Digest of Justinian. It was time that this reproach should be in some measure removed from the Lombard nation, and accordingly on November 22, 643, King Rothari published to the world his "Code" in 388 chapters, written by the hand of the notary Answald. The Prologue of this monument of barbarian jurisprudence is worth quoting:

"In the name of our Lord Jesus Christ begins the Edict which with God's help the most excellent man Rothari, king of the Lombards, hath renewed, with the nobles who are his judges. In the name of Almighty God, I, Rothari, most excellent man and king; and seventeenth king of the nation of the Langobardi; by the blessing of God in the eighth year of ray reign, and the thirty-eighth of my age, in the second Indiction; and in the seventy-sixth year after the Langobardi marching under Alboin, at that time their king, were brought by divine power into the province of Italy; prosperously given forth in my palace at Ticinum:

"How great has been our care and anxiety for the welfare of our subjects, the tenor of the following Edict will declare: both on account of the constant oppressions of the poor, and also on account of the extravagant exactions from those who are known to have larger property, but how they suffer violence we well know. Therefore, considering the compassion of Almighty God, we have thought it necessary to correct the present law, [inviting] our chief men to renew and amend it, adding that which is lacking, and removing that which is superfluous. And we have provided that it shall be all embraced in one volume, that each one may have permission to live quietly, according to law and justice, to labor against his enemies on behalf of his own opinion and to defend himself and his borders.

"Therefore, since these things are so, we have judged it useful to preserve to future ages the memory of the names of the kings our predecessors, from the time when kings first began to be named in the Lombard nation, as far as we have been able to learn them from ancient men, and we have ordered the Notary to affix them to this parchment".

Then follow the names of sixteen kings, with the families from which they sprang.

1. AGILMUND, of the family Regugiutus (Gugingus).
2. LAAJIISIO (LAJAMICHO).
3. LETH (LETHUC).
4. HILDEOCH (ALDIHOC).
5. GUDEOGH (GODEHOC).
6. CLAFFO.
7. TATO.
8. WACHO.
9. WALTHARI (WALTARI), son of WACHO.
10. AUTHARI or AUDOIN, of the family of Gaisus (Gausus).
11. ALBOIN, son of AUDOIN, who, as aforesaid, led the army into Italy.
12. GLEPH, of the family Beleos.
13. AUTHARI.
14. AGILULPH(ACQUO): a Thuringian of the family of Anawas.
15. ADALWALD.
16. HARIWALD (AROAL), of the family of Caupus.

In the seventeenth place he names himself, "I, who as aforesaid am in God's name King Rothari", and he recounts the uncouth names of his progenitors belonging to the family Harodos through twelve generations.

USTBORA
MAMMO
FRANCHONO
WEO
WEHILO
HILTZO
ALAMAN
ADHAMUND
NOCTZO
NANDINIG
ROTHARI

He then proceeds :
"And this general order we give lest any fraud creep into this Edict through the carelessness of copyists. But it is our intention that no such copies be received or have any credit except such as are written or certified (?) on request by the hand of Arswald, the notary who has written it by our orders".

The reader will not expect nor desire that in this book, which is not a law-book but a history, I should give a complete analysis of the 388 chapters, short as they are, which make up the Code of Rothari. I will only notice those provisions of the Code which illustrate the condition of Lombard society, will quote some of the curious words which the barbarians from beyond the Danube added to the vocabulary of Latium, and above all will notice any provision—if such is to be found in the Code—which illustrates in the most remote manner the condition of the conquered Romans under their Lombard lords. The importance of calling attention to this point (which is connected with one of the most difficult questions in the whole history of the Middle Ages) will abundantly appear in a later chapter. The reader must not look for anything like orderly arrangement or scientific division of the field of law. It would not be the Lombard Code if it possessed either of these qualities.

The Code begins with offences against the person of the king and the peace of the state. The conspirator against his life, the inviter of his enemies into the kingdom, the harborer of brigands, the exciter of the soldiers to mutiny, the treacherous officer who deserts his comrades on the field of battle, are all to be punished with death.

But on the other hand, the man who takes counsel with the king himself concerning the death of one of his subjects, or who actually slays a man by the royal order, is to be held guiltless, and neither he nor his heirs are to suffer any disquietude by reason of the murder, "because the king's heart is in the hand of God, and it is not possible for a man to escape whom he has ordered to be slain". If one man accuses another of a capital offence, the accused may appeal to the *camfio* or wager of battle. If he fail his life may be forfeited, but if his accuser fail he must pay the *guidrigild*, or price of blood, of which half shall go to the king, and half to the man whom he has slandered This word *guidrigild* is explained shortly after. If two free men without the king's order have plotted together as to the death of a third, and have carried their intention into effect, he who was the actual murderer shall compound for the dead man according to the price fixed, "that is to say, his *guidrigild*". If many persons of honorable birth have conspired together to kill a man, they shall be punished in *angargathungi*. This barbarous word is explained as meaning that they shall compound for the murder according to the rank of the person slain. If they have carried off plunder from the dead man's body, that is a plain case of *ploderaub*, or robbing the dead, and must be atoned for by a payment of 80 solidi.

"If any of our barons", says Rothari, "wishes to come to us let him come and go in safety and unharmed. Anyone doing him any injury on the road shall pay a composition according to the terms set forth below in this Edict". We note this early appearance of the word "barons" without venturing to define its exact value.

Laws 26-28 provide for the security of travelers by the highway, under the strange title, "De *Wegworin* id est *horhitariam*". The German word (derived from *wec* = way, and *werran* = to block or hinder) explains itself pretty easily as an obstruction of the high road. Its Latin equivalent is the aspirated form of the word which we use for the *orbit* of a planet. As to those sturdy rogues who do violence to travelers on the highway, the law is that "if any one shall place himself in the way before a free woman or girl, or do her any injury, he shall pay 900 solidi, half to the king, and half to her to whom the injury shall have been done, or to the person to whom the right of protecting her (*mundium*) belongs". This *mundium*, or claim to represent the rights of a female relative, is a word which we shall meet with again later on.

"If any one shall place himself in the way before a free man, he shall pay him 20 solidi, always supposing that he has not done him any bodily injury. If he have, he shall pay for the wounds or blows which he has inflicted according to the rate to be hereafter mentioned, and shall also pay the 20 solidi for stopping him on the highway".

"If any one shall place himself in the way before another man's slave or handmaid, or *Aldius*, or freed-man, he shall pay 20 solidi to his lord".

This word *Aldius*, which we shall meet with again in the laws of Rothari, might introduce us to a long and difficult controversy, which I shall not enter upon at this time. It is clear that the *Aldius* was in a state of imperfect freedom. He is named between the slave and the freedman, and his claim for damages from the highway robber is not paid to himself, but handed over to his lord. It is suggested that the vast mass, of formerly free Romans, or non-Lombard inhabitants of Italy, were reduced by the conquest to this condition of *Aldionate*, a suggestion which for the present shall neither be accepted nor rejected, but which I will ask the reader to bear in mind when next the word *Aldius* meets him in Rothari's Code.

Law 31 is headed *De Walapauz*: "If any man shall unjustly do violence to a free man by way of *walapauz*, he shall pay him 80 solidi. *Walapauz* is the act of one who stealthily clothes himself in the garments of another, or changes the appearance of his head or face with the intention of thieving". Apparently the modern burglar, who with blackened face breaks into a house by night, is guilty, though he knows it not, of the crime of *Walapauz*.

And this leads us to a curious custom which prevailed when a man was found, with however innocent intentions, by night in another man's courtyard. "If a free man shall be found by night in the courtyard of another, and shall not give his hands to be tied—if he be killed, no claim for compensation shall be made by his relations. And if he shall give his hands to be tied, and shall be bound, he shall pay for himself 80 solidi: because it is not according to reason that a man should enter in the night-time silently or stealthily into another man's courtyard; but if he have any useful purpose or need of his own, let him cry out before he enters".

Similarly a slave found at night in the courtyard of a householder, and not giving his hands to be tied, if he be slain shall furnish no claim for compensation to his lord : and if he give his hands, and is bound, shall be set free on payment of 40 solidi.

Scandalum, that is, an act of violence committed in a church, was to be atoned for by a special fine of 40 solidi, laid on the altar of the church. Within the king's palace it was a capital offence, unless the culprit could move the king's soul to mercy. *Scandalum* committed by a free man in the city where the king was abiding, required a fine of 12 solidi, even if no blow were struck; of 24 solidi in addition to the ordinary tariff for wounds if the brawler had struck a blow. In the case of a slave these fines were diminished one half. One half again all round was the abatement, if the city in which the brawl took place were not one in which the king was residing.

We now come to the laws fixing the fines that were to be paid for all sorts of bodily injuries, and these will be best exhibited in tabular form. We begin with the cases in which the injured person is a free man:

Blows struck in sudden quarrel causing a wound or bruise . . 3 solidi apiece up to 12 solidi. "If more blows are inflicted they are not to be counted, but let the wounded man rest content with himself".

Blow with the fist ... 3 solidi.

Blow with the palm of the hand ... 6 solidi

Blows on the head, only breaking the skin ... 6 solidi up to 18.

Blows on the head, breaking bones: (per bone) 12 solidi (no count to be taken above 36 solidi). "But the broken bones are to be counted on this principle, that one bone shall be found large enough to make an audible sound when thrown against a shield at 12 feet distance on the road. The said feet to be measured from the foot of a man of moderate stature, not the hand".

The deprivation of an eye is to be atoned for by the payment of half the fine due for actual homicide, "according to the quality of the person injured".

The cutting off of the nose to be atoned for by half the fine for homicide.

Cutting the lip ... 13 solidi.

If so cut that one, two, or three teeth appear ... 20 solidi.

Knocking out the front teeth ... 16 solidi per tooth.

Knocking out the grinders ... 8 solidi per tooth

Cutting off an ear—a quarter of the fine for homicide.

Wound on the face ... 16 solidi.

Wound on the nose, causing a scar ... 16 solidi.

Similar wound on the ear ... 16 solidi.

Fracture of the arm ... 16 solid'.

Wounding without breaking the arm ... 8 solidi.

Blow on the chest ... 20 solidi.

Piercing the rib ... 8 solidi.

Cutting off a hand—half the fine for homicide; if so stricken as to cause paralysis, but not cut off— a quarter of the full fine.

Cutting off a thumb—a sixth part of the fine for homicide.

Cutting off the second finger ... 17 solidi.

Cutting off the third finger (which is the middle one) ... 6 solidi.

Cutting off the fourth finger ... 8 solidi.

Cutting off the fifth finger ...16 solidi.

Cutting off a foot—half the fine for homicide.

Cutting off the great toe ... 6 solidi.

Cutting off the second toe ... 6 solidi.

Cutting off the third toe ... 3 solidi.

Cutting off the fourth toe ... 3 solidi.

Cutting off the fifth toe .... 2 solidi.

At the end of this curiously minute tariff of penalties for injuries to the person, we have the following interesting exposition of the motive of the law:

"For all the wounds and blows above mentioned, which may pass between free men, we have purposely ordained a larger composition than was in use among our ancestors, in order that the *faida* (feud), which is enmity, may be postponed after the receipt of the above-mentioned composition, and that more may not be required, nor any thought of guile be harbored in the heart; but let the cause be finished between the parties, and friendship remain. And should it happen that within the space of a year he who was wounded dies of the wounds themselves, then let the striker pay an *angargathungi*, that is [the full fine for homicide] according to the quality of the person injured, what he was worth".

The Increased wealth of the Lombards after the settlements in Italy evidently had made them able to pay a higher sum for the luxury of vengeance on an enemy, and justified the sufferer in demanding an ampler compensation for his wounds. At the same time, the motive of the royal legislator in lightening his penal code is clearly apparent. As the Lombard nation was putting off a little of its old savagery in the light of Roman civilization, it was becoming more and more necessary that feuds should cease, and that the old right of private war and the notion of vengeance as the inalienable right of the kinsmen of a murdered man should be restricted within the narrowest limits, and if possible should vanish out of the nation's life. A provision follows for the case of a man who has unintentionally caused the death of an unborn child. It is said that if the mother of the child is free, and has herself escaped death, her price shall be fixed as that of a free woman according to her rank in life, and the half of that price shall be paid for her dead child. If she dies, her composition is paid apparently without any compensation for the death of her offspring. And as before, let the feud cease because the injury was done unwittingly. This provision, that the composition shall be paid according to the mother's rank in life, seems again to point to a table of compositions graduated according to the sufferer's place in the social hierarchy, which appendix to the laws of Rothari we no longer possess.

The twenty-six laws which next follow deal with household injuries inflicted on another man's *Aldius*, or household slave At first sight we might think that *Aldius* and *Servus Ministerialis* were equivalent terms: but remembering the way in which *Aldius* was used in a previous law along with "slave" and "freedman", cannot doubt that we have here to deal with two classes of men differing in their degree of dependence, whose services, generally speaking, were of the same value to their lord. The one is the *Aldius*, the client or serf, generally perhaps a member of the vanquished Roman population; the other is the household slave, who may belong to any nationality whatever, who by the fortune of war or the stress of pestilence or famine has lost his liberty, and like our countrymen the boys from Deira who excited the compassion of Gregory, has been brought to Italy by the slave-dealer, and sold to a Lombard master.

For a member of either of these two classes, the composition for wounds and bruises (paid doubtless to his master, not to himself) was generally about a third of that which was payable for a similar injury to a free man. In the case of the loss of an eye, a hand or a foot, the fine was half of that for homicide, the same proportion but not the same amounts as in the case of the corresponding injury to a free man. And for many of the more important injuries it is provided that the culprit shall pay to the lord not only the fixed composition, but an allowance for the loss of the man's labor and the doctor's fees.

The next section, containing twenty-three laws, deals with injuries inflicted on a yet lower class—*servi rusticani*, the "plantation hands" of whom we used to hear in the days of American slavery. Here again the same general principle prevails : for serious injuries, the loss of an eye or a hand, half the fine for homicide : for others a composition which is generally about a sixth or an eighth of that which is paid for a free man, and in many cases compensation for loss of labor and the doctor's charges.

Any blow on hand or foot to either *Aldius* or slave which results in paralysis of the stricken member is to be atoned for as if it had been cut off.

All wounds and blows inflicted on the *Aldius*, the household slave or rustic slave, as also on the *Aldia* and the servant-maid, are to be atoned for according to the tenor of this decree. But if any doubt arise either as to the survival or the speedy cure of the injured person, let the lord receive at once half of the composition for the wound: the remainder being kept in suspense till the event be ascertained.

Within a year's space, if the man recovers, the balance unpaid for the wounds themselves shall be handed over to the lord; but if he dies the lord shall receive the whole composition for the dead man, allowing for that which has already been paid for the wounds.

The man who has inflicted a wound is himself to go and seek a physician. If he fail, then the wounded man or his lord is to seek the physician, and the other shall pay for loss of labor and doctor's fees as much as shall be adjudged by learned men.

Now at length, after all these minute details as to minor injuries inflicted on men of less than free condition, we come to the full composition to be paid in event of their actual murder:

He who kills another man's Aldius must pay (doubtless to the lord, though this is not expressly stated) 60 solidi.

He who kills another man's household slave "approved and trained" ... 50 solidi.

He who kills a household slave of secondary importance to the foregoing, who bears nevertheless the name of household slave ... 25 solidi.

He who kills a foreman swineherd who has two or three or more men in training under him ...50 solidi. For an inferior swineherd ..... 25 solidi.

He who kills a farm servant, a cowherd, a shepherd, goatherd or other herdsman, if a foreman ...20 solidi.

If one of his under-men ... 16 solidi.

He who kills a rustic slave under the farm-laborer ...16 solidi.

Anyone who by accident kills the infant child of a slave or farm-laborer shall be assessed by the judge according to the age of the child, and the money which it was able to earn, and shall pay accordingly.

The provision as to accidents connected with the craft of the forester has an interesting bearing on the current legal doctrine of "common employment". If two or more men are felling a tree which falls upon a passer-by and kills or injures him, they shall pay the composition for homicide or maiming in equal proportions. If the like accident befall one of the workers, they shall reckon one portion for the dead man, and pay the rest in equal shares. Thus, if two men were felling the tree and one were killed, the survivor would pay half the composition for his comrade; if three, each survivor would pay a third, and so on. And the feud shall cease inasmuch as the injury was accidental. In a later law (152) it is expressly enacted that if a man hires workmen, one of whom is drowned or struck by lightning, or crushed by a blown-down tree, his composition shall not be claimed from the hirer of his labor, provided the death was not directly caused by the hirer or his men.

A curious little group of laws on poisoning next comes before us. The free man or woman who mixed a cup of poison for another, but never found an opportunity to administer the fatal dose, was fined 20 solidi. If the poison were administered, but without a fatal result, the fine was half the composition for homicide. If death ensued, of course the whole composition was paid.

So, too, if a slave presented the poisoned cup, but failed to kill his victim, the master of the slave must pay half the composition which would have been due in case of death; and the whole composition if death ensued. In either event, however, the slave was to be handed over to be put to death, and the master had a right to deduct his market value from the penalty which he paid for the slave's crime.

But all this machinery of the *quidriqild*, however carefully worked, would sometimes fail to efface from the mind of the sufferer the memory of his wrongs. The retaliatory blow would after all be struck, and the terrible *faida* would begin once more. In order to guard against this recrudescence of the blood-feud, it was enacted that anyone who, after he had received the composition for a slaughtered relative, and after accustomed oaths of mutual amity had been sworn, took vengeance with his own right hand and slew the murderer, should, besides paying the ordinary composition for the new homicide repay twice the composition which he had received; and similarly, if it were only a wound or a bruise which had been inflicted upon him, he should repay double the composition paid him for that injury.

Again, we are brought by the next pair of laws face to face with one of the most difficult questions of modern legislation, that of "employers' liability". If we rightly interpret the words of the code there was a guild of master masons who took their name from the town of Como, the headquarters of the building trade of that day. According to Muratori, even down to the middle of last century troops of masons from the Italian lakes used to roam over the other provinces of Italy, seeking employment as builders. Possibly the fact previously noticed that the Lake of Como was for so many years a stronghold of the dying Imperial cause in Upper Italy, may have had something to do with this continued existence of an active building trade in the hands of the *Magistri Comacini*. However this may be, it was enacted that if in the course of their building operations the fall of material caused a fatal accident either to one of the workmen, or to a passer-by, the composition should not be payable by the owner of the house, but by the *Comacine Master*. For after by the contract he has received good money for his hire, it is not unreasonable that he should bear the loss.

Laws as to fire-raising follow. The man who has intentionally and with evil mind kindled a fire in his neighbor's house must repay the damage threefold; the value of the burnt property to be assessed by "neighboring men of good faith". An accidental fire caused by a man carrying burning coals nine feet or more away from his own hearth was to be compounded for by a payment merely equivalent to the value of the things destroyed

From fire the legislator passes to mills, probably water-mills. Any one breaking down another man's mill was to pay 12 solidi to the injured miller. For some reason or other, judicial fairness was more than usually doubtful in cases of this kind, and accordingly a judge who delayed his decision, or wrongfully gave leave for the destruction of a mill, was to pay 20 solidi to the king's palace. On the other hand, wrong might be done by building as well as by destroying a mill. There were men who did illegally what the "free selectors" of Australia do in virtue of the laws of the colony—who settled themselves down on another man's land and built a mill beside his stream. In such a case, unless the intruder could prove his right, the mill and all the labor that he had expended upon it went to the rightful owner of the soil.

We now come to the section of the Code which deals with the laws of inheritance. The feature which to our ideas seems the most extraordinary, and which is, I believe, peculiar to the Lombard laws, is the provision which is made for illegitimate alongside of legitimate children. If a Lombard left one legitimate and any number of illegitimate sons, the former took two-thirds of his property at his death, the latter all together one-third.

If he left two sons born in wedlock, they inherited each two-fifths, the collective bastards one-fifth. If there were three of the former class, they took each two-sevenths, and one-seventh was divided among the bastards.

If there were four, the bastards took a ninth; if five, an eleventh; if six, a thirteenth; if seven, a fifteenth. Beyond this point apparently the law-giver would not go in providing for the division of the inheritance.

In all cases where there was legitimate male issue, the daughters took nothing; but if a man left one daughter born in wedlock, and a number of illegitimate sons, the former took one-third of the inheritance, the latter one-third, and the remaining third went to the other next of kin. If the daughters were two or more in number they took a half, the bastards a third, and the next of kin a sixth.

Where there was no next of kin to claim under these provisions, the king's court claimed the vacant inheritance. As relationship did not count beyond the seventh generation we may believe that in that barbarous age, and with a roving population, the king's court was not seldom a successful claimant.

No man might declare his illegitimate sons legitimate, or put them on an equality with the sons born in wedlock, except with the consent of the latter given after they had attained "the legitimate age". This was reached, however, at the early period of twelve years. As with the Romans, so with the Lombards, a father had not absolute power over the disposal of his property. Except in the case of certain grievous crimes against filial duty (if a son had purposely struck his father, or plotted his death, or committed adultery with his stepmother), no father might disinherit his son, nor even *thing* away to another in his lifetime the property that should rightly devolve upon him. And the obligation was a mutual one : except to his own offspring, the son might not *thing* away his property to prevent it from being inherited by his father. The Latinized German word *thingare*, which meets us in this and many other Lombard laws, gives us an interesting glimpse into the political life or primeval Germany. In an earlier chapter of this work a slight sketch was attempted of the Folks-Thing, or national assembly of the Germans. Referring to that chapter for a fuller discussion of the subject, I may add that not many miles from the place where I am now writing there was discovered about ten years ago an altar which bore the inscription DEO MARTI THINGSO, and which, in the opinion of some of the best German archaeologists, was dedicated to Mars, the god of the assembly, in whose name the priests commanded silence and punished the offenders who were brought up for judgment Thus from a bare hillside in Northumberland has come in recent years a testimony to the widespread institution of the *Thing* among our Teutonic forefathers. Before such an assembly it was the custom of the Lombards that all transactions connected with property (especially perhaps property in land) should take place, and it was for this reason that a too generous (or perhaps spiteful) father was forbidden *thingare* his property to the detriment of his natural heirs.

From this custom of making every donation of property in the presence of the *Thing*, the donation itself came to be called *Thinx* or *Gairethinx*. As *ger* in the Old High-German language signifies a spear, and as we know that the Germans always came armed to their assemblies, it is suggested that the *gairethinx* or spear-donation may have been an especially solemn form of transfer of property. One of the laws of Rothari said, "If any man wishes to thing away his property to another, let him make the *gairethinx* itself not secretly, but before free men, inasmuch as both he who things and he who is the receiver are free men, that no contention may arise in future".

Now however solemnly a childless man might have *thinged* away his property, when for any cause he despaired of having issue of his own, if he afterwards begat legitimate sons, the previous *thinx* was utterly null and void, and the sons succeeded to the property as if it had never taken place. And even daughters and illegitimate children ousted the claim of the receiver of the *thinx* to all but a fraction of the inheritance

On the other hand, a childless man who at the solemn thing should pronounce the word *lidinlaib*, thereby expressing that the donee was to enter upon the property at his death, incurred obligations which, if he continued childless, he could not lightly set aside. He became in fact, what our lawyers call "tenant for life", and not "without impeachment of waste", for he must thenceforward confine himself to the reasonable use of the property, and must in no wise fraudulently dissipate the same. If, however, necessity came upon him, and he found himself compelled to sell or mortgage the property with the slaves upon it, he might appeal to the receiver of his *thinx* : "You behold under what compulsion I am about to part with that property which I gave to you at my death. If it seem good to you, help me now and I will preserve this property for your benefit". If the donee of the *thinx* thus called upon refused to help his benefactor, then any alienation or encumbrance of the estate made by the latter remained valid in spite of the donation.

We now come to the marriage laws of Rothari, an interesting section of the Code. But before entering upon it we must notice one important law which governs the whole relations of Lombard womanhood, whether married or single : "It shall not be lawful for any free woman, *living* according to the law of the to Lombards under our sway, to live under the power of *mundium* her own free will, or as it is called to be *selpmundia*, but she must always remain under the power of men, if not a husband or relative under that of the king's court, nor shall she have the power of giving or alienating any property, moveable or immoveable, without the consent of him in whose *mundium* she is living". The principle here laid down was recognized by most, if not all the German tribes whose laws have come down to us, though none deals quite so minutely with this question of the guardianship of women as the Lombard Code. The wording of the law may seem at first sight inconsistent with that high honor in which the Germans from the time of Tacitus downward are said to have held their women. But on reflection we perceive that the institution of this *mundium* or guardianship is chiefly intended for the woman's protection, and is a necessary consequence of the barbaric character of the rest of the Code. In a state of society where the *faida* or blood-feud was still a recognized principle, slowly and with difficulty giving way to the scarcely less barbarous *guidrigild*; under a system of laws which, as we shall see, tolerated the *camfio*, or wager of battle, as the test of right and wrong, what chance would a poor weak woman, if self-championed (*selpmundia*), have had of maintaining her rights? It was evidently necessary that she should have some male protector and representative, who if he had to assume responsibility for her acts, must have the deciding voice in the disposition of her property: and accordingly under the *mundium* of some man the Lombard woman lived from her cradle to her grave; if not under the *mundium* of a father, under that of a husband or a brother; if all these failed her, then under the *mundium* of the king's court. At the same time, though the institution of the *mundium* may have been originally designed for the woman's protection, it was undoubtedly sometimes a coveted prize. The regulations in the Lombard Code as to the division of the *mundium* among the brothers, even the illegitimate brothers, of the daughters of the house show that this view was taken of the guardian's position: and when the king's court came in and claimed the *mundium* of a wealthy heiress, we can well believe that some of the abuses of the right of wardship and marriage which prevailed in feudal times may have been in measure anticipated by the Lombard rulers. This, however, is a mere conjecture, not supported so far as I know by anything that is to be found in the scanty documents that have come down to us.

I must direct the reader's attention to one clause in the sentence above quoted from the 204th law of Rothari: "Any free woman living under our sway *according to the law of the Lombards*". This passage clearly implies that King Rothari had subjects who were not living according to the law of the Lombards. This has a bearing on a very wide and important controversy which will be referred to in a subsequent chapter.

Meanwhile our business is with the Lombard law alone, and we may now trace by such indications as that law affords us the history of the courtship and marriage of a Lombard woman. We must not, however, expect that the Code will reveal to us the sentimental aspect of a Lombard marriage : on the contrary, some of the provisions will remind us of the discussions which take place in many a French farmhouse at the present day concerning the precise amount of the dot of the daughter of a thrifty *propriétaire*.

When a Lombard suitor asked for the hand of a woman in marriage, if her guardian accepted him, a ceremony of betrothal was solemnized, and a written contract (*fabula*) was drawn up between the parties. The suitor covenanted to give a price which was called the *meta*; and some substantial guarantor joined in the covenant with him. If all went well, and the course of the matrimonial negotiations flowed smoothly, the father or brother in whose *mundium* the bride had hitherto been gave, probably on the eve of the wedding, a certain dowry to the bride which was called her *faderfio* (father's money) To this was added on the morning after the marriage a substantial present from the newly-wedded husband to his wife, according to the universal custom of the German tribes; and this present, which was called the *morgangebe* by the Alamanni, and the *morgengifa* among our Anglo-Saxon ancestors, was modified into *morgincap* among the sharp-speaking Lombards

But if the progress of the suit were not prosperous, and if the solemn betrothal did not ripen into marriage, the laws of Rothari had much to say about that contingency. If for two years after the betrothal the suitor kept on delaying the fulfillment of his promise, the father or brother, or he who had the *mundium* of the affianced woman, might exact from the guarantor the payment of the *meta*, and might then give the damsel in marriage to another. But perhaps the reluctant suitor alleged as a reason for his refusal that the woman had lost her chastity. In that case her parents must get twelve neighbors or kinsfolk to swear with them that the accusation was false. If they could do this the woman's reputation was considered to be cleared, and the suitor must either take her to wife, or pay a double *meta* as a penalty for the wrongful accusation.

If, however, for her sins it should happen that a woman was sorely afflicted after her betrothal, if she became a leper or a demoniac, or lost the sight of both eyes, then the suitor might reclaim his *meta*, and was not bound to take her in marriage. If, on the other hand, the guardian of a woman, after solemnly betrothing her to one man, connived at her marriage to another, he had to pay twice the *meta* to the injured suitor.

Once married, the woman passed under the *mundium* of her husband, and if she survived him remained under the *mundium* of his representative. If she had a son grown to adolescence it seems probable that he would be her guardian, but of course this would often not be the case, and she would then be under the *mundium* of some brother or kinsman of her late husband, who might be indisposed to relinquish the profitable trust. The royal legislator therefore clearly stated that the widow had the right to betake herself to another husband if he was a free man. In this case the second husband was bound to repay to the heir of the first, half of the *meta* which had been paid on the first espousals, and if the latter refused to accept this, then the wife might claim her whole *faderfio* and *morgincap* and she returned under the *mundium* of her parents, who might give her in marriage to whom they would.

We have several indications that this enforced *mundium* of the widow under her late husband's heir led sometimes to strained and painful relations. Anyone having the *mundium* of a free wife or maiden who falsely accused her of adultery, or called her a witch or conspired against her life, lost the *mundium* unless he were the father or the brother of the injured woman; and in this and several other cases the *mundium* went, in default of relations, to the king's court. Lastly, to end the story of the matrimonial life of the Lombard woman, if a man slew his wife for any cause which was not sufficient in law to justify her death, the murderous husband had to pay 1200 solidi, half to her parents or relations, and half to the king. If the murdered woman had left sons, these inherited the *morgincap* and *faderfio*: if not, they went to her parents, or failing them, to the king's court. But if the wife plotted against her husband's life, she was at his mercy and he might do to her whatsoever he would. If she slew him, she was herself to be put to death, and her property, if she left no children, went to the husband's heirs. Always, even in presence of the ghastliest domestic tragedies, the Lombard legislator keeps a cool head, and remembers to say what shall be the destination of the *faderfio* and the *morgincaq*.

Interspersed with the marriage laws of which I have spoken are some which deal somewhat more with the moral side of the relation between the sexes. Thus the seduction of a free woman was punished by a fine of 20 solidi, which was increased to 100 solidi if the seducer refused to marry his victim. If a man persuaded the betrothed bride of another to marry him he had to pay 20 solidi to the parents as penalty for seducing their daughter from her duty and 20 more in order to end the feud (*faida*) caused by his misconduct. Moreover he had to pay to the injured affianced suitor twice his *meta*. These comparatively light punishments fell on him who had by gentle means won the forbidden prize. Crimes of violence were rightly punished much more severely. Forcible compulsion of a woman to marry subjected the offender to a fine of 900 solidi, half of which went to the parents of the damsel, and half to the king's court. The injured wife was at liberty to go forth from the offender's house with all her possessions, and might place herself under the *mundium* of a father, a brother, an uncle, or the king, as she might choose.

In this connection we meet with a law which has given rise to much discussion: " If any man shall commit fornication with a female slave belonging to the nations, he shall pay to her lord 20 solidi. If with a Roman, 12 solidi".

It Is only in this casual reference to an act of immorality that we find in all the laws of Rothari the slightest express reference (doubtless there are many implied references) to the great mass of the subject population of Italy who called themselves, and were called by their conquerors, by the once proud name of Roman. And this reference carries us but a little way. The poor bondwoman of Roman extraction is evidently compared unfavorably with her fellow slave of "Gentile", that is of Teutonic or Slavonic origin, the kinswoman it might be of the Anglian lads whom Gregory saw in the market-place. But, after all, it is not her wrong, but the injury done to her master, that is in the mind of the legislator. It is to him that the fine is paid, and all that we learn from this passage is that the stout, strong "gentile" woman who had come across the seas or from the countries beyond the Alps was a more valuable possession to her master than one of the oppressed, emaciated, famine-wasted daughters of Italy.

Acts of immorality committed chiefly against women of servile condition are dealt with in laws 205-214, and we then come to the interesting subject of marriages contracted between persons of unequal status, one free, the other unfree.

In these marriages the general rule seems to have been that which also prevailed in the Roman law, that the issue of the marriage shared the condition of the mother. Thus if an *Aldius* married a free woman, on his death she and her sons might go forth from his house free, but on condition of renouncing the *morgincap* which her late husband had given her, and giving back to his lord the sum which he had once paid to her parents for her *mundium*. If a slave married a freed woman or an *Aldia* she lost the qualified freedom which she had possessed, during the marriage, but might reclaim it on her husband's death, and go forth free with her children. If an *Aldius* married an *Aldia* or a freed woman the sons became *Aldii* on the estate of their father's lord. If he married a female slave, the children of the marriage were slaves of their mother's master. But if he ventured to lift his eyes to a free woman, and make her his wife, he ran the risk of hearing sentence of death pronounced upon him. The relations of the woman who thus demeaned herself had the right to slay her, or to sell her for a slave into foreign parts, and divide her substance among themselves. If they failed to do this, the king's officers might lead her away to the king's court, and set her to work among: the female slaves at the loom. So jealous was the Lombard law of the honor and reputation of the free woman

But, lastly, there was the possible alternative case, that a free man might wish to marry one of his own female slaves. For such a union the law had no such terrors as those inflicted in the converse case of the marriage of a free woman with a slave. But he might only marry her on condition of first enfranchising her, which he must do in a solemn manner by way of *gairethinx* before the assembly of the people. The enfranchised slave, who was now declared to be *wurdi-bora*, might now become her late master's lawfully-wedded wife, and could bear him legitimate sons, with full claim to succeed to his inheritance.

From this subject, by a natural transition, the legislator passes to that of the manumission of slaves.

Of this manumission, as he informs us, there were four kinds.

(1) The fullest and most complete was that which was practiced when a man wished to give his male or female slave absolute freedom to go where he pleased, and dispose of his property as he would. To accomplish this, he first handed over the slave by solemn *gairethinx* to another free owner; that second owner to a third, and the third to a fourth. This last owner led the slave to a place where four roads met, handed him in the presence of witnesses an arrow the free man's weapon, murmuring a certain form of words which had been handed down from dim antiquity, and then pointing to the crossroads, said, "You have unfettered power of walking whither you will".

A slave or *Aldius* thus enfranchised became folk-free (that is, a sharer in the freedom of the Lombard people), and entirely out of his late master's *mundium*. If he died without natural heirs, neither his patron nor his patron's heirs succeeded to his property, but it went to the king's court.

(2) The second form of manumission was that of the slave who was remitted *impans*, that is, "to the king's wish". This passage remains hopelessly dark to us, but we are told that the slave thus liberated was *amund* (perhaps, however, not folk-free).

(3) The third form of manumission made its subject folk-free, but not *amund*. He lived like a free Lombard in the family of his late master, and under his *mundium*. He had received the "liberty of the four ways", and could go where he willed, and do what he pleased, but his property, in default of natural heirs, went to his late master.

(4) The fourth form of manumission, an incomplete and partial affair, not accompanied with "the liberty of the four ways", left its subject only an *Aldius*, that is, as we have seen, it left him in a semi-servile condition, not folk-free on the one hand, but on the other able to contract a valid marriage with a free woman, and probably not liable to the indignity of personal chastisement

The section on manumission ends with the following law, which has an important bearing on the question hereafter to be discussed, of the condition of the subject Romans under the Lombards :

"All freedmen who shall have received their liberty from Lombard lords ought to live under the laws of their lords, and for their benefactors, according to the concession which shall have been made to them by their own lords".

This provision certainly looks as if for some persons, and at some times, the *living* according to the law of the Lombards was not a privilege to be sighed for, but a duty, to be if possible evaded. But more of this hereafter.

The law of vendors and purchasers comes next in order but there is not much here that need claim our attention, except that we notice that the period required to give a prescriptive title to property is very short, only five years. So short a prescription perhaps points to a semi-barbarous state of society still existing among the Lombards, and to frequent changes of ownership by violence. If a man had been left as long as five years in undisturbed possession of land, or slaves, or jewels, it might be presumed that he was the rightful owner.

Also we observe that no slave, and even no *Aldius*, could sell property of any kind without the consent of his master or patron. An exception was necessarily made in the case of a slave who had charge of a farm (*servus massarius*), whose business it was to sell off the young stock, and who did not require the formal consent of his master for each transaction of this kind.

Six laws follow concerning the removal of boundaries the usual punishment for which offence was a fine of 80 solidi in the case of a free man; a fine of half that amount or death in the case of a slave. It is interesting to observe that a frequent method of marking the boundaries was by notching the forest trees.

The slave who thus falsified the markings on the forest trees was punished by amputation of his right hand; and here, with that delightful discursiveness which characterizes the Lombard code, we learn that the same punishment was inflicted on anyone who, without the king's order, stamped gold or coined money, and also on any one who forged a charter or other document.

A measure of police, for the peace and good order of the cities, follows. "If any free man enters any city or village *by the wall*, or leaves it in the same manner, without the cognizance of his magistrate he shall pay the king's court a fine of 20 solidi. An *Aldius* or slave committing the same offence is to pay a fine of 10 solidi. If he commits a robbery he shall pay the fine for such robbery imposed by this edict in addition.

Then follow some obscure and difficult laws which I will not presume to interpret, as to the custom of *pignoratio*, which was a sort of distraint upon the goods of a debtor executed by a creditor on his own responsibility. He was not allowed to resort to this process of self-compensation till after he had on three successive days called upon the debtor to pay his debt, and if he made any mistake in executing it (for instance, if he took the slave of A as security for the payment of the debt of B), he might have to restore eight times the value of the pledge so taken, unless he could swear that he had done it inadvertently. So too the man who had given a pledge (*wadia*) for the maintenance of an action and failed to redeem it within six days was fined 12 solidi.

The section of the edict which deals with theft contains eleven short and simple laws; the next section, that which is concerned with the case of fugitive slaves, is about twice as long, though it contributes only thirteen laws to the collection. Evidently under the Lombard kings, as under the Presidents of the United States who reigned before Abraham Lincoln, the recapture of fugitive slaves was a matter which occupied a considerable part of the thoughts of the local magistrates.

As for theft, if the article stolen was of the value of 10 *siliquae*, the thief, if a free man, had to restore the value of the object ninefold, and to pay a fine of 80 solidi. He might, it is true, escape from this heavy fine by accepting the penalty of death. For the slave the fine was 40 solidi, the rest of the punishment was the same. The free woman (if folk- free) arrested in the act of theft was only called upon to pay the ninefold value. No other fine was to be exacted from her, but she was to go back to her home and muse on the injury which she had done to her reputation by attempting so indecent an action. Any one finding gold or an article of raiment on the highway, and raising it higher than his knee, if he did not declare what he had discovered to the magistrate was to restore ninefold.

We pass to the laws which deal with the case of slaves escaping from their masters. If such a slave or a free man escaping from justice were caught, it was the duty of the magistrate of the place where the capture occurred to hand over two solidi as a reward to the captor, and keep the slave that he might restore him to his master, or the fugitive that he might restore him to his pursuers. Did such a fugitive, having once been caught, escape, his keeper must swear that he had not intentionally released him, but had guarded him to the utmost of his power. Otherwise (apparently) he made himself responsible for the consequences of his escape. If the fugitive, when challenged and summoned to surrender, did not give his hands to be tied, the pursuer slaying him was not to be held answerable for his death

All men were bound to hinder the slave in his flight, and to assist in detaining him. If a ferryman rowed him across a stream he was put on his defence, and unless he could swear a solemn oath that he was ignorant of the fugitive slave's condition, he was compelled to join in the quest, and if that were unsuccessful, to pay to the owner a sum equal to the slave's value, and a fine moreover of 20 solidi to the king's court. If the slave took refuge in a private house, the owner was justified in breaking into it, the fury of the pursuing master being deemed sufficient justification for the technical offence against the rights of property. If anyone knowingly harbored a fugitive slave, or supplied him with food, or showed him the way, or gave him a lift on his journey, the man who had thus helped the fugitive was bound first of all to go forth and find him, and if he failed to do that must pay the value of the slave; and of any property which he might have carried off with him, together with compensation for the work which had been damaged by the slave's flight.

As a rule, any one in whose house a slave sought shelter was bound to send a message to the master announcing the fact. If he failed to do so, and kept the slave more than nine nights he was responsible for any injury that the slave might commit, or for the loss to the owner caused by his death.

These rules applied to all classes. Even the officers of the king's court, the *Gastaldius*, or Actor Regis, the dignitaries of the Church, a priest or a bishop might not permanently shelter a fugitive slave, but having been summoned three times were bound to surrender him to his lord. If it happened, however (as seems often to have been the case), that the householder with whom the slave had taken refuge came forth and made peace between the slave and his master, persuading the latter to receive him back in favor and peace, and if afterwards the master, breaking his promise, avenged himself on his slave for his flight, he must for such violation of his plighted word pay to an ordinary householder 20 solidi, or twice that amount to one of the king's officers, or to a dignitary of the Church, if it was one of these whose intercession had thus been rendered of no avail. In the last case, that of broken faith with a bishop or priest, the forty solidi were to be deposited on the sacred altar where the injury had been done.

The general tenor of these laws seems to show that the sympathy of the whole community, not of the semi-servile rustics only, but also of the rich and powerful, was wont to be on the side of an escaping slave, and that the royal legislator must raise his voice loudly to secure a hearing for the rights of property in human flesh as then recognized by the law.

We come to a short section of the Code which deals with offences against the public peace. To enter another man's house in wrath and passion was such an offence, and was called *hoveros*, a word which perhaps signifies "house-storming". The penalty for such an offence, if committed by a man, was 20 solidi, but a woman cannot commit the offence of breach of the house-peace, which is *hoveros*: because it seems to be absurd that a woman, whether free or bond, should be able, like a man, to do violence with arms.

The next two laws point to the danger to the State arising from the oppressed condition of the slaves or *coloni*.

"If the slaves, by the advice of the country-folk (rusticani), shall enter a village with an armed band wretched to do mischief, any free man under the sway of our kingdom who shall put himself at their head shall run the risk of losing his life, and shall at all events pay 900 solidi, half to the king, and half to him to whom the injury was done. If the leader be a slave, and not a free man, let him be put to death. The slaves are to pay 40 solidi, to be divided as aforesaid".

The second law deals with something like a resisted eviction. Here the *rusticani*, whom I take to be equivalent to *coloni*, are the movers in the tumult, and their punishment is less heavy than that of slaves.

"If for any cause the country-folk shall collect together to make a conspiracy and a sedition, and shall threaten any one or forcibly carry off a slave or a beast which the lord may have wished to remove from the house of his slave, then he who has put himself at the head of the rustics shall die, or redeem his life according to his fixed price, and all who have run into that sedition to do evil shall pay 12 solidi, half to the king, and half to him who has suffered from the act of violence". Assaults committed by the rustics on the lord attempting to recover his property are to be compounded for according to the before-mentioned tariff. If any of the rustics be killed, no claim for compensation is to arise.

These two laws are of considerable importance for their bearing on the question hereafter to be discussed as to the extent of the application of these laws of Rothari; whether meant for Lombards alone, or for Lombards and Romans equally. It will be noticed that the words of the first law are very general—"any free man under the sway of our kingdom". These words should certainly cover the case of a free but subject Roman as well as of a Lombard. But then it is enacted that he shall be put to death, or shall at least pay a fine of 900 solidi. It may be argued that while the free Roman was to be put to death without question, the free Lombard was to have the chance of redeeming himself by a fine. A somewhat similar alternative is offered in the next law to the ringleader of the rustics, perhaps in view of the same difference of nationality.

The seventy-three laws which follow take us over a wide field, and I regret that the space at my disposal does not allow me to copy in detail the picture which they give us of the economic and social condition of the Lombards. More than we might have expected from the inhabitants of a land so rich in cities as Italy, these laws seem to bring before us a population of country-dwellers, I had almost said of country-squires, who still, like their ancestors in the first century, "shun the continuous row of houses, and settle, scattered over their various homes, as the fountain, the moor or the grove may have caught the fancy of each". We see them fencing round their meadows with planks or quickset hedges, and often trying to claim more than they can thus encompass. One lawless neighbor breaks down the fence entirely, and is fined 6 solidi: or he pulls out one plank or one bough, and has to pay 2 solidi; or whole squares of lattice-work and pays 3 solidi. Another with unjust mind hacks to pieces the woodwork of a plough (which our Lombard kinsmen called *plovum*), or steals the bell from a horse's neck, or the yoke or the harness-thongs from the patient ox. The fine for the first of these misdeeds is 4 solidi; for the other acts, and for most of those offences against rural peace which are about to be enumerated, the fine is 6 solidi.

The elaborate laws for the protection of vines show that the Lombards appreciated that slender and delicate tree which is married so happily to the elm everywhere in the rich plain of Lombardy, and by the fame of whose joyous fruitage they themselves, according to the Saga, had been tempted into Italy. But we read with astonishment that though the wayfarer might help himself to three grapes without offence, for any taken above that number he must pay the regulation fine of 6 solidi.

The announcement that the maker of a hedge by which man or beast is injured or slain will be held responsible for the injury, or even for the homicide, strangely reminds us of modern controversies about barbed wire-fencing; but he who digs a ditch round his plot of land is liable to no claim for compensation for man or beast injured by falling into it, "because he did it for the safety of his field, and not with guile"; and the same exception applies to the digger of a well, "because the well-water is a common gift for the benefit of all"

We find a similar allusion to natural right in the laws relating to the taking of honey. If a man steal a bee-hive with the bees inside it he pays 12 solidi; if he find a swarm of bees on a tree on which the owner has set his mark, he pays 6 solidi; but if there be no mark on the tree he may take the honey and keep it "by the law of nature". Only this "law of nature" does not apply to the *gahagia* or game-coverts of the king; and even in other forests, if the lord chances to come riding by, the finder of the honey must give it up to him, but shall not be liable to any further blame for taking it.

A similar rule applies to the finding of young falcons on an unmarked tree. Here, too, the finder may keep them unless the lord of the forest comes upon the scene. But if on any pretence, from trees marked or unmarked, he takes young falcons from the nest in the king's *gahagium*, he must pay a fine of 12 solidi.

The Lombards were apparently a nation of horsemen, and many laws are devoted to questions connected with matters equestrian. To knock out a horse's eye, or cut off its ear, or do it any other bodily injury, subjected the offender to the penalty of restoring another horse of equal value to that which he had maimed. To cut off the hairs of its tail was punished with a fine of 6 solidi. To make any disfiguring marks upon it, whereby the owner might be prevented from knowing his own, was so obviously the next step to theft that it was punished accordingly by a fine of ninefold the horse's value. To mount another man's horse and ride it about in the neighborhood was an offence punishable with a fine of 2 solidi; but to take it off on a journey without the owner's leave was virtual theft, and punished by the ninefold fine. But sometimes a man would find himself quite innocently in possession of a horse that did not belong to him. It had come straying into his courtyard, and was doing damage there. What must an honest Lombard do in such a case? He must take the horse to the local magistrate or to the congregation assembling at the church door four or five times, and must make proclamation to all men by the voice of the crier : "I have found a horse and I know not whose it is". Having done this, if no owner appeared, he might safely keep it and ride it as his own; but when the horse died he must keep a note of the markings on its skin, that he might have somewhat to show to the owner should he at last make his appearance. If he complied with these regulations he was free from all further responsibility; if he failed in any of them he was liable to the ninefold fine.

Perhaps a man who had lost his horse would entrust the quest for it to a servant, telling him the marks by which to know the missing animal, and the searcher would in his ignorance lay hands upon the wrong horse and ride it off to his master's stable. Thereupon the real owner of the second horse appears upon the scene and brings a charge of horse-stealing. Then let him in whose keeping the horse is make solemn oath that the mistake was involuntary, and if he have treated the horse well while it was in his stables he shall be subject to no further action.

The laws respecting the pursuit of game are numerous, but except for those previously quoted, which imply that the king's own *gahagium* was strictly preserved, they do not seem to indicate that jealous monopoly of the pleasures of the chase which was characteristic of feudal times. If a stag or any other wild creature has been shot by a man it becomes his, but the right of property in it lasts for only twenty-four hours. If a passer-by finds a wild beast wounded by a hunter or caught in his snares, it is his duty to carry the prize to the hunter, for which he shall be rewarded by the right shoulder and seven ribs. If he conceals the capture, he shall pay the hunter a fine of 6 solidi. If he be injured by a wild beast which has been caught in a snare, he has a right to compensation from the setter of the snare. But if of his own free-will and out of desire of gain he goes to such a wild beast, either ensnared or surrounded by dogs, and tries to make it his prey, then the consequences are on his own head, and he has no redress against the first huntsman

If a beast being wounded by the hunter meets a man, and slays him in its fury, the hunter will be held answerable for homicide. But this holds good only so long as the hunter is actually pursuing his quest with his dogs and his artillery. When he has given it up, and turned homewards, he ceases to be liable for the consequences of the rage of the wounded animal.

This whole section with which we are now dealing is concerned mainly with laws relating to animals, but after reading that he who strikes a cow in calf, and causes her to miscarry, must pay one *tremissis* (the third part of a solidus), and he who does a similar injury to a mare in foal shall pay one solidus, we are shocked to find that he who strikes another man's female slave, thereby causing abortion, pays only 3 solidi, only half the fine for stealing a horse's baiter, or pulling the hairs out of its tail. There is nothing in the Code of this strange semi-barbarous people which goes so far to justify St. Gregory's phrase "nefandissimi Langobardi" as this.

Incidentally to the discussion of injuries wrought by animals (which must, as a rule, be compounded for by their masters) we learn that "if, as a punishment for his sins, a man becomes rabid or demoniac, and does damage to man or beast, compensation shall not be claimed from his heirs", and conversely, if he himself be killed while in that state of frenzy, his heirs shall not be entitled to claim *guidrigild* on his behalf.

The various laws about swine and swineherds show that the unclean creature which Virgil does not condescend to notice in the Georgics played an important part in the husbandry of the Lombards. If a man found a herd of swine rooting about in his meadow, he might kill one, and not be asked to compensate the owner. If not in a meadow, but still feeding on land which was not their owner's, he might keep one as a hostage, and claim compensation for the rest at the rate of 3 *siliquae* (amounting to the eighth of a solidus) per pig. The champion boar of one of these great herds of swine was a valuable animal and went among the Lombards by the name of *sonorpair* and the theft of this hero among swine was punished by a fine of 12 solidi. But it was ordained that unless the herd consisted of at least 30 swine, its champion should not be considered to have attained to the dignity of a *sonorpair*. The swineherds (*porcarii*) were evidently a quarrelsome class of men, themselves often the slaves of serfs, and two laws are devoted to the special question of the quarrels with "assault and battery" which arose among them.

Lastly, to close this agricultural section of the Code, it is ordained that "no one shall have liberty to deny to travelers the right of grazing their horses, except it be in a meadow at haytime, or in a harvest-field. But after the hay or other crops have been gathered in, let the owner of land only vindicate the possession of so much of it as he can surround by a fence. For if he shall presume to remove the horses of travelers from the stubbles or from the pastures where other cattle are feeding, he shall pay the ninefold fine for these horses because he has dared to remove them from the open field which is *fornaccar* (land that has yielded its crop). We ask ourselves here what it was that the churlish Lombard landowner had to repay in *ahtugild*. It seems hardly credible that it can have been the actual value of the horse to which he had denied a meal. Was it the computed value of the horse's grazing?

From these pastoral and agricultural provisions we pass to the laws which regulate the judicial procedure of the Lombards. A rude and primitive kind of procedure it was, one from which the barbarous "wager of battle" was not yet entirely eliminated, but in which that appeal to brute force was being gradually superseded by a rough, but generally effective appeal to the conscience of the accused person and his friends. For we have now to deal with that system of combined swearing to the truth of a fact, or the falsehood of an accusation, which is generally called compurgation, and out of which probably sprang the Anglo-Saxon jury. But as the word "compurgation" is a term of later introduction—unknown, I believe, to any of the barbaric codes—and as the functions of a modern jury are altogether unlike, almost opposed to those of the fellow-swearers of the Lombard law, we shall do well to avoid the use of either term, and confine ourselves to the word *sacramentales*, which is that always used in the Codes not only of the Lombards, but of the Alamanni, the Frisians, and the Bavarians. The Lombard name for these persons seems to have been *Aidos*, a word obviously connected with the Gothic *Aiths*, the German *Eid*, and the English *Oath*, and meaning swearers; but the Lombard legislator writing in Latin prefers to use the words *sacramentum* and *sacramentalis*, connected of course with the modern French *serment*. The principle involved in this judicial process, so unlike our modern ideal of judicial investigation, but so widely spread through all the Teutonic nations, was evidently this:

One free German warrior accuses another of a certain offence, say of having stolen his horse, or murdered his slave. The accused man denies the fact; a multitude of his friends gather round him, and echo his denial; it seems as if there would be a bloody quarrel between the two parties. In earlier centuries the matter would have been thus settled by the strong hand, but now in the age of the migration of the peoples, a somewhat clearer vision of a possible "Reign of Law" has dawned upon the Teutonic mind. In order to prevent the interminable *faida* (blood-feud) from breaking out upon this trivial occasion, it is ordained that a given number of the friends of each disputant shall by solemn oath, either upon the Holy Gospels or upon their weapons of war consecrated by a Christian priest, assert their belief in the truth of the statements made by him whose cause they favor. It may be said, "And how much further does that process carry you? Of course each group will swear till sunset to the truth of its own side of the question". Apparently it was not so; there was still much reverence for truth in these rough, Rome-conquering Teutons. They were not like some modern party-politicians, or like a jury of Celtic farmers. They recognized in some degree the inviolable claims of truth, and this old pagan virtue of theirs was reinforced by the awful sanctions of the Church and by the dread of endless torment awaiting him who swore falsely on the Holy Gospels or the consecrated arms. Some rough examination or discussion of the facts of the alleged offence probably took place among the *sacramentales*, and at length it was generally found (this must have been the case, or the practice would have fallen into disuse) that on one or other side a "swearer" yielded to the force of evidence, and admitted either that the plaintiff had failed to make good his attack, or the defendant his defence. When this was done, when either one of the litigants or any of his supporters said "I no longer dare to swear to the truth of our cause", then the *sacramentum* was said to be broken, and the beaten party must pay his *guidrigild* if defendant, or if plaintiff must renounce his claim

These appear to be the general principles which governed the trial by *sacramentum*. It has been already remarked how utterly it differed from the trial by jury, which is in a sense its offspring. The modern juror is chosen expressly as a disinterested and impartial person: the *sacramentales* were chosen because they were friends and relatives of one or other of the litigants. The modern juror is exhorted to dismiss from his mind all previous knowledge that he may have acquired of the case, and to judge only on the evidence before him. The *sacramentalis* judged from his previous knowledge, and almost from that alone. Unanimity is required of a modern English jury, and one obstinate juror who holds out against the remaining eleven is an object of general dislike, and is labored with till he can be brought to a better mind. The one *sacramentalis* who yielded to conviction, and declared that he durst not swear to the truth of his principal's assertion, was in the teutonic institution the hero of the day, and it was his act of "breaking the sacramentum" which decided the right and wrong of the dispute.

Having thus described the general principle of trial by *sacramentum*, let us briefly consider the manner in which such a trial was conducted according to the legislation of Rothari.

As soon as a matter of dispute arose between two free Lombards, the plaintiff (who was called *ille qui pulsat*) called upon the defendant (*ille qui pulsatur*) to furnish security for the satisfaction of his claim. The defendant then gave some material pledge (*wadia*), probably of no great value, and "found bail", as we should say, or in other words prevailed on some one of his friends to act as guarantor (*fidejussor*) that the plaintiff's claim should be duly met. Twelve nights (in Teutonic phrase) were allowed him in which to appear and rebut the claim by his oath, and if, by reason of illness or for any other cause, he failed to do so, twelve more nights were allowed, and so on as excuse was pleaded. But if, on one pretext or other, he evaded his obligation for a whole year, judgment went against him by default. And similarly, he who made the claim, if he delayed for a whole year to establish it by means of *sacramentales*, lost all right to speak of the claim thereafter, and presumably had to restore the *wadia*. For the rule was, "Let him who is prepared to give the *sacramentum* have firm possession of the matter in dispute". If neither party thus made delay, and the cause came on for trial, it was the duty of the plaintift (if the case were a grave one, affecting values of 20 solidi or upwards) to nominate six *sacramentales* from among the near kindred of the defendant. In thus nominating, however, he might not choose any man who was known to be at enmity with his kinsman—for instance, any one who had struck him a blow, or conspired for his death, or who had *thinged* away property to another to which that kinsman had a claim. The defendant associated himself with these six men, and then apparently these seven chose five others, of whom it is only enacted that they should be free men. We should have expected to find that these last five were to be all kinsmen of the plaintiff, to match the six kinsmen of the defendant, but the law is not so written. The group of twelve *sacramentales* thus collected then proceeded to swear as to the rights of the case on the Holy Gospels, and it would seem that they must have gone on swearing until the strain upon the conscience became too great to be borne, and the *sacramentum* was broken by the defendant or one of his kinsmen refusing to swear any longer. If this did not happen, we must suppose that judgment was given for the defendant. Truly a strange way of arriving at truth in litigation, and one which seems unduly to favor the defendant, but in practice it cannot have been a complete failure, or men would not have continued to use it for centuries. If the cause were less important, represented by a value between 12 and 20 solidi, there were only six *sacramentales*, three chosen by the plaintiff, and two by the defendant, who himself became the sixth. And the whole number swore, not on the Gospels, but on the consecrated arms If the matter in dispute were of less value than 12 solidi there were only three *sacramentales*, the defendant, the nominee of the plaintiff, and a third chosen by both. They swore simply *ad arma*, apparently without any special religious rite. There are various provisions with which I need not now weary the reader, for the case of the death of a litigant or a *sacramentalis* before the cause was decided, but the following law is worth quoting entire : "If a man be attacked (*pulsatus*) by another on account of any fault, and denies it, let it be lawful for him to justify himself (*se idoniare*) according to the law and the gravity of the accusation (*qualitatem causae*). But if he shall openly proclaim that he committed it, let him pay composition according to that which is set down in this Edict; for it shall not be allowable for any man after he has openly confessed, afterwards to deny by *sacramentum* the guilt which he has once admitted. Because we have known many in our kingdom who have set up such wicked contentions. These things have moved us to correct them by the present law and bring them to a better state of mind".

Besides this system of trial by *sacramentales*, there evidently still survived the older and yet more barbarous system of the *camfio*, the warrior who offered what our forefathers called "wager of battle". As to this practice the laws unfortunately give us scarcely any information. We are told, however, that certain questions, such as the legitimacy of a son, the murder of a wife by her husband, the right to the *mundium* of a married woman, were to be decided by free *sacramentales*, because it appears to us unjust that so grave a matter should be disposed of in battle by the resisting power of one man's shield. On the other hand, the man who has in anger called a free woman (in another man's *mundium*) a harlot or a witch, if he repeats the charge in cold blood and maintains its truth, must prove it by a *camfio*. The woman accused of plotting the death of her husband may prove her innocence either by the *sacramentum* or by persuading some *camfio* to fight in her behalf.

It was ordained that no *camfio* in going forth to the judicial combat should presume to carry upon his person magical spells or anything of that kind. "Let him bring only the stipulated arms, and if any suspicion arise that he is privily wearing articles of magic, let enquiry be made by the judge; and if any such be found upon him, let them be torn out and cast away. And after these enquiries let the *camfio* himself lay his hand in the hand of his comrade in the presence of the judge, and declare in a satisfactory manner that he has nothing pertaining to enchantment on his person. Then let him go to the encounter".

An important law defines the position of the *ware-gango* (or foreigner who has come to settle in the land under the shield of our royal power). It is declared that men of this class ought to live according to the laws of the Lombards, "unless they have obtained from our piety the right to live according to some other law. If they have legitimate sons, let them be their heirs just like the sons of the Lombards; but if they have no legitimate sons, they shall have no power to filing away their property, or to alienate it by any other form of conveyance without the king's command". The language of this law clearly shows that there were other laws besides those of the Lombard invaders prevalent within the peninsula; but here, as in a previous enactment, "living according to the laws of the Lombards" seems to be spoken of as rather a duty than a privilege. Probably the explanation at any rate of this law is, that the king's court was determined to keep its grasp on the property of these wealthy *waregangi* in the event, perhaps a frequent event, of their dying without legitimate male issue.

This tendency of the king's court to enforce and exaggerate all pecuniary claims against the private individual (a tendency which may be partly excused by the fact that apparently there was no regular system of taxation in the Lombard state) is further manifested by laws 369 to 373. In all cases in which the king is interested as plaintiff, the composition payable to him is to be double that payable to a subject, the only exceptions being that of forcible abduction and marriage of a woman, or murder, in both of which the already heavy fine of 900 solidi is not to be exceeded. If a slave of the king commit murder, the king's court will pay the prescribed *guidrigild*, and the slave will then be hung over the dead man's grave; but in all cases involving the fine of 900 solidi the king's court is not to be called upon to pay the fine, though the slave will incur the risk of capital punishment.

Then, further, for the protection of the officers of the court who are executing the orders of their lord, it is enacted that if a *sculdhaizo* (which we may perhaps translate "justice of the peace") or other agent of the king is killed or assaulted in the performance of his duty, the offender shall, over and above the ordinary *guidrigild*, pay a fine of 80 solidi to the king's court. But in order to guard against those abuses of official position for the sake of private gain, which in the days of the Roman Republic made the government of the provinces a byword, it was enacted that no *gastaldius* receiving any gift by *gairethinx* from a private person during his tenure of office should be allowed to retain such gift except by a special precept of the king's indulgence. Without such express sanction any property acquired by him during his administration went straight into the grasp of the king's court.

The Lombards, as may be discerned from the character of their early sagas related to us by Paulus, were a somewhat superstitious people, haunted by the fearful and shadowy forebodings of the German forest-life, and especially afraid of the mysterious might of women who were in league with the powers of darkness. Hence the words *striga* and *masca*, signifying "witch", were terms of deadliest insult; and it was ordained (as we have seen) that any man (except a father or a brother) who had the *mundium* of a woman, forfeited that profitable guardianship if he called her by either of these opprobrious names. Apparently some of the strange old superstitions about blood-sucking vampires increased the horror of these words, for, says the legislator, "Let no one presume to kill another man's *Aldia* or female slave on the ground of her being a *striga*, which is commonly called *masca*. It is a thing not to be conceived of by Christian minds as possible that a woman can eat a living man from inside him. Therefore the penalty for any such offence shall be 60 solidi, in addition to the ordinary *guidrigild*; half of the fine to go to the owner, and half to the king's court. And if any judge shall have ordered the man to do that wicked deed, he shall pay the above-written penalty out of his own pocket".

Some curious belated laws about the fines for various forms of bodily injury form the conclusion of the Code. I will not describe them here, but will end with one strange provision as to the death of a brawling woman:

"If a free woman rushes into a brawl where men are striving, and receives a wound or a blow, or is slain, she shall be paid for according to her nobility; and the composition shall be so paid as if it had been the woman's brother against whom the offence had been committed. No further blame (on account of her being a woman) shall be attached to the offender, nor shall the (regular) fine of 900 solidi be exacted, seeing that she herself rushed into the quarrel, because it is an indecent thing for a woman so to do".

It will be seen that here the expression is used that the slain woman is to be compounded for "according to her nobility"; and in several of the laws of Rothari, especially the later laws, we have a similar expression: "let him be compounded for according to his computed price". These words raise one of the most difficult questions in connection with Lombard jurisprudence. In most of these barbarian codes, as is well known, we have a nicely graduated table of social distinctions, with corresponding varieties in the *weregild* paid for each. Thus according to the Alamannic Code, the life of a member of the most noble class (*Priorissimus Alamannu*) is appraised at 240 solidi; of the middle class of nobility (*medianus Alamannus*) at 200 solidi; of the *minoflidis*, or simple free man, at 160 solidi. Among the Salian Franks the murderer of an *antrustion* or *grafion* (men belonging to the two highest classes of nobility) had to pay 600 solidi; of a *sagiharon* or legal assessor of the court 600 or 300 solidi, according to his rank; and of a Roman *conviva regis* (king's guest) 300 solidi. Among the Ripuarian Franks the *weregild* of a bishop was 900 solidi; of a priest 600; of a deacon 500; of a sub-deacon 400; and so in several other instances. Now these words, "according to her nobility", and "as he shall have been appraised", clearly point to some such gradations of *guidrigild* among the Lombards also, but it is not easy to find it in the Code. We have, it is true, the distinction between the compositions for a free man, an *Aldius*, and a slave, but there the differentiation apparently ends. What is the reason of this strange silence? An Italian commentator, whose main thesis is the utter subjugation and servitude of the Romans under the Lombard yoke, maintains that the silence was intentional, and veiled one of the state secrets (*arcana imperii*) of the conquerors. He calls that secret the *variable guidrigild*, and asserts that the composition to be paid for a slain Lombard noble being written down in no code, remained hidden in the breast of the governor, and might be imposed by him according to his will. This *variable guidrigild* he asserts to have been one of the main instruments used by the conquering tribe to "keep their vanquished neighbours in a state of semi-servitude". This theory may be true, but I confess that I have not yet met with any adequate proof of it. To me it seems more probable, either that the tariff of composition for a slain or wounded noble has been omitted for some reason or other by the copyists of Rothari's manuscript, or that it was never inserted in the Code because it was so well known to all men that its rehearsal seemed unnecessary.

We come now at last to the conclusion of the whole matter; to the "Peroration of King Rothari", which, like the Prologue, shall be translated in full:

"We now confirm this Edict, which by God's grace we have composed after earnest study and long vigils. By the Divine favor we have persevered in our task, enquiring into and calling to remembrance the ancient laws of our fathers. Those which were not written we have nevertheless learned; and we have added to them those things which seemed to be expedient for the common welfare of all, and of our own race (in particular); acting herein with the advice and by the consent of the nobles, the judges, and all our most prosperous army; and we now order them to be written down on this parchment, with this one reservation, that all things which by the Divine clemency have been ascertained by our own accurate enquiry, or which old men have been able to remember concerning the ancient laws of the Lombards, are to be subjoined to this Edict. We add, moreover, hereto our confirmation by *gairethinx*, that this law may be firm and enduring, and that both in our own most prosperous times and in all time to come it may be kept inviolably by all our successors.

"Here ends the law which King Rothari with his noble judges has renewed".

There is, however, appended to the Edict a provision that all causes already decided shall be left undisturbed, but that any which are still in progress on that twenty-second day of November, of the second Indiction (643), shall be decided according to the provisions of the Edict. Also that no copies of the Edict are to be deemed authentic but those which are written or attested by the hand of Answald the notary.

Thus then did King Rothari, standing on a spear, or holding a spear in his hand, in the assembly of the chiefs of his nation in the palace at Pavia, solemnly confirm by the ceremony of *gairethinx* the Code which contained the laws and customs of his barbaric forefathers, with such additions as the statesmen of his kingdom, after seventy-six years of residence on the soil of Italy, deemed it advisable to append thereto. But he and they were dwelling in a land which had witnessed the birth and development through nearly a thousand years of the most comprehensive and the most scientific system of jurisprudence that the world has yet seen. The Roman Law, as codified by Justinian, was then in force at Ravenna and at Naples, as it is now, with necessary modifications, in force at New Orleans and at Batavia. Yet to this Code, one of the most splendid achievements of the human intellect, King Rothari and his peers do not refer in one line of their Edict. Their only mention of the great name of Rome, as has been already pointed out, is in that passage where an injury done to a Roman female slave is assessed at a lower rate than a similar injury to her Teutonic fellow-sufferer. And so the Lombard invaders, like children, repeat the lessons which they have learned from their forefathers of the forest, and try to fit in their barbarous law terms into the stately but terribly misused language of Latium. Throughout, Roman ideas, Roman rights, the very existence of a Roman population, are not so much menaced or invaded, as calmly ignored. The Code of Rothari, promulgated on the sacred soil of Italy, in a land which had once witnessed the promulgation of the Code, the Institutes, and the Digest of Justinian, is like the black tent of the Bedouin pitched amid the colonnades of some stately Syrian temple, whose ruined glories touch no responsive chord in the soul of the swart barbarian.

CHAPTER VI.

GRIMWALD AND CONSTANS

The central figure of Lombard history in the seventh century is (as I have already said) King Grimwald. It is true that his reign (662-671) was not a long one, but it was filled with important events, and included the most serious encounter with the power of the Eastern Empire that had been witnessed since Alboin entered Italy. Moreover, the events of his early and middle life attached a kind of romantic interest to his career which powerfully affected the imaginations of his countrymen. No name, we may safely say, except those of Alboin and Authari, was dearer to the Lombard minstrel than that of Grimwald, and if he has therefore invested him with a robe of beautiful Saga, every fold of which may not accurately correspond to the truth of history, we can easily pardon the illusion for the sake of at last finding a man who is something more than a mere name in a pedigree. Telling the tale as it is told us by Paulus, I have already related how Grimwald, son of Gisulf, duke of Friuli, was carried captive by one of the terrible Avar horsemen,—how, though little more than a child, he slew his unsuspecting captor and rejoined his flying brethren; how, after his two elder brothers had been basely assassinated at Opitergium by a treacherous Exarch, Grimwald and his brother Eadwald, disdaining to be subject to their uncle, who succeeded to the duchy of Friuli, betook themselves to the court of the old friend of their family, Arichis, duke of Benevento. It has also been told how Aio, the hypochondriac son of Arichis, after a short reign (641-642) was slain by the Slavonian invaders, and how he was succeeded by his kinsman and friend, Radwald (642-647), and he in turn by Grimwald, who reigned for fifteen years (647-662) as duke of Benevento. We have now to trace the course of events which made the fugitive prince of Friuli and the guest-friend of Benevento king in the palace at Pavia, and lord of all Lombard Italy.

Rothari, the legislator of the Lombards, died in the year 652 and was succeeded by his son RODWALD, whose short and inglorious reign (of five months and seven days) was ended by the sword or the dagger of a Lombard whose wife he had seduced. He was succeeded by ARIPERT, nephew of the great queen Theudelinda, whose family, as has been before said, was the stock from whence most of the Lombard kings were drawn throughout the seventh century. Of the reign of Aripert, which lasted nearly nine years (653-661), all that we learn is that he built, adorned, and richly endowed a church in honor of the Saviour outside the western gate of Pavia, which was called Marenca. On his death he was succeeded by his two sons, Perctarit and Godepert, who reigned, the one at Milan and the other at Pavia. It was the first time that the Lombards had tried the Frankish plan of a royal partnership; and that without the justification which might be supposed to exist in the case of the vast Frankish Empire, for the two royal cities of the Lombards were only twelve miles asunder. The experiment answered as ill with the sons of Aripert as with any of the fratricidal posterity of Clovis. Jalousies and suspicions soon arose between the two brother kings, and the discord, fanned by artful councilors on both sides, broke out into an open flame of war. Hereupon, Godepert sent Garipald, duke of Turin, to sue for the help of Grimwald, duke of Benevento, promising him the hand of his sister as a reward for his championship. But Garipald, dealing deceitfully with his master, suggested to Grimwald that he should himself strike a blow for the Lombard crown, pointing out, with some truth, that a strong, experienced and fore-seeing ruler like himself would be better for the nation of the Lombards than these weak youths who were wasting the strength of the realm by their unnatural contest. The temptation was listened to, and Grimwald, having nominated his son Romwald to the duchy of Benevento, set forth for Pavia with a chosen band of warriors. Everywhere on the road he gathered friends and helpers for his now scarcely veiled designs on the supreme power. Transamund, count of Capua, being sent through the regions of Spoleto and Tuscany, collected a band of zealous adherents in those two duchies, with whom he met Grimwald on the Aemilian Way. So the host, with ambiguous purpose, rolled on through the valley of the Po; and when Grimwald had reached Piacenza, he sent the traitorous Garipald to announce his coming to Godepert.

"And where shall I receive him?" asked the inexperienced and misdoubting king.

"You have promised him the hand of your sister", answered Garipald, "and cannot do less than assign him quarters in the palace. Notwithstanding, when the solemn interview takes place between you, it might be prudent to put on a coat of mail under your royal robes, for I fear that he has designs on your life".

With similar words did the cunning deceiver poison the mind of Grimwald: "Go to the interview well armed; be vigilant; I doubt the designs of Godepert. I hear that he wears a coat of mail under his mantle".

Accordingly, Grimwald and his followers entered the palace of Pavia, and on the next day the duke of Benevento was ushered into the hall of audience. The two men met apparently in friendly embrace, but even in the act of embracing, Grimwald felt the coat of mail under the regal mantle of his host. The dark suggestions of Garipald seemed in that moment to be verified; and, slaying that he might not be slain, he drew his sword and killed the hapless Godepert. All disguise was then thrown off, and Grimwald reigned as king in Pavia. The infant son of Godepert, named Raginpert, was conveyed away to some safe hiding-place by the trusty servants of the late king, and Grimwald, despising his tender years, made no effort to arrest him.

When Perctarit, reigning at Milan, heard the tidings of his brother's murder, fearing that he would be the next victim, he left the country with all speed and sought refuge at the barbarous court of the Khan of the Avars. His wife Rodelinda and his little son Gunincpert fell into the hands of Grimwald, who sent them for safe-keeping to Benevento. Except for the one foul deed, the murder of Godepert, into which he was entrapped by the perfidious counsels of Garipald, the hands of Grimwald were unstained by innocent blood.

As for Garipald, the contriver of all this wickedness he did not long rejoice in the success of his schemes. He had indeed deceived his employers all round, for he had embezzled some part of the presents which he had been ordered to carry to Benevento. The discovery of this fraud would probably before long have alienated from him the new king's favor, but more speedy vengeance overtook him. A certain dwarfish retainer of Godepert, born at Turin, burned to avenge the murder of his master. Knowing that Duke Garipald was coming on Easter Day to pray in the basilica of St. John, he hid himself in the church, climbing up above the baptistery, and holding on by his left arm to the column which supported the canopy. When the duke entered the church the little Turinese drew his sword, but kept it concealed under his robes. As soon as Garipald came under the place of his hiding, up flew the robe, out flashed the sword, wielded with all the strength of which the dwarf was capable, and the head of Garipald rolled on the pavement of St. John's basilica. All the followers of the duke rushed upon the dwarf, and pierced him with many wounds. But the little champion died happy, for he had avenged his master.

Grimwald, now, without a rival, king of all the Lombards, took for his second wife the sister of the slain Godepert, who had been betrothed to him before he set out from Benevento. He was probably twice as old as his new queen, but he was a man who, if there had not been that stain of kindred blood upon his hands, might have won the love even of a young bride. Tall, with well-knit limbs, with bald head and full flowing beard, he was, by the admission of all, a man of absolutely dauntless courage, and as great in counsel as in war. Secure in the affections of the Northern Lombards, he sent back the mass of his Beneventan army to their homes, enriched by great gifts, but retained a few of the leaders at his court, endowing them with large possessions.

But though Grimwald was not by nature cruel or suspicious, the thought of the exile Perctarit could not but sometimes threaten the solidity of his throne. He sent an embassy to the Khan of the Avars, offering him a *modius* full of golden coins if he would surrender the fugitive into his hands. But the barbarian, who had sworn by his idol to Perctarit that he would never abandon him to his foes, replied, "Without doubt the gods would slay me if I sacrifice this man whom I have sworn in their presence to protect".

Another embassy came, not this time offering gold, but warning the Khan that the peace which had now long time subsisted between the Avars and the Lombards would not endure unless Perctarit departed from his borders. Evidently the Avars were weaker or the Lombards stronger, than in the day when Grimwald's own home was ravaged, and himself all but carried into captivity by these terrible barbarians from the Danube. And now the Khan, while still faithful to the oath which he had sworn in the presence of his idol, and refusing to surrender Perctarit to his foes, appealed to the generosity of his guest to go whither he would, but not to involve him in war with the Lombards. Thus adjured, Perctarit determined to return to Italy, and throw himself on the clemency of the new king, for all men said that Grimwald was merciful. Having arrived at Lodi, he sent forward a faithful henchman named Unulf, who announced to Grimwald Perctarit's approaching arrival, and received an assurance that since he thus trusted to the king's honor, he should suffer no harm. When admitted to the royal presence Perctarit sought to throw himself at Grimwald's feet, but was gently restrained from that humiliation, and received the kiss of peace. Said Perctarit, "I am thy servant. Knowing thee to be most Christian and kind, I determined, instead of continuing to dwell amongst Pagans, to trust thy clemency, and come to throw myself at thy feet". The king renewed his promise, and sealed it with his accustomed oath: "By Him who gave me life, since thou hast come into mine allegiance, no harm shall happen to thee, and I will arrange that thou shalt have the means of living in comfort". He then invited the weary fugitive to rest in a spacious dwelling, ordering that all his needs should be sumptuously supplied from the public treasury. But when Perctarit reached the guest-house provided for him by the king, troops of the citizens of Pavia waited upon him to renew their old acquaintance. Whispering tongues reported these visits to Grimwald, assuring him that Perctarit was forming so large a party in the city that he would undoubtedly deprive the reigning king of his crown and life together. Again Grimwald listened to the fatal suggestion, "Slay or be slain", and forgetful of his sworn promise, began to plan the death of the innocent and unsuspecting Perctarit. The deed was to be done on the morrow, and meanwhile Perctarit was to be intoxicated that he might not perceive his danger and escape. A great banquet was prepared in Perctarit's dwelling, and was shared by many guests. Costly meats and various kinds of wine were brought from the king's table to Perctarit, and he feasted right royally. But one of his father's old servants bringing to the guest a portion from the royal table, bowed so low in salutation that his head went below the board, and then whispered, "The king has a purpose to slay you". At once Perctarit gave a sign to the butler who waited upon him to fill his silver goblet with water only. Messenger after messenger brought generous wines from the king, and Perctarit seemed to drink them eagerly, while really imbibing only water. The servants carried back to the king the tidings that Perctarit was drinking heavily, to which Grimwald coarsely replied, "Let that drunkard drink today: tomorrow he will disgorge the wine mingled with blood". Meanwhile Perctarit found means to communicate with Unulf, and tell him of the impending danger. Then Unulf sent a servant to his own house with orders to bring his bedding from thence, and spread his couch beside that of Perctarit. The guards whom Grimwald had by this time stationed to watch the doors of Perctarit's abode saw the slave enter with the bedding, and then after the supper was ended and all the other guests departed, they saw Unulf emerge, attended apparently by a young slave, whose head and neck were covered by the bed-clothes, the counterpane and the bearskin, under the weight of which he staggered. His brutal master urged him on with blows and curses, and more than once the overloaded youth fell to the ground while trying to escape from the blows. When they came to the place where the king's sentries were posted, these naturally enquired what was the matter. "My rascal of a slave", said Unulf, "spread my couch in the chamber of that tipsy Perctarit, who has filled himself with wine, and now lies like a corpse on the floor. But I have followed his mad courses long enough. So long as my lord the king lives, I shall henceforward stay in my own house". When the guards heard this they were glad, and let Unulf and the slave (who of course was Perctarit in disguise) pass without further question. Meanwhile Perctarit's valet who was the only other person that had been left in the house, made fast the door, and all was settled for the night. But Unulf let Perctarit down by a rope from a corner of the city wall overlooking the river Ticinus, and he, meeting with some of his friends, galloped away with them on some horses which they found grazing in the meadows, and the same night reached the city of Asti which had not yet submitted to Grimwald, but still held out for the lost cause. Thence one rapid journey to Turin; and the fugitive disappeared over the ridges of the Alps into the friendly country of the Franks. "Thus", says Paulus, "did Almighty God by His merciful providence deliver an innocent man from death, and at the same time preserve from blood-guiltiness a king who really desired to do what was right".

Morning came; the guards still paced up and down before the dwelling of Perctarit; at last the messengers of the king came and knocked at the door. The valet answered from within, "Have pity on him, and let him sleep a little longer, for he is weary with his journey and is wrapped in deep slumber". The messengers returned and told their tale to the king, who at once attributed Perctarit's heavy sleep to the potations of the preceding evening. "But it is time to rouse him now, and bring him to the palace", said the king. The messengers returned, knocked louder at the door, and were again entreated by the valet to let his master sleep a little longer. "The drunkard has slept long enough", said they in a rage, kicked open the door of the chamber, and rushed to the bedside. Finding no Perctarit there, and having hunted for him all over the house, they asked the valet what had become of his master. "He has fled", said the servant, who saw that further evasion was impossible. In their fury they seized him by the hair, and with many blows they dragged him into the presence of the king, clamoring loudly for his death as an accomplice in the flight of Perctarit. But the king ordered them to loosen their hold of the prisoner, and commanded him to tell the whole story of the escape. When the tale was ended, Grimwald said to the bystanders, "What think you ought to be done to the man who has wrought such a deed as this?". They all with one voice exclaimed that killing was not enough for him, but he ought to be put to death with many torments. "By Him who gave me life", said Grimwald, "the man is worthy of great honor who feared not to expose himself to death for the sake of his master. Let him be taken into my service as a valet". And with that he promised him great gifts, exhorting him to render to himself the same faithful service that he had rendered to his late lord. Unulf, for whom the king then enquired, had taken refuge in the church of St. Michael, but, receiving the royal promise of his safety, came forth, entered the palace, and threw himself at the feet of the king. From him, too, Grimwald would fain learn the whole story of the escape, and when he heard it he greatly commended his prudence and fidelity, and issued an order that he should be left undisturbed in the possession of all his property. After some time had elapsed, the king asked Unulf whether he now ever regretted not being with Perctarit, to which he answered with a solemn oath that he would rather die with Perctarit than live anywhere else in uttermost delights. The valet gave the same answer when asked whether he would rather be with the king in his palace or with his late master in his wanderings. Their words met with a kindly reception from Grimwald, who praised their loyalty to their lord, and bade Unulf take from his palace what he would, slaves or horses or household furniture, and hasten to the master of his choice. The valet, too, received the same gracious dismissal, and with the help of the king's safe-conduct, and loaded with his generous presents, they entered France, and were again with their beloved Perctarit.

It may possibly have been the flight of Perctarit into Frankish territory that disturbed the peaceful relations of the two kingdoms; but, whatever was the cause, an army of the Franks, the first that had been seen in Italy in that century, crossed the Maritime Alps, and threatened the throne of Grimwald. They were defeated by an easy stratagem, which speaks ill for the discipline to which they had been subjected. Grimwald having pitched his camp near to theirs, feigned panic and flight, leaving his tents with all their treasures, and especially with good store of wine, open to the invaders. They came, they plundered, they drank, and at night, while they were stretched in the heavy slumber of drunkenness, Grimwald and his warriors came upon them and slew so great a multitude that few found their way back to their own land. The slaughter—battle it can hardly be called—took place at Frenchmen's River, a village not far from the walls of Asti. Thus the "walls of avenging Asta", as Claudian called them, a second time witnessed the repulse of an invader.

But a more formidable foe than the weak Merovingian king or his Mayor of the Palace was to trouble the repose of Lombard Italy. Constans II, the son of Heraclius, and the heir of his grandfather's fitful energy and of some of his grandfather's genius, conceived the idea of becoming in fact as well as in name Emperor of Rome. It will be desirable here briefly to retrace the earlier stages of his career, and at the same time to take up some dropped stitches in the history of the Popes and Exarchs during the years preceding his invasion of Italy. Constans II (or, as he is more correctly called, Constantine IV) was born in the year 631, and in 642, when only a boy of eleven, found himself by the death of his father, the dethronement of his uncle and the exile of his grandfather's widow, the ambitious and unscrupulous Martina, sole Emperor of the Romans. A military *pronunciamiento* had prepared the way for his accession, but in the speech which he made to the Senate of Constantinople after the downfall of his rivals, he expressed his desire that he might have the Senators as his counselors, and judges of that which should be for the welfare of his subjects. This probably means that during the early years of his sovereignty the government was practically in the hands of a council of regency composed of the leading members of the Senate. Constans, however, grew up into a strong, self-willed man, and we may presume that while yet in early manhood he brushed aside his senatorial counselors, and governed as well as reigned. He could not wholly arrest—probably not the strongest of his Imperial predecessors could have arrested—the onrush of the children of Arabia, who wrested Armenia from the Empire, and made a temporary conquest of Cyprus and Rhodes. But he fought in person in the great naval engagement with the Saracens off the coast of Lycia, in which, though defeated and compelled to fly for his life, he seems to have inflicted enough damage on the enemy to prevent their fulfilling their intention of besieging Constantinople. Shortly afterwards came that great schism between the two rival claimants for the caliphate, Ali and Moawiyah, which still rends the Moslem world asunder, and which gave a welcome breathing-time to the hard-pressed champions of the Empire.

In ecclesiastical matters Constans II showed himself a hard-headed, unsympathetic, indifferent man of the world, determined that his Empire should not be harassed, if he could help it, by the speculative controversy which his grandfather had unwisely raised about the divine and human wills of Jesus Christ. The *Ecthesis* of his grandfather Heraclius had asserted the Monothelete doctrine, or as it is now decided to be, the Monothelete heresy, that there was but one will in the heart of the Saviour, and this doctrine had been eagerly upheld by successive Patriarchs of Constantinople, and as eagerly denounced by successive Popes of Rome. Popes and Patriarchs were excommunicating each other—in one case, to give greater solemnity to the transaction, the Pope descended to the crypt which contained the body of St. Peter, and dipped his pen in the consecrated chalice, that he might thus write the damnation of his enemy in the blood of Christ—and all the miserable wrangle of the Monophysite controversy seemed about to be renewed with greater bitterness than ever, at a time when the very existence of Christianity and of the Empire was threatened by the swords of the followers of Mohammed. Utterly weary of the whole dispute, and sympathizing apparently neither with his Monothelete grandfather nor with his Dyothelete father, the young Emperor Constans (he was then but seventeen years of age) ordered the removal of the *Ecthesis* from the doors of the great church at Constantinople, and put forth the famous document called the *Type*, in which he attempted the impossible task of imposing silence on warring theologians. "Inspired by Almighty God", said Constans, "we have determined to extinguish the flame of this controversy, and will not allow it any longer to prey upon the souls of men. The Sacred Scriptures, the works of the Fathers, the decrees of the Five General Councils are enough for us. Why should men seek to define beyond these? Therefore no one shall be allowed to speak of one will and one operation, or of two wills and two operations in the person of Christ. Any one transgressing this command shall, if a bishop, be deposed from his see; if a clergyman, from his clerical office; if a monk, he shall be confined, and banished from his monastery. If he holds any dignity or office, civil or military, he shall be deprived of it. If he is a nobleman, all his property shall be confiscated; if not noble, he shall not only be beaten with stripes, but further punished by perpetual banishment; that all men being restrained by the fear of God, and dreading the condign punishments with which we thus threaten them, may keep unmoved and untroubled the peace of the holy Churches of God".

Vain hope, by decrees and banishments and chastisements to silence the subtle ecclesiastical intellect when once engaged in a war of words like that aroused by the *Ecthesis*! Bad as that Imperial document had been accounted by the See of Rome, the *impiissimus Typus* was soon discovered to be even worse. Pope Martin, who had just succeeded Theodore 653 (the excommunicator of Pyrrhus), convened a council of one hundred and five Italian bishops, who met in the Lateran palace, anathematized the Patriarchs of Alexandria and Constantinople, "the most impious *Ecthesis*, the wicked *Type* lately put forth by the most serene Emperor Constans", and all receivers and defenders of the same.

The Pope had the Italian bishops and the general allies sentiment of the West on his side, but otherwise he stood alone against the Emperor and all the great Eastern Patriarchates. There are indications of his turning to the Frankish kings Clovis II and Sigibert II for aid, for moral at least, if not for physical support. Did he also invoke the assistance of the Arian king of the Lombards, Rothari, against the author of the Type, and the close confederate of the heretical Patriarch of Constantinople? This was charged against him, and in the difficult circumstances of his position it could not be imputed to him as a crime; but the meager annals of the period do not allow us to pronounce on the justice of the accusation. However, whether on religious or on political grounds a high-spirited young sovereign such as Constans II was not disposed to tolerate the insubordination of the Pope, who was still in theory only a subject of the most Serene Emperor. He sent his chamberlain Olympius as Exarch to Italy with orders to protect and cherish all bishops who accepted the Type, to sound the disposition of the army, and if he found it favorable, to bring Pope Martin a prisoner to Constantinople, after which display of power it was hoped that all the other bishops of Italy would readily subscribe the Imperial decree. If, however, he found the army hostile, he was to say as little as possible about the *Type*, and simply to strengthen his military hold on Ravenna and Rome. Arriving in the City with these somewhat ambiguous instructions, the new Exarch found all the bishops and clergy of Rome enthusiastic in their defence of the Pope and their condemnation of the Monothelete doctrine. Probably also the army shared the general enthusiasm, for the Exarch renounced the perilous attempt to seize the Pope in the midst of his flock. An after generation, however, believed the improbable story that Olympius ordered the assassination of the Pope in the very act of celebrating Mass at the church of S. Maria Maggiore but that the soldier who was commissioned to do the unholy deed was struck by a supernatural blindness which prevented him from seeing Pope Martin when he was in the very act of handing the chalice to the Exarch, and thus the murder was prevented.

Whatever the truth may be as to this alleged attempt on the Pope's life, there is no doubt that Olympius completely renounced the attempt to force the Imperial *Type* on the Roman Church. A reconciliation took place between Exarch and Pope, so complete as to give some color to the charge that Olympius aimed at making himself Emperor, and that Martin countenanced him in his treason. But the next step taken by the Exarch showed no disloyalty to the Empire. He crossed over with his army into Sicily in order to combat the Saracens, whose invasions of that island (which were to be continued with more or less intermission for more than four centuries) had already begun. "For their sins", however, as we are told, the greater part of his army perished, apparently by sickness, not by the sword; and Olympius himself died also, probably a victim to the same pestilence which had ravaged his camp.

The death of Olympius enabled Constans to resume his plans for the arrest of the Pope and the forcible promulgation of the Type. Theodore Calliopas, who arrives in was sent a second time to Ravenna as Exarch, appeared in Rome with an army on June 15, 653. The position of affairs was not unlike that which had been seen more than a century before, when Belisarius received orders for the deportation of Pope Silverius. Now, as then, the ecclesiastical motive for the *coup d'état* and the unslumbering jealousy between the sees of Rome and Constantinople were veiled by the imputation of political crimes. Martin was accused of having corresponded with the Saracens (doubtless the Saracen invaders of Sicily), as well as of being irregularly elected, of changing the faith delivered to the saints, and of showing insufficient reverence to the Virgin Mary.

At first the Exarch temporized; professed that he desired to come and adore his Holiness, but he was wearied with his journey, and he was afraid that Pope Martin had filled the Lateran with armed men; an insinuation to which the Pope replied by inviting the Exarch's soldiers to make a visit of inspection, and see if they could find a weapon or a stone therein. The Pope, who with better reason feared violence, and who had been for eight months in weak health, had his bed placed before the altar in the Lateran Church. Thither came the soldiers of the Exarch in full armor, with swords and lances, and bows with the arrow on the string. "They there did unutterable things", says the horrified Pope; but though their conduct was doubtless indecorous, its atrocity seems somewhat diminished when we find that the only recorded detail relates to the overthrow of the candles, which fell all over the church like leaves in autumn, and the crash of the stricken candelabra, which filled the church with a noise like thunder. Desiring to prevent the effusion of Christian blood, the Pope came from his sanctuary, the people shouting as he emerged from the church, "Anathema to all who say that Martin has changed a jot or a tittle of the faith. Anathema to all who do not remain in his orthodox faith even to the death". So the Pope wended his way through the City up to the palace of the Exarch, which apparently still stood where the palace of the Caesars had stood, on the Palatine Hill. Multitudes of the clergy and laity, who declared that they would live and die with the Pontiff, on the invitation of the Exarch swarmed after him into the palace. They had hoped if he were banished that they would be allowed to share his exile, but soon after midnight on the morning of Wednesday, the 19th of June, Pope Martin, while all his adherents were kept under close ward in the palace, was hurried on board a little ship which was lying at Portus, his only companions being six acolytes and one household servant.

On the 1st of July, the ship, slowly sailing, arrived at Misenum, but neither at Misenum nor any of the other cities of beautiful Campania (already called by the equivalent of its modern name, Terra di Lavoro), nor at any of the islands at which they touched was the exile from the Lateran palace allowed to leave the bark, which he felt to be indeed his prison. At last they reached the island of Naxos, where he was detained for more than a year, and there as a great favor he was permitted to reside in an inn in the city, and was twice or thrice indulged with the luxury of a bath. Possibly the Imperial Court hoped that if his courage were not broken as that of Vigilius had been by arrogance and insult, his sickly frame, known to be enfeebled by gout, would sink beneath the hardships which he endured. But the spirit and the bodily frame of the heroic Pope alike disappointed their expectations, and at length, on the 17th of September (654), he was brought into the harbor of Constantinople. There for ten hours on his pallet-bed on the deck of the vessel lay the venerable Pope, racked with gout, wasted by constant diarrhea, and feeling the nausea consequent on his long voyage. His adoring companions saw him thus "made a spectacle unto angels and to men"; but the populace of Constantinople, "men with wolfish faces and evil tongues", crowded round him, crying out that he was not fit to live. At sunset a squad of guards came, who placed him in a litter, and carried him off to a prison called *Prandiaria*. For ninety-three days he languished in this dungeon, deprived of all the comforts which were now necessaries to a high-bred Roman ecclesiastic. On the 19th of December (654) he was brought into the presence of the Sacellarius or Lord High Treasurer, who had summoned a meeting of the Senate for his trial. He was ordered to stand in the presence of his judges, and when the attendants pointed out that he was unable to stand, the Sacellarius thundered forth, "Then let two of you support him, one on each side, for he shall not be allowed to sit".

The examination, which was conducted through the medium of an interpreter, for the Pope was as ignorant of Greek as his persecutors were of Latin, turned entirely on political matters. The absurd accusation of complicity with the Saracens, which only derived color from the fact that the Pope had sent money to be distributed as alms among the Sicilian poor, seems now to have been tacitly abandoned, and the only charge which was vehemently pressed against him was one of complicity with the treasonable designs of Olympius. Rough and illiterate soldiers from the Exarch's army were brought to prove this charge; and the Pope asked in vain that they might be allowed to give their evidence unsworn, that they might not imperil their souls by perjury. The Pope began his answer to the charge against him thus :—"When the *Type* was prepared and sent to Rome by the Emperor..."— but the Prefect Troilus at once stopped him—"Do not bring in any questions about the faith. We are Romans and Christians and Orthodox. It is about the rebellion that we are examining you". The Pope's constant answer was that he had no power to resist the Exarch, who had the whole army of Italy at his disposal. "Was it I who made him Exarch, or you at Constantinople? But work your will upon me, and do it speedily". After this he seems to have tried to give a long harangue, which was faithfully interpreted by an African nobleman named Innocent; but the Sacellarius roughly interrupted, "Why do you interpret what he is saying? We do not want to hear it". With that he rose up, and all they that were with him, and going into the Emperor's chamber announced that they were ready to pass sentence upon the Bishop of Rome.

That sentence appears to have been a capital one, for the Pope was dragged through the streets of the city with a drawn sword carried before him; but if such a sentence was pronounced it was commuted into imprisonment and exile. He was forced to stand for some time in the Hippodrome, as a spectacle to the people, the guards as before supporting him on either side, and the young Emperor looking on through the lattice-work of his banqueting-hall at the humiliation of his great spiritual rival. Little could either persecutor or victim foresee how cruelly, more than five centuries later the indignities offered to the Roman Pope would be avenged on the Eastern Emperor by the sack of his own city of Constantinople.

The Sacellarius then came forth from the banqueting-hall and said, "See how the Lord has delivered thee into our hands. What hadst thou to hope for that thou shouldest strive against the Emperor? Thou hast abandoned the Lord, and He has abandoned thee". He ordered one of the guards to cut the strap which bound round his neck the satchel in which the Pontiff was accustomed to carry the sacred books, and then he handed him over to the Prefect, saying, "Take him, my lord Prefect, and cut him limb from limb".

Loaded with irons, with torn robes, but surrounded by a crowd not now shouting execrations, but saddened and awestruck at what was being done, the successor of St. Peter was dragged through the streets of Constantinople to the prison of Dioniede, in the Praetorian Prefect's palace. As he climbed up the steps of the prison, which were rough and steep, his swollen feet left upon them the stain of blood. He was then thrust into a cold and dreary cell, where the irons clanked upon his shivering limbs. One young ecclesiastic who had followed him, as Peter followed his Lord was permitted to share his dungeon, but the keeper of the prison was also always present, bound to the Pope by a chain, as was the custom in the case of culprits under sentence of death. There were, however, two kind-hearted women, mother and daughter, related apparently to the keepers of the prison, who succeeded in removing the chilled and exhausted Pontiff from the dungeon cell and from the continual presence of the gaoler. They carried him to their own bedroom, and laid him in a comfortable bed, where however he lay speechless till the evening. When evening came, Gregory, a eunuch and Grand Chamberlain, sent his majordomo with some scanty refreshment, who whispered words of intended comfort, "In all our tribulations we put our trust in God. Thou shalt not die". The Pope, however, who was worn out and longed for speedy martyrdom, only groaned. The heavy iron chains however were taken off from him and not again imposed.

One cause which led to some alleviation of the Pope's physical sufferings was the troubled conscience of Paul, the Patriarch of Constantinople, who had been fiercely anathematized by successive Popes, but who, being now upon his death-bed, could not endure the thought of the indignities which the remorseless Emperor was heaping on their common enemy. When Constans visited him the day after the trial, and told him what had been done, Paulus turned his face to the wall, and said with a groan, "Ah me! this too will be added to the number of my sins". At his earnest request, the capital sentence passed on the Pope was remitted by Constans, and the rigor of his confine was somewhat lessened.

To the patriarch Paul (who died December 26, 654) succeeded Pyrrhus, who, as we have seen, had once himself been a fugitive at Rome, had there renounced the Monothelete heresy, and had then returned, as the orthodox said, "like a dog to his vomit" when he found himself in the atmosphere of Monothelete Ravenna. This temporary departure from the ruling creed was however objected against him now, when he sought to recover the Patriarchal throne on which he had once before been seated. He declared that he had subscribed to the Pope's libellus (1) because he was his guest, and (2) under duresse. On these two somewhat inconsistent pleas the imprisoned Pope was now examined by an Assistant-Treasurer who bore the great name of Further Demosthenes. The Court minion, when he entered the prison, said with an unworthy sneer, "Our lord the excellent Emperor has sent us to thee, saying. See in what height of glory thou once wast placed, and to what a depth thou now hast fallen. For all this thou hast only thyself to thank". To which the Pope only replied, "Glory and thanksgiving in all things to the only King, Immortal and Invisible". Demosthenes then proceeded to cross-question him about his reception of the fugitive Patriarch Pyrrhus. "Whence did he draw his subsistence when he was in Rome?" "From the Roman Patriarchate" [the Lateran Palace]. "What was your object in thus supplying him with provisions?" "My good lord, you do not understand the ways of the Roman Church. For I tell you plainly, St. Peter does not repel any one, however poor and miserable, who comes to claim his hospitality, but gives them the whitest bread and divers kinds of wine. If then this is done even to miserable outcasts, in what guise ought we to have received one who came as the honoured bishop of the great see of Constantinople?" Then came the question as to duresse, the heavy wooden chains which were said to have been fastened on the Patriarch's limbs, and the many grievous things that had been done to him. To which answered the Pontift, "All this is utterly untrue, and there are men in Constantinople who were then in Rome, and who know how false is the accusation. There is Plato, once Exarch, who sent his messengers to Pyrrhus at Rome. Ask him, and if fear does not prevent him from speaking the truth, he will tell you. But I am in your hands. Tear me if you will, limb from limb, as the Treasurer said to the Prefect that he ought to do unto me. Work your own will upon me: but I will not communicate with the Church of Constantinople".

After eighty-four days's confinement in the prison of Diomede, the unfortunate Pope was again put on ship-board and delivered to the mercies of the stormy Euxine. What object the guards can have had in keeping their unhappy prisoner so long exposed to the miseries of sea-sickness we know not: but it was not till May 15, two months after his embarkation, that he was permitted to land at Cherson, a place which was not the same as the modern city of Cherson, but was situated in the Crimea, then called the Tauric Chersonese. Here he languished for four months, and then died worn out by disease and hardship. From two letters which he wrote to his friends at Rome, we receive a most melancholy impression of his state during these last four months of his life. He complains bitterly of the lukewarmness and forgetfulness of his Roman friends, who wrote him no letters, and sent him no alleviations of his distress. Almost the only news which he did receive from Rome was the unwelcome intelligence that, yielding to Imperial pressure, the Roman clergy had acquiesced in his deposition, and elected another Pope, Eugenius I, as his successor. The inhabitants of the country to which Martin was exiled were, according to his accounts, barbarians and heathens, and he suffered from want not only of the comforts, but almost of the necessaries of life. His only chance of buying corn was in small quantities from vessels which came thither laden with salt from the southern shores of the Black Sea, and then he had to pay for it at the high price of one solidus for a bushel.

Pope Martin died on September 17, 655. He was buried in that wild Crimean land, and miracles, of which there had been some mention during his life, were believed to be wrought at his tomb. On the whole, he must be pronounced one of the noblest figures in the long line of Roman Pontiffs. The querulous tone of the letters of his exile contrasts somewhat unfavorably with the utterances of that other victim of Imperial persecution,

St. Chrysostom. And, as I have before suggested, it is possible that there may have been some foundation for the political charges on which ostensibly his condemnation was based. But on the other hand there can be no doubt that if he had been willing to strike his flag to the Monotheletes, or to accept that arbitrary 'End of Controversy', the Type of the worldly-minded Emperor Constans, he might at once have ended his weary exile and had returned to the comforts and the splendors of the Lateran Palace. This he refused to do for conscience' sake, and he is therefore entitled to rank as one of the few martyrs who have sat in the chair of St. Peter.

Chronological notes

I must remind the reader, in returning to the course of Lombard history, that all the events with which we have been recently dealing occurred before the accession of Grimwald. Heraclius published his *Ecthesis* in 638, two years after the accession of Rothari. The *Ecthesis* was taken down, and the *Type* was substituted for it by Constans II in 648, four years before the end of Rothari's reign. When Rothari died (in 652), Martin had been for three years Pope. Exarch Olympius died in that year, and his successor's capture of the Pope occurred in the following year, the date of Aripert's accession to the Lombard throne. Aripert during his reign must have heard of the death of Martin in exile at Cherson, of the death of his successor Eugenius (June, 657), and of the elevation of his successor Vitalian, whose long pontificate (657-672) covers the whole of the reign of Grimwald. Under the rule of this Pope the Monothelete dispute seems to have slumbered. Fairly amicable relations existed between the patriarchates of Rome and Constantinople: Vitalian, though not going as far as Honorius in acceptance of Monothelete doctrine, was apparently willing to leave the question undiscussed, and as this was the very result most desired by Constans, a politician but no theologian, there was peace and the exchange of outward courtesies between Emperor and Pontiff.

Thus we come down to 662, the year of Grimwald's accession. Towards the close of this year Constans II formed the resolution to quit for ever his capital by the Bosphorus, and to try his fortune as a re-establisher of the Empire in the Western lands. To his contemporaries, accustomed to think of the Roman Augustus as immovably settled in the East, the resolution seemed like a madman's dream. Even the virtues of this Emperor (for he had some virtues), his rough energy, his broad view of the needs of the Empire, his abhorrence of theological disputation, as well as his undoubted vices, made him unpopular with the enervated, wordy inhabitants of New Rome. Two years previously he had put to death his brother Theodosius, whom he had before forced into holy orders, and now it was said that Theodosius continually appeared to him in the visions of the night, arrayed in the dress of a deacon, and offering him the sacramental cup, saying, "Drink, my brother!" The Imperial dreamer would take the cup, see that it was filled with blood, and awake with a cry of anguish. This story, however, comes from a very late and doubtful source and perhaps attests only the animosity of Church historians against a Monothelete heretic and the persecutor of Popes. The cruel tortures inflicted on the Abbot Maximus, the great champion of orthodoxy, and two of his disciples, who were flogged, had their tongues and right hands cut off, and were banished to the inhospitable neighborhood of Poti, doubtless kindled the resentment of many of the Emperor's subjects against him. But after all it was perhaps statesmanship quite as much as passion which determined Constans to quit his native city and seek his fortune in the West. His grandfather Heraclius had come from Carthage to found his dynasty. He was himself called Emperor of Rome, yet Rome and Italy, were daily slipping from his grasp, the city to the Pope, the country to the Lombards. Constans would revive the great projects of Justinian, and be in fact as well as in name Emperor of Rome. We need not therefore believe the late and legendary story that when Constans was standing on the deck of his cutter, he turned round to look at the receding towers and domes of Constantinople, and spat at the Imperial City. Better vouched for, however, is the fact that he was obliged to take his departure alone, and that when he sent from Sicily for his wife and his three sons, the citizens (perhaps represented by the Senate) refused to allow them to depart.

Constans went first to Athens, where he apparently sojourned for some time, and then, probably in early part of 663, crossed over into Italy, landing at Tarentum. Both by his landing-place and in various other ways his expedition reminds us of that other attempt which Greece made 944 years before, under Pyrrhus king of Epirus, to conquer Italy. Like that Aeacid prince, Constans sought to ascertan by supernatural means the event of his enterprise. He asked, not the priestess at Delphi, but a certain recluse who was believed to have the spirit of prophecy. "Shall I vanquish and hold down the nation of the Lombards which now dwells in Italy?" The holy man's answer, vouchsafed after a night of prayer, was less ambiguous than the response of the oracle to Pyrrhus. "The nation of the Lombards cannot be overcome, forasmuch as a pious queen, coming from another land, has built a basilica in their territory to the blessed John the Baptist, who therefore pleads without ceasing for that people. But the time will come when that sanctuary shall be held in contempt, and then the nation itself shall perish". The historian who records this prediction considered that he saw its fulfillment when the fall of the Lombard monarchy followed the simoniacal ordination of unworthy and adulterous ecclesiastics in the great basilica of Monza.

Undismayed by this unfavorable answer—if he ever received it—the Emperor pressed on from the region round Tarentum, where he still found subjects loyal to the Empire, and invaded the duchy of Benevento where Romwald the son of King Grimwald ruled. "The high nest of Acherontia", as Horace called it, a frontier fortress on one of the outlying buttresses of Monte Vulture, resisted all his attacks, but Luceria, "a wealthy city of Apulia", was captured, sacked and leveled with the ground. Certainly the Emperor of Rome practiced a strange method of delivering Italy. He then marched to Benevento, which he surrounded and tried hard to carry by storm. Young Romwald, sore pressed, sent his tutor Seswald to entreat his father's aid. On receipt of this message King Grimwald at once set out with a large army to the help of his son. Many of the Northern Lombards, however, deserted on the march. The jealousy or suspicion between Pavia and Benevento was too strong to be overcome even by the presence of the Roman Emperor on the soil of Italy: and the men of the northern provinces said to one another, with self-gratulations on their own superior wisdom, "The southern duke has helped himself to all that was best worth having in the palace at Pavia, and now he is going to Benevento to help his son. You will see that he will never return".

Meanwhile the Imperial army was pressing the siege of the city with all those engines of war the use of which the dexterous Greek understood so much better than the barbarian. By frequent sallies the gallant defenders inflicted grievous losses on the enemy, but the straitness of the siege was great, and day by day they looked for tidings of the approach of the Lombard king. At length they saw the messenger Seswald drawing near to the walls, but, alas! as a prisoner led by the Imperial generals. For while he was hovering near to the city seeking how he might enter, he had been captured by the enemy's scouts, who had brought him into the Emperor's presence. From him Constans learned of the near advent of Grimwald with a large army, and these tidings decided him to end the siege by all means as speedily as possible. Seswald was therefore allowed to approach the walls, having promised that he would assure the garrison that Grimwald could not help them. If he failed in this he was told that death awaited him. When the captive tutor was close to the walls, he asked to see his pupil, and as soon as Romwald came to the battlements he cried with a loud voice, "Stand firm, lord Romwald : thy father is at hand and will soon bring thee help. He is already at the river Sangro (about fifty miles from Benevento), and pitches his camp there tonight with a strong army. Have pity, I pray thee, on my wife and children, for I know that this perfidious race will not suffer me to live". As soon as he had finished his speech, the Emperor bade that they should cut off his head, and hurl it into the city from a catapult: an ungenerous revenge, and one in which a Teutonic warrior would have hardly permitted himself to indulge. The well-known features were kissed by the grateful lips of Romwald, and the head was deposited in a worthy shrine.

After all, no battle was fought under the walls of Benevento. Constans was now anxious to depart, and Romwald, whose troops were probably already suffering severely from famine, made "a bridge of gold for a retreating foe", handed over his sister Gisa to him as a hostage, and made peace on some terms, the nature of which is not recorded. Constans then started for Naples, where he was secure of a friendly reception, as that city belonged to the Empire; but on his way he was attacked by Mitola, count of Capua, at a place by the banks of the Galore (which a hundred years after was still called Pugna), and was defeated there with much slaughter. This skirmish (for it was probably nothing more) apparently broke the truce concluded under the walls of Benevento. One of the Byzantine nobles, named Saburrus, asked the Emperor to entrust him with the command of 20,000 men with whom he made no doubt that he should vanquish the young duke of Benevento. He set forth, and pitched his camp at Forino, about twenty-five miles east of Naples, which city was now the Emperor's headquarters. When Grimwald, who had by this time joined his son, heard the tidings of the Imperial general's approach he thought to go forth also and fight with him, but with something of the spirit of a young knight of later days, Romwald begged that he, with only a portion of his father's army, might have the glory of this day's encounter. Accordingly Romwald and Saburrus with their small selected armies met on the field of battle. From four different sides sounded the trumpets of Saburrus, as the Imperial forces rushed to the fray.

But in the thick of the battle, a stalwart Lombard named Amalong, who bore "the king's wand" (probably a spear from which fluttered the royal banner), struck one of the little Greek soldiers through the body with his weapon, which he held stoutly with both hands, and lifting him from his saddle, held the spear high in air, with his victim writhing upon it. The sight of this deed so disheartened the Greeks that they turned to flight, and in that flight the army was cut to pieces. Romwald returned to his father with the glory of victory, and the boaster Saburrus brought back few of his 20,000 men to his master.

"Constans", says the Lombard historian, "seeing Rome that he could avail nothing against the Lombards, turned all his threats and all his harshness upon his own partisans, that is, the Romans". This may have been the secret reflection of the trembling clergy and citizens when the stern Monothelete Emperor came among them, but the outward signs of mutual amity were observed on the visit which Constans now paid to Rome. It was certainly a memorable event. Three hundred and seven years had elapsed since the awe-stricken Constantius gazed on the glories of yet unruined Rome: nearly two centuries since any person calling himself Emperor had stood upon the Palatine Hill: one hundred and thirty-seven years were yet to elapse ere a barbarian king was to be acclaimed with shouts of *Carolus Imperator* in the streets of Rome. Meanwhile here is this successor of Augustus, who bears by full right the title of Emperor of the Romans, but who is Greek by language, Greek by education, and who, it is to be feared, "does not hold the Catholic verity in his heart, since by that arrogant *Type* of his he forbids us even to make mention of the Two Wills in Christ. He has accomplished but little against the terrible Saracens : he has done nothing to deliver Italy from the unspeakable Lombards: we must receive him as our rightful lord, but our hearts fail us when we ask ourselves what he will do in Rome". Such were probably the feelings of Pope Vitalian and his clergy as they went forth along the Appian Way six miles from the gates of the City to meet the Emperor Constans. But his first devout behavior probably somewhat allayed their terrors. It was Wednesday, the 5th of July (663), when he entered the Eternal City, and he at once proceeded to worship at the great basilica of St. Peter, leaving there a gift upon the altar. On Saturday he went to the church of S. Maria Maggiore, and there, too, he offered his gift. On Sunday the church of St. Peter's was filled with the Greek soldiers. All the clergy went forth with due pomp of lighted tapers to meet the master of that glittering host who was present at the celebration of Mass—doubtless receiving the consecrated elements from St. Peter's successor—and again offered his gift upon the altar; this time a *pallium* stiff with gold. On the next Saturday he visited in equal state the Lateran Church, the home of the great Western patriarchate; he bathed in the porphyry font, which legend, then or at a later day, declared to have been used for the baptism of Constantine the Great, and he dined in the spacious banqueting-hall which was known as the Basilica of Vigilius. Lastly, on the second Sunday of his visit, he again attended High Mass at St. Peter's, and took a solemn farewell of Pope Vitalian on this the last day of his sojourn in Rome.

Twelve days was the length of the Emperor's visit, but his time was not wholly occupied in hearing Mass and offering gifts on the altars of the churches. Gold and silver had apparently long vanished from all places but the sacristies of the churches, but there was still much copper on the buildings and in the statues of the City. Between his visits to the basilicas the Emperor usefully employed his leisure in stripping the City of all these copper adornments, even proceeding so far as to strip off the copper tiles which covered the dome of the Pantheon, now the church of St. Mary of the Martyrs. These spoils, and much else, probably some works of art, possibly some of the treasures of the libraries, were put on shipboard and consigned to Constantinople, at which city however, as we shall shortly discover, they never arrived. It was certainly an unworthy mode of celebrating the Roman Emperor's visit to the City which gave him his title; and the abstraction of the roof of the Pantheon must have reminded Romans who knew anything of the history of their City of the similar procedure of Gaiseric and his Vandals upon the gilt roof of the temple of Jupiter Capitolinus. But the necessities of the Empire were great : some of its richest provinces were in the hands of the Saracens; and the robberies of Constans were probably not for himself but for the State. Had there been any blood spilled or any sacred vessels abstracted during the Imperial visit to Rome, we should assuredly have heard of such atrocities. Upon the whole, we may presume that when, on the 17th of July, Constans finally turned his back on the Imperial City, Pontiff and people alike congratulated themselves that they had not suffered greater evils at the hands of their stern sovereign.

From Rome he went to Naples, and from Naples by land to Reggio. He must have remained some weeks in Southern Italy, for it was in September (if not later) that he crossed over from Reggio into Sicily. He remained in that island for five years, 663-668, making Syracuse his headquarters. The object of this long sojourn in Sicily evidently was that he might use it as his base of operations against the Saracens, who were overrunning the provinces of Northern Africa. He did indeed temporarily recover Carthage, but this success was counterbalanced by a severe defeat which his troops sustained at Tripoli. In Sicily as elsewhere he showed himself grasping and impecunious. The cultivators of Sicily and Sardinia, of Calabria and of the province of Africa, long remembered the oppressive procedure of the tax-gatherers of Constans. So inexorable were their demands that, to satisfy them, husbands were sold into slavery away from their wives, and children from their parents, and, under this intolerable tyranny, life seemed not worth the living. Now too, if we may believe the papal biographer, who writes in great bitterness of spirit against the Monothelete Emperor, Constans exceeded even his Roman exploits by his sacrilegious spoliation of the churches. All over the two islands, and the two provinces which have been named, sacred vessels and other precious ornaments dedicated to the worship of the sanctuary were carried off by the command of the Emperor and by the avarice of the Greeks

At length the hard and oppressive reign came to an end, but that end seems to have come rather from the sudden rage of an insulted menial, than from any deep-laid popular conspiracy. One day when Constans entered the bath which was called Daphne, at Syracuse, the valet who attended him, a certain Andreas, son of Troilus, while the Emperor was scrubbing himself with Gallic soap, lifted high the box in which the soap was kept, smote his master on the head with it, and ran away. As the doors of the bath-house remained long unopened, the attendants who stood without at length burst them open, and found their master lying dead upon the floor. If there had been, as seems probable, no conspiracy, it was nevertheless easy to foresee that the existence of a conspiracy against so harsh and unpopular a monarch would be easily suspected. It was probably in order to guard themselves against the certain vengeance of the Heraclian house that the courtiers determined to raise a new Emperor to the throne. Their choice fell on a certain Armenian named Mizizius, who much against his will accepted the dangerous diadem. He had calculated the chances of success more truly than those who forced the honor upon him. From all parts of Italy, from Istria and Campania, from Africa (the old home of the Heraclians), even from the island of Sardinia, soldiers flocked to Syracuse to suppress this ridiculous rebellion. When the young Constantine, the son of Constans, arrived in Sicily with a great fleet, he found the work already done, and the rival Emperor Mizizius slain. The pretender's head was taken to Constantinople, and with it many of the civil servants of the Empire who had taken part in the rebellion, and who, according to the cruel fashion of Byzantium, were mutilated before they were placed on board the ships which were to convey them to the place of execution.

Events such as these naturally weakened the resisting power of the Empire. We hear without surprise that the Saracens suddenly appeared with a large fleet in the Sicilian waters, entered Syracuse, made great slaughter among the people (a remnant of whom fled to fortified camps and the tops of the mountains), and then returned to

Alexandria, bearing with them immense booty, including the brazen ornaments, and all the other precious things which Constans Augustus had carried off from Rome.

As for King Grimwald's daughter Gisa, whom the Emperor had borne off from Benevento as a hostage, she too was taken by him to Sicily, and died there. The way in which Paulus mentions her fate inclines us to suppose that it was in some way connected with the troubles of the Saracen invasion.

The remaining events of the reign of Grimwald may be briefly told, and all relate to three out of the four great duchies, whose history in an earlier chapter was brought down to this point. The duchy of Trient is not noticed here.

In SPOLETO, on the death of Duke Atto (663), Grimwald conferred the duchy on his old ally *Transamund,* count of Capua, to whom he was largely indebted for his success in winning the Lombard crown. Transamund, who married a daughter of Grimwald, appears to have governed the Umbrian duchy for about forty years, and his descendants, to the third generation, sat on his throne.

At BENEVENTO, young Romwald seems to have remained ever in cordial love and loyalty to his the duchy father, and we may conjecture that the kingdom and the duchy were more closely confederate together during the reign of Grimwald than at any other period of their joint existence. The chief event of the young duke's reign seems to have been the arrival of a colony of Bulgarians in Italy under their duke Alzeco, who, "with all the army of his duchy", came to King Grimwald, and promised faithful service on condition of being allowed to reside in his land. Him Grimwald passed on to his son, desiring the latter to provide suitable habitations for him and his people. They were heartily welcomed by the young duke, who assigned to them for their residence a spacious region to the north of his capital, which had lain desert until that time, and which included the cities of Bovianum, Sepinum, and Aesernia. The fact that this broad reach of territory (situated, it is true, among the highlands of Samnium) should have remained desert till these Bulgarians from the Danube country came to occupy it, tells its own sad story of the desolation of Italy. The Bulgarian Alzeco coming thus into the territory of Duke Romwald, in a relation which in a later century would have been described as that of vassalage, had to forego the title of duke which he had hitherto borne, and be content with that of *gastald,* a title which, as we shall hereafter see, expressed more of personal dependence on the sovereign than the title of duke. Even down to the days of Paulus, that is, for a full century after the settlement, though the descendants of these settlers had learned the Latin tongue, the rude Bulgarian speech was still heard in these cities and villages round the skirts of Monte Matese.

Meanwhile in the duchy of FRIULI, the old home of Grimwald, disastrous events were occurring. Grasulf, Grimwald's uncle, after apparently a long reign, had been succeeded by *Ago,* of whom Paulus has only to tell us that a certain house called *Domus Agonis* was still visible at Forum Julii.

Duke Ago was followed by *Lupus,* an ambitious Duke and untrustworthy man. Instigated possibly by the patriarch of Aquileia, he led a band of horsemen by a highway cast up in old time across the sands to Grado, plundered that island city, and carried off the treasures of its church. Whether he deposited any of these treasures in the mother and rival church of Aquileia we are not informed. After this came the invasion of Italy by Constans, Romwald's cry for help to his father, Griniwald's rapid march to succor him. Before setting out the king committed his palace and all its treasures to Lupus of Friuli, perhaps an old Companion of his boyhood. But Lupus shared the general opinion of the northern Italians, that the Beneventan interloper, having once set his face towards the south, would never return to Pavia. He carried himself insolently in his delegated office; and perhaps—though this is not expressly told us—aimed at winning the kingdom for himself. When he learned that Grimwald was returning, Lupus, conscious of his misdeeds, retreated to his duchy of Friuli, and there openly raised the standard of rebellion.

On receipt of these evil tidings, Grimwald, unwilling to stir up a civil war between Lombards and Lombards, resorted to the strange and desperate expedient of inviting the Avars, the savages who, fifty years before, had slain his father and ravaged his home, to come and attack the rebel duke. The Chagan came with a great army, and was met by Lupus apparently on the old battle-ground of Theodosius by the Cold River below the pass of the Pear-tree.

For three days Lupus kept the savage horde at bay, at first with brilliant success, winning decided victories, and carrying great spoil out of their camp. But each day the number of his killed and wounded soldiers rose higher and higher, and still the apparently undiminished Avar horde rolled on towards him. On the fourth day Lupus was slain, and the remnant of his array scarcely succeeded in saving themselves by flight.

The surviving Lombards shut themselves up in the fortified cities, while the Avars as aforetime roamed over the duchy, carrying fire and sword through the wasted land. To Grimwald's ambassadors who came with a gentle suggestion that it was now time to cease from ravage, they replied that they had won Forum Julii by their arms, and did not mean to quit it. Hereupon Grimwald saw himself compelled to assemble an army for the expulsion of the Avars from Italian soil. But according to the *saga,* he effected his purpose not by force but by guile. The Chagan's ambassadors came and feasted at his board ere all his army was yet collected, but he dressed up the same squadrons in different attire on each succeeding day, and made them defile before the eyes of the ambassadors, leading them to suppose that each day fresh reinforcements were coming to his standard. "With all these multtudes", said he, "shall I burst upon the Avars and their Chagan, unless they speedily vanish from the territory of Forum Julii". The message carried back by the deluded ambassadors struck such terror into the heart of the Chagan that he made all haste to return to his own land.

The daughter of Lupus, Theuderada, was given in marriage to Romwald of Benevento, and in her new home, as we learn from the life of St. Barbatus, she played a part like that of Theudelinda in winning over the still half heathen, and wholly irreligious, Lombards of Benevento to the Christian faith.

His son Arnefrit sought to win his father's duchy, but fled at the approach of Grimwald, and took refuge with the Slovenes of Carinthia. Afterwards seeking by the help of these barbarians to recover possession of his duchy, he was slain by a sudden onset of the men of Friuli at a place called Nemae (now Nimis), about fifteen miles northwest of Cividale.

As the new duke of Friuli, Grimwald appointed *Wechtari,* a native of Vicenza, a man who had evidently already reached middle life, and who was, we are told, "a kind man, gently ruling the people". Though Arnefrit was dead, his Slavonic allies still troubled the duchy, and hearing that Duke Wechtari, of whom they stood in great awe, had gone to Pavia—doubtless in order to concert measures of defence with King Grimwald—they came with a strong body of men, and pitched their camp at a place called Broxae, not far from the capital. It happened providentially that Wechtari had on the previous evening returned from Pavia, and hearing of this insolent advance of the

Slovenes, he went forth with twenty of his followers to attack them. Seeing so small a troop issue from the city, the Slovenes said with jeers, "Lo, here come the patriarch and his clergy". But when they came to the bridge over the Natiso, on the other side of whose deep gorge the invaders had pitched their camp, Wechtari took off his helmet and showed his bald head and his well-known countenance to the foe. A despairing cry of "Wechtari! Wechtari!" ran through their ranks, and they all began to think of flight rather than of battle. Then Wechtari, perceiving their panic, charged upon them with his scanty band, and inflicted such slaughter, that out of 5000 Slovenes, few returned to tell the tale in Carinthia. So runs the *Saga* of Wechtari.

Throughout the long life of Grimwald he seems never to have forgotten the treachery practiced by the Patrician Gregory against his brothers Taso and Cacco. The Avars, as we have seen, he could forgive, he could even welcome as allies, but the Romans never. Especially did his anger burn against the city of Opitergium, in which the foul murder was committed. Not satisfied with the partial demolition of that city which had been accomplished some twenty or thirty years before by order of Rothari, he now utterly destroyed it, and parceled out the citizens who were left in it among the three neighboring cities of Forum Julii, Ceneta, and Tarvisium (Cividale, Ceneda, and Treviso). To this day the low estate of the little town, scarcely more than a village, of Oderzo, testifies to the vengeance of the Lombard king.

Equally hard was the fate of the city on the Emilian Way, twenty miles south of Ravenna, which still, in a slightly altered form preserves its classical name of Forum Populi. Many times had its inhabitants harassed his messengers going and coming in time of peace between Pavia and Benevento. Watching his opportunity, he burst, in the days of Lent, through the unguarded passages of the Apennines, came upon the city on Easter Sunday itself, when the children were being baptized, and slew the citizens with wide and indiscriminate slaughter, not sparing even the deacons who were officiating in the baptistery, and whose blood was mingled with the water of ablution. Then he beat down the chief buildings of the city, and left therein but a very few of its former inhabitants. Certainly the Lombard, even after a century's sojourn in Italy, fell far below the Visigoth in capacity for civilization. Alaric at Pollentia well-nigh ruined his cause by his unwillingness to fight on Easter-Day, the same day which Grimwald chose for a treacherous revenge and a cruel massacre.

At length the strong, hard, self-reliant man came to a characteristic end. He had been bled, probably for some trifling ailment, by the royal surgeons, and was resting in his palace on the ninth day after the operation. A dove flew past; he longed to reach it with his arrow; he took the bow and shot, but in doing so opened again the imperfectly closed vein, and died of the ensuing hemorrhage. The suggestion that his doctors had mingled poison in their drugs seems unnecessary to explain the death of so self-willed and impetuous a convalescent. He was buried in the basilica of St. Ambrose which he himself (evidently an orthodox Catholic by profession) had reared in the royal city of Ticinum.

It should be mentioned that in July 668, in the sixth year of his reign, Grimwald made a short addition to the code of Rothari. It will not be necessary here to examine this additional code minutely. It may be sufficient to say that it shows a general disposition to uphold the prescription of thirty years, whether against a slave claiming pardon, or against a free man resisting the attempt to reduce him to slavery; that wager of battle is discouraged, and trial by *sacramentum* as much as possible substituted for it; and that there are some stringent provisions against the offence, then evidently increasing, of bigamy. The law of Grimwald also imports from the Roman law the principle of representation of a father by his children in the event of his having died before the ancestor whose property is being divided. From the stress laid on this principle by Grimwald we must suppose that it had been imperfectly recognized by the tribunals of Rothari.

THE STORY OF ST. BARBATUS.

THE life of St. Barbatus, the most eminent apostle of Catholic Christianity in Southern Italy, has an important bearing on the history of the duchy of Benevento in the seventh century, and especially on the invasion of Constans; but hagiology has a character of its own, and refuses to be wrought in harmoniously with secular history, even in that picturesque and saga-like form which that history assumes in the pages of Paulus. I have decided therefore to relegate to a note the condensed narrative of the saint's life and works.

This narrative is derived from two documents published in the great Bollandist collection of the Acta Sanctorum under the date 19th of February. One of these lives, we are told, is extracted from an ancient codex written *in Lombard characters* belonging to the Benedictine monastery of St. John at Capua. The other, an expanded and paraphrastic copy of the first, comes from the archives of the church at Benevento. Waitz, who has edited the life of the saint in Scriptores Rerum Langobardicarum (M. G. H.), mentions eleven MSS., most of which he has consulted, and three of which are "litteris Beneventanis exarati". He considers that even the earlier form of the history cannot have been written before the ninth century, and follows Bethmann in rejecting as valueless the later and paraphrastic form which he attributes to the tenth or eleventh century. From some slight indications (chiefly the description of the invading Emperor as "Constantinus qui et Constans appellatur"), I should be disposed to believe that there is a foundation of contemporary tradition for the earlier document. The following is a greatly condensed translation of the Life:

Barbatus (who was born in the year 602) became famous when Grimwald held the reins of the Lombard kingdom, and his son Romwald ruled the Samnites.

The Lombards, though baptized, worshipped the image of a viper; and moreover, they devoutly paid homage in most absurd fashion to a certain "sacrilegious" tree not far from the walls of their city. From the branches of this tree was hung a piece of leather; and all those who were to take part in the ceremony, turning their backs to the tree, rode away from it at a gallop, urging on their horses with bloody spurs. Then suddenly turning round, they hurled their lances at the leather, which quivered under their strokes; and each one cut out a little piece thereof, and ate it in a superstitious manner for the good of his soul. And as they paid their vows at this place, they gave it the name *Votum,* which [says the scribe] it still bears.

All these superstitious practices greatly distressed the soul of Barbatus, who told the people that it was vain for them thus to try to serve two masters. But they, in their blind and beastlike madness, refused to abandon this equestrian form of worship, saying that it was an excellent custom, and had been handed down to them by their ancestors, whom they mentioned by name, and declared to have been the bravest warriors upon earth.

However, by his miracles, Barbatus began to soften the hearts of the rude people, who even by drinking the water in which he had washed his hands after celebration of the Mass, found themselves healed of their diseases.

Then "Constantius, who is also called Constans", desiring to restore the kingdom of Italy to his obedience, collected an innumerable multitude of ships, arrived at Tarentum, and ravaged nearly all the cities of Apulia. He took the very wealthy city of Luceria after severe fighting, and by the labor of his robber-bands leveled it to the earth. Then he went on to Beneventum, where Romwald abode, having a few very brave Lombards with him, and the holy father Barbatus remained there with them. Terrible was the attack of Constans, who harassed the defenders with ever-fresh bands of assailants. This lasted long, but Romwald, magnanimous and unterrified, made a brave resistance, now fighting from the walls, now making a sudden sally and hasty return into the city, for he was not strong enough to fight in the open plain. Still, though he had slain many of the assailants, his own ranks were thinned, and the inhabitants began to weep and wail, thinking that they would soon be destroyed by the robber-bands of Constans. As for Romwald, he, growing weary of fighting, gave a counsel of despair to his soldiers:—"It is better for us to die in battle than to fall alive into the hands of the Greeks, and so perish ignominiously. Let us open the gates of the city, and give them the hardest battle that we can". Perceiving this discussion, St. Barbatus said, "Never let so many brave young men be given over to destruction, lest they perish everlastingly. Good were the boldness of your hearts, if your minds were not so empty, and your souls so weak". Said Romwald, "What dost thou mean by emptiness of mind, and weakness of soul? Prithee, tell us". Thereupon Barbatus, promising them the palm of victory, if they would follow his counsels, preached a long sermon against idolatry, and exhorted his hearers to the steady and serious worship of Christ

Hereupon Romwald said, "Only let us be delivered from our foes, and we will do all that thou biddest us, will make thee bishop of this place, and in all the cities under our rule will enrich thee with farms and *colonies*".

Barbatus answered, "Know for certain that Christ, to whom ye have now turned in penitence, will set you free, and the assaults of Caesar and his people shall not penetrate the streets of Beneventum, but with changed purpose they shall return to their own borders. And that thou mayest know that I am telling thee the very truth, which shall shortly come to pass, let us come together under the wall. There will I show thee the Virgin Mary, the most pious Mother of God, who has offered up her health-giving prayers to God for you, and now, having been heard, comes to your deliverance".

After public prayers and solemn litanies, and after earnest private prayer offered up by Barbatus in the Church of the Virgin, the people, with Romwald at their head, assembled at the gate which is still called Summa. Then Barbatus desired them all to bow down to the dust, for God loveth a contrite heart, and went, in conversation with Romwald, close under the wall. Then suddenly appeared the Mother of God, at sight of whom the Prince fell to the earth and lay like one dead, till the holy man lifted him from the ground and spoke words of comfort to him who had been permitted to see so great a mystery.

On the following day the besieger, who had refused to be turned from his hostile purpose by an immense weight of silver and gold and a countless quantity of pearls and precious stones, now, receiving only the sister of Romwald, turned his back on Beneventum and entered the city of Neapolis. The blessed Barbatus at once took a hatchet, and going forth to Votum, with his own hands hewed down that unutterable tree in which for so long the Lombards had wrought their deadly sacrilege: he tore up its roots and piled earth over it, so that no one thereafter should be able to say where it had stood.

And now was Barbatus solemnly chosen bishop of Beneventum. Of all the farms and *coloniae* wherewith Prince and people offered to endow him, he would receive nothing, but he consented to have the house of the Archangel Michael on Mount Garganus, and all the district that had been under the rule of the bishop of Sipontum transferred to the See of the Mother of God over which he presided.

Still Romwald and his henchmen, though in public they appeared to worship God in accordance with the teaching of Barbatus, in the secret recesses of the palace adored the image of the Viper to their souls' destruction; wherefore the man of God, with prayers and tears, besought that they might be turned from the error of their way.

Meanwhile Romwald's wife, Theuderada, had forsaken the way of error, and was worshipping Christ according to the holy canons. Often when Romwald went forth to hunt, Barbatus would come to visit her, and discourse with her concerning her husband's wickedness. In one of these interviews she, heaving a deep sigh, said, "Oh! that thou wouldest pray for him to Almighty God. I know that it is only by thine intercession that he can be brought to walk in the path of virtue".

Barbatus.—"If thou hast, as I believe, true faith in the Lord, hand over to me the Viper's image, that thy husband may be saved".

Theuderada.—"If I should do this, I know of a surety that I should die".

Barbatus.—"Remember the rewards of eternal life. Such death would not be death, but a great gain. For the faith of Christ thou shalt be withdrawn from this unstable world, and shalt attain unto that world where Christ reigneth with His saints, where shall be neither frost nor parching heat, nor poverty nor sadness, nor weariness nor envy, but all shall be joy and glory without end".

Moved by such promises she speedily brought him the image of the Viper. Having received it, the bishop at once melted it in the fire, and by the help of many goldsmiths made of it during the prince's absence a paten and chalice of great size and beauty, for the offering up of the body and blood of Jesus Christ.

When all was prepared, on the sacred day of the Resurrection, Romwald, returning from hunting, was about to enter Beneventum, but Barbatus met him, and persuaded him first to come and assist in celebration of the Mass in the church of the Mother of God. This he did, receiving the communion in the golden vessels made, though he knew it not, from the image of the Viper. When all was done, the man of God approached the prince, and rebuked him sharply for tempting God by keeping the Viper's image in his palace. Should the terrible day of the Divine vengeance come, in vain would he flee to that idol for protection. Hearing these words, Romwald humbly confessed his sin, and promised to give up the image into the bishop's hands. "That thou needest not do", said the saint, "since it has already been changed into the vessels from which thou hast received the body and blood of the Lord. Thus what the Devil had prepared for thy destruction is now the instrument through which God works thy salvation".

Romwald.—"Prithee tell me, dearest father, by whose orders the idol was brought to thee".

Barbatus.—"I confess that I, speaking in much sorrow to thy wife concerning thy spiritual death, asked her for the image, and received it at her hands".

Thereat one of the bystanders burst in, saying, "If my wife had done such a thing as that, I would without a moment's delay cut off her head". But Barbatus turned to him and said : "Since thou longest to help the Devil, thou shalt be the Devil's slave". Thereupon the man was at once seized by the Devil and began to be grievously tormented by him. And that this might be a token and a warning to the Lombard nation in after times, the saint predicted that for so many generations [the biographer is not certain of the exact number] there should always be one of his descendants possessed by the Devil, a prophecy which, down to the date of the composition of the biography, had been exactly fulfilled.

Struck with terror, all the other Beneventans abandoned their superstitions practices, and were fully instructed by the man of God in the Catholic faith, which they still keep by God's favor.

Barbatus spent eighteen years and eleven mouths in his bishopric, and died on the eleventh day before the Kalends of March (19th of February, 682), in the eightieth year of his age.

This curious narrative, however little worthy of credence as a statement of facts, is a valuable piece of evidence as to the spiritual condition of the Lombards of South Italy in the seventh century. We may safely infer from it that conversion to Christianity was a much more gradual process in the south than in the north of Italy. Lupus of Friuli is neither saint nor hero in the pages of Paulus, but his daughter Theuderada is like another Clotilda or Theudelinda to the barbarous, half-heathen rulers of Benevento.

In another Life, contained in the *Acta Sanctorum*, that of St. Sabinus, we have a slight notice of Theuderada as a widow. After the death of her husband she ruled the Samnites in the name of her young son [Grimwald II], and during her regency a certain Spaniard named Gregory came to Spoleto in order to find the tomb of St. Sabinus, who had died more than a century before (in 566). Not finding the sepulcher there, he persuaded the Princess Theuderada to go and seek for it at Canusium. She found the tomb, and on opening it perceived that pleasant odor which often pervaded the sepulchers of the saints. She also found in it a considerable weight of gold, which the biographer thinks had been stored there in anticipation of that invasion of the barbarians which St. Sabinus had foretold. Unmindful of the commission which Gregory had given her to build a church over the saint's tomb, she carried off the gold and returned in haste to Benevento. But when she arrived at Trajan's Bridge over the Anfidus, by the judgment of God her horse slipped and fell. She was raised from the ground by her attendants, but recognized in the accident the vengeance of the saint for her forgetfulness. She hastened back to the holy man's sepulcher, built a church with all speed, roared over his body a beautiful marble altar, and made chalice and paten out of the gold found in the tomb. To the end of his life Gregory the Spaniard ministered in the church of St. Sabinus.

CHAPTER VII.

THE BAVARIAN LINE RESTORED.

PERCTARIT (672-688).

KING GRIMWALD died, leaving a grown-up son Romwald, his successor In the duchy of Benevento, and a child Garibald, the nominal king of the Lombards under the regency of his mother, the daughter of King Aripert. It was not to be expected, however, that the banished Perctarit would tamely acquiesce in his exclusion from the throne by his sister's infant son : and in fact, if the story told by Paulus be true, he appeared upon the scene even sooner than men had looked for him. One of the latest acts of Grimwald's reign had been to conclude a treaty of alliance with the king of the Franks, and a chief article of that treaty had been the exclusion of Perctarit from the Frankish realms. The hunted exile had accordingly taken ship for "the kingdom of the Saxons" (that is to say, probably the coasts of Kent), but had only proceeded a short distance on his voyage when a voice was heard from the Frankish shore, enquiring whether Perctarit was on board. Receiving an affirmative answer, the voice proceeded, "Tell him to return into his own land, since it is now the third day since Grimwald perished from the sunlight". Hearing this, Perctarit at once returned to the shore, but found no one there who could tell him anything concerning the death of Grimwald, wherefore he concluded that the voice had been that of no mortal man, but of a Divine messenger. Returning in all haste to his own land, he found the Alpine passes filled with a brilliant throng of courtiers surrounded by a great multitude of Lombards, all expecting his arrival. He marched straight to Pavia, and in the third month after the death of Grimwald was hailed as king by all the Lombards. The child Garibald was driven forth, and we hear no more of the further fortunes of him or his mother. Rodelinda, the wife of Perctarit, and Cunincpert his son, were at once sent for from Benevento. Romwald seems to have given them up without hesitation, and to have peaceably acquiesced in the reign of the restored Perctarit, whose daughter eventually married his eldest son.

For about seventeen years did "the beloved PERCTARIT" rule the Lombard state; a man of comely stature, full habit of body, gentle temper, kind and affable to all, and with a remarkable power (attested in the history of his wanderings) of attaching to himself the affections of those beneath him in station. He was a devout Catholic, and one of the first acts of his reign was to build and richly endow a convent for nuns called the "New Monastery of St. Agatha", in that part of Pavia which adjoins the walls whence he had made his memorable escape. Queen Rodelinda also built a basilica in honor of the Virgin outside the walls of Pavia, which she adorned "with many wonderful works of art", of all which unfortunately not a trace now remains.

The only exception that we can find to the generally mild character of Perctarit's rule is his treatment of the Jewish people. Like the Visigoths, the Lombards would seem to have written their adhesion to their new faith in the blood and tears of the Hebrew. We learn from the rude poem on the Synod of Pavia that Perctarit caused the Jews to be baptized, and ordered all who refused to believe to be slain with the sword.

In the eighth year of his reign Perctarit associated with himself his son Cunincpert, with whom he reigned jointly for more than eight years.

The only break in the generally peaceful and prosperous reign of Perctarit was caused by the seditious movements of Alahis, Duke of Trient, who for some years was a great troubler of the Lombard commonwealth. This Alahis had met in battle and signally defeated the count or *gravio* of the Bavarians, who ruled Botzen and the neighboring towns. Elated by this victory he rebelled against the gentle Perctarit, shut himself up in Tridentum, and defied his sovereign. The king marched into the valley of the Adige and commenced a formal siege, but in a sudden sally Alahis broke up his camp, and compelled him to seek safety in flight. No victory after this seems to have restored the honor of the king's arms, but by the intervention of the young Cunincpert the rebel duke was induced to come in and seek to be reconciled to his lord. Not forgiveness only, but a great increase of the power of Alahis was eventually the result of this reconciliation. More than once had Perctarit decided to put him to death, but he relented, and at the earnest request of Cunincpert (who pledged himself for the future fidelity of his friend), the great and wealthy city of Brescia, full of noble Lombard families, was added to the duchy of Alahis. Even in complying with this often-urged request, Perctarit told his son that he was compassing his own ruin in thus strengthening a man who would assuredly one day seek to upset his throne.

The kings of the Bavarian line appear to have been great builders. About this time Perctarit built, "with wonderful workmanship, a great gate to the city of Pavia, which was called Palatiensis, because it adjoined the royal palace. And when, soon after, his time came to die, he was laid near the church of the Saviour which his father Aripert had built in Pavia.

CUNINCPERT (688-700), who had already, as we have seen, ruled for some years jointly with his father, was now sole king, and his reign lasted till the end of the century. A strangely compounded character, this large-limbed muscular man, of amorous temperament, and apt to tarry too long over the wine-cup, was also apparently a devout Catholic, a friend of the rulers of the Church, an "elegant" man, and famous for his good deeds. He had married a Saxon princess named Hermelinda, probably a relative of the king of Kent, in whose dominions he had been on the point of taking refuge. Hermelinda, who had seen in the bath a young maiden of the noblest Roman ancestry, named Theodote, incautiously praised in her husband's presence her comely figure and luxuriant growth of flaxen hair, descending almost to her feet. Cunincpert listened with well dissembled eagerness, invited his wife to join him in a hunting expedition to the "City" forest in the neighborhood of Pavia, returned by night to the capital, and gratified his unhallowed passion. How long the intrigue lasted or by what means it was brought to a close we are not told, but when it was ended, he sent her to a convent at Pavia, which long after bore her name. It was apparently soon after Cunincpert's accession that that "son of wickedness", Alahis, forgetful of the great benefits which he had received from the king, forgetful of his old intercession on his behalf, and of the faith which he had sworn to observe towards him, began to plot his overthrow. Two brothers, powerful citizens of Brescia, Aldo and Grauso, and many other Lombards, entered into the plot, for which, doubtless, there was some political pretext, perhaps Cunincpert's inefficiency as a ruler, perhaps his drunken revelries, perhaps his too great devotion to the interests of the Church. Whatever the cause, Alahis entered Pavia during Cunincpert's temporary absence from his capital, and took possession of his palace and his throne. When tidings of the revolt were brought to Cunincpert, he fled without striking a blow to that "home of lost causes", the island on Lake Como, and there fortified himself against his foe.

Great was the distress among all the friends and adherents of the fugitive king, but pre-eminently among the bishops and priests of the realm, when they learned that Alahis, who was a notorious enemy of the clergy, was enthroned in the palace at Pavia. Still, desiring to be on good terms with the new ruler, Damian, the bishop of the city, sent a messenger, the deacon Thomas, a man of high repute for learning and holiness, to give him the episcopal blessing. The deacon was kept waiting for some time outside the gates of the palace; he received a coarse and insulting message from its occupant; and, when at last admitted to his presence, he was subjected to a storm of invective which showed the deep hatred of the clerical order that burned in the heart of Alahis. That hatred was mutual, and the bishops and priests of the realm, dreading the cruelty of the new ruler, longed for the return of the banished Cunincpert.

At length the overthrow of the tyrant came from an unexpected quarter. Alahis was one day counting out his money on a table, while a little boy, son of his Brescian adherent Aldo, was playing about in the room. A golden *tremisses* fell from the table and was picked up by the boy, who brought it to Alahis. The surly-tempered tyrant, little thinking that the child would understand him, growled out, "Many of these has thy father had from me, which he shall pay me back again soon, if God will". Returning home that evening, the boy told his father all that had happened, and the strange speech of the king, by which Aldo was greatly alarmed. He sought his brother Grauso, and took counsel with him and their partisans how they might anticipate the blow, and deprive Alahis of the kingdom before he had completed his design. Accordingly they went early to the palace, and thus addressed Alahis : "Why do you think it necessary always to remain cooped up in the city? All the inhabitants are loyal to you, and that drunkard Cunincpert is so besotted that all his influence is gone. Go out hunting with your young courtiers, and we will stay here with the rest of your faithful servants, and defend this city for you. Nay more, we promise you that we will soon bring back to you the head of your enemy Cunincpert". Yielding to their persuasions, Alahis went forth to the vast forest already mentioned called the "City forest", and there passed his time in hunting and sport of various kinds. Meanwhile Aldo and Grauso journeyed in haste to the Lake of Como, took ship there, and sought Cunincpert on his island. Falling at his feet, they confessed and deplored their past transgressions against him, related the menacing words of Alahis, and explained the insidious counsel which they had given him. After weeping together and exchanging solemn oaths, they fixed a day on which Cunincpert, was to present himself at the gates of Pavia, which they promised should be opened to receive him.

All went prosperously with the loyal traitors. On the appointed day Cunincpert appeared under the walls of Pavia. All the citizens, but preeminently the bishop and his clergy, went eagerly forth to meet him. They embraced him with tears: he kissed as many of them as he could : old and young with indescribable joy sang their loud hosannas over the overthrow of the tyrant and the return of the beloved Cunincpert. Word was at the same time sent by Aldo and Grauso to Alahis that they had faithfully performed their promise, and even something more, for they had brought back to Pavia not only the head of Cunincpert, but also his whole body, and he was at that moment seated in the palace.

Gnashing his teeth with rage, and foaming out curses against Aldo and Grauso, Alahis fled from the Eastern neighborhood of Pavia, and made his way by Piacenza into the Eastern half of the Lombard kingdom, a territorial division which we now for the first time meet with under a name memorable for Italy in after centuries, and in another connection: the fateful name of AUSTRIA. It is probable that there was in this part of the kingdom an abiding feeling of discontent with the rule of the devout drunkard Cunincpert, and a general willingness to accept this stern and strenuous duke of Trient as ruler in his stead. Some cities, indeed, opposed his party. Vicenza sent out an army against him, but when that army was defeated, she was willing to become his ally. Treviso was visited by him, and by gentle or ungentle means was won over to his side. Friuli collected an army which was to have marched to the help of Cunincpert, but Alahis went to meet them as far as the bridge over the Livenza, at forty-eight Roman miles distance from Friuli. Lurking there in a forest hard by, he met each detachment as it was coming up separately, and compelled it to swear fidelity to himself, taking good care that no straggler returned to warn the oncoming troops of the ambush into which they were falling. Thus by the energetic action of Alahis the whole region of "Austria" was ranged under his banners against the lawful ruler.

It may be noticed in passing that the language of Paulus in describing these events seems to show that the cities were already acquiring some of that power of independent action which is such a marked characteristic of political life in Italy in the Middle Ages. The turbulent personality of Duke Alahis is indeed sufficiently prominent, but he is the only duke mentioned in the whole chapter. It is "the cities" of Austria that, partly by flattery, partly by force, Alahis wins over to his side. The citizens of Vicenza go forth to battle against him, but become his allies. It is the "Forojulani", not the duke of Forum Julii that send their soldiers as they supposed to assist King Cunincpert, but really to swell the army of his rival.

Thus then were the two great divisions of the Lombard kingdom drawn up in battle array against one another on the banks of the Adda, the frontier stream. Nobly desirous to save the effusion of so much Lombard blood, Cunincpert sent a message to his rival, offering to settle the dispute between them by single combat. But for such an encounter Alahis had little inclination, and when one of his followers, a Tuscan by birth, exhorted him as a brave warrior to accept the challenge, Alahis answered, "Though Cunincpert is a stupid man, and a drunkard, he is wonderfully brave and strong. I remember how in his father's time, when he and I were boys in the palace together, there were some rams there of unusual size, and he would take one of them, and lift him up by the wool on his back, which I could never do". At this the Tuscan said, "If thou darest not meet Cunincpert in single combat, thou shalt not have me to help thee in thy enterprise". And thereat he went over at once to the camp of Cunincpert, and told him all these things.

So the armies met in the plain of Coronate, and when they were now about to join battle, Seno, a deacon of the basilica of St. John the Baptist (which Queen Gundiperga had built at Pavia), fearing lest Cunincpert, whom he greatly loved, should fall in the battle, came up and begged to be allowed to don the king's armor, and go forth and fight

Alahis. "All our life", said Seno, "hangs on your safety. If you perish in the war, that tyrant Alahis will torture us to death. Let it then be as I say, and let me wear your armor. If I fall, your cause will not have suffered; if I conquer, all the more glory to you, whose very servant has overcome Alahis". Long time Cunincpert refused to comply with this request, but at length his soft heart was touched by the prayers and tears of all his followers, and he consented to hand over his coat of mail, his helmet, his greaves, and all his other equipments to the deacon, who being of the same build and stature, looked exactly like the king when arrayed in his armor.

Thus then the battle was joined, and hotly contested on both sides. Where Alahis saw the supposed king, thither he pressed with eager haste, thinking to end the war with one blow. And so it was that he killed Seno, whereupon he ordered the head to be struck off, that it might be carried on a pole amid the loud shouts of "God be thanked" from all the army. But when the helmet was removed for this purpose, lo! the tonsured head showed that they had killed no king, but only an ecclesiastic. Cried Alahis in fury, "Alas! we have done nothing in all this great battle, but only slain a cleric". And with that he swore a horrible oath, that if God would grant him the victory he would fill a well with the amputated members of the clerics of Lombardy.

At first the adherents of Cunincpert were dismayed, thinking that their lord had fallen, but their hearts were cheered, and they were sure of victory, when the king, with open visor, rode round their ranks assuring them of his safety. Again the two hosts drew together for the battle, and again Cunincpert renewed his offer to settle the quarrel by single combat and spare the lives of the people. But Alahis again refused to hearken to the advice of his followers and accept the challenge; this time alleging that he saw among the standards of his rival the image of the Archangel Michael, in whose sanctuary he had sworn fidelity to Cunincpert. Then said one of his men, "In thy fright thou seest things that are not. Too late, I ween, for thee is this kind of meditation on saints' images and broken fealty". The trumpets sounded again for the charge: neither side gave way to the other: a terrible slaughter was made of Lombard warriors. But at length Alahis fell, and by the help of God victory remained with Cunincpert. Great was the slaughter among the fleeing troops of Alahis, and those whom the sword spared the river Adda swept away. The men of Friuli took no share in the battle, since their unwilling oath to Alahis prevented them from fighting for Cunincpert, and they were determined not to fight against him. As soon therefore as the battle was joined, they marched off to their own homes.

The head and legs of Alahis were cut off, leaving only his trunk, a ghastly trophy: but the body of the brave deacon Seno was buried by the king's order before the gates of his own basilica of St. John. Cunincpert, now indeed a king, returned to Pavia amid the shouts and songs of triumph of his exultant followers. In aftertime he reared a monastery in honor of St. George the Martyr on the battlefield of Coronate in memory of his victory.

There is a sequel to this history of the rebellion of Alahis as told by Paulus, but the reader will judge for himself what claim it has to be accepted as history. On a certain day after the rebellion was crushed, King Cunincpert was sitting in his palace at Pavia, taking counsel with his *Marpahis* (master of the horse) how he might make away with Aldo and Grauso, aforetime confederates with Alahis. Suddenly a large fly alighted near them, at which the king struck with a knife, but only succeeded in chopping off the insect's foot. At the same time Aldo and Grauso, ignorant of any design against them, were coming towards the palace; and when they had reached the neighboring basilica of

St. Romanus the Martyr, they were suddenly met by a lame man with a wooden leg, who told them that Cunincpert would slay them if they entered his presence. On hearing this they were seized with fear, and took refuge at the altar of the church. When the king heard that they were thus seeking sanctuary, he at first charged his *Marpahis* with having betrayed his confidence, but he naturally answered that, having never gone out of the king's presence, nor spoken to any one, he could not have divulged his design. Then he sent to Aldo and Grauso to ask why they were in sanctuary. They told him what they had heard, and how a one-legged messenger had brought them the warning, on which the king perceived that the fly had been in truth a malignant spirit, who had betrayed his secret counsels. On receiving his kingly word pledged for their safety, the two refugees came forth from the basilica, and were ever after reckoned among his most devoted servants. The clemency and loyalty of the "beloved" Cunincpert need not perhaps be seriously impugned for the sake of a childish legend like this.

It was probably in the early years of Cunincpert's reign that a terrible pestilence broke out among the people, and for three months, from July to September, ravaged the greater part of Italy. Each of the two capitals, Rome and Pavia, suffered terribly from its devastation. In Rome, two were often laid in one grave, the son with his father, the brother with his sister. At Pavia the ravages of the pestilence were so fearful, that the panic-stricken citizens went forth and lived on the tops of the mountains, doubtless in order to avoid the malarious air of the Po valley. In the streets and squares of the city, grass began to grow: and the terrified remnant that dwelt there had their misery enhanced by ghostly fears. To their excited vision appeared two angels, one of light and one of darkness, walking through their streets. The evil angel carried a hunting-net in his hand: and ever and anon, with the consent of the good angel, he would stop before one of the houses, and strike it with the handle of his net. According to the number of the times that he struck it, was the number of the inmates of that house carried forth next morning to burial. At length it was revealed to one of the citizens that the plague would only be stayed by erecting an altar to the martyr St. Sebastian in the basilica of St. Peter ad Vincula. The relics of the martyr were sent for from Rome, the altar was erected, and the pestilence ceased.

Notwithstanding the interruptions of war and pestilence, the court life of Pavia during the reign of Cunincpert seems to have been, in comparison with that of most of his predecessors, a life of refinement and culture. At that court there flourished a certain renowned grammarian, or as we should say, a classical scholar, named Felix, whose memory has been preserved, owing to the fact that his nephew Flavian was the preceptor of the Lombard historian. To him, besides many other gifts, the king gave a walking stick adorned with silver and gold, which was no doubt preserved as an heirloom in his family.

It is noteworthy, as showing the increasing civilization of the Lombards under this king, that he is the first of his race whose effigy appears on a national coinage. His gold coins, obviously imitated from those of Byzantium, bear on the obverse the effigy of "Dominus Noster Cunincpert", and on the reverse a quaint representation of the Archangel Michael, that favorite patron saint of the Lombards, whose image the panic-stricken Alahis saw among the royal standards at the great battle by the Adda.

It was in the second year of the reign of Cunincpert, and doubtless before the outbreak of the rebellion, that he received the visit of a king from our own land, who not of constraint, but of his own free will, had laid aside his crown. This was Ceadwalla, king of the West Saxons, a young man in the very prime of life, who had, only four years before, won from a rival family the throne of his ancestors. In his short reign he had shown great activity after the fashion of his anarchic time, had annexed Sussex, ravaged Kent, conquered and massacred the inhabitants of the Isle of Wight, and given to two young princes of that island the crown of martyrdom. But in the attack on Kent, his brother Mul, a pattern of the Saxon virtues, generosity, courtesy, and savage courage, had been burned in a plundered house by the enraged men of Kent. Either the loss of this brother, or the satiety born of success, determined Ceadwalla to lay aside the crown, to go on pilgrimage, if possible to die. He was received with marvelous honor by King Cunincpert, whose wife was in a certain sense his countrywoman. He passed on to Rome, and was baptized on Easter Day by Pope Sergius, changing his rough name Ceadwalla for the apostolic Peter. Either the climate of Rome, the exaltation of his spirit, or the austerities which were practiced by the penitent, proved fatal. He died on the 20th of April, 689, ten days after his baptism, and an epitaph in respectable elegiacs, composed by order of the Pope, preserved to after-generations the memory of his high birth, his warlike deeds, the zeal which had brought him from the uttermost ends of the earth to visit the City of Romulus, and the devotion to the Papal See which had caused him to visit the tomb and assume the name of Peter.

Near the end of his reign Cunincpert summoned that synod at Pavia which brought about the reconciliation between the Patriarch of Aquileia and the Roman Pontiff, and closed the dreary controversy on the Three Chapters, as has been already told in tracing the history of the Istrian schism.

Cunincpert was generally on the most friendly terms with his bishops and clergy, but once it happened that John, bishop of Bergamo, a man of eminent holiness, said something at a banquet which offended him, and the king, condescending to an ignoble revenge, ordered his attendants to bring for the bishop's use a high spirited and ill-broken steed, which with a loud and angry snort generally dismounted those who dared to cross his back. To the wonder of all beholders however, as soon as the bishop had mounted him, the horse became perfectly tractable, and with a gently ambling pace bore him to his home. The king was so astonished at the miracle that he gave the horse to the bishop for his own, and ever after held him in highest honor.

The last year of the seventh century saw the end of the reign of Cunincpert. He must have died in middle life, and possibly his death may have been hastened by those deep potations which seem to have been characteristic of his race. But whatever were his faults, he had his father's power of winning the hearts of his servants. He was "the prince most beloved by all and it was amid the genuine tears of the Lombards that he was laid to rest by his father's side, near his grandfather's church of Our Lord and Saviour".

LIUTPERT (700),

the son of Cunincpert, succeeded his father, but being still only a boy, he was under the guardianship of Ansprand, a wise and noble statesman, the father of a yet more illustrious son, who was one day to shed a sunset glory over the last age of the Lombard monarchy. At this time Ansprand had little opportunity of showing his capacity for rule, for after eight months Raginpert, duke of Turin, the son of Godepert, whom Grimwald slew forty years before, a man of the same generation and about the same age as the lately deceased king, rose in rebellion against his kinsman; and marching eastwards with a strong army, met Ansprand and his ally, Rotharit, duke of

Bergamo, on the plains of Novara—a name of evil omen for Italy—defeated them and won the crown, which however he was not destined long to wear.

RAGINPERT (700). ARIPERT II (701-712).

The new king died very shortly after his accession, in the same year which witnessed the death of Cunincpert. The boy-king Liutpert and his guardian Ansprand had yet a party, Rotharit and three other dukes being still confederate together. Aripert II, son of Raginpert, marched against them, defeated them in the plains near Pavia, and took the boy-king prisoner. His guardian Ansprand fled, it need hardly be said to the Insula Comacina, where he fortified himself against the expected attack of the usurper.

Rotharit meanwhile returned to Bergamo, and discarding all pretence of championing the rights of Liutpert, styled himself king of the Lombards. Aripert marched against him with a large army, took the town of Lodi, which guarded the passage of the Adda, and then besieged Bergamo. The "battering rams and other machines", which now formed part of the warlike apparatus of the Lombards, enabled him without difficulty to make himself master of the place. Rotharit the pretender was taken prisoner: his head and his chin were shaved, and he was sent into banishment into Aripert's own city, Turin, where not long-after he was slain. The child Liutpert was also taken prisoner, and killed by drowning in a bath.

The boy-king being thus disposed of, the faithful guardian Ansprand remained to be dealt with and army, doubtless accompanied by something in the nature of a flotilla, was sent to the Insula Comacina. Learning its approach, and knowing himself powerless to resist it, Ansprand fled up the Splügen Pass by way of Chiavenna and Coire to Theudebert, duke of the Bavarians, who, for the sake doubtless of his loyalty to the Bavarian line, gave him for nine years shelter in his court. The island on Lake Como was at once occupied by Aripert's troops, and the town erected on it destroyed. Unable to reach the brave and faithful Ansprand, Aripert, now established in his kingdom, wreaked cruel vengeance on his family. His wife Theodarada, who had with womanish vanity boasted that she would one day be queen, had her nose and ears cut off. The like hideous mutilation was practiced on his daughter Aurona, herself apparently already a wife and a mother. Sigiprand, the eldest son, was blinded, and all the near relations of the fugitive were in one way or other tormented. Only Liutprand, the young son of Ansprand, escaped the cruel hands of the tyrant, who despised his youth, and after keeping him for some time in imprisonment, allowed him to depart for the Bavarian land, where he was received with inexpressible joy by his father.

Of the twelve years' reign of Aripert II we have but little information, except as to the civil wars caused by his usurpation of the crown. The inhabitants of Italy saw with surprise the increasing number of Rome. Anglo-Saxon pilgrims, noble and base-born, men and women, laymen and clergy, who, moved "by the instinct of a divine love", and also deeming that they thus secured a safer and easier passage to Paradise, braved the hardships of a long and toilsome journey, and came on pilgrimage to Rome. It was thus, during the reign of Aripert, that Coinred, king of the Mercians, grandson of that fierce old heathen Penda, came with the young and comely Offa, prince of the East Saxons, to Rome, and there, according to Paulus, speedily obtained that death which they desired Thus also, sixteen years later, Ine, king of Wessex, lawgiver and warrior, after a long and generally prosperous reign of thirty-seven years, forcibly admonished by his wife as to the vanity of all earthly grandeur, followed the example of his kinsman Ceadwalla, and, resigning his crown to his brother-in-law, turned his pilgrim steps towards Rome, where he died, a humbly clad but not tonsured monk.

King Aripert, however, did not greatly encourage the visits of strangers to his land. When the ambassadors of foreign nations came to his court, he would don his cheapest garments of cloth or of leather, and would set before them no costly wines, nor any other dainties, in order that the strangers might be impressed by the poverty of Italy. One might say that he remembered the manner of the invitation which, according to the *Saga,* Narses had given to his people, and was determined that no second invitation of the same kind should travel northward across the Alps.

Like the Caliph of the next century, Haroun al Raschid, Aripert would roam about by night, disguised, through the streets of the cities of his kingdom, that he might learn what sort of opinion his subjects had of him, and what manner of justice his judges administered. For he was, says Paulus, "a pious man, given to alms, and a lover of justice, in whose days there was great abundance of the fruits of the earth, but the times were barbarous".

Certainly the times were barbarous, if Aripert II was a fair representative of them. There is a taint of Byzantine cruelty in his blindings and mutilations of the kindred of his foes, of more than Byzantine, of Tartar savagery in the wide sweep of his ruthless sword. He was devout, doubtless, a great friend of the Church, as were almost all of these kinsmen of Theudelinda. We are told that he restored to the Apostolic See a large territory in the province of the Cottian Alps, which had once belonged to the Papal Patrimony, and that the epistle announcing this great concession was written in letters of gold. Admirable as are, for the most part, the judgments of character expressed by the Lombard deacon, it is difficult not to think that in this case a gift had blinded the eyes of the wise, and that Aripert's atrocious cruelties to the family of Ansprand are condoned for the sake of the generous gifts which he, like Henry of Lancaster, bestowed on the Church which sanctioned his usurpation.

At length the long-delayed day of vengeance dawned for Ansprand. His friend Theudebert, duke of Bavaria, gave him an array, with which he invaded Italy and joined battle with Aripert. There was great slaughter on both sides, but when night fell, "it is certain" says the patriotic Paulus, "that the Bavarians had turned their backs, and the army of Aripert returned victorious to its camp". However, the Lombard victory does not seem to have been so clear to Aripert, who left the camp, and sought shelter within the walls of Pavia. This timidity gave courage to his enemies, and utterly disgusted his own soldiers. Perceiving that he had lost the affections of the army, he accepted the advice which some of his friends proffered, that he should make his escape into France. Having taken away out of the palace vaults as much gold as he thought he could carry, he set forth on his journey. It was necessary for him to swim across the river Ticino, not a broad nor very rapid stream: but the weight of the gold (which he had perhaps enclosed in a belt worn about his person) dragged him down, and he perished in the waters. Next day his body was found, and buried close to the Church of the Saviour, doubtless near the bodies of his father and grandfather. His brother Gumpert fled to France, and died there, leaving three sons, one of whom, Raginpert, was, in the time of Paulus, governor of the important city of Orleans. But no more princes of the Bavarian line reigned in Italy, where, with one slight interruption, they had borne sway for a century.

CHAPTER VIII.

STORY OF THE DUCHIES, CONTINUED.

FOLLOWING the course of the chief highway of Lombard history, we have now emerged from the seventh century and have arrived at the threshold of the reign of the greatest, and nearly the last, of the Lombard kings. But before tracing the career of Liutprand, we must turn back to consider the changes which forty years had wrought in the rulers of the subordinate Lombard states, and also in the relations of the Empire and the Papacy.

I. Duchy of Trient.

Of one turbulent duke of Trient, namely Duke Alahis, we have already heard, and have marked his attempts, his almost successful attempts, to overthrow the sovereigns who ruled at Pavia by the combined exertions of all the cities of the Lombard Austria. Apparently the forces of the Tridentine duchy were exhausted by this effort, for we hear nothing concerning the successors of Alahis in the remaining pages of Paulus Diaconus.

II. Duchy of Friuli.

The story of the duchy of Friuli, perhaps on account of the historian's own connection with that region, is much more fully told.

The brave *Wechtari* from Vicenza was succeeded in the duchy by *Landari*, and he by *Rodwald.* These to us are names and nothing more, but Rodwald during his absence from Cividale was ousted from his duchy by a certain *Ansfrit*, an inhabitant (probably a count or *gastald)* of Reunia on the banks of the Taghamento (Ragogna, about thirty miles west of Cividale). Rodwald fled into Istria, and thence by way of Ravenna (evidently at this time there were friendly relations between king and exarch) he made his way to the court of Cunincpert. Ansfrit's invasion of the duchy of Friuli had taken place without the king's sanction, and now, not content with the duchy, he aspired to the crown, and marched westward as far as Verona. There, however, he was defeated, taken prisoner, and sent to the king. According to the barbarous Byzantine fashion of the times, his eyes were blinded and he was sent into exile. For some reason or other, probably on account of his proved incapacity, Rodwald was not restored, but the government of the duchy was vested in his brother *Ado,* who, however, ruled only with the title of Caretaker *(Loci Servator).* After he had governed for nineteen months he died, and was succeeded by *Ferdidf,* who came from Liguria in the West, a stirring chief, but somewhat feather-headed and unstable in whose occupation of the duchy a notable event occurred

The Slavs neighbors of Friuli were much given to cattle-lifting excursions across the border, by which the Lombards of the plain suffered severely. Apparently Duke Ferdulf thought that one regular war would be more tolerable than these incessant predatory inroads: or else it was, as Paulus asserts, simply from a vainglorious desire to pose as conqueror of the Slavs that he actually invited these barbarians to cross over into his duchy, and bribed certain of their leaders to support the expedition in the councils of the nation. Never was a more insane scheme devised, and the danger of it was increased by Ferdulf's want of prudence and self-control. A certain *sculdahis* or high-bailiff of the king, named Argait, a man of noble birth and great courage and capacity, had pursued the Slav depredators after one of their incursions, and had failed to capture them. "No wonder", said the hot-tempered duke, "that you who are called Argait can do no brave deed, but have let those robbers escape you" *(Arga* being the Lombard word for a coward). Thereat the *sculdahis,* in a tremendous rage at this most unjust accusation, replied, "If it please God, Duke Ferdulf, thou and I shall not depart this life before it has been seen which of us two is the greater *Arga!"* Soon after this interchange of vulgar abuse came the tidings that the mighty army of the Slavs, whose invasion Ferdulf had so foolishly courted, was even now at hand.

They came, probably pouring down through the Predil Pass, under the steep cliffs of the Mangert, and round the buttresses of the inaccessible Terglou. Ferdulf saw them encamped at the top of a mountain, steep and difficult of access, and began to lead his Lombards round its base, that he might turn the position, which he could not scale. But then outspoke Argait: "Remember, Duke Ferdulf, that you called me an idle and useless thing, in the speech of our countrymen an *Arga*. Now may the wrath of God light upon that one of us who shall be last up that mountain, and striking at the Slavs". With that he turned his horse's head, and charged up the steep mountain. Stung by his taunts, and determined not to be outdone, Ferdulf followed him all the way up the craggy and pathless places. The army, thinking it shame not to follow its leader, pressed on after them. Thus was the victory given over to the Slavs, who had only to roll down stones and tree-trunks on the ascending Lombards, and needed neither arms nor valor to rid them of their foes, nearly all of whom were knocked from their horses and perished miserably.

There fell Ferdulf himself, and Argait, and all the nobles of Friuli; such a mass of brave men as might with forethought and a common purpose have done great things for their country; all sacrificed to foolish pique and an idle quarrel.

There was indeed one noble Lombard who escaped, almost by a miracle. This was Munichis, whose two sons, Peter and Ursus, long after were dukes of Friuli and Ceneda respectively. He was thrown from his horse, and one of the Slavs came upon him and tied his hands; but he, though thus manacled, contrived to wrest the slav's lance from his right hand, to pierce him with the same, and then, all bound as he was, to scramble down the steep side of the mountain and get away in safety.

In the room of the slain Ferdulf, a certain *Corvolus* obtained the ducal dignity. Not long, however, did he rule the city of Forum Julii, for, having fallen in some way under the displeasure of the king (apparently Aripert II), he was, according to that monarch's usual custom, deprived of his eyes, and spent the rest of his life in ignominious seclusion. This and several other indications of the same kind clearly show that these northern dukes had not attained nearly the same semi-independent position which had been achieved by their brethren of Spoleto and Benevento.

To him succeeded *Pemmo,* and here we seem to reach firmer ground, for this is the father of two well-known kings of the Lombards, and we may yet read in a church of Cividale a contemporary inscription bearing his name. The father of Pemmo was a citizen of Belluno named Billo, who having been engaged in an unsuccessful conspiracy, probably against the duke of his native place, came as an exile to Forum Julii, and spent the remainder of his days as a peaceful inhabitant of that city.

Pemmo himself, who is highly praised by Paulus as a wise and ingenious man, and one who was useful to his fatherland, must have risen early to a high position by his ability, for ancestral influence must have been altogether wanting. He probably became duke of Friuli somewhere about 705 a few years before the death of Aripert II, and held the office for about six and twenty years. The history of his fall will have to be told in connection with the reign of Liutprand, but meanwhile we may hear the story of his family life, as quaintly told by Paulus.

Pedigree of Pemmo :

BILLO of Belluno.
PEMMO — RATPERGA.
Duke of Friuli.

RATCHIS, RATCHAIT. AISTULF,
744-749. 749-757

This Pemmo had a wife named Ratperga, who, as she was of a common and countrified appearance, repeatedly begged her husband to put her away and marry another wife whose face should be more worthy of so great a duke.

But he, being a wise man, said that her manners, her humility, and her shame-faced modesty pleased him more than personal beauty. This wife bore to Pemmo three sons, namely, Ratchis, Ratchait, and Aistulf, all vigorous men, whose careers made glorious their mother's lowliness.

Moreover, Duke Pemmo, gathering round him the sons of all those nobles who had fallen in the above described war [with the Slavs], brought them up on an exact footing of equality with his own children.

I have said that a single existing monument preserves the memory of Duke Pemmo in the city over which he bore sway. Leaving the central portion of Cividale behind him, and crossing the beautiful gorge of the Natisone by the Ponte del Diavolo, the traveler comes to a little suburb, of no great interest in itself, and containing a modernize church, the external appearance of which will also probably fail to interest him, the little church of St. Martin. The altar of this church is adorned with a bas-relief in a barbarous style of ecclesiastical art. A rudely carved effigy of Christ between two winged saints (possibly the Virgin and John the Baptist is surrounded by four angels, whose large hands, twisted bodies, and curiously folded wings show a steep descent of the sculptor's art from the days of Phidias. Round the four slabs which make up the altar runs an inscription, not easy to decipher, which records in barbarous Latin the fact that the illustrious and sublime Pemmo had restored the ruined church of St. John, and enriched it with many gifts, having amongst other things presented it with a cross of fine gold; and that his son Ratchis had adorned the altar with beautifully colored marbles. Here then, in this little, scarce noticed church, we have a genuine relic of the last days of the Lombard monarchy.

III. Duchy of Benevento.

Our information as to the history of this duchy during the period in question is chiefly of a genealogical kind, and may best be exhibited in the form of a pedigree.

ROMWALD I = **THEUDERADA,**
son of Grimwald, daughter of Lupus of Friuli.
662-671 with his father;

GRIMWALD II,   GISULF I,
687-689,   689-706,
married Wigilinda,   married Winiperga.
daughter of King Perctarit.
ROMWALD II
706-730 (?).

We hear again of the piety of Theuderada, the heroine of the legend of St. Barbatus, and we are told that she built a basilica in honor of St. Peter outside the walls of Benevento, and founded there a convent, in which dwelt many of the "maids of God". Her son, *Grimwald II,* married, it will be observed, a daughter of King Perctarit and sister of Cunincpert. Apparently, therefore, the strife between the royal and the ducal line, which was begun by the usurpation of Grimwald, might now be considered as ended.

After Grimwald's short reign he was succeeded by a brother, *Gisullf I,* whose name recalled the ancestral connection of his family with Friuli, and their descent from the first Gisulf, the *marpahis* of Alboin.

Gisulf's son, *Romwald II,* reigned at the same time as King Liutprand, and his story, with that of his family, will have to be told in connection with that king, whose sister he married.

Though we hear but little of the course of affairs during these years in the Samnite duchy, it is evident that Lombard power was increasing and the power of the Emperors diminishing in Southern Italy. Romwald I collected a great army with which he marched against Tarentum and Brundisium, and took those cities. "The whole of the wide region round them was made subject to his sway". This probably means that the whole of the Terra di Otranto, the vulnerable heel of Italy, passed under Lombard rule. Certainly the ill-judged expedition of Constans was well avenged by the young Lombard chief whom he thought to crush.

Romwaldis son, Gisulf, pushed the border of his duchy up to the river Liris, wresting from the *Ducatus Romae* the towns of Sora, Arpinum, and Arx. It is interesting to observe that in our own day the frontier line between the States of the Church (representing the *Ducatus Romae)* and the kingdom of Naples (representing the duchy of Benevento) was so drawn as just to exclude from the former Sora, Arpino, and Rocca d'Arce.

It was during the pontificate of John VI (701-705), and possibly at the same time that these conquests were made, that Gisulf invaded Campania with a large force, burning and plundering; and arriving at the great granary of Puteoli pitched his camp there, no man resisting him. By this time he had taken an enormous number of captives, but the Pope sending some priests to him "with apostolic gifts", ransomed the captives out of his hands, and persuaded Gisulf himself to return without further ravages to his own land.

IV. Duchy of Spoleto.

Here, too, we have little more than the materials for a pedigree, as the remarkable denudation of historical materials which was previously noticed still continues.

It will be remembered that Grimwald of Benevento, in his audacious and successful attempt on the Lombard crown (661), was powerfully aided by Transamund, Count of Capua, whom he ordered to march by way of Spoleto and Tuscany to collect adherents to his cause, and that soon after his acquisition of sovereign power, he rewarded this faithful ally by bestowing on him the duchy of Spoleto, and the hand of one of his daughters.

TRANSAMUND I,   WACHILAPUS.
previously Count of Capua,
663 (?)-703 (?).
Married a daughter of King Grimwald.

FARWALD II,
703 (?)-724.

TRANSAMUND II,
734-739, AND 740-743.

Transamund appears to have reigned for forty years (663-703). He was succeeded by his son *Farwald II,* evidently named after the famous Duke Farwald of an earlier day, the founder of the duchy, and the conqueror of Classis. Notwithstanding the long reign of Transamund, his son appears to have been young at his accession, and his uncle *Wachilapus* was associated with him in the dukedom.

The story of Farwald II, and his turbulent son *Transamund II,* will be related when we come to deal with the reign of Liutprand.

CHAPTER IX.

THE PAPACY AND THE EMPIRE, 663-717.

FROM the day when Constans entered Rome on his mission of devout spoliation, the fortunes of the Papacy were so closely linked, at least for a couple of generations, with those of the Empire, that we may without inconvenience consider them together. That visit of the Emperor may be considered to have been the lowest point of the humiliation both of the Bishop and the City of Rome. Vigilius and Martin had been indeed dragged away from their episcopal palace and their loyal flock, and had suffered indignities and hardships in the city by the Bosphorus; but it was surely a lower depth of degradation to stand by, as Vitalian must needs do in trembling submission, with a smile of feigned welcome on his lips, while Constans the heretic, the author of the *Type* against which the Lateran Synod had indignantly protested, alternated his visits to the basilicas with his spoliation of the monuments of Rome. It may well have been at such a time as this that some Roman noble poured forth his feelings of indignation in a short poem which was found by the industrious Muratori in the library of the Dean and Chapter of Modena, and which may be thus translated :

> Rome! thou wast reared by noble hands and brave,
> But downward now thou fall'st, of slaves the slave,
> No king within thee hath for long borne sway;
> Thy name, thy glory are the Grecians' prey.
> None of thy nobles in thy courts remains,
> Thy free-born offspring till the Argive plains.
> Drawn from the world's ends is thy vulgar crowd,
> To servants' servants now thy head is bowed.
> "The New Rome"—such Byzantium's name today,
> While thou, the old Rome, seest thy walls decay.
> Well said the seer, pondering his mystic lore,
> *Rome's love shall fail, she shall he Rome no more.*
> But for the Great Apostles' guardian might.
> Thou long ago hadst sunk in endless night.

However, from this time forward there was a steady progress on the part of the people of old Rome towards independence of their Byzantine rulers, and in this successful Struggle for freedom the Popes were the more or less avowed and conscious protagonists. The day was passing away in which it was possible for the Eastern Caesar to send a policeman to arrest the Pope and drag him off to a Byzantine prison. We shall see one Exarch after another attempt this invidious duty in obedience to his master's mandate, and one after another will fall back disheartened before the manifestations of the popular will, which in the end will take the shape of an armed and organized National Guard.

This result is the more remarkable, as the Popes who presided over the Church during the period in question were for the most part undistinguished men, generally advanced in years—this must have been the cause of their very short average tenure of the see—and with so little that was striking in their characters that even the Papal chronicler can find scarcely anything to say of them except that they "loved the clergy and people", or "gave a large donation to the ecclesiastics and to the poor". In order not to burden the text with a multitude of names which no memory will wisely retain, I refer the reader for the Popes of the seventh century to a list at the end of this chapter and will mention here only those who took a leading part in the development of doctrine and the struggle with the Emperors.

A Sicilian ecclesiastic named Agatho, who occupied the chair of St. Peter for two years and a half (678-681), had the glory of winning a great ecclesiastical victory, and of settling the Monotheletic controversy on the terms for which Martin and all the Popes since Honorius had strenuously contended.

The young Emperor Constantine IV (668-685), whom we last met with in Sicily avenging his father's murder and who received the surname Pogonatus (bearded) from the populace of Constantinople, astonished to see their young lord returning to his home with the bushy beard of manhood, was occupied in the early years of his reign by matters too weighty to allow of his spending his time in theological controversy. For five years, 673-677, as has been already said, the great Saracen Armada hovered round the coasts of the Sea of Marmora, and the turbans of the followers of the Prophet were descried on the Bithynian shore by the defenders of Constantinople. Delivered from that pressing danger, the Emperor had leisure to consider the unhappy condition of the Church, distracted by that verbal disputation concerning the will of the Saviour for which his grandfather had unhappily given the signal. Constantine Pogonatus appears to have taken personally no decided line in this controversy, but to have been honestly anxious that the Church should decide it for herself. Four successive Patriarchs of Constantinople, generally supported by the Patriarchs of Antioch and Alexandria, had upheld Monothelete doctrine, and struggled for the phrase "one theandric energy". But the ecclesiastics of Constantinople probably saw that the mind of the Emperor was wavering, and that the whole West was united under the generalship of the Pope in a solid phalanx against them. It was understood that George, the new Patriarch of Constantinople, was willing to recede from the Monothelete position, and the Emperor accordingly issued an invitation to the Pope to send deputies to take part in a Conference for the restoration of peace to the Church. Pope Agatho before replying (27th March, 680) summoned a synod of Western bishops in which Monotheletism was unhesitatingly condemned, the voice of the young Church of the Anglo-Saxons, as represented by Wilfrid of York and others, being one of the loudest in defence of the two wills of Christ. Agatho thereupon dispatched three legates of his own, and three bishops as representatives of that synod, to take part in the proceedings of the Conference, which gradually assumed a more august character, and became, not a mere

Conference, but the Sixth Ecumenical Council, the third of its kind held at Constantinople.

At this Council, which was held in a domed chamber of the Imperial palace, and which was therefore sometimes called *In Trullo,* 289 bishops are said to have been present, and the sittings of the Council lasted from 7th November, 680, to 16th September, 681. On the left of the Emperor sat the bishops of the West, and on his right the Patriarchs of Constantinople and Antioch and the bishops of the East. It was soon seen which way the decision of the Council would tend. Pope Agatho's legates complained of the novel teaching of the Monothelete Patriarchs of the East. Macarius, Patriarch of Antioch, the Abdiel of Monotheletism, upon whom fell the burden of the defence of the lately dominant doctrines, undertook to prove that the dogma of "one theandric energy" was in harmony with the decisions of the Fourth and Fifth Councils, and with the teaching of Popes Leo and Vigilius. The genuineness of some of his quotations was denied, the aptness of others was disputed. George, Patriarch of Constantinople, formally announced his adhesion to the cause advocated by the Roman Pontiff. An enthusiastic priest named Polychronius, who undertook to prove the truth of Monothelete doctrine by raising a dead man to life, whispered in the ear of the corpse in vain. At length all was ready for the definition of the faith as to the Two Wills of Christ; the ratification of the decrees of Pope Agatho and the Western Synod; the deposition of Macarius, Patriarch of Antioch, from his high office, and the formal anathema on the dead and buried upholders or condoners of Monotheletic heresy.

Among these condemned ones were included four Patriarchs of Constantinople one Patriarch of Alexandria Theodore, bishop of Pharan, and—most memorable fact of all—a man too wise and tolerant for his age, Honorius, Pope of Rome.

At this crisis of the Church's deliberations, the *Liber Pontificalis* tells us that "so great a mass of black spiders' webs fell into the midst of the people that all men marveled, because at the same hour the filth of heresy had been expelled from the Church". To the minds of men of the present day the incident would seem not so much an emblem of the extirpation of heresy, as of the nature of the dusty subtleties which seventh-century ecclesiastics, both orthodox and heterodox, were occupied in weaving out of their own narrow intellects and presumptuous souls.

Though Pope Agatho probably heard enough concerning the opening deliberations of the Sixth Council to be assured of the final triumph of his cause, he died many months before the actual decision, and the news of the triumph itself must have reached Rome during the long interval which elapsed between his death and the consecration of his successor. The relations between Rome and Constantinople continued friendly during the rest of the lifetime of Pogonatus; and Pope Benedict II (684-685) received, so it is said, a letter from the Emperor dispensing for the future with the necessity of that Imperial confirmation for which the elected pontiff had hitherto been forced to wait before his consecration could be solemnized. If such a letter, however, were actually sent, the concession seems to have been silently revoked in the following reign.

Of Constantine Pogonatus, who died in 685, we may still behold the contemporary portrait in mosaic on the walls of the solitary church of S. Apollinare in Classe (Ravenna). There he stands, with his two young brethren Heraclius and Tiberius beside him, and hands to Reparatus, the venerable Archbishop of Ravenna, a document marked PRIVILEGIUM. This document was probably meant to confer on the prelates of Ravenna, not entire independence of the Roman See, but the same kind of independence and patriarchal jurisdiction which was enjoyed by the bishops of Milan and Aquileia. It was originally given by Constans near the close of his reign, and was possibly afterward confirmed by Pogonatus and his colleagues.

The figures of the two stripling colleagues of the Emperor, Heraclius and Tiberius, suggest some melancholy thoughts as to their fate, thoughts only too much in keeping with the mournful expression so common in these venerable mosaics. Shortly after the accession of Pogonatus, in the year 669, they were declared Augusti, in obedience to the clamors of the soldiers of the Eastern Theme, who flocked to Scutari shouting, "We believe in the Trinity. We will have three Emperors". A great noble was sent to appease the mutineers, and to profess compliance with their demands. Through him Constantine invited the leaders in the movement to a friendly conference with the Senate at Constantinople, and when he had these leaders in his power he transported them to Sycae (the modern Pera) and hung them there. The two unfortunate and perhaps unwilling claimants for the Imperial dignity had their noses slit by their jealous brother, and were immured within the palace walls for the remainder of their lives. Such was the manner of man by whose nod deep questions concerning the nature of the Godhead were then decided.

Pogonatus himself had two sons, Justinian and Heraclius; and it was a mark of his friendly feeling towards the Pope that in the last year of his reign he sent some locks of their hair as a present to Rome, and this valuable offering, accompanied by an Imperial letter, was received with all fitting reverence by the Pope, the clergy, and the "army" of Rome.

Of the younger of these two princes, Heraclius, we hear nothing : perhaps he, too, like his uncles, passed his life confined within the precincts of that palace which has witnessed so many tragedies. But Justinian II, who succeeded his father in 685 and in whom the dynasty of Heraclius expired, was a man who left a bloody and ineffaceable imprint on the pages of Byzantine history. He was in all things almost the exact opposite of the great legislator whose name he bore. Justinian I was timid, cautious, and calculating. The second of that name was personally brave, but rash, and a blunderer. The first had apparently no temptation to be cruel, and carried his clemency almost to excess. The second was, at any rate in later life, and after opposition had embittered him, as savage and as brutal as an Ashantee king or a bullying schoolboy, a tiger such as Nero without Nero's artistic refinement. Lastly, Justinian I was exceptionally fortunate or extraordinarily wise in his selection of generals and counselors. His namesake seems to have suffered, not only for his own sins, but for the grievous faults and errors committed by the ministers to whom he gave his confidence.

In the year of the young Emperor's accession Pope Benedict II died, and after the short pontificate of John V there was a contest as to the choice of his successor, the clergy desiring to elect the Archpresbyter Peter, and the army favoring the claims of a certain Theodore, who came next to him on the roll of presbyters. This statement, that the army took such a prominent part in the Papal election, strikes us as something new in Roman politics, and taken in conjunction with the events which will shortly be related, perhaps points to the formation of a local force for the defence of the City, something like what in after-ages would be called a body of militia.

In this case the clergy had to meet outside the gates of the great Lateran church as the army kept guard at the doors and would not suffer them to enter. The military leaders themselves were assembled in the quaint circular church of St. Stephen. Messengers passed backwards and forwards between the parties, but neither would give way to the other, and the election seemed to be in a state of hopeless deadlock. At length the chief of the clergy met, not in the Lateran church, but in the Lateran palace and unanimously elected an old and venerable Sicilian priest named Conon to the vacant office. When the old man with his white hairs and angelic aspect was brought forth to the people, the civil magnates of the City, many of whom probably knew the calm and unworldly life which the simple-hearted old man had led, gladly acclaimed him as Pope. So, too, did the leaders of the army, in whose eyes the fact that Conon was himself a soldier's son may possibly have been some recommendation of his merits. It took some time before the rank and file of the army would abandon the cause of their candidate Theodore, but at length they too came in, and submissively greeted the new Pope, whose unanimous election was, according to the custom of that time, announced by a special mission from all the three orders to the court of the Exarch Theodore

The election of Conon had been a politic expedient for allaying domestic strife, but he was so old and in such weak health that he could scarcely officiate at the necessary ordination of priests, and after only eleven months' pontificate he died.

Again there were rival candidates and a contested election, before the long and memorable pontificate of Sergius could be begun. The Archdeacon Paschal had already, during Conon's lifetime, been intriguing with the new Exarch John Platyn in order to obtain by bribery the succession to the Papal Chair. He had a large party favoring his claims, but Theodore, now Arch-presbyter, had also still his zealous supporters among the people. The army does not appear to have conspicuously favored one candidate more than another. The Lateran palace itself was divided into two hostile fortresses, the outer portion being garrisoned by the adherents of Paschal, the inner by those of Theodore. Neither party would yield to the other: clergy, soldiers, and a great multitude of the people flocked to the Lateran palace, and debated with loud and anxious voices what should be done. At length the expedient of a third candidate was again proposed, and obtained the concurrence of the vast majority. The person proposed was Sergius, a man of Syrian descent, whose father Tiberius had apparently emigrated from his native Antioch in consequence of the Saracen conquest, and had settled at Palermo in Sicily. The young Sergius, who came to Rome about the year 672, was a clever and industrious musician, and sang his way up through the lower orders of the Church, till in 683 he was ordained presbyter of the *titulus* (parish church) of St. Susanna, where he distinguished himself by the diligence with which he celebrated mass at the graves of the various martyrs. He was now presented to the multitude, and greeted with hearty acclamations. His followers being much the stronger party, battered down the gates of the Lateran palace, and the two candidates stood in the presence of their successful rival. The Archpresbyter Theodore at once submitted, and gave the kiss of peace to the new Pope : but Paschal stood aloof, in sullen hardness, till at length constrained and confused, he entered the hall of audience, and with his will, or against his will, saluted his new lord.

Paschal, however, though outwardly submissive, in his heart rebelled against the Syrian Pope, and continuing his intrigues with Ravenna, sent to the Exarch, promising him 100 lbs. of gold if he would seat him in the Papal chair. On this John Platyn came to Home, accompanied by the officers of his court, but not apparently at the head of an army. He came so suddenly and so quietly, that the Roman soldiery could not go forth to meet him with flags and eagles according to the usual custom when the Emperor's representative visited Rome. Finding on his arrival that all orders of men concurred in the election of Sergius, he abandoned the cause of his client Paschal, but insisted that the promised 100 lbs. of gold should be paid him by the successful candidate. Sergius naturally answered that he had never promised any such sum, nor could he at the moment pay it: but he brought forth the sacred chalices and crowns which had hung for centuries before the tomb of St. Peter, and offered to deposit them as security for the ultimate payment of the required sum. The beholders were shocked at the duresse thus laid upon the Church, but the stern Byzantine persisted in his demand: the 100 lbs. of gold were somehow gathered together, the Imperial sanction to the election was given by the Exarch, and Sergius became Pope.

As for his rival Paschal, he after some time was accused of practicing strange rites of divination, was found guilty deposed from his office of archdeacon, and thrust into a monastery, where, after five years of enforced seclusion, he died, still impenitent. The new Pope, who held his office for fourteen years Sergius, (687-701), was a younger man, and probably of stronger fiber than some of his recent predecessors; and well it was for the Roman See that a strong man filled the chair of St. Peter, for another conflict with the self-willed Caesars of Byzantium was now to take place.

In the year 691 Justinian II convened another Council, not this time for the definition of doctrine, but for the reformation of discipline. The reason for so much zeal on the Emperor's part for the purification of the Church morals is not very apparent: but it has been suggested that it was part of the younger Justinian's audacious attempt to rival the fame of his great namesake. On the part of the Eastern bishops who formed the overwhelming majority of the Council, there was perhaps a desire to retrieve in some measure the undoubted victory which the West had gained in the condemnation of Monotheletism, by showing that the East, unaided, could do something to reform the discipline of the Church. The assembly, which was meant as a sort of supplement to the two preceding Councils, received the grotesque name of the Quinisextan (fifth-sixth) Council, but is more often known as the Council of the Domed Hall *(in Trullo),* a name which was derived from its place of meeting, but which applied to its immediate predecessor as much as to itself.

The canons of this Council, 102 in number, touched, as has been said, on no point of doctrine, but were entirely concerned with matters of Church discipline, such as the punishment of ecclesiastics who played at dice, took part in the dances of the theatre, kept houses of ill-fame, lent money on usury, or without sufficient cause were absent from church on three consecutive Sundays. They showed, however (as might perhaps have been expected from the almost exclusively Oriental character of the Council), a disregard of Western usage, and of the claims of the See of Rome, which almost amounted to intentional discourtesy. By inference, if not directly, they pronounced against the Papal decision with reference to the second baptism of those who had been baptized by heretics in the Triune Name. They expressly condemned the strict Roman usage as to married presbyters, and they denounced the custom of fasting on Saturday in Lent, which had long prevailed in the Roman Church. And in a very emphatic manner the thirty-sixth canon renewed the decrees of the Second and Fourth Councils declaring "that the patriarchal throne of Constantinople should enjoy the same privileges as that of Old Rome, should in all ecclesiastical matters be entitled to the same pre-eminence, and should count as second after it". The third place was assigned to Alexandria, the fourth to Antioch, and the fifth to Jerusalem. The decrees of this Council received the signature of the Emperor, and of the great Patriarchs of the East, but the blank which was left after the Emperor's name for the signature of the Roman pontiff was never filled up nor has the Council *in Trullo* ever been unreservedly accepted by the Latin Church. In fact, the leaning shown by it towards toleration of a married clergy is at this day one of the points in which the "Orthodox" (Greek) differs from the "Catholic" (Latin) Church.

When the six volumes containing the decrees of the Quinisextan Council reached Rome the Pope not only refused to sign them, but forbade their publication in the churches. Thereupon Justinian in his wrath sent a messenger with orders to punish the Pope's councilors for disobedience to the Imperial edict. The holy man John, bishop of Portus, and Boniface, a *Consiliarius* of the Apostolic See, both of whom had probably made themselves conspicuous by their opposition to the Council, were carried off to Constantinople, where we lose sight of them.

It remained only to punish the chief offender, and to drag Sergius, as Martin had been dragged away, to buffetings and hardships in prisons by the Bosphorus. With this intent Justinian sent a huge life-guardsman named Zacharias to Rome. But as he passed through Ravenna, and there, no doubt, disclosed the purport of his mission, the inhabitants of that city (already perhaps inflamed with wrath against their tyrannical and high-handed sovereign) angrily discussed the meditated outrage on the head of the Roman Church. The "army of Ravenna"— evidently now a local force, and not a band of Byzantine mercenaries—caught the flame, and determined to march to Rome. The soldiers of the Pentapolis and the surrounding districts took part eagerly in the holy war: there was but one purpose in all hearts— "We will not suffer the Pontiff of the Apostolic See to be carried to Constantinople". Thus, when the life-guardsman Zacharias, accompanied probably by a slender retinue, reached Rome, it was not to inspire fear, but to feel it. The throng of soldiers surged round the City walls. He ordered the gates to be closed, and trembling, sought the Pontiff's bed-chamber, beseeching him with tears to shield him from harm. The closing of the City gates only increased the fury of the soldiery. They battered down the gate of St. Peter, and rushed tumultuously to the Lateran, demanding to see Pope Sergius, who, it was rumored, had been carried off like Martin by night, and hurried on board the Byzantine vessel. The upper and lower gates of the Pope's palace were closed and the mob shouted that they should be leveled with the ground unless they were promptly opened. Nearly mad with terror, the unhappy life-guardsman hid his huge bulk under the Pope's bed, but Sergius soothed his fears, declaring that no harm should happen to him. Then the Pope went forth, and taking his seat in a balcony outside the Lateran, he presented himself to the people. They received him with shouts of applause: he addressed them with wise and fitting words, and calmed their tumultuous rage. But though calm, they were still resolute; and they persisted in keeping guard at the Lateran till the hated Zacharias, with every mark of ignominy and insult, had been expelled from the City. So the affair ended. Justinian II, as we shall soon see, was in no position to avenge his outraged authority. The Imperial majesty had received its heaviest blow, and the successor of St. Peter had made his longest stride towards independent sovereignty.

The only other notable event in the long pontificate of Sergius was a Council which towards its close, and doubtless by his authority, was held at Aquileia to terminate the controversy of the Three Chapters. This Council (of which we have very little further information) was thus the counterpart, in Eastern Italy, of that which has been already described as held at Pavia by order of King Cunincpert.

Meanwhile, the Emperor was wearing out the patience of his subjects by his exactions and his cruelties. Possibly (as has been already hinted) in the first part of his reign, the blame of his unpopularity should be assigned, not so much to himself as to his ministers. Of these there were two named Stephen and Theodotus, especially odious to the people. Stephen was a Persian eunuch, who was appointed Imperial Treasurer, and distinguished himself by his zeal in raising money for that extravagant palace building, which was the passion of the two Justinians, as it has been the passion of so many later lords of Constantinople. Either because she thwarted his financial schemes, or for some other reason, the Emperor's own mother, Anastasia, incurred the eunuch's displeasure, and he had the audacity to order her to be publicly chastised like a refractory schoolboy. Theodotus was a monk, who had previously led the life of a recluse in Thrace, but was now made a logothete, apparently chief of the logothetes, and gave full scope to his imagination, no longer in devising the self-tortures of a rigid anchorite, but in planning the torture of others. Men were hung up by their wrists to high-stretched ropes, and then straw was kindled under their feet; and other punishments, which are not particularly specified, but which we are told were intolerable, were inflicted on some of the most illustrious subjects of the Emperor.

At length, after ten years of this misgovernment, the day of vengeance dawned. A certain nobleman from the highlands of Isauria, named Leontius, who had long and successfully commanded the armies of the East, had been for some cause or other detained in prison for three years by the Emperor. Then, changing his mind, the capricious tyrant decided to make him governor of Greece but ordered him to depart for his new province on the morrow of his liberation from prison. That same night he was visited by two monks, Paul and Gregory, who had, it would seem, formerly prophesied to him that he should one day wear the diadem. "Vain were all your prognostications to me of future greatness", said the melancholy man, "for now I go forth from the city, and soon my life will have a bitter end". "Not so", replied the monks; "even now, if you have courage for the enterprise, you shall win the supreme power". He listened to their counsels, hastily armed some of his servants, and went to the palace. The plea being put forward of urgent business with the Emperor, the prefect of the palace opened the door, and at once found himself bound hand and foot. Leontius and his men swarmed through the palace, opening the prison doors to all the numerous victims of Imperial tyranny who were there confined, and some of whom had been in these dark dungeons for six, or even eight years, having furnished these willing allies with arms, they then scattered themselves through the various quarters of the city, calling on all Christians to repair to the church of St. Sophia. Soon a tumultuous crowd was gathered in the baptistery of the church, and there Callinicus the Patriarch, constrained by the two monks and the other partisans of Leontius, preached a sermon to the people on the words, "This is the day that the Lord hath made : let us rejoice and be glad in it". The long-repressed hatred of the people to Justinian now burst forth in all its fury: every tongue had a curse for the fallen Emperor, and when day dawned an excited crowd assembled in the Hippodrome, calling with hoarse voices for his death. Leontius, however, mindful of past passages of friendship between himself and the Emperor's father, now spared the son, and after mutilating him in the cruel fashion of Byzantium, by slitting his nose and cutting out his tongue sent him away to banishment at Cherson, the scene of Pope Martin's exile. The two chief instruments of his tyranny, Stephen and Theodotus, were seized by the mob without the new Emperor's orders, dragged by the feet to the Forum of the Bull, and there burned alive.

The reign of Leontius was a short one (695-698), and he does not seem to have displayed as Emperor any of that ability or courage which he had shown as general of the Eastern army. The eyes of all loyal citizens of the "Roman Republic" were at this time turned towards the province of Africa, where the city of Carthage, recovered by the valor of Belisarius from the Vandal, had just been captured by the sons of Islam. A great naval armament was fitted out under the command of the patrician John. It sailed westward, it accomplished the deliverance of the city from the Saracen yoke, and for one winter John ruled in the city of Cyprian as Roman governor. The Saracen commander, however, was not disposed to acquiesce in his defeat. He returned with a larger army, expelled the Imperial garrison, and recovered Carthage for Islam and for desolation. The great armament returned, as that of Basiliscus had done more than two centuries before, shamefaced and sore at heart to Constantinople. At Crete, the troops broke out into open mutiny against both their general and the Emperor. John was apparently deposed from the command; a naval officer named Apsimar was proclaimed Emperor: the fleet sailed to Constantinople, which was at that time being wasted by a grievous pestilence: after a short siege, the sentinels on the walls of Blachernae, the northern quarter of the city, were bribed to open the gates to the besiegers: Leontius was dethroned, and Apsimar, who took the name of Tiberius, reigned in his stead.

During the seven years' reign (698-705) of this ineffective and colorless usurper the Papal chair—with whose occupants we are now primarily concerned—again became vacant. The comparatively long and successful pontificate of Sergius came to an end, and a Greek, who took the title of John VI, was raised to the papacy.

In his short pontificate the Exarch Theophylact came by way of Sicily to Rome. By this time the mere appearance of the Exarch in the City by the Tiber seems to have been felt almost as a declaration of war. The soldiers (again evidently a kind of local militia) from all parts of Italy mustered in Rome with tumultuous clamor, determined, we are told, "to tribulate the Exarch". The Pope, however, interposed in the interests of peace and good order. He closed the gates of the City, and sending a deputation
of priests to the improvised camp in which the mutineers were assembled, with wise and soothing words quelled the sedition. There were, however, certain informers whose denunciations of the citizens of Rome had furnished the Exarch with a pretext for unjust confiscations, and these men apparently had to suffer the vengeance of the people before order could be restored.

It was during the pontificate of this Pope that the previously described expedition of Gisulf I of Benevento into Campania took place, and it was John VI who, out of the treasures of the Papal See, redeemed the captives of the Samnite duke.

Another short pontificate of another John followed. The new Pope, John VII, was, like his predecessor, of Greek extraction. His father, bearing the illustrious name of Plato, had held the high office of Cura Palatii, an office which in Constantinople itself was often held by the son-in-law of the Emperor. Plato had in that capacity presided over the restoration of the old Imperial palace at Rome, which was now the ordinary residence of the Exarch's lieutenant. The future Pope was, so late as 687, administrator (rector) of the Papal patrimony along the Appian Way. His portrait in mosaic, which was formerly in the Oratory of the Virgin at St. Peter's, is still visible in the crypts of the Vatican.

The election of Pope John VII nearly coincided in time with the return of the fierce tyrant Justinian II to his capital and his throne after ten years of exile. Of his wanderings during these ten years we have a short and graphic account in the pages of Nicephorus and Theophanes. Cherson rejected him, fearing to be embroiled for his sake with the reigning Emperor. He roamed from thence into that region in the south of Russia which—it is interesting to observe—was still called the country of the Goths. Here he threw himself on the hospitality of the Chagan of the Khazars, a fierce tribe with

Hunnish affinities, who had come from beyond the Caucasus, and were settled round the shores of the Sea of Azof. The Chagan gave him his sister in marriage, and she was probably baptized on that occasion, and received the name of Theodora. With this barbarian bride the banished Emperor seems to have lived in some degree of happiness at Phanagoria by the straits of Yenikale, just opposite Kertch in the Crimea. But Tiberius, who could not "let well alone", sent messengers to the Khazar chief offering him great gifts if he would send him the head of Justinian; still greater if he would surrender him alive. The barbarian listened to the temptation, and under pretence of providing for his brother-in-law's safety, surrounded him with a guard, who, when they received a signal from their master—that is probably when the promised gifts were safely deposited in the Chagan's palace—were to fall upon the exile and kill him. A woman's love, however, foiled the treacherous scheme. Theodora learned from one of her brother's servants what was being plotted, and warned her husband, who, summoning the Chagan's lieutenant into his presence, overpowered his resistance, fastened a cord round his neck, and strangled him with his own hands. In the same way he disposed of the Prefect of the Cimmerian Bosphorus, apparently an officer of the Empire through whom the negotiations with the Chagan had been carried on : and then, after sending his faithful wife back to her brother's court, he escaped to the Straits of Yenikale, where he found a fishing smack, in which he sailed round the Crimea. At Cherson he had many enemies, but he had also powerful friends, and in order to summon these he lay to at a safe distance from the city. As soon as they were on board, he again set sail, passed the lighthouse of Cherson, and reached a place called the Gates of the Dead, between the mouths of the rivers Dnieper and Dniester. Here, or soon after they had passed it, a terrible storm arose, and all on board the little craft despaired of their deliverance. Said one of the ex-Emperor's servants to his master, "See, my lord, we are all at the point of death: make a bargain with God for your safety. Promise that if he will give you back your Empire you will not take the life of any of your foes". Thereupon Justinian answered in fury, "If I consent to spare any one of those men, may God this moment cause the deep to swallow me". Contrary to all expectation they escaped from the storm unhurt, and before long made the mouth of the Danube. They sailed up the stream, and Justinian dispatched one of his followers to the rude court of Terbel, king of Bulgaria. Rich gifts and the hand of the Emperor's daughter in marriage were the promised rewards if Terbel should succeed in replacing him on his throne. The Bulgarian eagerly accepted the offer: oaths were solemnly sworn between the high contracting parties, and after spending a winter in Bulgaria, Justinian with his barbarian ally marched next spring against Constantinople.

Again the attack was directed against Blachernae, the northern end of the land wall of Constantinople, and evidently the weakest part of the fortifications. For three days the Bulgarian army lay outside the walls, Justinian vainly offering to the citizens conditions of peace, and receiving only words of insult in return. Then, accompanied by only a few of his followers, he entered the city, as Belisarius had entered Naples, by an aqueduct, and almost without fighting made himself master of that part of it in which was situated the palace of Blachernae, where he took up his abode. The complete conquest of the city probably occupied some weeks: but it was at last effected. Tiberius III, now once again known by his old name of Apsimar, left the city, and sought to flee along the coast of the Euxine to Apollonia, but was brought back in chains to Constantinople. His brother and generalissimo Heraclius, who had fought bravely in the wars against the Saracens, and all his chief officers and bodyguards were hung from high gallows erected on the walls. For Apsimar himself yet deeper degradation was in store. His old rival Leontius, whom he had dethroned seven years before, was brought forth from the monastery to which he had consigned him, and the two fallen Emperors, bound in chains, were paraded through the fourteen regions of the city, a mark for all the scoffs and taunts of a populace ever ready to triumph over the fallen. Then it was announced that great chariot races would be exhibited in the Hippodrome. The people flocked thither, and saw the restored Emperor sitting on his lofty throne. His two rivals, still loaded with chains, had been thrown down before his chair, and each one of his purple sandals rested on the neck of a man who had dared to call himself Augustus while he yet lived. The slavish mob, who deserved to be ruled over by even such a tyrant as Justinian II, saw an opening for pious flattery of the successful cause, and shouted out, in the words of the 91st Psalm, "Thou hast trodden on the Asp and the Basilisk : the Lion and the Dragon hast thou trodden under foot". The Asp was meant to drive home the sense of his humiliation to the heart of Apsimar: the Lion was an insult for the fallen Leontius. After some hours of this humiliation they were taken to the place of public execution, and there beheaded.

The vengeance which filled the soul of Justinian while he was tossing in his skiff off the coast of Scythia enemies, had now full play. The patriarch Callinicus, who had preached the sermon on his downfall, was blinded and sent in banishment to Rome—a wholesome warning to Pope and citizens of the fate which might befall those who resisted the might of the World-Emperor—and in his place a monk named Cyrus, who had predicted the restoration of Justinian, was made Patriarch of Constantinople. Citizens and soldiers past counting perished in the reign of terror which followed. Some were sewn up in sacks and thrown into the sea. Others were, with treacherous hospitality, invited to some great repast, and as they rose up to depart were sentenced either to the gallows, or to execution by the sword. The Emperor's fury raged most wildly of all against the citizens of Cherson, who had dared to cast him forth from their midst, and had, as he considered, treacherously intrigued against him with Tiberius III. But the story of this revenge belongs to the latest years of the Imperial fiend. Our immediate business is to describe his dealings with the Pope of Rome and the citizens of Ravenna.

After the returned exile had been for a little more than a year in the possession of his recovered dignity, mindful still of his coveted glory as an ecclesiastical legislator, he sent two bishops of metropolitan rank, bearing the same Tome which had been before addressed to Pope Sergius, but bearing also a 'sacred' letter (the letters of Emperors were always thus styled), in which Justinian exhorted the Pope to convene a synod, to which he should communicate the Acts of the Quinisextan Council, confirming all the canons that seemed to him worthy of approbation, and deleting those which he deemed inexpedient. The timid Pope, John VII, probably an elderly man, who had learned habits of obedience as a civil servant before he was an ecclesiastic, and who had no doubt looked upon the sightless eyeballs of the Patriarch of Constantinople, blinded by this terrible autocrat, shrank from the responsibility of convening a synod, shrank from suggesting what canons in the Imperial Tome were deserving of censure, and in fact, through "weakness of the flesh", returned the Tome by the hands of the metropolitans to the Emperor, saying that he had no fault to find with any part of it. Soon after this unworthy concession Pope John VII died, and was succeeded by a Syrian named Sisinnius, who was, we are told, so afflicted by gout—an especially Papal malady—that he was obliged to employ the hands of others to convey food to his mouth. His short pontificate—of only twenty days—is noteworthy only for the fact that he set the lime-kilns at work to make mortar for the repair of the walls of Rome. An evil precedent truly. How many of that silent population of statues which once made beautiful the terraces of Rome have perished in these same papal lime-kilns!

The short pontificate of Sisinnius was followed by the long one of Constantine (708-715), the last Roman pontiff, apparently, who visited Constantinople. In his pontificate the ecclesiastical feud with the Archbishop of Ravenna, which had slumbered for thirty years, broke out afresh. Archbishop Theodore (677-691), whose quarrels with his clergy about money matters are quaintly described by Agnellus, had apparently reconciled himself with Rome in order to protect himself against the hatred of Ravenna; and his successor Archbishop Damian (692-708) had accepted the peace thus made, and had consented to journey to Rome for his consecration. So, too, did his successor, Archbishop Felix (708-724), but when the consecration was accomplished, the old rupture between the sees was recommenced on the question of the bonds *(cautiones)* for future obedience which the Pope exacted from the Archbishop. The profession of faith according to the decrees of the six councils, and the promise to abide by the canon law, were perhaps given in the accustomed form by the new Archbishop, but the third document required of him, which was a promise to do nothing contrary to the unity of the Church and the safety of the Empire, he claimed to express in his own language, and not in that prescribed by the Pope, and he was apparently supported in this resistance by the civil rulers of Ravenna. Such as it was, the bond was deposited in St. Peter's tomb, and not many days afterwards, says the Papal biographer it was found all blackened and scorched as if by fire. For this resistance to the authority of the Roman See, the Papal biographer considered that the Archbishop and his flock were worthily punished by the calamities which now came upon them through the furious vengeance of Justinian.

What was the reason for the frenzied Emperor's wrath against Ravenna does not seem to be anywhere stated. We might conjecture that he remembered with anger the opposition which the citizens had offered some ten years before to his arrest of Pope Sergius, but in that case Pope Constantine would surely have shared in the punishment. It seems more likely that there is some truth in the obscure hints given us by Agnellus that certain citizens of Ravenna had taken part in that mutilation of the sacred person of the Emperor which accompanied his deposition. Probably also the city had too openly manifested its joy at Justinian's downfall, and had too cordially accepted the new order of things established by Leontius, and afterwards by Apsimar. Whatever the cause, the rage of the restored Emperor turned hotly against the devoted city. "At night", says Agnellus (who perhaps exaggerates the importance of his own native place), "amid the many meditations of his heart his thoughts turned constantly to Ravenna, and he said to himself perpetually, "Alas! what shall I do, and how shall I begin with my vengeance on Ravenna?"

The actual execution of his scheme of revenge, however, seems not to have been difficult. He summoned the general-in-chief, a Patrician named Theodore, and ordered him to collect a fleet and sail first to Sicily (possibly in order to repel some assault of the Saracens), and afterwards to Ravenna, there to execute certain orders, as to which he was to preserve impenetrable silence. When his duty in Sicily was done, the general sailed up the Adriatic, and when he beheld Ravenna afar off, burst forth, if we may believe our monkish chronicler, into a pathetic oration, in which, with Virgilian phrase, he lamented the future fate of that proud city: "the alone unhappy and alone cruel

Ravenna, which then lifted her head to the clouds, but should soon be leveled with the ground". Having arrived at the city, and been greeted with the pomp due to the Emperor's representative, he pitched his tents, adorned with bright curtains, in a line of a furlong's length by the banks of the Po. Thither came all the chief men of the city, invited, as they supposed, to a banquet in the open air, for which the seats and couches were spread on the green grass. But as they were introduced, two and two, with solemn courtesy into the general's tent, at the moment of entrance they were gagged, and their hands bound behind their backs, and they were hurried off to the general's ship. When the nobles of the city and the Archbishop Felix had all been thus disposed of, the soldiers entered Ravenna, and amid the loud lamentations, but apparently not the armed resistance, of the citizens, set some of the houses on fire.

When the captives from Ravenna were landed at Constantinople they were brought into the presence of Justinian, who was seated on a golden throne studded with emeralds, and wore on his head a turban interwoven with gold and pearls by the cunning hands of his Khazar Empress. All the senators of Ravenna were slain, and Justinian had decided to put the archbishop also to death. But in the visions of the night he saw a youth of glorious appearance standing by Felix, and heard him say, "Let thy sword spare this one man". He gave the required promise in his dream, and kept it waking by remitting the penalty of death on the archbishop; but according to the cruel Byzantine custom he ordered him to be blinded. A silver dish was brought and heated to incandescence in the furnace. Vinegar was then poured upon it : the archbishop was compelled to gaze at it long and closely, and the sight of both eyes was destroyed.

The reflection of the Papal biographer on these events is as follows:—"By the judgment of God, and the sentence of Peter, prince of the Apostles, those men who had been disobedient to the apostolic see perished by a bitter death, and the archbishop, deprived of sight, receiving punishment worthy of his deeds, was transmitted to the region of Pontus".

Of the events which followed at Ravenna it is impossible to extract any rational account from the turgid nonsense of Agnellus. We can just discern that Joannes Rizocopus, apparently the newly-appointed Exarch, after visiting Naples and Rome, reached Ravenna, and there for his wicked deeds, by the just judgment of God, perished by a most shameful death. This is generally supposed, but perhaps on insufficient evidence, to have happened in a popular insurrection. On his death apparently the citizens of Ravenna elected a certain George (son of a learned notary named Johanices, who had been carried captive to Constantinople and slain there) to be captain over them. He harangued them in stirring speeches (full of Virgil), and all the cities round Eavenna, Sarsina, Cervia, Forlimpopoli, Forli, placed themselves under his orders, garrisoned the capital, and defied the troops of the Emperor. Doubtless the Insurrection was quelled, but how and when, and whether after a long interval of civil war or no, the chronicler, who gives us a multitude of useless details about the equestrian performances and spirited harangues of the rebel captain, quite fails to inform us. We learn, however (and here the better authority of the Papal biographer coincides with that of Agnellus), that after the death of Justinian the poor blinded Archbishop Felix returned from exile, resumed possession of his see, gave all the required assurances to the Pope, and died (725) at peace with the See of Rome.

Meanwhile Pope Constantine was visiting Constantinople, by the Emperor's command, in very different guise from that in which his predecessor Martin had visited it half a century before. He set sail from the harbour of Rome on the 5th of October,

710, accompanied by two bishops and a long train of ecclesiastics, among whom the future Pope Gregory II is the most interesting figured. When he arrived at Naples, he found the Exarch Joannes Rizocopus, come, if our former conjecture be correct, to take possession of his new government. Their paths crossed: Joannes went northwards to Rome, where he put to death four ministers of the Papal court—a mysterious act of severity which, unexplained, seems to contrast strangely with the diplomatic courtesies then being interchanged between Rome and Constantinople,—and then he proceeded on his way to Ravenna, where, as has been already said, a shameful death awaited him.

As for the Pope, he proceeded on his way to Sicily, where Theodore, patrician and general, the executor of Justinian's vengeance on Ravenna, met him with deep reverence, and was healed by him of a sickness which had detained him in the island. The Papal galleys then coasted round the southern cape of Italy, touching at Reggio, Cotrone, Gallipoli (where Bishop Nicetas died), and at last arrived at Otranto, where they wintered. Here they were met by the *regionarius* Theophanius, who, we are told, brought a document under the Imperial seal, ordering all Imperial governors of cities to receive the Pope with as much reverence as they would show to the Emperor's own person. Crossing over at length into Greek waters, and arriving at the island of Ceos, the Pope was there met with the prescribed reverence by Theophilus, patrician and admiral. From thence he proceeded to Constantinople. The Emperor himself was not there, having perhaps purposely withdrawn to Nicaea, but his little son and child-colleague Tiberius, offspring of the Khazar bride, came out to the seventh milestone, escorted by Cyrus the Patriarch of Constantinople, the Senate, and a long train of nobles and clergy, to meet the pontiff of Old Rome. All the city made holiday, and shouts of gratulation rent the air when the Pope, clad in full pontificals such as he wore in the great processions at Rome, entered the city mounted on one of the Imperial palfreys, with gilded saddle and gilded reins, which the servants of Justinian had brought to meet him.

The Emperor, on hearing of the Pope's arrival, was, we are told, filled with joy, and sent a 'sacred' letter to express his thanks, and to ask Constantine to meet him at Nicomedia in Bithynia, to which city he himself journeyed from Nicaea. When they met, the Papal biographer assures us that "the most Christian Augustus, with his crown on his head, prostrated himself and kissed the feet of the pontiff. Then the two rushed into one another's arms, and there was great joy among the people, when all of them beheld the good prince setting such an example of humility". From all the other information which we possess as to the character of Justinian II, grave doubts arise whether that "good prince" really humbled himself so far as to kiss the feet of his guest: but we can well believe that he received the Communion at the pontiff's hands, and besought his prayers that he might obtain much needed pardon for his sins. Some sort of discussion took place, for the deacon Gregory, the future Pope, "when interrogated by the Emperor Justinian concerning certain chapters, gave an excellent answer, and solved every question". We are told also that Justinian "renewed all the privileges of the Church", which suggests that something had taken place which might seem to infringe them. On the whole we are compelled to believe that there is here a dishonest suppression of facts on the part of the biographer, that the canons of the Quinisextan Synod were again laid by the Emperor before the Pope, and were (possibly with some modifications, for which deacon Gregory successfully contended) accepted by him.

On his departure from Nicomedia, the Pope was enfeebled by frequent attacks of sickness, but he was at length enabled to accomplish his return journey, and landing at

Gaeta, arrived on the 24th of October, 711, at Rome, where, after his year's absence, he was received with loud shouts of joy by the people.

Probably even if the Pope did yield in the matter of the Quinisextan Council, that concession was worth making for the sake of the increase of dignity which such a journey and such a reception in the Eastern capital brought to his office. After all deductions have been made for the exaggerations of the Papal biographer, there can be no doubt that the reception was a splendid one, and that the remembrance of the contumely heaped on Pope Martin might well be effaced by the sight of the reverence paid to Pope Constantine.

Scarcely had the Pope completed his return voyage, when the Emperor who had received him with such signal honor was slain. The chroniclers give us a very detailed, but also a singularly obscure history of the events which led to his downfall, but one thing is clear through all the confusion, that in his really insane fury of revenge against the inhabitants of Cherson, Justinian overreached himself, and almost compelled his most loyal servants to conspire against his throne.

Three expeditions were successively sent against Cherson, with orders to accomplish the utter destruction of the city. The first was fairly successful: the leading citizens were sent to Justinian for him to wreak his vengeance upon them; some of the nobles were tied to stakes and roasted before a slow fire; others were tied into a barge filled with heavy stones, and so sunk in the sea. But Justinian was not satisfied: he accused his generals of slackness in executing his orders, superseded them, and sent out others, who in their turn—partly owing to the energy with which despair had filled the Chersonites, partly owing to the interference of the Chagan of the Khazars, who came to defend the threatened city against a Roman Emperor more barbarous than himself—gave up their bloody commission in despair, and then for mere self-protection joined the party of revolt.

This party of revolt clustered round a certain Bardanes, an Armenian, to whom a Monothelete monk had long before prophesied that he would one day be Emperor of Rome. At each successive revolution, when Leontius and when Apsimar were raised to the throne, Bardanes had sought his monkish friend, who said each time, "Be patient; the day is not come yet; but when it does come, be sure that you restore Monotheletism, and undo the work of the Sixth Council". Bardanes talked imprudently of these prophesying to his comrades, and rumors of them reached the ears of Apsimar, who banished him to the island of Cephalonia. Justinian, to whom Apsimar's enemy probably seemed a friend, permitted Bardanes to return from banishment; and now, for some reason which is not clear to us, permitted him to accompany the first expedition to Cherson. Helias, whom Justinian appointed governor of Cherson, when he found that he had incurred his master's displeasure, proclaimed Bardanes Emperor under the less barbarous name of Philippicus, and the cause of this rival claimant to the throne was eagerly embraced by the despairing citizens of Cherson, and by one after another of the generals whom Justinian sent against them, and who feared to return to their master with his vengeance unsated. When Justinian heard of the elevation of Philippicus, his fury became more terrible than ever. Every one of the children of Helias was massacred in its mother's arms, and she herself was handed over to the dishonoring embraces of an Indian cook of the Emperor, a man of hideous ugliness.

The upshot of the whole matter was that the remnants of all three expeditions returned to Constantinople bent on dethroning Justinian, and placing the diadem on the head of Bardanes-Philippicus. Justinian again sought the help of Terbel, king of the

Bulgarians (with whom he had had many quarrels since he was restored to the throne by his aid), but obtained from him only three thousand men. He fixed his camp at Damatrys, and himself proceeded to Sinope, the nearest point to the Crimea on the coast of Asia Minor. Here he perhaps expected the hostile fleet to land, but he saw instead the sails of the mighty armament which he had himself fitted out, bearing off westward to Constantinople to accomplish his doom. He returned, "roaring like a lion", on the road to the capital, but his enemy had arrived there before him. Philippicus reigned in Constantinople: every avenue to the city was carefully guarded by his troops. Back fled Justinian to his camp at Damatrys, but there too his enemies were beforehand with him. The man whom he had so cruelly wronged, Helias, the life-guardsman and governor of Cherson, had marched with a strong body of troops to Damatrys, and opened negotiations with the soldiers of Justinian. On receiving solemn assurances of their personal safety, they abandoned their cruel master's cause and consented to shout for Philippicus Augustus. Helias, filled with rage at the remembrance of his wrongs, hunted down the fallen Emperor, made bare his throat, and with one blow from the short sword which hung by his side severed his head from his body. The ghastly trophy was, carried by a guardsman named Ptomanus to Philippicus, who forwarded it by the same messenger to Rome.

And how was the messenger there received? The Papal biographer says, "After three months the melancholy tidings resounded through the City that Justinian, the most Christian and orthodox Emperor, was murdered, and the heretic Philippicus had reached the summit of Imperial power". Into what strange world of Manichean confusion have we strayed, a world in which good and evil have no meaning in themselves, but stand merely as the watchwords of two parties of equally balanced power; a world in which it is possible for a monster like Justinian Rhinotraetus to be mourned as "a most Christian Emperor"?

To finish the story of Justinian's downfall, the pathetic end of his little son Tiberius must also be recorded. The little child, still only six years old, had been taken for refuge to the church of the Virgin, in the quarter of Blachernae. There he sat, with one hand holding a pillar of the holy table, and with the other clasping some fragments of the true cross, which his great ancestor had recovered from the Persians. Other sacred relics were hung round the child's neck, and Anastasia his grandmother sat near him. Maurus, the leader of the third expedition against Cherson, and now a partisan of Philippicus, strode up to the altar. The aged Empress threw herself at his feet, and implored him not to lay hands on the child, who at any rate was unsoiled by his father's crimes. But while Maurus was thus detained by Anastasia, his comrade and fellow-patrician, Joannes Struthus, forcibly wrenched away the little Tiberius from the altar steps, took the fragments of the cross from his hand and laid them upon the altar, hung the other relics round his own neck, and then, carrying the child out to the porch of another church, stripped him of his clothes, laid him on the threshold, and "cut his throat", says the chronicler, "as if he had been a sheep". With the death of that innocent child at the church-porch ended the dynasty of the great Heraclius. They had borne rule (610-711), in the Roman world, with two slight interruptions, for one year more than a century.

The fall of the Heraclian dynasty was followed by a period of unsettlement and revolution which lasted for six years. Philippicus (or Bardanes), who reigned from the autumn of 711 to the spring of 713; Anastasius, the chief secretary, who reigned from that date till the autumn of 715; Theodosius, whose reign ended in March, 717, are little more than shadow-Emperors, with whose troubled careers the historian of Italy need not concern himself. Only it is to be noted that under Philippicus there was a temporary recrudescence of that which had seemed safely dead and buried, the theory of the nature of Christ. True to the promise which he is represented as having given to the monk who had prophesied his accession to the throne, Philippicus convened a council of Monothelete bishops and abbots, who declared the decision of the Sixth Council to be null and void. The 'sacred' letter which he at the same time addressed to the Pope showed too plainly his heretical opinions. The Roman mob, who seem by this time to have acquired considerable skill in theological controversy at once took the alarm, and under the Pope's guidance assumed an attitude of something more than passive opposition. An "image" (perhaps something like a mediaeval reredos), containing a representation of the six Ecumenical Councils, was set up in St. Peter's by way of reply to the defiance hurled at the Sixth of those Councils by Philippicus. On the other hand, no picture of the heretical Emperor was allowed to be erected in any of the churches; his name was omitted from the Mass; his decrees were treated as waste paper, and golden *solidi* bearing his effigy obtained no currency. At length there was actual civil war in the streets of Rome. A certain nobleman named Peter came from Ravenna, armed with a commission to assume the office of Duke of Rome, deposing Christopher, who then held it. As Peter's commission ran in the name of the hated Philippicus, the people rallied to the side of his rival. Blows were struck, and more than thirty men were killed in the Via Sacra, within sight of the official residence on the Palatine; but the Pope sent some priests bearing the gospels and the cross down into the fray, and these succeeded in allaying the tumult, by persuading "the Christian party" to retire. Things, however, looked gloomy for orthodoxy and the defenders of the Sixth Council, when, about the middle of 713, tidings came by way of Sicily that Philippicus—had been deposed. He was seized by conspirators while taking his siesta in the palace, and like most deposed sovereigns of Constantinople, deprived of sight, and the orthodox Anastasius reigned in his stead.

This was the last flicker of the Monotheletic controversy, which had disquieted the Empire for just three-quarters of a century (638-713).

CHAPTER X.

THE LAWS OF LIUTPRAND.

FROM the story of the subordinate duchies, and the disputes of Popes and Emperors, we return to the main stream of Lombard history.

The wise and loyal Ansprand survived his return from exile and his elevation to the throne only three months. When he was upon his deathbed, the people of the Lombards raised his son LIUTPRAND to the throne as his partner while life still remained to him, his successor when death supervened; and the tidings of this event, which apparently was the result rather of popular enthusiasm than of any deep-laid political scheme, brought great joy to the heart of the dying king. For we must always remember that Liutprand, though the greatest and most powerful of Lombard sovereigns, and though no other king so nearly succeeded in welding the state into one homogeneous monarchy, had only the slenderest of hereditary claims to occupy the palace of Pavia. To talk of usurpation would be altogether out of place, since the element of popular election common to most of the Teutonic royalties was still strong in the Lombard kingship; but for more than a century all the wearers of the Iron Crown, with one exception had been connected by blood or by marriage with the family of the revered, almost sainted Queen Theudelinda, and to the glory of this descent the son of the Milanese noble Ansprand could lay no claim.

Of the year of Liutprand's birth we have no precise information, but as in 701 he was still a very young man, contemptuously allowed to live by the jealous tyrant Aripert II, when he mutilated or put to death all the rest of Ansprand's family, we can hardly suppose him to have been more than twenty-eight years old when, eleven years afterwards, he mounted the throne. He was a man of great personal strength and courage, and in his reign of thirty-one years he had the opportunity of displaying on a wide, one might almost say on a European theatre, the large gifts of statesmanship with which nature had endowed him. In these early centuries, after the disruption of the Roman Empire, no other ruler save Theodoric the Ostrogoth came so near to founding a real kingdom of Italy: but like Theodoric, his work perished because he had no son to succeed him.

At the very outset of his reign he narrowly escaped death by domestic treason. For some reason or other, his cousin Rothari conspired against his life, and invited him to a feast, at which he was to have been slain by armed men concealed in the banqueting-hall. Being warned of the plot, Liutprand summoned his cousin to the palace. He came, wearing a coat of mail under his mantle, which the king's hand discovered in the act of exchanging salutations. The tragedy of Grimwald and Godipert was again performed, with slightly different circumstances. When Rothari saw that he was discovered, he drew his sword and rushed at the king. Liutprand drew his too, but before either could strike, one of the king's lifeguards, named Subo, attacked Rothari from behind. He turned round and wounded his assailant in the forehead, but the interruption probably saved the king's life. The other bystanders fell at once upon Rothari, and slew him. His four sons, whose disappearance from the capital caused them to be suspected of complicity in their father's designs, when discovered were put to death.

As an illustration of the personal courage of the new king, Paulus tells us another story, which probably belongs to a later period of his reign. Being told that two squires had plotted his death, he ordered their attendance upon him, and rode with them and with no other escort into the densest part of the forest. Then drawing his sword and pointing it towards them, he upbraided them with their murderous designs, and called upon them, if they were men, to come on and slay him then and there. Stricken by "the divinity which doth hedge a king", the caitiffs fell at his feet and implored his pardon, which was granted to them as to many others who at different times conspired against him, for great was this king's clemency.

The reign of Liutprand naturally divides itself into two parts. The first fourteen years of that reign the reign (712-726) are almost bare of events. Doubtless he was during all that time, consolidating the forces of his kingdom; and the numerous laws which, during this period, were passed at the yearly assemblies of his armed fellow-countrymen, show his anxious care for the good government of his people. In 726, with the outbreak of the great Iconoclastic controversy, the scene changes, and an almost bewildering succession of wars, alliances, conquests, restorations of territory, interviews with Popes, and negotiations with Exarchs, fills up the remaining seventeen years of his reign.

Reserving for the next chapter the intricate, but momentous history of those eventful years, I propose now to summarize those additions to the Statute Book which attest Liutprand's activity as a legislator, and which were made in great measure, though not entirely, before the Iconoclastic controversy set Italy in a flame.

On the 1st of March for fifteen out of the thirty-one years of his reign, Liutprand, "the Christian and Catholic" King, by the advice and with the consent of the "Judges" of his realm and of the rest of his faithful Lombards, put forth his little volume of laws "for the settlement of any points of controversy which had arisen between his subjects, and which seemed to be insufficiently provided for by his most robust and most eminent predecessor Rothari", or by the "most glorious Grimwald".

At the very outset of his reign the young king claims high authority for his utterances as a legislator. He has conceived the idea of framing these laws, not by his own foresight, but by the will and inspiration of God : because the king's heart is in the hand of God, as is witnessed by the wisdom of Solomon, who said, "As the rush of water, so is the heart of the king in God's hand: if He shall keep it back, everything will be dried up, but if He in His mercy gives it free course, everything is watered, and filled with health-fullness". So too the Apostle James in his Epistle says, "Every good gift and every perfect gift is from above, and cometh down from the Father of lights".

This highly theological statement of the king's functions is no doubt due to the ecclesiastic employed by him to express his thoughts in that which was supposed to be the Latin language, and it is probably to the same official that we owe the following strong statement of the supremacy of the Roman Church, which is contained in the law against marriage with a first cousin's widow.

After enacting that any man offending against this law shall forfeit all his property, and his children shall be treated as illegitimate, the royal legislator adds, "This ordinance have we made because, as God is our witness, the Pope of the City of Rome, *who is the head of the Churches of God and of the priests in the whole world,* has exhorted us by his epistles in no wise to allow such marriage to take placed". But notwithstanding these expressions, and though the prologues to the laws lay a strong emphasis on the now Catholic character of the Lombard nation, it cannot be said that they exhibit any trace of that obsequious servility towards the Church which is characteristic of the laws of the Visigothic kings a little before this date, nor is there any vestige in them of that furious persecution of the Jews which was the especial disgrace of Spanish Christianity, and which paved the way for the Moorish conquest of Spain.

It must be noticed in passing that the Latin in which King Liutprand's statutes are clothed is barbarous, often to the verge of incomprehensibility, more barbarous than that of Gregory of Tours, more barbarous even (and this is worth noticing) than the laws of Rothari. Evidently during the seventy or eighty years that had elapsed since that king's accession, the light shed by the torch of learning had been growing dimmer and dimmer, and the Church had been losing even the feeble hold which she once had upon the wisdom and the culture of buried Paganism.

Taking a general survey of the laws of Liutprand and comparing them with those of Rothari, we see at laws once that the Lombards have entered upon a new phase of social life. The laws of the later legislator breathe far less than those of his predecessor the atmosphere of the forest and the moorland. The laws about falcons, and stags, and swarms of bees, have disappeared from the statute book, or at least require no fresh additions to be made to them, but instead thereof we have elaborate provisions for the enforcement of contracts and the foreclosure of mortgages.

One great and striking change made by King Liutprand shows the increasing value set upon human life, as the Lombards were putting off their barbarous customs and settling down into a well-ordered commonwealth. This was the virtual abolition of the *guidrigild,* and the substitution of absolute confiscation of the offender's property, in cases of murder. It will be remembered that, under the earlier legislation, the shedder of blood, according to a common custom among the Teutonic nations, had to pay to the representatives of the murdered man a compensation, which varied according to his rank of life, and which (though our information on the subject is not so precise as we could desire) was probably small, when the victim was a man of low social position. Now, however, the king ordained that in all cases where one free man killed another, not in self-defense, but of malice aforethought, he should lose his whole property. The heirs of the murdered man took only his old *guidrigild,* and the balance left over went to "the King's Court", the residuary legatee of all fines and compositions. If, on the other hand, the murderer's property was insufficient to pay even the old *guidrigild,* he was handed over to the heirs of the murdered man, apparently not to be put to death by them, but worked as a slave.

Of course, even this punishment falls far short of those which our modern civilization assigns to the crime of murder. Still we can see that, especially in the case of the rich and powerful, the effect of the new punishment would be far more deterrent than the old. Probably under the code of Rothari a Lombard noble might have killed a dozen free men of inferior position without seriously impairing his fortune, whereas now, after the first deed of violence of such a kind, he found himself stripped of everything. And thus the change introduced by Liutprand tended towards the equality of all men before the law, and was in the best sense of the word democratic. At the same time, while the *guidrigild* lost some of its significance on one hand, gained it on the other. If it was less important as protection against violence, it became more important as a penalty for crime. In the case of a nun's guardian who consented to her marriage ; of men who aided and abetted in an insurrection; of forgery of a document; of the preparation of a legal instrument by a scribe ignorant of the law; of breaking troth-plight, and giving to one man the affianced bride of another, the offender was bound to pay his *guidrigild,* which went in some cases to the King's Court, in others to the person injured by his offence. So, too, the officer of the crown who molested men in the enjoyment of their just right the master of a fugitive slave who presumed to drag him away from the altar of a church the man who committed an indecent assault upon a woman or who stole her clothes while she was bathing, the man who dared to marry the wife of another still living husband each had to pay the full *guidrigild* which, under the old law, would have been payable by his murderer. There seems to be a certain sense of justice, rough perhaps, but still justice, in this provision of the Lombard legislator, who says in effect to the wealthy and noble members of the community, "We will protect your persons by inflicting a heavier fine on him who assaults or molests you than on the assailant of a person of lesser rank : but on the other hand, if you transgress our laws, the penalty which you must pay shall be in the same proportion heavier".

In the laws of Rothari we had to regret the absence of any clear indication of the amount of *guidrigild* payable for the violent death of a member of each of the various classes of the community. King Liutprand gives us this missing detail, and as he does not profess to abrogate the law of his predecessor, he perhaps only re-states the previously existing custom. The law' is so important that it will be well to quote it entire:

"We remember that we have already ordained that he who [of malice] kills a free man shall lose the whole of his property; and that he who kills in self-defense shall pay according to the rank of the person slain. We now wish to ordain how that rank is to be estimated.

"The custom is, that if the slain man is a person of the lowest rank, who is proved to be a member of the [Lombard] army, the manslayer shall pay 150 solidi : for an officer 300 solidi. As concerning our followers let him who is lowest in that rank be paid for, when slain, at the rate of 200 solidi, simply because he is our servant; and those of higher position, according to the dignity of their office, in an ascending scale up to 300 solidi".

From this law we can at last form some idea of the estimation in which the lives of the different members of the Lombard community were held. We can hardly be wrong, however, in supposing that the "army man" of King Liutprand's edict is necessarily a member of the conquering nation : and thus we get no nearer to the solution of the old question, "What *guidrigild,* if any, was paid by the murderer or the unintentional slayer of a free Roman?"

But though on this point the laws of Liutprand fail to give us the desired information, they do not so entirely ignore the existence of a non-Lombard population as was the case with those of Rothari. In the first place, it is noteworthy that nearly all the laws which relate to inheritance begin with the words *Si quis Langobardus,* evidently implying that there were other persons than Lombards in the country to whom these laws did not apply, and we naturally conjecture that these persons are the old Roman population, still working, as far as their own internal affairs are concerned, by the laws of Theodosius and Justinian.

This conjecture becomes almost certainty when we read in Liutprand's law *De Scribis*, "We have ordained that they who write deeds, whether according to the law of the Lombards (since that is most open, and known by nearly all men), or according to the law of the Romans, shall not prepare them otherwise than according to the contents of those laws themselves. For let them not write contrary to the law of the Lombards or that of the Romans. If they do not know the provisions of those laws, let them ask others who do, and if they cannot fully learn the laws, let them not write the deeds. Let any one who presumes to act otherwise pay his own *guidrigild*, unless there is some express understanding [of an opposite kind] arrived at by the parties"

It is quite in accordance with the indications thus furnished us, that we find it provided that if any of a Roman married a Lombard woman, and acquired the *mundium* over her, she thereby lost the status of a Lombard woman. The sons born of such a union were Romans like their father, and had to "live by his law"; and in case of her marrying a second husband without the consent of the heirs of the first husband, they had no right to claim damages *(anagriph)*, nor to start a feud *(faida)* with the presuming consort.

We thus see that, under the Lombard kings, a beginning at any rate was made of the system of "personal law", a system which attained its full development under the Carolingian kings, under whom the various members of the same community, Franks, Lombards, Romans, each had the right of living under their own ancestral code of laws. Signs of Lombard jurisprudence, though still crude, and in some respects barbarous, had evidently some germs of progress and improvement. We can perceive on the part of Liutprand an anxious desire to govern his subjects justly, and to carry their reason along with him in his various decisions. We see with satisfaction that he is prepared to accept for himself the same measure which he metes out to others. Thus, having ordained that a lad under the age of eighteen cannot, except under certain special circumstances, make a valid alienation of his property to another man, he passes a special law enacting that not even to the king shall such a donation be valid.

As the power of the king had increased, that of his representatives had increased also, and with their power, the temptations to corruption, the vices of civilization beginning to take the place of the vices of barbarism. There are many laws against oppression and exaction by the king's stewards *(actores)*; and the penalties on the judge who merely delays the administration of justice are exceedingly severe. Two classes of judges are here enumerated, the *sculdahis,* and above him the *judex.* If a *sculdahis* delayed for four days to administer justice when called upon to do so, he had to pay 6 solidi to the plaintiff, and 6 to the *judex* above him. If the cause was too high for the *sculdahis,* and was brought before the *judex,* he had six days' grace given him, and at the end of that time, if he had not pronounced judgment, he had to pay 15 solidi to the plaintiff. Or, if it was a case which ought to be transferred to the King's Court, and the *judex* delayed doing so for twelve days, he had to pay 12 solidi to the plaintiff, and 20 to the king. Even the vast fortune of Lord Chancellor Eldon would scarcely have been sufficient to meet the continual levy of fines like these.

The old barbarous wager of battle *(pugna per camfiones)* still existed, but was viewed with suspicion and dislike by Liutprand. He does not scruple to imagine and provide for a case in which a man accused of theft has been vanquished in single combat, but stricter enquiry afterwards made by the king's representative *(publicus)* has established his innocence. He declares that wicked persons would sometimes challenge a man to the combat in order to annoy and worry him, and therefore prescribes the form of oath which the challenger might be forced to take, and which was to the effect that he had reasonable grounds of suspicion, and did not give the challenge in malice, in order to weary him by the battle. And in a very curious law about accusations of poisoning he expresses himself even more strongly, saying in substance, "We have now ordained that the punishment for the murder of a free man shall be the loss of the whole of the murderer's property: but certain men, perhaps through hardness of heart, have accused the relations of a man who has died in his bed of having poisoned him, and have therefore, according to the old custom, challenged them to single combat. It seems to us a serious matter that the loss of a man's whole property should be caused by the weakness of a single shield: and we therefore ordain that in case any accusation of this kind should be brought in future, the accuser shall swear on the gospels that he does not bring it in malice, but has good grounds for his suspicion. Then he may proceed to battle according to the old custom, but if the accused person or his hired champion is defeated, let him pay, not his whole fortune, but a composition, as under the whole law, according to the rank of the murdered man:—For we are uncertain about the judgment of God, and we have heard of many persons unjustly losing their cause by wager of battle. But on account of the custom of our nation of the Lombards we cannot change the law itself".

In connection with these allusions by Liutprand to the decaying jurisprudence of his ancestors, it will well to notice one passage in which he quotes the ancient customs of his nation. Law 77 enacts, "If two brothers, or a father and son, have divided their estate by solemn *thinx*, and one of them shall die without sons or daughters, let the King's Court succeed to him. We have ordained this because, though it be not precisely so set down in the edict (of Rothari), nevertheless all our judges and faithful subjects have declared that so the ancient *cadarfida* has ever been, down to our own time". The passage is interesting, because we have here a glimpse of that unwritten common law of the Lombards, known by this strange and somewhat mysterious name *cadarfida,* by which, according to the *Chronicon Gothanum*, legal disputes were generally decided until Rothari arose, the first codifier of Lombard law.

Space fails me to enumerate all the interesting particulars as to the social and domestic life of the Lombards, which may be gleaned from the laws of Liutprand. In particular, the numerous edicts relating to *women* would be well worthy of special study, showing as they do a decided upward tendency in the estimation in which they were held.

Another proof of increasing softness of manners is afforded by the laws about *slaves*. Of course, the unfree condition of the slave and the *Aldius* still continues, but a new and effectual form of manumission is introduced, according to which the owner gives the slave into the hands of the king. The slave by the intervention of the priest is then "led round the sacred altar", and after that dismissed free. This solemn act of manumission, in which king and priest were associated on behalf of freedom, was to have as great efficacy as if the slave had been declared "folk-free" by a regular *thingation.* The slave who, after he had in this or any other way received his "full freedom", continued to serve his old master (out of gratitude or for wages), was warned that he would do well to make frequent opportunities for showing forth his freedom to the judge and to his neighbors, lest in time to come the fact of his emancipation should be called in question. And if the owner of married slaves wronged the husband by committing adultery with the wife, he thereby emancipated both, as fully as if he had by solemn *thinx* given them their freedom. But in order that there might be no doubt of their emancipation, they were desired to come to the palace, prove their case, and receive their freedom at the hand of the king.

Though, as I have said, we have far fewer laws relating to the forest and the farmstead than in the code of Rothari, it is evident that *horses* were a valued possession, and their ownership, as in all civilized communities, was a frequent cause of litigation.

"If a man wishes to buy a horse, he ought to do it in the presence of two or three men, and not secretly. Then, if afterwards any one should claim that horse, he will have these witnesses to appeal to, and shall not be liable to a charge of horse-stealing. But if the claimant of the horse does not believe such witnesses, let the defendant confirm his case by putting them on their oath, unless they be that kind of men whom the king or the *judex* would believe even without an oath. But if he cannot produce any witnesses in whose presence the transaction took place, and can but repeat simply "I bought it", *or if he says that he bought it from some Frank, or nobody knows whom,* he will have to pay the fine for horse-stealing.

We find in the code of Liutprand one or two interesting indications of the *religious* condition of the Lombards. Especially we have some almost savage legislation against soothsayer's *(arioli),* whether male or female. Any one who himself consults such persons, or sends his slave to receive their answers, is to pay half of his own *guidrigild* to the king. The same heavy fine shall be paid by any *judex* or *sculdahis* or inferior functionary in whose district these soothsayers shall be lurking, if for three months he fail to discover and punish them. And if, when they have been detected and denounced, such functionary, either for a bribe, or out of pity, or for any other reason, lets them go, he shall pay not the half, but the whole of his *guidrigild* to the king. As a further incentive to diligence, the *judex* is ordered to sell the convicted soothsayer out of the province as a slave, and allowed to put the proceeds of the sale into his own pocket.

In the course of this legislation we are informed that (as at Benevento in the time of St. Barbatus) there were still some country folk who worshipped a tree or a fountain, calling it their *sacramentum;* and the punishment for these superstitious rites was the same as that for consulting soothsayers, the payment of half a man's *guidrigild* to "the sacred palace".

It is time to draw this slight and imperfect sketch of Liutprand's legislation to a close, but the reader may be interested by three or four of the most characteristic laws, which seem to show us the great king sitting in council with his judges, and hearing and resolving the harder cases which were brought before him.

Law 138. Incitement to murder by a slave.— "We have been truly informed that a certain man, by the instigation of the devil, said to another man's slave, 'Come and kill thy lord, and I have it in my power to grant thee whatsoever favor thou shalt desire'. Persuaded by him, the lad entered into the evil design, and the tempter was wicked enough to say in the very presence of the victim, 'Strike thy lord'. For his sins the slave struck the blow, and the other said, 'Strike him again. If thou dost not, I will strike thee'. Then the lad turned round and struck another blow, whereupon the master died. In the requisition for blood, it was argued [on behalf of the tempter] that he ought to pay only the composition for conspiring against life [consilium mortis, the fine for which was 20 solidi], but we and our judges were not at all satisfied with this argument, reflecting that conspiracy is a hidden thing, which sometimes attains its end, and sometimes misses it. But this murder was instigated in the actual presence of the victim, and we do not call it consilium when a man points to another, present before him, and says in so many words, 'Strike that man'. Therefore the instigator of the crime shall be punished, not for consilium mortis, but for murder itself; and, according to our recent edict, shall forfeit the whole of his property, of which half shall go to the heirs of the murdered man, and half to the King's Court".

Law 135. *Insult to a woman.*—"It has been reported to us that a certain perverse man, while a woman was bathing in a river, took away all the clothes which she had for the covering of her body; wherefore, as she could not remain in the river for ever, she was obliged to walk home naked. Therefore we decide that the hateful man who has been guilty of this presumptuous deed, shall pay his whole *guidrigild* to her whom he has offended. We do so for this reason, that if her father, or brother, or husband or other near male relative had found that man, there would undoubtedly have been a breach of the peace *(scandalum),* and the stronger of the two would probably have killed the other. Now it is better for the wrongdoer to live and pay his own *guidrigild,* than to die, and cause a *faida* to those who come after him, or to kill and lose the whole of his property".

Law 113. *Testamentary power.*—"If any Lombard should wish to make any special provision for a son who has served him well, he may have power to do so to the following extent. If he has two sons, he may favor the one who has shown him godly obedience by an extra third of the property; if he has three sons, by a fourth; if four, by a fifth, and so on. And if they have all served him equally well, let them partake equally of their father's substance. But if perchance the father have married a second or a third wife, and have issue both by the earlier and later marriages, he shall not have the power of thus preferring any one of the children of the later marriage during their mother's lifetime, lest any should say that it is done at her instigation. But after her death he shall have power to prefer as aforesaid. For we think it is according to God's will (and to right reason), that if, even between slaves, he who serves his master well is more rewarded than he who serves him badly, the father should have a similar power of distinguishing between his sons, and rewarding them according to their deserts".

Law 141. *Women incited to brawling by their husbands.*—"We have been informed that some faithless and crafty men, who do not dare themselves to enter a neighboring house or village and raise a disturbance there, for fear of the heavy composition to which they are liable for such an offence, have called together all the women over whom they had power, both free and bond, and have sent them against a weaker body of men. Then these women, attacking the men of such town or village, have inflicted blows upon them, and made greater disturbance, and done more mischief than even men would have done in their place. But when enquiry was made into the tumult, the men who were on the defensive, and could not help themselves, were called to account for their unwilling violence.

"Therefore we decree that should the women dare to act in this manner in future:

(1) Those who have defended themselves against them shall not be answerable for blows or wounds, or death itself, either to the husbands or the *mundwalds* of the women

"(2) Let the magistrate *(publicum)* in whose district the tumult has happened, catch those women, and shave their heads, and distribute them among the villages round about, that henceforward women may learn not to do such presumptuous deeds.

"(3) Should the women in such a brawl inflict blows or injuries on any one, their husbands must pay for them according to the tenor of [King Rothari's] edict.

"Our reason for making this ordinance both as to the chastisement of the women and as to the payment of their compositions is, that we cannot liken such a [craftily planned] assemblage of women to a faction fight, or sedition of peasants, since in those outbursts men act, not women"

I will end this chapter with two little incidents of village life drawn from the laws of Liutprand. —

Law 136. Death by misadventure at a well— "It has been told us that a certain man had a well in his courtyard; and above it (according to custom) a fork and a balance-weight for drawing water. Now while one man was standing under the balance-weight, another, who came to draw water, incautiously let the balance-weight go, and it came upon him who was standing there, and caused his death. When enquiry into the death took place, and a demand for the composition was made, it was held by us and our judges that the man who was killed, as he was not a mere animal, but had sense and reason, ought to have considered beforehand where he would take up his station, and what was the weight which he saw over his head. Therefore two-thirds must be deducted from his composition, and the third part of the sum at which he is valued, according to the tenor of the edict, shall be paid by him who drew the water carelessly, to the sons or nearest relations of the dead man : and so let the cause be finished without guile and without *faida,* since the deed was done unwittingly. Let there be no charge brought against the owner of the well, for if such a charge be admitted, no one hereafter will allow others to draw water from his well; in which case, since all cannot be the owners of a well, many poor persons will die, and wayfarers also will suffer great hardship".'

Law 137. Death of a child from a horse's kick.—"It has also been reported to us that a certain man lent his mare to another man to draw his wagon, but the mare had an unbroken colt which followed its mother along the road. While they were thus journeying, it chanced that some infants were standing in a certain village, and the colt struck one of them with his hoof, and killed it. Now when the parents brought the matter before us, and claimed compensation for the infant's death, we decided, after deliberation with our judges, that two-thirds of the child's guidrigild should be paid by the owner of the colt, and the remaining third by the borrower of the mare. True it is that, in a previous edict it was ordained that if a horse injures any one with his hoof, the owner shall pay the damage. But inasmuch as the horse was out on loan, and the borrower was a reasonable being, and might, if he had not been negligent, have called out to the infants to take care of themselves,—therefore, as we have said, for his negligence he shall pay the third part of the child's price".

With this sensible decision we take leave of Liutprand the legislator and the judge, and turn to consider the events of the age in which he had to play his part as a warrior and a statesman.

CHAPTER XI.

ICONOCLASM

IN tracing the history of the Lombard kings and that of the contemporary Popes and Emperors we have now overstepped the threshold of the eighth century. I do not propose to give an outline of the European history of this century as I did of its predecessor: in fact, only half of it will be traversed before the end of this volume is reached: but something may be said here as to the four greatest events by which it was distinguished. These are the Mohammedan conquest of Spain, the assumption of the title of King of the Franks by an Austrasian Mayor of the Palace, the conversion of the Germans beyond the Rhine, and the Iconoclastic Controversy. On examination we discover that almost all of these events had a close connection with one another, and that they unconsciously conspired towards one great result, the exaltation of the power of the Roman pontiff. St. Boniface, Charles Martel, Muza, and Leo the Isaurian, each in his different sphere co-operated towards the creation of that new, mediaeval Europe at the head of which was the Pope of Rome, a very different person politically from his predecessors, all of whom, whether great or small, had been the submissive subjects of the Eastern Caesar.

In 711, a year before Ansprand returned from his long exile in Bavaria and wrested the kingdom from Aripert, Tarik with his host of Arabs and Moors crossed the Straits which have ever since borne his name, defeated Roderic king of the Visigoths in the battle of Xeres de la Frontera, and began that conquest of Spain which was completed by his superior the Arabian Emir of Cairwan, Muza. We cannot help feeling some surprise at the small apparent effect produced on the rest of Europe by the loss of so important a member of the great Christian commonwealth. Paulus Diaconus devotes but one short dry sentence to the conquest of Spain, and the *Liber Pontificalis* mentions it not at all. One would say that the heresy of the Emperor Philippicus and his disfigurement of the picture of the Sixth Council at Constantinople affected the minds of the people of Rome more profoundly than the conquest by Asiatics of one of the finest regions of Western Europe. And yet that slow and difficult reconquest of Spain by the refugees in the mountains of the Asturias, which, as we know, did eventually take place, can hardly have been foreseen by these writers, since it was more than three centuries before half of the peninsula was recovered, and nearly eight centuries before "the last sigh of the Moors" bewailed their expulsion from their lovely Granada.

In the first fervor of their conquering zeal the Saracen the Pyrenees and made the Gothic provinces of Septimania their own. Many students of history hardly realize the fact that for something like half a century parts of Languedoc and Provence were actually subject to the Moorish yoke, that Narbonne, Arles, and Avignon all heard the Muezzin's cry, and called at the hour of prayer on Allah the Merciful and the Mighty.

It did not however need fifty years to reassure affrighted Europe by the conviction that Gaul would at any rate not fall as easy a prey as Spain to the turbaned hordes of the believers in the Prophet. Already in 721 the valiant Eudo of Aquitaine defeated them in a bloody battle under the walls of Toulouse, and eleven years later, after he himself had been vanquished, the remnant of his troops shared in the glorious victory which the stout Austrasians from beyond the Rhine achieved under the leadership of by Charles Martel on the plains of Poitiers, not far from the spot where, two hundred and twenty-five years before, the battle of the Campus Vogladensis gave to the Frank instead of the Visigoth the dominion over Southern Gaul.

This battle of Poitiers was, as every one knows, one of the decisive battles of the world, as important as Marathon or Salamis for the decision of the question whether Europe was to be the chosen home of empire in the centuries that were to follow. And for the victory thus won by Christendom over Islam, Europe was mainly indebted (and well did she know her obligation) to the bright and vigorous personality of Charles, surnamed the Hammer. When his father Pippin of Heristal died (714), the Frankish kingdom seemed to be falling asunder in ruin, a ruin even more hopeless, as springing from internal dissensions, than the collapse of Visigothic Spain. Aquitaine, Thuringia, Bavaria, all the great subordinate duchies were falling off from the central monarchy; Neustria and Austrasia were becoming two hostile kingdoms; and, to complete the confusion, the aged Pippin, passing by his son Charles who was in the vigor of youthful manhood, had bequeathed the Mayoralty of the Palace, as if it had been an estate, to his little grandson Theudwald, a child of six years old, under the regency of his mother Plectrude, by whose evil counsel this unwise disposition had been made. A Merovingian king incapable as all these later Merovingians were of doing a single stroke of business on his own account, a baby Prime Minister, with a greedy and unscrupulous woman as regent over him,—these were certainly poor materials out of which to form a strong and well-compacted state. But the young Charles, whom his stepmother had only dared to imprison, not to slay, first escaped from his confinement, then defeated the rival, Neustrian, Mayor of the Palace got hold of a Merovingian child and in his name ruled, like his father, as Mayor of the Palace over the three kingdoms, Austrasia, Neustria, and Burgundy. He subdued the savage Frisians, set up in Bavaria a duke who was willing to be his humble dependent, chastised Eudo of Aquitaine (who was aiming at independence and had well-nigh acquired it), and then having chastised, assisted him as we have seen, and protected his territory against the overflowing flood of Moorish invasion. Consolidator of France and saviour of Europe, Charles Martel was the real founder of the Arnulfing or Carolingian dynasty. But warned by the fate of his great-uncle Grimwald he did not himself stretch forth a hand to grasp the regal scepter. As long as his puppet lived, he left him the name and the trappings of royalty. When that puppet died, he did not indeed think it worth while to replace him by a successor, yet he did not change his own title. For the last four years of his life (737-741) there was literally "no king in the land"; a Mayor of the royal Palace, but no king inside it.

The reign, for such we may truly call it, of Charles Martel was nearly contemporaneous with that of Liutprand, with whom he had much intercourse, all of a friendly kind. The chain of events which enabled Pippin to assume the name as well as the reality of kingly power, and which brought him over the Alps to interfere in the affairs of Italy, will have to be related in a future volume. We only note them here as truly central events in that eighth century upon which we have now entered.

Politically the eighth century is one of the least interesting in English history. The great days of the Northumbrian kingdom are over, and the day of Wessex has not yet dawned. But from a literary or religious point of view the century is more attractive. During the first third of its course Baeda, decidedly the most learned man of his time, perhaps we might say the most learned man of all the early mediaeval period, was compiling his text-books, his commentaries, and his Ecclesiastical History of the English nation. And at the same time the English, who so lately had been receiving missionaries from Rome and from Iona, were sending out missionaries of their own, able, energetic and courageous men, to convert the still remaining idolaters of Germany. Chief among these missionaries were the Northumbrian Willibrord, who for forty years labored for the conversion of the Frisians, and the Devonshire-man Winfrith, who received from the Pope the name of Boniface, and who from 718 to 753 wrought at the organization of the half-formed Churches of Bavaria and Thuringia, preached to the heathen Hessians, hewing down an aged oak to which they paid idolatrous reverence, directed from his Archiepiscopal see at Maintz the religious life of all central Germany, and finally in his old age received the martyr's crown from the hands of the still unconverted Frisians. This great work of the Christianization of Germany is alien to our present subject, and must not here be further enlarged upon, but it may be noticed how closely it was connected with the other leading events of the eighth century. It is not improbable that the zeal of these English missionaries was partly quickened by the tidings of the rapid advances of Mohammedanism. It is certain that the work of proselytism was aided by the arms of Pippin and Charles Martel. As their frontier advanced across the Rhine, Christianity went forward: where it fell back for a time, heathenism triumphed, and the missionaries became the martyrs. The close connection of the German mission with the exaltation of the Arnulfing house is symbolized by the fact that Boniface either actually took part in the coronation of Pippin, or at least used his powerful influence with the Pope to bring about that result. And lastly, it is obvious how greatly the addition of the wide regions between the Rhine and the Elbe to the area of Western Christendom must have strengthened the authority of the Pope. The Byzantine Emperor in his dwindling realm, hemmed in by Saracens and Bulgarians, might issue what decrees he would to his servile Greek diocesans. Here in Western Europe, in England and in Germany, were mighty nations, young and full of conscious strength and promise of the future, who had received their Christianity from the hands of devoted adherents of the Pope, and would recognize no authority but his.

This thought brings us to the last great event of the eighth century, the outbreak of the Iconoclastic Controversy. This will need a somewhat more detailed notice than the others.

To the shadow-Emperors whose reigns filled six anarchic years after the death of Justinian II succeeded, in March, 717, Leo III, commonly called Leo the Isaurian. Here was at last a man at the helm of the State, and one who, though his name is scarcely ever mentioned without a curse by the monkish chroniclers of the time, came at the fortunate—I would rather say at the Providential—moment to save Eastern Europe from the Saracen yoke, and to preserve for Christianity in any shape, whether enlightened or superstitious, some influence on the future destinies of Europe. Leo (whose original name is said to have been Conon) was borne in Asia Minor, either at Germanicia in Commagene, or, as is more probable, in those Isaurian highlands which in the fifth century sent adventurers to Constantinople to disturb and trouble the Empire but now sent a race of heroes to deliver it. The year of his birth is not apparently mentioned, but we may conjecture it to have been somewhere about 670. In his youth he and his parents were removed from their Asiatic home to Mesembria in Thrace, and here, when Justinian was marching with his Bulgarian allies to recover his throne, Leo met him with a present of 500 sheep. The grateful Emperor rewarded him by a place in his life-guards, and announced that he regarded him as one of his "true friends". Before long, however, jealousy and suspicion entered his soul, and he sent his "true friend" on a desperate mission to the Alans in the Caucasus, a mission which occupied several years, and from which only by the exercise of extraordinary ingenuity as well as courage did he at last return alive. When he returned to the abodes of civilized men he found Justinian deposed and Anastasius reigning, who appointed him general of the Anatolian theme. In this district, which comprehended the central portion of Asia Minor, Leo for some years, by guile rather than force, kept at bay the Saracen general Moslemah, brother of the Caliph, who was threatening the city of Amorium.

It was known that the Saracens were preparing for a grand assault on Constantinople, and it was generally felt that the so-called Theodosius III, a government clerk who had been forced against his will to assume the purple, was quite unable to cope with the emergency. In the autumn of 716 Leo proclaimed himself a candidate for the diadem and the avenger of his patron Anastasius, who had been deposed by the mutinous authors of the elevation of Theodosius. After defeating the Emperor's son at Nicomedia, and apparently spending the winter in Bithynia, he moved on to Constantinople, where the Patriarch and the Senate welcomed him as Emperor. There was no further conflict: Theodosius recognized his unfitness for the diadem, and having with his son assumed the clerical garment, retired into safe obscurity.

The change of rulers had come only just in time to save the state. By the 1st of September, 717, the fleets and armies of the Saracen Caliph, constituting an armament apparently more formidable than that which Moawiyah had sent against the city forty years before, appeared in the Sea of Marmora. It is not necessary to give here the details of this memorable siege, in which, as in Napoleon's Russian campaign, fire and frost combined to defeat the forces of the invader. The besieged sent their ships laden with "Greek fire" into the fleet of the affrighted Saracens, burning many of their vessels and striking panic into the crews which escaped. The wind blew cold from Thrace; frost and snow covered the ground for a hundred days, and the camels and cattle of the besieging army perished by thousands. Famine followed as the natural consequence; the Saracens fed on disgusting preparations of human flesh, and pestilence of course followed famine. Upon the top of all their other calamities came an onslaught of the Bulgarians, who in this extremity of danger were willing to help their old foe, the Caesar of Constantinople. At length on the 15th of August, 718, the remnants of the once mighty armament melted away; the cavalry from the Bithynian plain, and the ships from the waters of the Bosphorus. Constantinople was saved, and the Paradise promised to the first army of the faithful that should take the city of Caesar was not yet won.

It was no marvel that such a great deliverance should be attributed to supernatural causes, and especially, by the monkish historians, to the prayers of the Mother of God.

But it is certain that the statesmanlike foresight, the mingled astuteness and courage of the great Isaurian Emperor, had also much to do with the triumph of Christendom. As soon as the Saracen invader was repelled, he began that reorganization of the Empire to which adequate justice was not rendered till our own day, and one of the chief monuments of which is the *Ecloga,* a kind of handbook of Imperial law for the use of the people, which has lately attracted the careful and admiring study of European jurists

This early in his reign Leo was called upon to face the rebellion of a Western province, the result doubtless of the miserable anarchy into which the State had been plunged by his predecessors. The Duke of Sicily, who was an officer of high rank in the Imperial guard named Sergius, hearing of the siege of Constantinople by the Saracens, decided to create an Emperor of his own, and invested with the purple a certain Sicilian, sprung from Constantinople, named Basil, to whom he gave the Imperial name of Tiberius. For a short time the new Emperor played at promoting officers and appointing judges under the advice of his patron Sergius; and then Paulus, the *cartularius* of the Emperor Leo, arrived, apparently with a single ship and with a letter from his master, in the harbour of Syracuse. The mere news of his arrival was sufficient. The conscience-stricken Sergius escaped to the Lombards of Benevento. The Sicilian army was collected to hear the 'sacred' letter read, and when they received the tidings of the destruction of the mighty armaments of the Saracens they burst into loud applause and gladly surrendered Basil and his new-made courtiers into the hands of Paulus. The usurper and his general-in-chief were at once beheaded. Of his adherents, some were flogged, others were shaved as priests, others had their noses slit, others were fined and sent into banishment, and thus order reigned once more in Sicily.

The first eight years of the reign of Leo seem to have passed, with the exception of this trifling rebellion in Sicily, in internal peace and tranquility, though not undisturbed by wars with the Saracens, notwithstanding the repulse of their great Armada.

Thus far he had done nothing to tarnish his fair fame to which he was entitled from ecclesiastical historians as a zealous defender of the Christian world against the warriors of Islam; nay, he had even given proof of his orthodoxy after the fashion of the age by vain attempts to compel Jews and heretics to enter the fold of the Church. The Jews outwardly conformed, but in secret washed off the water of baptism as an unholy thing. The Montanist heretics, in whom still lived the uncompromising spirit of their great predecessor Tertullian, solemnly assembled on an appointed day in their churches, and gave themselves over to the flames, rather than abandon the faith of their fathers.

At last in the ninth year of his reign Leo began that warfare against images by which, even more than by his gallant defence of Constantinople, his name is made memorable in history. Strangely enough this attempted revolution in ecclesiastical polity seems to have been connected with, perhaps derived from, a similar attempt on the part of a Saracen ruler. Yezid II, the Ommiade Caliph of Damascus (720-724), had received, according to Theophanes, an assurance from a Jewish magician of Tiberias that his reign should be prolonged for thirty years if he would only compel his Christian subjects to obliterate the pictures in their churches. His brother and predecessor, Caliph Omar II, had already enforced on the Christians one precept of the Koran by forbidding them the use of wine, and now Yezid would enforce another of the Prophet's commands by taking away from them temptations to idolatry. His attempt failed, and as his promised thirty years ended in an early death after a reign of only four years, his son Welid II put the lying soothsayer to death. The story is probably more or less fabulous, but contains this kernel of truth—that it was the contact with Mohammedanism which opened the eyes of Leo and the men who stood round his throne, ecclesiastics as well as laymen, to the degrading and idolatrous superstitions that had crept into the Church and were overlaying the life of a religion which, at its proclamation the purest and most spiritual, was fast becoming one of the most superstitious and materialistic that the world had ever seen. Shrinking at first from any representation whatever of visible objects, then allowing herself the use of beautiful and pathetic emblems (such as the Good Shepherd), in the fourth century the Christian Church sought to instruct the converts whom her victory under Constantine was bringing to her in myriads, by representations on the walls of the churches of the chief event of Scripture history. From this the transition to specially reverenced pictures of Christ, the Virgin and the Saints, was natural and easy. The crowning absurdity and blasphemy, the representation of the Almighty Maker of the Universe as a bearded old man, floating in the sky, was not yet perpetrated, nor was to be dared till the human race had taken several steps downward into the darkness of the Middle Ages; but enough had been already done to show whither the Church was tending, and to give point to the sarcasm of the followers of the Prophet when they hurled the epithet "idolaters" at the craven and servile populations of Egypt and Syria .

It was in the year 725, according to Theophanes, that "the irreligious Emperor first began to stir the question of the destruction of the holy and venerable images". In the following year, about harvest-time, volcano burst forth in the Archipelago close to the island of Thera. A heavy cloud of vapor hung over the Aegean, and pumice-stones were hurled over all the neighboring coasts of Asia Minor and Macedon. In this portent Leo saw the rebuke of Heaven for his slackness in dealing with the sin of idolatry, and the decree which had been before talked of was now formally issued. There can be little doubt that this decree was for the actual destruction of the idolatrous emblems. The statement which is generally made, that the Emperor's first decree only ordered that the pictures should be raised higher on the walls of the churches to remove the temptation to kiss and idolatrously adore them, is in itself improbable (for most of the pictures at this time were mosaics, which could not be so easily removed), and rests apparently on very doubtful authority. On the contrary, Leo seems to have set about his self-imposed task with an almost brutal disregard of the feelings of his subjects. Undoubtedly there are times in the history of the world when the holiest and most necessary work that can be performed is that of the Iconoclast. The slow deposit of ages of superstition encrusts so thickly the souls of men that the letters originally traced thereon by the Divine Finger are not at all or but dimly legible. In such a case he who with wise and gentle hand applies the mordant acid and clears away the gathered fallacies of ages may do as useful a work, even as religious a work, as he who brings a fresh revelation from the Most High. But even in doing it he must remember and allow for the love and reverence which for generations have clustered round certain forms or words against which it may be his duty to wage war; and he will, if he is wise, gently loosen the grasp of faith, rather than with ruthless hand break both the worshipped image and the heart of the worshipper.

Such, unfortunately, was not the policy of the Isaurian Emperor, inheriting as he did the evil traditions of four centuries of Imperial legislators, whose fixed principle it had been that whithersoever the Emperor went in the regions of religious speculation or practice, thither all his subjects were bound to follow him. The destruction or obliteration of the sacred images and pictures was promptly begun, and all opposition was stamped out with relentless severity. One tragic event which occurred at

Constantinople was probably the counterpart of many others of which no record has been preserved. Over the great gateway of the Imperial palace (which from the brazen tiles that formed its roof had received the name of Chalcé) had been placed a great effigy of Our Saviour, which, perhaps from the refulgent mosaics of which it was composed, had received the same name of Chalcé .The command went forth that this picture, probably one of the best known and most revered in all Constantinople, was to be destroyed; and hatchet in hand an Imperial life-guardsman mounted a ladder and began the work of destruction. Some women who had clustered below called out to him to cease his unholy work. In vain: the hatchet fell again and again on the loved and worshipped countenance. Threat the women (likened by later ecclesiastical writers to the devout women who carried spices to the tomb of the Saviour) shook the ladder and brought the life-guardsman to the ground. He still breathed notwithstanding his fall, but "those holy women" (as the martyrologist calls them), with such rude weapons as they may have had at their disposal, stabbed him to death. Something like a popular insurrection followed, which was suppressed with a strong hand, and was followed by the deaths, banishments, and mutilations of the women and their sympathizers.

The news of this attempted religious revolution deeply stirred the minds of the subjects of the Empire. In Greece and the islands of the Archipelago there was an immediate outburst of insurrectionary fury. A great fleet was prepared, a certain Cosmas was named Emperor, and on the 18th of April, 727, the rebels arrived before Constantinople. But the "liquid fire" which had destroyed the Saracen Armada proved equally fatal to the Image-worshippers. Cosmas and one of his generals-in-chief were beheaded; the other escaped execution by leaping, clad in full armor, into the sea: the cause of Iconoclasm was for the time triumphant. In the year 729 Leo called what Western nations would have described as a Parliament, but what the loquacious Greeks quaintly named a *Silentium,* in order to confirm and regulate the suppression of image-worship. At this assembly, Germanus the Patriarch of Constantinople, with whom Leo had been for five year vainly pleading for assistance in his religious war, formally laid down his office. "I am Jonah", said the aged Patriarch; "cast me into the sea. But know, oh Emperor! that without a General Council thou canst not make any innovations in the faith". Germanus was deposed and allowed to spend the remainder of his already ninety years of age in peace. His private chaplain, Anastasius, whom the old man had long felt to be treading on his heels, but who seems to have been sincere in his professions of Iconoclasm, was made Patriarch in the room of Germanus, and for fifteen years governed the Church of Constantinople. During the remaining ten years of the reign of Leo III we do not hear much as to the details or the Iconoclastic Controversy. The Emperor's attention was probably occupied by the repeated Saracen invasions of Asia Minor, but there is no reason to suppose that he abandoned the Iconoclastic position, though martyrdoms and mutilations of the Image-worshippers are little spoken of. Apparently the latter party had for the time accepted their defeat, and those who were most zealous on behalf of the forbidden worship emigrated in vast numbers to Southern Italy and Sicily. It is for us now to consider what effect the religious war thus kindled by the Isaurian Emperor had on the fortunes of Italy.

CHAPTER XII.

KING LUITPRAND

THE Iconoclastic decrees of the Emperor Leo probably reached Italy in the course of the year 726. Let us glance at the life and character of the man upon whom, as head of the Latin Church, the responsibility rested of accepting or rejecting them.

Gregory II, who succeeded to the chair of St. Peter on the death of Pope Constantine, was, like his great namesake, of Roman origin, and was the son of a man who bore the true Roman name of Marcellus. He had been brought up from a child in the Papal palace, was made subdeacon, treasurer and librarian, under the pontificate of Sergius, and had attained the position of deacon (687-701) when, as we have already seen he accompanied Pope Constantine to Constantinople, and bore the brunt of the discussion with Justinian the Noseless, as to the canons of the Quinisextan Council. His pure life, great knowledge of Scripture, ready eloquence, and firmness in defending the rights of the Church, all marked him out as a suitable successor to the Pope in whose train he had visited the New Rome. He continued the work of restoration of the walls of Rome, and set the destructive lime-kilns at work in order to aid in the process.

It was probably in the year after the consecration of Gregory that a Bavarian duke, "the first of his race" said the people of Rome, came to kneel at the shrine of St. Peter. This was the venerable Duke Theodo (probably a collateral descendant of Theudelinda), who had already divided his wide-spreading dominions among his three sons, and two of whose granddaughters about this time married the two chief rulers of the West, Liutprand and Charles Martel. Duke Theodo's visit was probably connected with a dark domestic tragedy which had ended in the mutilation and death of a Frankish bishop who had visited Bavaria, and it undoubtedly led to a closer dependence of the young and rough Church of the Bavarians on the See of Rome. This was yet more firmly knit when in the year 718 our countryman Boniface, as has been already said, offered himself to the Pope as the willing instrument of the spiritual conquest of Germany.

With Liutprand and the Lombards the relations of Gregory II seem in the early years of his pontificate to have been upon the whole friendly. We have seen how the Lombard king in the prologues to his yearly edicts delighted to dwell on the fact that his nation was "Catholic" and "beloved of God": and we have heard the remarkable words in which he announced to his subjects that he drew tighter the restrictions on the marriage of distant relations, being moved thereto by the letters of the Pope of the City of Rome, "who is the head of all the churches and priests of God throughout the world". It is entirely in accordance with the relation thus signified between the two powers that we find Liutprand at an early period of his reign renewing and confirming the mysterious donation of King Aripert II, of "the patrimony in the Cottian Alps".

It was a sign of the increased gentleness of the times and of the more friendly feeling between the Church and the Lombards that, after 130 years of desolation, the hill of St. Benedict was once more trodden by his spiritual children. About the year 719, Petronax, a citizen of Brescia, came on pilgrimage to Rome, and by the advice of Pope Gregory journeyed onward to Monte Cassino. He found a few simple-hearted men already gathered there, he formed them into a regular community, and was elected by them as their abbots. The fame of the new community spread far and wide: many, both nobles and men of meaner birth, flocked to the remembered spot, and by their help the monastery rose once more from its ruins, perhaps ampler and statelier than before. Years afterwards, under the pontificate of Zacharias, Petronax again visited Rome, and received from the Pope several MSS. of the Scriptures and other appliances of the monastic life, among them the precious copy of the great "Rule" which Father Benedict had written with his own hand two centuries before. These treasures, as we have seen, had been carried by the panic-stricken monks to Rome when Duke Zotto's ravages were impending over them.

But the Lombards, though now dutiful sons of the Church, had by no means ceased from their quarrel with the Empire. About the year 717 Romwald II, duke of Benevento, took by stratagem, as we are told, and in a time of professed peace, that stronghold of Cumae of which we last heard as taken by Narses from the Goths in 553. "All in Rome", says the Papal biographer, "were saddened by the news", and the Pope sent letters of strong protest to the Lombard duke, advising him, if he would escape Divine vengeance, to restore the fortress which he had taken by guile. He offered the Lombards large rewards if they would comply with his advice, but they "with turgid minds" refused to listen to either promises or threats. Thereupon the Pope turned to the Imperial Duke of Naples, stimulated his flagging zeal by the promise of the same large rewards, and by daily letters gave him the guidance which he seems to have needed. This duke, whose name was John, with Theodimus, a steward of the Papal patrimony and sub-deacon, for his second in command, entered the fortress by night. The Lombards were evidently taken by surprise, and there was little or no fighting. Three hundred Lombards with their *gastald* were slain: more than five hundred were taken as prisoners to Naples. The reward which the Pope had promised, and which was no less than 70 lbs. of gold, was paid to the victorious duke. Such events as this make us feel that we are on the threshold of the age in which Central Italy will own not the Emperor but the Pope for its lord, but we have not yet crossed it.

It was probably not long after this that Farwald II, duke of Spoleto, repeated the achievement of his great namesake and predecessor by moving an army northward and capturing Classis, the sea-port of Ravenna. But again, as before, the conquest which we might have expected almost to end Byzantine rule in Italy, produces results of no importance. Liutprand, whose aim at this time seems to be to keep his own house in order and to live at peace with the Empire, commands Farwald to restore his conquest to the Romans, and the command is obeyed. Whether these transactions have anything to do with the next event in the internal history of Spoleto we cannot tell, but we are informed that Transamund, son of Farwald, rose up against his father, and making him into a clergyman usurped his place. This revolution, which happened probably in 724, gave Liutprand, instead of an obedient vassal, a restless and turbulent neighbor, who was to be a very thorn in his side for nearly the whole remainder of his days.

It was perhaps the new duke of Spoleto who about this time obtained possession of the town of Narni, which place, important for its lofty bridge over the Nar, we have already learned to recognize as an important post on the Flaminian Way, and a frontier city between Romans and Lombards. The conjecture that it was Transamund of Spoleto who made this conquest is confirmed by the fact that we are expressly told in the next sentence of the Life of Gregory II that it was King Liutprand who put the host of the Lombards in motion and besieged Ravenna for many days. He does not appear however to have taken the city itself, but he repeated the operation of the capture of Classis, from whence he carried off many captives and countless wealth.

We are now approaching the time when the Isaurian Emperor's edicts against Image-worship may be supposed to have reached Italy. To those edicts alone has been generally attributed the storm of revolution which undoubtedly burst over Italy in the years between 727 and 730. But though a cause doubtless of that revolution, the Iconoclastic decrees were not the sole cause. Already, ere those decrees arrived, the relations between Byzantium, Rome, and Ravenna were becoming strained. The reader will have observed that for the last half century the popular party both in Ravenna and Rome had manifested an increasing contempt for the weakness of the Exarchs, hatred of their tyranny, and disposition to rally round the Roman pontiff as the standard-bearer not only of the Catholic Church against heresy, but also of Italy against the Greeks. Now, at some time in the third decade of the eighth century, there is reason to believe that financial exactions came to add bitterness to the strife.

The Emperor had been doubtless put to great expense by the military operations necessary to repel the great Saracen invasion, and he might think, not unreasonably, that Italy, and preeminently the Roman Church, the largest landowner in Italy, ought to bear its share of the cost. At any rate he seems to have ordered his Exarch to lay some fresh tax upon the provinces of Italy, and in some way or other to lay hold of the wealth of her churches. It would seem that some similar demand had been made in the East, and had been quietly complied with by the subservient Patriarch of Constantinople. The Pope however was determined to submit to no such infraction of the privileges of the Church. He probably ordered the *rectores patrimonii* throughout Italy and Sicily to oppose a passive resistance to the demands of the Imperial collectors, and this opposition stimulated the other inhabitants of Imperial Italy to a similar refusal

This defiance of the Emperor's edict naturally provoked resentment at Constantinople and Ravenna. The Exarch probably received orders to depose Gregory, as Martin had been deposed, and carry him captive to Constantinople. It is not necessary to charge the Emperor (as the Papal biographer has done) with ordering the death of the resisting pontiff. Such a command would have been inconsistent with the character of Leo, who showed himself patient under the long resistance of the Patriarch Germanus to the Iconoclastic decrees, and it is generally disbelieved by those modern writers who are least favorable to the Isaurian Emperors. It is very likely however that the satellites of the Byzantine government, perceiving the opposition between Emperor and Pope, concluded, as did the murderers of Becket, that the surest way to win their sovereign's favor was "to rid him of one turbulent priest"; and thus it is that the pages of the biography at this point teem with attacks on the life of Gregory, all of which proved unsuccessful.

A certain Duke Basil, the *cartularius* Jordanes, and a subdeacon John surnamed Lurion (that is to say, two Imperial officers and one ecclesiastic, who was probably in the service of the Lateran) laid a plot for the murder of the Pope. Marinus, an officer of the life-guards, who had been sent from Constantinople to administer the *Ducatus Romae,* gave a tacit sanction to their design, for the execution of which however they failed to find a fitting opportunity. Marinus, stricken by paralysis had to relinquish the government of Rome and retire from the scene; but when Paulus the Patrician came out as full-blown Exarch to Italy the conspirators obtained, or thought they obtained, his consent also to their wicked schemes. The people of Rome however got wind of the design, and in a tumultuary outbreak slew the two inferior conspirators, Jordanes and Lurion. Basil was taken prisoner, compelled to change the gay attire of a duke for the coarse robes of a monk, and ended his days in a convent.

Again a guardsman was sent by the Exarch, this time only with orders to depose the pontiff: and as he apparently failed to execute his commission, Paulus raised such an army as he could in Ravenna and the neighboring towns, and sent it under the command of the count of Ravenna to enforce the previous order. But the Romans and—ominous conjunction—the Lombards also, flocked from all quarters to the defence of the pontiff. The soldiers of the duke of Spoleto blocked the bridge over the Anio by which the Exarch's troops, marching on the left bank of the Tiber along the Salarian Way, hoped to enter Rome. All round the confines of the *Ducatus Romae* the Lombard troops were clustering, and the count was forced to return to Ravenna with his mission unfulfilled.

Thus then the political atmosphere of central Italy was full of electricity before the decrees against Image worship came to evoke the lightning flash of revolution. It will be well here to quote the exact words of the *Liber Pontificalis,* which is our only trustworthily authority for the actual reception of the decrees in Italy:

"By orders subsequently transmitted the Emperor had decreed that no image of any saint, martyr or angel should be retained in the churches; for he asserted that all these things were accursed. If the Pope would acquiesce in this change he should be taken into the Emperor's good graces, but if he prevented this also from being done he should be deposed from his see. Therefore that pious man, despising the sovereign's profane command, now armed himself against the Emperor as against a foe, renouncing his heresy and writing to Christians everywhere to be on their guard, because a new impiety had arisen. Therefore all the inhabitants of the Pentapolis and the armies of Venetia resisted the Emperors, declaring that they would never be art or part in the murder of the Pope, but would rather strive manfully for his defence, so that they visited with their anathema the Exarch Paulus as well as him who had given him his orders, and all who were like-minded with him. Scorning to yield obedience to his orders, they elected dukes for themselves in every part of Italy, and thus they all provided for their own safety and that of the pontiff. And when [the full extent of] the Emperor's wickedness was known, all Italy joined in the design to elect for themselves an Emperor and lead him to Constantinople. But the Pope restrained them from this scheme, hoping for the conversion of the sovereign".

From this narrative, which has all the internal marks of truthfulness, it will be seen that Gregory II, while utterly repudiating the Iconoclastic decrees and arming himself (perhaps rather with spiritual than carnal weapons) against the Emperor as against a foe, threw all his influence into the scale against violent revolution and disruption of the

Empire. In fact, we may almost say that the Pope after the publication of the decrees was more loyal to the Emperor, and less disposed to push matters to extremity, than he had been before that change in his ecclesiastical policy. The reason for this, as we may infer from the events which immediately followed, was that he saw but too plainly that revolt from the Empire at this crisis would mean the universal dominion of the Lombards in Italy.

Having given this, which appears to be the true history of Gregory's attitude during the eventful years from 725 to 731, we must now examine the account given by Theophanes, which, copied almost verbatim by subsequent Greek historians, has unfortunately succeeded in passing current as history. *Anno Mundi* 6217 [=A.D. 725]. "First year of Gregory, bishop of Rome. [Gregory's accession really took place ten years earlier.] In this year the impious Emperor Leo began to stir the question of the destruction of the holy and venerable images; and learning this, Gregory the Pope of Rome stopped the payment of taxes in Italy and Rome, writing to Leo a doctrinal letter the effect that the Emperor ought not to meddle in questions of faith, nor seek to innovate on the ancient doctrines of the Church which had been settled by the holy fathers.

(A.M. 6221; = A.D. 729.) After describing the steadfast opposition of Germanus, Patriarch of Constantinople, to the wild beast Leo (fitly so named) and his underlings, Theophanes continues, "In the elder Rome also Gregory, that all-holy and apostolic man and worthy successor of Peter, chief of the Apostles, was refulgent in word and deed; who caused both Rome and Italy and all the Western regions to revolt from their civil and ecclesiastical obedience to Leo and the Empire under his rule".

He then relates the deposition of Germanus and the elevation to the Patriarchate of Anastasius falsely so called: "But Gregory the holy president of Rome, as I before said, disowned Anastasius by his circular letters refuting Leo by his epistles as a worker of impiety, and withdrew Rome with the whole of Italy from his Empire".

The reader has now before him the passages in the history of Theophanes on the strength of which Gregory II is generally censured or praised (according to the point of view taken by the narrator) for having stimulated the revolt of Italy and stopped the payment of the Imperial taxes. They are quite irreconcilable with the story of the *Liber Pontificalis*, and every historian must choose between them. For my part, I have no hesitation in accepting the authority of the Papal biographer, and throwing overboard the Byzantine monk. The former was strictly contemporary; the latter was born seventeen years after Gregory was in his grave. Theophanes wrote his history at the beginning of the ninth century, when the separation of the Eastern and Western Empires through the agency of the Popes was an accomplished fact, and he not unnaturally attributed to Gregory the same line of policy which he knew to have been pursued by his successors Hadrian and Leo. He was moreover, as we have seen, outrageously ill-informed as to other Western affairs of the eighth century. It is easy to understand how the refusal of taxes, which was really an earlier and independent act in the drama, became mixed in his mind with the dispute about images, and how he was thus led to describe that as a counter-blow to the Iconoclastic decrees, which was really decided upon ere the question of Image-worship was mooted.

Theophanes is probably right in saying that the Pope sent letters to the Emperor warning him against interference in sacred things. Unfortunately these letters have perished, for the coarse and insolent productions which have for the last three centuries passed current under that name are now believed by many scholars to be forgeries of a later date. Much confusion is cleared away from the history, and the memory of a brave but loyal Pope is relieved from an unnecessary stain, by the rejection of these apocryphal letters.

Anarchy and the disruption of all civil and religious ties seemed to impend over Italy when the Emperor and the Pope stood thus in open opposition to one another. There was a certain Exhilaratus, duke of Campania, whose son Hadrian had some years before incurred the anathema of a Roman synod for having presumed to marry the deaconess Epiphania. Father and son now sought to revenge this old grudge on the Pontiff. They raised the banner of obedience to the Emperor and death to the Pope of Rome, and apparently drew away a considerable number of the Campanians after them. But the Romans (probably the civic guard which had been so conspicuous in some recent events) went forth and dispersed the Campanians, killing both Exhilaratus and his son. Another Imperial duke named Peter was arrested, accused of writing letters to the Emperor against the Pope, and, according to the cruel fashion which Italy borrowed from Byzantium, was deprived of sight.

At Ravenna itself something like civil war seems to have raged. There was both an Imperial and a Papal party in that city, but apparently the latter prevailed. The Exarch Paulus was killed (probably in 727 and it seems probable that for some time Ravenna preserved a kind of tumultuary independence, disavowing the rule of the Emperor, and proclaiming its fidelity to the Pope and the party of the Image-worshippers.

Meanwhile out of all this confusion and anarchy the statesmanlike Liutprand was drawing no small advantage. In the north-east he pushed his conquests into the valley of the Panaro, took Bologna and several small towns in its neighborhood, invaded, and perhaps conquered the whole of the Pentapolis and the territory of Osimo. It would seem from the expression used by the Papal biographer that with none of these towns was any great display of force needed, but that all, more or less willingly, gave themselves up to the Lombard king, whose rule probably offered a better chance of peace and something like prosperity than that either of the Exarch or the Exarch's foes.

At the same time Liutprand also took (by guile, we are told) the town of Sutrium, only thirty miles north of Rome, but this, after holding it for one hundred and forty days, on the earnest request of the Pope he gave back to the blessed Apostles Peter and Paul, without however restoring the booty which had rewarded the capture.

On the death of Paulus, the Eunuch Eutychius was appointed Exarch. He was apparently the last man who held that office, and though there is a provoking silence on the part of all our authorities as to his character, we may perhaps infer that he was a somewhat stronger and more capable man than many of his predecessors. But that is very faint praise.

The new Exarch landed at Naples—perhaps on account of the disturbed state of Ravenna—and from that city began to spread his net for the feet of the Pontiff. If the biographer may be trusted (which is doubtful), he sent a private messenger to Rome instructing his partisans to murder both the Pope and the chief nobles of the City. The citizens got hold of the messenger and his letters, and when they perceived the cruel madness of the Exarch they would fain have put the messenger to death, but the Pontiff hindered them. However, all the citizens, great and small, assembled in some sort of rude and unconscious imitation of the old *comitia* (held probably in one of the great Roman basilicas), wherein they solemnly anathematized Eutychius and bound themselves by a great oath to live or die with the Pontiff, "the zealot of the Christian faith and defender of the Churches". The Exarch sent messengers to both king and dukes of the Lombards, promising them great gifts if they would desist from helping Gregory II, but for a time all his blandishments were unavailing; Lombards and Romans vying with one another in declaring their earnest desire to suffer, if need were, a glorious death for the defence of the Pope and the true faith. Meanwhile the Pope, while giving himself up to fastings and daily litanies, bestowed alms on the poor with lavish hand, and in all his discourses to the people, delivered in gentle tones, thanked them for their fidelity to his person, and exhorted them to continue in the faith, but also warned them not to cease from their love and loyalty towards the Roman Empire. Thus did he soften the hearts of all and mitigate their continued sorrow.

But though the Exarch was at first unsuccessful both with the king and the dukes of the Lombards, there came a time (probably in the year 730) when Liutprand began to listen to his words and when a strange sympathy of opposites drew the Lombard King and the Greek Exarch into actual alliance with one another. If we attentively study Liutprand's career we shall, I think, see that the one dominant feature in his policy was his determination to make himself really as well as theoretically supreme over all Lombard men. In his view, to extend his territories at the expense of the dying Empire was good, and he neglected no suitable opportunity of doing so. To pose as the friend and champion of the Pope was perhaps even better, and he would sometimes abandon hardly-won conquests in order to earn this character. But to gather together in one hand all the resources of the Lombard nationality, to teach the half-independent dukes of Benevento and Spoleto their places, to make Trent and Friuli obey the word of a king going forth from Pavia, this was best of all: this was the object which was dearest to his heart. Thus what Ecgberht did eighty years later for England, Liutprand strove to do, not altogether unsuccessfully, for Italy.

From this point of view the rally of Lombard enthusiasm round the threatened Pope was not altogether acceptable to Liutprand. It was a movement in which the central government at Pavia had had little share. Tuscia and Spoleto, preeminently Spoleto, had distinguished themselves by their enthusiasm at the Salarian Bridge in repelling the invading Greeks. We are not informed of the attitude of Benevento, but we can see that the whole tendency of the movement was to substitute an independent Central Italy, with Rome as its spiritual capital, for the confessedly subordinate duchies of Clusium, Lucca, Spoleto, and the like.

As for Spoleto, there can be little doubt that Transamund, the undutiful son who had turned his father into a priest, was already showing his sovereign that he would have a hard fight to keep him in the old theoretical state of subservience and subjection. At Benevento also the forces of disorder were at work and, as we shall see a little later, a usurper was probably ruling the duchy of the Samnites.

In order then to accomplish his main purpose, the consolidation of Lombard Italy, Liutprand formed a league with the Exarch Eutychius, and the two rulers agreed to join their forces, with the common object of subjecting the dukes of Spoleto and Benevento to the king, and of enabling the Exarch to work his will on the Pope and the City of Rome. In accordance with this plan, Liutprand, who was of course far the stronger member of the confederacy, marched to Spoleto, received from both the dukes hostages and oaths of fidelity, and then moving northward to Rome encamped with all his army in the Plain of Nero, between the Vatican and Monte Mario. The combination of the Imperial deputy and the Lombard king, the might of Right, and the right of Might, seemed to bode instant destruction to the Roman Pontiff; but he repeated, not in vain, the experiment which his great predecessor Leo, three centuries before, had tried on

Attila. He went forth from the City, attended doubtless by a long train of ecclesiastics; he addressed one of his soothing and sweet-toned addresses to the Lombard, and soon had the joy of seeing him fall prostrate at his feet and vow that no harm should befall him through his means. In token of his penitence and submission Liutprand took off his mantle, his doublet his belt, his gilded sword and spear, his golden crown and silver cross, and laid them all down in the crypt before the altar of St. Peter. Solemn prayers were said; Liutprand besought the Pope to receive his ally the Exarch into favor, and thus a reconciliation, at least an apparent reconciliation, was effected, and the ominous alliance between King and Exarch was practically dissolved, never to be again renewed.

While the Exarch, now as it would seem an honored guest of the Pope, was tarrying at Rome, a wild and hopeless attempt to bring the opposition to Leo III to a head, by setting up a rival Emperor, was made and easily defeated. The pretender, whose real name was Petasius, assumed the name of Tiberius. This was, as we have seen, the appellation by which not only the Emperor Apsimar, but also Basil the pretender to the Empire who arose in Sicily, had elected to be called. We must suppose that some remembrance of the popular virtues of Tiberius II had obliterated the odium attaching to the name of Tiberius I. However, only a few towns in Tuscany swore allegiance to the usurper, and the Exarch, though troubled at the tidings of the insurrection, yet being comforted by the assurances of the Pope's fidelity, and receiving from him not only a deputation of bishops, but also the more effectual help of a troop of soldiers, went forth to meet the pretender, defeated him, and cut off his head, which he sent as a token of victory to Constantinople. "But not even so", says the Papal biographer, "did the Emperor receive the Romans back into full favor".

On February 2, 731, the aged Pope died. He was a man with much of the true Roman feeling which had animated his great namesake and predecessor, but with more sweetness of temper, and he had played his part in a difficult and dangerous time with dignity and prudence, upholding the rights of the Church and the claims of the Holy See as he understood them, but raising his powerful voice against the disruption of the Empire. By a hard fate his name has been in the minds of posterity connected with some of the coarsest and most violent letters that were ever believed to have issued from the Papal Chancery, letters more worthy of Boniface VIII than of the "sweet reasonableness" of Gregory II.

The new Pope, whose election was completed on March 18, 731, and who took the title of Gregory III, was of Syrian origin, descended doubtless from one of the multitude of emigrants who had been driven westwards and Romewards by the tide of Mohammedan invasion. He has not been so fortunate in his biographer as his predecessor, for the imbecile ecclesiastic who has composed the notice of his life which appears in the *Liber Pontificalis* is more concerned with counting the crowns and the basins, the crosses and the candlesticks, which Gregory III presented to the several churches in Rome, than with chronicling the momentous events which occurred during the ten years of his Pontificate. It is clear however that the third Gregory pursued in the main the same policy as his predecessor, sternly refusing to yield a point to the Emperor on the question of Image-worship, but also refusing to be drawn into any movement for the dismemberment of the Empire. In his relations with Liutprand he was less fortunate. He intrigued, as it seems to me unfairly, with the turbulent dukes of Spoleto and Benevento : and he was the first Pope in this century to utter that cry for help from the other side of the Alps which was to prove so fatal to Italy.

Gregory III was evidently determined to try what ecclesiastical warnings and threats would effect in changing the purpose of Leo. He wrote a letter charged with all the vigor of the Apostolic See, and sent it to the Emperor by the hands of a presbyter named George. But George, moved by the fear natural to man, did not dare to present the letter and returned to Rome with his mission unaccomplished.

The Pope determined to degrade his craven messenger from the priestly office, but on the intercession of the bishops of the surrounding district assembled in council, he decided to give him one more chance to prove his obedience. This time George attempted in good faith to accomplish his mission, but was forcibly detained in Sicily by the officers of the Emperor, and sentenced to banishment for a year.

On November 1, 731, the Pope convened a Council, at which the Archbishops of Grado and Ravenna and ninety-three other Italian bishops were present, besides presbyters, deacons, consuls and members of the commonalty. By this Council it was decreed, "that if hereafter any one despising those who hold fast the ancient usage of the Apostolic Church should stand forth as a destroyer, profaner, and blasphemer against the veneration of the sacred images, to wit of Christ and his Immaculate Mother, of the blessed Apostles and the Saints, he should be excluded from the body and blood of Jesus Christ, and from all the unity and fabric of the Church".

With this decree of the Council was sent to the Emperor a *defensor* named Constantine, who, like his predecessor, was forcibly detained and sentenced to a year's exile. The messengers from various parts of Italy who were sent to pray for the restoration of the sacred images were all similarly detained for a space of eight months by Sergius, Prefect of Sicily. At last the *defensor* Peter reached the royal city of Constantinople and presented his letters of warning and rebuke to Leo, to his son Constantine (now the partner of his throne), and to the Iconoclastic Patriarch Anastasius.

Here the Papal biographer breaks off, and we have to turn to another source to learn what answer the Emperor made to the remonstrances which had been addressed to him with so much persistence.

Theophanes (who knows nothing of the accession of the third Gregory) gives us the following information under date of 732:

"But the Emperor raged against the Pope and the revolt of Rome and Italy, and having equipped a great fleet, he sent it against them under the command of Manes, general of the Cibyrrhaeots. But the vain man was put to shame, his fleet being shipwrecked in the Adriatic Sea. Then the fighter against God being yet more enraged, and persisting in his Arabian [Mohammedan] design, laid a poll-tax on the third part of the people of Calabria and Sicily. He also ordered that the so-called *patrimonia* of the holy and eminent Apostles [Peter and Paul] reverenced in the elder Rome, which had from of old brought in a revenue to the churches of three and a half talents of gold, should be confiscated to the State. He ordered moreover that all the male children who were born should be inspected and registered, as Pharaoh aforetime did with the children of the Hebrews, a measure which not even his teachers the Arabians had taken with the Eastern Christians who were their subjects".

A few facts stand out clearly from this somewhat confused narrative. The maritime expedition which was frustrated by the storm in the Adriatic was no doubt intended to enforce the Iconoclastic decrees throughout Imperial Italy, perhaps to arrest the Pope. Apparently after the failure of this attempt it was never renewed. Financial grievances (probably the financial exigencies of the Imperial treasury) are again, as in our previous extracts from the same author, confusedly mixed up with religious innovations. But we may fairly infer that the sequestration of the Papal patrimonies, which would take effect chiefly in Sicily and Calabria, was meant as a punishment for the Pope's contumacy in respect of the decrees against image-worship : and if maintained, as it seems to have been, it must have seriously diminished the Papal splendor. The poll-tax and its necessary consequence the census of births, which is so absurdly compared to the infanticidal decree of Pharaoh, was doubtless a mere attempt—whether wise or unwise we cannot judge—to balance the Imperial budget. The fact that it was confined to Sicily and Calabria seems to show that all the territory in Northern and Central Italy which had lately belonged to the Empire was still seething with disaffection. Possibly even Ravenna itself was yet unsubdued, and in the possession of the insurgents.

At the same time, by an important ecclesiastical revolution, all the wide territories east of the Adriatic, which as part of the old Prefecture of Illyricum had hitherto obeyed the spiritual jurisdiction of Rome, were now rent away from the Latin Patriarchate: truly a tremendous loss, and one for which at the time it needed all the new conquests in England and Germany to make compensation.

With the facts thus gleaned from the pages of Theophanes our information as to the transactions between Emperor and Pope for the ten years of Gregory's pontificate comes to an end. Let us now turn to consider Liutprand's dealings with his subject dukes during the same period.

Affairs of Friuli

First we find our attention drawn to the region of the Julian Alps, where for some six and twenty years Pemmo, the skillful and ingenious, the tolerant husband of the ungainly Ratperga, the founder of one of the earliest schools of chivalry had been ruling the duchy of Friuli. It was somewhere about the point which we have now reached in the reign of Liutprand that this wary old ruler came into collision with that king's power, and lost both duchy and liberty. The cause of the trouble was ecclesiastical, and came, as almost all ecclesiastical troubles in that reign did come, directly or indirectly, from the controversy about the Three Chapters.

The synods which were held under Cunincpert at Pavia and Aquileia had reunited the Church of North Italy in the matter of doctrine, but the vested rights of the two Patriarchates which had been created in the course of the schism, remained, and were fixed in the established order of the Church, when, at the request of King Liutprand, Gregory II sent the *pallium* of a metropolitan to Serenus, Patriarch of Aquileia. Grado, which was within range of the fleets of Byzantium, had hitherto been the sole patriarchate in Venetia and Istria recognized by Rome. Now Aquileia, not ten miles distant from Grado (from whose desolate shore the campanile of the cathedral is plainly visible), Aquileia, which in all things was swayed by the nod of the Lombard king, was a recognized and orthodox Patriarchate also. A singular arrangement truly, and one which was made barely tolerable by the provision that, while maritime Venetia, including the islands in the lagunes, now fast rising into prosperity and importance, was to obey the Patriarch of Grado, continental Venetia, including Friuli and the bishoprics and convents endowed by its Lombard dukes, was to be subject to the rule of the Patriarch of Aquileia.

Dissensions of course arose, or rather never ceased, between the two so nearly neighboring spiritual rulers. They are attested by two letters of Pope Gregory II, one to

Serenus of Aquileia, whom he calls bishop of Forum Julii, warning him not to presume on his new *pallium* and on the favor of his king in order to pass beyond the bounds of the Lombard nation and trespass on the territory of his brother of Grado; the other to Donatus of Grado telling him of the warning which has been sent to Serenus.

It will be noticed that in the superscription of the letter to Serenus he is spoken of as bishop of Forum Julii. This can hardly have been his contemporary title, but it describes that which was to be his position in later times. As the Lombard duke was his patron, power naturally gravitated towards him, and Aquileia, always somber in its wide-reaching ruins, and now exposed to attack from the navies of hostile Byzantium ceased to be a pleasant residence for the Patriarch who took his title from its cathedral. At first he came only as far as Cormones, a little *castrum* half way on the road to Friuli. To the capital itself he could not yet penetrate, for, strangely enough, there was already one somewhat intrusive bishop there. From Julium Carnicum (Zuglio), high up in the defiles of the Predil pass, Bishop Fidentius had descended to Cividale in search of sunshine and princely favor, and receiving a welcome from some earlier duke had established himself there as its bishop. To him had succeeded Amator : but now Callistus, the new Patriarch of Aquileia, who was of noble birth and yearned after congenial society, taking it ill that these Alpine bishops should live in the capital and converse with Duke Pemmo and the young scions of the Lombard nobility, while he had to spend his life in the companionship of the boors of Cormones, took a bold step, forcibly expelled Bishop Amator. and went to live in his episcopal palace at Cividale. But Pemmo and the Lombard nobles had not invited Amator to their banquets to see their guest-friend thus flouted with impunity. Having arrested Callistus, they led him away to the castle of Potium overhanging the sea, into which they at first proposed to cast him headlong. "God, however", says Paulus, "prevented them from carrying on this design, but Pemmo thrust him into the dungeon and made him feed on the bread of tribulation".

The tidings of this high-handed proceeding greatly exasperated Liutprand, in whose political schemes the new orthodox Patriarch of Forum Julii was probably an important factor. He at once issued orders for the deposition of Pemmo and the elevation of his son Ratchis in his stead. No great display of force seems to have been needed for this change; probably there was already' a large party in the duchy who disapproved of the arrest of Callistus. Pemmo and his friends meditated an escape into the land of the Slovenes on the other side of the mountains, but Ratchis persuaded them to come in and throw themselves on the mercy of the king. At Pavia King Liutprand sat upon the judgment-seat, and ordered all who had been concerned in the arrest of Callistus to be brought before him. The fallen Duke Pemmo and two of his sons, Ratchait and Aistulf, came first. Their life was yielded as a favor to the loyal Ratchis, but they were bidden—perhaps in contemptuous tones—to stand behind the royal chair. Then with a loud voice the king read out the list of all the adherents of Pemmo, and ordered that they should be taken into custody. The ignominy of the whole proceeding heated the mind of Aistulf to such rage that he half drew his sword out of the sheath, and was about to strike the king, but Ratchis stayed his arm, and the treasonable design perhaps escaped the notice of Liutprand. All Pemmo's followers were then arrested and condemned to long captivity in chains, except one brave man named Herfemar, who drew his sword, defended himself bravely against the king's officers, and escaped to the basilica of St. Michael, which he did not leave till he had received the king's (faithfully kept) promise of pardon.

Ratchis justified the choice made of him for his father's successor by an irruption into Carniola, in which he wrought much havoc among the Slovenic enemies of his people, delivering himself from great personal peril by a well-aimed blow with his club at the chief of his assailants.

Of the after-fate of Pemmo and whether he lingered long in imprisonment we hear unfortunately nothing. He was certainly not restored to his duchy. From the whole course of the narrative we can at once perceive that a much stronger hand than that of the Perctarits and the Cunincperts is at the helm of the state, and that Liutprand is fast converting the nominal subjection of the great dukes into a very real and practical one.

Affairs of Benevento

Of the yet more important affairs of the great southern duchy of Benevento we have unfortunately but slender information. We have seen that before the death of Gregory II (731) Liutprand formed an alliance with the Exarch, in order that he might repress the rebellious tendencies of the dukes of Benevento and Spoleto. The duke of Benevento against whom this alliance was pointed is generally supposed to have been Romwald II, who had married Gumperga, niece of Liutprand. That theory cannot be disproved, but as Romwald seems to have reigned in peace with his great kinsman for many years, and as his death possibly occurred in 750, I am disposed to conjecture that it was the troubles arising out of that event which necessitated the interference of Liutprand. Paulus tells us that "on the death of Romwald there remained his son Gisulf, who was still but a little boy. Against him certain persons rising up sought to destroy him, but the people of the Beneventans, who were always remarkable for their fidelity to their leaders, slew them and preserved the life of their [young] duke". This is all that the Lombard historian tells us, but from an early catalogue of Beneventan dukes preserved at Monte Cassino we learn that there was actually another duke, presumably an usurper, named *Audelais,* who ruled in Benevento for two years after the death of Romwald II. It is clear therefore that Liutprand's work at Benevento was a difficult one, probably not accomplished without bloodshed. Having doubtless fought and conquered Audelais, he installed in the Samnite duchy his own nephew Gregory (who had been before duke of Clusium) and carried off his little kinsman Gisulf to be educated at Pavia. Here in course of time he gave him a noble maiden named Scauniperga to wife, and trained him for the great office which he was one day to hold.

Gregory is a man of whom one would gladly hear something more, for it would seem that he must have been a strong and capable ruler, who in such a difficult position kept the Beneventan duchy so long quiet and apparently loyal: but all that we know is that after ruling for seven years he died, apparently a natural death, and that *Gottschalk* was raised to the dukedom, evidently as an act of rebellion against the over-lordship of Pavia. Of Gottschalk also we hear very little except that his wife was named Anna, and from the emphatic way in which this lady is mentioned one conjectures that it was feminine ambition which urged Gottschalk to grasp the dangerous coronet. Three years, 739-742, he reigned, and then at last Liutprand, having put in order the affairs of Spoleto and other matters which needed mending, drew near to Benevento. At the mere rumor of his approach Gottschalk began to prepare for flight to Greece. A ship was engaged, probably at Brindisi or Taranto, and laden with his treasures and his wife, but ere the trembling duke himself could start upon his hasty journey along the great Via Trajana, the Beneventans who were loyal to young Gisulf and the house of Romwald rushed into his palace and slew him. The lady Anna with her treasures arrived safely at Constantinople.

King Liutprand arriving at Benevento seems to have found all opposition vanished, and to have settled all things according to his will. He installed his great-nephew Gisulf as duke in his rightful placed and returned victorious to Pavia. The reign of *Gisulf II* lasted for ten years, and overpassed the life of Liutprand and the limits of this volume.

In order to give a connected view of the changes which occurred at Benevento, it has been necessary to travel almost to the end of the reign of Liutprand. We must now return to the year 735, three years after he had suppressed the usurpation of Audelais of Benevento. It was apparently in May of this year that a strange event happened, and one which as it would seem somewhat overcast by its consequences the last nine years of the great king's reign. He was seized with a dangerous sickness, and seemed to be drawing near to death. Without waiting for that event, however, the precipitate Lombards, perhaps dreading the perils of a disputed succession, raised his nephew Hildeprand to the throne. The ceremony took place in that Church of the Virgin which the grateful Perctarit erected outside the walls in the place called *Ad Perticas*. When the scepter was placed in the hand of the new king men saw with a shudder that a cuckoo came and perched upon it. To our minds the incident would suggest some harsh thoughts of the nephew who was thus coming cuckoo-like to make use of his uncle's nest; but the wise men of the Lombards seem to have drawn from it an augury that "his reign would be a useless one". When Liutprand heard what was done he was much displeased, and indeed the incident was only too like that of the Visigothic king who in similar circumstances was made an involuntary monk, and so lost his throne. However, after what was perhaps a tedious convalescence Liutprand bowed to the inevitable and accepted Hildeprand as the partner of his throne. He must have been a man with some reputation for courage and capacity, or he would not have been chosen by the Lombards at such a crisis; but nothing that is recorded of him seems to justify that reputation. Both as partner of his uncle and as sole king of the Lombards, the word which best describes him seems to be that chosen by the historian, *inutilis.*

Of the years between 735 and 739 we can give no accurate account. They may have been occupied by operations against Ravenna. There are some slight indications that Transamund of Spoleto was making one of his usual rebellions. It was perhaps during this time that the strong position of Gallese on the Flaminian Way, which had somehow fallen into the hands of the Lombards and had been a perpetual bone of contention between Rome and Spoleto, was redeemed by the Pope for a large sum of money paid to Transamund a transaction which may have laid the foundation of the alliance between that prince and Gregory, and at the same time may easily have roused the displeasure of Liutprand. But the most important event in these years was probably Liutprand's expedition for the deliverance of Provence from the Saracens. His brother-in-law Charles Martel, with whom he seems to have been throughout his life on terms of cordial friendship, had sent him his young son Pippin that he might, according to Teutonic custom, cut off some of his youthful locks and adopt him as *filius per arma* The ceremony was duly accomplished, and the young Arnulfing having received many gifts from his adoptive father returned to his own land. He was one day to recross the Alps, not as son of the Mayor of the Palace, but as king of the Franks, and to overthrow the kingdom of the Lombards. But now came a cry for help from the real to the adoptive father of the young warrior. The Saracens from their stronghold in Narbonne had pressed up the valley of the Rhone. Avignon had been surrendered to them; Arles had fallen; it seemed as if they would make Provence their own and would ravage all Aquitaine. At the earnest entreaty of Charles Martel, who sent ambassadors with costly presents to his brother-in-law, Liutprand led the whole army of the Lombards over the mountains, and at the tidings of his approach the Saracens left their work of devastation and fled terrified to their stronghold.

In 739 the storm which had long been brewing in Central Italy burst forth. Transamund of Spoleto went into open rebellion against his sovereign. Gottschalk, as we have seen, in this year usurped the ducal throne of Benevento, and Pope Gregory III having formed a league with the two rebel dukes defied the power of Liutprand. The king at this time dealt only with Spoleto. He marched thither with his army; Transamund fled at his approach, taking refuge in Rome. In June, 739, Liutprand was signing charters in the palace of Spoleto and appointed one of his adherents named *Hilderic,* duke in the room of Transamund. He then marched on Rome, and as Gregory refused to give up his mutinous ally he took four frontier towns (Ameria, Horta, Polimartium, and Blera) away from the *Ducatus Romae* and joined them to the territory of the Lombards, whose border was now indeed brought perilously near to Rome. Having accomplished these changes Liutprand returned to Pavia.

The policy, perhaps we ought to say the intrigues, of Gregory III had so far been a failure. By his alliance with the rebellious dukes he had only made the most powerful man in Italy his enemy, and had lost four frontier cities to the Lombards. Help from distant and unfriendly Byzantium, help from the Exarch who was himself trembling for the safety of Ravenna, if not actually an exile from its walls, were equally unattainable. In these circumstances Gregory III entered again upon the policy which Pelagius II had pursued a century and a half before, and called on the Frank for aid. Writing to "his most excellent son, the *sub-regulus* lord Charles", he confided to him his intolerable woes from the persecution and oppression of the Lombards. The revenues appropriated to the maintenance of the lights on St. Peter's tomb had been intercepted, and the offerings of Charles himself and his ancestors had been carried off. The Church of St. Peter was naked and desolate; if the Frankish "under-king" cared for the favor of the Prince of the Apostles and the hope of eternal life, he would hasten to her aid.

As this letter was ineffectual, another was dispatched in more urgent terms. "Tears", said Gregory, "were his portion night and day when he saw the Church of God deserted by the sons who ought to have avenged her. The little that was left of the papal patrimony in the regions of Ravenna, and whose revenues ought to have gone to the support of the poor and the kindling of the lights at the Apostolic tomb, was being wasted with fire and sword by Liutprand and Hildeprand the Lombard kings, who had already sent several armies to do similar damage to the district round Rome, destroying St. Peter's farm-houses and carrying off the remnant of his cattle. Doubtless the Prince of the Apostles could if he pleased defend his own, but he would try the hearts of those who called themselves his friends and ought to be his champions. "Do not believe", urges the Pope, "the false suggestions of those two kings against the dukes of Spoleto and Benevento, as if they had committed any fault. All these stories are lies. Their only crime is that last year they refused to make an inroad upon us from their duchies and carry off the goods of the Holy Apostles, saying that they had made a covenant with us which they would keep. It is for this cause that the sword rages against them, and that those most noble dukes are degraded, and the two kings are making their own wicked followers dukes in their room. Send we pray you some faithful messenger, inaccessible to bribes, who shall see with his own eyes our persecution, the humiliation of the Church of God, the desolation of His property, and the tears of the foreigners (who are dwelling in Rome). Before God and by the coming judgment we exhort you, most Christian son, to come to St. Peter's help, and with all speed to beat back those kings and order them to return to their own homes. I send you the keys of the chapel of the blessed Peter, and exhort you by them and by the living and true God not to prefer the friendship of the kings of the Lombards to that of the Prince of the Apostles, but to come speedily to our aid, that your faith and good report may be spread abroad throughout all the nations, and that we may be able to say with the prophet, 'The Lord hear thee in the day of trouble, the name of the God of Jacob defend thee'."

The passionate appeals of the Pope failed of their effect. Charles Martel, as we have seen, was not himself morbidly scrupulous in the respect which he paid to the property of the Church. He probably did not believe, as posterity has not believed, that the sole fault of the two dukes was their refusal to invade the Roman territory. He rather saw in them two rebellious servants who were trying to sanctify their own turbulent courses by a pretence of defending the property of St. Peter. He himself was Liutprand's kinsman, his son had lately received a hospitable welcome at his court, his own cry for help against the Saracens had been generously responded to by the Lombard king. Decidedly he would not interfere against him, nor leave the plains of Provence a prey to the Saracens of Narbonne in order to win back for the angry Pope the towns which he had lost by his own rash meddling in the game of politics.

This being so, Transamund determined to try what he could effect by his own power, aided by the militia of the *Ducatus Romae.* He and his allies divided themselves into two bands, one of which invaded the southern part of the duchy, marching by the old Via Valeria, through the country of the Marsi and Peligni, passing the northern border of the Fucine lake, and receiving the submission, but not the willing submission, of the chief towns in this part of the duchy. The other troop, which was probably led by Transamund himself, marched along the Salarian Way, received the submission of Reate, and made all the old territory of the Sabines subject to the rebel duke. By December Transamund was again in his old palace of Spoleto, had slain his rival Hilderic, and resumed all his former audacity of rebellion against his king.

Affairs of Spoleto

The open alliance of the Pope and the rebel dukes, the easy reconquest of Spoleto, the always disloyal attitude of Gottschalk at Benevento caused Liutprand the Pope, and his Lombard counselors great anxiety. As the Papal biographer says, "There was great disturbance of spirits between the Romans and the Lombards, because the Beneventans and Spoletans held with the Romans". The unnatural alliance however was of short duration. Solemnly as Transamund had promised that if he recovered his duchy he would restore the four lost cities to the *Ducatus Romae,* when he was once securely seated in the palace of Spoleto he broke all his promises, and the towns which had been lost for his sake by the Romans continued Lombard still. On this the Pope withdrew the aid, whatever it was worth, which he had afforded to Transamund, and left Liutprand to deal with the two rebel dukes alone.

For some reason, however, possibly on account of the events hereafter to be related in connection with the capture and reconquest of Ravenna, something like two years elapsed after Transamund's expedition before Liutprand set forth to recover

Spoleto. During this Gregory III died (December 10, 741), and was succeeded after an unusually short interval by Zacharias, a Pope of Greek origin, whose memorable pontificate lasted ten years. Liutprand marched through the Pentapolis, and on the road between Fano and Fossombrone in the valley of the Metaurus sore peril overtook him. The two brave brothers of Friuli, Ratchis and Aistulf, both now loyally serving the Lombard king, commanded the van of the army, and when they reached a certain forest between those two towns they found the Flaminian Way blocked, and a strong force of Spoletans and Romans posted to dispute the passage. Great loss was inflicted on the advancing army, but the prowess of Ratchis, his brother, and a few of their bravest henchmen, on whom all the weight of battle fell, redeemed the desperate day. A certain Spoletan champion named Berto called on Ratchis by name, and rushed upon him with lance in rest, but Ratchis unhorsed him with his spear. The followers of Ratchis would have slain him outright, but he, pitiful by nature, said "Let him live", and so the humbled champion crawled away on hands and knees to the shelter of the forest. On Aistulf, as he stood upon the bridge over the Metaurus, two strong Spoletans came rushing from behind, but he suddenly with the butt end of his spear swept one of them from the bridge, then turned swiftly to the other, slew him, and sent him after his comrade.

Meanwhile the new Pope Zacharias had contrived to have an interview with the Lombard king, and had received his promise to surrender the four towns. Upon this the Roman army followed Liutprand's standards, and Transamund (according to the Papal biographer), seeing this conjunction of forces against him, recognized the hopelessness of the game, and surrendered himself and his city to Liutprand, who set up his nephew Agiprand as duke in his place. Like Gregory of Benevento, Agiprand had been duke of Clusium before he was thus promoted to the rule of a great semi-independent duchy. As for Transamund, his turbulent career ended in the cloister. He was made a cleric, that is probably monk as well as priest, and exchanging the adventurous and luxurious life of a Lombard duke for the seclusion of the convent had abundant leisure to meditate on his conduct towards his father, upon whom eighteen years before he had forced the same life of undesired religiousness. From Spoleto Liutprand proceeded to Benevento, and, as we have seen, expelled the rebellious occupant from that duchy also.

And here we must interrupt our survey of the changes which occurred in Central and Southern Italy, in order to notice an event of the greatest importance, the to which unfortunately we are unable to assign a precise date. I allude to the conquest of Ravenna by the Lombards and its recovery by the Venetian subjects of the Empire. Thrice during the two centuries of Lombard domination had the neighboring port of Classis been captured by the armies of Spoleto or of Pavia; but Ravenna herself, the city of the swamps and the pine-forest, had retained that proud attribute of impregnability which had made her ever since the days of Honorius the key-city of Northern Italy. Now she lost that great preeminence, but how we know not. When one thinks how even Procopius or Zosimus, to say nothing of Thucydides or Xenophon, would have painted for us that fateful siege, it is difficult not to murmur at the utter silence of the Grecian Muse of History at this crisis. Even a legend of the capture from the pen of the foolish Agnellus might have shed forth a few rays upon the darkness, but Agnellus seems never to have heard of this disaster to his native city. All that we have certainly to rely on is contained in the following sentences from Paulus, which come immediately after his account of Liutprand's expedition against the Saracens of Provence:

"Many wars, in truth, did the same King Liutprand wage against the Romans, in which he ever stood forth victorious, except that once in his absence his army was cut to pieces at Ariminum, and at another time when the king was abiding at Pilleus in the Pentapolis, a great multitude of those who were bringing him gifts and offerings and presents from various Churches were either slain or made captive by the onrush of the Romans. *Again, when Hildeprand the king's nephew and Peredeo duke of Vicenza were holding Ravenna, by a sudden onset of the Venetians Hildeprand was made prisoner, and Peredeo fell fighting bravely.* In the following time also, the Romans, as usual swollen with pride, came together from all quarters under the command of Agatho duke of Perugia, hoping to take Bologna, where Walcari, Peredeo and Rotcari were abiding in camp. But these men rushing upon them, made a terrible slaughter of their troops, and compelled the others to take flight". Paulus then goes on to describe the revolt of Transamund, which happened "in these days".

This paragraph of Paulus is dateless, unchronological, and confused beyond even his usual manner. It will be seen that he makes Peredeo come to life again, and work havoc among the Romans after he has fallen fighting bravely with them. But with all its blemishes the paragraph is a most important addition to our knowledge. It shows us that Ravenna was actually captured by the Lombards in the reign of Liutprand, for if it had not been captured it could not have been "held by his nephew and Peredeo". And further we learn that the city thus lost to the Empire was really and truly recovered for it *by the Venetians*. As Paulus wrote in the latter part of the eighth century, when the Venetians were still but a feeble folk, clustering together at the mouths of the Adige and the Piave, we may receive his testimony as to this brilliant exploit on their part without any of that suspicion which must attach to the vaunts of the chroniclers of a later day, the patriotic sons of the glorious Queen of the Adriatic.

Venetia in the eight century

In speaking of the Venetians as performing this feat, we must remember that though the race might last on unchanged into the Middle Ages, their home did not so continue. The network of islands bordering the Grand Canal, on which now rise the Doge's Palace, the Church of S. Maria della Salute, and all the other buildings which make up the Venice of today, may have been but a cluster of desolate mud-banks when Liutprand reigned in Pavia. The chief seats of the Venetian people at the time with which we are dealing were to be found at Heraclea, Equilium, and Methamaucus. The first of these cities, which according to some authors was named after the Emperor Heraclius, was probably situated five miles from the sea, between the mouths of the Livenza and the Piave, but even its site is doubtful, for the waters of the marsh now flow over it.

Equilium, which was for centuries the rival of Heraclea, and was partly peopled by fugitives from Opitergium when Grimwald executed vengeance on that city, was about seven miles south of Heraclea and not far from Torcello. It too is now covered by the waters, partly the fresh water of the river Sile, partly the salt water of the Adriatic. All the long-lasting hatreds of these two neighbor towns sleep at last beneath the silent lagune.

As for Methamaucus, which was in the eighth century a considerable city, it is now represented only by the few houses erected on the long island of Malamocco. The

Venice of the Middle Ages built on the various islets which bore the name of Rivus Altus (Rialto) was not founded till nearly seventy years after the death of Liutprand.

Somewhere about the year 700 the inhabitants of the various islands which formed Venetia Maritima seem to have tightened the bonds of the loose confederacy which had hitherto bound them, and for the "tribunes" who had hitherto ruled, each one his own town or island, substituted a "duke", whose sway extended over the whole region of the lagunes, and who was the first of the long line of the Doges of Venice. We say that the Venetians did this, and reading the events of 700 by the light of eleven centuries of later history we involuntarily think of the Venetian people as the prime movers in this peaceful revolution, and we invest the first duke, *Paulitio Anafestus* with the bonnet and mantle of his well-known successors, the Dandolos and Foscaris of the Middle Ages. Yet we may be sure that the ruler of the *Ducatus Venetiae* was at this time a much more insignificant person than his successors of the eleventh and twelfth centuries; and we might perhaps admit into our minds a doubt whether he was anything else than an official selected for his post by the Emperor or the Exarch, and whether popular election had anything whatever to do with his appointment in those early days.

However this may be, the new office seems at first to have successfully accomplished the purpose for which it was created. Paulitio of Heraclea, the first duke, reigned for twenty years in peace. His fellow-townsman and successor, Marcellus (who seems to have held under him the important office of Master of the Soldiery), had also a peaceful reign of about nine years. But Ursus, also a citizen of Heraclea, who according to the accepted chronology ruled the Venetian state from 726 to 737, met with a violent death, the cause of which we can only conjecture, but which may possibly have been connected with the bitter disputes that seem to have been constantly occurring between the two neighbor cities of Heraclea and Equilium. It is clear, however, that there was something like a revolution in Venetia Maritima.

"The Venetians", says the chronicler, "who, moved by bitter envy, had slain Ursus, for the space of five years determined to remain subject only to Masters of the Soldiery The revolt evidently was against the authority of one man raised for life above the level of his fellow-citizens; and the revolution had for its object the substitution of yearly magistrates, whom, now at any rate, after the partial disruption of the bonds which united Italy to the Empire, we may speak of as elected by the people. For five years (737-741 according to Dandolo) the Masters of the Soldiery performed their brief functions: their names being Leo, Felix surnamed Cornicula, Deusdedit (son of the murdered Ursus), Jubianus (or Jovianus) surnamed Hypatus (the Consul), and Joannes Fabriacus. At the end of the year's Mastership of the last named (742?), his eyes were torn out, and "the Venetians, abominating the office of Master of the Soldiery, again as before created for themselves a duke in the island of Malamocco, namely Deusdedit, the son of the aforesaid Ursus Hypatus, and his reign lasted for thirteen years".

It has been necessary to give this glance at the obscure and intricate subject of primitive Venetian history in order to introduce the only other early authority besides Paulus who mentions the capture and recovery of Ravenna. This is Joannes Diaconus (formerly called Sagorninus), who wrote near the end of the tenth century, that is to say 250 years after the events of which we are now speaking, but whose testimony is for many reasons worthy of consideration. After describing the election of the fourth Master of the Soldiery, Jovianus Hypatus, he says :

"In his days the Exarch, the foremost man of Ravenna, came to Venetia and earnestly entreated the Venetians to give him their help to enable him to guard and defend his own city, which Hildeprand, nephew of King Liutprand, and Peredeo, duke of Vicenza, had captured. The Venetians, favoring his petition, hastened with a naval armament to the aforesaid city of Ravenna; whereupon one of them [the Lombard invaders], namely Hildeprand, was taken alive by them, but the other, named Peredeo, fell fighting bravely, and the city was thus handed over in good order to the aforesaid Exarch, its chief governor; on account of which thing Gregory also, the Apostolicus of the City of Rome, desiring with all his heart the succor of the said city, had written with his own hand a letter to Antoninus, Patriarch of Grado, telling him that he ought with loving entreaty to induce the Venetians to go to the defence of the same city :

"Gregory to his most beloved brother Antoninus :

"Since, as a punishment for our sins, the city of Ravenna, which was the head of all things, has been taken by the unspeakable nation of the Lombards, and our son the excellent Lord Exarch tarries, as we have heard, in Venetia, your brotherly Holiness ought to cleave unto him, and in our stead strive alongside of him, in order that the said city of Ravenna may be restored to its former *status* in the holy Republic and to the Imperial service of our lords and sons the great Emperors Leo and Constantine, that with zealous love to our holy faith we may by the Lord's help be enabled firmly to persevere in the *status* of the Republic and in the Imperial service.

"May God keep you in safety, most beloved brother"

So far Joannes Diaconus, whose narrative, as I have already said, is really the only information that we have, except the few meager sentences in Paulus, as to an immensely important event, the capture of Ravenna by the Lombards and its recovery by the Venetians. It is true that we have in the history of Andrea Dandolo a repetition of the same story, with slightly different circumstances. In that version the event takes place some ten years earlier, and the chief actors are not Gregory III and the Master of the Soldiery, Jovianus, but Gregory II and the Duke, Ursus. But Dandolo published his *Chronicon* in 1346, and though it is a noble work, invaluable for the history of Venice in her most glorious days, it must remain a matter of doubt whether for this earliest period he had any other trustworthy materials before him than those which three centuries and a half earlier were at the disposal of Joannes Diaconus. Referring the reader to a Note at the end of this chapter for a fuller discussion of this question, I will briefly summarize the results at which we have arrived with reference to the sieges of Ravenna by the Lombards in the eighth century.

Summary

Somewhere about the year 725, or perhaps earlier, Farwald II, duke of Spoleto, took the port of Classis, but at the command of Liutprand restored it to the Empire.

A little later Liutprand again took Classis and besieged Ravenna, but apparently failed to take it.

Towards the end of the fourth decade of the century, probably after 737, Liutprand's nephew and colleague, Hildeprand, with the assistance of Peredeo the brave duke of Vicenza, besieged Ravenna, and this time succeeded in taking it. The Exarch (who was probably Eutychius, but this is not expressly mentioned) took refuge in the Venetian islands, and sought the help of the dwellers by the lagunes to recover the lost city. Pope Gregory III added his exhortations, which he addressed to the Patriarch of Grado, the spiritual head of the Venetian state. A naval expedition was fitted out: Hildeprand was taken prisoner, his comrade Peredeo slain, and the city restored to the

Holy Roman Republic. This recapture took place, if we may depend on the somewhat doubtful Venetian chronology, in the year 740.

We now return to the main stream of Lombard history as disclosed to us by the Life of Pope Zacharias in the Liber Pontificalis.

In the year 742 Liutprand was at the zenith of his power, unquestioned lord of Spoleto and Benevento and on friendly terms with the Pope. He, however, or seemed to linger, over the fulfillment of his promise to restore the four frontier towns which he had taken, three years before, from the *Ducatus Romae*. Zacharias therefore determined to try the expedient of a personal interview, and set forth, attended by a large train of ecclesiastics, for the city of Interamna (Terni), where the king was then residing. It was necessary for the party to pass through Orte, one of the four cities for whose restoration he was clamouring, and there they were met by a Lombard courtier named Grimwald, whom Liutprand had courteously sent to act as the Pope's escort. Under Grimwald's guidance they reached the city of Narni, with its high Augustan bridge; and here they were met by a brilliant train of nobles and soldiers, who accompanied them along the eight miles of road up the valley of the Nar to where Terni stands in the fertile plain and listens to the roar of her waterfalls. It was on a Friday that they thus in solemn procession entered the city where Liutprand held his court, and were met by the king himself and the rest of his courtiers at the church of the martyred bishop Valentinus. Mutual salutations passed, prayers were offered, the two potentates came forth from the church together, and then the King walked in lowly reverence beside the Pope for half a mile, till they reached the place outside the city where the tents were pitched for both host and guest. And there they abode for the rest of the day.

On Saturday there was again a solemn interview. Zacharias delivered a long address to the Lombard king, exhorting him to abstain from the shedding of blood and to follow those things which make for peace. Touched, as the ecclesiastics believed, by the eloquence of their chief, Liutprand granted all and even more than all that was asked for. The four cities and their inhabitants were given back, but not, if we may believe the biographer, to Leo and Constantine the Emperors, but to the holy man, Zacharias, himself. Large slices of the Papal patrimony which had been lost in the earlier and troublous times were now restored. One such slice, in the Sabine territory, had been withheld from the Papacy for near thirty years. The others were at Narni and Osimo, at Ancona and the neighboring Humana, and the valley which was called Magna, in the territory of Sutrium. All these possessions were solemnly made over by Liutprand to "Peter prince of the Apostles", and a peace for twenty years was concluded with the *Ducatus Romae*. There were many captives whom Liutprand had taken from divers provinces of the Romans and who were now detained in the fortresses of Tuscany or the region beyond the Po. Letters were sent by the king ordering that all these should be set free. Among these liberated captives were certain magnates of Ravenna, Leo, Sergius, Victor, and Agnellus. All apparently bore the title of Consul, and Sergius was possibly the same who was afterwards Archbishop of Ravenna.

This last statement certainly seems to confirm the theory that the capture of Ravenna by the Lombards had taken place not many years before the treaty of Terni. Is it not probable that the illustrious prisoner on the other side who had been captured at the reconquest of the city, Hildeprand the king's nephew and colleague, was restored at the same time, and that the possession by the enemy of so important a hostage had something to do with the wonderfully yielding-temper of Liutprand? Such is the very reasonable suggestion made by an eminent Italian scholar, but it should not be regarded as anything more than a conjecture.

On Sunday there was a great ecclesiastical function in the church of St. Valentinus. At the request of the King, the Pope ordained a bishop for a town in the Lombard territory .The King with all his dukes and *gastalds* witnessed the rite of consecration, and were so much moved by the sweetness of the Pope's sermon and the earnestness of his prayers that most of them were melted into tears. Then when mass was ended the Pope invited the King to dinner. The meats were so good, the mirth of the company so genuine and unforced, that, as the King said, he did not remember that he had ever eaten so much and so pleasantly.

On Monday the two great personages took leave of one another, and the King chose out four of his nobles to accompany the Pope on his return journey and hand over to him the keys of the surrendered towns. They were his nephew Agiprand duke of Clusium, a *gastald* in immediate attendance on his person, named Tacipert, Ranning, *gastald* of Toscanella, a frontier town of the Lombards, and Grimwald, who had been the first to meet the Pope by the bridge of Narni. All was done as had been arranged. Amelia, Orte, Bomarzo, with their citizens, were handed over to the Pope's jurisdiction. In order to avoid the long and circuitous route by Sutri, the combined party struck across the Lombard territory by way of Viterbo (here the presence of the *gastald* of Toscanella was important for their protection), and so they reached the little town of Bieda thirty miles from Rome, which Grimwald and Banning formally transferred to the keeping of Zacharias.

The Pope returned to Rome as a conqueror, and the people at his suggestion marched from the Pantheon to St Peter's singing the Litany. This expression of gratitude to Almighty God took the place of the old triumphal march of Consul or Imperator along the Sacred Way and up the Clivus Capitolinus.

In what capacity were these cities given to the Pope? Was he recognized as their sovereign, or as their proprietor? Were they still as absolutely part of the Empire as they were before Alboin entered Italy, although belonging to the Patrimony of St. Peter? or were they the germ of that new Papal kingdom which certainly was on the point of coming into existence? It is easy to suggest these questions, hard to answer them, especially for such a troublous time as that of the Iconoclastic controversy, when *de jure* and *de facto* were everywhere coming into collision. One can only say that the words of the Papal biographer, if he may be depended upon, seem to imply sovereignty as well as ownership.

The events just related seem to have filled the page of Lombard history for 742. In the following year Liutprand resumed his preparations for the conquest of Ravenna and the region round it. Terribly indeed had this little fragment of the Roman Empire in the north of Italy now shrunk and dwindled. Cesena, only twenty-five miles south of Ravenna, had become by the loss of the Pentapolis a frontier city, and even Cesena now fell into the hands of the Lombards. Eutychius the Exarch, John the Archbishop, and all the people of Ravenna, with the refugees from the Pentapolis and from the province of Aemilia, sent letters to the Pope imploring his assistance. Thereupon Zacharias by the hands of Benedict bishop of Nomentum and Ambrose chief of the notaries, sent gifts and letters to Liutprand, entreating him to abandon his preparations for the siege and to restore Cesena to the men of Ravenna. The embassy however returned, having accomplished nothing, and thereupon Zacharias determined once more to try the effect of a personal interview.

Handing over the government of Rome to Stephen, duke and patrician, he set forth along the great Flaminian Way to visit the theatre of war. At the church of St. Christopher, in a place called Aquila, the Exarch met him. All the inhabitants of Ravenna, men and women, old and young, poured forth to greet the revered pontiff, crying out with tears, "Welcome to our Shepherd who has left his own sheep and has come to rescue us who were ready to perish".

Zacharias sent his messengers (again the chief notary Ambrose, who was accompanied by the presbyter Stephen) to announce his approach to the king. When they crossed the Lombard frontier at Imola they learned that some forcible resistance would be attempted to the Pontiff's journey. He received a letter from them to this effect, conveyed by a trusty messenger under cover of the night, but undismayed he determined to press on after his messengers, whom, as he rightly conjectured, Liutprand would refuse to receive. On the 28th of June he came to the place near Piacenza where the Via Aemilia crosses the Po. Here the nobles as before met him and conducted him to Pavia. Outside the walls was a church of St. Peter named the Golden-ceilinged (*ad coelum aureum*), and here Zacharias celebrated Mass at 3 P.M. before he entered the city.

The following day, the 29th of June, was that on which the Church had long celebrated the martyrdom of St. Peter and St. Paul, and Zacharias had no doubt had this in view when he so timed his journey that his interview with the king should take place on that day. Again a Mass was celebrated with great magnificence in St. Peter's basilica in the presence of the King. Then mutual salutations were exchanged; and they entered the city together. Next day there was a formal invitation to the Pope brought by the chief nobles of the kingdom, and then a solemn meeting in the royal palace. The Pope earnestly entreated the King to desist from his further enterprises against the city of Ravenna and to restore the conquests already made. For some time Liutprand showed himself obdurate, but at length he consented to restore the country districts round Ravenna of which he had made himself master, and along with them two-thirds of the territory of Cesena. The remaining third, and perhaps the city of Cesena itself, were to remain in Liutprand's hands as a pledge till the 1st of June in the following year, by which time it was hoped that an embassy which he had dispatched to Constantinople would have returned with a favorable answer.

On the Pope's departure, Liutprand accompanied him as far as the Po, and sent with him certain dukes and other nobles, some of whom were charged to superintend the surrender of the territories of Cesena and Ravenna. "Thus", says the biographer, "by the help of God the people of Ravenna and the Pentapolis were delivered from the calamities and oppressions which had befallen them, and they were satisfied with corn and wine".

The interview with the Pope at Pavia was one of the last public acts of the great Lombard king. In January, 744, after a reign of thirty-one years and seven months, Liutprand died, and was buried by the side of his father in the church of St. Adrian. He was elderly, probably more than sixty years old, but not stricken in years. Had his wise and statesmanlike reign been prolonged for ten years more, Italy had perhaps been spared some disasters.

We read with regret the song of triumph which the Papal biographer raises over the death of "the intriguer and persecutor Liutprand". His own recital shows how utterly inapplicable are these words to the son of Ansprand. He had in fact carried compliance with the Papal admonitions to the very verge of weakness and disloyalty to his people.

There was evidently in him a vein of genuine piety of sympathy with men of holy life, illustrated by the fact that when the Saracens invaded Sardinia and profaned the resting place of St. Augustine, Liutprand sent messengers who at a great price redeemed the body of the saint and transported it to Pavia, where it still reposes.

In some respects the statesmanship of Liutprand seems to me to have been too highly praised. I do not find in the meager and disjointed annals of his reign which I have with great difficulty tried to weave into a continuous narrative, the evidence of any such carefully thought-out plan with reference to the Iconoclastic controversy as is often attributed to him. To say that he presented himself as the champion of the Image-worshippers, and in some sort, of the independence of Italy, as against the tyranny of the Iconoclastic Emperors, seems to me to be making an assertion which we cannot prove. The one aim, as I have before said, which he seems to have consistently and successfully pursued was the consolidation of the Lombard monarchy and the reduction of the great dukes into a condition of real subjection to his crown. He availed himself (and what Lombard king would not have done so?) of any opportunity which offered itself for cutting yet shorter the reduced and fragmentary territories which still called themselves parts of "the Roman Republic". But both from policy and from his own devout temperament he was disinclined to do anything which might cause a rupture with the See of Rome, and the Popes perceiving this, often induced him to abandon hardly-earned conquests by appealing to "his devotion to St. Peter".

I cannot better close this chapter than by quoting the character of Liutprand given us by the loving yet faithful hand of Paulus Diaconus in the concluding words of that history which has been our chief guide through two dark and troubled centuries :— "He was a man of great wisdom, prudent in counsel and a lover of peace, mighty in war, clement towards offenders, chaste, modest, one who prayed through the night-watches, generous in his almsgiving, ignorant it is true of literature, but a man who might be compared to the philosophers, a fosterer of his people, an augmenter of their laws.

"In the beginning of his reign he took many places from the Bavarians, ever trusting to his prayers rather than to his arms, and with the most jealous care maintaining peaceful relations with the Franks and the Avars".

CHAPTER XIII.

POLITICAL STATE OF IMPERIAL ITALY.

Now that we have reached the end of the dominion of the Eastern Caesars over all but a few detached fragments of Italy, and that we are also close upon the end of the dominion of the Lombard kings in the same country, it will be well for us to gather up such fragments of information as the scanty records of the time supply to us concerning the political institutions and social condition of the peninsula during the two centuries of their blended and conflicting rule.

The records, as I have said, are scanty, and the indications which they furnish are faint and difficult to decipher; but they have been scanned with eager scrutiny by great jurists and eminent historians, because in them lies, in part at least, the answer to one of the most interesting questions which were ever presented for solution to a political philosopher. That question is as to the origin and parentage of the great Italian Republics of the Middle Ages.

When we think of the rich and varied life displayed by the commonwealths of Italy from the twelfth to the fifteenth century, of the foreign conquests of one, the worldwide commerce of another, the noble architecture of a third, the wealth of artistic and poetic genius which seemed to be the common heritage of them all, and when we remember that in the earlier period of their history these great gifts of the intellect were allied to not less noble qualities of the soul, fortitude, self-devotion, faith, we are ready to say, perhaps with truth, that never has the human race worked out the problem of self-government in nobler forms than in these glorious republics, greater than the Athens of Pericles by reason of their spiritual capacities, greater than the Rome of the Scipios by reason of their artistic culture. We know, indeed, how soon that splendid dawn was overcast, how rapidly and how fatally the Italy of the *Communi* degenerated into the Italy of the Tyrants. Still the enquiry must ever be one of deepest interest to every student not merely of Italian, but of European history—Whence did the cities of Italy derive those thoughts of freedom which made them for a time the torch-bearers of human progress in the midst of the anarchy and darkness of feudalism?

One school of learned and able enquirers says that this torch was kindled from Rome, not the Rome of the Emperors, but the far-away, yet unforgotten, Rome of the Republic. Another school, equally learned and equally able, denies that there was any possibility of continuous historic development from Rome to Florence and Siena, and maintains that the republican institutions of Italy in the twelfth century were either absolutely self-originated or were the result of contact with Teutonic freedom. I cannot promise the reader that we shall be able to come to any definite solution of this great controversy, much of which of course lies centuries beyond our horizon; but he will at least understand how great the controversy is, and how it lends importance to questions at first sight paltry and pedantic, as to the names and functions of the governing authorities of Italy during these centuries of transition.

Though profoundly unfortunate for the country itself both then and in many after-ages, the division of Italy into two sections, one of which still formed part of the Roman Empire, while the other, under the sway of Lombard kings or dukes, was generally hostile to the Empire, and always independent of it, aids the scientific discussion of the problem before us. The actual course of events enables us to eliminate in great measure the barbarian factor from the former section, and to trace the history of Roman institutions by themselves, where no Teutonic element enters into the equation. In this chapter, therefore, we will deal with the questions of government, law, and social relations as affecting Imperial Italy alone.

Let us briefly recapitulate the facts as to the geographical boundaries of the Imperial territory, which it will be remembered was almost exclusively a sea-coast dominion. Starting from the north-east, we find the Istrian peninsula undoubtedly Imperial. But when we reach the head of the Adriatic Gulf, the ancient capital of Aquileia with its Patriarch is under Lombard rule, while the little island city of Grado, in which the rival Patriarch has set up his throne, still clings to the Empire. From the mouth of the Tagliamento to that of the Adige a long strip of the coast is for some time retained by the Emperors, and probably bears the name of *Ducatus Venetiae.* But in the earliest years of the seventh century Patavium and Mons Silicis (Padua and Monselice) were won for the Lombards by King Agilulf: soon afterwards Concordia fell into their power, and when in 640 Opitergium and Altinum were taken by King Rothari, the Eastern Caesar can have had few subjects left in this part of the country, except the indomitable islanders, who between sea and sky were founding upon the lagunes that cluster of settlements which was known by the name of Venetia Maritima.

The mouths of the Po, the city of Ravenna, and a great stretch of the Via Aemilia, with "hinterland" reaching up to the skirts of the Apennines, formed the large and important district known as the *Exarchatus Ravennae.* Further inland, Mantua, Cremona, Piacenza, and a few cities on the southern bank of the Po remained for a generation subject to the Empire, but were detached from it in the earliest years of the seventh century by King Agilulf, rightly incensed by the Exarch's kidnapping of his daughter. We travel down the shore of the Adriatic and come to the Duchy of the *Pentapolis,* consisting of the five flourishing maritime cities of Ariminum, Pisaurum, Fanum, Senegallia, and Ancona. Another inland Pentapolis, called *Annonaria* or *Provincia Castellorum,* included the cities of Aesis, Forum Sempronii, Urbinum, Callis, and Eugubium (Jesi, Fossombrone, Urbino, Cagli, and Gubbio). These two provinces together sometimes went by the conjoint name of Decapolis. A long stretch of coast, ill-supplied with harbors and therefore not belonging to the Empire, marked the spacious territory abandoned to the Lombards, and ruled by the dukes of Spoleto and Benevento.

Then rounding the promontory of Mount Garganus, we come to the town of Sipontum, which was Imperial till near the middle of the seventh century and then to the heel of Italy, from the river Aufidus to the Bradanus, comprising the seaport towns of Barium, Brundusium, Hydruntum, and Tarentum (Bari, Brindisi, Otranto, and Taranto). All of this region was Imperial land till Romwald of Benevento (between 665 and 675) rent the greater part of it from the Empire, leaving to the Caesar little besides the city of Otranto, which, though once for a moment captured by the Lombards, remained permanently Imperial, and was at a later period the base of important operations by the Greeks for the reconquest of Southern Italy. As the "heel", so also the "toe" of Italy, from the river Crathis to the Straits of Messina, remained during the whole of our period in the possession of the Empire. So, too, did the important island of Sicily, full of Papal "patrimonies", and forming a stronghold of Imperial power. Though harassed more than once by the invasions of the Saracens, it was not till the ninth century that they seriously set about the subjugation of the island : and in fact for half a century after the fall of Ravenna, the "Patrician of Sicily" was the highest representative of the Emperor in the western lands, the duke of Naples himself being subject to his orders.

Proceeding northwards along the shore of the Tyrrhenian Sea, we find in the ancient province of Lucania only Acropolis, and perhaps its near neighbor Paestum, left to the Empire. Entering Campania, we discover that the *duke of Naples* ruled over a small though wealthy territory, reaching from Salernum at one end to a point due west of Capua (itself a Lombard city) on the other. But the duchy reached very little way inland, and we might probably say with safety that from every part of the region which he ruled, the duke of Naples could behold the crater of Vesuvius.

Of much wider extent was the *Ducatus Romae,* which reached from Gaeta on the south-east to Civita Vecchia on the north-west, including practically the whole of the ancient province of Latium, a corner of the Sabine territory, and the southern end of Etruria. The changes of fortune that befell the Tuscan and Umbrian cities, by which Rome and Ravenna sought to keep up their communications with one another along the Flaminian Way, the cities of Todi, Perugia and Tadino, have been sufficiently described in earlier chapters.

Lastly, the beautiful Riviera (*di Ponente* as well as *di Levante*),from the river Magra to Mentone, remained a province of the Empire until about 640, when King Rothari the legislator took Genoa and all her sister cities, razed their walls (like Gaiseric the Vandal), and turned the region into the Lombard duchy of Liguria.

Of the islands of Sardinia and Corsica little is known during this period save that their fortunes were not closely interwoven with those of Italy. As they had once been subject to the Vandal kings of Carthage, so now, though restored to the Empire, they were still ruled by the Exarch of Africa. The invasions of these islands by the Lombards, of which we heard in the letters of Pope Gregory the Great, do not seem to have resulted in any abiding settlement. When the Emperor Constans was ruling or misruling Sicily, Sardinia was one of the districts which felt the heavy hand of his tax-gatherers and soldiers coming from Sardinia as well as from Africa and Imperial Italy deprived his successor, the usurper Mizizius, of his throne and life. In the eighth century Sardinia as well as Corsica suffered grievously from the incursions of the Saracens, though it does not appear that these invaders succeeded in formally detaching those islands from the Empire.

From these outlying dependencies we return to the contemplation of Imperial Italy, that we may enquire into the nature of the political organization by which the

Emperors dwelling in distant Constantinople maintained their hold upon the maritime regions of the peninsula. To begin at the very beginning of our present period, let us listen to the words in which the Emperor Justinian reasserts his dominion over the recovered land. In August, 554, the year after the death of Teias, the year of the final defeat of the Alamannic brethren, Justinian issued a solemn *Pragmatic Sanction* for the government of Italy. This decree, singularly enough, purports to be issued in reply to the petition of Pope Vigilius "the venerable bishop of the elder Rome", though that much-harassed pontiff had certainly left Constantinople, and most probably had died before its promulgation. The Emperor first solemnly confirms all dispositions which have been made by Athalaric, or his royal mother Amalasuntha, or even Theodahad, as well as all his own acts, and those of his spouse Theodora of pious memory. Everything, on the other hand, done by "the most wicked tyrant Totila" is to be considered absolutely null and void, "for we will not allow these law-abiding days of ours to take any account of what was done by him in the time of his tyranny".

Many laws follow (which seem to be well and wisely framed) as to the length of prescription requisite to establish a claim after "the years of warlike confusion which followed the accession of the tyrants". There is also an evident attempt made to lighten the burden of taxation, and so to guard against any future oppressions by men like Alexander the Scissors, which might goad the provincials to madness. Especially it is ordained that the tribute due from each province shall be exacted by the governors of that province only, and that the great Imperial ministers at headquarters shall not assist in the process. Some precautions are taken for lightening the burden of *coemtio*. Each province is only to be called upon to furnish tribute in kind out of that sort of produce which naturally grows there, and such tribute when rendered is to be taken at the current market price of the day. Moreover, the landowners of Calabria and Apulia, who have already commuted their *coemtio* into a money payment *[superindictitius tituliis)*, are not to be called on to pay that *titulus* and provide *coemtio* as well. And any senator or large tax-payer is to have free leave and license to visit the court at Constantinople in order to lay his grievances before the Emperor, as well as to return to Italy and tarry there as long as he will for the improvement of his estate, since it is difficult for absent owners to keep their property in good condition, or to bestow upon it the cultivation which it requires.

The two most important sections of the decree, however, in reference to our present subject are the 33rd and the 12th.

The 33rd runs as follows : "We order that all law-suits between two Romans, or in which one Roman person is concerned, shall be tried by *civil* judges, since good order does not permit that military judges shall mix themselves up in such matters or causes".

A "Roman person" is evidently a native of Italy in contradistinction to the horde of foreigners who served in the armies of the Empire. The intention of the legislator is that wheresoever the rights of such a Roman person are concerned, whether as plaintiff or defendant, his cause shall be heard before a civil judge, probably the *praeses* of the province, and not before the harsh and unsympathetic officer of the army, who, however, is recognized as the right person to try matters in dispute between one "military person" and another.

Sect, 12 relates to the mode of appointing these civil governors or *judices provinciarum* : "More over we order that fit and proper persons, able to administer the local government, be chosen as governors *(judices)* of the provinces by the *bishops and chief persons of each province from the inhabitants of the province itself*". This appointment is to be made without any payment for votes; and the letters patent of the office *(codicilli)* are to be handed to the new governor by the minister whose business it is *[per competentem judicem)* [free of charge]. On these conditions, however, that if they (the *judices provinciarum)* shall be found to have inflicted any injury on the taxpayers, or to have exacted anything in excess of the stipulated tribute, or in the *coemption* to have used too large measures, or unjust weights for the solidi, or in any other way to have unrighteously damnified the cultivators, they shall make good the injury out of their own property.

We see here an earnest endeavor to remedy the abuses of provincial administration. The governor of the province is to be a resident therein. This makes it less likely that he will incur the odium of oppressive acts, committed in a district of which he is a native, and where he will spend the remainder of his days. He is to be appointed without *suffragium,* the technical term for the payments, often of enormous amount, which had been hitherto made to the members of the Imperial household and the great functionaries of Constantinople, in order to secure their influence on behalf of the aspirant to office. Of course, where this *suffragium* had been paid, the new governor's first care was to recoup himself by wringing it out of the miserable provincials. But further, the governor is to be elected by the principal inhabitants of the province, instead of being merely nominated by the autocratic Emperor. We have here an important recognition of the principle of popular election, a great stride towards what we should call constitutional government. And a part, apparently a leading part in this election, is given to the bishop of the province. Here we have both a proof of the increased power of the higher ecclesiastics (since even the devout Theodosius would never have dreamed of admitting his bishops to a direct share in the government of the Empire), and we have also a pathetic confession of the Emperor's own inability to cope with the corruption and venality of his civil servants. He seems to have perceived that in the great quaking bog of servility and dishonesty by which he felt himself to be surrounded, his only sure standing-ground was to be found in the spiritual Estate, the order of men who wielded a power not of this world, and who, if true to their sacred mission, had nothing to fear and little to hope from the corrupt minions of the court.

The experiment of popular election of the provincial governors answered so well in Italy, that it was extended by Justinian's successor in 569 to the Eastern portion of the Empire. But as we shall soon see, it was but short-lived in either the East or the West.

Before we part from Justinian's Pragmatic Sanction we must notice one more section, the 19th, which deals with the subject of Weights and Measures: "In order", says the legislator, "that no occasion for fraud or injury to the provinces [of Italy] may arise, we decree that produce be furnished and money received according to those weights and measures which our Piety hath by these presents entrusted to the keeping of the most blessed Pope and the most ample Senate". Another indication this, of the purely secular business which, by reason of the general respect for his character and confidence in his uprightness, was being pushed off upon the Head of the Church by the Head of the State; and at the same time an interesting evidence that after all its sufferings at the hands of Totila and Teias, the Senate of Rome still lived on, if it were only to act as custodian of the standard yard and the standard pound.

The edict, which is addressed to the Illustrious Grand Chamberlain Narses, and to the Magnificent Antiochus, Prefect of Italy, ends thus: "All things therefore which our Eternity hath ordained by this divine Pragmatic Sanction, let your Greatness by all means carry into effect and cause to be observed, a penalty of 10 lbs of gold impending over all violators of these our commands". On the whole, the Pragmatic Sanction, notwithstanding its tone of ill-tempered railing at the defeated heroes of the Gothic nation, was a wise and statesmanlike measure; and I, who have in an earlier volume been compelled to say many hard things concerning the character and administration of Justinian, gladly recognize that here, in the evening of his days, he makes a generous effort to lighten the burdens of his Italian subjects, and to admit them to a share in his power. But "in the clash of arms laws are silent". Even as Pitt's well-meant scheme for Parliamentary Reform foundered in the stormy waters of the great French Revolutionary War, so the perils with which the Empire was soon surrounded, from Lombards in the West, from Avars, Persians, Saracens in the East, destroyed the faint hopes of freedom in the Roman Empire of the sixth and seventh centuries. It is at all times difficult for even the most enlightened despot to unclothe himself of the power with which in the course of generations the holders of his office have come to be invested, and in the face of menacing foreign foes that which was before difficult becomes impossible. We who have lived through the middle of the nineteenth century know what those ominous words "The city is proclaimed in a state of siege" betoken, how when they are uttered popular liberties are suppressed and all classes lie prostrate under the heel of a military despotism. We remember how even in the greatest democratic republic that the world has ever seen, "the War-Power" enabled President Lincoln practically to assume the position of an autocrat, wise and patriotic doubtless, but still an autocrat. And so, in the Empire, the tremendous dangers to which it was exposed, from the time of Justin II to the time of the Iconoclastic Emperors, led to the concentration of all power, civil and military, in the hands of one class of men who were virtually the military lieutenants of the Emperor. In the East, this tendency found its fullest expression in the change of the provinces into *themes,* which was begun by Heraclius and completed by Leo III. The word *theme* meant a regiment of soldiers, and thenceforward the military district or theme became the chief administrative unit of the Empire.

In Italy there was perhaps no such sudden and definite change, but all writers are agreed that there was a change, the result of which was to annul the division between civil and military functions which had been created by Diocletian and Constantine and to make the commandant of the garrison in each city which remained faithful to the Empire the one great centre of power, judicial and administrative, as well as military, for that city and for the district of which it was the capital.

This change however, as I have said, was probably a gradual one, and with the poverty of the materials before us we cannot precisely say when it began or when it ended. To make the further discussion of the subject clearer, it will be well to subjoin a table of the military and civil officers, as far as they can be ascertained, before this change had taken place which led to the practical absorption of the latter by the former.

MILITARY.	CIVIL.
EXARCH (Patricius Italiae).	Praefectus Italiae . . . Praefectus Urbi (or Praepositus Italiae).
Magister Militum or Dux.	Vicarius Italiae . . . Vicarius Urbis.
Tribunus or Comes.	Praeses Provinciae.

The hierarchy of civil offices, it will be seen, was still cast in the mould which was made at the beginning of the fourth century. So long as they retained any official vitality at all we must suppose the holders of them to have been concerned with the trying of causes in which private citizens of Italian birth (as opposed to military men and foreign followers of the camp) were concerned; with the collection of revenue; with commissariat business; and perhaps with the maintenance of roads and aqueducts. But already, in the time of Gregory the Great, the position of these civil rulers was declining in power and luster, so that we find the benevolent Pope compassionately relieving the necessities of an ex-governor of Samnium by a yearly pension of four solidi, and a gift of twenty *decimati* of wine. The slenderness of our information does not enable us to say definitely when this civil hierarchy finally vanished from the scene, but, to use the simile of a "dissolving view", we may conjecture that all through the seventh century their names were growing fainter and fainter, and those of the military rulers were growing stronger and stronger on the screen of Italian politics

The Exarch.

I turn then from these shadowy survivals of a great organization to direct the reader0s attention to the other half of the table of dignities, the military rulers who were more and more assuming all the functions of government to themselves, as the delegated servants of the Emperor.

High over all, and practically supreme over Imperial Italy was "the Most Excellent EXARCH". We shall probably get a good idea of his position by comparing him to the Governor-General of India, only that we must add to the civil functions of that high officer the military functions involved in the absolute personal command of the army. He seems to have uniformly borne the title of *Patricius* added to that of *Exarchus,* and he not unfrequently held high rank in the Imperial household, as *Cubicularius* (Grand Chamberlain) or *Cartularius* (Keeper of the Records). He was supreme judge in Italy; he made peace and war on his own responsibility, apparently without the necessity of consulting the Emperor; he nominated all the military officers below him, the dukes and tribunes and the like; perhaps also the civil governors, the prefects and the vicars, though of this there does not appear to be any direct proof. After the middle of the seventh century he was, what the Prefect had been till then, the supreme head of the financial department of the state. This ruler, whose exalted power gave effect to the will of the Pious Emperor was approached with servile prostrations by the subjects of his delegated reign. At Ravenna he dwelt doubtless in the palace of the great Theodoric. When he visited Rome, clergy, magistrates, soldiers, all the civic militia of Rome poured forth to meet him with their crosses and their standards, and led him with jubilations up to the Palatine Hill, where still in faded magnificence rose the cluster of buildings which has given its name to every other palace in the world.

Not the least important, assuredly, of the prerogatives of the Exarch, was the right transferred to him by his Imperial master of confirming the election of the Pope by the clergy and people of Rome. But notwithstanding this prerogative, and although in a certain sense the Bishop of Rome, as the Emperor's subject, might be held to be under the rule of the Imperial vicegerent, there can be little doubt that, at least from the time of Gregory the Great, the Pope, if he were a man of at all commanding personality, was, and was felt to be, a greater man in Italy than the Exarch. The Exarch was a foreigner, the minion of a court, sometimes holding office for no very long period, recalled and reappointed at the Emperor's pleasure. The Pope was an Italian, often a Roman citizen, speaking the noble old language of statesmanship and war: he alone could awe turbulent Lombard kings and dukes into reverent submission; round him gathered with increasing fervor, as the seventh and eighth centuries rolled on their course, not only the religious reverence, but the national spirit, the patriotic pride of the Roman people.

I shall briefly discuss the difficult subject of the origin of the Exarch's title, and then review the history of the men who bore it.

The Greek word Exarchus seems to have come into use in the days of Justinian, if not before, to denote a military officer of a very high rank and it may perhaps be looked upon as corresponding to our word "marshal". It is apparently in this sense only that the term is applied by Theophanes to Narses, whom he calls "Exarch of the Romans". For the persistent non-user of the term Exarch in connection with Narses by all contemporary writers seems clearly to show that he was not in his lifetime called the Exarch of Italy.

Neither, as far as we can discover, did *Longinus*, who ruled Imperial Italy from 567 to 585 and whose feebleness seems to have had much to do with facilitating the conquest of the Lombards, ever bear the title of Exarch. In fact, he is expressly called *Prefect of Ravenna* by Paulus, for which we may doubtless substitute *Prefect of Italy* as his true title. He was therefore, strictly speaking, only a great civil functionary, with no military command, and this may have been one reason for his failure to cope with the dire necessities of his position.

His successor *Smaragdus* twice held supreme power at Ravenna, his first tenure of office being probably from 585 to 589. And here we do at last get a contemporary use of the title Exarch. In a letter of Pope Pelagius II to his *apocrisiarius* Gregory at Constantinople, bearing date October 4, 584, we have a sentence saying that "*the Exarch* writes he can give us no help, for he is hardly able even to guard his own district". Here then we have the great military governors, who bore the title of Exarch for 170 years, fairly installed in the palace of Ravenna. It may be a question indeed whether Smaragdus was the first who bore that title. JM. Diehl suggests that *Baduarius*, the son-in-law of the Emperor Justin II, who came in 575 with a great army to Italy, and was defeated by the Lombards, may have been the first of the Exarchs, but we have no contemporary evidence of the fact, and the theory is at best but a plausible hypothesis.

Smaragdus, as the reader may remember, after his highhanded proceedings towards the Istrian schismatics, became insane, and was recalled by his Imperial master, who appointed Romanus Exarch in his stead.

Romanus, who ruled probably from 589 to 597, was a perpetual thorn in the side of Pope Gregory; unable, according to that Pope's representations, to defend him from the Lombards, and unwilling to make with the invaders a fair and honorable peace. Probably the fact was that now for the first time, with such a Pontiff as Gregory sitting in St. Peter's chair, the Exarch began to feel how completely he was overshadowed by the Bishop of Rome, and showed too manifestly to all men his ill-temper and his discontent at the anomalous situation in which he found himself placed.

On the death of Romanus (596 or 597) *Callinicus* (or, as Paulus calls him, *Gallicinus)* was appointed to the vacant post, which he held till about the year 602. Though he was more acceptable to the Pope than his predecessor, his dastardly abduction of the daughter of Agilulf, the signal punishment which the injured father inflicted on him, and the damage thereby done to the Imperial cause in Italy, marked his tenure of the high office of the Exarchate with dishonor.

Smaragdus (602-611), a second time Exarch of Italy, seems to have risen with the rise of the usurper Phocas, and fallen with his fall. It was evidently an especial delight to him to grovel before that base and truculent usurper; since besides the well-known statue and column in the Roman forum, he erected another statue to Phocas at Carthage.

Joannes (611-616), after an uneventful rule of five or six years, perished, apparently in a popular tumult.

Eleutherius, an eunuch (616-620), punished the murderers of his predecessor, suppressed the rebellionof Joannes Compsinus at Naples, visited Rome, himself tried to grasp the Imperial diadem, and was slain by his own mutinous soldiers at Luceoli.

Into one of these periods we possibly ought to interpolate the Exarchate of *Gregory,* "patricius Romanorum", who, as we learn from Paulus foully murdered the two sons of Gisulf, duke of Friuli, after luring them into the city of Opitergium by a promise to adopt the elder of them, Taso, as his "son in arms".

We have also to speak with great uncertainty of the tenure of office of *Eusebius,* who may not have been an Exarch at all, but an ambassador of the Emperor, but who in some strange way fascinated the young Lombard king Adalwald to his ruin. After this interval of uncertainty we come to *Isaac,* "the great ornament of Armenia", and the husband of "that chaste turtle-dove Susanna". His rule, which lasted probably from 625 to 644, was chiefly marked by the loss of the Riviera to the Lombards under Rothari.

Of the Exarchs who immediately followed Isaac, as before remarked we know extremely little. *Theodore Calliopas* may have ruled for the first time from 644 to 646.

Plato (646-649), a Monothelete, induced the Patriarch Pyrrhus to break with the Pope and return to Monotheletism.

Olympius (649-652), Grand Chamberlain, was employed by the Emperor Constans II in his first abortive attempt to arrest Pope Martin, desisted therefrom, was reconciled to the Pope, led his army to fight against the Saracens in Sicily, and died there, probably of camp fever.

Theodore Calliopas, sent a second time as Exarch to Ravenna (653-664), signalized his rule by the forcible arrest of Pope Martin.

Gregory, whose tenure of office perhaps extended from 664 to 677 is apparently only known by the occurrence of his name in the "Privilegium" of Constans II, given in 666 to Maurus, archbishop of Ravenna, confirming his independence of the See of Rome. In this Privilegium *Gregorius Exarchus noster* is mentioned as suggesting the issue of such a document, and is ordered to assist in giving effect to its provisions.

Another *Theodore* (probably different from Theodore Calliopas) dwelt in the palace at Ravenna from about 677 to 687. The monastery which he built near his palace, his receipt of the news of the election of Pope Conon, the three golden cups which he presented to the church of Ravenna, and the part which he took in the quarrel between his namesake Archbishop Theodore and his clergy, are all recorded in the pages of Agnellus.

Joannes, surnamed *Platyn* (687-702), contemporary with Pope Sergius (687-701), being appealed to in connection with the disputed Papal election of 687, appeared suddenly in Rome with his soldiers. He acquiesced in the election of Sergius, but insisted on taking toll of the Church to the amount of 100 lbs. of gold.

Theophylact (702-709), contemporary with Pope John VI (701-705), returning from Sicily to Rome, was assailed by the mutinous "soldiers of Italy", and hardly escaped through the Pope's intervention. I am not sure that we ought not to recognize in *Theodore,* "the patrician" and "primicerius" of the army of Sicily, an Exarch of

Ravenna. To him was entrusted the command of the expedition of vengeance directed by Justinian II against the city of Ravenna in 709.

Joannes, surnamed *Rizocopus,* about 710 met Pope Constantine at Naples, on his way to Constantinople; himself proceeded to Rome, put four eminent ecclesiastics to death, and, returning to Ravenna, died there shortly after "by a most disgraceful death, the just judgment of God on his wicked deeds".

Scholasticus (713-726), Grand Chamberlain and Exarch, transmitted to Pope Constantine, probably in 713, the letters of the shadow-Emperor Anastasius, in which he assured the Pope of his perfect orthodoxy.

Paulus (726-727) was sent by Leo III to enforce the iconoclastic edicts in Italy, and to arrest Pope Gregory II. He was prevented by the joint efforts of Romans and Lombards from executing the second part of this order, and was killed in an insurrection by the citizens of Ravenna.

Eutychius (727-752), the last Exarch of whom we have any mention, has figured both as a confederate with Liutprand, and as his antagonist, in the preceding history. He may have been still ruling when Ravenna fell before the assault of Aistulf, but of this we have no certain knowledge.

This brief summary of the deeds of the Exarchs is derived, we must remember, chiefly from hostile sources. An Exarch who lived on good terms with his ecclesiastical neighbours left no mark in history, while one who quarreled with Pope or Archbishop was sure to have his name mentioned unfavorably by the Papal biographer or by Agnellus of Ravenna. Still, even on the one-sided evidence before us we may fairly pronounce the Exarchs to have been a poor and contemptible race of men. They evidently felt themselves to be strangers and foreigners in the land; and taking no interest in the welfare of Italy, their chief thought probably was how to accumulate sufficient treasure against the day of their return to Constantinople. Feebly oppressive, they were neither loved nor greatly feared by their subjects or their soldiers. Three of them were killed in insurrections or mutinies, and a fourth only just escaped the same fate through the intervention of the Pope. One tried to grasp the Imperial scepter, but failed, and perished in the attempt. There is no trace of any great work undertaken by them, or of any wise and statesmanlike scheme for lessening the unhappiness of Italy. Even for their own proper business as soldiers they showed no special aptitude. City after city was lost by them to the Lombards, and not regained; and the story of their incompetent rule is at last ended by the capture of the hitherto impregnable city of Ravenna.

Consiliarus

The most important person on the staff of the Exarch was his *Consiliarius,* who was addressed by the title of "Most Eloquent", or "Magnificent". This minister was still probably in theory what he was in the days when this office was held by the historian Procopius, whom I have ventured to call "Judge-Advocate" to Belisarius. A general like Belisarius, who as general had according to Roman usage the power of trying causes (even though not of a purely military kind) in which soldiers were concerned, required a trained lawyer as his assessor, and such an assessor Belisarius found in the young legist, educated at Berytus, who, fortunately for posterity, was not a mere lawyer, but had also a true historical genius, and wrote for us the story of the wars of his chief.

But as the Exarch, though still in theory a military officer, gradually drew to himself more and more of the functions of a civil governor, of course the power and the responsibility of his legal assessor were proportionately increased, and it does not surprise us to find the *Consiliarius* (perhaps in the absence of his lord) himself sitting on the judgment-seat, and giving decisions on his own account

Next however to the Exarch in the great official hierarchy stood the *Magistri Militum,* or *Duces.* These titles had, by a complete deviation from the usage of the times of Constantine, become practically interchangeable. At that time the Magister Militum was a very important minister of State—notwithstanding the division between Masters of the Horse and Masters of the Foot, there were only eight Masters altogether throughout the whole width of the Empire—and the *Dux* was a comparatively obscure military officer, merely *Spectabilis,* and standing below the *Comes* on the official ladder.

Now, in accordance with the general tendency of affairs under the Eastern Empire, the title of *Magister Militum* has become cheapened so that there are very likely a dozen of them in Italy alone, but the title of *Dux* has been raised in dignity, so that he is now distinctly above the *Comes*. Referring to that which has been said in a previous chapter as to the reasons which may have induced the barbarian nations to place the *Heretoga* above the *Graf,* we may now perhaps not too rashly venture the suggestion that the usage of the barbarians caused a change in the usage of the Empire, and that the dukes of Campania and Sardinia shone in the reflected glories of the dukes of Benevento and Spoleto.

Cartularius.

In the same way as the Exarch was supreme throughout Imperial Italy, so the *Dux* was, or became, during the period which we are now considering, supreme in the province which was under his rule, commanding the troops, nominating all the civil functionaries, fixing the taxation of the province, and constituting in himself the highest court of judicial appeal both in civil and criminal causes, subject always doubtless to an appeal from his decision to that of the Exarch.

In close proximity to the *Dux* we find an officer of high rank called the *Cartularius*. In a letter of Pope Stephen III, \written in 756, the *Cartularius* is mentioned between the *Dux* and the *Comes*. Gregory the Great desires a correspondent to bring the necessities of Rome before the "Magnificent Man, lord Maurentius the *Cartularius"*. And in the year 638 we find Maurice the *Cartularius,* apparently the chief Imperial officer in Rome. He Incites the Roman soldiers to rebellion by pointing to the stored-up treasures of the Lateran, out of which their wages might well be paid: he enters the Lateran palace along with the civil rulers, seals up all the treasures of the sacristy, and sends word to the Exarch Isaac, inviting him to come and divide the spoil. Later on *(circa* 642) he foments a rebellion against Isaac himself, which is suppressed by Donus, *Magister Militum*; he flies to S. Maria ad Praesepe for shelter, is dragged thence, and sent to Ravenna for execution.

In all these transactions the *Dux Romae* is never mentioned. I am disposed to conjecture that what the *Consiliarius* was to the Exarch, the *Cartularius* was to the *Dux;* his assessor, and chief legal adviser, who in his absence acted as his representative, and who may perhaps during some casual vacancy of the office have pushed himself into a position of supremacy, and maintained it by the arts of the military demagogue, till it became necessary for the Exarch to remove him by force.

Dukes of Rome and Naples

Before we part from the *Dux* and his staff, we must take particular notice of two dukes, who from the scene of their administrative labors possess an especial interest for us. The *Dux Romae* is not mentioned by that name in the letters of Gregory, but it is probable that in the course of the seventh century the *Magister Militum* at Rome was addressed by that title. For an express mention of a Duke of Rome we must wait till the beginning of the eighth century (711-713), when a large part of the Roman populace refused to receive Peter as duke because he was the nominee of the heretical emperor Philippicus, and with arms in their hands vindicated the claim of his predecessor Christopher. Evidently by that time the *Ducatus Romae* had become a well-known office in the state. After the events of 726, and the uprising of the Roman population against the decrees of the Iconoclastic Emperor, the Duke of Rome, though still keeping his high office, seems to have more or less broken off his connection with Ravenna, and become for the remainder of the century the humble servant of the Pope.

So too the *Duke of Naples,* though ruling over a very limited territory, became at an early period, owing to the remote and detached position of his duchy, comparatively independent of the Exarch at Ravenna. This tendency is perhaps indicated by the insurrection of Joannes Compsinus (about 618), though we have no distinct authority for calling him duke, and though his rebellion was soon suppressed. But in the eighth century, though the dukes of Naples did not break off from the Eastern Empire, and in fact fought against the Roman insurgents on behalf of the Iconoclasts, there was an evident tendency on their part to become hereditary nobles instead of mere nominees of the Emperor, holding office at his pleasure. The Duke of Naples at this time seems to be generally called *Consul,* as well as *Magister Militum.* About 768 he joins the office of bishop to that of duke, and in the following century (but this is beyond our horizon), the descendants of this duke-bishop almost succeed in making both dignities, the spiritual and the temporal, hereditary in their family.

It should be noticed that from the early part of the eighth century onwards, probably because of the weakened hold of the central government upon them, there was a tendency in the duchies to split up into smaller districts, each of whose rulers assumed the coveted title of *Dux*. The Papal biographer as we have seen, describes the result of the iconoclastic decree to have been that "all men throughout Italy, spurning the Emperor's orders, chose dukes for themselves, and thus provided for the Pope's safety and their own". As a result, we find the number of dukes greatly increased. Perugia, Ferrara, Fermo, Osimo, Ancona, has each its duke, and probably fuller histories of the time would give us many more. How strongly this splitting-up of the duchies, coinciding with their liberation from Imperial control, would tend towards making the dignity of duke hereditary in certain families, and preparing the way for a feudal nobility in the Italy of the Romans, as well as in the Italy of the Lombards, will be at once perceived by a student of history.

Tribunes.

Of the *Tribuni,* the military officers with civil powers, who came next below the *Duces* in the Imperial hierarchy, we are not able to say much. The reader will not need to be reminded how completely in the Imperial age the word *Tribune* had lost that signification of a defender of popular rights which once belonged to it, and how it was ordinarily applied to a military officer ranking above the centurion, and corresponding pretty closely with our *Colonel*. No doubt, then, the Tribunes who commanded the detachments of troops in the various towns of the province of which the *dux* was governor, were essentially and in theory military officers; but we have abundant proof in the letters of Gregory I that already, by the end of the sixth century, they joined to their military functions all the ordinary civil duties of the governor of a town. The Tribunes, to whom Gregory writes (and who, though styled *magnifici* and *clarissimi,* are nevertheless addressed by him in a tone of patronizing condescension which he does not employ to *Duces* and *Magistri Militum),* are desired to redress financial grievances, to restore runaway slaves, to assist a niece to recover her uncle's inheritance, and so forth; all of them affairs entirely foreign to a military officer's duties. Thus we see here in a very striking manner how "the toga" was giving way to "arms", the officer stepping into the place of the civil servant in all the cities of Italy. Perhaps we may even say that the substitution took place earlier in the lower ranks of the services than in the higher; that by the time of Gregory the *Tribunus* had generally ousted the *Judex,* though the *Dux* had not yet entirely replaced the *Praeses.*

The Same officer who bore the title of *Tribunus* was also sometimes addressed as *Comes,* and we are tempted to say that these two titles were interchangeable, like those of *Magister Militum* and *Dux*; but it is difficult to speak with any certainty on this subject. It is certain (I borrow here some sentences from the latest French expositor) that from the beginning of the eighth century the exact hierarchy of titles begins to get into strange confusion; the ambition to wear a more sonorous name, the desire to amass a larger fortune by the *prestige* of an important post in the administration lead the chiefs of the Italian aristocracy to beg for dignities and titles from Byzantium, or to assume them on their own authority. Governors of towns call themselves Dukes, great proprietors intrigue for the functions of the Tribune, which become a hereditary title of nobility in their families; and administrative dignities go on multiplying, without any longer necessarily corresponding to real offices in the State.

The result of this examination into the political organization of Imperial Italy from the sixth to the eighth century throws an important light on the dark and difficult subject of the early history of *Venice.* As has been already hinted, we have exceedingly slight authentic and contemporary materials and a too copious supply of imaginative fourteenth-century romance for the reconstruction of that history. But, to repeat what was said in the preceding chapter, the uniform tradition of all the native historians, coinciding as it does with the contemporary letters of Cassiodorus, seems to prove that for two hundred years, from the close of the fifth century to the close of the seventh, the inhabitants of the islands in the Venetian lagunes were under the sway of rulers called *Tribuni* (Cassiodorus calls them *Tribuni Maritimi),* one for each of the twelve islands. About the year 697 they came together and chose one supreme ruler for the whole territory, who was called *Dux:* these *Duces* ruled the islands for about forty years, each one holding his office for life. Then annual magistrates, called *Magistri Militiae,* were appointed in their stead. This experiment, however, was found not to answer, and in 742 a *Dux* was again appointed, thus reinstating a line of elective life-magistrates, who for 1054 years ruled the cities of the lagunes, and for nearly 1000 years the one central queenly city of the Rialto, and whom history knows as the *Doges of Venice*. So much our inquiries into the contemporary history of Imperial Italy enable us easily to understand. The *Tribuni,* each one ruling in his own little island-town, are the Imperial officers whom we should expect to find there. If the islanders were from any cause detached from the rule of the *Dux Histriae et Venetiae* towards the close of the seventh century, during the troublous reign of Justinian II, it was natural that the inhabitants should elect a *Dux* of their own, hereby illustrating both the tendency towards a splitting-up of the great duchies into little ones, and the tendency towards popular election which became manifest when events weakened the hold of the Empire on the loyalty of the Italians. And what we have learned as to the almost equivalent value of the titles *Dux* and *Magister Militum* enables us readily to understand why, during the temporary obscuration of the life-ruling *Dux,* an annual *Magister Militiae* should be substituted in his place. The point on which we are not entitled to speak is as to the extent to which popular election may have entered into all these official appointments, especially into the appointment of the *Tribuni* who ruled in the several islands for two centuries. By analogy with the rest of Imperial Italy, we should expect these Tribunes to be nominated by a Duke or an Exarch, and so ultimately to receive their authority from Constantinople. It is possible that the peculiar circumstances which led to the foundation of the cities of the lagunes and their strangely strong geographical position may have rendered them more independent of the officers of the Empire than the other cities which still owned its sway. But, on the other hand, all our information about them comes to us colored by the fancies of men who lived long after Venice had thrown off the yoke of the Empire; nay, some generations after she herself had borne a share in the sack of Constantinople. Historians like Dandolo and Sabellico, with these thoughts in their minds, were sure to minimize the degree of their ancestor's dependence on the Empire, and to exaggerate the amount of independence possessed by their forefathers. Perhaps, too, even their knowledge of Roman history, imperfect as it may have been, led them to think of a Tribune as a sturdy champion of popular rights, like Tiberius or Caius Gracchus, rather than as the sleek, obsequious servant of an absolute master, who was really denoted by the term *Tribunus* in the sixth century after Christ.

We have now gone through all the higher members of the political organization of Imperial Italy during the Lombard dominion, and have certainly so far seen no germs of freedom which could account for the phenomena afterwards presented by the great Italian Republics. This is fully admitted by Savigny himself, who holds that all the higher ranks of the civil magistracy of the Empire disappeared under the waves of change, but thinks the minor municipal magistracies survived, partly by reason of their very obscurity. The question which thus presents itself for solution is whether the local senates or *Curiae* of the cities of Italy did or did not survive through those centuries of darkness, to the dawn of republican freedom in the twelfth century.

To prevent needless repetition I refer my readers an easier section of this history for a sketch of the rise and fall of the municipal system of the Empire. The reader, if he turns back to that section, will see how the once flourishing and prosperous town-councils of Italy and the provinces became transformed into life-long prisons, in which the unhappy members of a once powerful middle-class were penned like sheep, awaiting the "loud-clashing shears" of the Imperial tax-gatherer. At the time of Justinian the condition of these Senators (as they were called with cruel courtesy) was still unaltered. In a law passed in the year 536 the Emperor laments in his stately language that the Senates which were established in every city of the Empire, in imitation of the

Senate in the capital, are falling into decay, that there is no longer the same eagerness which there was in old time to perform public services to one's native city, but that men are willfully denuding themselves of their property, and making fictitious presents of it during their lifetime, in order to evade the statutory obligation to leave at least one-fourth of that property to members of the Senate. The Imperial legislator accordingly raises the proportion which must be thus left, to three-fourths. If a man leave legitimate children, they become perforce senators, and take the whole property with the burden. If he leaves only illegitimate offspring, they are to be enrolled in the Senate if they receive a bequest of this three-fourth fraction, otherwise it all goes straight to the *Curia*. If he leave only daughters, they must either marry husbands who are senators, or relinquish all claim to anything but one-fourth of their father's estate All these provisions show that we are still face to face with that condition of affairs in connection with the *Curia*—nominal dignity, but real slavery—which we met with a century and a half before in the legislation of Theodosius and his sons. We see from the letters of Pope Gregory that the same state of things continued half a century after the legislation of Justinian, for he forbids the ordination not only of bigamists, of men who have married widows, of men ignorant of letters, but also of those "under liability to the *Curia*", lest, after having received the sacred anointing, they should be compelled to return to business.

In the East, however, it is clear that, for some reason or other, not even as convenient taxing-machines could the *Curiae* be kept permanently in existence. It was perhaps the institution of a new order of tax-gatherers called *Vindices,* and the assignment to them of the functions formerly discharged, much against their will, by the Decurions, which brought about this change. Certain it is that about the year 890, the Emperor Leo VI, in an edict which I have already quoted abolished the last vestiges of the *Curiae,* which he described as imposing intolerable burdens, conferring imaginary rights, and "wandering in a vain and objectless manner round the soil of legality".

This having been the course of affairs in the Eastern Did Empire, we should certainly expect to find that the *Curiae* had not a longer life in the West. With war and barbaric invasion raging round them, with the tendency which we have observed in Imperial institutions to imitate those of the Germanic peoples, especially the tendency of offices to become hereditary and thus to prepare the way for a feudal nobility, we certainly should not expect these *Curiae,* the pale specters of long-dead republics, to maintain themselves in being for six centuries. The negative conclusion on this subject to which *a priori* probability leads us is that at which the majority of scholars have arrived as the result of *a posteriori* reasoning. But one great name, that of Carl Friedrich von Savigny, is inscribed on the other side of the question, and in deference to that opinion (from which no historical student differs without reluctance) we must look a little more closely at the constitution of the *Curiae,* such as they undoubtedly still subsisted on the soil of Italy at the end of the sixth century.

In the old and flourishing days of the Italian municipalities, as we have seen, the *Decurions* had been an aristocracy ruling their native city, and proudly holding themselves aloof from the *Plebeii* around them. It had been an honor eagerly sought after to have one's name inscribed in the *Album Curiae*. Here were to be found first of all the names of the *Patroni,* or, as we should call them, honorary members; either home-born sons of the *Curia,* who had passed through all the grades of office up to the highest; or eminent Italians outside the *Curia,* on whom it had bestowed, as we should say, "the freedom of the city". Here, too, were those who were serving, or had served, the office of *Duumviri* the office which imitated in each provincial town the position of the Roman Consulate, and which shared some of its reflected splendor. Here were other lower functionaries, who, as at Rome, bore the titles of *Aedile* and *Quaestor,* and here also was an officer called the *Quinquennalis,* appointed only once in five years, and whose dignity, corresponding to that of the Roman Censor, seems at one time to have overshadowed even that of the *Duumviri* themselves.

The Curator.

In the sixth century, the names, and hardly more than the names, of these municipal magnates still survived. The *Duumviri* appear to be alluded to under the more general term *Magistratus.* The continued existence of the *Quinquennales* depends on the rendering of a doubtful contraction in the papyrus documents of Marini. By a series of changes which even the patient labor of German scholars has hardly succeeded in fully developing, the power, such as it was, of the Italian *Curia* seems to have been concentrated in two officers, unknown in the third century, the *Curator* and the *Defensor.*

1. The *Curator* seems to have exercised those administrative and financial powers which we in England associate with the title of Mayor—perhaps adding thereto that of Chairman of the Finance Committee of the Corporation. The *Curator* of a large city like Ravenna was still an important person in the year 600. Gregory the Great addresses him as *gloria vestra,* consults him about important affairs of state such as peace with the Lombard king, asks him to obtain for certain soldiers their arrears of pay, recommends to his good offices the wife of the Prefect of Rome, who is visiting Ravenna If we may identify him, as seems probable, with the *Major Populi* whom we meet with at Naples, he had charge of the gates of that city, and vehemently resented the pretensions of a meddlesome and arrogant bishop to interfere with him in his work of guarding the city, and to raise up a party antagonistic to his government.

These last letters of Pope Gregory probably indicate to us one reason for the disappearance of the *Curator* from all our later historical documents. The bishop was rapidly becoming the most important person in all that related to the peaceful administration of the city. Between him and the military governor, the *Tribunus,* there was left but little room for the popularly-elected *Curator* or *Major Populi,* and so in the course of the seventh and eighth centuries he vanishes from the scene.

2. Similar, probably, was the fate of the *Defensor,* who at the beginning of our period stood at the head of all the local functionaries, taking precedence both of *Curator* and *Duumviri.* His office, however, was chiefly a judicial one, and we may therefore, recurring to our English analogy, call him the Recorder, as the *Curator* is the Mayor of the town. The *Defensor Civitatis,* that officer whom the Empire had called into existence in order to protect the humbler classes against the rapacity of its own instruments, had gradually grown into an important magistrate, with a court and official retinue of his own. He himself had become too often arrogant and oppressive, a wolf instead of a sheep-dog to the flock. Then, again, he too, though not one of the downtrodden *Curiales,* had declined in power and reputation, so that, as Justinian himself says in his 15th Novel, "The office of *Defensor* is so trampled upon in parts of our dominions, that it is considered a disgrace rather than an honor to possess it. For it is now sought after by obscure persons in need of food and clothing, and given to them as a matter of charity rather than of proved fitness. Then the governors remove them at

their pleasure for the most trifling fault, or for no fault at all, and put other persons in their room whom they call *place-keepers*, and this they do many times a year; so that the men of their staff and the rulers and inhabitants of the city hold the *Defensor* in utter contempt. Moreover, their judicial acts might as well never take place at all. For if the governors of the provinces order them to do anything in their official capacity, they generally do not presume to keep any record of their acts, looking upon themselves as the humble servants of the governor, whose nod they obey. Or, if they do make a record, in the first place they sell it [to one of the litigants], or secondly, as they have no place for storing their archives, the record is practically lost, and those who may desire to refer to it at a later day have to hunt it up from their heirs, or other successors, and generally find it worthless when they have obtained it".

In order to remedy all these abuses, Justinian ordained that the office of *Defensor* should be a biennial one, that he should be chosen by the bishop, clergy, and respectable citizens from among the more influential inhabitants of the city; that each one in his turn should be obliged to accept this public charge and that none, even of *Illustrious* rank, should be allowed to decline it. If any one after this enactment presumed to refuse to undertake the office, he was to be fined five pounds of gold, and was still to be compelled to act as *Defensor*. The *Defensores* were not to be removed from office, nor to have *place-keepers* appointed in their stead, by the ordinary provincial governors. If there were any complaint against their administration, the Praetorian Prefect alone was empowered to remove them. There were assigned to each *Defensor* from the staff of provincial servants, one reporter *(Exceptor)* to take minutes of his decisions, and two *Officiales* to carry them into effect.

To remedy the inconvenience which had arisen from the loss of documents in the *Defensor's* office, Justinian further ordered that a public building should be set apart in each city, in which he should store his records, under the care of an officer appointed for that purpose. It was hoped that thus the archives might be kept uninjured, and might be accessible to all men.

Under this law, *the Defensor* received, perhaps for the first time, the power of deciding civil cases up to the above-mentioned limit of 300 solidi. He had also summary criminal jurisdiction in all cases of slight importance, and the power of detaining graver offenders in prison, and sending them to the Praetor for trial. In short, his functions greatly resembled those of an English magistrate, with some of those which belong to a County Court Judge added thereto. Wills also, and voluntary donations, were registered in his court, and the provincial governor was not to seek to deprive him of this voluntary jurisdiction.

The Novel in question was evidently a serious and well-considered attempt to make this popularly chosen judge, who was to be elected from among the local magnates, a great and important part of the machinery of government. As far as it went, it was an attempt to decentralize administration, and to invite the wealthier provincials to take their share in the life of the state.

This attempt however, like those previously noticed in the same direction, probably failed under the pressure of the times. We cannot speak with any certainty on the subject, owing to the paucity of our materials, but the letters of Pope Gregory lead us to infer that in his day the office of *Defensor Civitatis* was not one of any political importance. He too, there is reason to think, found himself squeezed out between the Bishop and the *tribunus*. The Church and the Army so occupied the ground that there was no room for the delicate plant of local self-government to flourish between them.

If this is the general conclusion to which our historical materials, slender as they are, seem to lead us, what, it may well be asked, is the evidence by which Savigny could possibly be led to imagine a continuous life of municipal institutions, lasting on till the twelfth century? The answer is contained in the very interesting documents edited by Marini, which do certainly show that there was more tenacity of life in the old Curial organization than we should have supposed from the evidence mentioned above. We have here a nearly continuous chain of documents, reaching from the days of Odovacar *(circa* 480) down to 625, all showing the *Curia* as still existing as a *Court of registry for legal instruments.* We have here the records of sales, donations, the appointment of a guardian, wills, the discharge of claims under a will, and so on. The documents have almost all come from the archives of the Church at Ravenna, and relate chiefly to that city and its neighborhood, but there is no reason to doubt that every other city in Italy could show many others like them, had they been preserved with equal care. In these documents in Marini's collection, we meet with nearly all the names of magistrates that have been described above. The *Defensor,* the *Quinquennalis,* the *Magistratus* (who is no doubt equivalent to *Duumvir),* all figure in these papyri as witnesses to the various transactions recorded: and it is often expressly said that the persons concerned in them have asked that they may be inscribed on the proceedings of the *Curia.* The *Curator,* however, does not appear, an absence which is by some attributed to his being veiled under the title *Quinquennalis,* while another suggestion is that as an administrative officer he had no concern in these quasi-judicial proceedings of the *Curia.*

It is then on the strength of these most interesting documents that Savigny grounds his theory of the survival of the *Curiae* through the darkest part of the Middle Ages. It is true that the documents do not bring us down below 625, but it is perhaps fair to argue that this is an accident due to some special circumstances in the history of the Church of Ravenna, and that a more careful storage of the archives would have shown us some of a later date.

But even so, and without insisting too much on the great gap which intervenes between the seventh century and the twelfth, may we not fairly ask, what do these documents prove as to the political state of Italy? We have in them traces of certain courts still lingering on as mere courts of registration. These subscribing and attesting witnesses do not, for anything that the documents show us, possess any power in the city. Their functions are only what we call notarial functions, and it is but in accordance with what we might have expected that we find the word *Curialis* used in the ninth century (as Savigny himself admits) as a title equivalent to that of *Exceptor,* or registrar of the Court.

To me the nearest analogy to these *Curiae* of the seventh century, which Savigny regards with such romantic interest, and in which he sees the germs of the glorious Italian *Comuni* of the thirteenth century, is the "courts baron" and "courts leet", which still preserve a lingering existence in our own country. In the absence of a complete system of registration, these little Courts of ours have their value. The steward of the manor (generally a local attorney) and a few copyholders on the estate are aware of their existence, and can tell an intelligent inquirer when they will be held. But they are absolutely without influence on the political condition of the districts in which they meet, and the majority of the inhabitants would never notice their disappearance if they dropped absolutely out of existence. If we can imagine these faint survivals becoming once more great and powerful realities, or rather becoming greater and more powerful than they ever were in the noonday of the feudal system, if we can imagine them making and unmaking ministries, and determining the destiny of England, then, as it seems to me, we may also imagine the *Comuni* of Florence or of Siena descending from the *Curiae* of the Imperial age.

CHAPTER XIV.

POLITICAL STATE OF LOMBARD ITALY

We now turn to consider the political and social state of the much larger portion of Italy which was under the rule of the Lombard conquerors. Our enquiry into this part of the subject may be shorter than that which occupied us in the last chapter. Documentary evidence (except that furnished by the laws, which we have already examined) is scanty and obscure. The best evidence is that which is furnished by the actual history of the Lombard State as exhibited in the course of these two volumes, and from that evidence each individual reader can form his own conclusion.

Thus in the first place, as to him who stood at the head of the State, the king of the Lombards in his palace-hall at Pavia, we can feel instinctively what perhaps cannot be expressed scientifically, how the two elements of election and hereditary descent concurred, when the throne was vacant, towards the determination of its next occupant. The element of popular election, present in all these Teutonic monarchies, was there, but there was also a strong preference for the representatives of certain special lines of descent, especially during all the seventh century for the representatives of the sainted Theudelinda. Thus the succession to the throne, though much less strictly hereditary than that which obtained amongst the Franks, was much more so than that of the Visigoths. In Spain before the Moorish conquest and after the fall of the monarchy of Toulouse there was hardly a single royal family that succeeded in maintaining itself for more than two generations, whereas Aripert II, who got possession of the throne in 700, was descended in the fourth degree from the brother of Theudelinda.

The king of the Lombards, if he were a man of any force of character, was able to make his will felt very effectively, at any rate through all the north of Italy. He moved the national army whither he would: his favor could make or mar the fortunes of a subject: and the fabric of his wealth, the foundation of which was laid in the day when at the close of the interregnum the thirty-six dukes surrendered each one-half of his domains to the newly-elected Authari, was doubtless raised higher and higher by the confiscation of the property of rebellious nobles, and especially by the multitude of fines which, as we have seen in commenting on the laws of Rothari and Liutprand were payable to "the King's Court" or" the King's Palace"

"The king's rights" (I borrow here the language of a great German jurist) as limited by popular freedom were the following. The laws were devised by him in consultation with the great men and nobles of the land, then accepted by the collected army which formed the assembly of the people, and given forth in his name. He was the supreme judge, but, like other national judges, he was assisted by jurors in finding the verdict. From him went forth the summons to the host, but without doubt war, before being declared, was first talked over with the great men and approved in the assembly of the people, which was generally held on the 1st of March. The public domain, that is all the land that was not divided among private persons, was his, and was administered by officers specially named by him, the *gastalds*. It was he who safeguarded the peace of the community: therefore the highest criminal jurisdiction was in his hands, and was partly exercised by him directly, partly handed over to his own officers or to the heads of the people. The former mode was generally adopted when the disturbers of the peace were great and powerful persons. All crimes against the commonwealth, such as treason, disturbance of the national assembly, and the like, were punished by the king, either with death or with the maximum fine (900 solidi), and an equally heavy penalty avenged any breach of the peace which occurred in the king's palace. Even of the fines which were inflicted for injuries on private persons, one half [as a general rule] went to the king to atone for the breach of the public peace, while the other half went as solace and compensation to the injured party. Moreover the king exercised the highest police-jurisdiction, and took the necessary precautions for the safety of persons and property throughout the land. Without his permission, no free man accompanied by his clan *(fara)* might change his residence even within the kingdom [still less leave the country] : no one might exercise the craft of a goldsmith or coin money. Under his especial protection were all churches and convents with their appurtenances, as well as foreigners settling in the realm *(wargangi)*. He also represented the woman as against her guardian *(mundwald)*, the retainer as against his lord, and afforded a last refuge to men otherwise unarmed and unprotected. Out of these rights as universal patron or supreme guardian there arose for him various claims of inheritance which he exercised on behalf of the community when private heirs failed.

So far Hegel. But great as were the powers of the Lombard king when wielded by a strong and vigorous arm, it must not be forgotten that, as Hegel and other enquirers have pointed out, one influence which in other States did much to consolidate and strengthen royal power was wanting here. The Church, which undoubtedly did so much to establish the Frankish and the Saxon monarchies, seems to have been always cold towards that of the Lombards, nor could all the lavish gifts of kings and dukes to basilica and monastery do more than win a kind of grudging assent to the proposition that the *nefandus Langobardus* was somewhat less intolerable than aforetime.

Before we leave the subject of the Lombard kings, something must be said as to the chief emblem of their dignity, the far-famed Iron Crown. In the Church of St. John the Baptist at Monza is still to be seen that little golden circlet (15 centimeters in diameter, 5-3 centimeters high) which was guarded there among the most precious treasures of the Church for more than twelve centuries. It is made in six separate pieces, and it has in it twenty-two jewels of various kinds (chiefly pearls and emeralds), twenty-six golden roses, and twenty-four finely wrought enamels. But that which has given the crown its name and its special historic interest is not its precious gems, but the thin circlet of iron (only 3 oz. in weight and a centimeter high) which runs round the inside of the diadem. This iron rim is now said to be composed of a nail which was used in the crucifixion of Christ, and was brought from Jerusalem by Helena, mother of Constantine. With this precious ring of iron the crown of Constantine may have been adorned: it may have travelled from Constantinople to Rome: it may have been sent by Pope Gregory the Great to Theudelinda, though it is not probable that he would dare to give to a Lombard queen the emblems of Imperial sovereignty. But for all these conjectures, whether probable or improbable, there does not exist any shadow of proof: and, In fact, the theory of the connection of the Iron Crown with the sacred nail cannot be certainly traced back for more than three or four centuries, and is generally considered to have received its death-blow at the hands of Muratori. To one who, like the present writer, views with the utmost suspicion all the supposed discoveries at Jerusalem of the enthusiastic and credulous Helena, the question of one fiction less or more in connection with the sacred nails is not extremely interesting, and does not seem worth the tons of printed paper which have already been devoted to it. But the story of the Crown for its own sake, and as a great historic emblem, is undoubtedly interesting.

Till the twelfth century it appears to have been always called the *Corona Aurea;* after that, the name of *Corona Ferrea* gradually became more usual; and in the fourteenth century the Emperors Henry VII and Lewis the Bavarian being for some reason unable to obtain the precious so-called Iron Crown itself, are said to have been crowned with one made entirely of iron. This baser rival however soon vanishes from the scene, and the true Iron-Golden Crown reappears, and is used for the coronation of Charles IV, the author of the Golden Bull, and Charles V, the worldwide Emperor. Strangest of all the scenes in the history of the venerable ornament was that when, in the hands of a French Master of the Ceremonies, accompanied by the Archpriest and twelve citizens of Monza (dressed by their own especial desire in uniform), and escorted by fifty-six cavalry soldiers, it was transferred on the 18th of May, 1805, to the Cathedral of Milan, where eight days after, the son of a Corsican attorney placed it on his imperial brow, uttering the well-known words, "Dio me l'ha data, guai a chi la toccherà".

But though the Iron Crown still survives at Monza, a scarcely less interesting relic of Lombard domination has disappeared almost in our own days. Side by side with the Iron Crown were to be seen at Monza in the time of Muratori two other crowns, one of Agilulf and one of Theudelinda. The former, in some respects the most interesting of the three, was adorned with figures of Our Saviour, two Angels, and the Twelve Apostles, each standing in an alcove of laurel boughs. It had 65 carbuncles and emeralds and 158 pearls, and round the bottom of it ran an inscription recording that "Agilulf the glorious man, by Divine grace king of the whole of Italy, offered this crown to St. John the Baptist in the church of Monza". Unfortunately this most interesting historical relic must now be spoken of in the past tense. Having been carried off by Napoleon to Paris, it was kept there among the treasures of the Bibliothèque Nationale, but in January, 1804, it was stolen by one of the custodians named Charlier, and carried off by him to Amsterdam, the gold melted, and the jewels sold. The thief was captured and died in prison, but the crown of the noble Agilulf was irrecoverably lost.

As for the Iron Crown itself, after figuring in the coronation of two Austrian Emperors at Milan, it was after the battle of Solferino carried eastward to Venice, the last stronghold of Austrian power in Italy, and only after the war of 1866 was it brought back to its old home in Monza, where it may be hoped that it will now rest, to be used hereafter only for the coronation of the sovereigns of an united Italy.

The Duke

Passing now from the Royal to the Ducal office, we observe first a curious fact. The history of the interregnum and the high position attained by the rulers of Spoleto and Benevento, together with many other indications of the same kind, clearly show that the Duke was a most important person in the Lombard State, no foreign importation, but a homegrowth of the Teutonic genius, and yet we are entirely unacquainted with his true national name. *Dux* is of course Latin, taken over as we have seen from the Imperial hierarchy of office. Neither Paulus nor the laws of Rothari nor those of Liutprand give us the slightest indication how the office of Gisulf or Farwald was spoken of by himself and by his countrymen when no ecclesiastic was at hand to translate their language into the barbarous Latin of a legal document. We may conjecture that the Lombard name was some compound of *Ari,* the equivalent of army, and thus that it may have resembled the Anglo-Saxon *Heretoga* (Army-leader), but this can be only a conjecture, and raises the further question, Had the Lombards any word like *Ealdorman* to express the civil as distinct from the military duties of this great functionary, to describe the duke when sitting on the judgment-seat rather than when leading his warriors to battle?

The power and the possibilities of power residing in the office of the Lombard duke have been perhaps sufficiently indicated in the course of the preceding history. We have seen how an office which was at first delegated only for life, became in some cases virtually hereditary; how the perpetual rebellions of the Lombard dukes against their sovereign divided and enfeebled the State; how these rebellions were suppressed, and the dukes of Northern Italy were brought into comparative subjection and subordination before the end of the seventh century but how far harder even the great Liutprand found it to deal with the semi-independent dukes of Spoleto and Benevento. As to these latter princes and their relation to the central authority, our information is extremely vague. We can see that there was no close cohesion, but we are perhaps hardly entitled to assert that there was during the greater part of Lombard history absolute alienation and hostility between them. Matrimonial alliances between the families of king and duke are not uncommon: the sons of the duke are friendly visitors at Pavia : when occasion arises they can work together against Emperor or Exarch. Thus, though it is undeniable that the tie which bound the dukes of Spoleto and Benevento to the Northern kingdom was a somewhat loose one, and though commentators are right in calling attention to the pointed omission of the names of these dukes in the prologues to the laws even of the great Liutprand, it is not quite certain that we are right in deducing from this latter circumstance that they were really disaffected to the Lombard king. With the Flaminian Way still more or less blocked by Imperial troops, it might be unsafe for a great personage like the duke of Spoleto or Benevento to travel to Pavia without an escort, which would have been in fact an army. And it is noteworthy in this connection, that at none of the later diets held by Liutprand (not even when Benevento at any rate was loyal, being under the rule of the king's nephew Gregory) have we any express mention of the presence at these assemblies of nobles from either of the southern duchies.

The gastald

In connection with the ducal office generally, (passing on from the question of the larger semi-independent duchies), it will be well to notice an institution, peculiar, or nearly so to the Lombard State, that of the *gastaldat.* The *gastald,* whose name was probably derived from the Gothic word *gastaldan,* to acquire or possess, seems to have been a royal officer whose special business it was to collect the fines due to the king, and to administer the royal domain, distributed as it was through the various districts of Italy. It is a not improbable conjecture of Hegel, that when, at the restoration of the kingship, the dukes surrendered half of their territories in order to constitute such royal domain, this was a division of land, not of the revenues accruing from land, and that this may have been the occasion on which *gastalds* were appointed in order to safeguard the king's rights in the surrendered districts; to collect his rents and taxes; to judge the causes which arose within their *gastaldat*; and to lead forth to war the free Lombards who dwelt therein. Whether he lived in the same city as the duke we cannot say: probably in most cases he would fix his abode in a town of secondary importance. But it is essential to observe that the *gastalds* thus holding the king's commission were, and were meant to be, a check upon the power of the dukes, who though in theory themselves also the nominated servants of the Crown, were fast becoming hereditary rulers. Thus the two principles, what may be called by an anachronism the feudal principle and that of the centralized monarchy, being represented respectively by the duke and the *gastald,* were set over against one another, and exercised upon one another a reciprocal control. As was said in the laws of Rothari, "If a duke shall unjustly harass one of his men-at-arms, let the *gastald* relieve him until he find out the truth, and bring him to justice, either in the presence of the king, or at least before his duke". "If any *gastald* shall unreasonably harass his man-at-arms, let the duke relieve him until he shall find out the truth of his case"

It is to be noted, as a sign of the semi-independent position of the two great Southern dukes, that no royal *gastalds* appear to have existed in their dominions, but they appointed *gastalds* of their own, who seem to have been of somewhat inferior position to their namesakes in the rest of Italy, holding a delegated authority from the duke, each one in the little *actus* or township which formed the administrative unit in the duchy of Benevento, perhaps also in that of Spoleto. Meanwhile the duke himself lived almost in royal splendor at Benevento or Spoleto. His court was the centre of all power and all brilliancy. He had his chancellor *(referendarius),* his high constable *(marpahis),* his grand chamberlain and master of the robes *(cubicularius* and *vestararius),* and his grand treasurer *(stolesaz).* And, significant fact, in his charters and donations he always mentioned the year of his own reign, and forgot to mention that of his sovereign who was reigning at Pavia.

For Lombard Italy as a whole we find the number of *gastalds* apparently increasing, and that of the *duces* diminishing, as the seventh century wears on. In *civitates* such as those of Parma and Piacenza, which had been betrayed by their dukes to the Empire, it was natural that Agilulf, when he recovered them, should appoint not an aspiring duke but a subservient *gastald* to administer the affairs of the city, and that he should speak of these places as "cities of our royal house". Rothari too when he won from the Greeks the fair cities on the coast of the Riviera, probably put them under the rule of his *gastalds.* And in some of those cases in which the rebellion of a turbulent duke was with difficulty suppressed (as for instance in the case of Treviso), it seems probable that the king, while confiscating the private property of the duke, added his territory to the royal domain, and divided it up into *gastaldats.*

The sculdahis

Besides the *gastald,* there were other officers of the royal domain called by the general name of *actores regis,* the gradation of whose rank and various duties it is not easy to discover. It is interesting however to observe the important, even judicial functions of the The *saltarius* or forester. The *sculdahis,* or *sculdhaizo,* of whom frequent mention is made in the laws, seems to have been not unlike one of our justices of the peace. His title (the enforcer of obligations) seems to show that it rested with him to enforce obedience to the decisions of the court above; and the words by which Paulus Diaconus translates it *(rector loci)* show us that practically the *sculdahis* was the chief man in the little town or village in which he dwelt.

The particular *sculdahis* of whom Paulus speaks in this passage was that Argait whose unfortunate name, coupled with his want of success in capturing the Slovene robbers from over the mountains, exposed him to the clumsy banter of Duke Ferdulf of Friuli, and led to the loss of hundreds of Lombard lives through Argait's fool-hardy attempt to wipe off the stain upon his honor. But notwithstanding this error, Paulus tells us that he was "a noble man, powerful in courage and strength"; in fact, just like a stalwart, hot-tempered English squire, more terrible with that strong sword-arm of his, than successful in matching his wits against the shifty, nimble, petty thieves from over the border.

The organization of the Lombard State was undoubtedly crude and somewhat barbarous, though in the very quaintness of its barbarism there is a certain charm when we compare it with the pompous and effete hierarchy of Byzantine officialism. But the question which, as I have already often hinted, attracts while it continually eludes us is, What was the condition of the earlier population of Italy, of the men who though of various stocks all called themselves Roman, under these their Lombard conquerors? This question, as I have said, must attract us. After we have followed the history of the Imperial race from the hut of Faustulus to the glories of the Palatine and the Capitol, after gazing in many widely sundered lands on the handiwork of the Roman legionary and thus learning afresh in manhood the marvel of the schoolboy's commonplaces concerning "the lords of the world, the nation of the toga", how can we turn away from them in the day of their calamity, or fail to enquire how the sons of Italy, when their turn came to be enslaved, bore themselves in their bondage?

But the question, though it must be asked, cannot be satisfactorily answered. The pit of ruin into which Rome fell was so deep that scarcely a voice reaches us from its dark recesses. The Greek in similar circumstances would surely have told us something of his reverses. He would have written histories or sung elegies, or in some way or other coined his sorrows into gold. The Roman, always naturally unexpressive, endured, was silent, and died. The actual evidence as to the condition of the Latin population under their Lombard lords is scanty, and can soon be summarized for the reader. The conjectures with which we cannot help filling up the blank interstices of that evidence are endless, and a volume would be needed to discuss them thoroughly.

To begin with, there is the important statement by Paulus of the results of the Lombard conquest to which reference has already been made. In these Lombards, days [under the rule of the thirty dukes, just after the death of Alboin] many of the noble Romans were slain through avarice. But the rest being divided among their "guests" on condition of paying the third part of their produce to the Lombards, are made tributaries.

The general purport of this passage is clear enough. The largest land-owners among the Romans, the nobles who owned any *latifundia* which might still exist in Italy, were, as a rule, killed by the greedy Lombards, who probably portioned out their lands among them. The rest of the Roman inhabitants (for so surely we must understand the passage, not "the rest of the nobles") found themselves assigned as "hosts" to the new-comers who were their "guests", and bound to pay over to them one-third of the produce of their lands. The result of this revolution was of course in a certain sense to take away their freedom and make them tributaries (that is, not "tenants" but more nearly "serfs") to the invading Lombards. We have here therefore again nearly the same process which we have already watched in the Italy of Odovacar and Theodoric. The word *hospes* (host or guest) is a technical one in this connection, and expresses with unintended irony the relation in which the poor dispossessed Roman stood to his most unwelcome guest. Only we have to notice this difference, that whereas in Odovacar's and Theodoric's land-settlements and in that of the Burgundians and Visigoths a third or other fraction of the land itself was taken by the invader, here it was a third of the *produce* of the land to which he helped himself. This is an important difference, and at once raises the question, Was it a third of the gross produce of the soil, or was the "host" allowed to take subsistence for himself and those who helped him in the cultivation first, and then to pay a third of the net produce to his "guest"? If the latter, the tribute was, as such things went, fair and moderate : if the former, it is considered that it was equivalent to taking two-thirds of the net produce, and that it probably left but a narrow margin for the cultivator and his family. We have no means of deciding the question, but it seems on the whole most likely that the harsher view is the true one, and that the Lombard took his third of everything grown on the land before the Roman was allowed any wages for his labor.

However this may be, the following consequences seem necessarily to flow from the fact that the Lombards took from the previous inhabitants of Italy, not quota of land, but a quota of produce. In the first place, they were themselves thus exempted from the necessity of agricultural labor. They could live like gentlemen on the tribute paid by their down-trodden "hosts", could perhaps drift into the cities, or go hunting in the forests: in short, they missed that sobering, steadying influence which is given to the cultivator of the soil by his long annual struggle with Nature.

Secondly, the softening and harmonizing influence which is sometimes exercised by neighborhood and a common pursuit was necessarily here wanting. Cassiodorus says that Liberius, to whom was assigned the duty of marking out the Thirds in the Ostrogothic land settlement, so fulfilled his mission as actually to draw the men of the two nations closer together. "For whereas men are wont to come into collision on account of their being neighbours, with these men the common holding of their farms proved in practice a reason for concord". Doubtless this statement is colored by the official optimism which is characteristic of its author, but in the Lombard land settlement such a result was impossible. The Lombard *hospes* was a landlord, often probably an absentee landlord, and was hated accordingly.

For, thirdly, the necessary result of taking not land but a portion of his yearly produce from the Roman cultivator, was to make of him, as Paulus says, a "tributaries", and thus to deprive him, more or less, of his freedom. When the Ostrogothic or Rugian "guest" had with the high hand taken the allotted portion away from his Roman neighbor, it was nothing to him what that neighbor did with the rest. He might starve or grow fat on his diminished holding; he might drift away to Rome or Constantinople; he might enter the service of the Church, or join the army of diggers who by Theodoric's orders were draining the marshes of Terracina,—it was all one to the barbarian "guest" who had been quartered upon him. But the Lombard who had received not land but the arms of the subject-race for his portion, would undoubtedly insist that his "host" should remain upon the land and make it bring forth as plenteous crops as he could, and the whole force of the new rough barbarian kingdom would back his claim. Thus the Roman, lately perhaps a free cultivator, became not a tenant but a *tributarius,* and practically a "serf bound to the soil".

Hospites

We next come to a mysterious and difficult sentence of Paulus, which has been more discussed than anything else written by its author, and has given rise to almost as much controversy as the celebrated sentences of Tacitus as to the land-system of the Germans. After describing the period of the interregnum and how it was ended by the elevation of Authari to the throne, his assumption of the title Flavius, and the surrender by the dukes of half their property "to royal uses in order that there might be a fund out of which the king himself, his adherents, and those who were bound to his service by their various offices might be supported", Paulus says, *Populi tamen adgravati per Langobardos hospites partiuntur.* He then goes on to describe the happy estate of the kingdom of the Lombards under Authari, the absence of robbery and crime, the cessation of unjust exactions *(angaria),* and the fearless security with which every one went about his lawful business.

In the earlier pages of this history I have suggested as a translation of the above sentence, (in this division) the subject populations who had been assigned to their several Lombard guests were [also] included, that is to say, that along with the lands the tributary Roman populations settled upon them were handed over to the king. This seems to be the sense required by the general drift of the passage, but it must be confessed that it is difficult to get it out of the sentence as it stands. What seems an easier translation is offered by Marquis Capponi: "The tributary populations *(populi adgravati)* however are divided (that is remain divided) among their Lombard guests". This translation gives a good meaning to the word *tamen* (however), but it is difficult to get "remain divided" out of *partiuntur,* and it is also in itself improbable. For what would be the object of handing over to the king broad lands denuded of the tributary Roman who cultivated them, and what would the surrendering dukes do with the great populations thus thrown on their hands and deprived of the land from which they derived their sustenance?

On the whole, without going minutely here into the various and sometimes desperate devices which have been resorted to in order to obtain a satisfactory meaning from the passage, the safest course seems to be to acquiesce in the decision of Capponi, that, whatever may be its construction, it is too obscure to make it safe to resort to it for any fresh information as to the condition of the vanquished Romans. The subject with which Paulus is mainly dealing is the financial arrangements made between the dukes and their new sovereign. These it is probably hopeless now to understand, but it seems clear that the system by which the Roman landowner was made tributary to a Lombard *hospes* still remained in force, whoever that *hospes* may have been.

The Roman Population became Aldii

Having gathered such scanty information as we could from the pages of Paulus, let us now turn to consider what light is thrown by the Lombard laws on the condition of the vanquished Romans. The laws of Rothari, as we have seen, are eloquently silent as the Very name of Roman. Except for the one contemptuous allusion to the case of a Roman female slave *(ancilla Romana)* whose seduction was to be atoned for by a fine scarcely more than half that which was payable for the seduction of a Teutonic slave *(ancilla gentilis),* we might have supposed that Rothari and his counselors lived on a planet to which the fame of Rome had never reached. We find however in these very laws a large number of enactments. as to the rights and wrongs of the *Aldius,* a man who, as we discovered, occupied a position midway between the "folk-free" Lombard of the king's army and the mere slave. Everything seemed to show that we were here dealing with a man not greatly or essentially different from the Roman *colonus,* who cultivated the ground for a master and who could not change his condition or his home, but who on the other hand could not have his rent (if we call it so) raised arbitrarily upon him, nor be sold like the mere slave into distant bondage. In alluding, as I then did to the suggestion that among the *Aldii* of the Lombard law-book we had to look for the vast mass of the so-called "Roman" inhabitants of Italy who occupied it before the Lombard conquest, I proposed that we should for the time neither accept this theory nor yet reject it, but keep it before our minds and see how far it explained the phenomena which came before us.

Now, at the close of this enquiry, I ask the reader if he does not consider that the probability of this theory amounts almost to certainty? It is true we have not—would that we had—any distinct statement by Paulus or any other contemporary authority, "The Romans were made *Aldii"*; but we are told that they were made *tributarii,* and finding in the Lombard law-book continual allusions to a class of men—manifestly a large class—who are evidently *tributani,* we say with some confidence: "Surely the staple of this class is the vanquished Roman population". I may say that this theory is not the special discovery of any one student, though perhaps Troya has done more to establish its correctness than any other writer. It has by this time almost passed into one of the commonplaces of Lombard history; but it has seemed desirable to review the reasons by which it is supported and to show that they are likely to stand the test of further investigation.

If it be once admitted that the great mass of the Roman population are represented by the *Aldii* of the Lombard Codes, most of the desired information is ours. Almost all the events that could happen to them can be expressed (if we may speak mathematically) in terms of the *guidrigild,* which *guidrigild* however, we must always remember, was payable not to the *Aldius* himself but to his master. If a Roman cultivator was fatally injured by some truculent Lombard swashbuckler, it is not upon his injury or on his family's claims to compensation that Rothari meditates, but he argues that if his master is not indemnified for the loss of so profitable a drudge, there will be a *faida* between him and the homicide, and he therefore fixes the tariff of *guidrigild* to be paid by the homicide to the master.

Thus then, speaking generally, we may say if any one would know how the countrymen of Virgil and Cicero were faring during the latter part of the sixth and the seventh centuries and what sort of lives they lived, let him study the Lombard Codes and see what they say as to the position of the *Aldius* and *Aldia* in Lombard Italy. But there are two classes of persons to whom we cannot feel sure that this information applies.

The first are the handicraftsmen and dwellers in towns. Is there anything in the above-quoted words of Paulus about "paying the third part of their crops" (*frugum*) to the *hospites* which entitles us to say that a worker in metal living within the walls of a town was made subject to this tribute? It is generally conjectured by historical enquirers that this artisan class shared the degradation and the liability to tribute of their rural fellow-countrymen; but we cannot be said to have any proof of this proposition, nor is it so easy to understand how the quartering of the Lombard guest upon the Roman could be accomplished in the town as in the country.

And, secondly, the wealthy and leisured class apart from the mere land-owners, if there were any such class left in Italy,—how did they fare under the new system? I say, "if there were any such left", because the influences which had been at work in Italy to drain it of those whom we should call its gentlemen had been mighty and had been working for centuries. The impoverishment of the *Curiales,* the invasions of Alaric, of Attila, of Gaiseric, Odovacar and his Herulians, Theodoric and his Ostrogoths, preeminently the bloody revenges which marked the latter stages of the Ostrogothic war, the emigration to Constantinople, the tendency of all men of good birth and education to flock to the seat of officialism, whether at Ravenna or at Constantinople, in search of a career, the attractions of the Church for some, of the Convent for others,— all these causes had doubtless worked a terrible depletion of the rural aristocracy of Italy, even before the unspeakable Lombard came to hasten the process.

Still there may have been Roman gentlemen, as there may have been Roman artisans, who were no man's *Aldii,* and therefore stood outside the pale of express Lombard law, and if there were such I think we can only conjecture what amount of protection they received for life and property. My own conjecture would be that in the first generation after the conquest they received none at all. The sentence of Paulus, "In these days many of the noble Romans were slain through avarice", expresses, I suspect, the state of things not only under the lawless dukes, but even under Authari and Agilulf, at any rate in the earlier years of the reign of the latter monarch. Even under Rothari, if the son of a murdered Roman came to the King's Court and claimed compensation for his father's death, we can imagine the king's reply, "When Lombard has killed Lombard, we have ordered that a certain *guidrigild* be paid, *ut cesset faida,* to prevent a blood-feud. But how can any blood-feud exist between the Lombard and the soft weaponless Roman? No more than between a Lombard man and a woman. I cannot decree the payment of any *guidrigild,* but you can if you like try your fortune as a *camfio* in the dread wager of battle". And thereat, inextinguishable laughter would resound through the hall at the thought of the delicate Roman mounting horse and couching spear against the stalwart Lombard *exercitalis.*

Such would seem to have been the law, or rather the absence of law, in the earlier days of the Lombard state. But we saw in the laws of Liutprand that a stronger feeling against crimes of violence had then been growing up in the community. The conviction that murder was not merely a wrong to the relations of the murdered man, but a disgrace to the State, a breach, as our ancestors would say, of "the King's Peace", had evidently entered Into the mind of the legislator. It was under the influence of this conviction that he ordained that the murderer of "any free man" should atone for his crime by the loss of the whole of his property, part of which was to go to the murdered man's heirs and the rest to the King's Court. Here at first we think we have got the desired answer to our question as to the protection afforded by the law to the unattached Roman, who is no man's *Aldius*. As a free man he surely shares in the advantages of this law, and anyone who kills him *asto animo* (of malice prepense) will forfeit his whole property for his crime. But unfortunately, as has been already pointed out, a law which was passed four years later for the express purpose of explaining this law seems to limit those hopeful words, "any free man". It is true that the legislator here deals only with manslaughter in self-defense and does not expressly repeal any part of the law against premeditated murder. But when we find that the lowest *guidrigild* known to the legislator is for "the humblest person *who shall he found to be a member of our army"*, we feel that these words are probably to be taken as limiting the application of the earlier law also, and we fear that we may not infer that the truculent Lombard who of malice aforethought killed a free man of Roman origin was punished for the crime by the forfeiture of all his estates. Thus then, in the silence of the Lombard legislator, we are left to mere conjecture as to the condition of the Roman population. Individually I am disposed to conjecture that the increasing civilization of their conquerors had, at any rate by the time of Liutprand, perhaps long before, wrought great improvement in their condition, and that the murder or mutilation of a free Italian of non-Lombard descent was noticed and punished in some way by the Lombard magistrate, but how, to what extent, under the provision of what law, I do not think we have any evidence to show.

But while in criminal matters the man of Roman origin was thus at the mercy of the law, or rather the lawlessness, of his conquerors, in civil affairs we may reasonably suppose that he retained his own law, as far as he had knowledge and understanding enough to use it. Why, for instance, should the Lombard official trouble himself with the disposition of the Roman artisan's scanty savings among his descendants? Why should he care to impose upon him the Lombard principle of the exclusion of daughters in favor of sons, or the provision made by the laws of Rothari for illegitimate offspring? All these were surely matters far below the range of the Lombard duke or *sculdahis*; and so the men of Roman origin in their purchases and sales to one another, in making their wills, in dividing the property of an intestate, would go on, very likely clumsily and ignorantly enough, following, as far as they knew them, the provisions of the Digest and the Code. Thus we have at once a natural explanation of those passages already noticed in the laws of Liutprand where he uses emphatically the words "Si quis Langobardus" in treating of the laws of inheritance; of his refusal of the Lombard rights of *faida* and *anagriph* to the Lombard woman who has come under a Koman's *mundium*; and above all, of the important law *de scribis*, in which conveyancers are ordered, under very severe penalties for disobedience, to prepare their deeds either according to the law of the Lombards or according to the law of the Romans, and not to presume to alter either of these to suit their own convenience.

Thus we find that in the Lombard State, as in most of the other States founded by the barbarians on the ruins of the Empire, we have the germs of what is known as the system of Personal Law, as opposed to that of Territorial Law which is now universal in Christian Europe. Under this system, not only had the Barbarian one code of laws and the Roman another, but after the barbarian peoples had begun to get mixed with one another by wars and invasions, each separate barbarian nation kept its own laws, and thus, as Bishop Agobard said in the ninth century when writing to Louis the Pious, "you may see five men sitting or walking together, each of whom has his own law". We shall find this system in full operation under Charles the Great, and though undoubtedly it was less completely developed in Italy than in some of the other countries of Western Europe, owing to the attempt made by the Lombards to assimilate all other laws and customs to their own, Personal Law is there in the Laws of Liutprand, and it would probably have asserted itself more strongly had the life of the State been a longer one.

Here then for the present we leave the story of the Lombard settlers in Italy. They have succeeded in making good their position in the peninsula, notwithstanding all the efforts of Pope and Exarch, of Caesar and of Meroving to expel them. They have been steadily extending their frontier, and it seems clear that their final expulsion of "the Greeks" (as the Imperial forces are beginning to be called) is only a question of time, and not of any long time either. They have renounced their Arian Creed, have become great church-builders and convent-founders, and, as far as religious reasons go, there seems no cause why they should not live on terms of cordial friendship with the See of Rome. Lastly, they have been for more than thirty years under the sway of a hero-king—wise, courageous, merciful—who has done more than any of his predecessors towards welding their somewhat disorderly and discordant elements into one coherent and harmonious whole. "United Italy" appears full in view, and it seems as if by the arms of the rude Lombard this great victory will be won for humanity.

Why and how this fair promise failed, and how Europe organized herself at the expense of a hopelessly divided Italy, it will be my business to set forth in the concluding volume.

PART ONE

BOOK I
THE VISIGOTHIC INVASION
INTRODUCTION.
SUMMARY OF ROMAN IMPERIAL HISTORY.

CHAPTERS
I. EARLY HISTORY OF THE GOTHS
II. JOVIAN, PROCOPIUS, ATHANARIC.
III. VALENTINIAN THE FIRST
IV. THE LAST YEARS OF VALENS
V. THEODOSIUS
VI. THE VICTORY OF NICAEA
VII. THE FALL OF GRATIAN
VIII. MAXIMUS AND AMBROSE
IX. THE INSURRECTION OF ANTIOCH
X. THEODOSIUS IN ITALY AND THE MASSACRE OF THESSALONICA
XI. EUGENIUS AND ARBOGAST
XII. INTERNAL ORGANISATION OF THE EMPIRE
XIII. HONORIUS, STILICHO, ALARIC
XIV. ALARIC'S FIRST INVASION OF ITALY
XV. THE FALL OF STILICHO
XVII. ALARIC'S THREE SIEGES OF ROME.
XVIII. THE LOVERS OF PLACIDIA
XIX. PLACIDIA AUGUSTA
XX. SALVIAN ON THE DIVINE GOVERNMENT

PART TWO

BOOK II
THE HUNNISH INVASION

I. EARLY HISTORY OF THE HUNS.
II. ATTILA AND THE COURT OF CONSTANTINOPLE.
III. ATTILA IN GAUL.
IV. ATTILA IN ITALY.

BOOK III
THE VANDAL INVASION AND THE HERULIAN MUTINY

I. EXTINCTION OF THE HUNNISH EMPIRE AND THE THEODOSIAN DYNASTY.
II. THE VANDALS FROM GERMANY TO ROME.
III. THE LETTERS AND POEMS OF APOLLINARIS SIDONIUS.
IV. AVITUS, THE CLIENT OF THE VISIGOTHS.
V. SUPREMACY OF RICIMER. MAJORIAN.
VI. SEVERUS II, THE LUCANIAN. ANTHEMIUS, THE CLIENT OF BYZANTIUM.
VII. OLYBRIUS, THE CLIENT OF THE VANDAL. GLYCERIUS, THE CLIENT OF THE BURGUNDIAN. JULIUS NEPOS, THE CLIENT OF BYZANTIUM. ROMULUS AUGUSTULUS, SON OF ORESTES.
VIII. ODOVACAR, THE SOLDIER OF FORTUNE.
IX. CAUSES OF THE FALL OF THE WESTERN EMPIRE.

PART THREE

BOOK IV
THE OSTROGOTHIC INVASION.

I. A CENTURY OF OSTROGOTHIC HISTORY.
II. THE REIGN OF ZENO.
III THE TWO THEODORICS IN THRACE
V. FLAVIUS ODOVACAR.
V. THE FRIGIAN WAR
VI. THE DEATH-GRAPPLE.
VII. KING AND PEOPLE.
VIII. THEODORIC AND HIS COURT
IX. THEODORIC'S RELATIONS WITH GAUL.
X. THEODORIC'S RELATIONS WITH THE EAST.
XI. THEODORIC'S RELATIONS WITH THE CHURCH.
XII. BOETHIUS AND SYMMACHUS.
XIII. THE ACCESSION OF ATHALARIC.
XIV. JUSTINIAN.
XV. BELISARIUS.
XVI. THE LOVERS OF AMALASUNTHA.

BOOK V
THE IMPERIAL RESTORATION
535—553

I. THE FIRST YEAR OF THE WAR
II. BELISARIUS AT CARTHAGE AND AT NAPLES.
III. THE ELEVATION OF WITIGIS.
IV. BELISARIUS IN ROME
V. THE LONG SIEGE BEGUN.
VI. THE CUTTING OF THE AQUEDUCTS.
VII. THE GOTHIC ASSAULT.
VIII. ROMAN SORTIES.
IX. THE BLOCKADE
X. THE RELIEF OF RIMINI.
XI. DISSENSIONS IN THE IMPERIAL CAMP.
XII. SIEGES OF FIESOLI AND OSIMO.
XIII. THE FALL OF RAVENNA.
XIV. AFFAIRS AT CONSTANTINOPLE
XV. THE ELEVATION OF TOTILA.
XVI. SAINT BENEDICT (480 – 547)
XVII. THE RETURN OF BELISARIUS.
XVIII. THE SECOND SIEGE OF ROME.
CHAPTER XIX. ROMA CAPTA.
XX. THE RE-OCCUPATION OF ROME.
XXI. THE THIRD SIEGE OF ROME.
XXII. THE EXPEDITION OF GERMANUS.
XXIII. THE SORROWS OF VIGILIUS.
XXIV. NARSES AND TOTILA.
XXV FINIS GOTHORUM. THE LAST OF THE GOTHS

PART FOUR

BOOK VI.
THE LOMBARD INVASION.

I. THE ALAMANNIC BRETHREN.
II. THE RULE OF NARSES.
III. THE LANGOBARDIC FOREWORLD
1. Early Notices of the Langobardi by Greek and Roman Writers.
2. The Saga of the Langobardi
3. War with the Heruli
4. War with the Gepidae.
IV. ALBOIN IN ITALY.
V. THE INTERREGNUM.
VI. FLAVIUS AUTHARI.
VII. GREGORY THE GREAT.
VIII. GREGORY AND THE LOMBARDS.
IX. THE PAPAL PEACE.
X. THE LAST YEARS OF GREGORY
XI. THE ISTRIAN SCHISM.

BOOK VII
THE LOMBARD KINGDOM

A.D. 600-744

I. THE SEVENTH CENTURY.
II. THE FOUR GREAT DUCHIES.
I. The Duchy of Trient (Tridentum).
II. The Duchy of Friuli (Forum Julii).
III. The Duchy of Benevento (Beneventum).
IV. The Duchy of Spoleto (Spoletium).
Note A. Ecclesiastical notices of the Lombards of Spoleto in the Dialogues of Gregory the Great. Life of St. Cetheus.
III. SAINT COLUMBANUS.
IV. THEUDELINDA AND HER CHILDREN.
V. THE LEGISLATION OF ROTHARI.
VI. GRIMWALD AND CONSTANS.
The Story of St. Barbatus.
VII. THE BAVARIAN LINE RESTORED.
VIII. STORY OF THE DUCHIES, CONTINUED.
IX. THE PAPACY AND THE EMPIRE.
X. THE LAWS OF LIUTPRAND.
XI. ICONOCLASM.
XII. KING LIUTPRAND.
XIII. POLITICAL STATE OF IMPERIAL ITALY.
XIV. POLITICAL STATE OF LOMBARD ITALY.

PART FIVE

BOOK VIII.
FRANKISH INVASIONS.

I. INTRODUCTION. THE MEROVINGIAN KINGS. EARLY FRANKISH HISTORY.
II. THE EARLY ARNULFINGS
III. PIPPIN OF HERISTAL AND CHARLES MARTEL
IV. DUKES OF BAVARIA
V. THE GREAT RENUNCIATION
VI. THE ANOINTING OF PIPPIN
VII. THE DONATION OF CONSTANTINE
VIII. THE STRUGGLE FOR THE EXARCHATE
IX. THE PONTIFICATE OP PAUL I (757-767).
X. A PAPAL CHAOS.
XI. THE PONTIFICATE OF STEPHEN III.
XII. RAVENNA AND ROME.
XIII. THE ACCESSION OF POPE HADRIAN.
XIV. END OF THE LOMBARD MONARCHY.

BOOK IX
THE FRANKISH EMPIRE
774-814

I. THE PONTIFICATE OF HADRIAN I.
Frankish and Byzantine Affairs,
II. THE PONTIFICATE OF HADRIAN I.
Italian Affairs.
III. TASSILO OF BAVARIA.
IV. TWO COURTS : CONSTANTINOPLE AND AACHEN

V. POPE AND EMPEROR.
VI. CHARLES AND IRENE.
VII. VENICE.
VIII. THE FINAL RECOGNITION.
IX. CAROLUS MORTUUS.
X. THE LIFE OF THE PEOPLE

Printed in Great Britain
by Amazon